REVEL WITH A CAUSE

REVEL WITH A CAUSE

LIBERAL SATIRE IN POSTWAR AMERICA

Stephen E. Kercher

The University of Chicago Press Chicago & London

STEPHEN E. KERCHER is assistant professor of history at the
University of Wisconsin-Oshkosh.

The University of Chicago Press, Chicago 60637
The University of Chicago Press, Ltd., London
© 2006 by The University of Chicago
All rights reserved. Published 2006
Printed in the United States of America

15 14 13 12 11 10 09 08 07 06   1 2 3 4 5

ISBN: 0-226-43164-9 (cloth)

A portion of chapter 6 was published as "'We Hope You Like Us,
Jack': The Kennedy-Era Satire of Victor Navasky's *Monocle* and
Outsider's Newsletter" in *Studies in American Humor* New Series 3
(Winter 2001): 36–48.

Library of Congress Cataloging-in-Publication Data

Kercher, Stephen E.
    Revel with a cause : liberal satire in postwar America /
Stephen E. Kercher.
        p.   cm.
    Includes bibliographical references and index.
    ISBN 0-226-43164-9 (cloth : alk. paper)
    1. Satire, American—History and criticism. 2. Politics and
literature—United States—History—20th century. 3. American
literature—20th century—History and criticism. 4. Liberalism—United States—History—20th century. 5. Liberalism in
literature. I. Title.

    PS438.K47-2006
    817'.5409358—dc22   2005030535

♾ The paper used in this publication meets the minimum re-
quirements of the American National Standard for Information
Sciences—Permanence of Paper for Printed Library Materials,
ANSI Z39.48-1992.

TO MARLEY

Contents

Acknowledgments

The preparation of this book would not have been possible without the support of many people and institutions. Generous financial support sustained this project from its inception. While research grants and fellowships from the Graduate School, College of Arts and Sciences, and Department of History at Indiana University supported early stages of my research, a Faculty Development Grant from the University of Wisconsin-Oshkosh proved invaluable for the final preparation of the manuscript. I am particularly indebted to the Swann Foundation for Caricature and Cartoon and the Prints and Photographs Division of the Library of Congress, whose generous support assisted this project at a critical stage of its development.

While working on this project I have been assisted by many helpful archivists and librarians. I am indebted to Sara Duke and Harry Katz of the Library of Congress's Prints and Photographs Division, Lucy Caswell of Ohio State University's Cartoon Research Library, Randall Scott of Michigan State University's Comic Art Collection, and Mary Ellen Rogan of the New York Public Library for the Performing Arts. At Bowling Green State University I benefited from the expertise of Bill Schurk at the Music Library and Sound Recordings Archives and Allison Scott at the Popular Culture Library. I also wish to thank the librarians and staffs of the Special Collections at the University of Michigan Library, the Special Collections and Vincent Voice Libraries at Michigan State University, the Manuscript and the Motion Picture and Television Divisions of the Library of Congress, Yale University Library's Beinecke Collection, the

Department of Special Collections at the University of Pennsylvania Library, the Cinema-Television Library at the University of Southern California, the Museum of Television and Radio in New York, the University of Maryland's Library of American Broadcasting, the American History Museum at the Smithsonian Institution, the Chicago Historical Society, the Museum of Broadcast Communications in Chicago, the Polk Library at the University of Wisconsin-Oshkosh, and the wonderful public libraries of Ann Arbor, Michigan, and Neenah-Menasha, Wisconsin.

I owe great thanks to the many individuals who spent time with me in their homes and over the telephone discussing their role in fifties and early-sixties American satire: Nancy Ames, Del Close, Joan Darling, Robert Emmett, Pat Englund, Jules Feiffer, Theodore Flicker, Stan Freberg, Al Freeman Jr., Ed Friendly, Garry Goodrow, Mark Gordon, Stanley Grover, Barbara Harris, Buck Henry, Marshall Jamison, Tom Lehrer, Willard Levitas, Richard Lingeman, Arch Lustberg, Alan Myerson, Victor Navasky, Richard Neuweiler, Noel Parmental Jr., Sheldon Patinkin, Elliot Reid, Thomas Ryan, Bernie Sahlins, Herb Sargent, Dick Schaal, Avery Schreiber, Omar Shapli, David Shepherd, Larry Siegel, Paul Sills, Gloria Steinem, Calvin Trillin, and Saul Turteltaub.

I would like to thank Kelly Leonard and Andrew Alexander for providing me with access to The Second City's archives. Heartfelt thanks are also due Maria Reidelbach, who was willing to share her extensive collection of research materials on *MAD* magazine with me. Similar generosity and good cheer were provided by my history department colleagues at the University of Wisconsin-Oshkosh, Art Chimes, Art and Martha Harrison, Eric Jarvis, Dan McKeever, Mimi Minnick, Peter Tauber, Jeremy Mazner, John Benson, Nancy Godleski, Jacques Dutrey, Sarah Kaufman, Dennis Kitchen, Warren Debenham, Janet Coleman, Pat and Joe Howard, Lesli Johnson, Manning Fields, Caroline Stannard, Russell Zanca, Monica Eng, and Stella.

I have benefited from discussions and critical feedback from Jeffrey Sweet, Kim Thompson, Larry Mintz, David Pace, Tom Engelhardt, Paul Murphy, David Nordloh, Michael McGerr, Arthur Dudden, Ray Browne, Joseph Boskin, Paul Buhle, and Charlie McGovern. Casey Blake helped guide this project from the beginning and therefore deserves special credit for its accomplishments, whatever they may be. It is difficult to imagine how this study would have taken shape without his incisive feedback on early chapter drafts and, not least, his unflagging encouragement. Likewise, I consider myself fortunate to have worked with Douglas

Mitchell. The expert and friendly guidance he and the staff at the University of Chicago Press provided helped make this project a thoroughly enjoyable one.

Finally, I would like to express my gratitude to my family. I thank my parents, Ed and Ulla Kercher, and my two sisters, Anne and Lisa, for the support they have provided. Thanks also go to my daughter Petra and son Tristan, both of whom entered this world while I worked on this study. For my progeny, good humor is, thankfully, something much more than a topic of academic scrutiny. I am grateful for the joy and true revelry they have provided over the past several years. My deepest gratitude is reserved for their mother, without whose support, patience, and inspiration this study would not have been possible. I dedicate this book to her, with love and admiration.

Liberal Satire in Postwar America

The truth is that you cannot be memorably funny without at some point raising topics which the rich, the powerful and the complacent would prefer to see left alone. GEORGE ORWELL

We think the gods reveal themselves only to sedate and musing gentlemen. But not so . . . When I have been playing tomfool, I have been driven to exchange the old for a more liberal and catholic philosophy. HENRY DAVID THOREAU

Laughter can only make people a little more thoughtful. STANLEY KUBRICK

In the fall of 1958, the British critic Kenneth Tynan traveled to New York City, where he was engaged to begin writing theater reviews for the *New Yorker*. As his ship crossed the Atlantic Ocean, he made a list in his engagement book of those elements of American cultural and intellectual life he was most eager to encounter firsthand. In addition to "jazz," "beat," "*Dissent*," and "Zen," Tynan wrote the names of a magazine and a nightclub comedian familiar to many fans of American liberal satire—*MAD* and Mort Sahl. Tynan was excited about taking residence in the United States, a place he identified as "the prime incubator of nonconformist nightclub wit" since World War II. As a young man well attuned to avant-garde culture and sympathetic to left-liberal politics, Tynan was drawn to the satiric art and performance of Mort Sahl, Lenny Bruce, Mike Nichols and Elaine May, the Second City, and Jules Feiffer. In the late 1950s and early 1960s, he would describe their work in glowing terms to his British and American readers.[1]

This book explores the varieties of liberal satire that thrived in the United States in the two decades after World War II and attracted the interest of people like Ken Tynan. By *satire* I refer specifically to forms of humorous expression that, by definition, deploy irony to criticize vice and raise awareness. Spurred often by anger or scorn and informed by serious moral concern, satire is humor with a social purpose—protest, as Ken Tynan put it, "couched in wit."[2] I identify this satire as *liberal* because as a whole it corroborated the outlook and agenda of mid-twentieth-century liberalism and of the left wing of the Democratic Party in particular. So closely identified were liberal satirists with the Democratic Party by 1960 that Bob Newhart, one of several comedians who actively campaigned on behalf of Democrat John F. Kennedy, was on the mark when he unequivocally stated, "[t]here's no Republican Mort Sahl. Can't be."[3]

By and large, the satiric artists, performers, and writers under study here were born into progressive households, came of age during the Great Depression, formed early allegiances to Franklin Roosevelt and New Deal liberalism, and were shaped by the experience of World War II. A few maintained contact with the left-wing Popular Front culture of the 1930s and early 1940. After the war, they, like many other American liberals aligned with Americans for Democratic Action, supported an expanding welfare state, racial equality, and that key component of modern liberalism identified by historian Gary Gerstle—"expansive notions of individual freedom."[4] Together with a number of left-liberals and Popular Front holdouts, several were adversely affected by the postwar anticommunist movement. Others who did not suffer directly from McCarthyism deemed it an intolerable infringement on civil liberties. At the same time, however, many liberal satirists agreed with the prerogatives of the cold war and supported cold war Democrats Adlai Stevenson, John F. Kennedy, and Lyndon Johnson in presidential elections.

Though the satirists I am considering here demonstrated a fealty to American postwar liberalism, they readily criticized Democrats for failing to live up to liberal ideals. The moral position that liberal satirists adopted on liberalism's failures—and on Democrats' failure to push the issue of racial equality in particular—was in many cases an outgrowth of the marginal position they occupied as Jewish Americans or African Americans. While several important satirists were African American, a larger number were Jewish. Coming from an ethnic background that was historically persecuted and excluded from positions of cultural authority, raised in a culture that prized wit and deflationary humor, these thoroughly assimilated, articulate, determined, politicized young Jews proudly maintained the perspective of detached observers. As many of them have remarked, their Jewish consciousness contributed greatly to their identities as cultural renegades and facilitated the ironic distance necessary for their sharp and caustic humor. Both Jewish and African American satirists brought to their work elements of the critical, marginal perspective fostered within the urban minority subcultures in which they were raised.[5]

The satiric writers, performers, and artists I discuss in this book shared other important similarities. Like many of the young, educated, middle-class Americans who most appreciated their work, liberal satirists were drawn to the outlook of postwar existentialism. The sense of alienation liberal satirists felt toward mainstream American life fed their late modernist passions for truth and authenticity. In significant respects, liberal satirists resembled the young moderns of the 1920s who were committed to what Ann Douglas has identified as the ethos of "terrible honesty." Indeed, like the artists and writers who rebelled against the "feminine" and sentimental nature of Victorian culture, satirists prized "histrionic truthfulness above all else."[6] Participating in what Jackson Lears has called modernism's "discourse of authenticity," satirists often spoke of the necessity of exposing *reality*.[7] Indeed, for many of these artists and performers, humor did not provide an escape from reality but instead a momentary flight from the *unreality* of postwar American life. With remarkable consistency, in fact, the liberal satirists under survey here justified their social criticism on the grounds that it might help destroy the suffocating banality, artifice, and hypocrisy infiltrating American life and culture. To reveal through humor the *truth* behind the politics, religion, social mores, and culture of the day served as an important, if not primary, motive for many of them.

Of course, satirists' pursuit of truth was a thoroughly masculine enterprise. Indeed, with the significant exceptions of Elaine May and Marya Mannes, the liberal satirists who wielded the "weapon of wit" in the postwar years were all men. The discourse surrounding their work was saturated with notions of heroic male rebellion. With their concern over the deleterious effects of social conformity and their antipathy toward "feminine" consumer culture and American women in general, liberal satirists by and large represented the prerogatives and individualist ethos of the mid-century middle-class American male. It is little surprise then that they found one of their most enthusiastic supporters in *Playboy* publisher Hugh Hefner. In its revolt against the forces limiting white, middle-class American males' autonomy—namely, the white-collar world of corporations, the institution of marriage, and traditional familial obligations—*Playboy* considered satire a congenial medium for cultural revolt. Initiated in December 1953, *Playboy*'s remarkable rise in the publishing world coincided with the growing popularity that liberal satirists enjoyed. Like many liberal satirists, *Playboy* pledged to represent "truth," "honesty," and expressive freedom.[8] For the millions of servicemen, college students, and frustrated organization men who read *Playboy* in the 1950s, the brave, unsentimental satire published or discussed in their magazine had considerable appeal.

* * *

By focusing attention on a diverse range of satiric expression, including parody and "sick humor," this book aims to fill a large gap in the scholarship on twentieth-century American humor. The narrative accounts of Walter Blair, Hamlin Hill, and many other humor scholars have centered mainly on literary humor and have seldom addressed the fertile period of the "long fifties." The effect of such longstanding omissions has been to ratify the idea that, as historian Arthur Schlesinger Jr. argued in 1965, the decade of the fifties was "the most humorless period in American history." In years since, other writers and historians have similarly described the fifties as "essentially humorless" and "silent of laughter."[9] Ever since the 1960s, in fact, the Eisenhower era has more often struck observers as a *subject of* rather than a *source for* satire. Far from being mirthless, however, the two decades following World War II spawned satiric forms and techniques that have permanently altered the direction of modern American comic expression. It is difficult to conceive contemporary humor and comedy, for instance, without the influence of *MAD*, the Second City, and Lenny Bruce.

In addition to illuminating a recent chapter in the history of American humor, this study responds to a set of core issues within recent postwar American historiography. Ever since Eric Goldman wrote *The Crucial Decade* at the close of the 1950s, historians of the postwar period have called attention to its prevailing conservatism. Due in large part to the onset of the cold war and its domestic equivalent, the postwar anticommunist movement (what Ellen Schrecker correctly identifies as the "most widespread and longest lasting wave of political repression in American history"), the left-wing, Popular Front culture of the 1930s was wiped out, dissent was stifled, civil liberties curtailed, and traditional gender roles rigidly maintained. As a coalition of elites consolidated what Jackson Lears has termed America's postwar "corporate cultural hegemony," Americans, in their drive for security, safety, and material comfort, honored a host of postwar pieties including a belief in God, competitive individualism, private enterprise, and consumerism. Rather than question the assumptions behind the ideology and rhetoric of the cold war, upwardly mobile American intellectuals declared an "end of ideology" and generally shared in a celebration of consensus. In sum, the ideology of the day, as Stephen Whitfield has described it, was "not a lever with which the politically informed could act; it was more like a lounge chair in which they could repose." The "creedal imperatives of Americanism" suited many Americans just fine, and throughout the fifties tranquility, stability, and complacency reigned.[10]

Yet if the dominant mood in postwar America, particularly among America's expanding, suburban-dwelling middle class, reflected the era's affluence, stability, peace, and prosperity, it was continually disrupted by feelings of anxiety, alienation, and what sociologist C. Wright Mills in 1959 described as the "misery of vague uneasiness." Casting a large shadow over Americans' collective psyche was, of course, the looming presence of the Bomb. "Never before in human history have men consciously faced the knowledge that the mass extermination of the race is a distinct possibility," Lewis Coser noted in 1957, "never before has this eaten into the secret depths of human consciousness." A year later, the writer Margaret Halsey reflected on the mood shared by disillusioned liberals in particular. "The feeling does indeed deepen in many people," Halsey observed, "of being caught up in a sort of gangrenous sunset, brilliant with the streaky pyrotechnics of decay." At the same time they celebrated the Great American Way, then, Americans inhabiting what I. F. Stone called the "haunted fifties" struggled to make sense of the mixed signals that bombarded them, turned to the "crisis philosophy" of existentialism, and privately despaired over the possibility of instant annihilation.[11] Herein lies one of the great paradoxes of postwar American history.

In his introduction to the collection of seminal essays analyzing the postwar period, *Recasting America: Culture and Politics in the Age of Cold War* (1989), historian Lary May asked, "Did the transformation of intellectual and popular thought, along with the full flowering of a consumption economy, generate passivity in the face of a highly organized social order, or did it release new forms of creativity and liberation?"[12] Increasingly, historians have refuted the notion that postwar corporate liberalism and America's ideological consensus foreclosed the possibility of meaningful personal rebellion and have focused their attention on the ways Americans, particularly middle-class Americans, critically interpreted the context of their lives and even groped for "oppositional spaces" within American culture. By doing so, historians have departed from the traditional stress on the binary opposition between the staid fifties and turbulent sixties and increasingly identify continuities within the postwar era. This book is very much a part of that revisionist project.

*   *   *

Evidence that Americans and members of the educated middle class in particular sought confirmation of their disquiet and apprehension is abundantly clear in the popularity of *The Lonely Crowd, The Organization Man, The Power Elite,* and numerous other books of popular social criticism that appeared on bookshelves in the 1950s. The liberal and left-liberal intellectuals who inventoried the root causes of the malaise — most importantly, C. Wright Mills, Richard Chase, David Riesman, William Whtye, Paul Goodman, Betty Friedan, John Kenneth Galbraith, and Vance Packard — took aim at mass culture, advertising, the suburbs, social conformity, the corporate workplace, and traditional gender roles. Surveying the body of this work, historians such as Todd Gitlin and Daniel Horowitz conclude that America's middle class at midcentury was insecure and highly self-critical. "Relentless self-criticism," Morris Dickstein has written recently, "not complacency, was the real key to postwar culture." [13]

Recent cultural histories have further undermined assumptions about the success America's postwar "corporate cultural hegemony" enjoyed in "containing" dissent. In one of the best these studies, Daniel Belgrad relates how bebop jazz, abstract expressionist art, Beat prosody, and other kinetic arts created a "culture of spontaneity" that stood in direct opposition to the bureaucratic, rationalistic ethos of corporate liberalism. Other scholars practicing literary, media, and cultural studies have traced the lineaments of an oppositional culture through a wide range of sources — from the Greenwich Village avant-garde, to mass-circulation women's magazines, pre-1958 rock 'n' roll music, juvenile delinquency teenpics, paranoiac film noirs, revisionist Westerns, lurid Douglas Sirk melodramas, science fiction, and horror films. Young Americans who were part of what activist David McReynolds called the "disorganized disaffection" found inspiration in the rebellious pose struck by James Dean, Marlon Brando, and black jazz musicians. The Beats' romantic rejection of the banality of middle-class life likewise held wide appeal. Overall, then, there was no shortage of creative rebellion in the "other fifties." The remarkable expansion of America's postwar economy together with continuing advances in technology provided multiple "underground channels," as

Todd Gitlin describes them, "where the conventional wisdoms of the time were resisted, undermined, [and] weakened." Taken together, the products of these "underground channels" comprised what historian Margot Henriksen has labeled a "culture of dissent."[14]

In their zeal to read "against the grain," scholars decoding dissent in postwar American culture have occasionally courted tendentiousness and defied credulity. The same pitfalls await those who study postwar humor and comedy, but the very nature of comic expression, as Sigmund Freud has defined it, allows for slightly less strain. In *Jokes and Their Relation to the Unconscious,* Freud argued that the joke "represents a rebellion against . . . authority." As Ed Sikov demonstrates in *Laughing Hysterically: American Screen Comedy of the 1950s,* postwar Hollywood directors such as Frank Tashlin and Billy Wilder went to "wild lengths . . . to be rebellious" in the manner described by Freud and other comic theorists. The deliberate, antic affront to propriety delivered by postwar writers working in the traditions of black humor (Joseph Heller, Kurt Vonnegut Jr., and Terry Southern) and picaresque fiction (J. D. Salinger, Vladimir Nabokov, and Ralph Ellison) has caught the attention of numerous critics and literary scholars. Writing in reference to black humor fiction and film comedy, historian Margot Henriksen argues that "they matched both the explosive power and the deadly nihilism of the atomic bomb . . . [and] announced the dawn of the cultural revolution that . . . matched the transforming power of the bomb."[15] What eludes Henriksen and has escaped most cultural historians assessing cold war America are the challenges that other, specifically nonliterary humor and satire posed to the social and political status quo.

Given the abundant ironies, contradictions, and hypocrisies extant in cold war America, the two decades following World War II were wide open to satirists' cauterizing wit. As historian Jackson Lears notes in *Fables of Abundance,* "[i]n the end, the most effective response to the [fifties] relentless crusade for comfort was scabrous humor, which exposed the foolish pretensions of established authority and buried its representatives beneath the weight of their own technology." Few other professional historians beside Lears, Todd Gitlin, Joseph Boskin, and Howard Brick, however, have bent their ear to hear the strains of postwar laughter much less acknowledge the glint of the period's sparkling wit.[16] This neglect is particularly curious since American liberal satire was a subject of considerable critical and popular interest during this period. Among liberal and left-liberal critics such as Ken Tynan and an audience of educated, middle-class Americans, the type of satire that was found in comic strips and car-

toons, in small-circulation publications, and in nightclubs and small theaters represented some of the most engaging expressive forms available in
postwar America. The central purpose behind this study is to provide the
first comprehensive historical account and appraisal of this liberal satire.
By considering their humorous work seriously, I will demonstrate that
American postwar satiric writers, artists, and performers responded critically and creatively to concerns many middle-class Americans shared
over race relations, the cold war, McCarthyism, and the spread of hypocrisy and deceit. At its best, liberal satire boldly and intelligently challenged
cold war orthodoxy and demonstrated that dissent, when channeled
through satiric humor, was far from dead in the postwar period.

*   *   *

This study of postwar liberal satire begins by considering the postwar cartooning career of Bill Mauldin. Mauldin emerged from World War II as
one of America's foremost liberal cartoonists, but his hopes of using his
pen to speak out against the nation's postwar ills were severely chastened
by the politics of anticommunism. With his early retirement, the task of
translating moral anger at McCarthyism, Southern segregationists, and
the inertia of the Eisenhower administration into political cartoons, cartoon strips, and drawings fell to Herbert Block, Walt Kelly, and Robert
Osborn, the subjects of chapter 2. At a time when satiric cartooning was
in retreat, as many contemporary observers and critics noted, Mauldin,
Block, Kelly, and Osborn kept the tradition of angry graphic commentary
alive.

Chapter 3 concentrates on the strain of "sick" humor and satire that
aimed primarily at middle-class propriety and standards of "good" taste,
America's obsession with psychological normalcy, and the commercial underpinnings of consumer culture. Anchoring my discussion here are readings of Tom Lehrer's songwriting, the radio and television performance of
Ernie Kovacs, Sid Caesar, Henry Morgan, and Bob and Ray, the parody of
Stan Freberg, and, most importantly, Harvey Kurtzman's *MAD* comics.
The social satire produced by these liberal artists and performers was mirrored to an extent in the cartooning of Jules Feiffer, the stand-up comedy
of Bob Newhart, and the improvisational stage performance of the Compass and its descendants — Shelley Berman, Mike Nichols, and Elaine
May. The manner in which these satiric artists and performers addressed
relations between men and women, social conformity, and the stifling ef-

fect of America's mass culture industries are the subject of chapter 4. In chapter 5 I investigate improvisational stage performance further, demonstrating how the Second City, the Premise, and several British-based revues deployed spontaneous social criticism to pick at the root causes of the private and public anxieties that young, educated, middle-class Americans experienced in the late 1950s and early 1960s.

Aided in large part by the success of improvisational stage troupes, liberal satire during the Kennedy years reached new levels of popularity. Even political satire, once held at bay by the conservative cold war culture of the 1950s, appeared to rebound in this period. In chapter 6 I concentrate on the type of political satire that flourished during the "satire boom" of the early 1960s. The legitimacy that liberal satire enjoyed during this period indicates the extent to which American political culture had changed since the McCarthy and Eisenhower eras. Yet just how much liberal satire challenged the political status quo was very much open to question. At a time when the Kennedy administration itself reflected, as Christopher Lasch aptly put it, the "cultural tone of Broadway sophistication," liberal satire often did little more than reinforce the prejudices of the upper middle-class Americans who enthusiastically supported the Kennedy Camelot.

The fact that liberal satire found much of its support from Upper Bohemians and exurbanites — those Americans who became "flaming liberals," as critic Vance Packard caustically observed, "in the safety of their patios and favorite bars" — was not lost on the more politically astute, critically inclined satirists.[17] In chapter 7, I demonstrate how *Monocle* and the *Outsider's Newsletter,* Jules Feiffer, and comedian Mort Sahl began to realize the critical potential of liberal satire during the early 1960s. Chapter 8 describes how these and other liberal satirists extended their critique into the area of American race relations. Joined by three African Americans — cartoonist Ollie Harrington and comedians Godfrey Cambridge and Dick Gregory — these liberal satirists subjected one of the thorniest and most important challenges facing Americans to satiric scrutiny. Chapter 9, with its focus on the brilliant dark comedy *Dr. Strangelove, or: How I Stopped Worrying and Learned to Love the Bomb,* makes the case that liberal satirists at their frequent best not only highlighted the absurdity underpinning American race relations, they used their coruscating wit to strip bare the logic underpinning the cold war, the proliferation of nuclear weapons, and the Kennedy administration's machinations in Southeast Asia.

By the early 1960s, network television executives had begun to capitalize on the growing popularity of satiric entertainment among affluent
middle-class Americans by offering programs such as *The Bob Newhart
Show* and *Rocky and His Friends*. Chapter 10 closely examines the television
comedy that attempted to harness the critical spirit of liberal satire—
NBC's *That Was the Week That Was*. *TW3*, like the best and funniest liberal
satire, addressed pressing social and political issues but was in the end
compromised by the cowardice of network executives. Indeed, because
liberal satirists on *TW3* and elsewhere at times challenged social political
orthodoxy, addressed taboo subjects, and used language that might be
considered "offensive," they ran the risk of alienating their audiences and
business sponsors. By the early 1960s, a few performers and artists were
challenging the limits of satiric irreverence with material that was even
too indicting, despairing, or profane for the tastes of many educated,
middle-class audiences members. Chapter 11 focuses on the ways in which
Paul Krassner's satiric publication the *Realist* and "sicknik" comedian
Lenny Bruce finally and fatefully transgressed the bounds of liberal satire.

*　　*　　*

My choice of liberal satirists is necessarily selective. Some readers might
object to the omission of Roger Price, Orson Bean, Shepherd Mead, Al
Capp, and other comedic artists, writers, and performers who worked in
this fertile period.[18] I have chosen to concentrate on those satirists who
most skillfully and creatively responded to the concerns of their age. I betray nothing when I admit I find much of what they produced sharp and
wickedly funny. Yet at the risk of depriving satire of the "purely purgative"
license it demands—what typically happens when "an essentially anar-
chistic art," as critic Robert Brustein has remarked, is placed "into the
critical hands of liberal-humanists"—I have remained attuned to liberal
satire's limitations. Very little liberal satire spoke to the specific grievances of American women and various groups living on the margins of
American society.[19] Like most liberal intellectuals working at the high
tide of America's liberal consensus, satirists took America's postwar
affluence for granted and thereby avoided important issues of class. Indeed, taken as a whole, liberal satire played most directly to a small but
influential cohort of educated, middle- and upper-middle class liberals,
the self-conscious class who read the *New Republic*, fretted about the
"quality" of American life, and cast their ballots for Adlai Stevenson and

John Kennedy.[20] Liberal satire's market-mediated rebellion all too often conveyed a certain smugness. More than a few middle- and upper-middle class "hip" liberals who attended the satiric performances of the Second City or the comedian Mort Sahl considered themselves members on the same team aligned against the intolerant, unthinking enemy—the country rube, the racist Southerner, the fervent Goldwater supporter, the square accountant, the brainwashed suburban housewife.

Yet in the end liberal satire offered more than a confirmation of American liberals' worldview. At its best, liberal satire contributed a fierce social and political commentary, one in accord with the dissatisfactions voiced by the New Left and emerging counterculture. For young Americans who felt nearly overcome by the absurdity and hypocrisy that surrounded them, liberal satire proved a welcome tonic. By directly addressing what was too often ignored or left unsaid, satire had a cathartic effect. Evidence suggests that liberal satire also helped some Americans overcome feelings of isolation. Roger Bowen, one of the founding members of the Second City improvisational theater, echoed what many fans of satire felt when he remembered that to "see that there were a lot of [laughing] people who felt the same way you did . . . was a great tonic for the morale." The mutual enjoyment of satire, he continues, "increase[d] solidarity among the disaffected."[21] Four decades later, liberal satire retains the capacity to generate serious, penetrating commentary about our condition. This study was in fact initially conceived at a time when liberal satire was beginning to emerge from a long lull. Since then, Al Franken, Michael Moore, Jon Stewart, and Tom Tomorrow have demonstrated again that satire, drawn or written in the proper critical spirit, can indeed be "memorably funny" in the manner described by George Orwell.

PART ONE

THE POSITIVE USES
OF HUMOR

CHAPTER ONE

Bill Mauldin and the Politics of Postwar American Satire

At the start of the postwar era, comic strips, editorial cartoons, magazine "gag" panels, and various other forms of comic drawing and illustration enjoyed wide circulation in the United States. Even as broadcast television spread in the late 1940s and 1950s and began altering how Americans experienced culture, the visual vocabulary employed by these disparate forms of comic art continued to retain its strength and appeal. For some Americans living at midcentury, certainly, cartoons and line drawings represented the most effective and enjoyable vehicles for wit and satire. Fans of popular satiric cartooning, caricature, and illustration often recalled the tradition of Honoré Daumier, William Hogarth, James Gillray, and Americans such as Thomas Nast and Art Young—artists who over the past several centuries had used their art to express dissent and moral outrage. Borrowing from martial metaphors commonly used throughout World War II, these Americans valorized cartoons as "weapons of wit" capable of puncturing pomposity, deflating pretension, and exposing hypocrisy.[1]

Following World War II, few graphic artists working in the United States were in a better position to carry the tradition of satiric cartooning forward than the young Bill Mauldin. Mauldin, a native of the rural Southwest, emerged as one of America's most popular cartoonists during World War II while in his early twenties. While serving in the U.S. Army's 45th Infantry Division in Europe, he had contributed cartoons about soldiers and army life to the Division *News* and the soldier periodical *Stars & Stripes*. By 1944 his *Up Front* panel cartoon was distributed to seventy-nine newspapers back in the United States. With its thick line and gritty, comic realism, *Up Front* depicted the day-to-day travails of two unshaven, sardonic "dogface" GIs named Willie and Joe. Because these working-class characters belied the propaganda image of the clean-shaven, posture-erect infantrymen, because they occasionally issued impudent, derisive commentaries about army brass and military policy, General George Patton warned Mauldin privately against continuing his "seditious" cartoon.[2] For their part, many American soldiers prized *Up Front*'s irreverence as well as its refreshing candor and stark realism. As one infantryman stationed in Burma wrote his mother in 1945, the best part about Mauldin's cartoons was that "they are done by a man who knows the misery of the front and therefore shows it, not a decorated, pretty propaganda picture for home consumption." "The humor is bitter and hard," he explained, "yet there still is the sense of humor which is the saving point of all the American 'GIs.'"[3] A career army officer concurred, writing Mauldin in 1945, "I think your cracks at the 'brass hats' are perfectly grand—in spite of what Georgie Patton thinks."[4]

Many liberal and left-liberal readers and critics on the American home front were as adoring of Mauldin as they were his friend and benefactor, journalist Ernie Pyle. And since Mauldin used his cartoons to relate the unvarnished truth about the nature of military bureaucracy and life behind the lines, he was often identified with the great antiauthoritarian cartoonists of the early twentieth century. *New Republic* critic Herbert Lyons, for example, praised Mauldin for drawing "the kind of cartoons that have not been done by an American since the time of Art Young and the old *Masses*." "He is probably the only cartoonist of his generation," Lyons continued, "who owes nothing to the *New Yorker*"—the magazine some critics would later blame for setting the trend toward apolitical "gag" cartoons. By the final stages of World War II, Mauldin was one of the most famous and successful high school dropouts in the nation. At the ripe age of twenty-three, he had already earned five battle stars, a Purple Heart, the Legion of Merit, a Pulitzer Prize, and a cover feature in *Time* magazine. In addition, he had produced a best-selling Book-of-the-Month titled *Up Front* and then secured a movie deal for it with International Pictures (with Ring Lardner Jr. cooperating on the screenplay). More importantly, he had signed a lucrative cartooning contract with the United Features Syndicate. At the same time, he was flooded with writing and advertising offers. When Mauldin finally returned home to the United States, he was a national hero and a celebrity. Americans were so interested in the private affairs of the baby-faced veteran that a *Life* photographer was dispatched to the Mauldin home to document the moment when he was reunited with his wartime bride and infant son.[5]

Settling into his new civilian career, Mauldin first attempted to depict the challenges that he, his working-class characters Willie and Joe, and other GIs faced after they returned home and donned mufti: adjustments to family life, joblessness, the postwar housing crisis, and a lack of respect and recognition from the rest of society. In one early postwar cartoon, for example, a GI in uniform enters a room with elder local townsmen and is told, "Shut up, kid. You got no business discussin' serious matters." Mauldin addressed the housing crisis by picturing one GI seeking shelter for his family at a movie theater. "Matinee, heck," he tells the box office attendant, "we want to register for a week." In other cartoons, Mauldin summed up the bitter feelings shared by many returning servicemen— feelings that resonated elsewhere in American popular culture, particularly in William Wyler's 1946 film *The Best Years of Our Lives.* In one cartoon, a GI in a Veterans Administration hospital informs a blinded comrade, "We ain't no lost generation. We just been mislaid." In another, a bar patron spies a disconsolate GI and whispers to his buddy, "I can't tell whether he's a war-embittered young radical or a typical, 100 per cent American fighting man." All too often, Mauldin came to believe, they were one and the same.[6]

Before long Mauldin began banking on his celebrity in order to comment on other important social and political issues facing the nation. In significant respects he resembled his friend Marion Hargrove, the young GI author of the humorous wartime best seller *See Here, Private Hargrove* (1942) who, following his discharge in 1945, banked on his wartime celebrity in order to speak out on behalf of veterans' interests and an enlisted man's "Bill of Rights."[7] For Mauldin, as for Hargrove and many other (particularly African American) veterans, time spent in Uncle Sam's army made him, as he later remembered, "come out with a chip on my shoulder." It had taught him to distrust authority and not yield on matters of moral principle, particularly those relating to racial and religious tolerance. At a *New York Herald Tribune* forum in 1945, Mauldin related how his war experience had spurred his support of racial equality and civil liberties. If "it is true," he then argued, "that we were put into soldier suits to wipe out the Hitlers and the Mussolinis and the Hirohitos and the beliefs and the evils which they fostered, then we have not won the war—we have only won the battles." Speaking freely as a "civilian" no longer under the control of the military, Mauldin attacked the bigots and opportunists "who seek to realize their ambition under the guise of being 100 per cent Americans, of being patriots, and of protecting American interests."[8]

Motivated in large part by an innate rebelliousness (he had been a scrawny brawler since youth) and what he later described as his "peculiar sort of moral base," he began adapting his nationally syndicated cartoon as a vehicle for left-liberal satirical commentary.[9] As Mauldin explained his "radical" inclinations and the motivations behind his postwar cartooning in his 1947 anthology *Back Home:*

> Somewhere in my early childhood and in the army I developed a rather suspicious and rebellious attitude toward stuffed shirts, and since it has been my experience that more stuffed shirts are to be found in the higher ranks of wealth and position than anywhere else, I find myself more often in sympathy with the people who oppose the "elite" than not.[10]

By late 1945 and 1946, Mauldin had dropped his working-class characters Willie and Joe from the panel and instead substituted cartoons criticizing individuals, organizations, and trends that stirred his anger. Judging by the cartoons collected in *Back Home,* Mauldin disdained the idle rich and conservative patriot groups such as the American Legion and the Daughters of the American Revolution. He strenuously objected to postwar xenophobia and in particular the prejudice West Coast Americans shared toward the Nisei Japanese. "Naw—we don't hafta worry about th' owner comin' back," the new owner of a West Coast shop once owned by a Japanese American GI declares to a partner in one Mauldin cartoon from the period, "He wuz killed in Italy." Mauldin's wartime experience sensitized him to racial injustice, so he devoted a good number of cartoons decrying bigotry and the outbreaks of vigilante violence against African Americans in 1945 and 1946. In one of several cartoons commenting caustically on the Ku Klux Klan, a wife holds her husband's hooded robe and exclaims disgustedly, "Bloodstains again! And linens impossible to find!" And in several other cartoons Mauldin used his pen and brush to voice his concern over the military's appropriation of atomic energy. In one, a man informs his son as they make their way toward the "Army Proving Grounds," "Poppa is only a scientist, Junior. The *smart* men decide how to use my inventions."[11]

A survey of cartoons Mauldin drew between 1945 and 1947 reveals that what agitated the young artist most, with the possible exception of racial violence and discrimination, was what he identified as the "monstrous

"Investigate them? Heck, that's mah posse."

1. Bill Mauldin expresses his anger over the "monstrous witch hunt" taking place in the United States after World War II. Copyright by Bill Mauldin. Reprinted courtesy of the William Mauldin Estate.

witch hunt"—the postwar anticommunist movement. In dozens of cartoons from this period, Mauldin angrily attacked the shameless redbaiting deployed by conservative business interests, Southern racists, and politicians, particularly members of the House Committee on Un-American Activities (HUAC). One cartoon Mauldin included in *Back Home* pictures a member of HUAC informing another while pointing to the Bill of Rights, "Read 'em? I'm too busy protectin' 'em to read 'em."

Bill Mauldin and the Politics of Postwar American Satire

Other cartoons carried in syndication posited a connection between anti-communism and latent fascism. In one cartoon, Herman Goering's attorney approaches the war criminal's cell with a stack of newspapers screaming "Reds Menace" in their headlines, whereupon he asks the MP guard, "May I gif my client dis veek's papers? He needs cheering up."[12]

With his satiric cartoons aimed at racial bigotry and violence, right-wing red-baiting, the callousness of the privileged classes, and the weaponization of atomic power, the young Bill Mauldin betrayed not only what the *Atlantic Monthly* properly identified as "honest angry core" but a commitment to progressive, left-liberal political and social principles. Because of this, he was the subject of an adoring portrait in the left-liberal Popular Front newspaper *PM* and was the recipient of voluminous fan mail, much of it written expressing gratitude for what Mauldin's cartoons dared say at the dawn of the cold war. One man who identified himself as "a Negro American and Soldier" stationed "somewhere in Germany" congratulated Mauldin for using *Back Home* to deal "a well deserved blow to those who would have racial prejudice through out [sic] their hearts and then have the nerve to stand up and boast about what a good American they are, and yet criticize another nation about the things that go on in their land." "Keep up the good work," this soldier concluded, "and perhaps someday with the help of God America will wake up." Another man, a war veteran from Los Angeles, wrote Mauldin that he had read *Back Home* three times in seven years because he liked "something with guts and a message . . ." The chapters on bigotry and profiteers "touched me," he wrote, "because I could only say to my intimates what you were saying to the public." "I am not a red or an unhappy agitator," this man tried to explain, "I just like to face facts and give credit where it is due."[13]

Such praise was not, of course, universal. Several months after it honored Mauldin's cartooning on its front cover, *Time* magazine in September 1945 expressed concern that the young veteran had "gone slumming" by "digging for ideas" in Los Angeles taverns, veterans' service centers, and employment agencies. Over the next two years, as both the cold war and the domestic red scare intensified considerably, Mauldin's cultural influence and his outspoken support for progressive causes inevitably aroused suspicion. It is not surprising that one of the most effective and powerful arms of the anticommunist apparatus, the Federal Bureau of Investigation, initiated a dossier on Mauldin in 1946. Mauldin's FBI file commenced that year upon the publication of a "Willie and Joe" cartoon that ran in the *Washington Daily News*—a cartoon in which a sign posted on the door of a U.S. congressman reads, "Un-American Committee for Investigating Activities (Free Speech Division)." Also suspect in the eyes of FBI Director J. Edgar Hoover were cartoons ridiculing wiretapping, loyalty checks, and the Bureau's sluggish investigations into lynchings in Georgia. Although Hoover acknowledged that Mauldin was not a member of the Communist Party, he informed an agent that "it has been alleged that he is such without proof" and, moreover, that the cartoonist's "services have been sought by various communist front organizations . . ." Although Hoover did not order a formal FBI investigation, Mauldin was thereafter under suspicion for his politics and, among other things, his "expressed objection to the caste system in the Armed Forces." [14]

By this time, Mauldin's syndicate (United Features) and its customers around the country had grown nervous about the explicitly political, progressive direction his cartoons had begun to take. United Features began pointedly reminding Mauldin that it had originally sold his cartoon to 179 newspapers nationwide as an apolitical "gag panel," not as political or social satire. [15] With rights it had secured by contract, Mauldin's syndicate began to edit and alter the text of his cartoons. For example, United Features censors excised a Nazi swastika from the cartoon (mentioned above) that excoriated HUAC. Overall, Mauldin later claimed, United Features altered (and in many cases rendered meaningless) nearly twenty percent of his cartoons. The level of this aggressive censorship—much worse than what he experienced in the army—provoked such frustration and anger that Mauldin grew impudent, even reckless. "The more the syndicate censored me and the more the editors complained," he later explained in *Back Home*, "the more defiant I got." "Every time an editor bitched about my drawing a race-relations cartoon . . . I drew eight or ten of them in a row." [16] With his anger and frustration mounting, Mauldin occasionally "climbed on a soapbox and let fly with a sledge hammer," as he confessed, "when I should have used a needle." By forsaking humor and a sense of subtlety, Mauldin admittedly crossed the fine line separating satire from invective. [17]

Client newspapers responded to Mauldin's defiance by dropping his cartoon from their pages. At one point in 1946, newspapers canceled Mauldin's cartoon at the rate of one a day. Even the *St. Louis Post-Dispatch*, home of editorial cartoonist Daniel Fitzpatrick, opted out. With his fortunes declining rapidly, Mauldin appeared to be losing his confidence and his nerve. His ambitions for satiric, political cartooning were sadly humbled. In *Back Home* he admitted that his celebrity had "confused" him and that his use of heavy brushstrokes worked against his more subtle satiric intentions. Cartoons "have to be thrust gently," the chastened cartoonist confessed, "so that the victim doesn't know he's stabbed until he has six inches of steel in his innards." With a hint of contrition Mauldin told his readers that he was finding it "easier to adjust" himself to society and that his "radical years [were] almost over."[18] Coinciding with these public admissions, *Time* magazine reported in an article titled "Education of a GI" that Mauldin had remarried and, more importantly, had come around to a "drastic change in his . . . political thinking." Whereas the young cartoonist formerly was "playing a hard game of footsie with the far left," *Time* reported in its own inimitable way, he was now capable of criticizing the Soviet Union. "I guess I'm a disillusioned fellow traveler," Mauldin told *Time*. "We're all wrong, but Russia is wronger."[19]

Over the next several years, Mauldin managed to escape the control of his syndicate and began contributing cartoons to the *New York Star*, the left-liberal successor to *PM*. When the *Star* folded in 1949, however, Mauldin was finally forced to quit full-time editorial cartooning. By the early 1950s, Mauldin's "radical years" were most definitely behind him. Still a New Deal liberal, but one who now supported essential precepts of the cold war, Mauldin joined admirers such as Eleanor Roosevelt and Arthur Schlesinger Jr. in support of Adlai Stevenson's 1952 presidential campaign. Against his former army commander he enlisted Willie and Joe in the "Veterans for Stevenson" publicity campaign. After the election he occasionally donated cartoons to the *New York Post*, but he focused the bulk of his energies on writing. Except for a series of articles he produced for the liberal journal the *Reporter* in which he criticized the Eisenhower administration and, for *Collier's*, letters written from Joe to Willie reporting on the conditions of the Korea War, the majority of Mauldin's writing efforts during the period were unremarkable. Throughout this period, it is clear that Mauldin was being steered away from the type of satiric commentary toward which he was naturally inclined. "You can be as deflating as you want . . . if you feel that deflating is necessary," his editor at W. W. Norton wrote him in response to proposed project, "but what has to come through is the kind of relaxed zest you yourself showed about the whole business when you were talking to us."[20]

Mauldin found it impossible to submit to "relaxed zest" when he spoke out against Senator Joseph McCarthy. Mauldin remained an outspoken critic of the junior senator from Wisconsin throughout his four years in the public spotlight. During the presidential campaign of 1952, Mauldin publicly condemned McCarthy and his acolytes. Mauldin received criticism when he accused his former commander and Republican presidential candidate Dwight Eisenhower of welcoming the "friendship of the men who . . . represent the Nazis in the United States."[21] For several years thereafter, Maudlin continued to use his position as president of the liberal American Veterans Committee to speak out against Senator Mc-Carthy and conservative (what Mauldin called "reactionary") veterans groups such as the American Legion. For the *Reporter* in April 1953, Mauldin contributed an article ("A Reverie of Revenge") depicting a nightmare encounter in Prague with a racist gatekeeper named McCarranovichin and a mascaraed MVD (Soviet Ministry of Internal Affairs) border guard known as McCarthski. One woman who believed Mauldin was the country's "most important contemporary satirist of political events" informed the *Reporter* that this thinly veiled caricature of McCarthy, "with the glistening, black-lashed gangster's eyes, continues to haunt me, particularly on dark nights." For someone who knew the risks of making public criticisms of McCarthyism (he had admitted in *Back Home* that cartoons against red-baiting "got me into more trouble with the papers who bought my stuff, and the people who read it, than did anything else"), Mauldin's cartoon and his public criticisms were courageous but ultimately costly.[22]

When Mauldin decided to challenge conservative Republican Katherine Price Collier St. George (the first cousin of the late Franklin Delano Roosevelt) as a Democrat for the seat of the Twenty-Eighth Congressional District of New York in 1956, his strident criticism of anticommunism and what he called the "Era of the Cop," coupled with his past political affiliations, came back to haunt him. Though the *New York Times* compared Mauldin's campaign—a campaign that made use of a small airplane, novel singing commercials, and personal appearances by black-listed actor Burgess Meredith and musician Mitch Miller—to an impressive "off-Broadway production," it could not offset the ugly red-baiting deployed by his opponent. Proving Mauldin's contention that she "wears mink" but "throws mud," Katherine Price Collier St. George accused her challenger of communist leanings and cited as evidence his membership in numerous "left-wing organizations." In the end, St. George's tactic of painting Mauldin as a "subversive" and "egghead" proved devastating. After an ugly and often bitter campaign, she won the congressional seat with a plurality of nearly nine thousand votes.[23]

*   *   *

Retrospective accounts of Mauldin's life and career—including obituaries written after his death in 2003—have often interpreted the problems Mauldin encountered with his postwar cartooning career as a symptom of his immaturity and his struggles to adjust to his sudden celebrity.[24] While there is some truth in these assessments, it is important to also consider the substantial political pressure the young cartoonist experienced during the late 1940s. Unfortunately for Mauldin, his postwar cartooning career took off at the very moment that the right-wing anticommunist movement was beginning to deprive liberal and left-wing artists of their freedom to articulate their ideas openly. Mauldin, of course, was far from the only artist to feel the chill of the postwar cultural cold war. In the vast literature historians have devoted to the deleterious effects of McCarthyism in the late 1940s and early-to-mid-1950s, much attention has been duly paid to the hardships it imposed on writers, performers, and artists. Writers, directors, and producers working within Hollywood's film industry were particularly hard hit by HUAC's intense scrutiny and the lingering effects of the blacklist. Of concern to a number of liberal critics and intellectuals at the time were the inhibitions McCarthyism imposed not only on individuals working in Hollywood, but on satiric artists and performers as well. Arthur Schlesinger Jr., lamenting the loss of intellectual and creative freedom in the pages of the *Partisan Review* in 1953, pointed out that to "satirize the American businessman today . . . is to invite suspicion and attack; what was once satiric is now (in the business community, at least) subversive."[25] Certainly, as the careers of Bill Mauldin, Theodor Geisel, Al Capp, and Oliver Harrington suggest, satiric cartoonists were hardly immune from the climate of fear Schlesinger Jr. cited here.

Throughout World War II, Geisel (popularly known as "Dr. Seuss") supplied brilliant, whimsical cartoons pillorying fascists, the America First Committee, and enemies of Franklin Roosevelt's New Deal to the left-liberal newspaper *PM*. After the war, Geisel returned to more wide-ranging career interests, but the conservative, repressive political atmosphere taking root in the United States may have helped dampen his en-

2. For the July 1947 issue of the *New Republic,* Theodore Geisel (a.k.a. Dr. Seuss), the former *PM* political cartoonist, "came out of retirement, looked at the current American scene, and temporarily retired again." Courtesy of Dr. Seuss Enterprises, L.P.

thusiasm for political cartooning. In July 1947, the *New Republic*—the noted liberal publication that for a few years following the war carried the work of several Popular Front artists including illustrator Ben Shahn, former *New Masses* cartoonist Mischa Richter, and *PM*'s Melville Bernstein and Leo Hershfield—published Geisel's final political cartoon. In it, a befuddled Uncle Sam finds himself in a farcical, topsy-turvy world where men, women, and children point to each other wildly and charge, "Communist!" With this wry commentary on postwar anticommunist hysteria, the *New Republic* ruefully explained, Dr. Seuss had come "out of retire-ment, looked at the current American scene, and temporarily retired again" as a political cartoonist.[26]

Along with Geisel and Mauldin, Capp was perhaps the most notable and lamented casualty among satiric cartoonists during the early 1950s. Since 1934, his *Li'l Abner* strip had consistently delivered broad slaps at businessmen, politicians, and a host of American institutions. To many of Capp's fans, the character Li'l Abner was, in the words of one admirer, "a giant-killer, the declared enemy of the strong and evil, with a stone for Goliath always ready in his sling."[27] By the late 1940s, over forty million Americans regularly followed Capp's cornpone Candide in their newspa-pers, making *Li'l Abner* one of the most successful satiric strips ever to ap-pear in print.[28] But in the early 1950s, while *Li'l Abner* was still near the height of its popularity, Capp made a very public exit from the domain of satire. In a cover story he wrote for *Life* magazine in 1952, Capp explained that he was withdrawing from satiric cartooning because America had lost its "fifth freedom," the freedom to laugh. When he began receiving letters of protest from both liberals and conservatives, he claimed, "I was astounded to find it had become unpopular to laugh at any fellow Ameri-cans. In fact, when I looked around, I realized that a new kind of humorist had taken over, the humorist who kidded nothing but himself." With much fanfare and no apologies, Capp finally decided in March 1952 to "marry off" his longtime bachelor Abner. The best Capp could do in the 1950s, as he later claimed in a weak apologia, was to "sit McCarthy out and kid marriage." To "keep on with political satire—with things like Shmoos—would be to commit suicide," he argued. "[I]t's the duty of the satirist to stay alive . . . until it's safe to come out and possible to be useful again." By the time he announced his return to satire in 1963, his *Li'l Ab-ner* had begun to show signs of its age. Much to the regret of its former fans, many of whom never forgave Capp for his earlier failure of nerve, *Li'l Abner* never really regained its luster.[29]

Oliver Harrington was an African American artist based in Harlem who had contributed pithy, politically astute editorial cartoons, panel car-toons, and strips to black newspapers such as the *Amsterdam News* and *Baltimore Afro-American* since the mid-1930s. One of few black cartoonists whose work was published in the 1930s and 1940s, Harrington utilized an urban wise fool character named Bootsie to comment on the lives of Afri-can Americans and the racial injustice they faced in modern America.[30]

After securing a position (with the assistance of Eleanor Roosevelt) within the National Youth Administration, Harrington began serving a stint as art director and cartoonist for Adam Clayton Powell Jr.'s left-leaning weekly the *People's Voice*. While working for the *People's Voice*, Harrington's trenchant, at times fierce satiric attacks won the admiration of Paul Robeson, Richard Wright, Langston Hughes, and other African American writers active in the Popular Front.[31] During the war, he contributed his Bootsie panel (titled "Dark Laughter") and war correspondence to the *Pittsburgh Courier*.

Harrington was an outspoken critic of the way African American servicemen were treated in the army, and his calls for racial justice grew only more strident once the war against fascism concluded. Upon hearing the tragic story of Isaac Woodard, a black veteran who lost his eyes to police in South Carolina after challenging laws governing segregated bus transportation, Harrington accepted Walter White's invitation to direct the public relations office of the National Association for the Advancement of Colored People. As public relations director of the NAACP, Harrington assisted Orson Welles in the production of CBS radio broadcasts aimed at bringing the South Carolina policemen to justice. He also called U.S. Attorney General Tom Clark to account for not using the Department of Justice to halt the wave of postwar hate crimes perpetrated against African Americans.[32]

For his public criticism of the Truman administration, his associations within civil rights organizations, his support for left-wing intellectual and American Labor Party senate candidate W. E. B. DuBois, and, not least, his cartoon work for publications such as *Freedom*, Harrington became an object of suspicion for Clark and the FBI. When warned in 1951 that he was being investigated for his political ties, Harrington fled the United States for Paris, where he soon occupied a central position within the émigré community of left-wing, African American writers and artists. Since the FBI, the U.S. Bureau of Customs, and the Passport Division of the Department of State doggedly pursued Harrington in the early and mid-fifties and wanted him back in the United States so that he could answer for his "affiliation with the Communist movement," Harrington saw little reason to return to his country of birth. The imprisonment of his friend Benjamin J. Davis under the provisions of the Smith Act was an adequate incentive for prolonged exile. From Paris, Sweden, and then East Berlin, where he emigrated in 1961, Harrington eked out a living by contributing

artwork to various European publications. At the same time, he continued to draw his "Bootsie" cartoon for the *Pittsburgh Courier* and *Chicago
Defender.*[33]

Harrington clearly would have enjoyed an even larger audience and exercised greater influence — the type of influence he carried after the war—
had he not chosen to go into self-imposed exile. Operating on the margins
of his profession, Harrington enjoyed little access to the political and cultural institutions that might have allowed him to better showcase his considerable intelligence and talent. In the early 1970s, Harrington reflected,
"It's alright to live in Europe drawing and painting for personal satisfaction while turning out illustrations and cartoons for European publications for pork chops, but there is something missing somehow."[34] For
those African Americans who appreciated Harrington's sharp satiric
thrusts at American racism and his presence within Harlem's artistic and
intellectual community, clearly, Harrington's decision to leave the United
States was regrettable. Indeed, like other left-wing, Popular Front artists
such as Orson Welles, Charlie Chaplin, and Paul Robeson whose careers
were damaged (and in some cases destroyed) by their political commitments, Harrington was a casualty of the politically repressive climate settling over the United States in the late 1940s and early 1950s.

*   *   *

Poet Kenneth Rexroth and radio writer Reuben Ship, two other veterans
of America's marginalized Popular Front culture, certainly understood
the harm McCarthyism and America's cold war consensus culture imposed on satire and the tradition of radical humor itself. In a 1957 article
in the *Nation* titled "The Decline of American Humor," Rexroth mourned
the passing of "politically radical humor" and made special mention of
great cartoonists who once were published in the *Masses* and *New Masses.*
Lamentably, Rexroth opined, the satiric rage of Art Young and Robert Minor had been usurped by "*New Yorker* humor," humor "of, for and by the
great bulk of our population" which invariably hinges on "the whimsical
disaster[s]" that beset those who attempt to "do something as elemental
as driving a nail or mowing a lawn."[35]

Ship, a native of Montreal, began writing satirical material during the
1930s while a member of a small, traveling theatrical troupe. In the mid-
1940s he moved to Hollywood and was eventually hired by NBC to assist
in the writing of an ethnic radio sitcom titled *The Life of Riley.* He was sud-

denly fired by NBC in 1950, shortly before a colleague in the Radio Writers Guild identified him as a member of the Communist Party. Called before the House Committee on Un-American Activities in 1951, Ship proved a difficult witness. As the *New York Times* reported, Ship "vexed" Committee members when he protested the "shocking changes taking place in this country" and then began to quote Thomas Jefferson on the subject of intellectual freedom. A little more than a year later he was deported by the U.S. Immigration and Naturalization Service.[36]

Once back in Canada, Ship worked as a television scriptwriter and editor in the Toronto office of the advertising agency Young & Rubicam. His writing efforts there attracted little attention until the radio division of the Canadian Broadcasting Company broadcast his hour-long drama *The Investigator.* Originally aired on May 30, 1954, toward the end of the Army-McCarthy hearings, this program offered one of the most pointed satirical attacks aimed at Senator Joseph McCarthy during the fifties. It is little wonder that it was produced outside of the United States. Its plot—reminiscent of the brilliant 1946 British film *Stairway to Heaven* and, more obviously, Ship's painful experience with McCarthyism—concerned a nameless investigator (McCarthy) who, as a result of a plane crash, ends up "Up Here" on a temporary visa. Prior to being interviewed by the Permanent Investigating Committee on Permanent Entry, he is approached by a small faction of the Committee—among them, Titus Oates, Torquemada, and Cotton Mather—which was intent on using "the latest inquisitorial techniques" against the current Gatekeeper. With the eager assistance of the investigator, Oates and his co-conspirators oust the Gatekeeper and reopen residency hearings on "certain subversive individuals" who "have managed to infiltrate Up Here." It is when the investigator interrogates "subversives" such as Socrates and Jefferson that Ship's caricature of McCarthy turned vicious. Through a combination of double-talk, cunning, and intimidation, the investigator tramples his dignified victims and then has them deported "Down There." In the end, the investigator's co-conspirators realize he has become drunk on power. Even Satan ultimately objects to the investigator's purge because deportees such as John Milton, Martin Luther, and Karl Marx are urging inhabitants "Down There" to press for freedom and organize a union![37]

If broadcast today, *The Investigator* would undoubtedly strike the modern radio listener as hackneyed and heavy-handed. To many liberal Americans living in 1954, however, this program spoke a simple, powerful truth about the reckless dangers of McCarthyism. According to *New York Times*

Bill Mauldin and the Politics of Postwar American Satire

radio and television critic Jack Gould, *The Investigator* soon enjoyed "wide private circulation" in the United States, particularly in broadcasting and political circles. Even President Eisenhower and his cabinet were rumored to have savored Ship's ruthless depiction of McCarthy. By the end of 1954, bootleg recordings of *The Investigator* were made available to the general public and advertised by liberal critics such as Marya Mannes. Mannes, a columnist and part-time satirist for the *Reporter,* could not remember "a single political satire on current events" on American radio "since the war." Naturally, she greatly enjoyed Ship's satire and described it as "brilliantly savage."[38]

*　　*　　*

For Mannes, the fact that *The Investigator* was becoming an underground hit and was even beginning to be played on metropolitan radio stations was a sign that there might be light at the end of the tunnel. Still, there were numerous other liberal and left-liberal critics who worried publicly that the climate of fear that continued to pervade the United States through the midfifties was extinguishing the art of irreverent, satiric cartooning. Some of these critics and even a few outspoken cartoonists likewise complained that as a group America's cartoonists had succumbed to the great postwar celebration of American values and institutions and to the lures of prosperity. More astute commentators, such as Jerome Beatty Jr. of the *Saturday Review of Literature,* placed the blame for cartooning's growing timidity on the shoulders of the nation's magazine publishers. In a 1957 article for the *Saturday Review of Literature,* Beatty argued that the publishers and editors of large-circulation magazines such as the *Saturday Evening Post* and *Collier's,* afraid that they might offend readers and advertisers with material that challenged the status quo, routinely opted for the gentle, "domesticated" wit of *New Yorker*–style panel cartoons — cartoons typically devoid of topical content. Surveying typical cartoons from the nation's ten largest periodicals, Beatty concluded that "an elaborate system of institutionalized taboos . . . have destroyed the gag-cartoon's power to make any kind of realistic comment and/or funny comment on our society."[39]

Concern over the "decline" of satiric cartooning in the 1950s was more pronounced among editorial cartoonists working for newspapers than among purveyors of "gag" cartoons and comic strips. Speaking for more than a few of his colleagues, *Minneapolis Star & Tribune* editorial cartoonist Scott Long argued that he was "working . . . in a climate that is far different from anything we have known in the past." In "prosperous, insecure America," he complained, there "will be no rocking of the boat, please. No embarrassing questions. Just praise the dollar and pass the ammunition."[40] For Long and many of his colleagues, it was not just external political pressure but the changing structure of the American newspaper business itself that put editorial cartoons, traditionally prime exemplars of bold graphic satire, at risk. Indeed, in order to cut costs and increase profits, American newspapers in the 1950s increasingly subscribed to the work of nationally syndicated editorial cartoonists. As a result, a relatively small group of cartoonists served the nation's newspapers.[41]

For Long and his professional colleagues as well as a number of outside observers, syndication was just one of several factors leading to the decline of editorial cartooning in the 1950s. In their view, American editorial cartoons had begun to lose their critical bite ever since the 1940s. By the 1950s, they ruefully observed, editorial cartoons appeared to have reached their nadir. Indeed, diversity of opinion among professional editorial cartoonists appeared to have become extremely limited. Some critics complained that the symbols that editorial cartoonists routinely drew—hapless Russian pigs and bears, bewildered John Q. Publics, and Democratic donkeys—had become shopworn and clichéd. As a result, the vocabulary of editorial cartoons was incapable of communicating real criticism. Other critics charged that editorial cartoonists were merely illustrating or recycling the news, not prompting new insight. University of Wisconsin professor of journalism Henry Ladd Smith, in a widely noted 1954 article for the liberal weekly the *Saturday Review,* blamed editorial cartoonists directly for not taking advantage of the abundant opportunities for "social satire." Rather than using the cartoon as an "offensive weapon" like Thomas Nast, Art Young, and other great cartoonists of the past, Smith argued, many contemporary editorial cartoonists were only "wasting" editorial space.[42]

In response to this criticism, a cartoonist for the *Army Times* began organizing a professional organization that he hoped would help shore up the editorial cartoonists' image as tough, independent commentators. Chartered in 1957, the American Association of Editorial Cartoonists (AAEC) focused national attention on the craft of editorial cartooning and provided its overwhelmingly male membership with a valuable forum for addressing pertinent professional issues. Despite its service to the profession, however, the AAEC did little to encourage or facilitate more daring, satiric commentary. Indeed, the creation of the AAEC was more of a symptom of their profession's decline than a vehicle for its resurgence. As some cartoonists then realized, to truly revive the reputation of their profession, to recall the great American tradition of satiric cartooning and restore the cartoon's potential for social and political commentary, what AAEC members really had to do was follow the example that Bill Mauldin briefly set in the years after World War II.[43]

CHAPTER TWO

"We Shall Meet the Enemy"

HERBERT BLOCK, ROBERT OSBORN,
WALT KELLY, AND LIBERAL
CARTOONISTS' "WEAPON OF WIT"

By the early 1950s, it appeared to many liberal critics, artists, and observers that satiric cartooning in the United States was suffering from the ill effects of the country's conservative cold war culture. Since McCarthyism severely cowed liberals and, as historian Ellen Shrecker has recounted, "wiped out . . . the heart of the vibrant left-labor Popular Front that had stimulated so much social and political change in the 1930s and 1940s," it inevitably impacted American cartoonists, many of whom shared a liberal or left-liberal political bent. For these practitioners of one of the most overtly topical and political popular art forms enjoyed by the American public, the postwar Red Scare cast a dark pall and limited the cartoon's potential as a "weapon of wit."[1]

Yet although McCarthyism had a devastating impact on American cultural and intellectual life, as historians such as Shrecker, Stephen Whitfield, and others have ably demonstrated, it did not wipe out dissent altogether. While Federal Theatre Project playwright Arthur Miller vilified McCarthyism in *The Crucible* (1953), for example, director Don Siegel plotted his revenge in the science fiction thriller *Invasion of the Body Snatchers* (1956).[2] Neither did the second Red Scare entirely snuff out the critical potential of satiric cartoons, caricatures, comic strips, and illustrations. Despite the mounting evidence of editorial cartoons' decline, hard-hitting satiric cartoons were hardly absent from the American scene following Bill Mauldin's premature retirement in 1949. Even those observers who despaired over the low quantity and quality of American satiric cartooning conceded the existence of notable exceptions. British cartoonist Ronald Searle, for example, claimed in 1957 that as "bad as I think the majority of American cartoonists are, you have four or five who are probably finer than any in the world."[3]

Among the editorial cartoonists often singled out for praise were Paul Conrad of the *Denver Post* and Daniel Fitzpatrick of the *St. Louis Post-Dispatch*. These two men consistently produced cartoons that stood above the work of their colleagues. Their devastating caricatures of Senator Joseph McCarthy in the early 1950s were particularly noteworthy. One of Conrad's caricatures of McCarthy was reprinted on recall petitions that circulated throughout Wisconsin in 1954. McCarthy was reportedly so enraged by the cartoon's role in this "Joe Must Go" campaign that he sent an attorney to Denver to investigate the *Post*. McCarthy might have been similarly irked by the unflattering treatment he received from *New Yorker* cartoonist George Price in his 1951 book *Ice Cold War*. In a dramatic break from his usual work, Price here compiled a collection of caricatures—including caricatures of McCarthy, journalist Westbrook Pegler, and other red-baiters—and then juxtaposed them (with heavy irony) against quotes taken from the plays and sonnets of William Shakespeare. Fred Wright, a saxophone-playing jazzman who in 1949 became the staff artist for the United Electrical, Radio and Machine Workers of America and its *UE News,* used cartoons as sharp rejoinders to the Taft-Hartley Act, McCarthyism, and other postwar onslaughts against the American labor movement. Although class-conscious, prolabor cartooning left virtually no trace in mainstream publications in the two decades following World War II, the work of Wright and the United Auto Workers Ben Yomen circulated widely (through Federated Press syndication) in scores of local union publications. Equally significant were the pro–civil rights cartoons drawn by Bill Sanders, Clifford Baldowski, Robert York, and Tom Little—editorial cartoonists working for newspapers located in the upper South and border states—as well as the drawings and caricatures that artist Ben Shahn contributed occasionally to publications such as the *Nation*. For the *Nation* and, more memorably, the 1952 Adlai Stevenson presidential campaign (declaring, with a caricature of opposing candidate Dwight Eisenhower, "Watch Out for The Man on a White Horse!"), Shahn drew work that commented critically on America's swing toward conservative politics.[4]

While the satiric cartoons and drawings of Conrad, Wright, and Shahn could sting, their cultural influence did not compare with the work of three other cartoonists active in the early and mid-1950s: Herbert Block,

Robert Osborn, and Walt Kelly. From the pens, brushes, and grease crayons of these three liberal cartoonists came a body of work notable for its sharp critical perspective and wit. Although each of these men specialized in forms of cartooning that were markedly different in form and approach—Block worked in editorial cartoons, Osborn in caricature and cartoon illustration, and Kelly in newspaper comic strips—they resembled each other in significant respects. As a group they shared the view that cartoons and comic art in general had the ability to expose with spare, expressive economy the reality behind America's social and political ills. They also retained a strong allegiance to liberal political and social values. In their outlook toward the Soviet Union, each of them shared much in common with cold war liberals. But they also harkened back to the moral and political outlook of the New Deal. By insisting on the necessity of promoting civil liberties and racial justice, they fell in line with progressive wing of the postwar Democratic Party. And in their attempts to expose the "brutal truth" about how deception, hypocrisy, artifice, and sentimentality were creeping into American life during the 1950s, they found company with other satirists, artists, and intellectuals who later helped give shape to New Frontier and Great Society liberalism.

By focusing their attention on issues of social justice and power, these artists never lost sight of how their variety of satiric expression could be used to make straightforward, powerful moral arguments. For Jean Shepherd, the irreverent, late-night radio monologist who attracted large audiences of alienated young males along the East Coast during the mid- and late 1950s, cartoonists such as Block and Osborn were nothing less than "the last stronghold, carrying the small failing Zippo lighter of humor in America today." In the pages of the *Cartoonist,* the journal of the National Cartoonist Society (NCS), Shepherd encouraged cartoonists,

> As one who works, nay toils, in an industry that long ago gave up its sense of humor when it rejected Fred Allen and Henry Morgan . . . I can speak as one in a desert can of an ice cold martini, "We need you, boys, now more than ever before . . . Give 'em hell."[5]

It was their ability to "give 'em hell" that garnered these cartoonists the lavish praise they received from angry, frustrated liberals during the 1950s. According to Jules Feiffer, a key figure among the generation of satiric cartoonists who came of age during the late 1950s and early 1960s and who is given extended discussion in subsequent chapters, Block and his cohort played a vital role in the postwar years by reminding Americans of "the positive uses of anger . . ."[6] For Feiffer and large groups of other young, well-educated, liberal Americans, Herblock, Osborn, and Kelly provided an important cultural outlet while keeping the distinguished tradition of angry graphic satire alive during the postwar era.

*   *   *

In the opinion of a good number of editorial cartoonists active during the 1950s and early 1960s, Herbert Block (who signed his work as "Herblock") was the most skilled and influential member of their profession. To millions of other Americans who encountered his pointed, witty cartoons through the Hall Syndicate's distribution, Herblock ranked as one of the era's most incisive liberal satirists. As one critic argued in the early sixties, Herblock was the "angriest, funniest and most devastating satirist let loose on any editorial page in America." For many liberals during the early and mid-1950s, the height of the second Red Scare, Herblock stood out as one of the most important advocates for civil liberties and social justice in the United States. A Unitarian minister interviewed in 1956 by *Woman's Home Companion* spoke for many other fans of Herblock's direct, forceful cartoons by describing him as "undoubtedly the greatest preacher in America today."[7]

Like many of his fellow editorial cartoonists, Herblock was an artist whose sense of identity was closely tied to the intense, fast-paced, decidedly masculine world of print journalism. The excitement of the newspaper business lured him at an early age. As a boy growing up in Chicago, he emulated his brother, a reporter for the *Chicago Tribune*. With the encouragement of his father, a chemist and amateur cartoonist, Herblock developed a talent for drawing that was augmented through classes at the Art Institute of Chicago. This talent, coupled with his interest in journalism, eventually led him in the direction of editorial cartooning. By the summer of his sophomore year at Lake Forest College, he had decided to quit his formal education and begin working as a full-time editorial cartoonist with the *Chicago Daily News*—the paper that gave Art Young his start in cartooning several decades earlier.[8]

At the *Daily News,* Herblock occupied an office across the hall from one of Chicago's most celebrated editorial cartoonists, Vaughn Shoemaker. It was from "Shoes," who later instructed the young Bill Mauldin at the Chicago Academy of Art, that Herblock picked up on the vertical orientation, the heavy crayon shading, the clear, simple labeling, and other fundamentals of editorial cartooning that had been practiced by Shoemaker, Edmund Duffy, and Ding Darling. Herblock's progressive leaning was evident in the very first daily cartoon he produced for the *Daily News* in 1929 — a cartoon criticizing the environmental devastation caused by clear-cut logging. Herblock's cartoons became more consistently political and partisan during the early 1930s when he began working for the Newspaper Enterprise Association (NEA), a large syndicate operating out of Cleveland. In the Cleveland NEA office, surrounded by progressive columnists and editorialists, Herblock began to align himself with the political agenda of the New Deal as well as share the urgent antifascist outlook of the Popular Front. It was at this time that Herblock was beginning to understand and appreciate the demands of his unique calling. He defined this calling and his conviction as a satirist in a 1940 article for the *New York Times Magazine* in which he praised the memory of the late-nineteenth-century cartoonist Thomas Nast, a hero to Herblock from the time he had read his biography as a boy. "A cartoonist cannot be neutral," Herblock wrote of Nast, "he fights for a cause and his most powerful weapons are weapons of offense." None of Nast's followers, he added, "wielded the sword of righteousness with such crusading fervor." For the remainder of his career, Herblock's ambition was to translate the same anger and bold critical insight that Nast brought to his cartoons to modern readers.[9]

After serving as a cartoonist and publications editor in the army during the war, Herblock was hired by a struggling newspaper operating in the nation's capital, the *Washington Post*. Before long he acquired a reputation among the *Post*'s readers as a cartoonist committed to the liberal Democratic domestic agenda and the cold war foreign policy of the Truman administration.[10] In 1950, Herblock's cartoons won considerable critical praise and notoriety when they were put on display at Washington's Corcoran Gallery. Journalist Richard Rovere, reporting on the exhibition for the *New Yorker*, observed that Herblock at times "paraphrases Art Young's grim, unsettling humor" and as a result had become "possibly the country's best bet to revive an American art that can stand plenty of reviving."[11] A much larger reading public became exposed to Herblock's satiric drawings during the next decade when the prestige and circulation of the *Post* rose. By mid-1958 the *Post* and the Hall Syndicate were distributing Herblock's cartoons to 266 newspapers. At the same time, liberal periodicals such as the *New Republic* and the *Progressive* regularly reprinted Herblock's work in their pages.

Three popular cartoon anthologies Herblock produced during this period—*The Herblock Book* (1952), *Herblock's Here and Now* (1955), and *Special for Today* (1958)—provide a good sense of his prolific output during the 1950s. In addition to allowing Herblock to assemble and reprint a substantial quantity of his syndicated work, these collections afforded Herblock the opportunity to further explicate his views on domestic and foreign policy issues—views he was always forced to condense in the symbolic shorthand of his satirical cartoons. Like Bill Mauldin, Herblock enjoyed writing. "For a person who works mostly in drawings," he explained in his autobiography, "I'm fascinated and awed by the use and power of words."[12] The voice he adopted for his anthologies was plain and folksy, reminiscent of Mark Twain and Will Rogers. As with these and other American comic predecessors, Herblock's use of straight talk and simple language helped defuse what some might have considered subversive about his message. It was also well suited to the expression of traditional civic idealism that underwrote his satiric criticism. Throughout his anthologies' "free-style monologues," Herblock professed his support for a democratic public and what he regarded with reverence as "the people." In a tone reminiscent of the Popular Front democratic idealism of the 1930s he argued in *Special for Today* that it was "upon this faith [in 'the people'] that our government was founded—a faith that involves trust in each other, dedication to free inquiry, and confidence in the collective wisdom of an informed public."[13]

Herblock's belief in democratic principles prompted him to strike out repeatedly at corruption within the American political process. From his post in the nation's capital, Herblock was well positioned to observe and satirize affairs of state. At a time when American intellectuals boasted about the nation's political consensus and the smooth operation of what John Kenneth Galbraith described as "countervailing powers," Herblock's cartoons provided a corrective by illustrating the influence of moneyed interests within Washington. With a thick, bold line, clear labels, and a deft comic touch, Herblock often depicted the congressmen, government officials, and corporate lobbyists who wielded power within the federal government as overfed, duplicitous knaves on the take. As the Eisenhower administration further legitimated cooperation between American corporations and the federal agencies, Herblock warned of dangers private interests (particularly the "gas and oil interests") posed to the public good. A February 1958 Herblock cartoon, for example, pictured an elephant (the cartoon symbol of the Republican Party invented by Thomas Nast) in a three-piece suit scolding a fat-cat lobbyist wheeling a barrel full of cash ("With Continued Appreciation . . . From Your Gas and Oil Pals") into the "Administration" building. "I've Told You Fifty Times," the elephant exclaims angrily, "Not At The Front Door!"[14]

Ever the democratic idealist, Herblock argued in *The Herblock Book* that "corruption and subversion" in politics are dangerous, "but I don't know of any form of either that's more dangerous than the corruption and subversion of the democratic system itself—because when that's distorted the people don't have the full power to correct any other evils. That's why I do cartoons on some of these things that have been going on for years and that don't generally make big news."[15] In his most outspoken and impassioned anthology, *Herblock's Here and Now,* Herblock supplemented cartoons critical of Washington's obeisance to business interests with an imaginary "Business Letter" he wrote to the "Board of Directors, U.S. Policy Manufacturing Co." Speaking as a "small shareholder" who has "been with the Firm for over 45 years now," Herblock protested that "the Company" had "signed away" offshore oil properties and "our other properties, in parks, forests and public lands." "I haven't quite got it into a phrase or slogan yet," Herblock concluded with irony, "but what I have in mind is that this 'government' idea would be something for all the people."[16]

While retaining a commitment to ideals of democracy and social justice—ideals central to Progressive Era and New Deal liberalism— Herblock also devoted cartoons to concerns addressed increasingly by modern, postwar liberalism. These concerns, as defined by historian Eric Foner, included an "overriding preoccupation with civil liberties, including the right to personal privacy and the free expression of ideas, and a pluralist concern for the rights of racial and ethnic minorities."[17] Judging by the body of work he contributed in the dozen years after World War II, Herblock had an abiding interest in the fate of civil liberties in the United States. Throughout the late 1940s and early 1950s, Herblock was greatly disturbed by the hysteria of the postwar Red Scare and fretted over Americans' "dedication to free inquiry" and their right to dissent. In one brilliant June 1949 cartoon titled "Fire!" Herblock depicted a panic-driven man (labeled HYSTERIA) with a bucket of water in hand scrambling up a ladder in order to extinguish the torch held aloft by the Statue of Liberty. In other cartoons he railed against Senator Pat McCarran, his

3. "Fire!" Herblock's 1949 warning foretold the growing dangers of the postwar anticommunist movement. By permission of the Herb Block Foundation.

Internal Security Act, and his Senate Internal Security Subcommittee; FBI wiretapping and the Bureau's accumulation of secret dossiers on suspected communists; and the damage done to American foreign service and foreign policy by the loyalty programs initiated by the Truman administration.

Herblock's cartoons effectively registered the toll loyalty oaths, FBI investigations, and other elements of the second Red Scare took on Americans' psyches. In a 1948 cartoon, for example, Herblock pictured a man peering furtively out his kitchen window and whispering to his wife who is about to pour Russian dressing on the dinner salad, "Okay, Honey—Put It On." Several years later, when public criticism of the status quo might be considered "subversive" or "un-American," Herblock declared unapologetically, "I am one to criticize and have been doing it for years." "I can remember a time not so many years ago," he wrote in *Herblock's Here and Now,* "when criticism of government and jokes about public officials . . . were supposed to be good for us . . . I find it hard to believe that this stuff, which was until recently yummy . . . and sometimes even enriched with political arsenic, has now become bad bad bad, even in nontoxic form and comparatively mild doses." To combat this trend and help end the "Era of Feeling Numb," he proposed applying "a few grains of ordinary salt" and "some old-fashioned irritants" to his cartoons.[18]

Few of Herblock's satirical cartoons contained as much "salt" or pure anger as those he directed at Senator Joseph McCarthy. Herblock was an early and consistent critic of the junior senator and his red-baiting tactics. In March 1950—a month after McCarthy delivered his notorious Wheeling, West Virginia, speech identifying communists at work within the U.S. State Department—Herblock drew the cartoon that created the label "McCarthyism." Here Herblock depicted Ohio Senator Robert Taft and other complicit Republicans prodding the GOP elephant to ascend a teetering stack of tar buckets. "You Mean I'm Supposed to Stand On That?" the caption asks. For the next four years, until McCarthy's fall from grace, Herblock submitted him to rough satiric caricature. Typically, Herblock rendered the junior senator as a sinister, sleazy huckster with an unshaven face and a bucket of tar close at hand. In August 1951 Herblock depicted him with tar brush in hand and a squad of vigilante thugs in tow pursuing a pack of scurrying citizens (one of whom is identified with "Civil Rights") and government employees. A placard foisted by one of McCarthy's supporters reads, "If You Aint's For Franco and Chiang, You're Un-American." Nearby a bemused citizen scratches his head and asks Uncle Sam, "Say, What Ever Happened to 'Freedom-From-Fear'?"—a reference to one of the Four Freedoms promised by Franklin Roosevelt a decade earlier. And in a September 1952 cartoon bearing the caption "Nothing Exceeds Like Excess," Herblock pictured McCarthy at the wheel of

4. "Nothing Exceeds Like Excess," Herblock's 1952 pointed critique of Senator Joseph Mc-Carthy and the complicity of his fellow Republicans. From *Herblock: A Cartoonist's Life* (Times Books, 1998). By permission of the Herb Block Foundation.

large, leaking tar bucket truck accompanied by supporters who proclaim, "We're Against McCarthyism BUT—" and "We Believe in Decency BUT—."[19]

Cartoons like these were clearly fed by a sense of anger, but they were likewise nurtured by Herblock's civic idealism and reverence for democratic principles. Referring to McCarthy and other "Fear Dealers," Herblock wrote in 1952,

Well, I think what's been going on in this country has been a kind of unorganized Un-American Revolution, in which the smear-bucket brigade has been trying to sack our institutions while hollering at us to look farther and farther under the bed for subversives . . . I think we ought to award the badge of Un-Americanism to some of those who have tried so hard to pin it on others. They've earned it, and it's time we let 'em have it.[20]

The effect these cartoons and caricatures had on the American public is difficult to gauge. Historian Roger Butterfield was clearly exaggerating when he wrote in 1956 that Herblock's cartoons "helped end the menace of McCarthy, just as surely as [Thomas] Nast's tiger cartoons killed off Boss Tweed."[21] Nevertheless, Herblock's wickedly funny cartoons clearly provided many liberal Americans with a small measure of relief. If nothing else, they, like Edward R. Murrow's famous March 9, 1954, "See It Now" television broadcast, assured Americans that McCarthy's reckless behavior was not escaping critical scrutiny, that his worst excesses would not go unchecked. For Herblock, drawing these cartoons also served a valuable personal end. As he remembers in his memoir, "there was real pleasure in having an outlet for my anger [over McCarthyism] instead of imploding with it."[22]

Herblock's cartoons were almost equally severe in their depictions of the man he identified at the head of the "Dickey front" of anti-Communism, Vice President Richard Nixon. Herblock issued his first swipes at Nixon when he was a Congressional member of HUAC in the late 1940s. Herblock reviled the roughshod tactics of HUAC. In an October 1947 cartoon, he pictured two HUAC members in an automobile trampling a crowd of innocent bystanders. "It's Okay," one of the two men explains to a woman dodging out of their way, "We're Hunting Communists." The next year Herblock depicted Nixon and two HUAC colleagues dressed in Puritan garb exclaiming, "We Got To Burn The Evil Spirits Out Of Her" as they hurriedly heaped a pile of logs beneath the chained torso of Lady Liberty.[23] In subsequent cartoons Nixon appeared unshaven and dirty, often spattered with the tar that Herblock saw him hurl freely at others.

In both appearance and in gesture Herblock associated Vice President Nixon with Joseph McCarthy's worst excesses. In an October 1954 cartoon Herblock pictured Nixon lunging for a tar brush from Joseph McCarthy's outstretched hand. And in one of the most memorable and controversial cartoons Herblock drew for the fall campaign season of 1954, Nixon emerges from a city sewer hole to greet his enthusiastic supporters.

"We Shall Meet the Enemy"

5. "Here He Comes Now." In this 1954 cartoon, Herblock took delight in caricaturing Vice President Richard Nixon, the head of domestic anticommunism's "Dickey Front." By permission of the Herb Block Foundation.

Subsequent cartoons attacked what Herblock identified as Nixon's inauthentic, chameleon-like character. In a February 1956 cartoon, for example, Nixon muses, "Let's See—What'll I Wear Today?" while peering into a closet full of different guises. Taken together, Herblock's caricatures of Nixon were some of the most damaging images of the vice president to circulate publicly in the 1950s. Their effect did not escape the notice of the thin-skinned politician; Nixon was reportedly so upset by Herblock's jibes that he canceled his subscription to the *Washington Post.* Years later, Nixon conceded in an interview that Herblock's caricatures "got to me."[24]

Herblock's satiric treatment of President Dwight Eisenhower was more restrained, although hardly benign. Unlike the vast majority of editorial cartoonists in the 1950s, Herblock did not merely recycle the image liberals bequeathed Eisenhower—that of an affable, grandfatherly, golf-playing chief of state. Rather, Herblock pictured the popular president as an aloof clown whose neglect of the office had serious, negative consequences. Particularly when it came to checking McCarthy's excesses and handling the problem of racial integration, Herblock considered Eisenhower's lack of leadership inexcusable. In the cartoon he drew for syndication on March 4, 1954, Herblock pictured President Eisenhower confronting Senator McCarthy (wielding a bloody meat cleaver) with a feather drawn from his sheath. "Have A Care, Sir," the president responds feebly. It is clear that Herblock was frustrated and angered by Eisenhower's failure to respond to America's growing racial crisis. Herblock delivered one of his simplest, sharpest thrusts at President Eisenhower in an April 3, 1956, cartoon. The president, wearing the uniform of a fire chief

6. "The Helicopter Era." Hardly the grandfatherly caretaker of a nation blessed with affluence and consensus, Herblock's Eisenhower was an aloof clown dangerously out of touch with the pressing issues of the day. By permission of the Herb Block Foundation.

"We Shall Meet the Enemy"

and a blank, Daddy Warbucks–type expression, mutters, "Tsk Tsk— Somebody Should Do Something About That" to Uncle Sam as a "Civil Rights Crisis" burns uncontrollably in the near distance. Hardly the head of state whom some historians credit for exercising a "hidden hand" in domestic policy matters, Herblock's Eisenhower was inept and dangerously out of touch.[25]

Because of his longstanding interest in international affairs and the enormous stakes involved in the burgeoning cold war, Herblock subjected the Eisenhower administration's foreign policy and nuclear diplomacy to sustained satiric scrutiny throughout the 1950s. No other figure in the administration featured more prominently in Herblock's cartoons than Secretary of State John Foster Dulles, a man of stern countenance variously depicted as a "One-Man State Department," a peddler of "Frozen Attitudes," dispenser of both fright-inducing medicine and "Happiness Pills." Dulles, in Herblock's view, not only exacerbated the United States' misguided policy toward Asia (and its support of Chiang Kai-shek in particular), but his hard-lined diplomatic strategy toward the Soviets was dangerously provocative. Herblock registered his concern over Dulles's "brinkmanship" in a January 1956 cartoon. Here Dulles, dressed in a Superman outfit, pushes Uncle Sam to the edge of a cliff while issuing a weak assurance: "Don't Be Afraid—I Can Always Pull You Back." In other cartoons, Herblock lambasted foreign policy that Dulles, Secretary of Defense Charles Wilson, and others within the Eisenhower administration pursued—a foreign policy that, in the name of "realism," ignored the interests of people around the world who the United States pledged to protect. "By now I'm fed up to here," Herblock wrote in 1952, "with the kind of talk about 'national self-interest' which seems to imply that any policies that don't kick our neighbors in the teeth must be for selling our country down the river."[26]

Although Herblock consistently warned against the dangers of heightening tensions with the Soviet Union, he by no means refrained from satirizing Joseph Stalin, Nikita Khrushchev, and officials within the Kremlin. In this way, Herblock's often pointed caricatures and cartoons dovetailed with the outlook shared by most mainstream, anticommunist Democrats and cold war intellectuals. By condemning and at the same time legitimating elements of the cold war, Herblock's thinking appears paradoxical, ambivalent, or confused. Yet it is important to note that Herblock, as with the other liberal cartoonists and satirists considered here, may have been motivated by a pragmatic rationalization: in order to allow himself the opportunity to express his other, wide-ranging opinions, he would ridicule Stalin, Khrushchev, and other communist scapegoats and thus prove himself a "rational," "responsible," "clearheaded" commentator. In many cartoons throughout the late 1940s and 1950s, Herblock mocked the machinations of repressive communist regimes as well as the personal failings of leaders such as Khrushchev. Herblock's satirical criticisms of Stalin's perfidy were so good, in fact, that the U.S. State Department in the early 1950s distributed millions of them throughout the world in a pamphlet titled *Herblock Looks at Communism*.[27]

Even though Herblock presented himself as a "realist" on the cold war, he, like Bill Mauldin, nevertheless ran afoul of the zealots and crusaders propelling the anticommunist movement. For his unstinting satiric criticism of McCarthy, Nixon, and Eisenhower, Herblock had already earned the enmity of many American conservatives. His political enemies included Senator Pat McCarran, who attempted to excise $10 million from a State Department appropriation because of its publication of *Herblock Looks at Communism*. Several years later, a conservative congressman together with the American Legion convinced the CBS television network not to broadcast a series of fifteen-minute television programs (funded by the liberal Fund for the Republic) that were to feature Herblock as a humorous political commentator.[28] Far more numerous were the angry readers who bristled at Herblock's criticisms of Republican politicians and the domestic cold war security apparatus. It is impossible to know what kind of letters Herblock's opponents wrote to the local newspapers who carried his work in syndication. There is a good chance that they resembled the letters one chagrined newspaper reader wrote FBI chief J. Edgar Hoover in June 1957. Herblock "is striving to shake public opinion in favor of acts that our different government departments enact from time-to-time, against the Communist party," the correspondent complained. "He is trying, in his subtle manner, to create opposition to our use of the H-bombs, while Russia goes merrily on her way." "This bird needs looking into," this crackpot conservative urged. "I would at least have the fun of throwing him in the can."[29]

Although Herblock never made it "in the can" and never merited an official, full-scale FBI investigation, he was the subject of J. Edgar Hoover's persistent scrutiny. Throughout the 1950s, Hoover and FBI agents compiled a dossier on Herblock that included a reference to a private phone conversation under surveillance in which suspected individuals expressed admiration for the cartoonist's work. The Herblock file also contains a

"We Shall Meet the Enemy"

small collection of cartoons, most of them critical of Hoover and the FBI's abuse of authority. Of particular note is a July 1957 cartoon in which a congressman tramples on a citizen (a "Prayer Rug") while bowing before a godlike Hoover, who sits high atop a file cabinet. Earlier, Herblock had been assisted by Hoover and the FBI when he received anonymous, violent threats in response to his McCarthy caricatures. Judging by the "Prayer Rug" cartoon and others lambasting FBI wiretapping, Herblock did not believe he owed Hoover any favors. To a group of Cleveland journalists in 1957 Herblock called Hoover "a police chief so carried away by his own power that he attacks all who disagree with him." Hoover, for his part, appeared so rattled by Herblock's satiric pokes that he had an agent read his 1957 anthology *Special for Today* and then write a six-page report noting instances of "biting sarcasm" made at his expense.[30]

Had Herblock not earned recognition for his caustic cartoons on Soviet-style Communism, had he been a greater champion of organized labor or taken more radical stances on other issues, the FBI might have identified and treated him as something other than what he was — a member of what the FBI identified as the "liberal faction" of the *Washington Post*. On most issues, Herblock was indeed a committed liberal. He identified himself with the Democratic Party and steadfastly supported its two-time presidential candidate Adlai Stevenson. In 1952 he even temporarily ceased cartooning for the *Washington Post* when its management chose to back Dwight Eisenhower. Yet his support of Stevenson and other Democrats was hardly unqualified. Throughout the fifties he chided congressional Democrats for failing to rise above their Republican opponents. He was particularly frustrated by Democrats' inability to counter conservatives' attacks. "In their efforts to avoid criticism," he argued in the *New Republic,* many Democrats "have leaned over backward so far that they have fallen flat on their responsibilities." As a progressive, New Deal liberal, Herblock was unimpressed by Democratic compromise and "middle-of-the-road" solutions. The middle of the road, he argued, was often "the worst possible place to be. And in a choice between right and wrong, I think something better than a middle-of-the-road policy is needed."[31]

In the end, Herblock's ultimate fealty was to truth. Throughout his career, he considered himself a journalist as much as a cartoonist, and he was fond of reminding reporters and others in the newspaper business that their primary responsibility was to act as "watchdogs," to speak truth to power. Whether created to reveal the dangers of nuclear arms or the threats McCarthyism posed to Americans' civil liberties, Herblock's satiric cartoons used irony and comic exaggeration in order to jolt Americans awake from their slumber during the Eisenhower siesta. Their ultimate goal, as Herblock viewed them, was to point out hidden realities, to separate "truth" from the lies suffocating fifties America. "Truth," Herblock argued with a bluster and bravado characteristic of many postwar liberal satirists, is a "good weapon . . . for those who are willing to use it." Through "truth," Herblock hoped to begin "filtering out" from cold war America what he called "HP2x" — the "Miracle Ingredient . . . (Hocuspocus twice multiplied)." "HP2x," he complained in 1955, "performs a slick-as-a-whistle conversion of ordinary hogwash into rich sudsy stuff which produces an authentic-looking luster, sparkling with simulated sincerity. I don't like it, and . . . I object when the product runs a poor second to the packaging, and when the appearance of quality or sincerity takes the place of quality and sincerity." [32]

*   *   *

Robert Osborn, one of the most influential satiric illustrators working in the 1950s, shared Herblock's aversion for sham and pretense. In a tribute to his friend and fellow cartoonist for the *New Republic* in 1956, Osborn singled out Herblock's ability to delineate the "unvarnished truth" every day of the week in newspapers around the country. "This is a great relief to a LOT of people," Osborn wrote. "We are so hag-ridden by the singing Hucksters," "so surfeited with counterfeit presentations — from car design to the fake eroticism of whispered weather reports — that Herblock affects all of us about the way a sound buoy affects the fog-bound sailor. We shout for JOY!" Herblock, Osborn continued, used his pen as a "saber or needle, stabbing with deadly precision at sham, cheating, bombast, greed, complacency and any organized folly." [33]

Like Herblock, Osborn acquired the moral convictions that became integral to his satiric cartooning when he was young. Osborn also grew up in the Midwest, though far removed from Herblock's Chicago neighborhood. As the son of a prosperous lumberman, Osborn was raised in the mill town of Oshkosh, Wisconsin. It was in his comfortable childhood, he remembered in his autobiography, that he acquired a taste for simplicity, an appreciation of what he termed the seasons' "gentle moments," and a lifelong devotion to nature and rural life. From an early age, Osborn's mother nurtured his imagination and encouraged him to develop his native drawing talent. Overweight and unathletic, he emulated his hero Charlie Chaplin and began capturing people's attention through humor. Like Bill Mauldin and Herblock, Osborn discovered as a boy how to combine his drawing skill and love of humor into cartooning. As a pupil he contributed primitive political cartoons (such as one supporting the League of Nations' execution of "Autocracy") for his school's annual publication, and he even began submitting cartoons and drawings to *Life,* the popular humor magazine. He continued to hone his talent for cartooning while working for the student newspaper at the University of Wisconsin. When he transferred to Yale University after his freshman year, he shifted his attention away from cartooning and set his sights on becoming a painter like the great Paul Cézanne, whose work he had admired while on visits to the Chicago Art Institute.[34]

Though trying hard to concentrate on becoming a "serious" artist, Osborn could never shake his love of humorous cartooning. While at Yale in the mid-1920s, he collaborated with his classmate and friend Dwight Macdonald on the campus humor magazine, the *Yale Record.* He contributed political cartoons for the *New Haven Register* and even began submitting single-panel cartoons to Harold Ross at the *New Yorker.* Ross encouraged Osborn to devote himself to gag cartooning, but Osborn in the end decided to deny his native talent and instead pursue a more respectable career path as a professional painter. For a decade following his graduation from Yale, Osborn spent much of his time training and working in Europe. Unfortunately, his artwork brought him more frustration than success. By the time he finally decided to return to the United States in the late 1930s he was thoroughly discouraged, in poor health, and, as he later remembered, "slowly coming apart within." In desperation, he followed the advice of a close female friend and wrote the Swiss psychiatrist Carl Jung for help. Jung's three-page reply apparently provided Osborn with some solace and a much-needed sense of direction. As Osborn later wrote his friend Lewis Mumford, his correspondence with Jung had finally forced him to "drop all pretense" and admit "with palms up to any dagger wound of Reality . . . the whole tenor of my life and feelings . . . To release To open out To seem real again . . . AND my life once again became SIMPLE." In order for him to achieve psychological balance and "seem real again," Osborn realized in the late 1930s that he had to abandon his hopes of becoming a successful painter and instead concentrate on the skill that brought him satisfaction and recognition. On one wall of his apartment

Osborn resolved in big letters, "Look into becoming a GREAT cartoonist."[35]

Successful sales of three humorous cartoon books he produced shortly after his return to the United States—*How to Shoot Ducks* (1939), *How to Shoot Quail* (1939), and *How to Catch Trout* (1939)—confirmed Osborn's talent for drawing spare, expressive, entertaining cartoons. Osborn's drawing talent would also afford him the opportunity to contribute to the war against fascism. Living in Europe in the 1930s Osborn witnessed the rise of fascism firsthand. The sight of Adolf Hitler at a Nazi rally in the mid-1930s so unnerved Osborn that he shortly thereafter attempted to join Spanish Republican troops fighting General Francisco Franco. Several years later, Osborn volunteered to serve in the Canadian Royal Air Force. On both occasions he was turned down because of a recurring duodenal ulcer. When the United States went to war, the navy was willing to overlook Osborn's medical ailment and enlist his services as a cartoonist within its Bureau of Aeronautics. At a desk next to his Bureau colleague Edward Steichen, Osborn poured out several thousand cartoon training manuals and posters for aviators and mechanics. The characters Osborn developed for these instructional materials, including the dangerously inattentive pilot named Dilbert, became widely recognized in and out of the navy. In addition to bolstering Osborn's reputation as a cartoonist, his work for the navy greatly influenced his emerging style. Forced to produce a large number of cartoons quickly, he developed a swift, simple line, which conveyed both motion and feeling very effectively. "What I discovered in the Navy," Osborn later wrote, "was that I had an ability to quickly comprehend a problem, organize its components, and then produce the drawings that explained what needed to be known."[36] Marked by its fluidity and linear simplicity, the distinctive style of drawing that Osborn perfected while in the navy stretched the traditional boundaries of cartooning (Osborn himself preferred to be called a "drawer" rather than a "cartoonist") and would soon become widely imitated by American illustrators.

Osborn's wartime experience influenced the subject matter as well as the technique of his future drawing. While touring the Pacific theater obtaining information for his cartoon work, Osborn encountered the horrors of war firsthand. On the deck of an aircraft carrier he witnessed the pilot who had taught him to fly go down with his wounded plane at sea. As "we all watched," he remembered four decades later, "he simply flew away, leaving the task force and his friends continuing on into the dusk of that alien sea. I cannot resolve this image in my mind even today: the view of a young man departing to death." This and other experiences with war and the military prompted Osborn to draw the first of what would become many satiric cartoons critical of war and the military. Assembled in a collection he titled *War Is No Damn Good!* (1946)—the title inspired, no doubt, from William Steig's well-known, cynical cartoon commentary on mankind, "People Are No Damn Good" (1942)—these simple cartoons and drawings attempted to depict what Osborn called the "miseries" of warfare. Several cartoons were explicitly critical of the callous authority exercised by military commanders and politicians and therefore betrayed an irreverent attitude somewhat reminiscent of Bill Mauldin's wartime cartoons. The book's most memorable drawing, a skull-shaped mushroom cloud titled "Atom Bomb," appeared on the last page. Drawn less than two weeks after the bombing of Hiroshima, it grimly warned of future wars' possible consequences. In the opinion of critic Steven Heller, *War Is No Damn Good!* was a milestone in the history of American cartoon art. The "first antiwar book of the nuclear age," Heller suggests, *War Is No Damn Good!* recalled the nightmarish vision of Otto Dix, George Grosz, and Francisco de Goya. With "Atom Bomb" in particular, Osborn approximated the stark expressiveness and fierceness of Mexican illustrator José Guadalupe Posada, an artist whom Osborn greatly admired.[37]

As *War Is No Damn Good!* confirmed, cartoons and drawings had become the vehicles through which Osborn could best articulate his moral convictions. Like Mauldin and Herblock, however, he realized that opportunities for pursuing a career in satiric cartooning in postwar America were limited. Addressing what he called the "emasculation of American humor" in a 1957 issue of the *Saturday Review,* Osborn argued that "over here . . . we [American cartoonists] tend to try to please everyone, to try not to hurt anyone's feelings. But the implication of this is that we want everyone to conform to a general pattern: the principle of being nice to everybody is a kind of insult to the human race." Osborn decided in the early 1950s to go against the prevailing trends in American cartooning and not play it safe. He resolved to "speak clearly with pictures" and exercise his "comic impulse"—an impulse he defined as "basically poetic-rhapsodic—radiant & orgiastic and supremely disdainful."[38]

Throughout the 1950s and early 1960s Osborn managed to escape the pressures of syndicated cartooning and contribute his work to magazines and book publishers on a freelance basis. Fortunately for Osborn, editors

such as the *New Republic*'s Michael Straight and *Harper's* Russell Lynes became admirers of the distinctively simple, yet effective line rendered by
his charcoal pencil. Lynes, an irreverent and witty liberal social commentator who in *Surfeit of Honey* (1957) famously catalogued America's debilitating drift toward comfort and conformity, recognized the unusual
power of *War Is No Damn Good!* With this book, Lynes later wrote, Osborn
had become "something a good deal more deadly" than a cartoonist. "He
had become," he said of his friend Osborn, "one of the most furious
satirists of our time. In his hand a pencil had become a bull whip with
which he struck out at pompousness and pretension, at human waste and
indignity, at loss of individual identity, and at all kinds of simpering self-
satisfaction."[39]

With the help of editors like Lynes, Osborn's satiric cartoons and illustrations began appearing in a wide variety of publications in the 1950s, including *Life, Harper's,* the *Reporter, Esquire, Horizon, Fortune,* and the *New
Republic.* During this heyday of magazine and book illustration, Osborn's
simple, modern graphic technique was in great demand. He became the
illustrator of choice for writers of parody, satire, and liberal social criticism. To magazine articles and books written by Dwight Macdonald,
Walter Goodman, S. J. Perelman, A. C. Spectorsky, John Keats, Marya
Mannes, Eve Meriam, Peter Blake, C. N. Parkinson, and Russell Lynes,
Osborn's expressive cartoons served as the perfect complement. In the
opinion of cartoonist Garry Trudeau, Osborn's cartoons bore a kind of
critical insight into contemporary life unmatched by any contemporary. "No finer interpreter of mores and manners," Trudeau has argued,
"no deadlier chronicler of genius and grace, was working in American
graphic arts."[40]

Osborn's boldest satiric cartoons found two outlets during the 1950s,
the *New Republic* and two self-illustrated books—*Low & Inside* (1953) and
Osborn on Leisure (1956). It was in the liberal journal the *New Republic* in
particular that Osborn returned to concerns that he had outlined earlier
in *War Is No Damn Good!* Osborn contributed cartoons to the *New Republic* that warned against the outbreak of hostilities between the world's
superpowers. To some extent, Osborn, a man who shared the period's
obsession with Freudian psychology, viewed the outgrowth of tensions
between the United States and the USSR during the cold war as a manifestation of mankind's innate aggressive instincts. He made this plain in
the drawings and hand-lettered text he supplied for *Low & Inside,* a book
devoted to elucidating what Osborn understood as the "steady plight of

MAN." Osborn joined Herblock in ridiculing the machinations of the Soviets, but the American government and Eisenhower administrations in particular were more consistent targets of his satire. In his first cartoons for the *New Republic,* submitted at the dawn of the cold war when the journal reflected the outlook of progressive Democrat Henry Wallace, Osborn pictured Winston Churchill as a jack-in-the-box gesticulating wildly at Fulton, Missouri (the site where he had declared that an "iron curtain" had descended on the East), and an American, clad in armor and kneeling in prayer, with the caption "Only We Have the Bomb."[41] In later years, Osborn singled out Secretary of State John Foster Dulles in satiric cartoons. Osborn pictured Dulles as a man in a black frock coat poised as a bomber plane ("Dulles flies NOW . . . *You* pay later!") or stiff, cobwebbed statue ("No Man Is An Island Entire Of Itself"). Possessed with a sour and reckless sense of self-righteousness, Osborn's Dulles in an October 1956 spread walks a tightrope while clumsily balancing bags of money, a gun, and a club. "Dulles," the caption reads, "The Threat of Force . . . The Lure of Dollars."[42]

In many of these cartoons Osborn pictured President Dwight Eisenhower as ineffectual junior partner carried in tow, as if a child, by his Secretary of State. Like Herblock, Osborn was quick to associate the president with the game of golf (often picturing Eisenhower's head itself as a dimpled golf ball) as a way of highlighting his connections to moneyed interests and his perceived dereliction of duty. During the election season of 1956 in particular, Osborn hit hard at Eisenhower, his wealthy Wall Street supporters within the Republican Party, and his vice president, Richard Nixon. For covers of *Harper's* and the *New Republic* in 1955 and 1956, Osborn had already hinted at Nixon's dark, secret self by stripping him of facial features. For a special illustrated feature, "Osborn Views the Campaign," published in the October 15, 1956, issue of the *New Republic,* Osborn pictured Nixon and Eisenhower in a boxing ring against their beefed-up opponent Adlai Stevenson. When Eisenhower asks whether Stevenson has "put on quite a lot of weight since the last fight?" his running mate responds, "I'd better get the smear brush!" In an adjoining cartoon, Nixon intones, "And . . . *This* time we're going to DO LOTS for schools & the Aged, & Farmers & Small Business in the next four years . . . maybe . . . & Hogs right Now . . . 'till Election—honest!!!"[43]

The only other Republican politician to receive more of Osborn's contempt than Richard Nixon in the 1950s was Joseph McCarthy. When Osborn attempted to caricature his fellow Wisconsinite in the early 1950s,

7. During the climax of the 1954 Army-McCarthy hearings, Robert Osborn contributed fierce caricatures of his fellow Wisconsinite to the *New Republic*. By permission of the Osborn family.

his emotions, he later remembered, "simply couldn't be brought under usable control." When he illustrated Richard Rovere's article "The Adventures of Cohn and Schine" for the *Reporter* in July 1953, he rendered a slightly simian McCarthy in a robe with a dagger at his side. A year later, when *New Republic* editor Michael Straight asked Osborn for a drawing to illustrate his article "The Fanaticism of Joe McCarthy," Osborn depicted McCarthy as a thick-browed Neanderthal with a menacing sneer and razor sharp teeth. This proved a bit too strong for Straight, who opted instead for drawings of McCarthy as a wildly flailing, hydra-headed beast and, for this issue's cover, a man with slightly effeminate features.[44]

Osborn's uniquely abstract, expressive technique was particularly well adapted to criticize the climate of fear and repression that McCarthy had helped create. In *Low & Inside* Osborn alluded darkly to the Red Scare's menace in a pair of drawings captioned "spectre of suspicion" and the "censorship of ideas." Later, when asked to illustrate Michael Straight's *Trial by Television* for Beacon Press, Osborn drew "Silence Dissenters,"

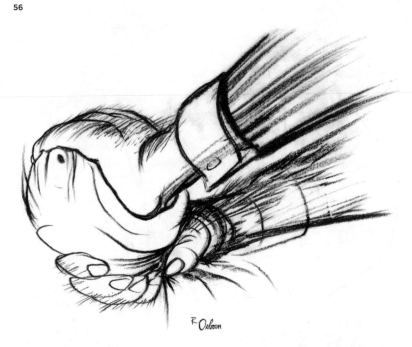

8. "Silence Dissenters," Robert Osborn's commentary on McCarthyism's suppression of civil liberties. Library of Congress, Prints & Photographs Division, Caroline and Erwin Swann Collection of Caricature & Cartoon, LC-DIG-ppmsca-07747. By permission of the Osborn family.

perhaps the most forceful graphic indictment of the anticommunists' attack on civil liberties to come out of the McCarthy era. Here Osborn depicted a hand of an anonymous man clutching the throat of a dissenter while the palm of his other hand presses hard against his victim's mouth.[45]

Osborn's depiction of free speech violently gagged conveys brilliantly a sense of motion as well as Osborn's intense moral repulsion against McCarthyism. It serves as a prime example of Osborn's unique ability to translate emotion, and in this case a palpable sense of anger, into a simple cartoon or drawing. As even his admirers would admit, Osborn's satiric drawings often lacked subtlety. But Osborn's ability to distill moral outrage into a simple line was unmatched. "The one thing I think I may do," Osborn claimed in 1958, "is the direct and easy release of the unconscious and its image, and then having seen the feeling—and knowing it—I try to fix it simply and sincerely." In Osborn's hands, cartoons emerged with a brooding fury. They became "so alive," Osborn's friend Robert Motherwell later commented, "that they seemed to writhe on the page with an uninhibited energy." They were often expressions of raw, spontaneous, unconscious emotion. "I draw what I feel," Osborn once explained, "it is as simple as that, and the stronger the feeling the better the picture. The drawings I like best seem to come right out of my unconscious—full-blown and no changes made—and they are, of course, what I am." With a visceral power rare in comic art, Osborn succeeded in producing what one admirer appropriately labeled "tornadoes of personal protest."[46] Like Bill Mauldin and Herblock, Osborn helped preserve the tradition of American graphic satire during the 1950s and demonstrated how the cartoon, simple and clear in outline, could harness moral outrage and anger.

*　　*　　*

The moral force behind Osborn's satiric cartoons appealed greatly to Walt Kelly, the creator of the syndicated *Pogo* newspaper comic strip. Reporting on the field of cartooning in 1959, Kelly praised Osborn's work for having the "imagery and symbolic terrorism of [William] Blake." This was a compliment Kelly paid to few of his contemporaries. With the exception of Osborn, Herblock, and a few other cartoonists, in fact, Kelly considered most of his colleagues timorous and overly cautious. For a time in the early 1950s he clearly understood the reasons for their timidity. In an article he contributed to the *New York Times Book Review* in 1952 titled "A Crying Need for the Cleansing Lash of Laughter," he claimed that the "true humorist has found it well nigh impossible to laugh . . . while peering over his shoulder." Those "few who sense a few cracks in the masterpiece called Man," he argued, "are intimidated by the perfectionists into quiet thumbsucking."[47]

Although he recognized the climate of fear in which cartoonists operated during the postwar years, Kelly nevertheless believed that the "true humorist[s]" must vigorously search "for the hidden absurdities, the implicit pomposities, and . . . [put] the bright light of daytime on them." Privately, Kelly expressed disappointment over the retreat his boyhood friend and fellow comic strip artist Al Capp made during the 1950s. To an assistant of the cartoonist Charles Schulz, Kelly privately complained that Capp was "looking over his shoulder and breathing hard." "Not me," Kelly continued. "I never look back OR front. I run blind. I'm my own man." In a 1958 issue of the *Progressive,* Kelly admonished his colleagues: "With very few exceptions the cartoonists of this country should be ashamed of themselves. While a man named Herbert Block . . . runs the

9. "The true humorist has found it well nigh impossible to laugh while peering back, over his shoulder." Walt Kelly's illustration for his 1952 *New York Times Book Review* article proclaiming "A Crying Need for the Cleansing Lash of Laughter." © 2006 Okefenokee Glee & Perloo, Inc. Used by permission.

broken field practically unaided, slashing the enemy . . . most of the rest of us are sitting on the sidelines resting." "Many of us," he continued, "eke out a slender but comfortable living gratifying our egos by squeaking, for peanuts, the safe message that all is right with the world which none of us created and few of us deplore." Cartoonists "who bark at the contemporary," he argued earlier in the *Saturday Review,* "are too often toothless. And without the proper dental equipment, it is hard to understand how anyone can bite off or chew, much less digest, the real meat of the day." True humor or satire, Kelly maintained in an interview, was a mode of expression ideally suited for "social comment." How "are you going to have humor without [it]?" he asked. "The only thing left is slapstick, and that gets tiresome quickly."[48]

Kelly argued repeatedly throughout the 1950s that cartoonists ought to be well-read and "subversive" and that they should act as "watchdog[s]" for society. Humorists in general, he claimed, "must be relentless and ruthless . . . quick of mind, light of hand, and fleet of foot." Like his fellow liberal satirists, Kelly believed humor could help see through and unmask the conservative opposition. The "satirist or humorist—as opposed to a jokester—is a liberal," Kelly remarked in 1963, "against all the redundancies and stupid conservatism of the big landowners. To be a real humorist you must have skirted the edges of poverty. You must be able to look at the entrenched and say we don't like those guys."[49]

Together with Mauldin, Herblock, and Osborn, Kelly also drew from the heroic, male-centered discourse of authenticity in order to delineate satire's critical objectives. In Kelly's opinion, satire (or as he occasionally labeled it, "true humor") was one of the most effective vehicles for communicating the "truth" and conveying the "real." As opposed to the "gags" and the "wisecracks" which, as he noted, Americans take great pride in producing, "true humor" is "something that clears the air" and "makes life more real . . ." In a revealing twelve-page, unpublished essay on the mechanics of humor and his *Pogo* strip, Kelly argued that the expression of "truth" lies at the root of humor. The "difference between entertainment and true humor," Kelly claimed, "is the difference between the streetwalker and the wife." The "closer [humor] comes to expressing the truth," he claimed, "the more worthwhile becomes the medium" of comic expression.[50]

In significant respects, Kelly viewed cartooning as a species of news reporting. On several occasions he explained that the key to cartoons' power was their ability to pursue, capture, and then communicate ideas.

Like his good friend Herb Block and Bill Mauldin, in fact, Kelly strongly identified with reporters and the world of print journalism. Lecturing audiences across the country in the 1950s, he repeatedly lauded the press as one of the few remaining heroic voices of freedom in the world. He considered the newspaper and its comics and editorial pages in particular some of the few remaining venues for honest, forthright expression. Nearly all of his best friends were reporters and editors, and he was often seen with them inhabiting Costello's, Moriarty's and other watering holes popular with New York's publishing world. It was in the thoroughly masculine milieu of print journalism that Kelly, like most editorial cartoonists, felt most at home.[51]

Kelly's love of newspapers began when he was a child. As he proudly claimed later in life, he grew up in a multiethnic, working-class neighborhood of Bridgeport, Connecticut, the son of a theatrical scene painter. Like Bill Mauldin, Herblock, and Robert Osborn, Kelly developed a skill and affection for cartooning at an early age and first published his work in school publications. As a teenager, he began reporting and, later, cartooning for his hometown paper, the *Bridgeport Post*. After brief stints as a caseworker for the Welfare Department and a laborer at a local undergarments factory, he began working full time in the *Post*'s art department. "When it eventually dawned on the young that the old conservatism, the old Horatio Alger formula, was not operative any longer," he remembered years later, "many of us became the stuff of the New Deal." While at the *Post* in the early 1930s, he even drew cartoons in support of Bridgeport's socialist candidate for mayor. In 1935 he moved to California and began work at the Walt Disney Studio. It was in the intense and highly productive atmosphere of the Disney "factory" that he mastered the techniques of cartooning and sequential narrative. He remained at the Disney studio until the bitter, nine-week strike there in 1941 forced him "through a picket line," he later wrote (in customary third person), and "back to New York with his coat tails smoking." Though Kelly was always very cagey about his politics, it is clear that the hard-line, antilabor, red-baiting stance that the Disney management adopted toward the studio unions was a searing experience for Kelly (and a number of other very talented colleagues)—an experience that helped shaped his liberal outlook.[52]

Back east in the early 1940s, Kelly contributed work to several large comic book companies and, after the war broke out, helped illustrate foreign language guides for the U.S. Army Education Branch. He also began to develop a new comic feature relating the swampland adventures of an

African American child named Bumbazine, an alligator named Albert, and a possum character named Pogo. Throughout this period he maintained close ties to New York newspapers. In 1948 he joined the staff of *PM,* which was succeeded shortly thereafter by the *New York Star.* At the *Star,* Kelly served as art director and drew editorial cartoons (including several that supported an interracial hospital) reflecting the newspaper's left-liberal, prolabor politics. Throughout the summer and fall of 1948 Kelly took aim at the intensifying anticommunist crusade by caricaturing HUAC Chairman J. Parnell Thomas as a hapless Sherlock Holmes who is accompanied by a wiretapping bloodhound labeled "Investigating Committee." His most notorious cartoons from that year depicted New York governor and Republican presidential candidate Thomas Dewey as a "Mechanical Man." Like Bill Mauldin, whom he hired to join the staff of the *Star* in 1948, Kelly was forced to quit editorial cartooning when the newspaper finally folded in 1949. Throughout the early 1950s Kelly joined Mauldin in occasionally drawing editorial cartoons critical of Senator McCarthy and other Republicans.[53]

While at the *Star,* Kelly introduced his *Pogo* comic as a strip. By this time he had dropped the Bumbazine character and had begun to feature Pogo, the gentle, innocent possum, more prominently. After the *Star* folded, Kelly's strip was picked up by the Post (later Publishers-Hall) Syndicate. Thereafter it became one of the fastest growing strips in the syndicate's history. It appeared in over four hundred newspapers only four years after it began its run. By 1958, an estimated fifty million readers followed *Pogo* in five hundred newspapers worldwide. *Pogo* also reached millions of American readers through two dozen anthologies published by Simon and Schuster in the 1950s and early 1960s. The quadrennial "I Go Pogo" presidential campaigns that Kelly initiated in 1952—campaigns intended to parody presidential candidates and their campaigns—became sizeable high school and college fads. The 1952 "I Go Pogo" campaign lampooning Adlai Stevenson and Dwight Eisenhower's "I Like Ike" slogan touched off mock student demonstrations on several American campuses. In Cambridge, Massachusetts, 1,200 Harvard students' innocent homage to Pogo's candidacy precipitated a "wild" confrontation with Boston police—one of the few events that stirred Harvard's somnolent student body during the 1950s.[54]

The range of Kelly's talents and the supply of his creative energy exceeded what he produced in *Pogo.* The demand for his work was great, and it very nearly exhausted him physically. In addition to various television

10. Walt Kelly, creator of *Pogo,* in 1953. Library of Congress, Prints & Photographs Division, *Look* Magazine Photograph Collection.

projects, he was offered (and with few exceptions, rejected) numerous merchandising and advertising deals. In 1954, the NCS—which three years earlier had anointed him "Cartoonist of the Year"—elected Kelly president of the organization. At the critical moment when the comic strip industry was in danger of being censored, Kelly's leadership was pivotal to the NCS's strong defense.[55] Throughout the 1950s, Kelly also wrote articles and reviews for various publications, delivered scores of lectures to college and civic groups, and appeared on television programs (including NBC's coverage of the 1956 political conventions) as a commentator. As cartoonist, editor, and freelance artist and writer throughout the 1950s and early 1960s, Kelly remained a public figure of some prominence.

Defining how the creation that made Kelly most famous, the syndicated *Pogo* comic strip, appealed to Americans in the 1950s and early 1960s is no easier than explaining the complicated genius of its creator. *Pogo*'s fans no doubt enjoyed the dreamy, slightly surrealistic setting Kelly created amid the backwaters of the strip's setting, the Pogofenokee Swamp. *Pogo*'s cast of characters, cleverly rendered with Kelly's skillful brush technique, invited readers into an imaginative landscape rare in comic strips of the period. Not since George Herriman's "Krazy Kat," in fact, had the medium offered such a rich, anarchic fictional world. In addition to indulging in slapstick, vaudevillian action, the fractured parallel universe of *Pogo* evoked elements of postwar existentialism and absurdist theater. The éclat *Pogo* enjoyed with liberal intellectuals no doubt stemmed, at least in part, from its depiction of modern anomie and angst. Equally appealing to fifties' audiences were its meandering, unpredictable, spontaneous plotlines. Few contemporary comic strip artists in fact came close to matching Kelly's virtuosity in the techniques of storytelling. Kelly involved his readers intimately into the affairs and intrigues of the community of animals populating this rural Arcadia. Many *Pogo* fans cherished the complex, idiosyncratic personalities of the strip's nearly 150 anthropomorphic characters—the poet turtle Churchy La Femme, the stuffy Howland Owl, the sourpuss Porkypine, the braggart Albert the Alligator, and the innocent fool/hero Pogo. Through his training at the Disney Studios, Kelly learned how to give these animal characters masterful form and a broad range of expression. Shades of Mark Twain, William Faulkner, and Lewis Carroll were also evident in Kelly's creative use of language. Kelly provided his characters with a colorfully aural, polyglot Southern syntax that many *Pogo* fans enjoyed imitating. The facility with dialect and love of language Kelly acquired as a child also helped shape *Pogo*'s offbeat, nonsense poetry.[56]

All of these elements contributed to *Pogo*'s broad appeal, but it was Kelly's incorporation of sharp yet subtle satire in particular that won over a considerable audience of educated, middle-class Americans. When he addressed the satire at play in his strip, Kelly was often deliberately and mischievously evasive. Like other chastened left-wing and left-liberal artists of the 1950s, he remained wary of revealing too much about the political motivations and meanings behind his work. Kelly in fact claimed that he was nothing but a "Keystone Cop and throwin'-pie humor man" and that people (especially "highbrows") should not look to *Pogo* for satire. "Every once in a while some grinning gargoyle of a dedicated liberal searching for meaning," he wrote in *Ten Ever-Lovin' Blue-Eyed Years with Pogo* (1959), "comes grinning at me with teeth set like a jack-o'-lantern and says, 'Walter, tell me, what are you trying to do? What's behind the strip?'" Kelly's answer to such questions was that "there is altogether too much searching for meaning in this world" and that he was only "trying to have fun and make money at the same time." When one man from New York asked Kelly earnestly whether his satire was "deliberate" or just a way of making money, Kelly responded with typical playfulness: "I feel the world is a funny place and merely try to report on it thru [sic] the comic strip medium. By inclination I am a burglar but find drawing a lot easier. This explains nothing, but what does?" Yet despite issuing such mischievous denials, Kelly clearly viewed his strip as a source for critical comment. On occasion he admitted that there was indeed "meaning" in his strip. When asked by one frustrated high school senior from Pennsylvania if the "small bits of satire" he found in *Pogo* were an apparition, Kelly informed him, "Unless I have lost my grip entirely, I would say that if you did not see some meaning in the strip, POGO, something would be wrong. That's the very reason that I work at it. It may seem strange but the meaning is intentional."[57]

Evidence that Americans from many walks of life actively pursued and actively negotiated the meaning of Kelly's satire in the 1950s and early 1960s exists abundantly within the correspondence he maintained during this period. "Speaking of 'meaning,'" a young man from New York wrote Kelly, "as social satire, it seems to me, 'Pogo' is unexcelled. The parodies you've done on the election were superb." Like other fans who wrote Kelly, this young man offered a few suggestions for future targets:

> The skill and unerring aim with which you direct your shots prompt me to ask you to undertake a few good satirical thrusts at the following more-than-worthy targets: psychoanalysis . . . Marxism's "economic determinism" . . . and Hollywood itself (for example: the inevitable bare chest of the Kirk Douglas opera; the one-blow knockout by the good guy of the bad; the makeup and plunging necklines of the glamour queens, etc.).[58]

In an admiring review of Kelly's work, *New York Post* writer Murray Kempton claimed that *Pogo* was "an idol among the eggheads." Fan letters written to Kelly reveal that *Pogo*'s satire was indeed adored by an audience of well-educated, liberal Americans — the type of people who enthusiastically backed Adlai Stevenson for president in 1952 and 1956. Not since *Krazy Kat* or Crockett Johnson's *Barnaby* had a comic strip appealed to such an identifiably "highbrow," liberal readership. In the opinion of many educated American liberals, Kelly was one of the few popular artists working in the 1950s who, through satire, consistently attempted to reflect and comment upon contemporary reality. Minnesota Senator Hubert Humphrey spoke for many other liberal Americans when he praised Kelly for his "imaginative style and his courage in lampooning everything phony and dishonest . . ."[59]

Some of the people who wrote Kelly related how they participated with other Pogophiles in "Pogo" reading groups. Such clubs proudly devoted themselves to penetrating, with the aid of certain acquired exegetical skills, the strip's hidden messages. Indeed, the ability to decipher the meaning of *Pogo*'s satire conferred membership to a marginal, somewhat exclusive group of people. One former University of Chicago sociology student informed Kelly, for example, that she and her friends "used to classify people into two-classes—those who appreciated 'Pogo' and the others, who weren't worth mentioning." For many precocious young Americans, one's devotion to *Pogo* became a badge of honor, a statement of one's identity as a "thinking" liberal. A boy from Bronxville, New York, requested a Pogo button from Kelly so that he could, as he explained, "make clear [his] political convictions" to the "rather outspoken Republican schoolchildren" in his neighborhood.[60]

The satire of *Pogo* appealed to Americans for many reasons. To many, it undoubtedly represented a voice of common sense in an age of hysteria. Despite its many fantastic elements, *Pogo* was grounded in reality. Letters to Kelly indicate that readers cherished its rich allegory and its subtle allusions to real life. "Thank you, thank you, thank you for Pogo," a Chicago housewife wrote Kelly, and "in particular for his meditation upon the preservation of mankind in this, our phony world." Unlike much commercial, popular culture in the 1950s, *Pogo* also challenged its readers' moral imagination. It respected its audience's intelligence and steered clear of formula. One high school student spoke for many other fans when he told Kelly that after "so many love stories, Bugs Bunny type stories, and wild western adventures, 'Pogo' is a pleasant relief."[61]

Many Americans followed *Pogo* because it addressed, in its satiric manner, the complex nature of personality and human motivation. The object of *Pogo*'s subtle criticism was often the failings and weaknesses of individual character. Kelly intended his readers to recognize their own pride, greed, and prejudice within the animals roaming the swamp. *Pogo* was not, he admitted to himself, a "panorama of popular human types" but the "projection of all the characteristics" that "can be found within one person." "So humor and perhaps Pogo can deliver to us truths," Kelly hoped, "which we will accept more willingly because they are more palatable and comprehensible." When explaining the "underlying philosophy" of *Pogo* in the *Saturday Review* in 1958, Kelly admitted that after "a lumpy lifetime of searching for the hilarious truth in others, any rickety raconteur is delighted to find that he need not go outdoors to discover the drollness and frailty of man. In fact, the best bits of boobery can be found within one-self." The "great final joke," according to Kelly, could prove to be "that in our search for the summit we never explored the crags of our individual consciences." In the end, Kelly argued that the real symbol of the cold war was elusive and "dimly seen," an "Abominable Snowman" of ignorance and fear.[62] To readers who were aware of the intractability of America's social and economic inequalities, Kelly's inward, psychological orientation might have appeared hollow and politically naive. But correspondence between Kelly and his fans reveals that many Pogophiles understood and appreciated his complex allegorical examination of human motive. One New Hampshire man who grasped the subtle intent of *Pogo* wrote the editor of his hometown paper and explained that although *Pogo* is "confined to a somewhat limited medium of expression . . . it shows a great deal of penetration into the make-up of people and the forces that control our behavior." "So much satire in any age," he continued, "is written or drawn by gifted misanthropists . . . But Kelly has a humanity, a breadth of sympathy, a capacity to forgive without condoning the frailties of his fellow man that lifts his comment upon our follies . . . [to] the level of high art."[63]

According to several contemporary critics, Kelly's compassionate understanding of his fellow man muted *Pogo*'s anger and, in the opinion of one Harvard *Crimson* reviewer, made it "shad[e] off into whimsy and gentleness." Yet while *Pogo*'s satire did reflect, as one commentator has argued, a "calmer wisdom," it lacked neither nerve nor ferocity. On several notable occasions in the early and mid-1950s, in fact, Kelly used his strip to lash out at organizations, individuals, and events that disturbed him. During its first year in circulation, *Pogo* eschewed satiric, topical commentary. By mid-1950, however, the former editorial cartoonist Kelly found it difficult to ignore the events of the day. "I finally came to understand that if I were looking for comic material, I would not ever have to look long," Kelly later explained. "We people manufacture it every day in a hundred ways. The news of the day would be good enough . . . After all, it is pretty hard to walk past an unguarded gold mine and remain empty-handed."[64]

Beginning in 1950, Kelly developed several notable satiric episodes aiming squarely at Senator Joseph McCarthy and the intensifying Red Scare. Given Kelly's liberal politics, his outspoken support of civil liberties, and, not least, his bitter experience with the antilabor, red-baiting tactics used against striking cartoonists at the Disney Studio in 1941, it is not surprising that he responded critically to the postwar anticommunist hysteria. While with the *New York Star* he, like Bill Mauldin, had derided HUAC's investigations through editorial cartoons. In June 1950, thick clouds of suspicion, much like those whipped up by HUAC, began to settle over the innocent realm of the Pogofonokee Swamp. When Pup Dog turns up missing, the denizens of the swamp blame Albert the Alligator and his notoriously indiscriminate appetite. Unproven assertions of Albert's guilt are abetted by two "brave investigators"—a dog and pig that comics scholar H.C. Harvey claims were caricatures of conservative, anticommunist newspaper publishers Robert McCormick and Randolph Hearst—and the severely austere, ultrapious Deacon Mushrat. At Albert's trial, his accusers label the Declaration of Independence "un-constitutable" and otherwise resort to innuendo to impugn his character. Albert the Alligator was eventually exonerated and good will was restored, of course, but the atmosphere of paranoia lingered on.[65]

In the spring of 1951, just as Julius and Ethel Rosenberg were convicted for espionage, Kelly initiated a more direct satiric attack on conservatives' anticommunist crusade by introducing the vigilante Audible Boy Bird Watchers Society. Led by Deacon Mushrat and three bat recruits named Bewitched, Bothered, and Bewildered, the Audible Boy Bird Watchers became comic equivalents of the period's self-righteous communist hunters. In late October and early November 1951, the Deacon declares the turtle Churchy LaFemme a "*dangerous* menace" who must therefore be "watched, watched, watched." When asked by the Boy Bird Watchers if that meant that they should "snoop" on Ol' Turtle (a member of an "*underwater group*" engaged in "*sub*mersive *activities*"), the frock-coated Deacon responds (rendered in Gothic lettering within his speech balloons), "Snoop?! Goodness, what a horrid word! No, we'll make dignified intelligence reports." Shortly thereafter the Ladies of the Vigilante Auxiliary (the swampland's equivalent of the DAR) learn that Churchy LaFemme has been implicated by a bit of "devious" cryptic poetry and by the memoir of a "beautiful spy queen" titled *I Was an Ex-Member of the Underground*—allusions to the prominent professional anticommunist witness Elizabeth Bentley and to the type of *mea culpa* written by former communists such as Whittaker Chambers's soon-to-be-published *Witness*. Unshaken by the rapidly changing series of charges, one member of the Ladies Auxiliary, Miz Stork, confesses all too humanly: "*Well,* 'taint my affair—I mind my own business an' stay *comfy* . . . *an*' out of trouble."[66]

Sly references to the ongoing anticommunist crusade ("he mought be the tool of a *foreign power!*") continued to creep into *Pogo* throughout 1952.

And in the spring of that year, Kelly introduced a pair of black cowbirds, holdovers of the doctrinaire Communist Party who are quick to denounce "imperious discrimination," "utter deviationism," "benighted paternalistic infantilism," and "absentee landlordism," among other outrages. When Pogo defends their right to be cowbirds, he is labeled guilty by association. In September, the cowbirds follow the trajectory of many ex-communists who renounced their former associations. "We've *changed!*" the cowbirds cry. "We suddenly saw how *vile* we'd been when *Pogo protected our rights* . . ." In March 1953, the Deacon, Boy Bird Watchers, and cowbirds were joined by a new character, the Honorable Mole MacCarony, a near-blind mole whose twin obsessions were "bird watching" (communist hunting) and the eradication of germs (a clear allusion to cold war America's manic fear of disease, foreign ideologies, and "deviant" sexual practices). When Mole MacCarony warns that the germs "of all nations swarm unchecked thru the entire air" he betrays not only his paranoia but his xenophobia as well. Indeed, MacCarony served as a stand-in for the ultraconservative senator from Nevada, Pat McCarran, chairman of the Senate Internal Security Subcommittee and sponsor of the McCarran-Walter Immigration and Nationalities Act, which Congress passed over President Harry Truman's veto in 1952. More than a caricature of one influential senator, Kelly later explained, the introduction of Mole MacCarony "was an attempt to find a symbol for another wad of bug-eyed greed which was typified by our sudden worry about who was coming into the country as a refugee or an immigrant and who, for that matter, was going to be allowed to stay here."[67]

The tragicomic events unfolding in the Pogofonokee Swamp up to this point certainly did not please all *Pogo* readers. A New York woman wrote Kelly at the time to express her "dismay at the bogeyman-like quality [his] strip . . . assumed in the last few issues of the *Post.*" "I object very strongly," she wrote, "to villains like the ones we have met there recently." Kelly responded, "Inasmuch as Pogo is an attempt at satire there will be occasions when caricatured villains will show up . . . Hope you will bear with me through the bitter as well as the sweet." Despite the complaints some readers and newspaper publishers had begun to register, Kelly by mid-1953 had set the stage for what would become his most sustained and angry satiric criticism of McCarthyism. By this time, Kelly could clearly no longer contain his outrage over what Joseph McCarthy himself was doing as chair of the Permanent Subcommittee on Investigations within the Senate's Government Operations Committee. Like Herblock, Mauldin, and Osborn, Kelly despised McCarthy. "As one who sniffed the breeze in Germany in 1930," Kelly wrote privately in 1952, "I would say [the stench invading America] smells like a sorcerer's apprentice trying to render Wisconsin cheese into political gold."[68]

On May 1, 1953, Kelly introduced a villainous, shotgun-toting bobcat named Simple J. Malarkey who was called to assist Mole MacCarony and Deacon Mushrat with the "growing peril" and "dangers" lurking within the swamp. Just as Deacon introduces Malarkey to the Boy Bird Watchers and then prepares to "read an account of his past . . . activities," Malarkey interrupts with a loud shotgun blast. "Objection sustained, Mr. Malarkey," the shaken Deacon responds. For the next six weeks Malarkey ran roughshod over the investigations of the Boy Bird Watchers and even changed their name to the "Bonfire Boys." Compared with Malarkey, even the Deacon and Mole MacCarony appear sensible and sympathetic. "Your methods are too crude," MacCarony tells Malarkey, "you should have *dignity* and *law* on your side." Meanwhile, Albert and Pup Dog conspire to trick Malarkey by masquerading as "Arf an' Nonny," a parodic reference to conservative cartoonist Harold Gray's strip "Little Orphan Annie." When their plan is foiled, Malarkey proposes to tar and feather them. "Make 'em *all* birds," says Malarkey. "*Then* when we identifies birds we'll know what's what . . . They'll be what we say . . . *accurate* . . . no more hearsay."[69]

Malarkey's malice eventually causes the Deacon to take flight and seek safety with Pogo aboard his boat, the HMS *Herbert Block*—a tribute to the friend and fellow cartoonist whose stand against Joseph McCarthy was winning Kelly's admiration. Ever the voice of reason, Pogo tells the Deacon, "They aint' gone scare nobody if nobody listens at 'em . . . An' they is got perty doggone hard to *listen* to."[70] Momentarily receptive to the wisdom dispensed by Kelly's swampland creatures, the Deacon is scolded by Uncle Porky:

> *You* brung in them two expert birdwatchers . . . sayin' it was to keep us from makin' *dern fools* of ourselves . . . whereas it's the *in*herent right of *all* to make dern fools of theirselves . . . It ain't a right held by you *official* types alone . . . The rest of us might not have the sheer ability at it but us *do* got the right . . . So don't mess with it . . .[71]

In the end, the Deacon devises a scheme for Malarkey and his partner to fall into their pot of tar ("I always say: Give one of these sharpers enough rope and . . . he'll hang himself . . ."), and after a series of slapstick mishaps Malarkey is tarred and feathered. Turning now against Mole MacCarony,

11. In his *Pogo* strip for March 3, 1953 (top), Walt Kelly introduced readers to Mole MacCarony, a reference, in part, to Nevada Senator Pat McCarran. Two months later (below), Kelly depicted the menacing presence of Senator Joseph McCarthy in another new character, Simple J. Malarkey. Library of Congress, Prints & Photographs Division, uncatalogued and LC-USZC4-13082. © 2006 Okefenokee Glee & Perloo, Inc. Used by permission.

Malarkey, on June 12, 1953, exited the strip wielding an ax and chasing his former partner from the scene.

Malarkey returned to the swamp in August 1954, shortly after Senator Joseph McCarthy's nationally televised fall from grace. The main purpose behind Malarkey's reappearance was to introduce his new sidekick Indian Charlie, a badger bearing a remarkable resemblance to Vice President Richard Nixon. Several months later Kelly thrust Malarkey onto the stage one final time in order to retaliate against an ultimatum that was laid down by the publisher of a Providence, Rhode Island, newspaper. When the paper threatened to drop *Pogo* if Kelly once again showed the faces of Malarkey and Indian Charlie, Kelly had them don sacks over their heads when they come into contact with Miss Boombah, a "Rhode Island red" rooster from Providence. "What with the concern in the strip with Miss Boombah, already established as being a R.I. Red," Kelly later remarked, "it was easy to have Malarkey and I. Chas. put K.K.K. type garb on, which identified their kind a little more, and yet live up to the letter of this [ultimatum]."[72]

As a result of Kelly's impish ploy, the Providence paper moved *Pogo* where many of its detractors felt it belonged, onto the editorial page. Before that, at least one newspaper, the *Orlando Florida Sentinel,* dropped *Pogo* altogether following Malarkey's appearance. Despite the objections of several editors, however, it appears that Kelly's satiric jabs at Pat Mc-Carran, Joseph McCarthy, and the zealots behind the second Red Scare cost Kelly little. Kelly's widow claims that the FBI tapped Kelly's phone in 1948, and it appears that J. Edgar Hoover, acting on a tip from a Cincinnati resident, ordered FBI cryptanalysts to examine the dialogue of the *Pogo* strip for evidence of coded Soviet criticism of the Bureau. No evidence suggests that Kelly was the subject of a full-scale FBI investigation, however. If anything, Kelly's topical commentary won over an expanding fan base of liberal Americans frustrated by mainstream American culture's timidity during the early 1950s. Liberal journalist Murray Kempton, for one, argued that since Capp had married off Li'l Abner ("to appease the customer"), Kelly was the only strip artist remaining who was capable of "working over Joe McCarthy, heedless of animal cries from the gallery."[73]

In the opinion of other fans, Kelly's Malarkey caricature captured Mc-Carthy's evil with frightening clarity. Cartoonist Bill Watterson remembers how Malarkey revealed McCarthy for what he was, a "soulless menace." Kelly's strips on McCarthy made a particularly strong impression on

Jules Feiffer, who was then just beginning his career as a satiric cartoonist. Feiffer recalls that Kelly's political cartoons and his early *Pogo* strip hit him "like a bolt of lightning." "I remember thinking 'this guy's angry.'" Kelly, Feiffer adds, "brought rage back to the editorial page in a way that I hadn't seen since the cartoonists of the *Masses*." "He put rage back into the political cartoon" and "brought a kind of moral indignation to the form, pure and with a degree of zealotry that I admired." Kelly's "wrath was scathing and monumental," Feiffer states. "I thrived on his satire in those early cold war years." Indeed, Kelly's caricatures of McCarthy and Nixon, like those created by Herblock, stuck in the minds of Feiffer and many other Americans. The term "Malarkeyism" itself even came to symbolize the recklessness and maliciousness of the second Red Scare.[74]

People who resented what opportunistic politicians like Joseph McCarthy and Richard Nixon had done to poison America's political culture were particularly pleased with Kelly's caricatures. A physicist from New York, for example, wrote Kelly to inform him that he was grateful for "more than the mere fun which is Pogo." This man continued,

> I refer to your political satire on the "terrorists" (if I may use the term understandably in this way) . . . My gratefulness lies in being reminded that such satire is still possible. Recently I have found the "hog-calling," the "piping up of the rats" by the "terrorists" intensely depressing. Your strip reminds me that we're not so far gone as that, and that we've had them before.[75]

In a second letter this man wrote that he envied "the Kellys, [and] the Herblocks . . . those who have a public voice, and who use it well. The private citizen who may feel the need to speak up in defense of such slippery concepts as the 'individual,' the 'private opinion,' the 'unconformed' finds his single voice lost in the general shriek."[76]

For this physicist and for many other liberal Americans who followed *Pogo,* Kelly's strip demonstrated that satiric cartooning and drawing were far from dead in the 1950s. Like the best work of Bill Mauldin, Herblock, Robert Osborn, and a few other cartoonists, Kelly gave voice to a moral, dissenting perspective that was in short supply during the postwar years. For their liberal fans and followers, these cartoonists signaled proof that there were other people in the country who shared their sense of anger and dismay. Kelly clearly recognized this, and on occasion he even acknowledged a sense of solidarity with his angry readers. To the earnest New York physicist who complained of the "single voice lost in the general shriek," Kelly wrote back, "It is hardly embarrassing at all to know that many of us are as one. It has been ever true and will remain: From the depths of humility comes decency and the real security. Some of us will rear children who will never be ashamed."[77]

Like his friends and colleagues considered here, Kelly provided an important voice for moral outrage but did not yield to a sense of despair or cynicism, a point not lost on his liberal supporters. As one woman told Kelly in 1958, "during [the] horrors of the late Senator McCarthy's irresponsible and evil inquisition your strip was one of the very, very few places in the United States regularly and outspokenly devoted to the criticism of stupidity and intolerance." "So help me, Kelly," another woman wrote in 1953, "the MacCaroney [sic] thing is the most wonderful thing that has ever happened to journalism in this country!" As "long as you can create (and have published) stories like [your MacCarony series]," she continued, "and as long as a significant segment of we who read it can cheer it . . . hope springeth eternal."[78]

This woman and *Pogo* fans like her had good reason to cheer Kelly's penetrating and daring satire. The MacCarony, Boy Bird Society, and Malarkey episodes were published in newspapers across the country long before CBS newsman Edward R. Murrow first questioned McCarthy's tactics on the *See It Now* television broadcast of October 1953. Ten weeks later, Murrow featured an interview with Kelly on his *Person to Person* program, at which time he offered a nationwide television audience a preview of Simple J. Malarkey's role in his soon-to-be-published book, *The Pogo Stepmother Goose* (1954). When on March 3, 1954, Murrow closed his second and more damning *See It Now* expose of Senator McCarthy by quoting Shakespeare's *Julius Caesar* ("Cassius was right. 'The fault,' dear Brutus, 'is not in our stars but in ourselves . . . '") he might well have repeated instead words Kelly provided for the introduction to his previous bestselling anthology *The Pogo Papers* (1953):

> It is just unfortunate that in the clumsy hands of a cartoonist all traits become ridiculous, leading to a certain amount of self-conscious expostulation and the desire to join battle. There is no need to sally forth, for it remains true that those things which make us human are, curiously enough, always close at hand. Resolve then, that on this very ground, with small flags waving and tinny blasts on tiny trumpets, we shall meet the enemy, and not only may he be ours, he may be us. Forward![79]

The anticommunist movement of the late 1940s and 1950s may have muffled dissent within the United States, but it also incited the moral anger and wit of cartoonists such as Walt Kelly. The cartoons, caricatures, drawings, and comic strips that he and his fellow cartoonists Herbert Block, Robert Osborn, and Bill Mauldin produced in the dozen years after 1945, though quite different in structure and orientation, shared the ability to distill liberals' outrage and produce a body of hard-hitting and at times wickedly funny satire. Wielding their "weapons of wit," these artists kept alive a tradition of irreverent commentary that ran through Mark Twain, Sinclair Lewis, and Charlie Chaplin and lambasted those political personalities and forces that undermined civil liberties, the spread of civil rights, and other causes liberals continued to hold dear during the fifties.

PART TWO

THE CLEANSING LASH OF LAUGHTER

CHAPTER THREE

Comic Revenge

PARODIC REVELRY AND "SICK" HUMOR IN
THE 1950S SATIRIC UNDERGROUND

In the introduction to his 1955 cartoon anthology *Here and Now,* Herbert Block complained that Americans were "living in an era of slogans, symbols and smooth talk which may well go down in history as the Genuine Simulated Golden Age." "Every time you turn on the radio or television," he continued, "somebody is telling you how you, yes *you,* can get this wonderful, yes wonderful, gadget *now,* yes *now, yes* you can get it *now*—until you feel like hollering, 'No, no, *no*—never!" In the "Era of Feeling Numb," as Herblock put it, sincerity, authenticity, and truth had succumbed to a "miracle ingredient" called HP2x, or "Hocus-pocus twice multiplied."[1]

While Herblock and many of his fellow liberal political cartoonists focused mainly on HP2x's effects on the political arena, they also took the opportunity to direct critiques at mass culture and the increasing "slickness" of American life in general. By doing so they joined a good number of postwar liberal intellectuals who throughout the fifties remained preoccupied with mass culture's deleterious effects on American life. American intellectuals, writers, and artists living and working during this increasingly affluent period devoted much of their attention to explicating the ways mass culture, the spread of suburbia, and the consolidation of large-scale bureaucratic organizations afflicted the inner lives of the middle-class American male. While intellectuals such as David Riesman and William Whyte assailed social conditions that compromised the individuality of middle-class American men, writers of fiction stretching from J. D. Salinger and Vladimir Nabokov through Terry Southern, William S. Burroughs, and John Updike excoriated the hypocrisy and the pretense, the insincerity and fakery—the HP2x—that they saw suffusing middle-class Americans' private and public lives during the fifties.[2]

Liberal satirists of the Eisenhower era worked in a similar spirit. Through various modes of rough, critical parody—collectively labeled "sick humor" by its detractors—a number of satiric writers, artists, and performers pursued a type of satiric revenge on the stale commercial formulas and whitewashed realities at the heart of postwar consensus culture. Irreverent and at times aggressively masculine, these satirists— Henry Morgan, Bob and Ray, Stan Freberg, Ernie Kovacs, Sid Caesar, Tom Lehrer, and Harvey Kurtzman—worked within the traditions of American comic realism and twentieth-century modernism, both of which deployed brutal truth or "terrible honesty" to counteract the spread of artifice and feminine sentimentality.[3] From their point of view, the decade of the fifties—a period that heavily promoted the virtues of domesticity and what *McCall's* magazine in 1954 coined "togetherness," witnessed a tremendous expansion of mass consumer culture and advertising and institutionalized the mythology of the Great American Way—cried out for what Walt Kelly called the "cleansing lash of humor." As such, it proved a particularly fertile period for parodic revelry and the brutal truth telling of "sick" humor.

*   *   *

The variety of bawdy, antisentimental, aggressively masculine parody and satire that became popular during the fifties had strong roots in American popular culture. In the comic tales of popular nineteenth-century rogues such as Simon Suggs and Sut Lovingood, for example, Americans encountered, as Jesse Bier has written, a "wellspring of contempt for a veritable system of falsifications." During the early decades of the twentieth century, the "vulgarly realistic style" that Bier identifies with the frontier humorists found expression in college humor magazines. Subsisting largely on parody and directed at the concerns of male undergraduates—namely, the hypocrisy of elders, alcohol, sex, and sports—college humor magazines flourished during the teens and twenties.[4] During the Depression, the type of irreverent parody that marked college humor magazines surfaced in two significant, though short-lived publications: *Americana* and *Ballyhoo*. The former, edited by Alexander King, lasted only thirteen issues but featured the work by satiric artist George Grosz, poet e. e. cummings, and novelist Nathanael West. *Ballyhoo* was edited by former *Judge* and *Life* editor Norman Anthony and published by George Delacorte. With its comic features and, most notably, ad parodies for products such as the "Smilette"—a device worn around the head that by pulling up the corners of the mouth forced an illusory smile (APPLY NOW AT YOUR CHAMBER OF COMMERCE OR THE REPUBLICAN NATIONAL COMMITTEE)—*Ballyhoo* became a short-lived sensation at a time when Americans had grown naturally wary of consumer capitalism's promises.[5]

Shortly thereafter, radio comedians Fred Allen and Henry Morgan emerged as two of the preeminent satirists in the United States. Allen in particular is remembered as one of the few satiric geniuses to emerge in the medium of radio. Ever since the Boston-born Irish American began broadcasting *Town Hall Tonight* on NBC during the mid-1930s, he distinguished himself from a large field of radio comedians with his use of biting, intelligent, satiric wit. Unlike the self-effacing Jack Benny, the topical comedian Bob Hope, or many other comics operating in the popular sitcom format, Allen was widely recognized and admired as a satirist, a performer who was unafraid to spoof celebrities, the profit motives of the entertainment industry, inane quiz and talent programs, ad agencies, business executives, politicians, and the broadcast networks. Allen's barbed comments regarding censorship and the doltish, spineless organization men who staffed ad agencies and networks understandably prompted concern on the part of his parent network. As radio historian Michele Hilmes relates, NBC executives and censors in late 1946 grew incensed when Allen performed a scene titled "The Radio Mikado" in which he satirized NBC and a fictional ad agency by the name of Button, Burton, Bitten, and Muchinfuss. Six months later, NBC cut Allen off the air for thirty-five seconds because he refused to excise material aimed at its censors. Following this celebrated incident, NBC took what Hilmes has termed a "militant stance" toward Allen's brand of satire. To make matters worse, Allen's ratings during 1947 and 1948 began to suffer against the competition of *Stop the Music,* a musical game show broadcast on the fledgling ABC radio network. Finally, in 1949, NBC retired Allen and his brand of irreverent parody from the airwaves.[6]

Henry Morgan greatly admired Allen and resembled him in significant respects, particularly in his creative use of language and his scorn for the business side of radio broadcasting. Morgan has received relatively little attention from broadcast historians, but he was one of the most original, controversial, and daring personalities in radio during the 1940s. Born Henry Lerner von Ost Jr., he was raised by Jewish parents in the Lower

East Side of New York City. Though a rebellious spirit since his youth, he eventually managed to graduate (with some difficulty) from the Harrisburg Military Academy in Pennsylvania. During the 1930s he began working as an announcer for radio stations on the East Coast. For station WEBC in Duluth he later hosted an unorthodox program titled, significantly, *Strictly Masculine*. Here Morgan regularly played Chinese funeral music, conducted imaginary Man-on-the-Street interviews, and performed a host of other absurdist antics. By the time he initiated *Meet Mr. Morgan* on New York City's WOR in 1940 and, shortly thereafter, *Here's Morgan* on the Mutual Broadcasting System, he had acquired a reputation as a comic iconoclast, a man who had little respect for either network officials or station management. In one of his most celebrated stunts during the mid-1940s, for example, Morgan performed an on-air auction of the executive staff at Mutual Broadcasting. Like his friend Fred Allen, Morgan attracted much attention by relentlessly prodding stuffed shirts and the folly of network regulations.[7]

Throughout the early and mid-1940s, Morgan cultivated an image as radio's bad boy by routinely hurtling comic insults at the broadcast industry, network censorship, and the tired gimmicks of the period's radio programs. Unlike any other comedian then on radio, Morgan also railed against racism, predatory financial institutions, and the hazards posed by Senate investigations into "un-American" activities. Although he—like other innocent victims of McCarthyism—later declared himself "apolitical," his radio programs were often informed by a strong social and moral conscience. In addition to comic skits and radio parodies, one of Morgan's stock routines involved mock interviews in which he played thickly accented characters such as psychiatrist Heinrich von Morgan. Aside from his eclecticism and his smart, snappy style, what endeared Morgan to his fans and to intellectuals during this period was his relentless prodding of consumer culture, particularly mind-numbing hard-sell advertisements. Offering as an example of the fraudulent claims advanced by the manufacturers of consumer goods, Morgan once quipped that the chemical ingredients in toothpaste included "'primocarulated bromide'—the medical term for profit to the manufacturer."[8]

Like Harvey Kurtzman, Stan Freberg, and a number of satirists who succeeded him, Morgan held admen responsible for propagating consumer capitalism's deceits. Morgan considered advertisers "hucksters" and "idiots" intent on obscuring reality and, worse yet, bent on treating the American public as a thoughtless herd of sheep. He was renowned for

12. Shades of W. C.
Fields: radio's "bad
boy" satirist Henry
Morgan. Wagner Inter-
national Photos, Inc.,
New York.

tossing away or shredding the copy prepared by his sponsors' ad agencies and then delivering an improvised meditation on his sponsor's product. "I couldn't abide reading the junk the clients provided," Morgan recalled in his 1994 memoir, "so I ad-libbed them in kind of breezy, off-handed fashion that sometimes bordered on the insulting." At a time when the ultimate taboo in commercial broadcasting was to question the sanctity of a sponsor's product, Morgan's insults ultimately cost him a string of financial backers. Life Savers canceled their sponsorship of one of his programs after he suggested that the company was "mulcting the public" when it left a hole in the center of its candies. Similarly, candy bar maker Oh Henry! dropped its support of a Morgan program when he told parents that if they fed their children "enough Oh Henry . . . they'll get sick and die." [9]

With his contemptuous treatment of advertising, his W. C. Fields–inspired flouting of childhood innocence, mother, and femininity, and his penchant for relating the brutal truth about deceits rampant in the contemporary world, Morgan resembled many other male satirists popular in

Comic Revenge

postwar America. Like others within this cohort, Morgan was an aggressive and uncompromising male individualist. As his autobiography reveals, he was quick to brag about his sexual conquests and complain about his female partners, and he was prone to engaging in alcoholic excess. Urbane and cultivated, he was at the same time notoriously prickly, pugnacious, and unpredictable. He took pride in writing his own material and enjoyed the challenges of improvisation. Nourishing his iconoclastic image, he was quick to point out what separated him from mainstream comedians and humorists. "I'm a rebel," he told an interviewer in 1947. "My humor is based on rebellion against the foolishness of the world."[10]

Together with Herblock, Bill Mauldin, and other liberal cartoonists, Morgan was also a progressive and an outspoken advocate for the protection of civil liberties. As a member of the Progressive Citizens of America and the spouse of an actress and political radical named Isobel Gibbs, Morgan was invited to speak at the Veterans against Discrimination of Civil Rights Congress and a rally on behalf of the Stop Censorship Committee. Unfortunately for Morgan, his activities and Popular Front political sympathies provoked the ire of the radical anticommunists who had policed the American broadcast industry since the late 1940s. Three of the most powerful of these anticommunists were former FBI agents who cynically traded on fears aroused by the postwar Red Scare to enrich their small "consulting" firm, American Business Consultants. In their 1950 publication Red Channels—known in the entertainment industry as the "blacklisters' Bible"—Morgan was cited along with playwright Arthur Miller, folk singer Pete Seeger, director Orson Welles, conductor Leonard Bernstein, and other progressive artists and performers as a communist dupe and "subversive."[11]

Throughout the late 1940s and early 1950s, broadcast networks, advertising agencies, and sponsors, all of them vigilant about purging radical political and pro-union sentiment from popular entertainment, systematically discriminated against performers like Morgan. Through the influence of his friend and benefactor Fred Allen, Morgan continued broadcasting his unsponsored program on NBC through 1950. Despite taking steps to clear his name—following the instructions of an executive at the advertising agency Batten, Barton, Durstine, and Osborn, Morgan appeared on a television show hosted by Conrad Nagel, attended anticommunist social gatherings, and, to Morgan's eternal regret, made a speech to the American Federation of Television and Radio Artists in which he criticized the blacklisted actor and AFTRA member Philip Loeb—

Morgan thereafter had difficulty finding employment. His reputation for brashness and unpredictability certainly did not endear him to potential employers. According to media critic and historian Gilbert Seldes, Morgan had become less bankable by the early 1950s because he appeared bitter and angry. "He was making a personal vendetta out of his dislike for stupidity," Seldes wryly observed, "as if he were all alone in the battle for intelligence." At a time when sponsors and broadcast executives began relying on safe, predictable entertainment, Morgan's brand of spontaneous, irreverent comedy—the type of "completely uninhibited" comedy that, as *Variety* put it, "cause[d] more gray hairs to producers in a brief 15 minutes than most performers during an entire career"—was beginning to fall out of favor in broadcast radio and television.[12]

*   *   *

Network radio in the 1950s proved little more hospitable toward satirist Stan Freberg than it did toward Fred Allen and Henry Morgan. Like several satirists who emerged in the 1950s, Freberg was an admirer and student of these two radio comedians. In his autobiography Freberg relates how as a boy he wanted to "stand at a network-radio mike someday" and like his idol Allen, "skewer some of the absurdities I was already observing in the world . . ." He got his start in radio during the 1940s, working as a sound effects artist and actor on programs such as CBS's *Tell It Again*. He did not earn a reputation as a solo comic performer until the early fifties when he began making parody records for Capitol. In 1950, Freberg recorded a spoof of sappy, soap opera dialogue between a loving couple. Against the sentimental strains of background violins and organ, Freberg's John and Marsha repeat each other's names in various emotional pitches. Spurred by the remarkable success of "John and Marsha," Freberg kept his ears open for other possible targets to parody. "When something rankled me enough," Freberg recalls, "I leapt to my typewriter and knocked out a record on the absurdity."[13]

Given Freberg's animus against the sentimental formulas to which he (and other male satirists) believed teenaged girls and women were particularly prone, Freberg was quick to lampoon the swooning teen idol Johnnie Ray. It was the "absurdity" of the television detective series *Dragnet* that prompted Freberg's most successful parody record, "St. George and the Dragonet." Selling 900,000 copies in just two weeks, Freberg's spoof became the fastest selling single in the history of the American recording

13. Satirist Stan Freberg with fans in the studios of Capitol Records in 1959. Bill Bridges/ Time & Life Pictures/Getty Images.

industry up to that time. Soon after disk jockeys around the country be-gan spinning "St. George and the Dragonet" and his other Capitol spoofs, Freberg was hailed as the newest member of the Fred Allen–Henry Mor-gan school of wit. Like his fellow satirists, Freberg clashed with the radio networks' conservative management. According to Freberg, radio net-works banned their affiliate stations from playing two of his Capitol re-leases—"John and Marsha" and "Abe Snake for President," a 1952 parody of electoral politics.[14]

Freberg was a shrewd entertainer and self-promoter who knew how to parlay his confrontations with network bureaucrats in order to bolster his image as America's newest up-and-coming satirist. In a 1954 article for *Collier's* magazine titled "It Only Hurts When I Laugh," Freberg cited his bad experiences with network bureaucracy—particularly what he identi-fied as the "fungus called Music Clearance"—and Capitol Records attor-neys as proof that satire in postwar America was nearly extinct. According to Freberg, his parodies had rendered him an outcast among his peers, even his bebop musician friends! "There could be only one reason why many people choose to avoid me," Freberg claimed. "I am a satirist." Surveying the mood of caution within the entertainment industry, he lamented that the "fate of the satirist" is "harder now than ever before" and that "censorship, pressure groups and executives with no sense of hu-

mor threaten to shackle my type of satire forever." "This has become a society," he continued, "where slapstick is king but Fred Allen has suffo-
cated . . . and a great wit like Henry Morgan is exiled from the big time
because he dared to poke fun at someone besides himself." Repeating
a refrain often heard during the fifties, Freberg complained that Mc-
Carthyism and "conformity" seriously threatened to extinguish the nation's sense of humor, an alarming prospect since a healthy sense of humor
was vital to both American democracy and the task of coping with the
modern, "confused world."[15]

In the end, Freberg was able to reassure network officials that he was
"not a subversive" but someone who "just want[ed] to have a good
laugh."[16] In 1954, CBS offered him the opportunity to play the title role in
a radio sitcom titled *That's Rich*. This series ostensibly revolved around the
exploits of a naive, innocent young man who moved to Hollywood in
hopes of getting a break in show business, but through the use daydream
sequences Freberg managed to insert tame parodies of celebrities such as
Jack Webb and Eartha Kitt. Several months into the program, CBS reportedly threatened to cut all of Freberg's parody sequences. To Freberg,
this served as further evidence of the network's allergy to satire. CBS,
Freberg claimed, "is most anxious to keep word from getting out that I
am a satirist. Before meeting possible sponsors, I am always cautioned in
hushed tones, 'For goodness sake, don't tell them you're a satirist!' But
alas . . . I cannot hide it. I am a satirist."[17]

Given the acrimony and mistrust that reportedly developed between
Freberg and CBS over the failed *That's Rich* series, few would have predicted future collaboration between the two. But with the aid of a friend
who was an executive at the West Coast office of CBS Radio, Freberg arranged deals for two radio projects. The first was an "Analysis of Satire"
that Freberg produced for a 1956 installment of *CBS Radio Workshop*. The
second, a much larger commitment, permitted him to create, write, and
staff his own thirty-minute weekly comedy program during the summer
of 1957. Impressed by the success of Freberg's "Banana Boat" parody for
Capitol earlier that year, CBS evidently believed the young satirist had
enough talent to fill the void left by Jack Benny's recent departure. In addition to a generous budget, CBS gave Freberg a remarkably free hand in
the development of *The Stan Freberg Show*. It even permitted Freberg to
reject sponsors he considered immoral or in "bad taste." The only precau-
tion CBS insisted on taking was recording the program "live" and then
broadcasting an edited version several days later.[18]

Together with producer Pete Barnum, cowriter Howard Gossage, longtime associates June Foray, Peter Leeds, Daws Butler, Jud Conlon's Rhythmaires, the Billy May Orchestra, and a group of talented sound effects artists, Freberg aired the premiere of *The Stan Freberg Show* on July 14, 1957. Immediately, Freberg clashed with network censors over the material he chose to present on air.[19] On the August 18, 1957, broadcast of his program, Freberg took aim at network censors' timidity in a piece titled "Elderly Man River." Here, as he attempts to sing the popular tune from Kern and Hammerstein's *Showboat,* "Ol' Man River," Freberg is intermittently interrupted by a censor from the "Citizen's Radio Committee." Cautioned against using jargon, double negatives, and insensitive terms such as "old," Freberg is finally forced to sing a tame, yet ultimately unrecognizable version of the song.[20] In succeeding installments, the satiric thrust of *The Stan Freberg Show* was more muted. What followed were deadpan interviews, reprised Freberg song parodies, and spoofs of fifties phenomena such as variety shows, Lawrence Welk, and the hi-fi fad. Many segments had a smart edge, but more often Freberg's brief skits were vehicles for whimsy and baroque aural experimentation. It was not until October 1957, after CBS had decided not to renew his program, that Freberg began aiming satiric barbs at the institution that most annoyed him—advertising.

Advertising men and the business of advertising had always irked Freberg. In a 1953 *New York Times Magazine* profile, Freberg described admen as a "little army with Brooks Brothers suits and pea brains." Freberg's frustration with the advertising industry mounted when his radio program failed to find a sponsor even though it pulled an audience of five to six million. Because he rejected tobacco ads and sponsors who wanted only "spot" ads (he insisted, rather anachronistically, on having single sponsors underwrite his program), *The Stan Freberg Show* was doomed to failure. Nevertheless, Freberg blamed admen for his program's demise. On the final two original installments of *The Stan Freberg Show,* aired on October 6 and 13, 1957, Freberg took his revenge by depicting them as unthinking phonies and stiffs. In "Gray Flannel Hatful of Teenage Werewolves," a parody of various contemporary horror films, Freberg related the story of an inhabitant of Westchester County who was a werewolf by night and an advertising man by day. When this character metamorphoses into an adman, his hair recedes into a crew cut, he suddenly dons a gray flannel suit, his head is "filled with senseless metaphor," he begins spewing admens' clichés and exchanging sports lingo with his fellow jug-headed conformists at Batton, Barton, Rubicam, and Thompson, and finally he devises winning copy that claims, "Leading specialists agree that food is the number one cure for hunger." Another segment titled "Freberg in Advertisingland" followed Freberg as he searches for sponsors and advice at the World Advertising Corporation. While there, Freberg encounters a carnival-barking adman named Mr. Gambit who demonstrates how World Advertising represents clients such as the United States of America. Condensing the worst aspects of American cold war boosterism and advertising's hard-sell technique, Gambit's ad runs, "Yes, for people who know countries best it's America two to one!"[21]

*   *   *

Local radio and the nascent medium of television in the end proved more receptive to the type of parody and satire that Freberg aimed at American mass culture. Beginning in the early 1950s and continuing throughout the decade, a large number of the most innovative and interesting radio programs, whether they were devoted to comedy or rhythm and blues and rock-and-roll music, were produced by local or regional radio stations, not the national networks. Largely because of commercial television's success, radio stations not only grew in number during the 1950s, they also left greater room for experimentation and specialization, particularly in broadcast comedy. Nowhere was this more evident than at large, powerful, metropolitan stations such as WNEW, WMGM, and WOR in New York City. In 1952, WNEW, the first station to adopt a twenty-four-hour-a-day disk jockey format, began airing a live morning program featuring a tandem named Klavan and Finch. Throughout the 1950s and early 1960s, Gene Klavan and Dee Finch provided their morning listeners with a steady diet of ad-libbed repartee and comic nonsense. They prided themselves on their irreverent treatment of their station bosses, their sponsors, and the records they played on the air. In his account of this period, *We Die at Dawn,* Klavan bragged that he and his partner were "at times . . . satirical . . . and downright nasty" and that they believed in "stirring up a little trouble every so often . . ." Local New York stations also experimented with programming during the after-midnight hours. In 1952, WMGM hired Henry Morgan to broadcast live from a restaurant on West 55th Street each weekday from midnight to 3 A.M.[22]

Similar to Morgan with his smart, sly, offbeat approach was Jean Shepherd. Beginning in 1956, Shepherd played jazz records and delivered meandering stream-of-consciousness monologues after midnight on station WOR. With his stories about his hometown of Hammond, Indiana, his wry commentaries on American middle-class conformity, and his complaints against "smug, righteous day people," Shepherd played the comic pied piper for a large audience of hip adolescents and self-declared "night people" inhabiting metropolitan New York and areas along the eastern seaboard. The nature of Shepherd's complaints against the "straight" world is perhaps best revealed in a 1957 article he wrote for *MAD* magazine—a publication that, like the *Realist,* the *Village Voice* and, later, *Playboy,* welcomed his written contributions. In this article, Shepherd disparaged the conformist "'Day World' philosophy of 'Creeping Meatballism,'" a philosophy that foisted upon an unsuspecting public the idea that "contemporary people are slim, and clean-limbed, and they're so much fun to be with . . . because they drink Pepsi-Cola." To fight the deceits engineered by advertisers, television, and consumer culture in general, Shepherd counseled the development of a little "Night People" in everyone. "EVERY ONE OF US," Shepherd concluded,

> I don't care who he is, has a certain amount of "Night People" in him. Because, no matter how many refrigerators you buy from Betty Furness, no matter how many "custom" suits you buy, no matter how many cars with fins you buy, you're still an individual. And I'll say this: Once a guy starts *thinking,* once a guy starts *laughing* at the things he once thought were very real, once he starts laughing at T.V. commercials, once he starts getting a boot out of movie trailers, once he begins to realize that just because a movie is wider or higher or longer doesn't make it a better movie, once a guy starts doing that, he's making the transition from "Day People" to "Night People." [23]

Fortunately for nonconforming "Night People," postwar local radio offered up several other comedic performers for America's satiric underground. Bob Elliott, Ray Goulding, Steve Allen, and Ernie Kovacs all began their careers in local radio. Of these performers, only Elliott and Goulding, working together as "Bob and Ray," remained closely tied to the medium of radio. Like other innovative talents in radio, they were mainly heard on powerful stations based in New York City—during the mid-1950s they worked on WINS and for a several years prior to their first retirement in 1965 on WHN. They first began working together in 1946 as cohosts for a morning news and music program on the Boston radio station WHDH. At first they were expected to behave as traditional "straight" announcers, but it was not long before the pair began using the news segment as a springboard for off-the-cuff comic banter. Later, when WHDH granted them a twenty-five-minute program titled *Matinee with Bob and Ray,* they experimented with a broad range of humorous characterizations and parody. Listeners responded to Bob and Ray's offbeat comic routines with enthusiasm; by the late 1940s they had acquired a devoted following in the Boston area and earned a reputation as the most daring and inventive comic team in radio. They made their national debut in 1951 through a pair of NBC radio programs — one, a fifteen-minute program presented daily, and the other, an hour-long variety program airing on Saturday evenings — and a prime-time NBC television program. For NBC in 1952 and ABC in 1953, they created (with the assistance of veteran radio satirist Raymond Knight) and performed (with comic actress Audrey Meadows) several daytime and prime-time programs. None of the early-1950s incarnations of *The Bob and Ray Show* fared well on television, however. For the remainder of the decade the majority of their work was in radio.[24]

To the ears of many radio listeners during the 1950s, few radio performers were as inventive, spontaneous, or imaginative as Bob and Ray. In addition to providing voices for a wide cast of characters, the pair had the remarkable ability to improvise material while performing one of their skits or mock interviews on the air. Like accomplished jazzmen, the fellow native New Englanders collaborated instinctively. Their timing was often flawless, their use of language and their flights of fancy inspired. It is no surprise that they were the darlings of Jackie Gleason, Sid Caesar, and other period comedians who prized improvisation and spontaneity. In addition to their fresh technique, Bob and Ray provided listeners with varieties of parody and satire that were all too rare in commercial broadcasting in the 1950s. As with Depression-era radio comedians such as Raymond Knight and Stoopnagle and Budd, Bob and Ray often chose as their comic butts everyday Americans, people blind to their own stupidity and "engaged in enterprises," as Kurt Vonnegut has astutely observed, "which, if not contemptible, are at least insane."[25] In the opinion of those listeners who cracked their comic code and were "in" on their jokes, Bob and Ray were unusually adept at revealing the truth about the way "ordinary Americans" — the pretentious creeps and the phonies, the dullards and nincompoops, the crooks and frauds — behaved. In this way, Bob and Ray also resembled fellow East Coast radio satirists Fred Allen and

14. Throughout the 1950s, radio comedians Bob Elliott and Ray Goulding playfully lampooned advertising and American consumer culture. Photo by Larry Fried, reproduced by permission of Lauren Wendle.

Henry Morgan. Although less acerbic than either of these contemporaries, Bob and Ray nevertheless emulated their deft and literate satiric characterizations.

They resembled Allen and Morgan most when they satirized commercialism and the banality of American popular culture. Particularly in their scattershot parodies of radio commercials, Bob and Ray flashed elements of the same disdain that Morgan harbored toward advertisers and their phony merchandising gimmicks. Bob and Ray riddled promotions for fictional products such as Woodlo (the product "all America is talking about") and their Home Brain Surgery Kit (available at "laughably low prices" from their "over-stocked surplus warehouses") with the commercial pitch's worst clichés. And in regular features such as "The Life and Loves of Linda Lovely" and the much celebrated "Mary Backstayge, Noble Wife," Bob and Ray travestied the weepy sentimentalism and banal plotlines underwriting postwar soap opera dramas. In the same vein as *MAD* comics, Bob and Ray took comic revenge on a wide variety of public figures and national icons, transforming heroic males into jerks and pansies, macho detectives into incompetents such as "Hartford Harry,

Private Eye," Mary Margaret McBride into the vapid Mary Margaret Mc-Goon, Arthur Godfrey into the bore Arthur Sturdley, "Mr. Keen, Tracer of Lost Persons" into "Mr. Trace, Keener Than Most Persons," Jack Armstrong into "Jack Headstrong, the All-American American," and newsmen and sportscasters in general into the bumbling fool Wally Ballou and the inebriate Steve Bosco. Bob and Ray even made a foray into political satire during the 1954 Army-McCarthy hearings when they depicted the Wisconsin Senator (in episodes of their "Mary Backstayge, Noble Wife") as a bumbling official from Skunk Haven named Commissioner Carstairs.[26]

Like Jean Shepherd, Bob and Ray thrived best on local New York radio stations that permitted them the time and the autonomy to develop innovative comic material. Bob and Ray were also broadcast "from approximately coast to coast" on national networks: an evening program for Mutual in 1956, programs for NBC in 1951 and 1952, and beginning in 1955, brief spots for its weekend *Monitor.* Yet collaborations between the radio networks and performers such as Bob and Ray were often short-lived and difficult. Network radio, even when it could afford to take a few chances, had a difficult time accommodating offbeat talent. As the case of *The Stan Freberg Show* and the equally short-lived 1957 Henry Morgan vehicle *Sez Who* illustrated, the CBS radio network in particular had a tendency to mishandle satiric performers. Bob and Ray's fortunes with CBS proved no different. In 1959 they broadcast a daily fifteen-minute program on CBS, but it failed shortly after it was launched.

*   *   *

Local television, like local radio, nurtured a number of creative and original comedic talents during the early 1950s. On Chicago's WNBQ during the early fifties, Dave Garroway's *Garroway at Large* offered an intelligent, spontaneous comic style that would largely disappear from television by the middle of the decade. In other cities, local television stations recruited offbeat comics and disk jockeys to help fill the large blocks of daytime, non-network time that occupied their broadcast schedules. While Los Angeles's KNXT-TV hired an upstart named Johnny Carson to present a weekly program titled *Carson's Cellar,* Philadelphia's WPTZ-TV chose Ernie Kovacs, an antic, prank-loving New Jersey disk jockey, to host its afternoon cooking and fashion shows. Kovacs provided a manic, irreverent presence for these programs and his hit morning program *3 to Get*

Ready. This last program, which Kovacs and his small cast performed live with neither scripts nor studio audience, attracted Philadelphia viewers with its improvised, novelty shop prop shtick and parodic, behind-the-scenes peeks at television production.[27]

Kovacs was hired by NBC in 1951 but never really found a permanent home in the network's schedule. Between 1951 and 1957, he appeared on a long list of daytime, prime-time, and special programs, where he deployed a repertoire of television and advertising parodies, unpredictable blackouts, sly asides, and elaborate sight gags. Because many of the comic devices Kovacs deployed were dependent on absurd, unexpected visual tricks and on surrealistic juxtapositions of sight and sound, they defy easy explanation and, in the end, appealed to a limited audience. In the opinion of those devoted fans who appreciated spontaneous satire and irreverent parody more than the safe, homogenized domestic situation comedies churned out by the networks, the "dime-store guerilla theater" served up by this Hungarian saloon keeper's son constituted one of television's few redeeming features. Particularly in his self-referential and mocking send-ups of the medium of television itself, Kovacs was, in his own peculiar way, subversive. As critic J. Hoberman, the best interpreter of Kovacs's distinctive comedic genius, has observed, few acts in the history of television were as openly and comically antagonistic to the medium as the time when Kovacs closed the last, live performance of a canceled WPTZ program by dismantling its set with an ax.[28]

Steve Allen was also able to translate to 1950s network television elements of the inventive, improvisational comic style he had gained through his experience in radio. Allen, the son of an Irish vaudeville comedienne, began working on a variety of local and network radio programs during the late 1940s. He first caught the attention of CBS network executives with his popular, offbeat late-night radio program *Breaking All Records* for Los Angeles's KNX. In 1950, CBS brought Allen to New York. Following a period of uncertainty and numerous time slot changes, Allen eventually settled in with a nightly thirty-minute comedy program. Although critics enjoyed, as Allen later recalled, the "creative, experimental stunts" he performed on this program, CBS decided to cancel it in 1953. His network television career was revived when, as a temporary replacement for Arthur Godfrey on his *Talent Scouts* program, he deliberately fumbled a Lipton Tea commercial. According to Allen, his parody of Godfrey's famous Lipton's sales pitch caused the audience to go "wild" with laughter and, more importantly, brought his "abilities to the attention of many of the 'right' people." One of these "right" people was NBC president Pat Weaver, one of the few network presidents in the early history of television who had a good eye for comedic talent. In 1954 Weaver arranged for Allen to begin broadcasting his local program, *The Steve Allen Show,* on NBC with a new title, *Tonight!* For the next two years (except for a period during the fall of 1956 when he was assisted by Kovacs), Allen hosted *Tonight!* five nights a week during the network's late evening hours.[29]

Into a network time slot that had seen very little of interest or originality, Steve Allen inserted a wide assortment of parody sketches, irreverent banter, and spontaneous comic action. Most fondly remembered were his offstage, ad-libbed stunts, his interactions with audience members, and his "Man on the Street" segments. His appeal stemmed from a quick, smart edge that marked his conversational style and his relaxed, self-effacing manner. To American audiences during the fifties, he was the master of the "ad-glib," the hip square, the piano accompanist for Beat poet Jack Kerouac, the horn-rimmed television comic with the Madison Avenue account executive's wardrobe and the jazzman's cool, "cerebral" style. Like Kovacs and a few other experimentalists consigned to the margins of 1950s television comedy, Allen viewed television as a plastic medium, a fertile ground where experimentation, improvisation (one of his favorite bits was to compose melodies at the piano based on notes elicited by audience members), intimacy, and abstraction—important aesthetic elements of jazz performance—might take root. Allen also cultivated an image as the liberal "thinking man's comic" and later dedicated himself to using television as a medium to challenge and educate his audiences.[30]

*   *   *

One of early American television's most sustained and successful efforts at parody and satire was launched by two men who had no experience in radio, Max Liebman and Sid Caesar. Liebman, a veteran of vaudeville and an experienced producer of Broadway and Pocono Mountains resort revues, arranged a deal (once again with Pat Weaver) that provided NBC with a live stage revue every Saturday evening. Drawing from the large pool of comedic talent that was ethnically Jewish and native to New York City, Liebman assembled a cast of brilliant performers (Caesar, Imogene Coca, Howard Morris, and Carl Reiner) and writers (Lucille Kallen, Mel Tolkin, Tony Webster, Mel Brooks, and Joe Stein) who provided a weekly program akin to traditional, urban vaudeville—an impression given by Caesar's broad impersonations, antic performance style, and use of dialect comedy. More than vaudeville, however, what Liebman and Caesar intended to replicate—from their initial collaboration on the 1949 *The Admiral Broadway Revue* on—was "sophisticated" revue-style comedy.[31] In place of the patter and slapstick routines appearing on Milton Berle's *Texaco Star Theater,* Liebman, Caesar, and their staff created satiric routines based on the day-to-day, often domestic experiences of men and women in postwar America.

In his autobiography Caesar explains that he was pushed by the demands of creating new material every week and therefore compelled "to rely more and more on crazy ideas I got from seeing things on the street and in the subways, and from my relationship with [my wife] Florence." Equipped with their skills in pantomime, dialect, and character acting and informed by the insights of Freudian psychology—it is significant that most of *Your Show of Shows* collaborating writers and performers were undergoing psychoanalysis while working on the program—Caesar and Coca were able to lend a palpable sense of hostility, anger, and frustration to their satiric profiles of modern Americans. In their popular "Hickenloopers" sketches, Caesar and Coca addressed the hostile antagonism between husbands and wives, in much the same way Jackie Gleason's *Honeymooners* did later. Equally if not more popular than the "Hickenloopers" and "cliché" sketches, the monologues, pantomimes, and mock interviews lampooning pontificating authority figures were the parodies of high and low culture that Caesar, Coca, and their colleagues devised. Much in the style of Bob and Ray, Ernie Kovacs, and *MAD* magazine, *Your Show of Shows* travestied opera and ballet, modern art, television programs, and, perhaps most memorably, popular and esoteric "art" films.[32]

Your Show of Shows delivered a stream of parody and social satire that was remarkably consistent for a weekly, ninety-minute live broadcast. As a result, it ranked among the top ten network programs during the 1950–51 and 1951–52 seasons and routinely garnered critical praise in the mainstream press. Typical of the laudatory assessments heaped on *Your Show of Shows* at its peak was the assessment of *New York Times* critic Jack Gould who opined that it was "an island of engaging literacy in TV's sea of vaudeville mediocrity." Gilbert Seldes also greatly admired Caesar's talent, particularly his ability to comically depict the frustrations endured by the antiheroic modern American male. While Caesar and Coca collaborated together on *Your Show of Shows,* Seldes wrote in *The Public Arts* (1956), "not a single program of its quality, or anything near it, was attempted."[33] The program's novelty inevitably began to wear thin, and by late 1954 its audience share had begun to slip. In order to stem its high production costs ($220,000 per program) and reap a better return on its talent investment, NBC encouraged Caesar, Coca, and Liebman to pursue three different projects. Once Caesar and his colleagues went their separate ways, the collaborative chemistry and smart comic edge that *Your Show of Shows* had achieved largely disappeared from broadcast television.[34]

*   *   *

Throughout the early 1950s, American radio and television provided a large venue for the type of antisentimental, anticommercial parody practiced by Henry Morgan, Stan Freberg, and other satirists. Yet as their experience proved, mainstream commercial radio and television restrained the type of comic revenge they were capable of meting out. Because of the trepidations of the American broadcast industry, fans of irreverent, antiestablishment parody and humor—young American males in particular—turned to a growing satiric underground for comic relief. Within this subterranean culture, the taste for more aggressive and thoroughgoing affronts to propriety and consumer culture was more than met by sick jokes, the recordings of Tom Lehrer, the cartoons of men's magazines, and, most of all, *MAD* comics.

The first of these, underground sick jokes circulated widely at a moment in time when concerns about a growing collective neurosis were finding expression in the work of Beat poets such as Allen Ginsberg and in books such as Erich Fromm's *The Sane Society* (1955). Taken as a whole, they indulged in the perverse and defiantly and deliberately courted the impression of psychological sickness or maladjustment. In 1957, *Time* magazine broke the news to many concerned adults that "on college campuses and playgrounds, youngsters are laughing at a new kind of joke that has spread across the nation with appalling thoroughness." Known variously as "bloody marys," "hate" or "cruel" jokes, "gruesomes," and "meanies," sick jokes typically chose as their subjects the murder of friends and relatives ("Mommy, why are we out in our boat at night?" "Shut up, and tie that cement block around your leg."), mutilation ("Mommy, I can't move my foot." "Shut up, or I'll cut your legs off too"), cannibalism ("Mommy, I hate my sister's guts." "Shut up and eat what's put in front of you."), incest

("Mommy, what's an Oedipus complex?" "Shut up and kiss me."), degenerate parents ("Daddy, why are we celebrating Christmas in July?" "Well, you know you are dying of leukemia."), and all manners of disease and mutilation ("Can Bill come out and play?" "No, he's got leprosy." "Well then can we come in and watch him rot?").[35]

When called to explain this disturbing phenomenon, Freudian psychologist Martha Wolfenstein, the author of *Children's Humor* (1954), explained that it represented an aggressive reaction against "the noble sentiments that the public is constantly being asked to turn out." *Harper's* magazine editor Eric Larrabee likewise claimed that sick jokes represented a "rebellion of a people sated with piety, prosperity and snake oil." Sociologist David Riesman, coauthor of *The Lonely Crowd* (1950) and an intellectual much concerned with organizational society's deleterious effects on the male individual, argued that sick jokes assumed "violent and macabre forms" as a way of protesting the blandness of one's personal condition. In addition, several critics and intellectuals linked the rise of sick jokes to the underlying fear of atomic destruction. Columbia University professor Jacques Barzun speculated that sick jokes "act . . . as an antidote taken ahead of time against likely horrors," while author Philip Wylie conjectured that they helped "wipe away a little of the burden of terror put on us by living in this age."[36]

All of these explanations have some merit, yet they omit one of the most obvious satiric themes running throughout this joke cycle: the reversal of the "mother love" ideal. It is particularly odd that Philip Wylie, who in his satiric survey of American beliefs and customs, *The Generation of Vipers* (1942), leveled a vitriolic attack on mom and "momism," missed this connection. It is also clear that the enthusiastic trading of sick jokes provided young Americans with a way to react against the heavy demands of psychological normalcy. During the fifties, in fact, displaying signs of "sickness" and "madness" became a gesture of defiance for some young, middle-class Americans. Beginning with Holden Caulfield, the protagonist of J. D. Salinger's popular novel *The Catcher in the Rye* (1951), the figure of the alienated, disillusioned misfit who was "growing up absurd" compelled the sympathy and allegiance of young people who believed that psychological maladjustment was not an illness, as the squares and phonies of the adult world maintained, but a form of intuitive wisdom. As Daniel Belgrad has noted, the neurosis cultivated by Beat poets such as Allen Ginsberg was likewise intended as a "profound cultural query." Jack Kerouac summed up this strategy perfectly in *On the Road* (1957) when his protagonist Sal Paradise states, "The only people for me are the mad ones, the ones who are mad to live, mad to talk, mad to be saved."[37] Indeed, the enjoyment of sick jokes and Kerouac's mad pose shared a similar motive: both served to separate the intelligent individual from the great unthinking, "phony" masses.

Not surprisingly, the defiant pose that sick jokes and sick humor in general began to maintain in the 1950s rankled critics at both ends of the ideological spectrum. In the opinion of syndicated columnist Robert Ruark, who proposed that Americans "Nix the Sickniks" in a 1963 issue of the *Saturday Evening Post,* the sick humor of the 1950s "built itself off [a] state of inverted mental sickness, and it was only natural that it would descend to the barnyard in its eventual amplification." Jonathan Miller, an up-and-coming British satirist with the Beyond the Fringe troupe, addressed the phenomena of American sick jokes from a different perspective. Writing for the *Partisan Review,* Miller charged that sick humor was a merely a childish way of exploring "the outlines of a puzzling moral contour." Typically deployed, Miller reasoned, to test the tolerance (the "moral flexibility") and hipness of the person toward whom it is directed, sick humor provides the "self-styled liberal" who trades in this type of "jocular irony" an easy way to separate himself from the herd. The problem with sick jokes, Miller maintained, is that they "celebrate the very prejudice which the self-styled liberal claims to hate." In his wide-ranging assault on liberal satire's "New Irony," published in the *American Scholar* in late 1961, Amherst College professor Benjamin DeMott anticipated several of Miller's objections. Like Miller, DeMott interpreted much of the laughter spurred by sick humor as a gesture of "knowingness." "Exchanging conversational coin with [the ironist]," DeMott argued, "means entering a secret relation, accepting membership in an exclusive community, marking yourself off from fools." An even larger concern for DeMott was what he viewed as the cynicism underwriting sick jokes and humor. The "effect of the body of sick criticism," he wrote, "is to maintain that *all* postures toward issues in question are absurd." For DeMott, then, the appreciation of sick humor represented further proof that Americans were in a disturbing flight from "common pieties" and ideological commitment.[38]

In their critiques, critics like Miller and DeMott posed challenging questions about the orientation and true cultural effect of sick humor and liberal satire. It is certainly true, as we shall see in subsequent chapters, that these forms of irreverent comic expression encouraged a type of smug, self-congratulatory, in-group mentality among its liberal fans. Indeed, the consumption and appreciation of sick humor and liberal satire at times signaled more about the superiority of one's taste and intelligence than one's convictions about issues of social importance. The charge of cynicism that DeMott leveled against sick humor and satire also had some legitimacy. Yet both DeMott and Miller went too far in their dismissals. Both exaggerated sick humor's nihilism, just as *Time* magazine had done in its notorious and oft-quoted 1959 exposé on America's "sickniks."[39] Confusing cynicism with skepticism, Miller and DeMott, like other critics and intellectuals, were too quick to dismiss sick humorists as rebels without causes.

Postwar purveyors of sick humor, parody, and liberal satire walked a thin line between bleak cynicism and moral commitment. Undeniably, inevitably, their work shaded into the former; during the cold war years of the fifties and early sixties, the pull of despair was strong, despite what popular memory of the period often tells us. Yet as the cases of Harvey Kurtzman and other sick humorists and liberal satirists demonstrate, there were strong, at times intense moral motives behind their comedic critiques. Theater critic Robert Brustein reflected this awareness when he took stock of sick humor and satire for the *New Republic* in 1962. "For if the young seem negative and irresponsible," Brustein wrote of sick humorists and satirists at work in the fifties and early sixties, "then this may be because their positive and responsible elders have left them such a poisoned inheritance." "[It] is a measure of health, not sickness," Brustein concluded, "that their inevitable anger and resentment can still be disciplined within a witty, sharp, and purgative art."[40]

* * *

Even in the career of the sick songwriter Tom Lehrer, there were notable examples of outrage and social concern. Lehrer's career as a singing parodist dated back to 1942 when, at the age of fourteen, he performed a brief ditty about Adolf Hitler on the radio program of a family friend. Several years later, while pursuing graduate studies in mathematics and statistics at Harvard University, the precocious and prank-loving Lehrer began to gain notoriety for the song parodies he played at private parties and smokers. Performed in the style of popular songs from the 1930s—songs that he had learned to play on the piano as a kid growing up in New York City—Lehrer's parodic tunes offered an irreverent take on a host of sentimental ideals and sacred subjects. Lehrer so impressed Boston-area satirist Al Capp that in 1951 he was invited to contribute to Capp's short-lived television quiz program. A year later, Lehrer appeared at a Boston nightclub named Alpini's. Encouraged by his songs' popularity in and around Cambridge, Lehrer decided to cut an album at a do-it-yourself recording studio in Boston. In little more than an hour one day in January 1953, Lehrer recorded all but one of the songs in his repertoire. On the liner notes to his new album, *Songs by Tom Lehrer*, he declared, in the same self-deprecating manner Harvey Kurtzman would deploy in his *MAD* comics, that he was a "longtime exponent of the *derrière-garde* in American music." "Now at last some of the songs with which he has been revolting local audiences for years are available to all," Lehrer commented about himself tongue-in-cheek.[41]

The fifth cut on *The Songs of Tom Lehrer*, "I Wanna Go Back to Dixie," provided listeners with a glimpse of Lehrer's liberal social concerns. Delivered in a deadpan manner similar to that deployed by his idols and fellow New Englanders, Bob and Ray, this number poked fun at "the many delightful features of the South"[42]:

I wanna go back to Dixie
Take me back to dear ol' Dixie
That's the only li'l ol' place for li'l ol' me.
Ol' times there are not forgotten
Whuppin' slaves and sellin' cotton
And waitin' for the Robert E. Lee . . .

I wanna talk with Southern gentlemen
And put my white sheet on again
I ain't seen one good lynchin' in years . . .[43]

More characteristic of the sick parodic songs that made up Lehrer's early repertoire was "Old Dope Peddler," a mock ballad (based on sentimental fare such as "The Old Lamplighter") that celebrated an unlikely neighborhood do-gooder, and "My Home Town," an exercise in twisted nostalgia that recalled the "little girl next door" who "used to give [sex] for free," "Dan" who was "swell . . . and ground [his mother-in-law] up real well," and, finally, "the guy that took a knife, and monogrammed his wife, then dropped her in the pond and watched her drown." In "Be Prepared," Lehrer mocked the code of the all-American Boy Scouts: "Keep those reefers hidden where you're sure that they will not be found," Lehrer advised, and "Don't solicit for your sister, that's not nice, unless you get a good percentage of her price." The song then concluded,

Comic Revenge

If you're looking for adventure of a new and different kind
And you come across a Girl Scout who is similarly inclined
Don't be nervous, don't be flustered, don't be scared
Be prepared! [44]

While light and carefree about sex, Lehrer's parodic songs were pessimistic about the sustainability of romantic love. In "When You Are Old and Gray," Lehrer sang in the manner of a sentimental love song:

Since I still appreciate you
Let's find love while we may
Because I know I'll hate you
When you are old and gray . . . .

Your teeth will start to go, dear
Your waist will start to spread
In twenty years or so, dear
I'll wish that you were dead. [45]

Lehrer's comic negation of love and tenderness found its most sick expression in "I Hold Your Hand in Mine":

I hold your hand in mine, dear
I press it to my lips.
I take a healthy bite
From your dainty fingertips.

My joy would be complete, dear
If you were only here.
But still I keep your hand
As a precious souvenir.

The night you died I cut it off.
I really don't know why.
For now each time I kiss it
I get bloodstains on my tie.

I'm sorry now I killed you
For our love was something fine.
And till they come to get me
I shall hold your hand in mine. [46]

Priced at $3.50, the first four hundred copies of Lehrer's album sold rapidly around Harvard Square. Word of it spread quickly, and before long Lehrer was receiving orders from cities and campus towns across the

15. Backstage at the Palace Theatre in London, Tom Lehrer plays up his image as America's "Archpriest of Irreverence." Evening Standard/Hulton Archive/Getty Images.

United States. *The Songs of Tom Lehrer* eventually sold over 350,000 copies and became one of the most popular underground albums ever produced. Across the country in 1953, young Americans played it repeatedly and memorized its lyrics. A year later, national publications reported that a "Lehrer cult" was spreading among the nation's young people.[47] Lehrer's popularity continued throughout the midfifties, prompting him in 1957 (after two years of compulsory army duty) to drop his graduate studies and pursue a career as a professional performer. After playing his first concert at Hunter College in New York, Lehrer toured nightclubs, college campuses, and concert halls across the United States and the English-speaking world. In 1959, Lehrer gathered the songs that he had been performing over the past several years on his second album, *More Songs of Tom Lehrer*. With such ditties as "Poisoning Pigeons in the Park" and "Oedipus

Rex," Lehrer solidified his reputation as America's "Complete Iconoclast" and "Archpriest of Irreverence."

Lehrer's profane songs undoubtedly raised the hackles of some women, conservative traditionalists, and watchful parents. Yet since these songs, like sick jokes, operated under the cloak of humor and satire, because they fell in line with the work of Ambrose Bierce, W. C. Fields, and America's long tradition of violent, misogynistic humor and reflected the irreverent attitudes of contemporary male comedians and satirists such as Henry Morgan, Ernie Kovacs, and Bob and Ray they provoked no loud public outcries. Indeed, Lehrer's songs echoed "the true satirical note," as a *Boston Herald* critic appropriately noted, "of rampant [male] individualism." They also meshed perfectly with the antidomestic, antisentimental male rebellion underwriting *Playboy* magazine. Given the affinity between Lehrer's irreverent, masculinist outlook and *Playboy*'s editorial agenda, it is no surprise that Lehrer received his first feature-length notice in *Playboy*. Appearing in the magazine's May 1955 issue, Rolf Malcolm's admiring profile called Lehrer "a dangerous man, a shatterer of illusions, a mocker of traditions, a cruel deflator of our most jealously guarded shams and sentimentalities. This is, in short, that most feared of human fiends: a satirist." Distilling perfectly what *Playboy* and scores of Lehrer's young male fans appreciated most about Lehrer, Malcolm went on to claim that the "appalling (as well as appealing) thing" about his humor "is that its basic ingredient is nothing more than honesty." Looking back to the midfifties, Lehrer agrees that middle-class Americans were hungry for humor that attacked the hypocrisy and the inflated postwar idealism that surrounded their daily lives. "I think a lot of people," Lehrer remembers, "probably saw [my album] as an island of . . . what they regarded as sanity." [48]

The spirit of Lehrer's songs meshed with the sick jokes traded on playgrounds, and it found echoes in the stand-up comedy of Jonathan Winters and Theodore Gottlieb. Winters, an Ohio-born comedian who served in the marines during World War II, worked in local radio before he received his big break on network television in the mid-1950s. On programs such as *Omnibus* and *The Jack Paar Show,* Winters performed satiric characterizations of a wide range of people, from the small-town hick to the big-city pseudo intellectual. Off camera and in the confines of one of the "sophisticated" nightclubs that were opening their doors to the "new comedians," Winters's antic, at times dizzying caricatures broached homosexuality, violence, mental illness, and other "way out," suggestive material that courted critics' disapproving label of sick. In response to his critics, Winters in 1958 told *Time* magazine, "If you're not sick, you're a bore." "Who's to say who's sick?" In the minds of his detractors, Winters answered his own question the next year when he suffered a nervous breakdown while performing at the hungry i in San Francisco.[49]

Gottlieb, the son of wealthy German Jews who perished at Dachau, fled Europe for California (reportedly with the assistance of Sigmund Freud), where he worked as a laborer. He initiated his career as a performer when he began reading Edgar Allen Poe onstage in San Francisco. After moving to New York in the midfifties, he found bookings at small bohemian nightclubs in Greenwich Village. Billing himself as "Brother Theodore," Gottlieb offered patrons of his midnight program *Blossoms of Evil* ("a choleric commentary on our life and times") comic lectures, as he told *Playboy* in 1958, "on how to manufacture baby oil, using live babies; the joys of making love to a raincoat; and other commercial pap." "People say that I am mad," he responded to his critics, "but I have found that madness is a very healthy sickness. Without it, I would have gone insane long ago."[50] For individuals like *Village Voice* critic Jerry Tallmer who delighted in the macabre, Brother Theodore was "one of the most acrid satirists in his profession." Writing in 1958, Tallmer gushed, "To hear him vent his spleen on medicine, medicos, head shrinkers, faith-curers, führers, audiences, and in general the whole swinish race of mankind, is to hear it (and see it, for his physical acting matches the other) with all the vehemence of Carlyle and all the exactness of Swift."[51]

Shades of Lehrer's sick humor were also evident in the work of cartoonists such as Edward Gorey, Tomi Ungerer, William Shoemaker, Gahan Wilson, and Shel Silverstein—three of whom were regularly published in *Playboy*.[52] The cartoonist with whom Lehrer was most often compared, however, was Charles Addams. During the fifties, Addams's macabre gag panel cartoons found a wide audience through the *New Yorker*, where they had been published for two decades, and through popular anthologies such as *Homebodies* (1954), *Nightcrawlers* (1957), and *Black Maria* (1960). In a bizarre and fantastic fashion, Addams's panel cartoons narrated tales of murder and murderous desires (often between spouses), of cannibalism, and all sorts of odd, irrational phenomena. Addams was the anti-Disney, ritually performing his twisted comic reversals of values Americans held dear. Critic Dwight Macdonald accurately captured the essence of Addams's cartoons and the reasons behind their popularity in an appreciation for the *Reporter* in 1953. Macdonald here explained that they appeal to Americans because they "provide a healthy antidote to the saccharine treatment of the [family] in our advertisements and other forms of mass culture." "After the depressingly cheerful families of beer ads, the pious celebrations of marital bliss on the radio, the sentimental gushing over the kiddies everywhere except in the same," Macdonald continued, "it is wonderfully relaxing to see these themes treated with a reverse twist, a bend sinister."[53]

* * *

With its caustic references to "depressingly cheerful families" in beer ads and the "pious celebrations" to be found in soap opera dramas, Dwight Macdonald's comments would have certainly appealed to Harvey Kurtzman, a liberal cartoonist who harbored a deep distaste for "sentimental gushing" and the artifice emanating from postwar American culture. Like several other satirists who emerged during the fifties, Kurtzman was a child of East European Jewish immigrants. While growing up in the Bronx during the Depression, Kurtzman was deeply influenced by his left-leaning parents' support for labor unions and racial justice. As Kurtzman admitted in an interview with historian Paul Buhle, his mother and stepfather subscribed to the communist *Daily Worker* and were very much part of the Popular Front culture of the 1930s and 1940s. Kurtzman and his siblings were reared, as he recalls, with a "radical bent as regards things like race and labor unions." He began to develop his natural talent for drawing when, at his mother's insistence, he began attending children's classes at the Pratt Institute in Brooklyn. He was later accepted to study at the High School of Music and Art, a school for gifted children created during the 1930s by New York mayor Fiorello LaGuardia.[54]

While still at the High School of Music and Art, Kurtzman worked as an assistant to Louis Ferstadt, a cartoonist for Classic Comics and the *Daily Worker.* By this time, the teenaged Kurtzman had no trouble, as he wrote in his autobiography, "think[ing] of something satirical or biting to say." Like the progeny of many immigrants, Kurtzman was determined to abandon the Old World ways of his parents and assimilate himself to American society. The distinctive manner in which Kurtzman and other second-generation Irish, Italian, and Jewish kids growing up on the streets of New York engaged American popular culture was by saluting it with Bronx cheers. In the school lunchroom, Kurtzman and his schoolmates (three of whom, Will Elder, Al Jaffee, and John Severin, later collaborated with him on *MAD*) engaged in parodic revelry, rigorously needling contemporary radio programs and the formulaic Hollywood movies they viewed at their local theaters. Kurtzman recalls that, "all over New York there were Jewish guys in separate high schools doing the same routines." "We were a product of our Jewish backgrounds in New York," and as a result "the same kind of Jewish direction of thinking would come up with the same scene." "Sid Caesar eventually did all the routines we anticipated. And it was no coincidence. We were feeding off the *same material,* reacting to Hollywood the *same way,* coming to the *same conclusion.*"[55]

After attending Cooper Union and then freelancing for several large comics studios, Kurtzman was drafted into the army, where he contributed cartoons for the Department of Information and Education. Much relieved to finally end his wartime duty (he was based at various locations in the South and had great difficulty dealing with the native racism), Kurtzman moved back to New York and resumed his cartooning career.[56] Although he failed to find work at the newspaper *PM*—Walt Kelly, then *PM*'s cartoon editor, rejected his portfolio—Kurtzman was hired to work for Stan Lee's Timely Comics. In 1949, while struggling to keep the commercial art studio that he had opened with Will Elder above water, Kurtzman obtained his first work, an educational comic about the dangers of venereal disease, through E.C. Comics, one of the largest comics publishers in the United States. E.C.'s owner, Bill Gaines, immediately recognized Kurtzman's talent. With profits pouring in from the sales of his popular and graphically violent line of horror and suspense comic books, Gaines granted Kurtzman the license to produce *Two Fisted Tales* and *Frontline Combat.* Originally conceived during the Korean War as adventure comics, these two titles grew into gritty, naturalistic military dramas. By painstakingly rendering the conditions of modern warfare, Kurtzman was able to deny the glorification of combat and register his dissent against the average war comic's fixation with, as Kurtzman later described it, "Americans beating up little buck-toothed yellow men." In the process of completing the books, he "came . . . to the marvelous conclusion," as he later explained, "that it's the truth that one should be interested in, that if you aimed your thinking toward telling the truth about something, then you're doing something worthwhile."[57]

Kurtzman became further convinced of the critical potential of parody and satire after he read several college humor magazines. After experiencing their "irreverent sledgehammer satire," Kurtzman later remembered, he suddenly "became aware of a certain approach to humor." "College magazines had a lot of anger, a lot of satire," Kurtzman later explained. "Those magazines were outrageous in their approach to humor, and I wanted to be outrageous. They suggested to me not ideas but an attitude—a mood, something bigger than detailed ideas." When Kurtzman approached Bill Gaines with the idea of publishing a new, humorous comic book, Gaines assented.[58] With his new venture, a comic book he titled *MAD*, Kurtzman found the perfect vehicle through which he could marry his moral anger, his devotion to truth and authenticity, and his urban Jewish American wit.

When the first issues of *MAD* hit newsstands in the late summer of 1952, it promised "Humor in a jugular vein" for ten cents a copy. In its editorial statement, Kurtzman told his readers that they could expect a "comic magazine based on the short story type of wild adventure that you seem to like so well." At first, *MAD* stuck close to this description, yielding little more than crudely exaggerated genre parodies of science fiction and crime comics. In its second issue, however, *MAD* offered a glimpse of the type of popular culture parody that would soon account for its success. With "Melvin!" Kurtzman struck at the farfetched fantasy and racism behind Edgar Rice Burroughs's venerable *Tarzan*. In *MAD's* third and fourth issues, Kurtzman broadly lampooned the *Superman* comic books and *The Lone Ranger* and *Dragnet* television series. In the "Superduperman" and "Lone Stranger!" stories in particular, Kurtzman hit upon a formula that would sustain *MAD* for years to come, namely, the robust deflation of mythic, all-American heroes. In Kurtzman's hands, the Lone Ranger was depicted as a coward prone to falling off his horse. Superman, meanwhile, became a thug and a sellout who even used his broad chest as a commercial billboard. The climax of Kurtzman's comic revenge on Superman came in the last panels when the superhero reveals his true identity to Lois Lane, who then spits back, "Big deal. Yer still a creep!" Kurtzman's unprecedented affront to Superman so upset its publisher that it promptly threatened to sue *MAD* and its parent company. Undaunted by threats of litigation, Kurtzman searched for and eventually found an attorney who was willing to support *MAD's* legal right to parody.[59]

From this moment on, Kurtzman's *MAD* comics mercilessly lampooned a host of square-jawed, goyishe American tough guys, from the upright, virtuous marshal played by Gary Cooper in *High Noon* to Marlon Brando's motorcycle bad boy in *The Wild One*. At the mercy of *MAD's* twisted plotlines, comic book, television, and movie heroes would reveal themselves as venal knaves, cowards, narcissists, and lechers. From its inception, then, *MAD* was committed to seizing hold of postwar America's heroes, icons, and myths and violently turning them on their heads. Rather than bowing down to the cherished ideals underwriting 1950s consensus culture—togetherness, family, prosperity, upward mobility, and psychological normalcy, all of them powerfully reinforced by television, movies, and mass-circulation magazines—Kurtzman and his fellow *MAD* wise guys jokingly sided with the maladjusted, the twisted, sick, and insane. Commenting, in part, on the crusade psychologist Dr. Fredric Wertham had waged against E.C. suspense and horror comics, *MAD* plugged itself as "junk" and "garbage" that "poisoned" young minds.[60]

By its fourth issue, *MAD* had finally begun to find an audience and earn some money. "From then on," *MAD* publisher Bill Gaines recalled, it "just took off."[61] Before long, *MAD* spawned a host of imitators with titles such as *Wild, Whack, Flip, Nuts, Riot, Madhouse,* and *Bughouse.*[62] *MAD*'s rising popularity owed much to the type of comic hero deflation Kurtzman deployed in "Superduperman," but it was also largely due to the distinctive graphic style that *MAD*'s three main artists, Jack Davis, Wally Wood, and Will "Chicken Fat" Elder brought to each issue. All three men had assisted Kurtzman with his war comics but appeared better suited toward illustrating the type of irreverent parody he was supplying for *MAD*. Elder in particular thrived within *MAD*'s anarchic format; his influence on the style and tone of *MAD* was substantial. Since Elder was also a second-generation Jewish American raised in the Bronx and educated at the High School of Music and Art, he shared much in common with Kurtzman.[63] To a remarkable degree, Kurtzman and Elder operated on the same comic wavelength, much as Bob and Ray and, later, Mike Nichols and Elaine May did. Steeped in the same urban Jewish culture, Kurtzman and Elder together contributed many small verbal flourishes (words such as *potrzebie* and *furshlugginer*) and visual details (small signs or tchotchkes reading "post no bills" and "We got Borscht" plastered throughout) that defined the *MAD* comics' aesthetic.[64]

When working together in *MAD*'s creative hothouse on Lafayette Street, Kurtzman and Elder pushed each other to come up with ideas that were funny and outrageous. Typically it was Elder who took Kurtzman's plot and, as Kurtzman later recalled, "move[d] everything an inch to the left."[65] Under Elder's influence, Kurtzman allowed *MAD*'s panels to become densely packed with product logos, advertising slogans, pop culture images, and other bits of detritus taken from American commercial culture. Elder's panels recalled the phantasmagoric imagery of Flemish painter Peter Brueghel, Elder's favorite artist, and the irreverent sensibility of Dadaists such as Marcel Duchamp.[66] Most of all, Elder's work betrayed the influence of the manic, authority-deflating Marx Brothers comedies of the thirties. "I felt that if I could expose this zaniness, this bottled-up zaniness in me, in some kind of medium," Elder remembered of his early days with Kurtzman, "I would really burst forth, you know. Explode." Fortunately, he continued, "[Kurtzman] harnessed whatever energies I had into the proper channeling . . . I felt that all my wild energies had to be harnessed into saying something important, something where it needed to be said."[67]

More than anything else, what Elder and Kurtzman believed "needed to be said" was that the Great American Way, as legitimated by American corporate liberalism and translated through American movies, television, comics, and advertising, was riddled with a disturbing mix of deception, sentimentality, and condescension. Like Ernie Kovacs, Henry Morgan, Bob and Ray, Stan Freberg, and other satirists working in the male-centered tradition of twentieth-century modernism, Kurtzman and Elder attacked, in the name of "terrible honesty," all the cloying clichés and the smothering, sanctimonious ideals with which the American public was being bombarded. In a revealing interview conducted in 1976, Harvey Kurtzman looked back on the early years of *MAD* and observed that there "was a very fertile audience for reality stuff because [Americans] were bored with make-believe. It was the right time for a shift." Kurtzman continued,

> In the make-believe world, the fantasy world of Andy Hardy, of the early MGM movies, it's almost like taking dope or tranquilizers. It makes you feel good; it doesn't make you more aware of anything. So in a sense, it has a decadence about it . . . I think that's why the wave washed over us, over the country so violently—because for years, we had been living with make-believe humor, make-believe radio, make-believe movies. Suddenly came the age of reality art, of consciousness-raising.[68]

The manner in which Kurtzman and his colleagues used parody and satire to raise their readers' consciousness was at times simple and direct. One of his favorite devices was to contrast reality (or realistic art forms such as the modern novel) with the mass media's sanitized depiction of that reality. For the February 1955 issue of *MAD*, for example, Kurtzman juxtaposed the "movie and television version" of a cowboy—a handsome, clean-shaven man named, significantly, Lance Sterling ("Could you ever picture a cowboy hero called Melvin Poznowski?")—with John Smurd, a "100% genuine cowboy" who wore a "nauseating" walrus mustache. Unlike Lance Sterling, "old John Smurd worked like a horse" (and had no union), so he had little time or energy for "shooting it out with bad guys."[69] In later issues of *MAD* comics, Kurtzman developed an "American Scene Department," where he began to address the *real* joylessness of eating out at restaurants and the *real* hassles of shopping at "convenient" suburban supermarkets. He also initiated a feature titled "Scenes We'd Like to See!" in which male heroes *in reality* fail to save maidens and are slain by evil villains.

One of the most inventive and complex techniques that Kurtzman and Elder developed to catch their readers' attention involved a self-reflexive breakdown of boundaries and narrative frames, much in the manner of Ernie Kovacs's productions for early television.[70] In *MAD's* parody of *Alice in Wonderland,* Alice cries, "Lemme outta this *furshlugginer* place!" and finally calls "the super" to let her out of her dream with a passkey. A little while later she encounters Warner Brothers' cartoon figure Bugs Bunny and turns scared because she "realized from movies she'd seen [that] this rabbit was very dangerous to chase!" Upon waking, she complains about the story's corny "old 'dream' plot" and then is carted off to see a psychoanalyst. In other parodies, Mickey Mouse, Superman, Tarzan, Charles Atlas, and other pop culture figures routinely make unexpected visits and thereby further upset the order and continuity of the comic strip or movie being burlesqued. On occasion, characters abruptly abandon their involvement in their plot and begin registering their true feelings and their gripes directly with the reader. Frustrated by Wonder Woman's ability to fend off machine-gun bullets with her bracelets, the evil villain in *MAD's* April 1954 "Woman Wonder" parody suddenly yells, "Wait a minute! Wait a minute! Isn't this story getting kind of ridiculous?" After stepping out of a frame, he declares that he is quitting the story "until it makes more sense." Likewise, in his lampoon of the comic *Bringing Up Father,* Kurtzman had Mr. Jiggie gripe after being assailed by his wife's dishes, "By golly, let's face the facts! They think it's so funny when I get hit in the head to the accompaniment of a few stars drawn in! . . . There's just so much punishment the human comic-strip body can take!" In an act of female-directed comic revenge characteristic of many *MAD* plots, he then retaliates while asking, "How do *you* like the feel of the spinning dish cracked against the skull . . . ?"[71]

By using *MAD* as a vehicle to illuminate the "reality" behind certain events and institutions, Kurtzman and his liberal colleagues occasionally provided their readers with insightful social and political commentary. In *MAD*'s December 1954 issue, for example, Kurtzman took aim at the way the principal characters on the *Howdy Doody* children's show shamelessly pitched merchandise (in this case, Skwushy's "half-baked" bread and Phud cereal) to its innocent, trusting, juvenile audience. When Buffalo Bob asks some wise kid in the gallery what he would like to do someday, the kid responds with refreshing candor, "Of course . . . advertising and entertainment are lucrative fields if one hits the top brackets . . . much like 'Howdy Dooit' has! In other words . . . what I want to do when I grow up is to be a hustler like Howdy Dooit! I want to be where the cash is . . . The *green* stuff . . ." Television's blatant, unrelenting commercialism was also a target in "What's My Shine?," a lampoon of the popular CBS game show *What's My Line?* Written at the time of the Army-McCarthy hearings (though it appeared on newsstands several months later), the main point of this piece was to highlight Senator Joseph McCarthy's reckless red-baiting and bullying.[72]

McCarthy returned to *MAD*'s pages again in mid-1955 in a brilliant parody of Walt Kelly's *Pogo* comic strip. Here Kurtzman's Pogo goads his fellow animals to pursue "real politics like the Dixon-Yates contrac' or the Taft-Hartley Law!" only to have McCarthy (who, thanks to the newly wise Pogo, is no longer able to pass as Simple J. Malarkey) pop up and declare, "Now don't get cute! Don't . . . Don't get cute with me! It's very clear that by getting cute . . . and acting cute, you sneak across your senile ideas . . . You don't fool me for a minute! You're all [Southern] Democrats!" After being populated by a slew of world leaders (a comment on Kelly's sly introduction of caricatured politicians into his strip), Pogofenokee Swamp becomes the scene of global conflict and then nuclear annihilation. As they watch the atomic mushroom cloud form over Pogo's former tranquil backwater domain, Donald Duck, Goofy, and Mickey and Minnie Mouse defend themselves from accusations that they were the ones who implanted the idea of treating "real politics" in Pogo's head. "Learn *politics* and join a *party?*" Mickey exclaims, "Mercy no! That's the *kiss of death!* We didn't tell him that!"[73]

MAD readers had earlier caught a glimpse of a very un-Disney cynicism animating Mickey and his cohort in "Mickey Rodent!" Here a somewhat nefarious, bewhiskered Mickey plots to do away with his nemesis, Donald Duck. After successfully caging him, Mickey tells Donald, "For

16. With features such as "Howdy Dooit!" (excerpted here) Harvey Kurtzman, Bill Elder, and their colleagues at *MAD* took a swipe at the Walt Disney Company, *The Howdy Doody Show,* and shameless pitching at the heart of commercial broadcasting. *MAD* magazine.

years I've watched you pushing your way into my act . . . You and . . . them three noodnik ducks!" In addition to poking fun at the conventions of Disney comics, "Mickey Rodent!" called attention to the nature and scale of "Walt Dizzy's" postwar cultural empire. Not least, it exacted a little comic revenge on Walt Disney, a man whose reputation for union busting and conservative politics continued to inspire the anger of Kurtzman and many other liberal satirists at work in 1950s America.[74]

* * *

For someone like historian Paul Buhle, who experienced the fifties as a child growing up in the Midwest, reading "Mickey Rodent!" and other *MAD* satires made a profound impact on his consciousness. "I confirmed all my suspicions about the commercial colonization of the mind," Buhle has recounted, "by studying *MAD*'s satires as I had never studied my school books." *MAD*, Buhle states, "was the *only* subversive literature available." Cartoonist Art Spiegelman similarly remembers the effect that Kurtzman's *MAD* had on his young mind. "Mickey Rodent!" he claims, "changed my life. Something sinister was revealed below the sanitized surface of 1950s Disney America." Judging by the letters Kurtzman published in every issue of *MAD*, many other Americans were similarly impacted by *MAD* comics. Some readers clearly viewed *MAD* as a salvation and a signal that not all sanity had been lost in the Age of Eisenhower. Many particularly appreciated its challenge to the idiocies and banalities of American consumer culture. "*Mad* is by far the most intelligent and mature comic on the market, besides the generally wittiest," a man from New York wrote Kurtzman in 1955. "From the start, you have cleverly pointed out the stupidities, the idiocies, the hypocrisies of life today. You are the only comic that has dared to be subtle . . . to assume intelligence on the part of the reader." A Tufts College student similarly claimed a year earlier, "If intelligent satire can woo kids from stupid comic-books and television, *MAD* comics will carry us far along the way, and each one saved from imbecility will be a triumph for you." For many *MAD* readers, certainly, the ability to pick up on the coded critiques contained within *MAD*'s pages distinguished one from the great "unthinking" masses. One high school student from Brooklyn betrayed an element of the sense of superiority and conspiracy shared by denizens of the 1950s satiric underground when he cheerfully reported to Kurtzman, "It's no exaggeration to say that *MAD* is read by the most intelligent students in the school."[75]

In addition to offering a glimpse of how *MAD* was read and enjoyed, the letters Kurtzman published in "Mad Mumblings" provide us with a rough profile of *MAD*'s readership. It seems clear from this evidence that the overwhelming majority of *MAD*'s readers were male. This is not surprising since postwar American comic book subculture was largely a male domain. It is also reasonable to expect that *MAD* appealed to a male audience since it, like *Playboy,* Tom Lehrer, Bob and Ray, Stan Freberg, and Ernie Kovacs to one extent or another blamed "feminine" forces at large in society for the prudery, sentimentality, and deception at the heart of American consumer culture. *MAD*'s masculine orientation is also evident in the way it catered to the gaze of its male readers. To the delight of many males in the sexually repressive fifties, certainly, the pages of *MAD* were a visual delight, brimming with beautiful, buxom women and much girl chasing. The pages of *MAD* also provided readers a steady diet of comic violence, much of it directed at females. It was with glee that Kurtzman and his colleagues depicted Little Orphan Annie being chopped to bits by a train and Wonder Woman being beaten to a bloody pulp by her arch nemesis. As even Kurtzman acknowledged in "Julius Caesar!"—his self-reflexive parody of *MAD*'s parody—*MAD*'s "lampoon women" were either gorgeous or very ugly.[76] Indeed, in the work of occasional *MAD* contributor Basil Wolverton, all forms of feminine beauty were grotesquely caricatured.

MAD's frame of reference rendered it most coherent to city dwellers, particularly those residing on the East Coast. It appears clear, however, that readers from all parts of the United States fell for *MAD*'s antic humor as well as its use of intriguing and exotic phrases. On the whole, *MAD* comics appealed most to older boys, high school and college students, and young adults, but older adults were known to read it as well. Although liberal intellectuals were loath to express anything but contempt for popular culture in the mid-1950s, critic Robert Warshow, describing his son's enthusiasm for *MAD* in the journal *Commentary,* admitted that he had read it "with a kind of irritated pleasure." Kurtzman received letters from adults (from mothers in particular) who sternly objected to his efforts, but he also received letters of support. One man from rural Illinois wrote in 1954 to inform Kurtzman that "*MAD* is a publication that makes its readers stay on their toes to get all the humor." "You will find," he continued, "that the age-group that reads *MAD* is considerably older than that for any comic-book."[77]

Encouragement like this eventually helped convince Kurtzman that he ought to orient *MAD* toward a more adult readership. His ultimate ambition was to transform *MAD* from a newsprint comic book to a more expensive, higher-quality "slick" magazine. At the back of *MAD*'s twenty-third issue, Kurtzman was happy to announce the switch. "For the past two years now," he wrote, "*MAD* has been dulling the senses of the country's youth. Now we get to work on the adults."[78] From Kurtzman's perspective, converting *MAD* into a magazine would not only help legitimate his enterprise, it would guarantee that he would no longer have to face the censorship of the Comic Magazine Association's Code. Bill Gaines, whose horror comics were largely responsible for the creation of the Comics Code, agreed to follow Kurtzman's plan since *MAD* was by then one of the few moneymakers he had remaining in the E.C. line.

When the July 1955 issue of *MAD* magazine hit newsstands, Kurtzman's ambitious new strategy was immediately apparent. On the inside cover, he placed a full-page parody of Bufferin's well-known hard-sell advertising campaign. Meticulously rendered by Will Elder, *MAD*'s ad for "Bofforin" declared, "Why wait for old-fashioned cold relief? Go Kill yourself!" Elsewhere Kurtzman featured ad parodies of female products such as "Ironmaidenfit" brassieres and "Pund's" cold cream. Ad parodies were rare, though at times trenchant, in the *MAD* comic books. Now, in *MAD*'s new magazine format, ad parodies became one of the highlights. In addition to ad parodies, Kurtzman began adding substantial amounts of text, now supplied by outside contributors including fellow liberal satirists Ernie Kovacs, Stan Freberg, and Steve Allen. *MAD* then adopted the figure of Alfred E. Neuman from a 1930s humor magazine and designated him the magazine's official mascot. From this point on, this gap-toothed, impish imbecile—a spiritual cousin to Holden Caulfield and many other postwar malcontents "growing up absurd" during the fifties—and his slogan "What, Me Worry?" served as potent symbols of the ironic distance *MAD* and its "gang of idiots" would enjoy from the corrupt commercial world that surrounded them.

The evolution of *MAD* magazine by late 1955 boded well for fans of intelligent, incisive satire. With the inclusion of more text, MAD had been able to broaden the range of its targets while sharpening its barbs. After writing and editing just five issues of the new *MAD* magazine, however, Kurtzman decided to sever his ties with Bill Gaines and begin looking for a new publisher.[79] Fortunately for Kurtzman, *Playboy* publisher Hugh Hefner, a big fan of *MAD* comics, enthusiastically offered his financial assistance. With financing generously supplied by Hefner's publishing company, Kurtzman was finally able to produce the type of glossy, full-color, adult satire magazine that he had a long hoped for. When *Trump,* as the magazine was titled, made its debut in early 1957, it featured the work of fellow *MAD* defectors Will Elder and Jack Davis and talented gag cartoonists such as Arnold Roth, Frank Interlandi, R.O. Blechman, and Ed Fisher. Although *Trump* contained brilliant ad parodies and a good deal of other sharp and funny material, its high production costs and low sales prompted Hugh Hefner to withdraw his support after only two issues.[80]

*   *   *

Soon after Kurtzman left *MAD,* Bill Gaines replaced him with Al Feldstein. Feldstein was a logical choice as Kurtzman's successor. He had been loyal to Gaines, and as the former editor of *Panic, MAD's* sister publication at E.C., he had gained experience putting together a magazine of parody and satire. Feldstein wasted little time in gathering new artists and writers. Within a year he recruited Don Martin, Mort Drucker, George Woodbridge, Dave Berg, Joe Orlando, Kelly Freas, Norman Mingo, and Bob Clarke, all of whom helped continue *MAD's* reputation for graphic excellence. For writers he recruited Nick Megliola, Frank Jacobs, Paul Laikin, Tom Koch, and Gary Belkin. In the late fifties and early sixties he supplemented his staff with artists Antonio Prohias and Sergio Aragones and former *Trump* writers Al Jaffee and Larry Siegel. Following the example that Kurtzman had set earlier, Feldstein also began soliciting contributions from humorists and satirists sympathetic to *MAD's* irreverent point of view, people such as Sid Caesar, Ernie Kovacs, Bob and Ray, and Tom Lehrer.

By and large, Feldstein continued many of the elements that had made *MAD* such a remarkable success. Ad parodies, for example, remained an integral part of *MAD* under Feldstein's editorship. Following the same precise detail that Will Elder had demonstrated earlier, Kelly Freas contributed several notable ad parodies, including one that deftly deflated the sanctimonious "Great Moments in Medicine" ads sponsored by pharmaceutical company Parke-Davis.[81] At the same time that he consolidated the antic formula and nose-thumbing attitude that Kurtzman and his collaborators had coined, Feldstein worked hard to broaden *MAD's* appeal. Reflecting back on the decisions he faced after taking over the helm of *MAD,* Feldstein argues that Kurtzman "was trying to get very . . . arty and literary, and he had gone off on a very strange direction." "I wanted to keep *Mad* a satire magazine that would have a wide appeal . . . I was greedy. I wanted to make a lot of money."[82]

The surest way for Feldstein to expand *MAD*'s circulation was to more explicitly target the immense demographic of Americans under the age of twenty-one. Although *MAD* comics had appealed to teenagers, it never encouraged the type of generational identity that its successor did. As *MAD* magazine entered the sixties, its condemnation of hypocrisy was pointed not only at America's mass media but at American adults in particular. During the early sixties, *MAD*'s explicit appeal to teenagers was studied by numerous commentators, including Columbia University sociologist Charles Winick. After interviewing more than four hundred teenagers, Winick concluded that *MAD* was helping reinforce young people's membership in a kind of "ritual non-conformity." While reading *MAD*, Winick concluded, the "teenager may feel that he is learning to emulate 'gamesmanship' while laughing at it. He can be an inside 'dopester' while chivying inside dopesters." For Winick, *MAD*'s effect on America's youth was largely positive, particularly since *MAD* made "dissident theories . . . feel at home and helped to get them into millions of homes." For other observers, however, *MAD*'s lessons to America's youth were far less salutary. Critic T. J. Ross, writing in the radical journal *Dissent* in 1961, objected to *MAD*'s message of "gamesmanship" and further argued that rather than "voicing resistance to the oppressiveness of official culture, *MAD* expresses a savage acquiescence to it." "In the savagery of its acquiescence," Ross continued, "*Mad* shows its consumers how to be bastards à la mode." Dwight Macdonald, in his influential *New Yorker* articles on the emergence of teen marketing, similarly observed that "*Mad* expresses the teenagers' cynicism about the world of mass media that their elders have created—so full of hypocrisy and pretense, so governed by formula . . . [but it] speaks the same language, aesthetically and morally, as the media it satirizes; it is as tasteless as they are, and even more violent."[83]

MAD editor Al Feldstein, identifying himself as a liberal satirist, defended his magazine by claiming that it helped educate America's youth to the hypocrisies of their elders. "I was getting a great deal of satisfaction," Feldstein remembers, "because I thought that I was performing a kind of service for young people in my own way as a liberal in at least alerting them to what was going on around them in terms of advertising, politics, manufacturing, packaging, et cetera."[84] There is little question that Feldstein's message was getting through to American teenagers. By 1959,

Teen Age Survey Inc. reported that *MAD* magazine had become the favorite magazine of fifty-eight percent of American college students and forty-three percent of high schoolers.[85] In that year, *Mad* regularly sold over one million copies per issue. Despite competition from two new competitors, *Cracked* and *Sick, MAD* continued to increase its circulation over the next several years. Displaying an entrepreneurial savvy that was lacking in Harvey Kurtzman, Al Feldstein and Bill Gaines by 1960 had begun to sell *MAD* merchandise and even branch out to television.[86] A year later, Bill Gaines sold *MAD* for $5 million.

By 1964 *MAD*, with a circulation of several million, had itself become a sacred cow. In August of that year, *Esquire* magazine editor Harold Hayes, a friend and admirer of Harvey Kurtzman, and his staff devoted a five-page spread to a dead-on parody of *MAD*. In prefatory comments for its "Things We Would Like to See" in "Bad," *Esquire* mimicked,

> Hey, gang! Have you ever noticed how we are the leading magazine of satire and act brave about daring to poke fun at all kinds of sacred cows, but mainly we never satirize anything that really matters? Just imagine what it would be like if you picked up your monthly copy of *Bad* and found us dealing with subjects of genuine significance in America![87]

The impression that the post-Kurtzman *MAD* was missing its opportunity to comment on important issues of the day was shared by one New York high school student who in 1961 wrote cartoonist Jules Feiffer to complain about the magazine's trajectory. "I used to identify with *Mad* magazine," this young man confessed, "until I interviewed the editors last spring and they said they didn't satirize segregation or organized religion because it would hurt their circulation."[88] Although there was ample justification by this time to charge *MAD* with avoiding "subjects of genuine significance," it is difficult to deny the critical spirit that it had helped inspire among young, middle-class Americans coming of age in the fifties. Future Students for a Decomcratic Society (SDS) president and "Port Huron Statement" (1962) author Tom Hayden edited his own underground version of *MAD* titled the *Daily Smirker* while he was in high school. "'What, Me Worry?'" Hayden remarks, "could have been the motto of suburban America in the fifties."[89] The ironic temperament and irreverent edge that *MAD* and its ilk contributed were integral to the growing popularity and influence of liberal satire. Seizing on the same spirit of comic revenge and quest for authenticity that animated the work of Stan Freberg and many other male social satirists, *MAD* struck at the commercial practices, social conventions, and cultural institutions that underwrote postwar consensus ideology and the Great American Way. At its best, *MAD*, particularly in its earlier incarnation, invited a spirit of skepticism toward institutions (the mass media in particular) and dramatically broadened the range of subjects open to satiric scrutiny. By interrogating the "HP2x" extent in America's "Simulated Golden Age," it also helped pave the way for the revival of satiric stage performance and the proliferation of satiric cabarets and revues in particular.

CHAPTER FOUR

"Truth Grinning in a Solemn, Canting World"

LIBERAL SATIRE'S MASCULINE, "SOCIOLOGICALLY ORIENTED AND PSYCHICALLY ADJUSTED" CRITIQUE

During the early and mid-1950s, Americans who relished social and political satire had come to expect little from the American stage. In the eyes of many observers, satiric stage comedy, whether delivered through cabaret performance, musical revue, or more formal stage production, appeared to have disappeared in the postwar years along with the politicized Popular Front culture that had once nourished it. Whereas Americans living in 1930s and early 1940s had been able to enjoy Harold Rome's working-class musical revue *Pins and Needles* and the poignant political cabaret of Barney Josephson's Café Society, postwar audiences were left with light Broadway comedies such as *Time Out for Ginger* (1952), *A Date with April* (1953), and *The Tender Trap* (1954)—"unabashedly commercial" comedies, according to former *PM* drama critic Louis Kronenberger, restricted by the dictates of "winning" formulas and "factory methods." Stage director and Group Theatre cofounder Harold Clurman largely concurred with Kronenberger's grim assessment. From his post as drama critic for the *Nation,* Clurman traced stage comedy's decline (as well as the "decline of the satiric spirit") to the repressive atmosphere of the 1950s. It was during the age of McCarthy, Clurman made clear, that "[o]ur hopes were dissipated, rebelliousness was first frowned upon and then squelched." "Social criticism now seems to lack a base and the building of positive values appears to lack support in social realities," Clurman concluded. "We are not so much frightened, now that McCarthy has passed away, as transfixed, stuck, spiritually immobilized."[1]

The perennial disappointment Clurman, Kronenberger, and other liberal and left-liberal critics experienced during the 1950s was relieved periodically by the premiere of a fresh and slightly daring satiric comedy.[2]
Overall, however, the satire contained in these comedies was either too
sporadic or too light to please these critics, most of whom were all too
willing to concede playwright George Kaufman's bitter observation that
satire was "what closes on Saturday night." Yet for critics and for a growing audience of Americans who appreciated satirical commentaries on the
social mores and customs of the day, not all was lost. Signs of recovery
were beginning to emerge at mid-decade. By 1958, even Harold Clurman
was able to offer hope that the American stage would recapture the moral
vision and strong convictions it had once displayed in the 1930s. As models for this new theater, he pointed to the work of Albert Camus, Jean
Genet, Eugène Ionesco, and Samuel Beckett, European pioneers of what
Martin Esslin in 1961 labeled the "theatre of the absurd." Together with
their off-Broadway American counterparts (Edward Albee, Jack Richard-
son, Arthur Kopit, and Jack Gelber) and the new theatrical avant-garde
assembling in Julian Beck and Judith Malina's Living Theater and other
small Greenwich Village venues, these modernists brought an existentialist, darkly comic perspective to bear on what Esslin called the "the absurdity of inauthentic ways of life."[3]

Clurman would also take cheer in the development of a new school of
social satire performed by young improvisational troupes in small venues
located in Chicago, St. Louis, New York City, and San Francisco. Along
with the "button-down" "cerebral" satirist Bob Newhart and the cartoonists Jules Feiffer and Robert Osborn, performers in, and later spawned
from, Chicago's Compass Players delivered brutally honest, darkly comic
explorations into middle-class conformity, the troubled relationship between men and women, and a number of other issues relevant to young,
discontented, alienated Americans living in Eisenhower's America. Taken
together, these satirists ratified the perspective of a number of liberal sociologists and critics who throughout the fifties fretted over the growth
of large-scale bureaucratic organizations and the development of mass
commercial culture. Equally important, they demonstrated an affinity for
the work of European and American avant-garde playwrights, Beat poets,
and jazz musicians. The fertile social satire they created in the two decades after World War II betrayed a preoccupation with existentialist
angst, a fear of conformity, a belief in the primacy of authenticity and cre-

ative expression, and a devotion to what historian Daniel Belgrad has recently called "the aesthetic of spontaneity."[4]

*   *   *

Although improvisational satire became identified with the avant-garde cultural life of New York City and Greenwich Village during the early 1960s, it originated a decade earlier in Chicago. At first blush, Chicago during the early 1950s seemed an unlikely spawning ground for theatrical experimentation. As one local theater critic put it in 1953, Chicago during this period was "the theatrical equivalent of the place old elephants go to die."[5] Despite its dismal theatrical scene, however, Chicago enjoyed a reputation as a spawning ground for cultural experimentation and improvisational performance in particular. Postwar American blues and jazz thrived in the Windy City, and it was through Chicago television station WNBQ that the live and often unrehearsed programs *Studs [Terkel's] Place* and Burr Tillstrom's *Kukla, Fran and Ollie* were broadcast to NBC affiliates around the United States during the early 1950s. Chicago was also home to the University of Chicago, which under the leadership of Robert Hutchins had become one of the most progressive academic communities in the United States.

It was in the liberal intellectual milieu of the University of Chicago that two young theater enthusiasts named David Shepherd and Paul Sills initiated the Compass Players, the first important improvisational theater troupe to emerge in the postwar years. Shepherd, the son of a wealthy New York architect and a distant relative of the Vanderbilt family, was a graduate of Harvard (where, as a student, he had worked on the *Harvard Lampoon*) and a self-proclaimed socialist. By the early fifties, he recalls, he had become "infuriated" and "disgusted" with the East Coast theater establishment's "upper-class effetism [sic]." Having studied theater at Columbia University and the Sorbonne, he was anxious to transplant the traditions of Italian masked comedy (*commedia dell'arte*) and German cabaret onto American soil. His initial attempt at producing Molière comedies through a summer company failed. Finally, in 1952 he hitchhiked to the Midwest with his $10,000 inheritance and began making plans for a working-class, community theater in the stockyards of Gary, Indiana. After failing to ignite interest for such a theater among the proletariat of Gary, he moved to Hyde Park, the progressive neighborhood that was home to the University of Chicago's student and faculty intellectuals.[6]

In Hyde Park, Shepherd came into contact with a small, informal community of young theater enthusiasts interested in staging their own productions. In 1953, together with former University of Chicago students Paul Sills and Eugene Troobnick, Shepherd formed the Playwrights Theatre Club in a former Chinese laundry on North LaSalle Street. Over the next year and a half, Shepherd and his colleagues produced a body of highbrow classical and avant-garde plays at Playwrights, including works by Brecht, Chekov, and Büchner. Although Playwrights acquired a reputation as an innovative, avant-garde, left-leaning theater, Shepherd was not satisfied with its accomplishments. On May 25, 1954, he confessed to his journal that over the past year and a half he had "helped build a miserable self-centered arts club which talks over the heads of its bourgeois members at the same time it licks their feet for support."[7]

Based in part on what he had witnessed at Chicago's College of Complexes—an informal, irreverent theatrical enterprise headed by a former Wobbly named Slim Brundage—Shepherd proposed the creation of a new, thirties-style, Brechtian "people's theater," which he named "the Compass." Such a theater, Shepherd hoped, would "remove the glass curtain that's formed between the actors and the audience" and engage the "reality" of American life. In a January 1955 *Chicago* magazine interview, he harkened back to the days of the Popular Front by claiming that the Compass would appeal to the "man on the street." With an "intensity the stage hasn't known since Ibsen," Shepherd boldly announced, the Compass would "take the audience on a trip thru [sic] society. Maybe we'll show them what's happening in Malaya or some place." He pledged that his Compass theater would encourage audience members to "comment, applaud, hiss" and, significantly, "one night a week . . . tell the actors what story to play and how to play it." In the hands of the right actors, Shepherd hoped, the Compass might revive the type of breezy, irreverent, political cabaret that had thrived in the 1930s and was once again cropping up in Düsseldorf, Berlin, and other European cities.[8]

The most important stage technique Shepherd adapted for the new Compass was that of improvisation. Although he had become familiar with the concept and uses of improvisation through his studies of the *commedia dell'arte* tradition, it was not until he became acquainted with Paul Sills, his collaborator at Playwrights, that Shepherd grasped its true potential. Sills had first honed his interest in theater while a student at Chicago's progressive Francis Parker School. He was also the son of Viola Spolin, a theatrical maverick who had begun to develop improvisational "games" during the 1930s while teaching drama (under the auspices of the Works Progress Administration) at Chicago's Hull House Recreational Training School. Sills took the playful improvisational techniques developed by his mother and gave them a Brechtian twist. Like Shepherd, Sills agreed with Brecht's emphasis on the nonsubjective theatrical experience and the creative interchange between audience and actors. Sills also shared Shepherd's progressive social concerns. In his hands, improvisation was not merely an acting device, it was a tool that could assist in the process of raising awareness and of community building. Through the use of improvisation, Sills argued in a 1964 interview, actors could help build "communities that have real life."[9]

Sills's approach to improvisation appealed to Shepherd since it promised to generate "reality" and authentic, spontaneous contact between actors and audiences. Rather than commit entirely to improvisation, however, Shepherd preferred that the Compass work from written scenarios, as European *commedia dell'arte* troupes had done centuries earlier. In magazines as far afield as Britain's *Times Literary Supplement* and *New Statesman and Nation,* Shepherd began to solicit "Brechtian fables," "political satires," and "cabaret material" for his new theater. In a 1954 brochure for the Compass, Shepherd called for scripts "that would never be shown on Broadway, Hollywood or TV ... stories that move outside the family circle to show America's history and place in the world today." "At The Compass," Shepherd wrote, the playwright "won't be required to copy the surface of life—a poor kind of realism—if he prefers to dig through to find the real core of a person, or a story, or a society ... *All we ask for is a form that can be recognized by the man-in-the-street, and that is strong enough to stand up in a cabaret.*"[10]

Several months before the Compass officially opened, Shepherd staged a performance titled "Enterprise" at the University of Chicago's Reynolds Club. The performance was based on a scenario written by Roger Bowen, a young, liberal Ivy League graduate like Shepherd who was at the University of Chicago pursuing a graduate degree in English. Bowen's scenario related the plight of four working-class teenage boys who are conned by a used car dealer named "Crazy Jake." After wrecking the car that they had collectively purchased from Crazy Jake, the four innocents are forced to pay him off by selling junk jewelry to unsuspecting high school girls. Having learned the dubious ethics of American "enterprise" from Crazy Jake, the boys become successful and are eventually given a Junior Achievement Award. At the awards ceremony, the Junior Achievement president, Crazy Jake, pays homage to the automobile and America's "spirit of hustle." "America," Crazy Jake proclaims at the scenario's conclusion, "is a nation of hustlers."[11]

As Compass historian Janet Coleman has argued, "Enterprise," with its condemnation of American business ethics, provided Shepherd and his colleagues with the "substantive prototype" for subsequent scenarios. Though critical of economic exploitation, however, neither the content nor the tone of this scenario took a truly "Marxist angle" as Coleman suggests. There was nothing particularly "Marxist" about Bowen's portrayal of the avaricious used car dealer, the "typical do-gooder" Junior Achievement committeewomen, or the other Americans it caricatures. Moreover, when Bowen described the working-class teenagers as laggards who "regard going to work as the greatest danger in life" and as gullible consumers "hypnotized by automobiles," he betrayed the snobbery and condescension that would later occasionally mar Compass scenarios.[12] Despite its somewhat slipshod social analysis, "Enterprise" received a warm reception from the young, liberal University of Chicago students who had gathered to watch it. The laughter this thirty-five-minute production received, in fact, convinced Paul Sills that he ought to commit to Shepherd's venture.

On July 5, 1955, after several weeks of intense improvisational training led by Viola Spolin, the Compass made its debut under Paul Sills's direction. Joining Sills, Shepherd, and Bowen in the original Compass Players were an African American student, an industrial relations counselor, and a former Communist Party organizer. Also integral to the early Compass were a bright young woman named Barbara Harris and Andrew Duncan, a University of Chicago graduate student. Aside from Shepherd and Sills, perhaps the most important contributor to the early Compass was an intelligent and fiercely independent young woman named Elaine May. As the daughter of a Yiddish actor named Jack Berlin, May had grown up in the world of theater. Unlike her Compass colleagues, she had received little formal education. As a teenager she had married, had a child, and then divorced her husband. After briefly studying acting under Maria Ouspenskaya and then pursuing several occupations, she decided to lead the life of a bohemian rebel. She eventually hitchhiked to Hyde Park and then gravitated toward its amateur theater scene.[13]

May and her young Compass Players colleagues first performed in a small nightclub connected to the Compass Tavern. The Compass Tavern was located in a vibrant, eclectic area within Hyde Park, just down the street from the well-known Bee Hive jazz club. Like nearby campus bars and hangouts, the Compass Tavern attracted what writer Isaac Rosenfeld in *Commentary* described as "an interracial clientele of mixed types." Included within this diverse group were a few sober-minded business and engineering students (the "yaks") but even larger numbers of young, jazz-crazed hipsters, alienated, middle-class bohemians, and what Rosenfeld sarcastically called "retired students." Many of these young rebels were drawn to the Compass Tavern because talk of Kierkegaard and Nietzsche was thick in its air, a set of *Encyclopedia Britannica* lined its bookshelves, Beethoven and Vivaldi played on its sound system, and, not least, because Michelob flowed from its tap.[14]

Soon after the Compass Players began performing in the summer of 1955, they began drawing a capacity crowd of ninety, six nights a week. On a small, rudimentary stage backed by several colored, moveable panels, they developed and performed material at a frenetic pace. Under the direction of Shepherd and Sills, in fact, the Compass Players managed to produce a new show nearly every week. Typically, each performance began with a short piece and then proceeded with a "Living Newspaper," a segment clearly inspired by Federal Theater Project productions of the 1930s. With its "Living Newspaper" segment, Compass actors attempted to weave humorous dialogue and pantomime into newspaper articles they read onstage. David Shepherd recalls this popular portion of the Compass program: "It was about 'Hello. You're reading this shit [newspapers and magazines] every day. We're going to show you now what is behind this shit.'"[15] Following this segment, the Compass Players usually performed a longer scenario play and then ended with a few scenes and blackouts based on audience suggestions.

Although the ephemeral nature of Compass's improvised scenarios poses significant challenges of interpretation, it seems clear that those performed during the summer of 1955 developed comic themes along the lines of Bowen's "Enterprise." "The Drifters" and "The Fuller Brush Salesman" conveyed the message that, as Roger Bowen remembers it, "in this society, you either screw or be screwed . . ."[16] Elaine May's "The Real You" also attempted to demonstrate how popular, middle-class formulas for success—in this case, the "Human Potential" movement—ironically end up claiming innocent victims. In this scenario, May related a tale about five losers who are enticed to enroll in Joe Charm's School of Success. Each character there learns the importance of exaggerated enthusiasm and self-promotion. As a result of their personality training, however, all five characters end up intimidating and alienating the people they hoped to impress. Drawing inspiration from David Riesman's *The Lonely Crowd* and William Whyte's *The Organization Man* (two sociological critiques with which early Compass Players were well familiar) as well Arthur Miller's dramatic play *Death of a Salesman* (1949), scenarios such as May's satirized fifties consensus culture and Americans' obsession with "fitting in."[17]

Perhaps the most poignant scenario the Compass Players produced during the summer of 1955 was May's "Georgina's First Date." Unlike the great majority of scenarios and scenes that the Compass and its male-dominated successors performed in the 1950s and early 1960s, this piece focused solely on the experience of a female character. Its plot focused on an unattractive teenage girl named Georgina who is asked to the senior prom by Edward, one of her school's most popular boys. Edward cares nothing for Georgina and only invited her in order to please the members of the club he wishes to join. With the coaching of her sister and the prodding of her ambitious mother, Georgina desperately attempts to live up to her date's expectations. She becomes "so absorbed in her own effort to have 'personality,'" May's scenario suggested, "that she is unaware of what she is being used for." In the end, Georgina suffers through the prom and, in a tragic twist, is raped by Edward. Despite her trauma, she tells her mother when she returns home that she had a wonderful time.[18]

To be sure, the sober, brutal realism behind "Georgina's First Date" often mitigated the comic effect of Compass scenarios. It is likewise difficult to discern anything funny in Shepherd's "Five Dreams for Five Actors" scenario—a Freudian nightmare involving a wedding between an elderly grandfather and his granddaughter, a young business executive who is fated to wear a paper bag over his head, and, finally, another middle-class business man who murders his "castrating" wife with a carving knife.[19] Like other early Compass scenarios and scenes commenting on middle-class conformity and alienation, interpersonal and family conflict, marital discord, and emotional pain, "Georgina's First Date" and "Five Dreams for Five Actors" were in fact tinged with a sense of despair. In significant respects, Compass scenarios reflected the sense of anxiety, restlessness, and bleak pessimism that many middle-class Americans shared in the early and mid-1950s. At the exact moment when Americans were celebrating their remarkable affluence, the "end of ideology," and the triumph of the American Way, there remained strong undercurrents of dissent and dissatisfaction. Throughout the postwar period, this dissent was translated through a variety of subterranean cultural channels, from film noir and the "sick" satire of *MAD* to the work of Beat poets, absurdist playwrights, and the emerging school of "black humor" fiction writers. In keeping with this emerging counterculture of the 1950s, then, Compass Players spoke directly to the restlessness and nagging doubts of its young, educated middle-class patrons.

To many audience members, the idea of lampooning mothers and fathers, salesmen, hucksters, and professors freely onstage was liberating. The fact that Compass actors uttered obscenities and the undisguised names of national politicians confirmed that their enterprise was boldly out of step with the rest of 1950s cold war America.[20] From the perspective of Compass performer, Andrew Duncan, to engage taboo subjects onstage with a type of humor that was direct, honest, and irreverent was an exhilarating experience — for both performers and audience members. Duncan remembers,

> To suddenly find an applied form in which to get up and start expressing the things we were thinking about and feeling at that time, with all those repressed political, social, psychological feelings . . . I mean, the freedom! . . . A lot of what we did was very negative in that we were satirizing the establishment's institutions. But a lot of it, too, was an expression of how we wanted to live, crude and pioneering as it was. And we struck a responsive chord in our audience.[21]

The informality and comic spontaneity of Compass performances also contributed greatly to their appeal. For young, educated Chicagoans who had grown wary of the increasingly structured and bureaucratized patterns of postwar life and tired of the dull, formulaic nature of so much mainstream commercial culture, the Compass seemed an oasis of unpredictable, creative freedom. Nowhere else but the Compass, certainly, could Chicago audiences see male performers (often shirtless and smoking onstage) engaging in freeform comic antics onstage. People living in and around the liberal University of Chicago community were drawn to the Compass and its impudent, "reckless theatrics" for many of the same reasons that young, hip, alienated Americans throughout the United States were attracted to Jack Kerouac's "spontaneous bop prosody" and the improvised performance of jazz musicians. The association between the Compass and African American jazz in particular was manifest in the style and mood of Compass performances. Like the "new wave" comedians simultaneously emerging in Chicago, New York and San Francisco nightclubs, young Compass performers exuded the same spontaneous edge and liberating spirit that made the jazz aesthetic so appealing to white, middle-class audiences in the fifties.[22]

*   *   *

After its first several months of operation, the Compass altered its composition and its orientation significantly. During the fall of 1955, the Compass was forced to relocate off the University of Chicago campus. The Hyde Park amateurs who participated in performances during the Compass's first summer returned to their regular jobs. At the same time, Paul Sills, his wife Barbara Harris, and Roger Bowen took leave. To replace them, Shepherd recruited five actors, all of whom had professional experience in the theater. One of them, Mark Gordon, had been blacklisted during the early 1950s because of his involvement in left-wing political activities. Gordon shared Shepherd's interest in reviving thirties-style proletarian, community theater, and with Shepherd's blessing he took his revenge on McCarthyism in a scenario titled "The Fifth Amendment." But Gordon's influence on the type of satiric material the Compass would create onstage was limited. More integral to the future trajectory of the Compass Players' comic orientation were the addition of Severn Darden, Mike Nichols, and Shelley Berman. Shepherd later resented that these performers used his theater "as a training ground for 'The Steve Allen Show,'" but there is little doubt that these three performers, together with Elaine May, would help bring the Compass its greatest notoriety. Unlike the exceptionally WASPish Shepherd, these actors, along with Elaine May and most other Compass members, were informed to a large extent by their identities as Jews. Like the alienated, rebellious Compass goys (many of whom emulated and in some cases envied their Jewish colleagues), they were articulate outsiders well poised to observe the follies of America's middle class and the shallow promises of the American Way.[23]

With the addition of Berman, Darden and Nichols—none of whom shared Shepherd's interest in didactic scenarios and "proletarian theater"—the Compass began to wean itself from Shepherd's original formula for improvisational satire. In place of scenarios, Compass Players began to revise and perfect brief, snappy, well-polished comic scenes they had generated while improvising. This came as a relief to the educated, white-collar "upper Bohemians" who began infiltrating the audience when in mid-1956 the Compass relocated to the Argo Off-Beat Room, a chic 250-seat nightclub on Chicago's near North Side. The Argo's clientele clearly favored parodies and satires on subjects with which they were familiar—male-female relationships, middle-class family life, the suburbs, and popular culture—over "Brechtian fables." Freed somewhat from Shepherd's oversight, Darden, Nichols, May, and Berman indulged their audience's requests for send-ups of television programs, famous authors, and other staples of middlebrow American culture. Two scenes, "Mountain Climbing" (spoofing a sport made famous by Sir Edmund Hillary) and "Football Comes to the University of Chicago" (poking fun at effete young "U of C" intellectuals and their brawny coach's efforts to prepare them for the gridiron) became staples on the Compass stage and were later performed by the Second City. Parodies of intellectuals and high art continued to be quite common in Compass sketches and improvisations.[24]

Before long, the adroit and talented Compass Players acquired reputations as sassy, irreverent clowns—satiric renegades who with their quick wit and native intelligence devastated the lifestyles, hypocrisies and mores of suburban WASPs. Night after night they thrilled the partially inebriated Argo clientele with their taboo-breaking, "sophisticated" humor, their knowing references to Tennessee Williams and Nietzsche, and, above all, their improvisational feats. By all accounts, Nichols, May, Darden, and Berman evolved into brilliant and often hilarious performers. The material they developed together (and often in competition with one another) impressed many, including show business insiders. "After a few stiff ones," one impressed nightclub reviewer for *Playboy* magazine noted of the Argo Compass, "the new concept in theatre takes on a certain glow and the facile performers' agility in out-thinking and upstaging each other seems downright supernatural."[25]

What might have impressed the readers of *Playboy* most about the routines Berman, Nichols, and May developed during late 1955 and 1956 was their humorous treatment of the frustrations and obsessions haunting modern, middle-class American males. Of course, according to *Playboy,* one of the male's biggest threats came in the form of the domineering wife, the "man-eater" and "castrator." Elaine May, a woman whose intelligence, self-confidence, and physical attractiveness reportedly intimidated many of her male Compass colleagues, played this part perfectly. With her overt sensuality and biting, aggressive wit, May confounded the feminine stereotypes that were dominant in the fifties. As John Limon has commented, May was a "laughing Medusa," a comic heroine starkly at odds with domestic clowns such as Gracie Allen, Harriet Nelson, and Lucille Ball. In "The Lost Dime," one of the popular scenes she originally improvised with Berman and later performed with Nichols, May played an uncaring, nasal-toned telephone operator. Berman here calls her in desperation after his car has become stranded in the middle of nowhere. He pleads with her to grant him another call, but she is unmoved. On one level, this scene commented on the rigid bureaucracy of the phone company, yet what really drove it was the way May's character reduced her male customer into a pathetic, pouting child. Here as in several other popular Compass scenes, the male character became a victim, comically infantilized and "emasculated" by May.[26]

In addition to material involving men and women, Berman, Nichols, and May continued to develop scenes that parodied the culture and institutions of Middle America. In "Fuller Brush Man," for example, Berman demonstrated to Nichols how an enterprising young man ought to assert himself as a salesman. As with the earlier scenario "Enterprise," the Compass Players here used comic exaggeration to illuminate the vulgar side of America's business culture and success ethic. In another characteristic Compass scene, "PTA Open House and Fun Night," May lampooned that matronly symbol of goyish rectitude, the suburban PTA chairwoman. After elucidating her obeisance to American values and middlebrow culture, she introduces the headliner for her "Evening of Art," Mr. Alabama Glass, a homosexual playwright from the South—a cross between Tennessee Williams and Truman Capote. Played in a high-pitched voice by Nichols, Glass reports on his next play *Pork Makes Me Sick,* a pretentious melodrama in which one character commits suicide because he is accused of not being a homosexual.[27]

Other scenes Nichols, May, and Berman developed from Compass improvisations parodied, in a manner strikingly similar to *MAD* magazine, the clichés and the shallow formulas abundant in American mainstream culture. In one very popular routine they developed at the Compass, Mike Nichols played a slick disk jockey named Jack Ego. While interviewing a stupid young starlet named Barbara Musk (May), Ego engages in shameless name-dropping and self-promotion. Following his lead, the starlet eventually claims that she also knows "Al" Schweitzer, though she says, "I personally have not dated him . . ." By exaggerating the pretense behind the celebrity interview, Nichols and May attempted to highlight what many American highbrows considered one of the most cloying and superficial aspects of the modern entertainment industry.[28]

*   *   *

Despite winning the attention and praise of Chicago's smart set, the Compass struggled financially. In large part because of Shepherd's poor business management, it was finally forced to suspend operation in January 1957. In an attempt to rescue his troupe from extinction, Shepherd entered into a partnership with a twenty-five-year-old theatrical entrepreneur named Theodore Flicker. With the exception of his Jewish background, Flicker resembled Shepherd in many ways. Like Shepherd, he was raised in a wealthy family and had received his education at a private school and college. He too had studied theater in Europe and, upon returning to the United States, attempted to create a traveling "people's theater." When Flicker and Shepherd met, they shared ideas on how to adapt the Compass for an off-Broadway audience. Flicker was particularly intrigued by the possibilities of improvisation. As he later remarked, improvisation appeared to be the way to "do theater: cut out all the shit, get rid of all the managers and the agents and the Shuberts and all the unions and everything, it was just actors in direct contact with the audience. It was the most exciting thing imaginable."[29]

While Shepherd attempted to find backers for their new venture, Flicker brought the Compass Players—who now consisted of Severn Darden (a friend of Flicker's from Bard College) and three new recruits, Del Close, Nancy Ponder, and Jo Henderson—to St. Louis. St. Louis in 1957, Flicker remembers, was "one of the most exotic places I have ever been in my life." It was there that the Compass Players were booked by the nightclub owners Fred and Jay Landesman to perform in their new Olive Street establishment, the Crystal Palace. The Crystal Palace (or "C.P." as it was known by regulars) turned out to be the perfect venue for the reborn Compass. With its marble busts, brass monkeys, black brick walls, large crystal chandeliers, and other expensive bric-a-brac that the Landesmans supplied from their antiques gallery, the C.P. was St. Louis's oasis for hip sophistication, a place where advertising executives, and aspiring hipsters from the middle and upper-middle classes as well as "real swells" from prominent local families congregated to imbibe a little sassy avant-garde entertainment along with their cocktails. "There was something about all the darkness mixed with gold, crystal, whiskey and the tinkling of the piano," Jay Landesman remembered of the C.P., "that people found irresistible."[30]

Flicker, Close, and their colleagues in the new St. Louis Compass determined early on that they should concentrate their satiric attacks on male-female relationships, marriage and other middle-class American institutions. From the time they began performing together in April 1957 until they ceased seven months later, Flicker and his troupe created scenes onstage with such titles as "Magicless Marriage," "Adultery," and "For the Love of Sex." On Tuesday evenings, the designated "Love and Passion Night," Crystal Palace patrons were treated to Shepherd's "Dream of the Young Executive," "Blind Date," "Last of the Centaurs," and a number of Thurberesque scenes featuring, according to Close, a "poor picked-upon male, and a lot of misogyny." In "The Schnook Strikes," a scene in which a browbeaten husband bludgeons his wife with a kitchen knife, the Compass Players gave their Crystal Palace audience Walter Mitty with a sinister twist. When not propelled by masculine frustration and rage, Compass satires of marriage—informed, in some cases, by the troubled relationships of Compass Players' parents—were heavily laden with pathos. In a mime titled "Two Loves," for example, a male Compass actor courts and marries a woman and then falls in love with another. Despite motioning to each of his lovers to stay put while he runs back and forth between them, he is unable to prevent them from wilting and, ultimately, dying.[31]

According to Compass Player Del Close, the laughs he and his "tragically hip" colleagues received in scenes like "Two Loves" were definitely of the schadenfreude variety. "There was a kind of darkness about it all . . . 'well we're all the organization man, we're all trapped in this machine,'" Close recalls, "but it did get laughs." This apparently was not always the case. After witnessing Close and his colleagues perform a characteristically bleak improvisation on marital failure, the *St. Louis Post Dispatch* critic Myles Standish wrote that he "hastily ordered another quinine water to recover from the shock." When the Compass Players concluded their performance, Standish commented, he and his party "left groping a little in the mazes of our mind." Standish's review no doubt pleased Flicker and his Compass Players since their credo was to jolt the middle-class suburbanites who came to see them. For advertising copy Flicker once proposed, "FRANKLY, friend, if you are afraid of taking a good look into what you really are . . . you probably wouldn't like COMPASS THEATRE." Explaining the relationship between the Compass Players and the audience to *Variety*'s Abel Green, Flicker claimed with a hipster's characteristic contempt that he and his fellow performers were "outlaws . . . people who were different then [sic] the great gray middle-classes." Through their broad satiric portrayals of marriage, advice column writers, popular psychiatry, "Split-Level thinking," and, as Flicker put it, popular attitudes on "Art, Love, Ethics, and . . . almost every aspect of manufactured mass thinking," the young Compass Players, much like Beat poets and other cultural rebels emerging in the 1950s, registered their complaints against the "squares" and unhappily married corporate drones settling the wide suburban expanse of Eisenhower's America.[32]

For the benefit of its paying customers, Flicker and his colleagues were careful to offset the existentialist gloom of its scenes with a raucous, carnival atmosphere. In Flicker's hands, the Compass's improvisational satire became polished entertainment, a high-wire act intended to thrill and surprise Crystal Palace patrons. Flicker had his actors stop smoking onstage and replace their street clothes with tights. More importantly, he encouraged them to create scenes that were short and snappy. As "onstage director," Flicker assumed the role of ringmaster, introducing scenes, soliciting audience suggestions for improvised sets, and terminating action (through the all-important "blackout button") at the appropriate time.[33]

In the end, Flicker's formula for poignant yet playful satire proved effective in St. Louis. After Mike Nichols and Elaine May rejoined the Compass in July 1957, its prospects only improved. Despite the fact that the Compass was finally making money, however, Shepherd had grown unhappy with his partner. In Shepherd's opinion, the Compass had wandered far off course. Whereas Shepherd had coined the name Compass because he intended his troupe to point where American society was going, Flicker used it in reference to his troupe's playful willingness to follow and improvise from the audience's suggestions. In Shepherd's mind, the Compass in Flicker's hands had become little more than a parlor game for St. Louis's municipal opera crowd. Worst of all, the Compass Players seemed less and less interested in political issues and "stories that move outside the family circle." While Shepherd and Flicker argued over the Compass's future direction, they lost the trust and confidence of their colleagues, most of whom were working in St. Louis with the hope that a new Compass would soon open in New York City. When plans for a New York Compass fell through in October 1957, Nichols, May, Flicker, Close, and Shepherd scrambled for rights over the material they developed. In a letter to Darden (perhaps the only Compass Player aloof from the acrimony and deception that tainted the late Compass), Flicker vowed to "take what I want from COMPASS, The Compass that I made, and shall try and beat [Shepherd] to the punch here in NY."[34]

*   *   *

By the time the St. Louis Compass was beginning to disintegrate, Shelley Berman had already begun to demonstrate how the type of social satire he and his Argo Compass colleagues pursued together onstage could be adapted into a successful solo nightclub act. Initially in appearances at two Chicago jazz and folk music nightclubs, Mr. Kelly's and the Gate of Horn, Berman began modifying scenes he had developed in Compass improvisations into feigned phone conversations and various other monologues. With a stool, a couple of handkerchiefs, and a pack of cigarettes as his only props, Berman centered his audience's attention on the frustrations endured by his neurotic characterizations. Although his occasional use of sexual double entendres and grotesqueries tempted observers to group him with the up-and-coming "sicknik" comics, Berman's technique and subject matter clearly drew from his experience at the Compass. As would other former Compass Players, Berman parodied slick show business types, jibed intellectuals, highlighted the struggles and misunderstandings that take place between parents and their children, and portrayed the poor schlemiel's humiliation at the hands of women.

What won Berman most acclaim were his comic depictions of the obsessions, frustrations, and tiny embarrassments endured by the midcentury, middle-class American male. Most typical of the type of material he and Mike Nichols performed with the Compass was "Franz Kafka on the Telephone," a scene in which Berman is forced to confront a small contingent of "castrating" female telephone operators (including one named Miss Freud) in pursuit of a lost dime. In some of his most popular routines Berman spoke of his fear of flying and x-ray machines, and he revealed the angst that small irritations such as the "teeny black speck" that floats in a glass of milk provoke. As writer Max Lerner admiringly wrote in the liner notes of Berman's *The Sex Life of the Primate* album, Berman left the "political satire . . . to others" and contented "himself with the revealing trivia that show up the absurd in the wrack of daily life."[35]

In popular routines such as "Complete Neuroses," Berman used his vulnerable "everymanic-depressive" persona to lampoon the type of man "who is scared of fear itself." In this way, Berman was gently critiquing the private obsessions nurtured by the 1950s vogue of Freudian psychology. In doing so, however, Berman reflected and in a sense ratified the same therapeutic culture he ostensibly ridiculed. In effect, Berman's act itself mimicked a kind of therapy session. With his stool as his couch and his audience as his therapist, Berman wove his monologues with a pronounced confessional tone. To a reporter from *Time* magazine, he in fact admitted, "My whole act is confession. Every word I say, I'm admitting something." "Shelley Berman may not consider himself a therapist," the critic Louis Untermeyer wrote in the liner notes for Berman's popular album *A Personal Appearance*, "but he has the paramount ability to evoke the healing power of laughter. He makes his audiences forget the cost and calamities of modern life by recognizing—and, what is more, responding to—its absurdities."[36]

At a time when Freudian psychology, popular existentialist philosophies, and works of popular fiction directed middle-class Americans' attention toward the interior obsessions and anxieties of the self, Shelley Berman's inward comic explorations found considerable appeal. After a well-received appearance on *The Jack Paar Show*, Berman began playing clubs such as Max Gordon's prestigious New York venue, the Blue Angel. He then became a regular guest on *The Ed Sullivan Show*. In 1958, only a year after he began his solo act, Berman recorded *Inside Shelley Berman* for Verve Records. This album topped the American charts in 1959 and remained in the Billboard Top 40 for two and a half years. Together with his next two gold albums, *Inside Shelley Berman* helped spur a new wave of comedy LPs. By 1961, Berman was one of the most successful comedians in America and one of the most highly paid entertainers in the world, making $10,000 a week for appearances at the Empire Room in the Manhattan Waldorf Astoria.[37]

*　　*　　*

The gently satiric, inward-gazing comedic routines that Shelley Berman developed onstage helped prepare the way for Bob Newhart, one of several young "cerebral" stand-up comics who emerged during the early 1960s. At a time when middle-class Americans were enjoying unprecedented access to higher education, were taking pride in the spread of "sophistication" and "good taste"—in their acquisition of what sociologist Pierre Bourdieu identified as "cultural capital"—the emergence of Berman, Newhart, Nichols and May, and their cohort of social satirists was a salutary development. The sudden popularity of Newhart and these other "New Comedians"—comedians who eschewed borscht belt shtick for comic insight into contemporary mores—went hand in hand with the "sophisticated" style and cultural tone of the New Frontier and its patron President John Kennedy.

Like Berman, Newhart was a native Chicagoan, born on the city's West Side. An Irish Catholic, Newhart attended Loyola University where he earned a degree in accounting. After serving two years in the army, he briefly attended law school and then worked a series of unfulfilling office jobs. As a hobby, he and a friend would improvise and then record humorous dialogues in the manner of radio comedians Bob and Ray. With the help of a local Chicago disk jockey, Newhart came to the attention of several Warner Brothers executives who were eager to market an act similar to Berman's. Warner Brothers recorded Newhart live at a Houston nightclub and then released the album *The Button-Down Mind of Bob Newhart* in April 1960. Within twelve weeks Newhart's first recorded performance sold over 200,000 copies and had become the number one selling album in the country. Its stunning popularity—it eventually became the first spoken comedy album to sell over a million copies—helped Newhart garner three Grammy Awards in 1961 and spurred the release of several more albums including *The Button-Down Mind Strikes Back* (1960) and then *Behind the Button-Down Mind of Bob Newhart* (1961) and *The Button-Down Mind on TV* (1962). Aside from Shelley Berman, few other American comedians in 1961 were in greater demand on late-night television variety shows or in urban nightclubs.[38]

The key to Bob Newhart's wide appeal was rooted not only in the novel mode of telephone dialogue that he borrowed from Shelley Berman and his good sense of comic timing, but in his adaptation of the same Robert Benchley/James Thurber "little man" persona that served Berman and Mike Nichols so well. The picture that nightclub audiences and listeners of Newhart's albums formed of Newhart onstage was not of a *sphritzing* Milton Berle–type comic but of an educated, balding "button-down" accountant from the suburbs. With his diffident, easygoing manner and his three-button suit, there appeared to be little threatening about this fellow middle-class Organization Man. Though he was dismissed as "the Kingston Trio of the sick comics" by discerning critics such as Ralph Gleason, despite the fact that he was often quick to resist the occupational designation of "satirist," Newhart was nevertheless capable of delivering keen comic observations. He was clearly a man with a few gripes

17. Button-down
everyman Bob
Newhart performs one
of his imagined tele-
phone calls during the
early 1960s. Photofest.

to air, foremost among them the encroachment of corporate and governmental bureaucracy and the victimization of the lower-level, white-collar
male worker. In interviews he gave during the early sixties, Newhart confessed that he "resented corporations" since they "flatten personalities."
In his most succinct description of his comedic approach, Newhart
claimed, "I have a pet peeve [that] runs through my humor—the imper-
sonal corporate bigness in modern life, and the individual getting lost."[39]

Like the Compass Players, Shelley Berman, Bob and Ray, Stan Freberg,
Harvey Kurtzman, and other satirists of the fifties and early sixties,
Newhart used humor to ridicule the cant and hypocrisy rippling through
America's commercial and corporate culture. In one of his early signature
routines, Newhart fantasized what might happen if an office worker
named Charlie Bedloe really spoke his mind at his retirement party.
Newhart began this routine on an autobiographical note, explaining how
as an itinerant accountant he had attended his share of retirement parties
and how these parties were all the same. Slipping into character as Bruce

"Truth Grinning in a Solemn, Canting World"

Higgins, the stuffy department supervisor, Newhart proceeds to issue the standard, cliché-ridden thank you speech. To highlight how truly inauthentic was management's gratitude toward their loyal employee, he has the supervisor forget Charlie's name. In order to permit "'good old Charlie' [to] stand up and say what he actually felt instead of the phony things the departing one usually says," as Newhart later explained, he played him as if he were slightly inebriated. With refreshing candor, Newhart's Charlie remarks to his colleagues that his bosses' speeches made him want to vomit. "You put in your fifty years and they give you this crummy watch," Charlie blurts. "It works out to twenty-six cents a year . . . If it hadn't been for the $50 a week that I glummed out of petty cash, I wouldn't have made a thing."[40]

In another popular routine, Newhart demonstrated how a modern-day press agent might have attempted to manage Abraham Lincoln's image. As Shelley Berman did with many of his characters, Newhart played his press agent as if he were engaged in a telephone conversation. Like Mike Nichols's Jack Ego disk jockey, Newhart's slick PR man oozed insincerity. "Hi, Abe sweetheart," he begins. "How are you kid? How's Gettysburg?" When he finds out that Lincoln wants to change "Four score and seven" to "Eighty-seven," he protests, "Abe, that's meant to be a grabber. Abe, we test marketed that in Erie, and they went out of their minds."[41] Audiences and critics perceived something refreshingly honest, even slightly subversive about such routines. "Once he walks onstage and adjusts a microphone," the *Saturday Evening Post* noted, "he pricks bombastic balloons, disembowels stuffed shirts. He performs the operation so deftly the pompous are unaware they're being eviscerated." "What he does," critic Gilbert Millstein concurred, "is heavily satirical of sacred cows, so that the total Newhart can infuse a scarifying assault on the body politic with the ruddy glow of health or bite the hand feeding him and make it feel like a manicure."[42]

*   *   *

After Shelley Berman demonstrated how Compass material could be modified into a popular solo act, his former Compass colleagues Mike Nichols and Elaine May decided that they too would strike out on their own. In late 1957 they determined to develop their tandem act and then moved to New York City, obtained Jack Rollins as their manager, and almost immediately began playing established clubs such as the Blue Angel

18. Mike Nichols and Elaine May. Photofest.

and Village Vanguard. After appearing on *The Jack Paar Show* and *The Steve Allen Show,* Nichols and May were booked for a January 1958 episode of NBC's *Omnibus.* During the course of this "Suburban Revue" hosted by Alistair Cooke, the pair performed "Dawn of Love," a standard Compass scene in which a teenaged boy desperately attempts to make out with his date in the back seat of an automobile. The teenager begins by explaining his "urges" but eventually, after a protracted negotiation over intimacies, he squeals, "You can't imagine how *much* I would respect you." When she finally relents and begins reciprocating his affection, the boy turns scared and assumes his girlfriend's former reticence.[43]

The acclaim this televised scene brought Nichols and May, one of the first in American prime-time television to deal comically with teenagers' sexual behavior, was considerable. Almost immediately, the pair became celebrities. During the next several years, they, along with Shelley Berman and Bob Newhart, became some of the most well-known and highly paid satirists in America. Relying almost exclusively on material they and their Compass colleagues developed in Chicago and St. Louis, Nichols and May played elegant, "sophisticated" nightclubs all across the country, from the Mocambo in Hollywood to the Down in the Depths in New York City's Hotel Duane. In addition to making nightclub and television appearances, they released albums (*Improvisations to Music* [1958] and *Nichols and May Examine Doctors* [1962]), moved out to Hollywood where they briefly starred in an ill-conceived game show titled *Laugh Line,* and, beginning in 1960, recorded improvised scenes for the weekend NBC *Monitor* radio program. They reached the pinnacle of their success as a team in late 1960 when they brought *An Evening with Mike Nichols and Elaine May* to Broadway's Golden Theatre. Lavishly produced and promoted by Alexander Cohen and directed by Arthur Penn, *An Evening with Mike Nichols and Elaine May* was a smash hit. An album recorded from the show rose to number ten on the Billboard charts in 1961.

The arrival of Nichols and May on Broadway pleased no one more than those liberal critics who had earlier lamented the dearth of "sophisticated" comedy and satire in the American stage. The *New Republic*'s Robert Brustein, for example, marveled at the way "they employ[ed] extraordinary powers of observation to locate the clichés of conventional middle-class life." Brustein continued,

> Nichols and May, in short, are the voice of the outraged intelligence in a world given over to false piety, cloying sentiment, and institutionalized stupidity, and if this small voice can still be heard above the racket being produced all around us, then satire is still performing its traditional functions: to relieve that overwhelming sense of frustration, impotence, and isolation which afflicts the better spirits in our fatuous times.[44]

Brustein's remarks capture perfectly the sense of alienation and the spirit of conspiracy that liberal satire's ardent supporters shared during the late 1950s and early 1960s. It also reflects the unconscious snobbery that was an ineluctable part of satire's appeal to the "better spirits." Of all the satiric performers who made it big during this period, Nichols and May possessed perhaps the greatest snob appeal. It was not incidental that producer Alexander Cohen chauffeured guests for the October premiere of *An Evening with Mike Nichols and Elaine May* to the Golden Theater in Rolls-Royces. While on Broadway Nichols and May became the darlings of upper-middle-class, New York theater society. It was then that Nichols initiated friendships with Kenneth Tynan, Leonard Bernstein, Richard Avedon, and other luminaries in New York's cultural scene. Outside of New York, Nichols and May found admirers among statesmen such as Adlai Stevenson and the Shah of Iran. John Crosby was one of the few critics to temporarily suspend the hype Nichols and May generated

19. Facilitated by their quick wit and almost uncanny rapport, Elaine May and Mike Nichols improvise a sketch about a doctor and her patient for the NBC radio program *Monitor*. Library of Congress, Prints & Photographs Division, *Look* Magazine Photograph Collection.

by wryly noting that the pair had "started out taking pot shots at the sacred cows and now, after five years of solid success, they are in terrible danger of becoming one." [45]

The reasons for Nichols and May's popularity among well-educated, upper-middle-class urbanites are not difficult to discern. To begin with, their style was irresistibly "smart," witty, and inside. Their comic portraits of neuroticism, their parodies of therapists, and their frequent allusion to psychoanalysis struck a chord with New York—and by all accounts, largely Jewish—audience members, many of whom were well versed in Freudian vocabulary. Many who saw them perform were also impressed (and in some ways flattered) by their improvised references to playwrights and authors, both famous and obscure. Finally, seasoned theatergoers were undoubtedly impressed by the uncanny rapport Nichols and May enjoyed onstage. With the exception of one audience-suggested improvisation, all of the scenes they performed were well rehearsed. Nevertheless, all of their collaborative dialogues maintained a skillful spontaneity and unpredictability. Like a pair of seasoned jazz musicians, Nichols and May appeared capable of following each other on any riff. In "Pirandello," for example, they held the audience in suspense and disbelief as they transmogrified from two children pretending to fight like parents into a pair of feuding adults and, finally, just as the curtain for act 1 I was about to fall, back into Nichols and May.

Nichols and May's smart style and satiric characterizations did not appeal only to an upper-middle-class, urban, theatergoing audience. They brought the type of social satire performed by the Compass—irreverent, spontaneous, and self-critical—to the masses. The fact that the pair made promotional appearances on the *What's My Line?* and *Person to Person* television programs, that they were interviewed and profiled in major publications such as *Time* magazine, and, moreover, that their *Evening with Mike Nichols and Elaine May* album sold well across the country suggests that they also found (and targeted) a large mainstream and middlebrow audience. Indeed, as one writer suggested in a *New York Times Magazine* profile of the pair, Nichols and May enjoyed "both snob and mob appeal," just as Charlie Chaplin, Fred Allen and the Marx Brothers had earlier. Critics from magazines and daily newspapers gave a good indication for Nichols and May's widespread appeal and, more importantly, America's receptivity to liberal satire by 1960. Many of these critics particularly enjoyed the way Nichols and May opened their program. From opposite sides offstage, a white-collar commuter (Nichols) returning home after a day at work perfunctorily exchanges greetings with his suburban wife (May) and then asks her to mix him a dry martini. Only after the two meet each other onstage do they realize that the husband has accidentally entered the wrong home. "There is embodied here," the critic of the *New York Journal-American* marveled, "a commentary on the entire structure of suburbia." Likewise, other critics praised the satirists for holding up "life-sized mirrors to [Americans'] foibles, frustrations . . . and foolishness . . ." The *New York Morning Telegraph*'s Whitney Bolton characteristically suggested that "[t]hey murder what is sacred, hallowed and beloved in our free land and make you like it."[46]

Particularly for young people who had learned about patterns of courtship through their parents, popular fiction, soap opera dramas, instructional films, and other sources, the comic portraits of male-female seduction offered by Nichols and May appeared bold and honest. In one characteristic seduction scene, for example, Nichols played the part of a suave advertising man from "G.A.A. & P." who pulls out all the clichés and tricks of the modern-day playboy in order to get his secretary into bed.[47] In this and many other comic scenes, Nichols and May refuted fifties' stereotypes of marital bliss and domestic tranquility and portrayed through humor the way men and women attempt to con each other.

After seeing Nichols and May perform at Harvard Poet's Theatre in 1960, a young woman commented to her escort that "the best thing about them is that they're concerned with things that I didn't think anybody ever noticed but me."[48] This earnest judgment accords with what many young American adults felt about satirists like Nichols and May during the 1950s and early 1960s. In short, Nichols and May laid bare the precarious position sensitive, intelligent individuals—particularly modern males—occupied in a world given to cant, hypocrisy, middle-class conformity, and other social maladies neither acknowledged nor discussed in public. For those young, liberal middle-class adults who were felt estranged from American society during the Eisenhower era, Nichols and May and their cohort represented a breath of fresh air and a hopeful signal that individualism and the spirit of irreverence had not been extinguished from the land.

*   *   *

Nichols and May's comic scrutiny of courtship between men and women made a particularly strong impression on cartoonist Jules Feiffer.[49] Feiffer was born in 1929 and grew up in a largely Jewish neighborhood in New York's East Bronx. Both of his parents were Polish Jews who had immigrated to the United States when they were in their teens. Because his father was a failed and often unemployed salesman who lacked, as his son remembers, "the absence of ethics to be a successful businessman," his mother—an ambitious, well-educated fashion designer—was the family's breadwinner. From an early age he was convinced that the best way to "escape childhood" was to concentrate on cartooning. This was, he remembers, "the only skill I had that made me feel superior to the other kids." In a written tribute to Jerry Siegel, the creator of *Superman,* Feiffer has hinted how he decided to use his skills as a cartoonist to assimilate into mainstream American society. "If [Siegel] was at all like me (another Jewish boy in a different place at roughly the same time)," Feiffer wrote, "he sensed the difference, his otherness. We were aliens . . . [who] chose to be bigger, stronger, blue-eyed and sought-after by blond cheerleaders."[50]

To achieve success and recognition Feiffer decided to join Siegel and the fraternity of comic artists. "To me these men were heroes," Feiffer has remarked. "The world they lived in, as I saw it in those years of idolatry, was a world in which a person was blessedly in control of his own existence: wrote what he wanted to write, drew it the way he wanted to draw it—and was, by definition, brilliant." Feiffer made his first step toward his future career when, at the age of fifteen, his mother enrolled him in New York's Art Students' League. Upon graduating from high school in 1946, he lacked the necessary credits to enroll in college, so he continued his art studies at the Pratt Institute in Brooklyn. As with many other cartoonists, however, Feiffer's most valuable vocational training came on the job. Fortunately for Feiffer, he was hired by one of his idols, Will Eisner, to assist in the production of his newspaper comic insert, *The Spirit Section.* For the next five years, Feiffer worked closely with Eisner on *The Spirit* strip, eventually contributing a large portion of its writing and layouts. In 1949 Eisner rewarded his employee with a space to publish his own strip. Feiffer here introduced *Clifford,* a chronicle of a small boy's frustrated encounters with authority and the adult world.[51]

For three years following his discharge from the army in 1953, while either unemployed or working for some "schlock art house," Feiffer struggled to develop a style that was both meaningful and marketable. Prior to the 1950s, he had thought of producing his own weekly strip for syndication. By 1955, however, he was convinced that he would never achieve the virtuosity of his comic book artist heroes and that he should therefore find his own niche. He began formulating a type of comic expression that he believed was absent from the American scene—humor that was honest and truthful, humor that eschewed shopworn comic stereotypes and instead revealed something relevant about the mind-set and the anxieties of the middle-class, urban American living in the 1950s. After encountering the work of Robert Osborn and William Steig, he began to understand how simple, abstract drawings could render the true feelings and emotions of modern-day individuals. Like many other young cartoonists starting out in the 1950s, Feiffer had been greatly impressed by Osborn's line—a line that Feiffer said, "skittered, and soared, and turned scratchy, crabby, fluid as water, as if his circuits were wired to the insides of our brains." Few other cartoonists working during the Freudian fifties were better able to capture neurosis, anxiety and nervousness in their line. Feiffer was likewise drawn to the peculiar psychological orientation of Steig, who in his foreword to *The Rejected Lovers* (1951) stated that Americans were "a world of bewildered people—sad, lovelorn, full of pent-up emotions." Steig's *Agony in the Kindergarten* (1950) in particular made a lasting impression on Feiffer since it "revealed the secret thoughts of children and grown-ups" with "angst- and guilt-ridden imprints of the soul." "What a way to go, I thought," Feiffer later recalled. "And I went."[52] In a manner soon paralleled by the Compass Players and its descendents, Feiffer began to use humor to explore the self-doubts, private obsessions, and secret torments that afflicted Americans living in the age of Freud and Kierkegaard.

Like Osborn, Steig, and Mike Nichols, Feiffer struggled emotionally as a young man and turned to a form of Freudian psychoanalysis for help.[53] Feiffer committed himself to psychoanalysis for nine years, and he maintains that the process ultimately benefited him. But his experience, together with his contact with educated, middle-class New Yorkers who were preoccupied by psychological concerns (people who, as Feiffer put it, used psychoanalysis "as a topic of conversation" or a device to "prolong their illness"), also left him with serious reservations over psychoanalysis's social and political effects.[54] By late 1956, the analysand's obsessive concern with psychological "adjustment" was providing fodder for Feiffer's sharp, observational satire and laying the seedbed for his emerging cartooning career. In October of that year, Feiffer found the perfect venue for his psychologically attuned, existentialist satire—the *Village Voice.* Just then emerging as a politically-engaged, iconoclastic, underground publication and serving New York's young, hip "intellectuals" as well as denizens of what editor Daniel Wolf called the "Brooks Brothers underground," the *Voice* provided Feiffer with an audience that identified closely with Feiffer's characters. In a strip titled, tellingly, *Sick, Sick, Sick,* Feiffer began skewering the educated neurotic's proclivity for making histrionic statements about troubles "relating." Urban neurotics in the cast of "Feiffer's People" were, even more than the characters Mike Nichols, Elaine May, and Shelley Berman played onstage, pitiful creatures who tripped over their Freudian vocabulary as they struggled to gain coherence and contain their frustration. The subject of countless sociological studies and chronically "aware," the Village men and women that Feiffer scrutinized were often their own worst enemies. In one characteristic *Voice* strip from May 1958, Feiffer depicted a man lying on the ground paralyzed by indecision. Though he knows he must get up, this character is mired in his own introspection, caught in a circular trap of his own tortured self-analysis. While perfectly still and staring at the sky, he eventually discovers that he may be only "rationalizing" or somehow unaware of his true motivations. "I must dig! I must dig!" he finally declares. Still im-

20. Jules Feiffer, "the Hogarth of Bleecker Street," exposed the hang-ups and evasions of his urban peers in the borderless panels of his "Sick, Sick, Sick" strip. Photo by Dick DeMarsico. Library of Congress, Prints & Photographs Division, NYWT&S Collection.

mobile in the last panels, he pledges to start probing . . . after he counts to three.[55]

As clear as Feiffer was here in his animus against what he termed America's "analytically oriented environment," his strips clearly assumed their own therapeutic tone. At their heart, his strips—like the performances of the Compass Players, Nichols and May, and Bob Newhart—functioned (and were appreciated) as a type of Freudian therapy. Through them, the "truth" about middle-class Americans' self-delusions was revealed. Like Shelley Berman and his former Compass colleagues, Feiffer in many ways normalized the therapeutic mentality he set out to ridicule. Stylistically as well, his strips often operated in a therapeutic vein. When not revealing themselves through their private thoughts and conversations, Feiffer's characters addressed readers directly. Through this novel and intimate cartooning technique, Feiffer in effect had his readers assume the role of the analysand *and* analyst. Feiffer invited his readers to get into the heads of his lonely, misunderstood, self-deluded males and females in order to observe them work through their problems. As the title of his 1960 cartoon compilation suggests, Feiffer's characters were "explainers," neurotic, self-obsessed individuals in desperate need of someone who could take their attempts to rationalize and justify themselves seriously.

Feiffer's main intention, informed as it was by his left-liberal politics, was to warn that psychoanalysis had become a type of secular religion among Village inhabitants, that it was in effect making people like himself "over-aware." "Perhaps we have reached a point where we can explain it all and still know nothing," he worried privately at the time in his journal. Decades later, Feiffer recalled that his intention in his early work for the *Voice* was plainly to ridicule Freudian clichés and the "endless babble of self-interest, self-loathing, self-searching and evasion." Together with intellectuals Paul Goodman, David Riesman and C. Wright Mills, Feiffer scorned the psychology of social adjustment advocated by postwar neo-Freudians and shared their concern that Americans, in their rush to Freudian analysis, were depoliticizing important public issues. Mills, who argued in *The Sociological Imagination* (1959) that many "great public issues as well as many private troubles are described in terms of 'the psychiatric'—often, it seems, in a pathetic attempt to avoid the large issues and problems of modern society," would have surely appreciated Feiffer's March 13, 1957, strip in the *Village Voice*. Feiffer pictured here a middle-aged man soliloquizing about his suppressed political instincts. "I used to be a rebel in my youth," he tries to explain, but "I learned [that] rebellion is simply a *device* used by the immature to *hide* from his own problems." As a result, when he becomes aroused by a "civil rights case" or some other political issue he goes to his analyst and they "work it out." "You have no idea how much better I feel these days," he concludes complacently.[56]

Perhaps the clearest case that Feiffer made against the therapeutic mind-set was his illustrated article, "Couch-as-Couch-Can School of Analysis," published in the *New York Times Magazine* on May 18, 1958. In this piece, Feiffer demonstrated how a representative American male over the course of a lifetime suffered from the cumulative effects of Freudian psychoanalysis, pop psychology paperbacks, and what historian Christopher Lasch would later call "the helping professions." In the end, Feiffer's representative overanalyzed, emasculated middle-class American male meets a similarly neurotic female, and together they realize that they suffer from a "clear case of relationship-resistance due to anxiety needs, ego doubts and identity problems." "As a step in the right direction," Feiffer concludes ironically, "they get married" and have a ball "free-associating" and "examin[ing] each other's motives in blissful togetherness." "No one feels guilty any longer because who in this crazy kind of

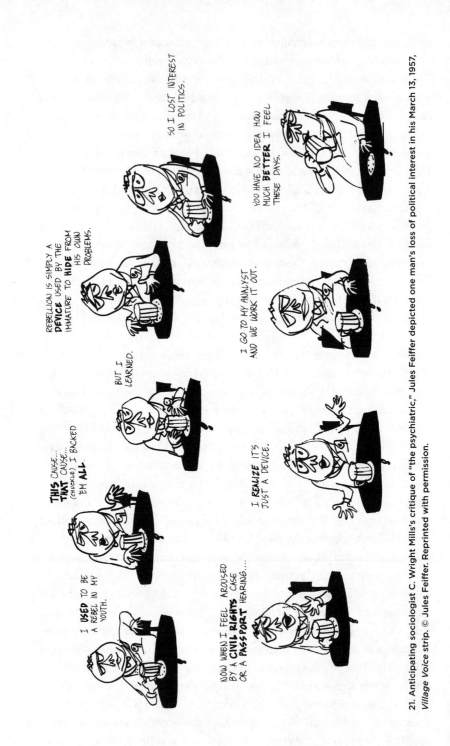

21. Anticipating sociologist C. Wright Mills's critique of "the psychiatric," Jules Feiffer depicted one man's loss of political interest in his March 13, 1957, *Village Voice* strip. © Jules Feiffer. Reprinted with permission.

H-Bomb world can be blamed for having problems? The idea is to look into one's self. The whole idea is to dig." [57]

The people most responsible for isolating and destabilizing Feiffer's representative young man are, notably, women: his obsessive mother, the young ceramics major he dated from Sarah Lawrence who interpreted what his "dreams of career, success, [and] glory . . . really mean," the former girlfriend who tells him that what he really wants is a mother, and "Big Mommy, the Ma Perkins of the psychiatry set," that "great surrounder of problems who while not solving them, will at least soften them into immobility." In addition to revealing Feiffer's animus toward psychiatry, "Couch-as-Couch-Can School of Analysis" addresses one of Feiffer's principal interests throughout the late 1950s and early 1960s — the troubled relationship between modern-day men and women. Like the Compass Players and Nichols and May, Feiffer well understood the potential for satirizing sex and gender relations, issues that were largely shrouded in secrecy during the 1950s. Like many Americans in the postwar years, Feiffer struggled to make sense of the way men and women interacted amid, as historian Elaine Tyler May describes it, the "sexual fallout of the atomic age." In the mid-1950s, Feiffer believed he was one of the few artists attempting to assess the way men and women struggled to relate to one another. When he saw Nichols and May perform their teenage make-out scene on the *Omnibus* television broadcast in January 1958, he suddenly realized he was not alone. Feiffer remembers that he was "absolutely bowled over" by the piece. "It was a breathtaking experience." "I couldn't believe what I was seeing because it was so close to what I was trying to do . . . and so absolutely perfect . . . real and honest . . ." "Mike and Elaine," Feiffer admitted in *Playboy* in 1961, "are the only ones in the field who go after one of the things that really interest me: the relation between boys and girls." Through his strips, Feiffer attempted to break through the postwar sexual containment—what he labeled "sexual McCarthyism"—and, like Nichols and May, force the subject of sex into public discourse. "There was no such thing as comedy about relationships, nothing about the newly urban and collegiate Americans," Feiffer insists. "What I was interested in was using humor as a reflection of one's own confusion, ambivalence and dilemma, dealing with sexual life as one knew it to be." [58]

Throughout the late 1950s and early 1960s, Feiffer subjected American males to some unusually tough satiric scrutiny, consistently caricaturing arrogant, lecherous male predators—the type of character that Mike Nichols portrayed in his "seduction" scenes with Elaine May and, in a later collaboration with Feiffer, the film *Carnal Knowledge*. Surprisingly, Feiffer contributed a number of these satiric strips to *Playboy* magazine, the house organ of aggressive masculinity during the 1950s and 1960s. On occasion, Feiffer used his *Playboy* strip (which he initiated in 1958) to demonstrate how two self-professed "lady-killers" (the suave "Stevie" and the leather-clad, Marlon Brando–like hipster "Huey") behaved toward women or, when alone, how they mused on the art of courtship. Both of these men were narcissists who shared an ugly contempt for women.[59] In the strip Feiffer contributed to the April 1961 issue of *Playboy,* for instance, he depicted Huey giving a friend a lesson on how to handle the "urban chick." "Make an urban chick feel *defenseless* and she'll confuse it with love," he advises. "To the urban chick brutality is a *status* symbol." Other *Playboy* strips commented on the American male's inability to appreciate a woman's whole self. In a strip ironically titled "The Lover" and published in the July 1960 issue of *Playboy,* Feiffer depicted a pathetic young gentleman describing to his friend how he had met the perfect woman on a date. Rather than concentrating on the pleasures of his date's company when he was with her, he confesses, the only thought he entertained was, "Wait till I tell the fellas."[60] Incapable of reciprocating true affection, numb to women's feelings, and blind to their indiscretions, the vain, often misogynist men Feiffer caricatured in his strips were ready targets.

As a brother to two sisters and as a keen observer of offensive male behavior, Feiffer was sympathetic to some of the frustrations borne by American women at midcentury. In this he resembled fellow cartoonist Robert Osborn, who included several memorable images of unhappy, overburdened housewives in his 1956 book *Osborn on Leisure.* Yet like Osborn and a great number of middle-class American artists and intellectuals, Feiffer also bought into the notion of the victimized, "castrated" male and what Arthur Schlesinger Jr. termed "the crisis of American masculinity." Reflecting the widespread concern among white-collar males in the 1950s over the definition and exhibition of masculinity in the increasingly standardized, bureaucratized corporate world and the demands placed upon men by the obligations of marriage, family, and the tender ideal of "togetherness" (what Schlesinger identified as the "the most sinister of present-day doctrines"), the "crisis of masculinity" helped give birth to a wide variety of cultural expression that served male fantasies of flight and rebellion.[61] In illustrations for *The Decline of the American Male* (1958) and articles such as "Husbands: The New Servant Class," Osborn himself pictured domineering wives running their spouses ragged. Though he shared much in common with Osborn, Feiffer directed his attention less at gender tensions in the suburban home than the plight of the urban, professional male—the type of reader targeted by the *Village Voice* and, to a greater degree, *Playboy*.

Playboy publisher Hugh Hefner was enthralled with Jules Feiffer's work when he encountered it in the *Village Voice* and a competing men's magazine titled *Rex*. In the latter, Feiffer had contributed a seven-page spread titled "Kept" for the December 1957 issue. Here an unattractive male named Basil revealed his secret for success with women: simply nodding his head and agreeing to the neurotic "gibble gabble gibble gabble gibble" spewing forth from female companions. In the *Voice*, Feiffer was prone to caricaturing women in one of two unflattering extremes: either as passive victims or aggressive "man-eaters." In the opinion of some female readers, many of his strips reflected a latent hostility toward women. This was perhaps most evident in a continuing series of strips Feiffer created around an insecure nebbish character named Bernard Mergendeiler. Inspired in part by Feiffer's experiences as a single man "trying to make out" in the late 1950s (and reminiscent of the poor schlemiels Shelley Berman was prone to play in his nightclub routine), Bernard was repeatedly spurned and embarrassed by women. In a *Voice* strip dating from July 1957, for example, Bernard professes sincere affection to a woman ("Do you *know* how *long* I waited to meet someone like *you*—a girl I could *talk* to . . . ?") only to have her reel away excitedly and flag the attention of an athletic hulk named Buzzy. In this and many other Feiffer strips of the period, kind, gentle, emotionally vulnerable men like Bernard finished last. As much as we like to tell ourselves that kindness and gentleness pay off in the end, *reality* dictates, Feiffer insisted, that tenacious, overbearing men are the ones who really get ahead, with women as with everything else. Moreover, most men suffer in the hands of domineering women—masters at the arts of intimidation and humiliation. In Feiffer's strips, even Superman was not immune from having his masculinity questioned and undermined by a female antagonist.[62]

In April 1958, Hefner wrote Feiffer that what he was contributing to the *Village Voice* "is exactly right for us" with perhaps "even more emphasis on urban living as apart from strictly Village living . . ." In the next several weeks, Hefner courted Feiffer, offering generous payments for "work done specifically for us," work that focused "first and foremost, of course, [on] the continuing male-female relationship . . ." "We're not particularly interested in political satire, international stresses, religious or racial issues, nor the family unit," Hefner informed Feiffer, "for we are an escapist magazine that treats the reader as though he were a bachelor and attempt to take him out of the cares and worries of the work-a-day world around him." Out of these early contacts a long-term collaboration between Hefner and Feiffer was established. For his part, Hefner, a frustrated cartoonist himself, offered Feiffer extended and at times dead-on editorial critiques of his work and, more importantly, granted Feiffer full freedom to pursue subjects of his own choosing. In return, Feiffer provided *Playboy* and its readers with a series of strips satirically deconstructing, from a male's point of view, sexual politics between men and women.[63]

The biggest obstacle facing the men and women in Feiffer's *Playboy* and *Village Voice* strips was often direct, honest communication. "I'm trying to explain in my work the complete breakdown in communications," Feiffer explained to an interviewer in 1959. "In sex, people who are on intimate terms are incapable of expressing themselves to each other, each living in a private world."[64] With men and women, as with all other relations governing American life, Feiffer suggested, communication was breaking down. Exacerbated by the infusion of psychiatric and sociological jargon, communication had become less effective, less reliable. Worse yet, American men and women were all too often using language as a tool for deceit rather a device to achieve mutual understanding.

With his ear for the way educated middle-class men and women communicated with each other, Feiffer resembled no one more than Nichols and May. Yet Feiffer's satiric take on relationships was on the whole much darker than that of his counterparts. The men and women Feiffer scrutinized, particularly in *Playboy*, were numb to each other's feelings, incapable of penetrating each other's protective armor or of negotiating the emotional terrain that divided them. When not analyzing or literally explaining their relationships to death, they talked past each other. At their very worst, they were quick to inflict their counterparts with abuse and psychological torment. Whether because of a man's hostility to women, a woman's need to dominate her mate, or a number of other causes, the sexual and marital relationships Feiffer caricatured throughout the late 1950s and early 1960s were unfulfilling and doomed to failure. In an October 1964 strip for the *Village Voice,* a man and his wife sit with their backs pointed toward the reader while they watch television in their reclining chairs. "Sometimes when I used to stroke you tenderly," the man tells his wife, "I used to think what if I slowly increased the intensity of my stroke—so that it would go: stroke, stroke, *stroke, POW!* Naturally I was horrified by such thoughts . . . [and] I began to wonder if I didn't have mixed feelings toward you . . . So to save us both from my impulses, I no longer go near you. That's why I watch all this television." "Me too, Sam," responds his wife as she reaches over to hold his hand.[65]

Taken together, the bulk of Feiffer's strips and writings from the late 1950s and early 1960s (including his picaresque novel *Harry the Rat with Women* [1963], serialized in *Playboy*), revealed a deep skepticism about the prospects of loving reciprocity and mutual giving between men and women. In retrospect, Feiffer confesses that at the time he simply "thought women were devouring and men hated women."[66] Although he opposed the "Playboy philosophy," his strips unwittingly ratified *Playboy's* deepest suspicions about marital commitment. Feiffer's *Playboy* and *Village Voice* cartoons, in short, may have awakened male readers to their own insensitivity, but they more likely legitimated their worst suspicions about the long-term viability of relationships between men and women.

*   *   *

By focusing on the frustrations and defeats of men in particular, Feiffer was able "to take the . . . Benchley hero," as he later recalled, "and launch him into the Age of Freud."[67] Through his strips, Feiffer gave voice to the alienated young men whom social critic Paul Goodman described sympathetically in *Growing Up Absurd* (1960), the male members of the "silent generation" of college students, the closet rebels and frustrated organization men. During the decade of the fifties, Feiffer recounts, America "cloned itself into a country made up of millions of Clark Kents. And day after day, you could hear them muttering to themselves: 'I'm not really like this. If they only knew my real identity.'" It was exactly this preoccupation with the "real identity" and integrity of the male personality that animated the Compass Players and Feiffer's strips on conformity. From the time they first began appearing in the *Village Voice* and (in a strip aptly titled *The Conformist*) *Playboy,* Feiffer's strips echoed the concern C. Wright Mills, David Riesman, William Whyte and other liberal social critics and intellectuals voiced over the threats they believed large-scale organizations posed to the integrity, freedom, and individuality of American males. A significant number of Feiffer's strips demonstrated how Riesman's "organization men" and gray flannel, middle-class denizens of the suburbs sadly succumbed to the prevailing consensus. In a May 1957 strip for the *Voice,* for instance, Feiffer depicted the progression of conformity in the life cycle of a Madison Avenue advertising man. Throughout his early life this man had been told by his mother to "play like everyone else," by friends to "join gangs like everyone else," and by his college advisor to "join a frat like everyone else." "And soon," he confesses while a rope binds his arms and legs, "you couldn't tell me from everyone else . . . Now they tell me I'm a conformist."[68]

Several strips ironically pointed out that warnings against conformity only encouraged more conformity. One such strip pictured a man on a stool informing readers how he had kept up with the sociological literature. "Well, in between being silent, conforming, belonging, acquiring and taking care of my leisure problem," he states with exasperation, "I haven't had a chance yet to seek status . . . I guess I'll fit it in somehow." In *Voice* strips throughout 1956 and 1957, Feiffer pointed out that Village bohemians inevitably lapsed into their own form of conformity. In these strips he indicted Village hipsters and beatniks—whom he later called "a bunch of aimless infants who stand for nothing"—for their shallow, false attempts at rebellion.[69] Echoing complaints that intellectuals such as Robert Brustein and Norman Podhoretz were then registering against the Beats and their followers, Feiffer, in a September 1957 strip for the *Voice,* pictured a hip young man sitting at a restaurant table with a date and defining what a "rebel" like himself is. He "don't talk up to no judge," this man rambles, "he *cuts out*—you know, man—he *withdraws* . . . and he says, '*squares* I do not *know* you' . . . And soon he's *so* withdrawn he only hears *himself.* So he writes it in a book. And the squares . . . *buy* his withdrawal and everyone makes a *mint. That's* rebellion man."[70]

Feiffer's antipathy toward the conformity bred by postwar white-collar, corporate culture was often pronounced. In several strips during this period, Feiffer took aim at the modern corporation, which he, like other contemporary critics, blamed for feeding cynicism and defeatism to young American males. The organization men Feiffer caricatured yielded their senses of identity, languished in boredom, suffered at the capricious whims of their bosses, and lost out to ambitious, backstabbing colleagues.

One victim of this system, a twenty-four-year-old "consultation assistant," told readers that despite having to attend "daily make up sessions with the morale department's psychoanalyst," despite relinquishing the loyalty of his family, he "could die for the company." Readers of such strips, many of whom were employees in large corporations, did not miss the sad irony of this young man's predicament.[71]

In much the same vein, Feiffer often used his cartoons during the late 1950s and early 1960s to satirize the shallow formulas and manipulative sensationalism that proliferated mass culture and advertising. In several strips from the late fifties and early sixties, Feiffer blamed writers, admen, market researchers, and executives for manipulating consumers and polluting public life with the dictates and values of the marketplace. In a world where the consumer was said to be king, his strips argued, anything was marketable—even anger. In a January 1958 *Voice* strip he caricatured a business executive who recommends to his colleagues, on the basis of customer research, the marketing of anger. "Take the *threat* out of anger," he tells the board. "This must be the *banner year* for anger, gentlemen. Remember, anger can be sold! . . . Next year we can go to tranquilizers." In another *Voice* strip an account executive, inspired by the Eisenhower administration's handling of the 1958 recession, proposes an animated commercial (with a jingle "Stop that crying! Keep 'em buying!") to spur consumption and, consequently, propel the nation's prosperity. Feiffer targeted mass culture's consumers as well. A man made numb to the world around him, for example, admits in a strip that he "can't tell *anything* anymore." In defeat, he sits in front of his television set and begins watching *Gunsmoke*. "What's the difference?" he concludes pathetically.[72]

*   *   *

In his attacks on advertising and mass culture, Feiffer's work was at times consonant with that of fellow cartoonist Robert Osborn. Throughout the fifties and early sixties, Osborn gave vent to his frustration with what he perceived as America's shallow materialism and its reckless disregard for the environment. In books such as *Low & Inside* (1953) and in drawings for the *New Republic* and the *Atlantic*, Osborn lampooned public relations, cupidity, and the wasteful excesses of American automobile design. In *Low & Inside*, Osborn utilized a wildly expressive calligraphy to help describe what he despairingly termed "the steady plight of MAN; the anarchy of his laughter and the terrifying lawfulness of his tragedies." In *Osborn on Leisure* (1956), Osborn supplied a brief narrative to criticize the coercive "teamwork" of the large-scale business organization and the debilitating effects of alcohol. By participating in modernity's "rat race," Osborn argued, Americans were sacrificing their opportunity for achieving autonomy, self-fulfillment, and meaningful leisure. As he had argued throughout the 1950s, Osborn stressed that "reality" must be restored to American life. Only the *"understanding* heart . . . *possessed of a psychic unity,"* he concluded with the type of punctuation Feiffer would emulate, "can comprehend the infinite possibilities of *Reality* and, being confident, can understand the hearts of other men and speak to them in turn with trust and clarity."[73]

With their satiric jabs on the causes and consequences of conformity, Jules Feiffer and Robert Osborn joined a group of liberal critics and intellectuals—men such as Lewis Mumford, John Keats, John Kenneth Galbraith, David Riesman, Russell Lynes, Vance Packard, A. C. Spectorsky and William Whyte—whose mid- and late-1950s jeremiads sold remarkably well to the middle-class American public. Osborn, certainly, shared these writers' preoccupation with the "softness," complacency, and dullness of postwar, middle-class, suburban American life. It was no coincidence that Osborn was the illustrator of choice for several of these liberal critics' books and articles. Like much of their social and cultural critique, Osborn's satire in retrospect appears overly dismissive, classbound, even somewhat elitist. When Osborn, a man who drove a British-made Riley and who lived in a home designed by Edward Larrabee Barnes, satirized the aesthetic confusion of mass culture and the grotesque automobile designs coming out of Detroit, he betrayed more than a hint of snobbism. As Richard Pells, Daniel Horowitz, and other cultural historians have pointed out, liberal American critics and intellectuals during the 1950s were more preoccupied by middle- and upper-middle-class cultural concerns—what Arthur Schlesinger Jr. famously identified in 1956 as "qualitative" issues—rather than issues of economic justice that animated the New Deal liberalism of the 1930s.[74]

Feiffer was not loath to portray the average middle-class citizen as a passive victim of shallow commercialism and America's vulgar mass culture, but his strips, at their best, were informed by a more searching critical spirit, one more attuned to the political consequences of conformity than an allegiance to "good taste." Like C. Wright Mills, the Columbia University sociologist whose writings during the 1950s inspired the New

Left, Feiffer demonstrated how the goal of social "adjustment," so commonly touted in fifties popular psychology, negated common sense, discouraged intellectual curiosity and, in the long run, suppressed Americans' disquiet with the logic of the cold war. As we shall see in a later chapter, Feiffer's satiric criticism of the cold war in particular penetrated the military industrial apparatus that worked to gain the consent of the American public.

*   *   *

With the exception of Walt Kelly, no other cartoonist working in the United States in the late 1950s and early 1960s did more than Jules Feiffer to bring penetrating satiric insight and contemporary relevance to the comic strip. Feiffer's use of borderless panels, spare backgrounds and hand lettering, coupled with a line "whose tautness and economy," as art historian Elizabeth Frank has stated, "suggest neat, brittle fury," contributed to a unique style that attracted much attention and won considerable praise. With his pen, Feiffer brilliantly captured hand gestures and body language, but it was his writer's gift for monologue and dialogue that allowed him to puncture the thought and behavior of his contemporaries. In Feiffer's strips, educated, middle-class urbanites were able to identify themselves and people they knew and laugh at the self-delusions, bad behavior, and uncomfortable predicaments they had experienced in common. "The general effect," critic George Melly wrote of Feiffer's strips, "is as disconcerting as hearing a playback on a tape recorder which had been hidden under a sofa . . ." Indeed, given the skill and influence of Feiffer's satire, the admission "I felt like a character in a Feiffer cartoon" became a standard in urban conversation.[75]

By 1958, the year Berman and Nichols and May began their meteoric rise to fame, Feiffer had already acquired a reputation as one of the smartest and most "hip" cartoonists working in America. Though he still received no payment for his *Voice* cartoons, he gained exposure when they were reprinted in magazines such as *Liberation*, *Madison Avenue* and *Anvil and Student Partisan*. Three years later, a *Cue* critic reported that "Feifferophiles are legion. The first were a small band of readers of the *Village Voice*, but the flock has now expanded far beyond the confines of 'hip' New Yorkers." By that time, Feiffer's weekly strip (now titled *Feiffer*) was being distributed by the Hall Syndicate to sixty-eight newspapers (including the

London Observer) as well as several dozen college papers. Together with the work of Robert Osborn, Herblock, and Bill Mauldin, Feiffer's strip was also published in the pages of the *New Republic*, a magazine noted for its small but influential liberal readership. In addition, Feiffer had published five compilations of his cartoons and a novel and had received the George Polk Memorial Award in Journalism for providing "insights into the frustrations of modern man."[76]

While "highbrow" liberal publications branded Feiffer a young "intellectual" or "sociologist" (*Harper's,* for example, claimed that Feiffer managed "to tell us more about the way we live in the mid-twentieth century than any half-dozen sociologists, two dozen popular novelists, and Vance Packard combined—and furthermore, [he] is funnier"), critics in mainstream publications marveled how this "mild-mannered intellectual" and self-proclaimed "court subversive," this "Hogarth of Bleeker Street" and "voice of the Floundering Fifties" had become "the only syndicated avant-garde satirical cartoonist in the United States . . ." One reviewer in the *New York Times Book Review* claimed that Feiffer's wide syndication was nothing less than "a startling event in the history of modern culture." "It is difficult," writer and self-professed "high-middlebrow" critic Russell Lynes said of Feiffer's growing celebrity in 1961, "to think of anyone in recent years who, speaking with such a quiet public voice, has made such a big noise." While Arthur Schlesinger Jr. called "Feiffer" "ruthless as a good piece of surgery," even the *Jackson (Mississippi) Daily News* could admit that its creator was "one of the most articulate of commentators on the contemporary scene . . ." The astute *Village Voice* critic Nat Hentoff, an enthusiastic supporter for the new, late-1950s social and political satire, credited Feiffer with going "beneath the surface of topicality into the marrow of our frustrations in a society of abundance inhabited by lonelier and lonelier people."[77]

Like Nichols and May, Feiffer won admirers among Manhattan's cultural elite, most notably Kenneth Tynan, the influential *London Observer* drama critic who was in residence at the *New Yorker* during the 1959 and 1960 theatrical seasons. A far larger segment of Feiffer's appreciative audience, however, was composed of college students and young, educated, urban middle-class males in their twenties. So popular was Feiffer with the former crowd that by the early 1960s he was routinely delivering lectures on college campuses across the country. Feiffer's appeal among the latter, the type of young males who read the *Village Voice* and *Playboy,* was perhaps more significant. These were the fans that reportedly carried their favorite Feiffer strips in their wallets. As Russell Lynes observed, they were "the pretentious and talented young . . . the sociologically oriented and the psychically adjusted," the "advertising men who work in what they call (but nobody else does) the 'creative' departments." More accurately yet, Feiffer's biggest fans were, as Gilbert Millstein reported for the *Saturday Evening Post,* "rebels posing as organization men," men who could not "resist pinning his cartoons on the office bulletin board when the boss is not looking."[78] As the poet Paul Carroll described "Feiffer people" in 1961,

> [they] belong to that generation who dropped in at the tail-end of the War and missed the glory and 'the piss-and-vinegar': who floundered or goofed through school on the GI Bill: who in the early Fifties tried on long pants at the first organization-man-type job and first neurotic love affair and first bout with the head-doctor: who drank too much and smoked too much at too many parties: who in macabre fascination watched the Eisenhower Administration progress from inanity to peevish stupidity to the brink of atomic war: who learned to live with the Bomb by believing in nothing: who waited and continue to wait for something to happen but know it never will: who are neither Angry nor Beat but who simply exist in a vacuum explaining and apologizing forever to ears that are not there.[79]

Along with those who laughed at the Compass Players, cheered Nichols and May, and purchased Bob Newhart's comedy albums, "Feiffer's people" appreciated the smart, irreverent, occasionally poignant insight social satire provided into middle-class life at midcentury. For middle-class men in particular, this social satire gloriously fulfilled the role prescribed for it by liberal playwright Gore Vidal in 1958. At its base, Vidal wrote in the *Nation,* satire was simply "truth grinning in a solemn canting world." To its fans, the satiric "truth" delivered from the stage of the Compass and the borderless panels of *Sick, Sick, Sick* came as a fresh, occasionally bracing breath of air and provided a sense of relief from the feelings of loneliness and isolation that resulted from living in the alienating, bureaucratic, "plastic" world of the fifties. Feiffer understood this well. In a *Playboy* interview Feiffer professed that his work "might be of help simply by showing other people who thought they were alone that they aren't alone." The public response to his work demonstrated, he later remembered, "that I was doing exactly what I wanted to be doing, which is to represent people who felt unrepresented and didn't think anybody in print spoke on their behalf." Indeed as a writer for *Commentary* observed in 1961, when one looked at a Feiffer cartoon or listened to "cerebral," "sick" comedians such as Nichols and May "one had the feeling that one was not isolated, that there was a widespread underground recognition that things were not 'jes fine.'"[80]

CHAPTER FIVE

Spontaneous Irony

THE SECOND CITY, THE PREMISE,
AND EARLY-SIXTIES SATIRIC
CABARET AND REVUE

During the mid- and late 1950s, the social satire produced onstage by the Compass Players and in cartoon strips by Jules Feiffer struck a chord with a growing audience of educated, middle-class Americans who shared anxieties over the spread of social conformity, the stifling of dissent, and tensions between the sexes. To their fans, these social satirists succeeded in using humor to broach subjects that were all too often ignored in public discourse. Equally appealing was the way these liberal satirists, much like the Beat poets, jazz musicians, and abstract expressionist painters of the fifties, had allowed improvisation to drive their creative approach. Insightful, spontaneous, and, at times, revelatory, the satiric commentary that the Compass Players, Nichols and May, and Jules Feiffer produced ultimately inspired several new cabarets and revues—most importantly, the Second City, the Premise, the Establishment, and *Beyond the Fringe*—that collectively expanded the range of satire's social and political criticism into the early 1960s.

*   *   *

By 1958 the remarkable success and popularity that Shelley Berman, Mike Nichols, and Elaine May had achieved made their former Compass colleagues more than a little envious. During the summer of that year a number of them decided to follow these performers' lead and capitalize on liberal satire's new vogue. After studying in Paris on a Fulbright Scholarship, David Shepherd created a Compass road company with Nancy Ponder and two young actors named Jerry Stiller and Alan Arkin. "I decided to go back into improvisational theater," Shepherd later admitted candidly, "[because] I wanted to make as much money out of it as other people had done." Del Close underwent analysis with Theodor Reik, began participating in LSD experiments for the U.S. Air Force, and then embarked on a career as a stand-up comic. After two years of "absolutely humiliating defeat" as a comic, he eventually won some attention with an eclectic, esoteric act in which he parodied psychoanalysis (the subject of his 1959 comedy album *The Do-It-Yourself Psychoanalysis Kit*) and existentialist philosophy, among other things. Severn Darden initiated his own offbeat solo act and began performing at the Gate of Horn, a Chicago nightclub that was then one of America's premiere venues for folk music and the "new comedy."[1]

Back in St. Louis, at the fashionable Park Plaza Gourmet Room, Theodore Flicker presented *Whadd'ya Want?*, a short-lived satirical revue that, according to one *Variety* critic, was "not for people from Squaresville." *Whadd'ya Want?* proved a commercial failure, but Flicker nevertheless managed to convince his benefactors, Fred and Jay Landesman, to open a new, more opulent Crystal Palace on Gaslight Square where he soon directed Darden, Close, and other former Compass Players in Samuel Beckett's *Endgame* and *Waiting for Godot*. Also for the new Crystal Palace, Flicker directed *The Nervous Set*, a musical parody of Beat poets based on Jay Landesman's unpublished recollections of Greenwich Village bohemian life. In 1959 Flicker brought a slightly sanitized version of *The Nervous Set* starring Del Close and Larry Hagman to Broadway. "Nothing on the local music stages this season has been so acid and adult," *New York Times* theater critic Brooks Atkinson wrote of it, "as the wry portrait of Greenwich Village beatniks it offers when the show begins." Despite this weighty endorsement and its playful poster ads—designed, significantly, by Jules Feiffer—*The Nervous Set* drew a small audience. Much to the disappointment of Flicker, his backers, and a handful of supportive critics, it closed after a three-week run.[2]

In the end, it was former Compass director Paul Sills, not David Shepherd or Theodore Flicker, who perfected the formula for a commercially viable, improvisational cabaret oriented toward social and political satire. While Shepherd and Flicker struggled with their respective enterprises, Sills met with Roger Bowen and Howard Alk to discuss plans for opening a new cabaret theater. Bowen had previously worked with Sills at the Compass and had recently returned from military duty in Japan. Alk, a film editor and former Trotskyist, had helped Sills manage the Gate of Horn nightclub. Together the three men originally discussed opening a West Coast–style hangout where, as Sills remembers it, "we would invite [Allen] Ginsberg and people of that sort to read and talk and sing." They eventually decided to convert the Compass along the lines of Café Society—the Depression-era cabaret theater once operated by Barney Josephson in New York's Greenwich Village. To help finance their venture, Alk, Bowen, and Sills turned to Bernard Sahlins, an entrepreneur who, like Sills, was a native Chicagoan and a graduate of the University of Chicago. Throughout the fifties, Sahlins, often with the help of Sills, had launched a series of short-lived classical and avant-garde theatrical productions in Chicago. A man with an eye for good investments, Sahlins pledged proceeds from the sale of his tape recording business to help support Sills's newest venture.[3]

In an ironic tribute to the witty, scathing three-part profile of Chicago that A. J. Liebling wrote for the New Yorker in 1952—a profile in which the writer labeled Sill's hometown a "not-quite metropolis" and his alma mater "the greatest magnet for neurotic juveniles since the Children's Crusade . . ."—Sills, Alk, Bowen, and Sahlins named their new improvisational theater the Second City. For performers, Sills and his partners recruited Eugene Troobnick, a former Playwrights member who was working as an editor for Playboy, and ex-Compass Players Barbara Harris, Severn Darden, and Andrew Duncan. These former University of Chicago students were soon joined by Alan Arkin, an actor and musician who had recently played with the Tarriers, a folksinging quartet, and David Shepherd's St. Louis Compass troupe; and Mina Kolb, an actress familiar to Chicagoans through the Rain or Shine with Ray Raynor television program.[4]

On December 16, 1959, Sills and his troupe opened their first performance, Excelsior and Other Outcries, in a 120-seat theater located on the fringe of Chicago's Old Town. From the beginning, Sills was aware that the Second City would need a more polished or "sophisticated" approach if its brand of satiric cabaret was to succeed financially. "We wanted a club where people would come," Sills remembers. To that end, Sills, Alk, and Sahlins determined to keep admission prices low and offer patrons espresso and hamburgers in addition to alcoholic beverages. Tapping Sills's "knowledge of nightclub business and modern decor—[on] what was 'in' in forty different directions," they decided to decorate the interior with red velour opera drapes, black painted phone booth doors, and round globe lighting fixtures. On the whole, Second City's intimate environment was designed to capture the ambiance of 1920s Berlin cabaret. According to Andrew Duncan, there was "something sexy about the look of the place. A sin kind of thing." Upon its carpeted stage, male Second City actors performed in dark corduroy three-piece suits. Harris and Kolb wore black frocks and pearls. In keeping with the Compass's minimalist approach, chairs (or "nesting boxes") were a few of the only props used on the Second City stage.[5] Also reminiscent of the early Compass was the sprightly musical accompaniment of jazz pianist Bill Mathieu.

The most noticeable departure the Second City made from the Compass, particularly the early, Chicago-based Compass, was its adoption of set scenes. Although Sills and his troupe still devised material through spot improvisations—either in rehearsals or in late-night sessions with an audience—they typically performed their program like a well-polished cabaret or revue. Only at two or possibly three moments during their two-act performance would Second City performers engage in "pure" improvisations based on audience suggestions. Following introductions and explanations by straight man emcee Andy Duncan, Second City scenes under Sills's direction proceeded at a snappy, well-timed pace.

The Second City may have differed from its predecessor somewhat in terms of its style and approach, but it pursued many of its same targets. Blackout sketches poking fun at Freud and psychoanalysis, for example, were steady fare at the Second City. Parodies of high and low culture also abounded. During its first several years of operation, Second City's various companies spoofed *True Confessions,* Dick Clark, Eugene O'Neill, *The Ted Mack Amateur Hour, Candid Camera,* and other television programs, folksingers, opera, toothpaste commercials, *Mother Goose,* and foreign films such as Ingmar Bergman's *Wild Strawberries.* With the Second City throughout the early 1960s, Severn Darden also continued lampooning Bruno Bettelheim and other University of Chicago intellectuals.

Like their predecessors at the Compass, Second City performers devoted much of their comic material to relationships within the family, particularly relationships between husbands and wives and parents and children. Quite unlike the idealized portraits of family life offered by television sitcoms, the Second City attempted to highlight what its predominantly male members perceived as the "brutal truth" behind traditional middle-class marriage. According to Paul Sills's assistant director Sheldon Patinkin, the Second City with its relationship (or "people")

22. Members of Second City's original troupe: (clockwise from left) Severn Darden, Paul Sand, Andrew Duncan and Barbara Harris. Photofest.

scenes was attempting to decipher "what we thought the human situation was." The *real* human situation, according to Patinkin and his colleagues, was not defined primarily by feelings of "togetherness"—an ideal highly touted in 1950s American consensus culture—but, rather, misunderstanding, alienation, and pain. Together with playwrights Tennessee Williams and Edward Albee, cartoonist Jules Feiffer, the artists and writers of *MAD,* and a host of other male satirists working during the 1950s and early 1960s, Second City's young performers refuted American mainstream culture's idealized, saccharine outlook on social harmony and the many satisfactions derived from marriage and a steady domestic life. In the blackout scene "Centaurs," the extinction of a mythical animal species was linked to the inability of wives to prepare themselves in time for important engagements—in this case the disembarkment of Noah's ship. In one of its darker jokes about marriage, "Just Rehearsing Dear" (a piece Del Close remembers as "wonderfully misogynistic"), a Walter Mitty–type man explains to an imaginary judge and jury why he had killed and dismembered his wife. When the shrilly offstage voice of his wife asks

"George, what are you doing down there in the basement?" the man shouts back, "Just rehearsing, dear."[6]

Second City scenes addressing the dark, secret lives of middle-class families often evinced a mood of pathos and sentimentality. In "First Affair," for example, Severn Darden and Barbara Harris played a father and teenage daughter who for the first time discuss the daughter's recent sexual awakening. Although the scene humorously played up the daughter's clichéd references to Sigmund Freud and Erich Fromm, its focus was on the understanding a father attempts to gain with his hip, yet emotionally immature child. Even with its emphasis on sympathy and compassion, however, "First Affair," like many other scenes performed by improvisational troupes and strips drawn by Jules Feiffer, betrayed a measure of doubt about the efficacy of interpersonal communication and the attainability of mutual understanding. The impression the critic for the *Christian Science Monitor* got when he saw this scene performed was that it "plung[ed] its two characters . . . into a mute impasse of despair and mutual isolation." Pointing out the harmful effects of familial and intergenerational misunderstanding was likewise the objective of "Family Reunion," a poignant, long scene performed during the Second City's 1963 *13 Minotaurs or Slouching toward Bethlehem* program. In this scene, informed by the painful experiences of at least one Second City performer, the mother, father, and brother of a young gay man named Warren pay him a long overdue visit in his Chicago apartment. Despite relaying multiple hints about his homosexuality, Warren's conservative Midwestern family refuses to acknowledge his true identity. As Warren comes close to disclosing the truth about himself, his brother, father, and mother brusquely depart, ironically informing him, "If you've ever got anything bothering you that you want to talk over, you know where we are."[7]

The subjects of dating and male-female relationships, also integral to the social satire of the Compass, Nichols and May, and Jules Feiffer, figured prominently in early-sixties Second City performances. In "The Tailor and the Model," "The Protest Marchers," "The Novelty Shop," "Don't I Know You?" and other scenes, Second City performers humorously surveyed how men and women struggle but ultimately fail to connect with one another. Perhaps the most popular and acclaimed example of this type of scene was "Museum Piece," created and performed by Alan Arkin and Barbara Harris in 1961. Set in the Art Institute of Chicago, it depicted an encounter between a beatnik and a young, uptight, middle-class woman who admits to having "numerous problems in the area of spontaneity." After listening to her explain what she has learned about avant-garde art in her humanities classes, the guitar-strumming beatnik encourages her to liberate her senses and begin appreciating paintings by first getting in touch with her feelings. After gradually shedding her bourgeois inhibitions, the young woman declares her new acquaintance "marvelously incoherent" and then begins a giddy free association reading: "Freedom, freedom, freedom . . . blue, green, orange, yellow . . . I hate my aunt." Sensing that he has prompted her breakthrough, the beatnik makes his move, whereupon she retreats in fright. In the end, as with many other Compass and Second City scenes, man and woman, separated by class and differences of outlook, fail to relate.[8]

In numerous comic scenes, the Second City dramatized the clash between the sensitive and intelligent (as represented by the Second City and its fans) and the "phony" other (the hypocritical do-gooder, the businessman and the suburbanite) — the type of clash that J. D. Salinger outlined a decade earlier in his novel *The Catcher in the Rye*. In "Lekathoy," performed during the 1961 program *Alarums and Excursions,* two former college roommates — one a successful financial broker and the other a student who, after twenty years, is still working on his degree — encounter each other by chance on a city street. With its caricatures of its bookish and boorish characters, this scene evoked laughter. Yet by highlighting the irreparable breach now separating these former best friends, the tone of "Lekathoy" was marked less by mirth than by melancholy. When the broker in the end accidentally breaks his former friend's precious Greek urn, he shatters all memories of the idealism and love of learning they used to share.[9]

With its caricature of the phony, anti-intellectual broker in "Lekathoy," the Second City repeated the type of complaint that *MAD,* the Compass Players, Jules Feiffer, and other liberal satirists repeatedly registered against the middle-class conformists and squares inhabiting 1950s America. Indeed, patrons of the Second City enjoyed a steady diet of satire directed at the mores, prejudices, and lifestyles of the American middle class — the social class to which most of them belonged. In 1961, for example, Second City reprised a David Shepherd "Dream" sequence (what a *Variety* reviewer appropriately labeled a "heavy handed . . . moody psycho-philosophical study of middle class conformity") in which troupe members wore paper sacks over their heads in order to signify and condemn the blind conformity of the bourgeoisie. That same year, Second City performers played a modified version of the Compass's "Exurbanites" in which a group of pretentious, culture-loving liberals living in the suburbs shun a working-class deliveryman at a house party. "Great Books," a popular Second City scene from the early 1960s, lampooned the way an adman, loud-mouthed housewife, and other suburban philistines might convert a classroom discussion on Dostoevsky's *Crime and Punishment* into a shamble of gossip and psychological jargon.[10]

While Second City performers shared the Compass Players' animus against middle-class suburban conformity, they were equally interested in depicting the difficulties individuals, particularly young, sensitive, intelligent men and women, had with "fitting in." As many Second City "people scenes" demonstrate, Paul Sills and his colleagues were preoccupied with the effects of modern-day alienation and loneliness. As Roger Bowen later admitted, the Second City under Sills consistently portrayed society as a "blind, meaningless, unintelligent automaton, and people would just get lost in it." In key respects, then, Sills and the Second City shared the existentialist preoccupations of many young, educated middle-class Americans during the fifties. By turning their attention to the quest for meaningful identity and authenticity, these "Satirists à la Sartre," as one admirer branded them, tapped into concerns that had inspired the poetry of Beats such as Allen Ginsberg and by the early sixties was giving shape to the student New Left.[11]

Versions of two characteristic Second City alienation scenes, "Vend-a-Buddy" and "Phono Pal," demonstrated the absurd, tragic lengths that lonely individuals might go in order to find understanding and a sense of acceptance. The former, introduced in 1962 (a moment when fears of automation were very much on the minds of Americans), dramatized an encounter between a disgruntled husband (Alan Arkin) and a coin-operated talking robot (Eugene Troobnick). Although initially skeptical of the robot's ability to understand his domestic problems, the man soon drops nickel after nickel with the desperate hope that he might wring some sympathy out of his automated acquaintance. More pathetic yet were the attempts Paul Sand and Barbara Harris made at winning friendship by playing a Dale Carnegie self-help-type "how to win a friend" album. Moved "beyond belief" after he witnessed someone reading Carnegie's book on a city bus, Sand conceived "Phono Pal" as a commentary on the loneliness individuals encountered in modern society. In the version performed by Harris, the electronic "phono pal" pauses long enough to allow her to spill forth her doubts and troubles. The phonograph finally interrupts with the promise that it will be her "boyfriend until the end, the end, the end," the needle now skipping, "the end, the end."[12]

More trenchant and wider in scope was a Second City scene titled "Peep Show for Conventioneers." Originally improvised by Del Close and Severn Darden, this scene was eventually expanded to the point where it comprised the entire second act of the Second City's 1963 *To the Water Tower* program. In it, two expense account businessmen (MacIntyre Dixon and Dick Schaal) out "looking for the action" are ushered into a seedy whorehouse, where they are met by a mysterious proprietor played by Del Close. Deploying visionary fantasies like those used in Jean Genet's absurdist masterpiece *The Balcony,* the proprietor, a master of illusion, projects images that cater to each man's subliminal desires. By encouraging fantasies involving, for example, a patriotic invasion of Cuba, Jackie Kennedy's bare legs, and the return of a childhood sweetheart, the proprietor sucks each man into his own frightening "psychic trap." In the end, each businessman's desire brings no satisfaction, only frustration and humiliation. Dreams of heroic service transform into ugly megalomania, the return of true love dissolves into a cheap ad for Salem cigarettes. With its shifting moods and its complex interposition of status obsession, paranoia, and lost innocence, "Peep Show" argued that modern-day America is a land of empty illusions, a place where, as the final slide announces against the backdrop of four American flags, "you can have . . . whatever you want . . . for a price."[13] With deeply ironic scenes such as "Peep Show," the Second City substituted the insipid, whitewashed reality offered by Doris Day movies, Pat Boone records, and Colgate toothpaste ads with bitter, poignant truths about the alienating effects of corporate liberalism and the emptiness of America's mainstream commercial culture.

Given Second City's attention to the alienating effects of modern consumer society, the drift toward middle-class conformity, and the barriers erected between individuals and men and women in particular, it is easy to see how cartoonist Jules Feiffer became one of its many fans. "When I saw [Second City's] work," Feiffer recalls, "I thought it was so akin to what I was doing . . . so sharp . . . and social and funny." So great was his admiration for the fledgling Second City, in fact, that he agreed to mount his first stage production, *The Explainers,* with Paul Sills on the Second City's sister stage (the Playwrights Theater) in May 1961. When Sills asked him to produce a longer piece for the show, he wrote his first short stage play, *Crawling Arnold,* a satire about a dysfunctional upper-middle-class suburban family and their bomb shelter.[14] Feiffer's strips also shared a number of aesthetic similarities with Second City performances. Feiffer and Sills pursued similarly stark and minimalist approaches to their work, approaches that were reminiscent of Samuel Beckett and other existential modernist playwrights. One of the most notable and innovative elements of Feiffer's strips, in fact, was the manner in which they isolated their alienated and confused characters against a bare backdrop. In this sense, the uncluttered, borderless panels Feiffer drew resembled nothing more than the propless stages on which Second City companies performed.

*　　*　　*

Like Jules Feiffer, former Compass director Ted Flicker was very impressed with the style of improvisational, cabaret theater that the Second City had created in Chicago. Shortly after his musical, *The Nervous Set,* closed on Broadway, Flicker initiated plans for opening a Second City–style improvisational cabaret theater in Israel. When the Israeli government failed to support his plans, however, Flicker returned to New York and again began searching for wealthy patrons willing to back a venture there. When he finally secured the necessary funds, Flicker purchased a Greenwich Village bar located on the busy corner of Bleecker and Thompson streets and converted it into an intimate cafe-theater named "The Premise." After interviewing several hundred actors, Flicker eventually hired three: Thomas Aldredge, George Segal, and Joan Darling. Flicker had learned with the Compass Players that he needed to find a way to secure the loyalty and, equally important, spur the productivity of his company. To that end, he offered members of the Premise's "permanent company"—a group that soon included James Frawley and Buck Henry—participation in a unique profit-sharing scheme.[15]

Flicker experienced considerable difficulty procuring liquor and cabaret licenses, so when the Premise opened in November 1960 it served only espresso, tea, hot chocolate, and other standard Village coffeehouse items. "With a cafe policy of only coffee-house style refreshments," the first Premise *Playgram* stated, "it hopes to maintain a relaxed atmosphere where the patron knows he can have a sophisticated evening of first-class theatre and sociable nourishment without breaking the family budget." The key to creating a "sophisticated evening" was for Flicker, as it was for Sills and the Second City, the presentation onstage of satiric, irreverent points of view. In an interview with *New York Herald Tribune* columnist and critic Judith Crist, Flicker whetted the appetite of satire fans in New York by promising that his troupe would "often of necessity" expose its satirical point of view "on subjects ranging from art through fox-hunting." Audience members who came to the Premise and seated themselves within its warm, intimate surroundings saw Flicker emerge onstage and heard him promise—for at least the first half of the Premise performance—satires of "cultural or sociological note." On occasion this meant that the Premise would begin by reprising old Compass scenes such as "The Magic Is Gone" and "Last of the Centaurs." The Premise also pioneered several of its own despairing, satiric portraits of male-female incompatibility. Overall, Flicker's audiences learned early on that the Premise was not a place one would go to find sentimental, Hollywood-style treatments of romantic love. What it and its male-dominated cohort offered instead were satiric portraits of marital discord and steady doses of female treachery and guile. The Premise's "Teenage Fantasy," for example, demonstrated for audiences what typically occurs when a young man asks a young woman out on a date. After presenting the idealized versions of this encounter from the perspective of both the boy and girl, Flicker—once again assuming the role of emcee and ringmaster—demanded that his players "Stop!" and then "play it the way it *really* happens . . ." After the boy says "Hi," the girl immediately snaps back, "Schmuck!" [16]

Like the Second City and Jules Feiffer, the Premise often satirized Freudian psychoanalysis and the plight of the obsessive, modern American analysand. "As with a lot of modern American humour," a critic for the British *Spectator* astutely observed of a Premise performance in 1962, "psychiatric disorder is the basis of much of the show's best material." Premise members, like Anthony Holland and several other Second City performers, excelled in yielding portraits of high-strung, urban neurotics. Thomas Aldredge in particular was, in the words of the same *Spectator* critic, "lean and quivering as a whippet . . . [and] expresse[d] the nervousness of his various characters by shooting his arms in gestures . . ." Like the Second City's Barbara Harris, Joan Darling excelled at lampooning neurotic, psychologically unbalanced characters. In one characteristic early Premise scene, "The Chess Story," Darling played a woman who is invited to play chess with a male stranger (George Segal) in Washington Square. Before long, she confesses that she is in therapy and therefore a bit indecisive and unstable. She translates every move in psychological terms and eventually accuses her patient challenger of being "*really* hung up on the rules." "Compromise is the basis of a healthy relationship," she begins to shout at him. "This is *not* going to be like all the others, with *give, give, give* on my side and *take, take, take* on the other!" [17] In the end she has thoroughly intimidated and infantilized her male acquaintance.

Whether played by Joan Darling, Elaine May, Barbara Harris, or one of Feiffer's "man-eaters," the psychoanalytically inclined, neurotic woman cast in late-1950s and early-1960s social satire was the sensitive, educated man's arch-nemesis. Running throughout "The Chess Story" and some of the satire that the Premise, Second City, and Jules Feiffer aimed at psychoanalysis was a male-centered critique of its "emasculating" tendencies. Despite the animosity they evidenced toward vogues in psychiatry, however, it appears clear that early-sixties satirists were not entirely unsympathetic to the therapeutic ethos infusing postwar American culture. Some of the satire that the Premise, the Compass, and the Second City in particular aimed at Freudian psychoanalysis amounted to little more than an affectionate ribbing—the type of ribbing enjoyed most by the numerous analysts who reportedly attended their performances. Performers in these troupes believed firmly enough in the benefits of psychoanalysis to submit to weekly sessions with a therapist. The Premise's Joan Darling, a skillful actress who thrived in her caricatures of neurotics, confessed to an interviewer that she hoped to become an analyst herself when her stage career was over.[18]

The tendency of performers such as Darling to focus on the self and on inner states of mind appealed to many urban audience members but frustrated others. In the opinion of Jonathan Miller, a member of the British troupe Beyond the Fringe, the obsession Darling and her cohort shared over psychoanalytic themes invariably led to predictable, banal conclusions. Miller likened the Second City's portraits of vulnerable, insecure urbanites to a "series of off-hour observations by a warm-hearted psychiatric social worker." The depths that the Second City, the Premise, and Nichols and May reached, Miller astutely observed, "are the curiously self-absorbed familial depths of the analytically oriented. They represent a section of American society which has grown up quite aware of the Oedipal situation and is very articulate about it." Noting that much of their satire "seems to be tied in with the Jewish family structure," Miller went on to suggest that "there are other ways in which one can be penetrating besides focusing on the syndromes caused by the mother who tried to overfeed her son with noodle soup."[19]

*　　*　　*

What redeemed the Second City and the Premise in the eyes of Miller and other critics was their quick-witted, energetic, and impromptu performance style. Like Jules Feiffer, performers with the Premise and the Second City embraced an aesthetic of spontaneity which, as Daniel Belgrad has ably demonstrated, appealed to a wide variety of postwar abstract expressionist painters, bebop jazz musicians, and Beat poets. Because they were committed to the "honesty" and "authenticity" tapped by the subjective, creative, unconscious mind, because they seized on improvisation as a "potent emblem of freedom," Second City performers in particular closely resembled many of the avant-garde artists and performers based in New York during the early sixties.[20] It was exactly this shared devotion to improvisation and spontaneity that explains why at least one member of New York's avant-garde theater community, the Open Theater's Joseph Chaikin, avowedly borrowed ideas from Viola Spolin (the mother of Second City director and cofounder Paul Sills) and why Larry Rivers, Frank O'Hara, and other New York artists and poets reportedly enjoyed attending Second City performances. It also accounts for the comparisons some observers drew between the Second City and the work of abstract expressionist painters. A writer for the *Chicago Daily News,* for example, compared the way Sills put a scene together with his Second City actors to the creation of a Jackson Pollock painting, "where seemingly insignificant, unplanned globs of paint, guided by some inner compulsion, are dropped onto a canvas that becomes a meaningful whole."[21]

It is difficult to overestimate the importance that Second City and Premise members attached to improvisation. For many, the improvisational method seemed a more spontaneous and authentic way to engage the circumstances of American life. With its accent on immediacy and honesty, it promised a unique access to personal and social truths. In addition to fulfilling the practical goal of originating satiric material, improvisation for Premise and Second City actors in fact worked as a tool for putting actors and audience members in touch with immediate reality, thus acting in accord with Gestalt psychology and with evolving tenets of encounter psychiatry. In the opinion of the more devoted and long-term members of the Premise and the Second City, improvisation, like encounter exercises, seemed capable of helping the individual restore spontaneous awareness. As Theodore Flicker has explained, he and his Premise actors used improvisation as a type of group therapy while in rehearsal. Flicker remembers that "this was before group therapy became a big thing, before encountering was even heard of, but we had to tell each other the truth. No matter how angry we were with each other, we had to speak that anger in the rehearsal or dressing room."[22]

Barbara Harris confirms that acting on the Second City stage served a therapeutic function. As she remembers,

> We could play all the antisocial and rebellious characters we wanted. All the obnoxious people that were aspects of us. We'd do it and it would be over with. If I had a mousy tendency, I'd play mousy women until it went away. I could make fun of myself and the parts of me that were superficial or pretentious. It was a place to ventilate obsession in the whole large scheme of society and politics.[23]

For Harris and her colleagues, improvisation facilitated the realization of personal freedom and, at the same time, a sense of community. The goal of forging community was particularly important to her former husband, Paul Sills, and his mother Viola Spolin. Spolin, who throughout the early 1960s led Second City members in consciousness-raising "theater games," outlined her credo on improvisation in her 1963 handbook, *Improvisation for the Theater*. Echoing the writings of philosopher John Dewey, Spolin here addressed the importance of "creative experience" to the individual and the integral role democratic, interdependent working relationships play in forging a "healthy group relationship." In order to realize creative experience, Spolin argued, we must once again seize what she called the "intuitive," that level of personal and group involvement that "comes bearing its gifts in the moment of spontaneity . . ." According to Spolin, it was only through moments of true, creative spontaneity that "personal freedom is released, and the total person, physically, intellectually, and intuitively, is awakened."[24]

Because improvisation prompted the participation of the audience, it contributed greatly to the unique sense of intimacy that existed between the performers and audience members. There is no question that the feelings of intimacy, solidarity, and even conspiracy that improvisational troupes shared with their audiences accounted for much of improvisational satire's success during the early 1960s. Jules Feiffer accurately evokes this feeling of solidarity that he and other fans of liberal satire shared in the late 1950s and early 1960s,

> My readers and I became conspirators. And it was in a spirit of conspiracy that I slunk down to the Village Vanguard to see Mort Sahl or Mike Nichols and Elaine May. Or skulked off to Chicago to see Second City. We were members of a comic underground, meeting in cabarets and cellar clubs, making startlingly grave and innovative jokes about virginity, Jewish mothers, HUAC and J. Edgar Hoover.[25]

Well-educated, conversant in the discourse of existentialist philosophy and Freudian psychoanalysis, politically progressive, and disproportionately urban and Jewish, the middle-class audiences attending Second City and Premise shows found their smart, spontaneous improvisational performances very appealing. Few forms of live performance in the United States encouraged such lively engagement on the part of its audience. Fewer still followed the Second City's example of inviting audience members to mingle with performers at the bar after the show.

In addition to fostering intimacy and a sense of community, the improvisation practiced by the Second City and the Premise had an affinity with the performance of some of America's most vital and exciting artists during the early 1960s—jazz musicians. In the liner notes for its 1961 Vanguard album, the Premise claimed that it was "as much a product of our own time, place and people as the wail of a blues trumpet or the cry of a saxophone."[26] It was only natural that the Second City relied heavily on their jazz pianists—Bill Matthieu (also a columnist for *Down Beat* magazine), Tom O'Horgan (later the director of the musical *Hair*), and William Bolcom—to help set the mood and pace of their performances. Individual performers in the Second City and the Premise, like their predecessors with the Compass, were quick to claim the inspiration of African American jazz musicians. Second City performances were "like verbal-physical jazz," performer Alan Arkin remembers. "I think we had the same kind of audience which appreciates good jazz musicians." Arkin and his colleagues played off each other's improvised dialogue in a manner similar to the way jazz musicians interacted during jam sessions. With their inhibitions dissolved by alcohol and their manic energy occasionally fueled by amphetamines, more than a few improvisational performers appeared to emulate the existential "White Negro" hipster famously outlined by Norman Mailer in the journal *Dissent*. Like Beat poets and other avant-garde artists, members of the Second City and the Premise were drawn to the vibrant style, oppositional stance, and personal habits of black jazz musicians. Looking back on the "hip," nonconformist persona he carried while with the Premise, Flicker states that he was "a raging, out-of-control iconoclast." In addition to wearing a goatee (like several members of the Second City), Flicker drew attention to his jazzman's sense of daring by frequently advertising the risk inherent in the Premise's improvisational technique. In the liner notes for the Premise's 1961 album, Flicker stated that he and his colleagues had "declared war to the bitter end: war against the huge stage machines . . . war against the playwrights who are themselves 'establishments' with phalanxes of agents, managers, advisers, gag writers and play doctors." The "radical step" Flicker and the Compass claimed to make was in "prod[ding] the audience out of its habitual somnolent passivity [and] making it think for itself and take part in the act of creation."[27]

By billing the Premise as a completely impromptu entertainment—an "improvisational revue," as Flicker put it, "with scenes performed as a result of suggestions by the audience"—he, more than anyone else, raised the stakes for satiric improvisation. In his standard introductory remarks before the audience, Flicker would explain, "Because [this program] is improvised, it can be the most exciting, the richest kind of theatrical experience that you have ever had the good fortune to view." Once the program had begun, Flicker worked hard to accentuate the excitement of improvisational performance. In one characteristic routine, he suddenly interrupted a parody of *A Place in the Sun* by yelling "FREEZE." He then had his actors resume their dialogue along lines called out by audience members. Although he seemingly allowed spontaneity to reign over Premise performances, Flicker actually exercised a fairly tight control over what transpired onstage. By controlling the all-important blackout switch, he was able to kill improvised scenes that began to lose direction. He also permitted Premise actors who were in trouble onstage to extricate themselves by committing some imaginary form of suicide. Through devices like these, then, Flicker was able to spare his audiences from improvised scenes that in hands of the more experimental Second City would occasionally seem to drag on for an eternity.[28]

The biggest step Flicker took to keep Premise scenes short, pungent, and entertaining was to have his actors rehearse them beforehand. Indeed, Nichols and May had already proven that to a considerable extent, well-polished, rehearsed scenes were almost certainly a prerequisite for commercial success. This lesson was no doubt reinforced when reviews of the Premise's premiere performance appeared in important newspapers such as the *New York Times*. Reflecting on what he had witnessed at the Premise, the critic for the *Times* pointedly mused whether "some advance thought and consideration on the material might not have proved helpful."[29] Over the next several years Flicker took pains to ensure that a set number of Premise scenes were well rehearsed and that performers prepared themselves in advance for the second set's improvisations. Years later, Flicker explained how he and his colleagues actually created their material,

23. During intermission, Premise members (from left) Joan Darling, George Segal, Tom Aldredge, and Theodore Flicker peruse newspapers in order to prepare for topical improvisations. Courtesy of the Theodore J. Flicker Collection, Cinema-Television Library, University of Southern California.

Somebody comes into rehearsal and says, 'I just saw a funny thing on the street and it reminded me of . . .' Or somebody comes in and says, 'How about what the mayor did today?' And somebody else says, 'Look what's on the headlines today. They're going to ask about it tonight. Let's invent something.'[30]

The Second City was similarly engaged in the practice of originating scenes at rehearsals. However, since this troupe was a bit more candid about its creative method—it stressed to its audiences that the majority of its scenes were "based on" rather than immediately derived from improvisations—it escaped charges of fraud and deception. Flicker and the Premise were not so lucky. Particularly among British critics who observed the Premise during its 1962 run in London, suspicions of dishonesty were rife. Although generally admiring in their reviews, these critics resented the fact that the Premise's improvised scenes were so obviously rehearsed. Some of these critics labeled improvisation a "gimmick" and suggested that the Premise revise its claims. Charles Marowitz, an American theater critic and stage director living in London, reported in a dispatch to the *Village Voice* that the Premise had turned "theatre into a kind of scintillating parlor trick." If its scenes are "prepatterned," Marowitz argued, "it is unfair for the Premise to recommend itself as free-wheeling, untrammeled improvisation and to announce ominously, 'Now we're going to take our lives in our hands and make something up for you,' a ruse which is accompanied by an elaborate show of prospecting for material, brandished clipboards, written suggestions, and the whole cozy little audience-participation lark." The Premise's "ruse" was not lost on some of its audience members either. One disgruntled patron of the Village Premise complained to Flicker that the second "improvised" performance he had paid to see was no different than the first. In reply, Flicker informed him, "I think your understanding of improvisation is in error. It does not mean that we invent what we do on our feet every night."[31]

Although some adherents of the Spolin-Sills school of improvisation were loath to admit it, "instant," pure or on-the-spot improvisation was a frail reed upon which to depend for sharp, insightful satire. Roger Bowen, the performer responsible for authoring some of the first scenarios and scenes for the Compass and Second City, was one politically oriented satirist who regarded the improvisational method with considerable suspicion.[32] In fact, both actors and audiences were at times embarrassed by improvisations that failed onstage. Andrew Duncan, who along with Eugene Troobnick attempted an improvised scene on nuclear disarmament one night during the early 1960s, has related just how Second City's improvised satire could fall flat. "We just didn't know what we were talking about," Duncan remembers of their unscripted commentary, "And it was terrible. And I remember Dwight McDonald [sic] was in the audience and he said, 'This is satire?' We missed because we got off into an area we didn't know enough about."[33] Even if an improvisational actor had read voluminously and was well informed about foreign and domestic issues, he or she was not necessarily capable of creating insightful, effective satiric material onstage. Sustained irony, the type of irony that underwrote the best Second City and Premise scenes, demanded a type of creative deliberation rarely inspired on the spot.

To the bulk of their audiences, whether or not the Premise or the Second City pursued "pure" improvisation mattered little in the end. As many educated audience members were no doubt aware, true on-the-spot improvisation was, ironically, rare in the improvisational arts. Even the best jazz musicians, after all, honed their licks in practice sessions. By and large, then, few Second City and Premise patrons expected that the improvisational satire that they paid to see be completely unrehearsed or perfectly on target. When an on-the-spot improvisation failed disastrously at the Second City, Chicago audiences still expressed appreciation for the actors' earnest and enthusiastic efforts. From their point of view, improvisational satire was at its heart uniquely capable of creating an atmosphere of intimacy, collegiality, and good fun. Judging by critics' evaluations appearing in a wide range of newspapers and magazines, the overall effect of the "instant theater" created by the Premise and Second City was exhilarating. One *Newsweek* critic, for example, noted of the Premise in 1961, "This sort of pertinent, impertinent improvisation is the first breath of fresh air to hit the theater world since the birth of The Method." After witnessing the spontaneous stage virtuosity of the Second City's Alan Arkin, Severn Darden, and Barbara Harris, *Village Voice* critic Andrew Sarris similarly gushed, "There are moments when you know that you are in the presence of professionals who can stagger you with a look."[34]

*   *   *

The lavish praise both *Newsweek* and the *Village Voice* extended to Second City and Premise improvisational satire found many echoes throughout the early sixties. At times, these favorable appraisals were informed by a nostalgia for revues such as *Pins and Needles* (1937), *Lend an Ear* (1948), Leonard Sillman's *New Faces of 1952,* and, in particular, *The Revuers,* the irreverent New York nightclub revue initiated in 1939 by Adolph Comden, Betty Green and Judy Holliday.[35] In addition to offering a reminder of what smart, socially relevant satiric cabarets and revues once offered American audiences, the Second City and the Premise gave hope that a mood of irreverence—nearly snuffed out by McCarthyism and Eisenhower-era mass conformity—was on the brink of revival. The *New York Herald Tribune*'s venerable critic John Crosby spoke for many when he observed in 1961 that since "television's great satirist, Sid Caesar, has fled to Las Vegas, the last refuge of satire and the satiric sketch seems to be the supper club, and the Greenwich Village basement." In his enthusiastic review of the Premise, Crosby wrote,

> Since Broadway has got so square—what few jokes you'll hear on Broadway sound thoroughly researched to be sure they won't offend anyone from Dubuque—the Greenwich Village basements, the Shelley Bermans, the Bob Newharts, the Nicholses and Mays are the only people who make comment on life around us, especially life around us right now.[36]

The idea that the Second City and the Premise were somehow filling a critical void in American culture was repeated several times in the liberal journal the *Nation*. In his 1961 review of the Second City, Robert Hatch, the *Nation*'s theater critic, referred back to the previous decade's dark ages and the "great search [that] was on in this country for social satire . . ." "Mr. Eisenhower's conduct of the Presidency defied caricature," he wrote, "and his immunity to acid wit seemed to cast a haze of solemn conformity over a nation previously celebrated for irreverence." Fortunately, Hatch argued, America now had the Second City, a troupe whose "best skits bring the heart-lifting promise that pomposity, hypocrisy, stupidity and the fashions in ideas and taste will no longer lord it over us, unscathed by laughter." Several years later, it seemed clear to another *Nation* contributor that the Second City and the Premise were indeed "largely responsible for an increased national interest in intelligent satire."[37]

From the perspective of many liberal critics writing in the early 1960s, the Second City and the Premise communicated a perspective on American life that was far more penetrating and honest than anything found in mainstream popular culture. In the context of theater and nightclub entertainment as well, these improvisational troupes distinguished themselves with the challenges they posed to their audiences. As one critic for *Cue* commented in 1963, there was a time, before the introduction of satiric cabaret and revue "when the tired businessman could relax, confident that *some* things always stayed the same—like the baggy pants comedian, the fancily undressed chorus girls, the loud music blaring through the fog and smoke and booze. Now, lest he take care, he may find himself watching instead a razor-sharp . . . revue by bright young people intent on pointing up the absurdities of what passes for American civilization—or the lack of it."[38]

Liberal, educated, middle-class audiences thrilled at improvisational satirists' spontaneous irony, and as a result Second City and the Premise enjoyed a level of success that David Shepherd and his various Compass companies could never have imagined. In Chicago, the Second City proved popular and profitable from its inception, attracting a steady crowd of Chicagoans, suburbanites, and out of towners. Between 1959 and 1964, various resident Second City companies performed a total of fifteen revues, all of them composed of scenes inherited from previous companies or devised anew during improvised sets and rehearsals. As one local observer proudly noted in the *Nation,* the "vibrant troupe of young comedians who . . . pooled their talents" at the Second City represented

"the newest and brightest manifestation of the Chicago comedy renaissance . . . a kind of Skidmore, Owings and Merrill of satire." [39] Throughout
the early 1960s, the Second City served as one of hippest hangouts in Chicago, routinely drawing visiting celebrities as well as hometown heroes
such as Nelson Algren and Studs Terkel. Second City performers were
themselves fixtures in Chicago's hip social and cultural scenes. Like other
local celebrities, they were frequent guests at Hugh Hefner's Playboy
mansion. [40]

In June 1961, Bernard Sahlins and Paul Sills set their sights beyond Chicago and booked the founding Second City company for an eight-week
gig at Los Angeles's Ivar Theater. Later that year, they teamed with Max
Liebman, the former producer of Sid Caesar's *Your Show of Shows,* and presented a thoroughly rehearsed version of their program in Broadway's
Royale Theater. Scenes from this production, *From the Second City,* comprised the second of two albums that the Second City recorded for Mercury Records. Several of the critics who expressed reservations about
the Second City's Broadway show correctly observed that the troupe
belonged not in the cavernous Royale Theater but in a more intimate,
cabaret-type setting. Many of them were therefore noticeably enthusiastic when in January 1962 a second company of the Second City began performing to sold-out crowds at Square East, a Greenwich Village nightclub
located across the street from Gerde's Folk City, the venue where Bob Dylan frequently played sets. Over the next three years, the Square East ran
eight consecutive Second City productions. Andrew Duncan, a member
of the first Second City troupe to play at Square East, recalls the enthusiastic reception he and his colleagues received there. "A lot of audiences
went crazy," Duncan remembers. "I never heard laughter like that in a theatre before." [41]

The heady success the Second City enjoyed in Chicago and New York
encouraged their business manager Bernard Sahlins to book appearances
in Toronto and London. During the summer of 1963, Sahlins even initiated an ill-advised and short-lived "suburban branch" of the Second City
at a Fire Island beachfront restaurant. Sahlins's ambition was matched
only by the Premise's Theodore Flicker. At its peak, the Premise's two
companies played sixteen shows a week, including three weekend night
performances and a Sunday "Hangover Matinee." Soon after winning the
1961 *Village Voice* Off-Broadway Obie Award and the Vernon Rice Award
(the latter "For creating on Bleecker Street an irreverent, brash and novel
form of entertainment") Flicker initiated plans to open a Premise branch

in Westport, Connecticut. He later organized touring companies for Washington D.C., Miami, and London and considered having the Premise perform its "instant theater" in Toronto, Puerto Rico, Manila, Boston, and Bangkok.[42]

*   *   *

The success that the Second City and the Premise attained in the United States was matched in Britain by a revue titled *Beyond the Fringe*. During the early sixties, the Fringe set the critical standard by which the Second City and other satiric cabarets and revues were often compared. Its cast was composed of four young men who had performed in revues while students at Oxford and Cambridge colleges—Dudley Moore, a jazz pianist; Alan Bennett, a history tutor at Oxford; Jonathan Miller, a pathologist at a London hospital; and Peter Cook, a comic writer and performer. All were admirers of American satirists such as Sid Caesar, Nichols and May, Mort Sahl, and Lenny Bruce. The success they achieved while performing at the 1960 Edinburgh Festival brought them a booking at London's Fortune Theatre. When *Beyond the Fringe* opened in May 1961, it struck London critics and audiences as daring and impudent. Compared with the mainstream musicals and comedies playing in London's West End—*My Fair Lady, Oliver!* and *Watch It, Sailor!* among others—this irreverent production presented audiences with a form of satiric entertainment that many considered revolutionary. With satiric scenes prodding Anglican clergymen, the mythologization of British wartime heroism, the pretensions of middle-class liberals, British royalty, the class system, and, most memorably, Tory Prime Minister Harold Macmillan, *Beyond the Fringe* hit sacred cows that until then had remained relatively unscathed.[43]

Although Kenneth Tynan, the influential, left-liberal theater critic for the London *Observer,* complained that *Beyond the Fringe* was "anti-reactionary without being progressive," he was blown away by it, describing it as the "funniest revue that London has seen since the Allies dropped the bomb on Hiroshima." Heralding their breakthrough as a portent of greater cultural freedom throughout England, Tynan declared, "Future historians may well thank me for providing them with a full account of the moment when English comedy took its first decisive step into the second half of the twentieth century."[44] Fringe members Jonathan Miller and Alan Bennet took Tynan's proclamation seriously, but it was Peter Cook, Macmillan's impersonator and the author of the majority of the material used in *Beyond the Fringe,* who seized on it as a mandate. More than anyone else in Britain, it was Cook who was responsible for giving shape to the Anglo-American "satire boom" of the early sixties. As *Beyond the Fringe* continued its run through 1961, Alan Bennett commuted to his teaching job at Oxford in a chauffeur-driven Rolls Royce and Jonathan Miller practiced medicine in a London hospital. Cook, meanwhile, began formulating plans for a satiric cabaret like those he had enjoyed while visiting Germany. He eventually converted an abandoned strip joint in Soho into a hip, cabaret-style satire and jazz nightclub that he named (with irony) the Establishment Club. In order to escape the oversight of Lord Chamberlain, the censoring authority for the British stage, Cook and his partner Nicholas Luard made the Establishment—billed as "London's First Satirical Nightclub"—a members-only club. As soon as it opened in October 1961, socialites, cabinet ministers, fashion models, intellectuals, and members of what would soon be known as "swinging London" clamored to gain entry and, while consuming a meal of roast beef and Yorkshire pudding, witness the sharp satiric revue put on by its resident company.[45]

Coinciding with the grand opening of the Establishment Club was the inauguration of *Private Eye,* an irreverent, sometimes scathing satiric magazine inspired by Harvey Kurtzman's *MAD* comics and *Help* magazine. Together with *Beyond the Fringe* and the Establishment Club, *Private Eye*—which Cook purchased in 1962—became the subject of endless debates in the British press concerning the nature and effect of the Anglo-American "satire boom." By 1962 these three satiric ventures had become the rage among young, progressive, middle- and upper-middle-class Londoners. Just as *MAD,* the Second City, and Nichols and May appealed to a new, more skeptical and world-weary generation coming of age across the Atlantic, *Beyond the Fringe* and its ilk spoke directly and powerfully to Britain's disaffected youth. According to Christopher Hitchens, someone who was "groping" his way to maturity in the early 1960s, "there were two handy ways of keeping your sanity . . . some of us were fortunate enough to find allies in the wider world. We found them by listening to *Beyond the Fringe* and by reading [Joseph Heller's novel] *Catch-22.*" "The Fringe and the Catch," Hitchens adds, "were passwords by which one could survive living in Absurdistan."[46]

Enterprising theater producers in the United States took note of the profound effect *Beyond the Fringe* and the Establishment Club had on segments of the British public. Two of these producers in particular, Alexander Cohen and David Merrick, were so eager to import the smart and "so-

24. Peter Cook's satiric troupe, The Establishment, in 1964 (from top to bottom): Jeremy Geidt, Carole Simpson, David Battley, Eleanor Bron, and John Bird. Photofest.

phisticated" satire of *Beyond the Fringe* to Broadway that they engaged in a small bidding war to obtain it.[47] In the end, it was Cohen, the producer who had earlier packaged the irreverent British duo Flanders and Swann and the team of Nichols and May on Broadway, who won the right to import *Beyond the Fringe*—the soon-to-be-dubbed "Beatles of Comedy"—to New York. As the Fringe prepared for their American tour, Peter Cook and Bernard Sahlins made arrangements for a two-month exchange between their respective cabarets. On October 7, 1962, a day after *Beyond the Fringe* made its American debut in Washington, D.C., resident performers at the Establishment (John Bird, Eleanor Bron, Jeremy Geidt, and John Fortune) took to the stage of Chicago's Second City. To capitalize further on the Anglo-American rage for satire, Cook had the Establishment players continue on from Chicago to Washington, D.C., and then to San Francisco. In January 1963, Cook established permanent residence for the Establishment in New York City at the Strollers Theatre Club on East 54th Street.[48]

Beyond the Fringe and the Establishment made very favorable impressions on critics and audiences throughout the United States. Undoubtedly, much of their popularity, like that of Nichols and May, was the result of a certain snob appeal. Even more than their American counterparts, the Oxbridge-educated British satirists evinced a manner of literate sophistication. One did not have to be an Anglophile to appreciate their felicitous use of the English language or their insouciant charm. Another reason for their widespread appeal may stem from the fact that they were mainly attacking British, not American institutions and class politics. American audiences were clearly kept at a safe remove from some of their more acerbic material. Yet the Establishment and the Fringe were also clearly capable of impressing critics and audiences with sharp, intelligent material. For example, when *Beyond the Fringe* premiered on Broadway in late October 1962, right at the height of the Cuban Missile Crisis, it presented a frightful, absurd scene involving nuclear war. Cook, Miller, and Bennett, playing the roles of expert panelists at a civil defense meeting, used their own unique brand of dark humor to expose the illogic of nuclear retaliation, the lunacy of individuals attempting to shield themselves from radiation, and, perhaps most effective of all, the flippant and casual disregard with which defense officials treat the possibility of nuclear annihilation. "If they won't allay your terror of the awful menace," *New York Times* critic Howard Taubman wrote of this scene, "they'll have you shaking so hard with laughter that you'll forget momentarily to tremble with fear." "What a pity one must return to the real world of disputatious winds and alarming trumpets," Taubman concluded, "where wonderfully talented Englishmen or Americans or Russians are not roaring with joyous irreverence."[49]

The immediacy and satiric acuity of scenes such as this helped win the Fringe and the Establishment much favor, particularly among critics writing for liberal publications such as the *Nation,* the *New Republic,* and *Hudson Review.* While Harold Clurman in the *Nation* praised the Fringe's "spitball assault," Robert Brustein in the *New Republic* called it "violently funny" and compared it favorably with the work of Jules Feiffer and Nichols and May. Like Feiffer and Nichols, in fact, members of *Beyond the Fringe's* original cast gained entry into New York's chic cultural and intellectual circles. Jonathan Miller, whose background (he was the son of a prominent Jewish physician) and career interests (stage directing) closely resembled those of Nichols, gained notice as a promising young liberal intellectual. In 1963 and 1964 he assumed the role of a critic when he began reviewing American films and television for the *New Yorker* and the *New York Review of Books.*[50]

*   *   *

In addition to paving the way for British imports such as the Establishment and *Beyond the Fringe,* the popularity and critical success that American liberal satire achieved during the late 1950s and early 1960s encouraged a notable proliferation of small-group, ensemble satiric performance throughout the United States. During this period, urban coffeehouses and cafes spawned dozens of satiric revues, both amateur and professional. Predictably, most of these satiric revues and coffeehouse cabarets operated in hip enclaves located within large cities such as Chicago (the Happy Medium on Rush Street), St. Louis (the Landesman's Crystal Palace), San Francisco (the North Beach nightclub the Purple Onion), and New York City (Phase 2 and Take 3 in Greenwich Village). Even Washington, D.C.—a city not known for its cutting-edge cultural fare—hosted three satiric revues, all operating on M Street in Georgetown. Based primarily on a scripted and musical format rather than Compass and Second City–style improvisation, these coffeehouse revues proved enormously popular among liberal, middle-class audiences who shared an appetite for the type of middle-class self-criticism satirists typically proffered onstage and, not least, a desire for keeping up with the newest tastes in popular entertainment. Applauding the emerging trend in 1959, the journal *Theatre Arts* stated that the "true satirical revue" was one of the few mediums available in America that could "give people an intelligent comic slant on the world at large." In its 1962 survey of "after dark satire," *Horizon* magazine likewise complimented the "groups of young people" performing in revues "who have learned to work comfortably together and who throw in a rehearsed or spontaneous gag at the moment they feel it will unstuff the greatest number of shirts." With "pointed instruments," *Horizon* stated approvingly, these revues explored "America's life and leisure, emblems and problems, arts and neuroses, excesses and successes . . ."[51]

The most self-consciously chic and "sophisticated" of the satiric revues to emerge during the late 1950s and early 1960s were those produced by Julius Monk. Monk, a flamboyant, suave Southerner and part-time fashion model, was, as *Show Magazine* put it, "virtually . . . the lone impresario of cabaret satire" during the 1950s.[52] In 1956, Monk helped create a new cabaret entertainment for Irving Haber's Downstairs Room on West 51st Street in New York City. Monk's first production, *Four Below,* became an unexpected smash hit. In this show and its two successors, *Son of Four Below* and *Take Five,* Monk carefully arranged cabaret material—acquired from aspiring songwriters such as Herb Hartig, Bud McCreery, and Ronny Graham—that lampooned Tennessee Williams, Beat poetry, seduction, the "international set," and a host of other subjects familiar to well-educated, urbane, upper-middle-class New Yorkers. With proceeds taken from these enormously lucrative ventures, Monk converted a townhouse once owned by millionaire businessman John Wanamaker into two new, extravagantly decorated venues, Upstairs at the Downstairs and Downstairs at the Upstairs. From 1958 to 1962, Monk there directed Jane Connell, Gerry Matthews, and Celia Cabot (and on one occasion, Del Close) in a run of irreverent but "tasteful" revues including *Demi-Dozen* and *Pieces of Eight.* Finally, from 1962 to 1964, Monk ran his increasingly inside and chic (and still spectacularly successful) revues in the Plaza Hotel's elaborately re-designed Rendezvous Room supper club. In 1963, Monk even exported a revue to Chicago, a city, he told the *New York Times,* "in need of more sophistication."[53]

Monk never intimated that his self-described "cerebral" and "intimate" nightclub act might help awaken audiences to important social or political issues. Delivered with a wink by Monk's perky and attractive performers, songs and skits from his renowned Upstairs at the Downstairs and Plaza 9 revues lightly parodied subjects such as folk singers, David Susskind's *Open End* television talk show, author Mary McCarthy, critic Vance Packard, James Bond, the Four Seasons, Harvard academics, designer fashion, and New York tap water. In an introduction to a book version of *Baker's Dozen,* the second "farinaceous farrago" he staged for the elegant Plaza 9, Monk explained that he emulated "the mid-Victorian supper rooms where the gentry sat, supped, and presumably applauded

Spontaneous Irony

the variety of players presented nightly." "The existentialists' Parisian cave and the politicized Munich cabaret with its caustic cautery," he further elucidated, "are as beyond our ken as is/was the West Coast School of iconoclasts . . ." "No one has a Pollyanna fixation around here," he conveyed to *The New York Herald Tribune* with characteristic hauteur, "but we do respect civilized propriety." "Any policy of sharp political satire would be defeatist, like trying to make Kafka into a Broadway show. I don't really understand the propensity for people to be evil on stage."[54]

Monk's imitators produced entertainment that generally fit the same mold. After Monk left the Upstairs at the Downstairs in 1962, Irving Haber, the nightclub's owner, hired revue veterans Rod Warren, Ben Bagley, and Ronny Graham to continue his venue's long and lucrative run of sassy, "cerebral" entertainment. In late 1963, Haber hired Compass founder David Shepherd to produce a new revue titled *Twice Over Nightly*. After several failed attempts at reviving the Compass's formula for sharp, improvisational satire, Shepherd appeared ready to produce comic entertainment devoid of politics. For performers, he recruited Jane Alexander, several Second City alumni, and Mary Louise Wilson, a star of former Julius Monk revues whose "mere presence," a *Cue* critic wrote, "touches any setting with class." All in all, Shepherd and his colleagues presented a tame revue that even Monk might have enjoyed. Critics for the *New York Times* and the *New York Herald Tribune* agreed that *Twice Over Nightly* yielded a "happy zest" "to relax at and smile with," a revue "just right for the holiday season" and tailored for those "who want a change of pace from the savage irreverence and topical sophistication of the better bistro shows."[55]

The *New York Times* critic was correct to distinguish Shepherd's classy entertainment from the "savage irreverence" staged by liberal satirists (including his former colleagues) during the early sixties. Likewise, it is important to recognize the differences in outlook that separated Paul Sills and Ted Flicker from Julius Monk. At both the Second City and the Premise, improvisational satire was not intended to replicate the "mid-Victorian supper room" but as a vehicle to engage the complex and rapidly changing social reality that performers and audience members shared in common. At its best, the spontaneous irony produced onstage at the Second City and the Premise confronted the bleak, unidentified social conditions that spawned feelings of alienation and anxiety among Americans coming of age in the fifties. Nevertheless, Monk's conscious appeal to "sophistication" and elite taste underscores an element of snobbery that to one degree or another infused late-fifties and early-sixties satiric revues and cabaret. With their esoteric in-jokes on subjects such as Freudian psychoanalysis, with their broad caricatures of the lifestyles and tastes of the suburban middle class, improvisational satirists played best to educated, urban white liberals from the middle and upper-middle classes.

In important respects, the material they presented onstage reflected the outlook, tastes, and prejudices of "new class" liberals—liberals who were ascendant in the late 1950s and who, with the election of John F. Kennedy, helped set the political and cultural mood of the early 1960s. Indeed, improvisational satire reached the peak of its popularity during the New Frontier, at the very moment when "intelligence," "culture," and "sophistication" served as potent bywords in the lexicon of "new class" liberals throughout the United States. Taken as a whole, the success that the Second City and its American and British cohorts enjoyed in the United States contributed significantly to the impression that liberal satire, once moribund, had entered a new golden era. Whether the political inflections of this satire would mirror the outlook of its benefactor in the White House or somehow break free to challenge the cold war and racial status quo became one of the central questions for those who deliberated the politics of laughter.

PART THREE

THE POLITICS
OF LAUGHTER

"We Hope You Like Us, Jack"

LIBERAL POLITICAL SATIRE, 1958–63

Although the Second City, the Premise, and their British counterparts appealed to audiences and critics with their spontaneous, witty commentaries on contemporary social conditions, what often won them their greatest acclaim was their willingness to probe important political issues of the day. In the opinion of a number of prominent liberal critics, certainly, the attention that the Second City and the Premise paid to domestic and international affairs were among their most noteworthy achievements. "For years," an enthusiastic *Cue* critic reviewing the Second City in 1962 wrote, "many of us have complained that our revues are lacking in biting political satire . . . hear ye, hear ye, here it is—the political revue in all its mordant glory." In a similar vein, former Group Theatre founder Harold Clurman in the *Nation* praised the Premise for reviving the type of native "fresh youthfulness, good-humored disrespect, healthy skepticism and wide-eyed shrewdness" that had been missing since the 1930s. Clurman, perhaps pining for the type of left-wing, politically engaged culture that thrived during the days of the Popular Front, added that the Premise's "tomfoolery" made points "more smartly" than "the long-faced editorials by our most earnest journalists."[1]

By the late 1950s and early 1960s, liberal critics such as Clurman who had several years earlier lamented political satire's passing enthusiastically greeted a resurgence of satiric political commentary. For a large and growing audience of Americans inclined toward liberal politics and the Democratic Party, the spread of topical, politically relevant improvisational satire, together with the emergence of a modern-day Will Rogers named Mort Sahl and, not least, the sharp-edged cartooning of Bill Mauldin, Herbert Block, Robert Osborn, and Walt Kelly, represented a refreshing break from the bland consensus and inertia of the Eisenhower era. For some liberal Democrats, certainly, the early sixties "satire boom" harkened back to the glory days of the Popular Front and the type of outspoken, irreverent commentary that animated its comic masterpiece, Charlie Chaplin's *The Great Dictator* (1940).

By the early 1960s, McCarthyism's grip on American culture had loosened significantly and a new breed of Democrat—one attuned to the importance of advancing equal rights, expanding civil liberties, and improving the lives of individuals throughout the free world—was ascendant. Represented best by their standard bearer John F. Kennedy, modern-day American liberals advocated a new moral awareness, called attention to quality-of-life issues, cultivated a sense of sophistication, and, with their continuing opposition to communist expansion, exuded masculine heroism. After Kennedy was elected president, smart, irreverent political commentary, long absent from the American scene, appeared poised to make a remarkable comeback. With the young, witty, urbane John Kennedy in the White House, satiric expression, long a resource for cultural dissent, became for many American liberals a source of affirmation and a sign of better days to come.

*   *   *

Judging by the despair that commentators, critics, and comedians made public throughout the mid-1950s, liberals' appetite for irreverent political satire went largely unmet during the Eisenhower era. Ever since the early days of the cold war, in fact, the place of humor's role in the "serious" sphere of politics remained very much in doubt.[2] Nowhere is this better illustrated than in the 1952 and 1956 presidential campaigns of Democrat Adlai Stevenson. On the campaign trail Stevenson sprinkled his speeches with funny asides and quips and thereby earned a reputation as an intellectual wit. As numerous commentators pointed out, Stevenson was clearly flouting "Corwin's Law," named after the late-nineteenth-century senator from Ohio who once reportedly admonished an aspirant of public office that he ought to be "solemn as an ass" if he wanted to win. Just how far Stevenson would get with his witty approach was very much open to question in 1952. As a Syracuse University professor of philosophy noted in the *New York Times Magazine,* "We are . . . about to witness a controlled experiment of just how far a candidate for President may dare to go in this country in putting a sense of humor on public display."[3]

Unfortunately for Stevenson and his supporters, Republican challenger Dwight Eisenhower used the Democrat's wit against him, claiming that it was symptomatic of his effete, "egghead" manner. In order to offset the concerns Eisenhower raised in 1952, Stevenson in 1956 attempted to shed his image as the congenital joker. Although he tempered his dry, sophisticated wit and gravitated instead toward a more self-deprecating style of humor, he occasionally aimed ridicule at Vice President Richard Nixon and Secretary of State John Foster Dulles. Stevenson's quips about these two—he once called Dulles "America's misguided missile" and described his foreign policy as "the power of positive brinking"—struck a chord with the well-educated, middle- and upper-middle-class American liberals who supported him. Stevenson, like these Americans and the liberal satirists who rallied to him in 1952 and 1956, believed there was integral role for ridicule, wit, and satire in American politics. Reflecting on his use of these comic devices on the campaign trail, he later remarked, "You get your nose rubbed into this solemnity and this seriousness of our time and it begins to have its effect on you, it buries your own natural spontaneity of personality." "I think ridicule, and the best of us do ridicule humorously," he steadfastly maintained, "is effective in our political scene."[4]

The minor controversy surrounding Adlai Stevenson's use of humor during the 1952 and 1956 presidential campaigns only added to the impression that American political humor had taken a toll since the onset of the cold war. While it was acceptable to ridicule political figures of foreign nations, particularly those located behind the iron curtain, it appeared dangerous during the early and mid-1950s to satirize politicians and authority figures at home. Bill Mauldin and other liberal political cartoonists were certainly aware of how the postwar period restricted the possibilities of satiric expression. Indeed, it was exactly this situation that prompted *Variety* to ask in the middle of the decade, "Why . . . aren't the comedians puncturing the inflated false fronts of some of the more preposterous politicos like they used to? What has brought on the new silence?"[5] Throughout the fifties, American critics and intellectuals repeatedly echoed *Variety's* lament.

Not surprisingly, many commentators singled out McCarthyism's chilling effect on dissent as the primary cause of political humor's postwar demise. Looking back on the decade of the fifties, Leon Harris, author of *The Fine Art of Political Wit* (1964), observed that during Senator Joseph

McCarthy's rise to prominence, "no one on the entire American political scene chose to bell the cat with humor or in any other way." In his *Treasury of American Political Humor* (1964), Leonard C. Lewin likewise described a "cloud of political repression" dimming "the wit of even the least intimidated" during the fifties. Historians Arthur Dudden and Arthur M. Schlesinger Jr. similarly blamed fear and repression for squelching political humor. Schlesinger, an avid supporter of Adlai Stevenson throughout the fifties and a man who, like his hero FDR, enjoyed a reputation as an ironic wit, argued that "laughing at the powerful" had begun "to grow risky" during the fifties, while Dudden claimed that it was "the growing pressure to bypass whatever is controversial or thought improper . . . that account[ed] for the decay of political humor." With the same gravity displayed by others addressing this topic, Malcolm Muggeridge, the former editor of Britain's satirical magazine *Punch,* insisted that "it may well be that those who seek to suppress or limit laughter are more dangerous than all the subversive conspiracies which the FBI ever has or ever will uncover."[6]

James Thurber, a writer very worried about what he called "the diminishing of political satire," blamed the ideological left as much as the political right for humor's woes. "The leftists have made a concerted attack on humor as an antisocial, antiracial, antilabor, antiproletarian stereotype," Thurber wrote in 1960, "and they have left no stereotype unused in their attacks, from 'no time for comedy' to the grim warnings that humor is a sickness, a sign of inferiority complex, a shield and not a weapon." Beat poet and critic Kenneth Rexroth agreed with Thurber that "true humor" was one of "the most effective mode[s] of courage," and he concurred that American radicals had long ago abandoned their sense of humor. Rexroth believed, however, that the principal cause of political humor's decline could be traced to America's spiritual malaise. "What is wrong with American humor is what is wrong with American life," Rexroth pointed out in an April 1957 issue of the *Nation*. "It is commercialism."[7]

In their effort to divine the source of political humor's decline, some writers even criticized President Dwight D. Eisenhower and his administration for establishing a political style that was too serious and somber. By the late 1950s, in fact, it appeared to some Americans that even Soviet Premier Khrushchev, who flashed his wit often during his 1959 tour of the United States, was more capable of using humor than the grim-faced president, his thin-skinned vice president Nixon or his secretary of state John Foster Dulles.[8] When Eric Goldman, a professor of history at Princeton

University, surveyed the political doldrums of the 1950s, he referred to President Eisenhower as a man who "persists in talking in platitudes straight out of the old days of the Rutherford B. Hayes Marching Societies." Never in history, Goldman wrote at the end of Eisenhower's term, "has a nation been more ripe, more begging for mockery, for satire, for wit." Goldman continued,

> Oh my God . . . where are the guffaws in this country, the purifying wit and humor, the catharsis of caricature, the outcries against all this unmitigated nonsense? They come here and there in a few publications or broadcasts, a few weary voices, a few groans or a few bright shafts, but for the most part the scene is unruffled and unruffable. Our faces are straight, our thoughts are doggedly constructive, our ramparts are high and wide against the man who belly-laughs. Sometimes I think the real menace to America is not Communism at all. Sometimes I think we are just going to bore ourselves to death.[9]

Goldman's comments accurately reflected the frustrations many American liberals and intellectuals harbored throughout the 1950s. For many of them, the time was nigh to unleash political satire again and thereby allow it to shed light on the fallibilities of America's conservative politicians. Margaret Halsey, writing in the *New Republic* in 1958, suggested, for example, "that against the ready-mix virtue of the 'new' Nixon, we do have weapons. Confronted with a potential President of such a stripe, we can lock up the spoons and the Constitution and treat morality with enough high seriousness to get the humorists out of hock and fetch the writers of comedy back from exile." Several months later, Gore Vidal echoed Halsey's remarks in the *Nation*. Vidal, a witty young novelist (and staunch Stevenson supporter) who began writing for television and for Hollywood during the 1950s, had experienced considerable success in 1956 and 1957 with his satiric play *Visit to a Small Planet*. After enjoying a long run on Broadway, Vidal's play toured numerous theaters throughout the United States. Given the troubles he encountered in getting his play produced, Vidal was moved to write that "satire ha[d] taken a beating." He questioned the nation's ability to foster satire, given its preoccupation with "uniting and exploring, pioneering and building, inventing and consuming." "Should a home-grown Hitler appear," Vidal warned the *Nation*'s readers, "whose voice amongst the public orders would be raised against him in derision?" Vidal, like Halsey, concluded that the time was ripe for satire as it was for truth, "for is not satire, simply, truth grinning in a solemn canting world." "Look at the targets," Vidal continued, "Christianity,

Psychiatry, Marxism, Romantic Love, Xenophobia, Science . . . You need only take your pick, and not worry about bad taste. If one can make the cautious laugh by clowning, half the work is done, for laughter is the satirist's anaesthetic: he can then make his incision, darting on before the audience knows what has been done to it."[10]

*   *   *

Throughout the mid-1950s, liberal critics together with a sizeable number of subscribers to liberal periodicals such as the *New Republic* could still count on the commentary of cartoonists Herbert Block, Walt Kelly, and Robert Osborn. The work of artists like these, in the judgment of the liberal journal *Saturday Review of Literature,* constituted "pretty nearly the last refuge of irreverence in the Eisenhower era." All three continued their pointed commentaries on the failures of President Eisenhower and his administration, the dangers of the cold war, and America's racial crisis. In 1958 they were joined by Bill Mauldin, who had been coaxed out of retirement in order to replace Daniel Fitzpatrick at the *St. Louis Post-Dispatch.* For forty-five years Fitzpatrick had been one of the most respected liberal editorial cartoonists working in the United States, so Mauldin was understandably apprehensive about filling his shoes. He also had misgivings about meeting the day-to-day responsibility of editorial cartooning. But Mauldin's writing income was lagging, and he considered the liberal *Post-Dispatch* one of the few newspapers in the country to which he could contribute in good conscience.[11]

A noticeable shift in Mauldin's cartooning style accompanied his new position with the *St. Louis Post-Dispatch.* Rather than rely solely on pen and heavy brush, Mauldin by late October 1958 began using grease crayon shading, a technique that, as Fitzpatrick had been demonstrating for decades, lent a greater tonal subtlety and contrast to editorial cartoons. Deploying the more direct, no-nonsense approach practiced by "Chicago school" cartoonists Vaughn Shoemaker and Herblock, Mauldin now rendered his cartoons with labels and succinct captions. A superb draftsman, Mauldin captured motion and the likeness of his subjects with a degree of precision uncommon among his peers. Mauldin's combination of artistic skill and sharp satiric outlook proved very effective, and within a year after taking up his new post with the *St. Louis Post-Dispatch,* he reestablished his reputation as one of the country's most talented political cartoonists. Daniel Fitzpatrick was so pleased with his replacement that he compared him to Herblock and explained "that's as high a compliment as you can pay." Indeed, in the late 1950s and early 1960s, Mauldin was widely recognized as Herblock's closest peer, his best competition. With the exception of Herblock, no other cartoonist in the United States had a wider reach or greater influence. By 1961, Mauldin's cartoons reached ten million readers in ninety-nine newspapers nationwide and were reprinted in publications such as the *New Republic* and *Dissent*. His position was further enhanced in 1962 when he was hired away from the *Post-Dispatch* in order to become a roving "cartoon commentator" for the liberal *Chicago Sun-Times*.[12]

It is easy to see why Mauldin and Herblock were so often compared to one another; the two men shared much in common. Like Herblock, certainly, Mauldin defined his role as cartoonist in heroic terms. The cartoonist, Mauldin told a reporter, "must peel back the veneer of hypocrisy and deception, stick pins in pompous windbags, puncture inflated egos, comfort the afflicted and afflict the comfortable, in a word, carry on the fight for the 'little guy' against greedy and vested interests, bigots and fakers, potential Caesars and misguided do-gooders . . ." "If it's big," went Mauldin's credo, "hit it."[13] In their critical stance, Mauldin's cartoons from the late 1950s also often mirrored those of his colleague's. On the Soviet Union, China, Cuba, and their communist leadership, for example, Mauldin consistently repeated Herblock's censorious jabs. Throughout the fifties, Herblock had satirized the Kremlin's heavy-handed, bumbling, yet threatening machinations. As if to dispel any lingering doubts about his views toward communism, Mauldin by the late 1950s even outdid Herblock, portraying Mao Zedong and Nikita Khrushchev as reckless thugs and associating them with tigers, snakes, and even Frankenstein. Mauldin's return to cartooning was in fact boosted significantly by his criticism of the Soviet Union. In 1958, soon after he took up his post at the *St. Louis Post-Dispatch,* he was awarded his second Pulitzer Prize for a cartoon criticizing the travails of artists and intellectuals within the Soviet Union. The winning cartoon depicted a bedraggled intellectual (a reference to writer Boris Pasternak) performing hard labor at a Russian gulag in the dead of winter. "I won the Nobel Prize for Literature," he tells his workmate. "What was your crime?"[14]

Although critical of the Soviet Union, China, and Cuba—he began taking shots at Fidel Castro in January 1959, soon after he and his rebels overthrew the corrupt pro-American dictatorship of President Fulgencio Batista—Mauldin repeatedly blamed the Eisenhower administration for

25. During the height of the Kennedy era "satire boom," Herblock, pictured here at his *Washington Post* office, used his pen and brush to ratify the outlook of cold war liberalism. Library of Congress, Prints & Photographs Division, *Look* Magazine Photograph Collection.

26. Shortly after reviving his career in 1958, Bill Mauldin was awarded his second Pulitzer Prize for a cartoon critical of the Soviet Union's treatment of dissident intellectuals. Library of Congress, Prints & Photographs Division, LC-DIG-ppmsca-03232.

its part in escalating the cold war. Mauldin and Herblock warned ominously about the threat of nuclear annihilation and the harmful effects
posed by radioactive fallout from bomb testing. They also targeted the
pro-bomb propaganda circulated by the Atomic Energy Commission as
well as what President Eisenhower in his 1961 farewell address identified
as the "unwarranted influence" of the "military-industrial complex." In
general, both men assailed the absurd logic of the cold war. In one
Mauldin cartoon, two boys representing the world's superpowers brawl
on the sidewalk and explain to an adult onlooker, "He started a preventive
war and I'm fightin' to end one." Another Mauldin cartoon pictured a high
military official bragging about the development of the newest addition
to the American arsenal: an "anti-anti-missile-missile." Mauldin commented on the occasionally ironic effects of U.S. foreign policy in a
May 1959 cartoon. In it, a citizen confronts a military official at the helm
of a tank labeled "U.S. Military Aid to Dictators," which has just trampled
innocent civilians, and asks, "You mean there's no other way to keep
them from going Communist?" More typical was the ridicule Herblock
and Mauldin directed at Secretary of State John Foster Dulles, a man
whom many liberals criticized for his hard-line diplomacy and ques-
tionable policy toward the Middle East, Taiwan, and Southeast Asia.
Mauldin caricatured Dulles often as a cowboy (the "fastest gun in the
West") and a reckless fool, a man willing to play Russian roulette with the
hydrogen bomb.[15]

Dulles's conduct of U.S. foreign policy symbolized for Mauldin,
Herblock, and many other American liberals the consequences of the
Eisenhower administration's failed and tired leadership. In both foreign
and domestic policy, Mauldin and Herblock argued through their cartoons, the Eisenhower administration was languishing. Echoing arguments liberal Harvard economist John Kenneth Galbraith put forth in his
influential book *The Affluent Society* (1958), Mauldin and Herblock complained that during the late stages of Eisenhower's watch the interests of
corporations and prerogatives of private gain were compromising the
country's commitment to social programs and education. A February 1959
Herblock cartoon pictured President Eisenhower explaining the reason
behind "inadequate school construction program" to a schoolchild. "It's
not the principle," Eisenhower explains feebly, "it's the money." Several
weeks later, newspapers ran a Mauldin cartoon in which three fat cats
(representing oil, gas, and insurance industries) frolic with bikini-clad
women in a desert pool labeled "tax relief." To a desperate man crawling

"We Hope You Like Us, Jack"

to the pool for relief, the oil industry representative barks, "Beat it! We're a mirage!"

*   *   *

Equally important to the prospects of postwar liberal political satire was the emergence of Mort Sahl, a young stand-up comedian from California. For liberal writers and intellectuals who complained habitually about the "decline" of American political satire, Sahl represented a rare glimmer of hope. While Gore Vidal paid tribute to the "curious magic" Sahl performed in front of paying customers, James Thurber wrote that "Perhaps Mort Sahl is the answer." "From what I have heard about him," Thurber wrote in 1958, "he will not be intimidated." Mort Sahl made his professional debut in 1953 at the hungry i, a small basement club catering to a crowd of "hungry intellectuals" and tourists in San Francisco's North Beach district. Billing himself as "Cal Southern from Southern California," Sahl initially emulated the folksy style of Will Rogers and the popular rural sage Herb Shriner. During his first few months onstage, Sahl entertained audiences with imitations of movie stars and observations about life in California. As he recalls, he initially "didn't dare to talk about what was really on [his] mind." By early 1954, however, he began to take swipes at political and social issues, foremost among them the corrosive effects of McCarthyism. One of his first onstage jokes to gain wide underground circulation involved his description of the new McCarthy jacket, a jacket that would improve upon the popular Eisenhower jacket, Sahl said, by including an additional flap "which buttons over the mouth." Other quips Sahl delivered on the hungry i stage commented on J. Edgar Hoover (and his new book *How to Turn Your Friends into the FBI for Fun and Profit*) and physicist Robert Oppenheimer, a man who, according to Sahl, was told by government officials to "turn in your brain, you're through." Sahl likewise observed that every time the Russians threw an American in jail, HUAC would throw an American in jail "to show them they won't get away with it."[16]

Sahl's early jokes on J. Edgar Hoover and the ironies of the cold war appear tame in retrospect, but they struck many Americans at the time as audacious and delightfully irreverent. At a time when many liberals considered voicing dissent in public risky business, the topical material Sahl presented in the small basement club in San Francisco represented a significant breath of fresh air. By mentioning public officials such as Hoover and Senator McCarthy by name and subjecting them to ridicule, contemporary critics often noted, Sahl was in fact helping bring a long period of public silence to an end. In the early sixties, critic Kenneth Allsop considered Sahl's impact retrospectively and argued that it was he "who blew the first holes in conformity and silence, the holes through which the new irreverence has since poured—and washed along with it the miasma of a neurotic time." Jonathan Miller, one of the many satirists in the United States and Britain who acknowledged a debt to Sahl, linked the comedian to the tradition of European cabaret, where actors reduced the aura surrounding powerful personalities by engaging in primitive "naming rituals."[17]

Not surprisingly, there were members of the hungry i's audience that bristled at Sahl's irreverent jokes on the cold war and issues such as racial segregation. Sahl was often heckled and called a "Jewish, Communist nigger-lover." He was also pelted with pennies and threatened with violence. On occasion, it was even necessary for hungry i owner Enrico Banducci to escort Sahl out of his club so that he would avoid injury. Sahl, possessing a combative personality and a healthy dose of masculine bravado, met early opposition with resolve. "I was really angry that anybody told me [that my kind of humor] couldn't be done," he remembers of his early career. "It became an end in itself." As he gained confidence, Sahl began to demonstrate a fierce determination to buck his conservative antagonists and restore politics back to the stage, to make theater an arena for free expression. A decade after he began his career in stand-up comedy, Sahl explained that the "mission of theatre is to *wake people up*. Make them feel something . . . There's an urgency about it."[18]

Sahl's determination reflected his strong-willed temperament and radical individualism, to be sure, but it was also inspired by his upbringing in a left-wing household. Like other liberal satirists who emerged in the 1950s and early 1960s, Sahl inherited a strong social and political conscience from his lower-middle-class Jewish parents. Sahl has called his father, a failed writer who worked as a clerk and court reporter in Los Angeles, a "dreamer" and a "moral leader." "My father and mother gave me a very radical orientation. They are people who refused to watch America turn 180 degrees after FDR." From an early age, Sahl developed an iconoclastic streak and a taste for satiric comedy—a taste satisfied in the 1940s by radio comedian Henry Morgan. Sahl's antiauthoritarianism was later severely tested when, at the age of eighteen, he enlisted in the U.S. Army Air Forces. While stationed at a base in Anchorage, Alaska, Sahl demonstrated a resistance to military authority by publicizing various forms of military payola in a newsletter he edited titled *Poop from the Group.* Sahl's brazen attempt at muckraking journalism earned him eighty-three consecutive days of KP duty. After completing his military duty, he attended the University of Southern California on the GI Bill, earned an engineering degree, and then began studies at USC's Graduate School of Public Administration. Although poised to pursue a career as a civil servant, like his father, Sahl had aspirations of becoming a writer. Eventually, a clash with the dean of the School of Public Administration helped motivate Sahl to leave Los Angeles (and a dead-end job as car salesman) and follow his girlfriend north to the University of California at Berkeley.[19]

As Sahl recounts in his 1976 autobiography *Heartland,* arriving in Berkeley was in "many ways . . . like being born again." Within Berkeley's coffeehouses, he recalls, there "was a cadre of left-wing-oriented Jewish kids with fervor. I just wandered around and listened." Throughout the early fifties, while bumming around the Berkeley campus and San Francisco's bohemian North Beach district, Sahl came into contact with many young Beats and other marginal characters. He occasionally read poetry in friends' homes, and he was even responsible for initiating the University of California's first "non-conformity club." Just as Paul Sills, Mike Nichols, and other early members of the Compass partook of the vibrant milieu surrounding Chicago's Hyde Park, Mort Sahl imbibed the rich left-liberal intellectual and cultural life of the Berkeley–San Francisco area.[20]

With Sills, Nichols, and their cohort of young, hip, Jewish stage performers, Sahl in fact shared numerous similarities. In addition to their Jewish ethnic backgrounds, left-liberal political upbringing, affinity for Popular Front political theater, and their relatively high levels of education, Sahl and the early Compass members evinced strong desires to escape the slick, artificial conventions of their craft and instead present themselves as informally, authentically, and spontaneously as possible. For Sahl, this first meant trading in the suit and tie or tux (the customary dress of the nightclub comic) for a sweater when he mounted the stage to perform. "It occurred to me," Sahl remembers of his break with tradition in early 1954, "you mustn't look like any member of the society you're criticizing. What could I be? I was twenty-six. I went out and got myself a pair of blue denims and a blue sweater and a white button-down shirt open at the neck: graduate student. Which I was. And I went out there and I did it and it worked. It let the audience relax." To complement his graduate student appearance and, equally important, help him remember his mate-

rial, Sahl carried with him onstage a newspaper stapled with notes. Every
once in a while, Sahl recalls, "I would digress because I had no discipline.
And when I digressed, I got my first laugh."[21] Before long, spontaneous
digressions governed a significant portion of Sahl's delivery onstage.

Early on Sahl structured his stand-up routines around anecdotes
concerning political figures or some other event or phenomena in
1950s America. He was fond of cutting back and forth between subjects
frenetically, informing his audience, "I'll get back to that in a minute"
and punctuating his delivery with humorous parenthetical remarks and
quick, ironic one-liners. Sahl commonly interjected his delivery with
questions—"you know about this?" or "is anybody listening?"—exclama-
tions—"Onward!"—and, on occasion, a self-satisfied bark of laughter. A
good illustration of Sahl's technique occurs when he relates to a hungry i
audience in 1960 an encounter he had with a group of New York juvenile
delinquents. When he told them that he wanted to join them, Sahl tells
the audience, they "panicked from the responsibility" and ran away. With
his pithy, topical observations, his informal dress, his departure from old-
school, Borscht belt comedians' "gags," and his appeals to intelligence,
Sahl appeared to be breaking nearly all of the conventions of stand-up
performance. Indeed, the loose, jazz-inflected performing style Sahl began to develop on the hungry i's stage in 1954 represented as big a departure from the conventions of modern stand-up performance as did the
Compass's break with mainstream commercial theater. Recalling the first
time he had witnessed Sahl's unique style at a New York nightclub during
the midfifties, comedian Woody Allen states,

> He was the best thing I ever saw. He was like Charlie Parker in jazz . . . There
> was a need for a revolution, everybody was ready for the revolution, but some
> guy had to come along who could perform the revolution and be great. Mort
> was the one. He was like the tip of the iceberg. Underneath were all the other
> people who came along: Lenny Bruce, Nichols and May, all the Second City
> players . . . He totally restructured comedy . . . He changed the rhythm of the
> jokes. He had different content, surely, but the revolution was in the way he
> laid the jokes down.[22]

The association Allen draws between Sahl and an improvising jazzman
such as Charlie Parker is one that critics made repeatedly during the
fifties. In the opinion of some contemporary observers, Sahl resembled a
nightclub comedian less than he did a jazz musician wailing onstage with
his "impressionistic yackety-yack" and using his rolled-up newspaper as

27. Mort Sahl, in his trademark casual attire, entertained patrons of Chicago nightclub Mister Kelly's in 1957. Grey Villet/Time & Life Pictures/Getty Images.

his "ax." When the influential *San Francisco Chronicle* columnist Herb Caen first saw Sahl perform in 1954, he was impressed by the manner in which Sahl mirrored "a jazz musician playing a chorus: toying with phrases, following the melody and suddenly losing it, trying for high notes that he sometimes splattered."[23] Others were struck by his "cascading stream of consciousness" and the jittery, nervous staccato of his delivery. Sahl solidified his connection to the West Coast jazz scene by touring college campuses with his friends Dave Brubeck and Paul Desmond. In the late fifties and early sixties, Sahl also performed at the Newport and Playboy Jazz Festivals and even wrote a column in *Metronome* magazine. Overall, then, Sahl betrayed a close identification with the jazz musician. Describing his delivery onstage in a 1963 interview, Sahl revealed,

> See, when I work, I feel a cadence, just like when you play, when you blow; I feel a certain cadence, and I feel it coming, I feel *rhythms* . . . you feel a cadence and you find it as you go. But I become impatient with it and want to start with something else, because *every word I do* is improvised. I don't rehearse anything . . . You just find it from night to night, and it starts to build up.[24]

Given Sahl's affinity with jazz and improvisation, his unorthodox style, his youth and background in San Francisco, it is easy to understand why critics were tempted to view Sahl as "the rebel without a pause" or, more commonly, "The Will Rogers of the Beat Generation." Yet while Sahl freely admitted his debts to the jazz world, he was quick to distance himself from the Beat movement. "There's no rebellion going to come out of the beat generation," he said in a 1958 interview, "the beat guys are all mystical as hell, and hedonists." Several years later he likewise argued that the "beatniks don't want to be involved with society, which is the antithesis of what I do." Contrasting himself against what he viewed as the "apolitical" beatniks, Sahl portrayed himself as a politically committed New Deal liberal. For Sahl, stand-up satiric expression became the vehicle through which he could defend the liberal politics of his parents' generation against the conservative postwar trajectory of American politics. Like other American liberal satirists active during the 1950s and early 1960s, Sahl aimed to do more than make people laugh; he believed he could use humor to prod people to think and help them distinguish the "reality" of their situation. "I never said I was a [comedian]," Sahl told reporters in 1960. "I just sort of tell the truth." Real humor, as Sahl defined it in 1954, "has a point of view and deals with reality—which in our time is funny enough to kill you." To the charge that he was a cynic, Sahl responded, "I consider myself a very moral man . . . if I criticize somebody it's only because I have higher hopes for the world. Revolutionists have hope."[25]

In truth, Sahl during the 1950s was less a revolutionist than a liberal Democrat. Together with the great majority of the satiric writers, performers, and artists who emerged in America during the 1950s and early 1960s, Sahl's politics fell in line with the "new class" or "qualitative" liberalism outlined by intellectuals such as John Kenneth Galbraith and Arthur Schlesinger Jr., the *New Republic,* and the Democratic candidates Adlai Stevenson and John F. Kennedy. Sahl's identification as a partisan Democrat was solidified in the late 1950s as he earned a reputation as the country's preeminent Republican basher. At performances throughout this period, Sahl obliged liberals' appetite for putdowns of President Eisenhower and his administration. If President Eisenhower "said something about a policy," Sahl later explained his strategy, "I would extend his logic to expose the innate absurdity of it." Sahl convulsed patrons of Los Angeles's Crescendo nightclub at the time of the U-2 imbroglio when he said that he saw Eisenhower and his inept administration in a passive, "female role." "I have a vision of them in Washington," Sahl told the crowd. "'Did [the Soviets] call today? Why doesn't [Premier Khrushchev] call today?" Playing on stereotypes of the First Couple as America's most powerful squares, Sahl joked that the president was the type of man who entertained the young jazz-loving king of Thailand by inviting the Guy Lumbardo orchestra to play at the state dinner. In addition to gibing President Dwight Eisenhower, Sahl took shots at his corporate-friendly cabinet and Secretary of Defense (and former General Motors president) Charles Wilson in particular. At the beginning of one routine, Sahl simply began reeling off the names of the Eisenhower cabinet while the audience reportedly "squealed in delight." Sahl also liked to target Secretary of State John Foster Dulles, but the political figure who received Sahl's sharpest barbs was Vice President Richard Nixon. In 1959, a nightclub audience rewarded Sahl with a gust of raucous laughter after he observed of the former HUAC member's recent visit to the Soviet Union, "He can't call anybody a Communist and hurt their career over there."[26]

Throughout the fifties, Sahl satirized Walt Disney and big business in general, along with the American Medical Association and the Daughters of the American Revolution. Included among Sahl's domestic concerns was the slow progress of racial equality. Like other liberal satirists, Sahl lambasted Southern segregationists. But he was not remiss in pointing out the serious failures of national political leaders as well. Trading on liberal cartoonists' comic stereotype of the president as an aloof, golf-playing clown, Sahl told audiences at the time of the Little Rock school desegregation conflict that President Eisenhower might walk a little black girl to school in Little Rock by the hand (as Senator Hubert Humphrey recommended) but faced the problem of "deciding whether or not to use an overlapping grip." "Last fall," Sahl elsewhere remarked in 1957, "Eisenhower said that he felt we should approach the problem *moderately.* But Stevenson said, we should solve the problem *gradually.* Now if we could just hit a compromise between these two extremes." Sahl also punctured the ironies of the cold war and took aim at the persistence of anticommunist ideology. Liberal audiences particularly appreciated Sahl's pointed observations about the American military establishment's nuclear strategy. Of the "missile gap" separating the world's superpowers that Democratic presidential candidate John Kennedy exploited on the campaign trail in 1960, Sahl memorably observed, "Maybe the Russians will steal all our secrets—then they'll be two years behind." The CIA has its own foreign policy, Sahl also quipped, "which sometimes coincides with that of the United States."[27]

*   *   *

By satirizing political issues and personalities in his informal, spontaneous manner, Mort Sahl first earned a devoted following in the San Francisco area. He came to the attention of audiences and critics throughout the United States in 1957, soon after he opened a long stand at Mister Kelly's in Chicago with jazz singer Billie Holiday. The following year Sahl headlined an eclectic revue titled *The Next President* on Broadway. Although *The Next President* closed after only two weeks, Sahl's Broadway debut earned him glowing reviews from some of New York's most important critics. Compared with the topical comedian Bob Hope, whose scattershot monologues hit politicians of all stripes but rarely penetrated beneath the skin, Sahl struck New York critics and audiences alike as hip, sharp, and intelligent. The *New York Herald Tribune's* Walter Kerr and John Crosby described Sahl's performance as if it were a portent of marvelous things to come. The fact that Sahl was able to "tease people into laughing out loud and quite frequently," Kerr wrote, "is an indication that something in our society has begun—after too many muddy and fearful years—to change. First thing you know, irreverence will be in vogue again, and even satire may wear its old, outrageous and becoming smile." Crosby concurred with Kerr's assessment, arguing that the Broadway audience who saw Sahl laughed "hungrily, as if they'd been waiting for something to laugh at for a long, long time, something more substantial than Perry Como's inability to read the cue cards which has been the big laugh-getter all year." "Frankly," Crosby continued, "I think the turning point has come. I could be over-optimistic but I think non-conformity is coming in, and that blandness is getting too bloody bland for all of us."[28]

Between 1957 and 1960, Sahl's unique brand of satiric comedy was made available to the American public through the release of six long-playing records. Aside from providing Sahl with handsome royalties, these popular recordings afforded Sahl a much wider reach for his satiric comedy. In 1960, Sahl explained that he made "records because I honestly believe that what I say in the clubs the rest of the country should hear." "Y'know," Sahl added, "people are very evangelistic about comedy records. They play them for one another, like we take out our best silver for our friends." The success of these records, which by the end of 1960 had sold in excess of 125,000 copies, helped kindle a new mania for recorded comedy albums.[29]

Sales of Sahl's records were undoubtedly boosted by the admiring coverage that they received in *Playboy* magazine. *Playboy* and its publisher Hugh Hefner were in fact some of the most enthusiastic and important supporters of Sahl's career. Hefner well understood the appeal Sahl's image as outspoken, liberal, hip iconoclast carried with *Playboy*'s young, affluent male readership and was quick to exploit their association. "A friend of jazz," *Playboy* said admiringly of Sahl, "he also digs such urban subjects as hi-fi and sports cars." Sahl's frequent dismissive comments about his challenges with "chicks" and his Feiffer-like skepticism of long-term, male-female relationships certainly ruffled no feathers in *Playboy*'s editorial offices. (It would appear that the Mort Sahl "Playbill" clutched in the hand of the May 1961 Playmate was no accident.) Beginning in 1958 and continuing through the early 1960s, *Playboy* published wildly enthusiastic reviews of Sahl's albums, reported on Sahl's visits to Hefner's Chicago mansion, invited Sahl to participate in *Playboy* roundtable discussions, and employed him as *Playboy* Jazz Festival emcee. In *Playboy*'s eyes, Sahl was indeed the "dean of hip wits."[30]

Sahl was also the subject of adoring profiles in liberal middlebrow publications such as *Holiday,* the *New Yorker,* and the *Reporter,* a good indication that, although he had gained a sizeable audience by 1960, the core of his support remained with educated, middle- and upper-middle-class American liberals. Throughout the fifties, Sahl had distinguished himself from the herd of blue-collar Borscht belt–Vegas–Hollywood gag men that had dominated mainstream American comedy since World War II. Like other liberal satirists, Sahl was very much in tune with the educated, middle- and upper-middle-class Americans' psychological obsessions. In a manner remarkably similar to that of cartoonist Jules Feiffer, Sahl poked fun at and, at the same time, validated middle-class Americans' interest in psychology. Sahl commonly laced his speech with references to "security symbols," "mental hang-ups," "group hostility," and "value judgments." In typical fashion, Sahl in 1958 told an audience about meeting a folksinger who lacked a navel, which he interpreted as the ultimate rejection of one's mother. On occasion Sahl used psychological references to joke about contemporary politics. In 1958, for instance, he observed that psychiatrists affiliated with the American Psychiatric Association were beginning to understand that mental hang-ups relating to the mother or father "may have been Roosevelt's doing all the time." Sahl even playfully described himself as a kind of analyst in the liner notes to one of his early albums. "Repeated plays [of this album] will produce previously undiscovered hostilities," Sahl wrote. "However, I cannot be responsible for changes in foreign policy . . . Kaleidoscope, free association, oral neuroses, call it what you will. I've attempted to touch upon areas in which you are insecure . . ."[31]

With his repeated use of pointed topical jokes, esoteric references, and self-referential parodies of intellectuals and their psychiatric and academic jargon, Sahl was casting himself squarely on the side of well-educated liberals who came to see him perform. By 1960, Sahl had become the literate voice of "outraged intelligence," the one comedian liberal "eggheads" could call their own. Of course, nightclub patrons unprepared for Sahl's virtuosity were left vexed and confused by his act. *Cue* in 1959 reported of Sahl's engagement at the New York Copa, for example, that "He rambled on and on and those diehards who were schooled to laugh at Durante, the Kean Sisters and Joe E. Lewis stared and stared and stared." A year later Henry Morgan described seeing Sahl lose "seventy per cent of the people in the room [who] didn't know what the hell he was talking about." Morgan continued, "He was using plain English and fairly short words—he was talking about these people and the time in which they live—and they acted as though the whole thing were being done under water on Saturn."[32]

In the end, Sahl's approach to comedy reinforced a sense of solidarity and, admittedly, superiority among his well-educated, middle- and upper-middle-class liberal fans—fans whom Sahl commonly referred to as "my people." At the conclusion of his performances he would congratulate his followers for their "attention span" and "individual perception." In interviews he defended them by arguing that they ought to be treated on a "better-than-twelve-year-old mentality level."[33] In the 1950s, Sahl's fans, like the fans of other liberal satirists, considered themselves an embattled minority amid America's great unthinking, materialistic masses. For them, Sahl's smart, at times acid political comedy represented a blow for intelligence, critical thinking, and liberal values.

*   *   *

Mort Sahl and two-time Democratic presidential candidate Adlai Stevenson shared much the same liberal constituency, so it is easy to see how the two men became friends and professional allies. Sahl was introduced to Stevenson in 1957 while he was appearing at Mister Kelly's in Chicago. According to Sahl, Stevenson thereafter caught his act often—much to Stevenson's delight, he was occasionally the subject of Sahl's ribbing onstage—and even entertained him at his estate in suburban Liberty-ville. For the 1960 presidential election Sahl remained loyal to Steven-son, though he ultimately agreed to help out his Democratic rival John Kennedy after the Massachusetts senator secured his party's nomina-tion.[34] Sahl had become acquainted with Kennedy the previous year and was even approached by his father, Joseph Kennedy, about supplying the Kennedy campaign with some political jokes. According to Sahl, Ambas-sador Kennedy phoned him one evening in 1959 and said, "I understand that you're preeminent in the field of political humor. I want you to write some things for Johnny." The elder Kennedy's request did not appear un-usual to Sahl since by this time he had already been approached by other prominent Democrats to appear at their-fund raising dinners. Over the next year and a half, Sahl honored Joseph Kennedy's request and for-warded—without a fee—a steady supply of jokes for his son, either through his West Coast courier Pat Lawford or his aides Pierre Salinger and Ted Sorensen. While Sahl was on the road, he telegraphed material to John Kennedy through Western Union. Although Kennedy reportedly never used Sahl's jokes about Eisenhower and Nixon, he did incorporate a quip intended to defuse concerns about his religious devotion. In re-sponse to charges that he would dig a tunnel to Rome if elected, Kennedy would jokingly respond, "I'm against public works progress of any kind."[35]

During the campaign season of 1960 Sahl reached the apex of his per-forming career and was one of the most recognizable figures in American show business. Throughout this period, Sahl kept a high public profile, ap-pearing not only as a comedian on the nightclub stage but as an actor in a Hollywood movie and emcee for the annual Academy Awards broadcast. In numerous magazine and newspaper stories about his career, Sahl was hailed as the dean of the new "cerebral comics" and "sickniks." As the sub-ject of a *Time* magazine cover story in July 1960, Sahl was labeled a "Will Rogers with Fangs." That same month, an ad in the *New Yorker* publiciz-ing Sahl's return to the hungry i in San Francisco branded him "America's only working philosopher." He also appeared in a two-page fashion spread for *Esquire* magazine modeling, what else, a selection of fine sweaters. In the autumn of 1960, Sahl embarked on a thirty-city tour that included many college campuses. On this lucrative venture, Sahl was capable of netting over $10,000 per night. By this time Sahl had also begun playing mainstream venues ranging from the Copacabana and Carnegie Hall in New York to the Flamingo in Las Vegas and the Fontainebleau in Miami.

Democrats were eager to parlay Sahl's celebrity on behalf of John Kennedy's campaign, and to a considerable extent Sahl appeared willing to oblige. At public appearances throughout 1960, Sahl rarely missed an opportunity to needle candidate Richard Nixon and his party. To patrons of Chicago's Mister Kelly's, for example, Sahl mimicked the vice president telling people at the 1960 Republican convention that home life for the Nixons involved wife Pat knitting a flag while he studied the Constitution. When asked of Nixon's chances in the election, Sahl liked to respond, "Pretty good, but what about ours?" Similarly playing up the dangers of a future Nixon administration, Sahl would tell nightclub audiences, "Kennedy is an inexperienced, boyish forty-three whereas in only three years Nixon will be fifty . . . if we're here." During the months leading up to the election, Sahl covered the political conventions in a syndicated newspaper column, cohosted (with David Susskind) "An Unconventional View of the Convention" for Los Angeles television station KHJ-TV, performed at the several events during the Democrats' convention in Los Angeles (where he told his partisan crowd, "we don't have time for jokes . . . We have to overthrow our government"), and accompanied Adlai Stevenson on campaign stops on behalf of John Kennedy. Just weeks before the election, Sahl and Stevenson appeared together with Melvyn Douglas—the husband of Helen Gahagan Douglas, an early victim of Richard Nixon's red-baiting—at a Broadway theater. Sahl delivered material critical of candidate Nixon but was apparently upstaged by Stevenson, whose "barbed witticisms" included a reference to the vice president's malleable political persona. "I don't think anyone has shown so many faces to the American public," Stevenson joked, "since the late Lon Chaney."[36]

An hour after Stevenson and Sahl's joint appearance, the Broadway theater hosting the event staged a production of Gore Vidal's play *The Best Man*. Set at a presidential convention in Philadelphia, this successful election-year drama—since opening in March it had enjoyed a long and lucrative run on Broadway—focused on the campaign of a high-minded though promiscuous presidential candidate named William Russell (a composite of Adlai Stevenson and John Kennedy), who, as played by actor Melvyn Douglas, is forced to confront the dirty politics of his rival Joseph Cantwell (a morally upright scoundrel and closet homosexual inspired, in large part, by Richard Nixon). Vidal's play was principally a melodramatic morality tale, yet it contained numerous witty and satiric remarks — remarks that made a strong impression despite having to be toned down in order to accommodate the political ambitions of its author. While *The Best Man* was running on Broadway, Vidal campaigned as a Democrat for a Congressional seat in upstate New York. Vidal could ill afford to offend the electorate with stinging satire, although his penchant for wit against his Republican challenger prompted one *New York Times* reporter to write that he "sounds like Mort Sahl."[37]

Vidal clearly delighted at the prospect of having Kennedy (to whom he was distantly related) in office, and he was quick to offer the young, witty candidate his assistance. During the Democratic convention in Los Angeles, Vidal hosted a Hollywood party for Kennedy that helped solidify ties between America's show business and political elites. At another moment during the 1960 campaign, Gore informed Kennedy that he would act as an emissary to Dutchess County neighbor Eleanor Roosevelt, a stubborn Stevenson supporter, and, as Gore wrote, "those liberal establishments [the *Nation,* the *Reporter,* and the *Partisan Review*] to which I have a key." Gore also advised that he "meet the various contiguous worlds of Norman Mailer, Philip Rahv, Trilling, etc." "They view you with suspicion," he continued, "but I have a hunch you could win them around."[38]

One important liberal intellectual whom Gore did help woo away from the Stevenson camp was historian Arthur Schlesinger Jr. Like his Harvard colleague John Kenneth Galbraith, Schlesinger believed strongly in the merits of political humor. In a January 1960 article for *Esquire,* Schlesinger linked the sensibility shared by Sahl and other satirists to the evolution of a "new mood in politics." Schlesinger here predicted that Americans, poised on the threshold of a new decade, were finally prepared to leave the Eisenhower era's "godly materialism" and the "politics of fatigue" behind them and once again commit themselves to a "larger national purpose." As proof of this new mood, he pointed to the "spreading contempt . . . for reigning clichés," a "new acerbity in criticism," and "dangerous tendencies toward satire and idealism . . ."[39]

* * *

Arthur Schlesinger Jr. could not have predicted how insurgent forces — the San Francisco demonstrations against HUAC and the new phase in the civil rights movement spurred by the Greensboro, North Carolina,

Woolworth sit-in, in particular—would change the American political landscape in 1960. Neither could he have guessed how successfully John Kennedy and his advisors would cultivate the candidate's reputation for wit that election year. John Kennedy's penchant for strong and sharply honed wit had become a notable feature of Kennedy's personality in the mid- and late 1950s, when he served Congress as a junior senator from Massachusetts. Later, with the assistance of comedians such as Mort Sahl and his aide Ted Sorensen, Senator Kennedy commonly interjected jokes and humorous illustrations into the body of his prepared speeches.[40] Sorensen remembers that Kennedy "believed topical, tasteful, pertinent, pointed humor at the beginning of his remarks [could] be a major means of establishing audience rapport; and he would work with me as diligently for the right opening witticism, or take as much pride the next day in some spontaneous barb he had flung, as he would on the more substantive paragraphs in his text." To aid his efforts, Sorensen kept a large "humor folder" from which he mined toastmaster stories as well as humorous works by Will Rogers and Finley Peter Dunne. The fruits of Kennedy's collaboration with Ted Sorensen and other contributors paid off handsomely in 1958 when, at the annual Gridiron Club Dinner in Washington, he delivered a ten-minute comic monologue that reportedly "brought the house down." Kennedy impressed many reporters as well as members of his party when he used humor here to help defuse concerns about his father's role in his political future. Reading from a fictional telegram that his "generous daddy," Joseph Kennedy, had sent from the French Riviera, Kennedy stated, "'Dear Jack, don't buy a single vote more than is necessary. I'll be damned if I'm going to pay for a landslide.'"[41]

As a presidential candidate in 1960, John Kennedy was careful to address weighty issues such as the "missile gap" in a direct, decisive, and specific manner. On matters concerning the cold war and the threat posed by communism, there was little that Kennedy found humorous. Yet he frequently used self-deprecating wit to help neutralize lingering concerns over his family's wealth, his youth and inexperience, and his Catholic faith. With the assistance of Sorensen, Richard Goodwin, and his "advance men" Joseph Kraft and John Bartlow Martin, Kennedy was also able to tailor witty remarks to the conditions of each area he visited on the campaign trail. As his confidence grew, Kennedy began to expand his use of humor in public speeches, often departing from his prepared text (he took pride in being a "textual deviate") with off-the-cuff quips, jokes, and comic putdowns. Gene Graham, a reporter for the *Nashville Tennessean*, followed John Kennedy across the nation in 1960 and was, as he remembers, "chuckling at every stop." Kennedy, Graham said, "had the remarkable ability to project at once the image of a deeply serious young man, anxiously concerned with his country's welfare, in a terrible hurry to rescue it—and all the while with a laugh on his lips." Many other reporters assigned to cover the 1960 presidential campaign took note of Kennedy's cool and relaxed style and considered it a welcome departure from the anxious and gloomy mood clinging to the Nixon camp. "To most of us ace reporters," the *San Francisco Chronicle's* Arthur Hoppe recalls, "it was the Shining Young Knight versus the Forces of Darkness. The Kennedy campaign was one big party, while the ambiance that loomed around Nixon was thick with sullen suspicion."[42] Like a number of other reporters, Hoppe was a Stevenson liberal who was initially wary of Kennedy but eventually warmed to him because of his good-humored, self-effacing, ironic manner.

For observers such as *Harper's* Washington correspondent William S. White, who early in 1960 stated that the "Humor Quotient may be the most important index to watch in the first Presidential campaign of a new and—hopefully—funnier decade," the contest between John Kennedy and Richard Nixon offered a few hopeful signs that humor and satire were returning to the serious sphere of politics. By the spring of 1960, even Vice President Nixon and the GOP appeared willing to follow the Democrats' cue and poke fun at themselves and their adversaries. Veteran UPI reporter Merriman Smith noted that Nixon, feeling somewhat compelled to "loosen up," began making joking references to the Checkers scandal that had previously dogged him. In an ill-advised move that the Kennedy campaign was quick to exploit, Nixon supporters hired comedian Jimmy "Professor Backwards" Edmondson to warm up an Omaha crowd with anti-Catholic jokes that connected Kennedy with the Pope.[43]

As their dislike of Nixon intensified, John Kennedy and his staff increasingly interjected satiric jabs into their speeches. In off-the-cuff remarks that Sorensen later admitted were perhaps "overly caustic and captious in their criticism," Kennedy began to hit at what he argued were Nixon's empty slogans and his desperate attempts to hang on to President Eisenhower's coattails. "What Mr. Nixon does not understand is that the President of the United States, Mr. Eisenhower, is not the candidate," Kennedy would tell an audience. "You have seen those elephants in the circus. Do you know how they travel around the circus? By grabbing the tail of the elephant in front of them [laughter]."[44] In television commercials, the Democratic National Committee further undermined the association between Nixon and his superior by rerunning the injurious (though unintended) remarks President Eisenhower once made about his vice president at a press conference. Other ads excerpted unflattering shots of Nixon taken from his first televised debate with Kennedy. As Kathleen Hall Jamison has cogently observed, these images of Nixon as the shifty-eyed, sweating, "bearded conspirator . . . appeared to be the gutter-dwelling Nixon of Herblock's cartoons given flesh."[45]

Not surprisingly, the Democratic National Committee and the Kennedy campaign received willing support from more than a few liberal satirists during the presidential campaign. Given America's growing racial crisis and the perception that the Eisenhower administration was failing to provide the leadership necessary to guide the country's domestic and foreign policy in the future, the election of 1960 became one of signal importance to many liberal artists, writers, and performers. In addition to Mort Sahl and Gore Vidal, a number of them cheerfully deployed forms of satiric criticism on behalf of Kennedy. More often than not, their satiric criticism was aimed directly at Nixon, a man whom many liberal satirists still bitterly resented for his postwar red-baiting. Indeed, during the campaign year of 1960, the image of Vice President Richard Nixon as a sinister and ruthless opportunist was reinforced not only in Herblock's cartoons but in nearly every vehicle of satiric art and performance extant. The defeat of Richard Nixon provided liberal satirists of all stripes a rallying point and sense of purpose. On the stage at the Second City, the hungry i, and other nightclubs and cafes hosting improvised and stand-up satire, Nixon was the object of much rough treatment. He was also an easy and tempting target for cartoonists Bill Mauldin, Herblock, and Robert Osborn.

Mauldin, who identified himself as an "ill-disguised Kennedy man" in a 1960 *Time* magazine profile, did not bother to conceal his political preferences. In March 1960, Mauldin drew a cartoon of President Dwight Eisenhower sitting at the rudder of "The ship of state" with the caption, "About time some young fellow took over here at the helm." Mauldin hit at Nixon hard, depicting him in one instance as a werewolf but more often caricaturing him as a sharp-beaked "Dickie Bird." In 1960, Nixon conceded that he needed to erase "the Herblock image" in order to win the presidency, but he would receive no help from Herblock himself. Herblock continued his unrelenting, unsparing caricatures of Nixon throughout that election year. In January, Herblock presented Nixon as a

"We Hope You Like Us, Jack"

witch brewing a noxious stew and muttering to a mirror, "Mirror, mirror, on the wall, who's the fairest one of all." As the election drew nearer, Herblock and Robert Osborn drew attention to what they perceived as Nixon's chameleon-like nature, his predilection for masks and false appearances. In June, for example, Herblock pictured five Nixon look-alikes as guests on the popular television game show *To Tell the Truth*. Running through a list of issues, panelist Nelson Rockefeller, a moderate Republican, asks "Will the real Richard Nixon please stand up?"[46]

In a series of cartoon drawings for the *New Republic* as the November election drew near, Osborn attempted to focus attention on Nixon's disreputable past, his reckless ambition, his deceitfulness, and his paranoia. Four years earlier Osborn admonished *New Republic* readers "Stick with Ike & get STUCK with Dick." Now he warned of "Nixon's Lullaby" ("Go to sleep my honey child. The goblins won't getcha if you don't watch out"), and his cynical embrace of "Home, Mother, the Flag . . ." ("The next thing you know he'll be talking about 'Exchequer' his DOG!"). Osborn obviously relished his job of caricaturing Nixon. Toward the later stage of the campaign he contributed a particularly vicious illustration of Nixon and his "instinct for the jugular" to the *New Republic* while instructing its editors, "as the going gets *rough* toward the end be ready with this."[47] The *New Republic* did not publish this cartoon, but in its last issue before the election it ran "The Fakes Progress," Osborn's scathing depiction of Nixon's transformation from politician to snarling hyena. During his metamorphosis, Nixon's soliloquizes,

> Am I worthy of the office . . . Yes! Pat & the girls & Mamie & Mother think that I am . . . the base is solid but now we'll build on it . . . I say this, I made lots of statesman-like decissions [sic] until Eisenhower couldn't remember them . . . I seem to be perspiring in here, its [sic] probably rigged . . . Make him up for this one so he doesn't look like a dishonest undertaker . . . Would you have our Chief apologize to Khrushchev? . . . I won't yield anything anywhere to anybody . . . Do you want Commies running the U.S.A? . . . etc. etc.[48]

Robert Osborn took the occasion of the fall election season to publish his most extended satiric critique of American life to date, *The Vulgarians*. While it did not explicitly endorse John Kennedy, it, like John Kenneth Galbraith's *The Affluent Society* (1958), reflected perfectly the concerns shared by liberal intellectuals and upper-middle-class voters aligned with the Democratic Party's "new class" constituency. Described by Osborn as a "satire in pictures and words on the decline of greatness and the rise of

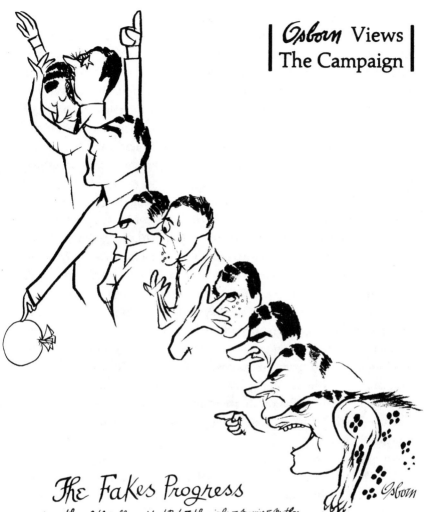

Osborn Views The Campaign

The Fakes Progress

Am I worthy of the office ··· Yes! Pat & the girls & Mamie & Mother think that I am ····· the base is solid but now we'll build on it ··· I say this, I made lots of statesman-like decisions until Eisenhower couldn't remember them ····· I seem to be perspiring in here, its probably rigged··· Make him up for this one so he doesn't look like a dishonest undertaker··· Would you have our Chief apologize to Khrushchev?····· I won't yield anything anywhere to anybody····· Do you want Commies running the USA?···· etc. etc.

28. As the 1960 presidential election approached, Robert Osborn gave vent to his strong feelings toward Richard Nixon in the *New Republic*. By permission of the Osborn family.

mediocrity in America," *The Vulgarians* attempted to delineate the ennui, artifice, and complacency that he believed were eroding the American spirit. In a letter he wrote to his publisher at the New York Graphic Society, Osborn defined the impetus behind his book: "I wrote and drew this book," he explained, "out of annoyance, dismay, and finally anger. About three years ago, perhaps four, one began to feel the jellyfish quality of American life and its easeful, uncertain drift . . . As the years wore on, the pile of our rank, apathetic materialism mounted and the examples of our clear, forceful and audacious leadership diminished to the vanishing point."[49]

More evident in *The Vulgarians* than in his previous work, Osborn had his calligraphic text carry the load of his invective. "Moisten your lips and we will examine the present corruption of our greatness," Osborn told his readers at the outset. See "to what ends our natural riches & our freedom have been put," he continued, "what over-weaning desire for money & comfort is doing to America." Hucksters and slick Madison Avenue "idea" men, a television spewing suds and "a culture of foaming nonsense," and billboards cluttering the countryside were a few of the many culprits Osborn identified in this compendium of rage. More than any other target, however, Osborn disparaged the tokens of inauthenticity—the "smile," the "nauseous coziness" and "giggly . . . cuteness & delight"—he saw enveloping the nation and drowning out "harsh REALITY." "We founder," he concluded regretfully, "in a pudge fudge . . . For the time being we have lost our way."[50]

Not surprisingly, *The Vulgarians* was heartily endorsed by the *New Republic* and liberal intellectuals such as Galbraith and Arthur Schlesinger Jr. I. F. Stone, the radical journalist who was positioned further on the political left, declared in a jacket blurb, "I wish I were a foundation: I would place a copy [of *The Vulgarians*] in every home in America. It could conceivably do us more good than putting a man in space." William Cole, in his review for the *New Republic,* compared Osborn to George Grosz and Art Young and stated that it was "shocking to think that we look *that* bad to one of our fellow-Americans."[51]

Although ignored by admiring reviewers, Osborn's satiric criticism in *The Vulgarians* and his other work of the late 1950s betrayed a measure of aesthetic snobbery and condescension. More seriously, Osborn's preoccupation with the effects of affluence also elided the problems of poverty and inequality. It ignored America's racial crisis altogether. In this sense, Osborn joined other 1950s liberal critics and intellectuals who seemed more concerned with automobile tailfins and the garish tastes of the working and lower middle classes than social and economic justice. At certain points within *The Vulgarians'* narrative, Osborn even appears to lose his critical balance and yield to despair and bitterness.

Yet like Herblock, the satiric artist he greatly admired, Osborn never forfeited his faith in democratic citizenship and his commitment to political change. To his credit, he avoided the cynicism and hopelessness that dogged some postwar liberals. In the end, he demonstrated that the animating force behind his satire was a commitment to democratic ideals. "If all this seems unduly critical & bleak—take HOPE," he advised at *The Vulgarians'* conclusion. With "a force like that of mounting Spring: DEMAND solution & begin to GENERATE once more a PUBLIC purpose to which our private works will be redressed . . . within the MEANING of our NATIONAL life!" Accompanying a drawing of a finger pointing at the reader on the last page, Osborn's text powerfully concludes,

> And the insurgent force will be YOU . . . pressing at every turn . . . [and] undertak[ing] on a SCALE WORTHY OF OUR GREATNESS such public purposes as . . . sufficient schools . . . desegregation, conservation, urban planning . . . to name a few—and once more WE shall look like a vigorous, revolutionary people![52]

With its concern over America's lapse into complacency and bad taste, its support for liberal public policies, its invocation of democratic idealism and getting America "moving again," Robert Osborn's *Vulgarians* reflected the message and spirit of the 1960 Kennedy campaign. Like Bill Mauldin and Herbert Block, Osborn had been a steadfast supporter of Adlai Stevenson throughout the fifties. Now, for the first election of the new decade, they shifted their allegiance to John Kennedy. When their candidate won, they took some satisfaction in the cumulative effect their work had on public opinion. But once Kennedy assumed office, Mauldin, Block, and Osborn, together with other liberal satirists, were confronted with the possibility that their work, which had thrived in large part because it stood in opposition to the conservative Republican administrations, would become less relevant with Democrats in power.

*   *   *

During the early days of the Kennedy administration, any concern that liberal satirists may have harbored about the viability of their art was overshadowed by the perception that the United States, now under the direction of bright, urbane, witty young men, had entered a new golden age of political humor. A new spirit of irreverence was afoot in the land, and more than a few critics and commentators traced this phenomenon directly to the young president himself. Americans had voted into office a man to whom writer Norman Mailer, in an *Esquire* essay published just several weeks shy of the election, memorably ascribed a "patina of that other life, the second American life, the long electric night with the fires of neon leading down the highway to the murmur of jazz." Vigorous, adventurous, hip, and "handsome as a prince," Kennedy was also in Mailer's estimation appealingly witty. Observing Kennedy up close, Mailer observed, significantly, that there "was a good lithe wit to his responses, a dry Harvard wit, a keen sense of proportion in disposing of difficult questions . . ."[53] With a cool, ironic, witty man in the White House, many liberal, educated, middle-class Americans hoped, the gray and depressingly glum years of the Eisenhower age might soon recede from memory.

Throughout his term in office, President Kennedy continued to impress entertainers, journalists, and segments of the American public with his instinct for spontaneous witticisms and satiric jabs. Historian Richard B. Morris was one of many observers who noted admiringly how, in "his first few months in the White House, President Kennedy has displayed a subtle and intellectual brand of humor that sets him apart from most of his predecessors." *Village Voice* critic Andrew Sarris joined numerous others who marveled at Kennedy's comic performance at his 1962 birthday bash at New York's Madison Square Garden. Even though acts on that occasion's bill such as Nichols and May were hard to follow, Kennedy appeared to be in "top form," as Sarris put it, when he "parodied the melodramatic utterances of his predecessors in office." "His whole bearing communicated a delight in satire," Arthur M. Schlesinger Jr. later remembered of President Kennedy, "and in his wake came an exuberant revival of American irreverence."[54]

*   *   *

Since much of the liberal satire produced during the Kennedy years ratified the cold war outlook and domestic policies of New Frontier liberalism, it is easy to understand why Arthur Schlesinger Jr., a close advisor to the president, would render such an innocuous appraisal of irreverence's "exuberant revival." Neither he nor anyone else within the Kennedy administration, certainly, was made to suffer much from liberal cartoonists' satiric sting. Relieved to have someone who appeared to share their liberal social and political views occupy the White House, Herblock, Mauldin, and Osborn saw themselves as allies rather than adversaries to the Kennedy administration. "Happily, in the New Frontier town of Washington," Herblock would later remember of the period, "Mr. Kennedy was on *our* side." Preferring to spend time with people who were "fighting the good fight," Herblock joined his *Washington Post* colleague Art Buchwald for social events at the Hickory Hill home of Attorney General Robert Kennedy. For both Herblock and Mauldin, John Kennedy was a sympathetic figure whose liberal social agenda stood little chance against the conservative political and economic forces arrayed against it. A January 1961 Herblock cartoon, for example, pictured Kennedy in the Old West, at the helm of a "New Frontier" covered wagon turning the bend toward "Committee Gulch." Lying in wait, dressed as Indian warriors, were "Conservative Democrat[s]" and members of the "G.O.P. coalition." In his own depiction of conservative stonewalling, Bill Mauldin pictured Kennedy as a cowboy spurring Congress (a horse named "Old Ironsides") to action but ultimately going nowhere. While it is true that numerous Kennedy administration initiatives (particularly those advancing domestic social programs) were stymied by the Republicans and conservative Democrats serving on the House Rules Committee and what Herblock labeled "Legislative Dead-Enders," liberal cartoonists' preoccupation with the conservative opposition obscured the complex political realities of the time. In general, by concentrating so consistently on enemies to the Kennedy administration—conservative Republicans, southern segregationists, and foreign communist regimes—liberal cartoonists often missed the opportunity to offer up the type of trenchant critiques the administration itself deserved.[55]

Throughout the Kennedy administration, liberal cartoonists continued their comic assaults on social and political conservatives. Because the early 1960s witnessed the growth of conservative grassroots movements such as the Young Americans for Freedom and the John Birch Society, liberal cartoonists had no shortage of targets. Still angry at the harm conservative red-baiters inflicted on him a decade earlier, Mauldin throughout the early sixties drew cartoons mocking Arizona senator Barry Goldwater, the John Birch Society, and the "G.O.P. ultra-right." In Mauldin's view, it was clear that Goldwater and his far-right supporters were prepared to overtake the Republican Party by deceit and even brute force if necessary. Just as Mauldin grouped the John Birch Society with the KKK and the U.S. Nazi Party in an April 1961 cartoon titled "Malice in Wonderland," Walt Kelly in his *Pogo* comic strip portrayed the organization as a thoroughly toxic influence in American politics. In a series of strips originally published in 1961, the bluenose Puritan Deacon Mushrat leads the Pogofonokee swampland's "Jack Acid Society" against "dangerous liberals and other scum." Pledging to stem "creeping democracy," Mushrat and his followers even create a "Black List" of subversives—a reference not lost on Kelly's readers. To those liberal readers irked by the rise of the John Birch Society, Kelly's tart satire of right-wing "patriot" groups came as welcome relief. A woman from Columbus, Ohio, spoke for many other liberal *Pogo* fans when she informed Kelly that his "utterly delightful spoofing of the John Birch tribe mentality gives us hope for America, and for a return to sanity in this country."[56]

Neither Mauldin nor any of his liberal colleagues exercised much restraint when commenting on America's cold war foes. Assuming the cold war stance they taken since the late 1940s, America's best-known satiric cartoonists caricatured Nikita Khrushchev, Fidel Castro, Mao Zedong, and other foreign communists. While Robert Osborn depicted Khrushchev with a Hitler mustache for a cover of the *New Republic,* Herblock and Mauldin relished equating Castro with a weasel, an octopus, a spoiled child, or, more commonly, a puppet controlled by Moscow. Mauldin, who called Castro a "psychopath," took special aim at the Cuban government, particularly its suppression of civil liberties. In May 1960, for example, Mauldin pictured Fidel Castro, with his feet propped up on his desk, lighting a cigar with a newspaper labeled "Free Press." Even Walt Kelly entered the fray in the early 1960s, portraying Khrushchev and Castro in his *Pogo* strip as, respectively, pig and goat.[57] In sum, the caricatures and cartoons Mauldin and his colleagues produced during the early 1960s captured the raw distrust Kennedy administration officials and cold war liberals felt toward foreign communists.

Many of the political issues and topics the Second City and the Premise addressed in their programs were consistent with those singled out by Herblock, Robert Osborn, and Walt Kelly. Like them, members of these troupes took delight in lampooning Richard Nixon, Barry Goldwater, and the John Birch Society. They also shared cold war liberals' antagonism toward communists. Much to the delight (and perhaps the relief) of their paying customers, the Premise and the Second City proved they were capable of ridiculing the humorless, totalitarian Cuban and Soviet leadership as ruthlessly as they did Republicans in the U.S. Congress. While the Premise mocked Fidel Castro, the Second City's Eugene Troobnick or Alan Arkin (in its popular "Kennedy-Khrushchev Press Conference" scene) impersonated Soviet Premier Nikita Khrushchev, answering audience members' questions in gibberish Russian. In response to one question about the Soviet's outlook on peace, Khrushchev, through his interpreter (usually the quick-witted Severn Darden), stated, "We are always for peace. Anybody who stands in the way of peace will be destroyed." Other Second City and Premise scenes lampooned Khrushchev as a hothead and a dissembler of truth. A blackout gag for the Premise in 1962, for example, had the Czechoslovakian ambassador to Moscow rush into Khrushchev's office to express his condolences on the sudden death of former Soviet Foreign Minister Molotov that morning, to which Khrushchev replies, "Thanks, but it's *tomorrow* morning."[58]

The scenes that the Second City and the Premise performed onstage in many respects mirrored the cartoons that Mauldin and his cohort published in liberal magazines and newspapers. With their antagonism toward communism and their support of civil rights, civil liberties, conservation, increased funding for education, expanded social services, and restraints on private industry, the scenes and cartoons produced by these satirists dovetailed neatly with New Frontier liberalism. Taken as a whole, they added significantly to the impression that the liberal wit and satire, what the *Nation* theater critic Robert Hatch identified in 1961 as a "new spirit of mischief," had surfaced in America shortly after "moving day at the White House."[59]

The newspaper journalism of Art Buchwald, Arthur Hoppe, and Russell Baker, like the work of liberal cartoonists and stage satirists, provides a good indication of the growing acceptance of and demand for irreverent political commentary during the early 1960s. All three of these men were born in 1925, served in the military or military reserves during World War II, and began careers as "straight" journalists, reporters, and columnists before they made their mark in the early 1960s as syndicated political humorists. Buchwald, the best known of the three, had worked in Paris as a celebrity interviewer and offbeat commentator for the *New York Herald*

Tribune during the 1950s. Shortly after moving to Washington in 1961, Buchwald began writing a satiric column (syndicated in two hundred papers around the world) that mocked American politicians, fads, and events of the day—often with a deceptively light touch. In one characteristic column titled "They Need Each Other," for example, Buchwald imagined a "hotline" telephone conversation between President Kennedy and Soviet Premier Khrushchev in which both confess how much they depend on each other's irrational cold war maneuvers abroad in order to obtain military appropriations at home. After Kennedy lodges a final complaint about the Soviet's "failure to subvert many neutral countries," he is told, "We're doing the best we can for you in Viet-Nam, Mr. Kennedy."[60]

Hoppe, named the "West Coast Buchwald" by *Newsweek* in 1963, began his career as a beat reporter for the *San Francisco Chronicle.* In 1960, just as America was emerging, as Hoppe recalls, "from the roseate glow of the Eisenhower years, where Norman Rockwell set the taste in satire," he initiated a humorous column that over the course of the next several years prodded capital punishment, Southern segregationists, the Christian Anti-Communist Crusade, and the crisis stirring in Southeast Asia. Like Hoppe, Russell Baker initially wrote as a political reporter but found his true calling as a humorous commentator. Much to the surprise of many observers, the traditionally staid *New York Times* in 1962 offered Baker the opportunity to satirize a wide range of political personalities and events on its prestigious op-ed page.[61]

In other areas of American mass communications during the early sixties, journalists and writers of all stripes began to engage political subjects in a refreshingly sardonic, satiric, and parodic manner. Throughout this period, one of the most popular newsmen on network television was David Brinkley, a man whose most notable gift was his dry wit. Teamed with his "straight man" Chet Huntley on NBC's *Huntley-Brinkley Report,* Brinkley delivered, as David Halberstam has noted, "an irreverence that the medium [of television] with its inherent overseriousness badly needed." By 1960, *Time* magazine declared, veteran newsman Edward R. Murrow was "still television's big news name; but his doom-edged, oracular school of reporting—better suited to war and disaster than to the gaudier side of U.S. politics—was rendered obsolete by the fresh wind from NBC." Whether in the conservative *National Review* or the liberal *New Republic,* writers such as William F. Buckley, Noel Parmentel Jr., and Murray Kempton infused their analysis of topical subjects and politics with irony and sharp wit. Perhaps the most notable mainstream venue for political humor during the early 1960s was *Esquire* magazine. It was here that Richard Rovere first published his controversial spoof "The American Establishment," Noel Parmentel Jr. contributed his New Right parodies "Folk Songs for Conservatives" and "The Acne and the Ecstasy," and John Kenneth Galbraith (writing under the pseudonym Mark Eparnay) lampooned social science, the "American Peerage," and American foreign policy.[62]

*   *   *

The early sixties also witnessed the maturity of a notable small-circulation satiric publication titled *Monocle*. *Monocle* owed its existence to a Yale University Law School student named Victor Navasky. The son of a Jewish businessman from New York, Navasky fell under the spell of left-liberal Popular Front culture while growing up in New York City. He attended Swarthmore College and served in the U.S. Army before beginning his legal studies in the mid-1950s. While in New Haven, Navasky began to have doubts about pursuing a future career in law. To satisfy his interests in politics, writing, and humor, he initiated *Monocle* as a magazine of political satire in 1957. As Navasky no doubt realized, the market for such publications was limited at the time. In 1956 a satirical magazine titled *Bounty,* which proclaimed itself "The American Satirical Magazine" and boasted an editorial board including such wits as Henry Morgan, lasted only three issues. Yet as a fan of political satire and a former editor of humorous publications in college and the army, Navasky was committed to his idea of launching *Monocle*. Having closely followed public discussions about the poor state of American wit under McCarthyism, Navasky in 1957 firmly believed that the time was "very ripe for satire." With *Monocle*, Navasky remembers, he aimed to use political satire both as a "form of dissent" and as a deterrent against conformity, "blandness," and the lingering effects of McCarthyism.[63]

In its inaugural issue, Navasky's *Monocle* defined itself as a "leisurely quarterly of political satire." "Our conscious policy," Navasky and his small volunteer staff wrote, "is to subject the political scene to the infinite approaches of satire." In particular, Navasky and his partners pledged to "provide new perspectives on the political problems of the day" by opening *Monocle*'s pages "to all manner of men and ideas," including anonymous heads of state.[64] While, during its first two years of operation, *Monocle* did feature satiric articles written by a State Department foreign service officer and other government insiders (all of whom used pseudonyms), it drew the bulk of its contributions and editorial assistance from graduate and professional students in and around New Haven—people such as Richard Lingeman, Jacob Needleman, Laurence Pearl, Charles Prentiss, Sid Zion, and Christopher Lehmann-Haupt.

After graduating from Yale Law School, Navasky left New Haven in order to join the staff of Michigan governor G. Mennen Williams. While working for Williams, Navasky and his collaborators managed to keep *Monocle* alive. In 1960, Navasky decided to withdraw from government service, move back to New York City, and convert *Monocle* into a national magazine. With $75,000 raised from shareholders such as a U.S. State Department public information officer, Hollywood director George Axelrod, and Mrs. Marshall Field of Chicago, Navasky was able to increase *Monocle*'s outreach and improve its overall quality.[65] The production of *Monocle* eventually rose from three to twenty-five or thirty thousand copies per issue, with a total of five thousand copies set aside for subscribers. In late 1962, Navasky and his principal partner Richard Lingeman—a man with whom Navasky had written a musical about anticommunist paranoia in 1959—initiated the *Outsider's Newsletter,* a satiric weekly advertised as *Monocle*'s "fearless, funny little brother" and whose parodic motto was "All We Know Is What We Don't Read in the Papers." At the same time, they, along with art editors Louis Klein and Phil Gips, accentuated *Monocle*'s unique graphic design. With its odd, railroad timetable size and its mid-nineteenth-century illustrations—taken mainly from woodcuts, engravings, and old issues of *Punch* magazine—*Monocle* from its inception resembled no other publication available in America. With the addition of cartoons and caricatures from some of the best graphic artists emerging in the country—artists such as Ed Sorel, R. O. Blechman, David Levine, Ed Koren, Robert Grossman, Lou Myers, Tomi Ungerer, Terry Gilliam and Seymour Chwast—*Monocle* took a large leap forward in terms of its visual style.

Its monocled mascot and its motto "In the land of the blind the one-eyed is king" recalled the spirit of the *New Yorker,* but *Monocle* was more overtly political and, therefore, less commercial than it and most other mainstream publications. Most notably, Navasky targeted *Monocle* at people knowledgeable about political issues and the operations of the

American government. Much more consciously *inside* than any other form of American satire popular during the 1950s and early 1960s, *Monocle* was directed at public policy intellectuals, liberal academics, members of the press, and people working within the ranks of the federal government in Washington—people whom Navasky and Lingeman jokingly identified as America's "subinfluentials." Clearly, *Monocle* was intended to appeal primarily to subinfluentials sympathetic to the left wing of the Democratic Party. Nearly all of the writers, cartoonists, and staff—including Michael Dukakis, Navasky's distributor in Cambridge, Massachusetts—working on behalf of *Monocle* were liberal Democrats. As Navasky has remarked, "we were mostly left-liberal Democrats with anarcho-syndicalist pretensions."[66]

Navasky and his collaborators maintained ties with other American liberal satiric writers and performers. Recalling his intentions, Navasky states that he had initially conceived *Monocle* "as part of a new ferment that expressed itself . . . through improvisational theater, the Second City group out in Chicago, Mort Sahl . . . Lenny Bruce coming up through the nightclub underground, [and] Paul Krassner doing the *Realist* . . ."[67] At various times throughout the late fifties and early sixties *Monocle* featured contributions from Second City member Richard Neuweiler; Chuck Alverson, Harvey Kurtzman's collaborator on *HELP!;* and John Putnam, the art director for *MAD* and editorialist for the *Realist. Monocle* also received advertising support from the *Realist,* and at one time the *Outsider's Newsletter* reprinted portions of Peter Cook's *Private Eye.*

By the early sixties Navasky's pool of contributing writers and editors included a host of liberal Yale law professors (Fred Rodell and Charles Lund Black) and English professors (Neil Postman, Reed Wittemore, and Robert Bone), senior editors at the *New Yorker, American Heritage,* and *Newsweek,* and a long list of journalists and free-lance writers including John Leonard, Kurt Vonnegut, David Cort, Karl Meyer, Nora Ephron, Dan Wakefield, Gerald Jonas, and Calvin Trillin. Notable among *Monocle's* liberal contributors and staff were several women: Vivian Scott; Karla Sideman Kuskin, an author and illustrator of children's books who wrote poetry for *Monocle* under the name of K*S*K; Eleanor Dienstag, a free-lance writer who worked as Navasky's assistant editor; Katherine Perlo, a poet who was the daughter of a Marxist economist and Roosevelt administration official; and Eleanor Rockwell Edelstein, a housewife who occasionally contributed to the *New Republic.*

The liberal political slant of *Monocle*'s editorial staff and contributors was most clearly manifest in their relentless ribbing of Republican politicians and conservative organizations. Throughout the late fifties and early sixties *Monocle* lampooned President Dwight Eisenhower and Vice President Richard Nixon, John Foster Dulles, New York governor Nelson Rockefeller and the concept of "dynamic conservatism." Nixon, a frequent target in the pages of *Monocle* and the *Outsider's Newsletter*, was variously depicted as the "Manchurian Candidate," a gang leader named "Dick Mildew," and a shameless opportunist who, following his 1962 defeat in the California gubernatorial race, was willing to disband his family ("breaking up the act," as Nixon's daughter Tricia described it) in order to make a "new start." *Monocle* and *Outsider's Newsletter* contributors also satirized conservative spokesmen and organizations such as *National Review* editor William F. Buckley, the John Birch Society, and the Young Americans for Freedom. While Dan Wakefield parodied the John Birch Society (the "Fred Spruce Fraternity") and other "Demagogues of the Far Center," New Jersey congressman Frank Thompson Jr. issued a Swiftian "Modest Proposal for the Return to Conservatism through Decentralization," which called for the elimination of National Parks, those wasteful "pockets of socialism." Throughout the early sixties, *Monocle* and its sister publication reserved their severest satiric scrutiny for Arizona senator Barry Goldwater. In various parodies and caricatures, their contributors depicted the future Republican presidential nominee as a Tarzan from "The Lost Safari," the "Son of King Kong," and "that Phoenix cowboy . . . [with] the fascist gun in the west!"[68]

By publishing contributions from Democratic congressman Frank Thompson Jr. as well as John P. Roche, the National Chairman for Americans for Democratic Action, and Sam Brightman, the Democratic National Committee's Deputy Director of Public Affairs, Navasky and his colleagues demonstrated clearly their fealty to liberal politics and the Democratic Party. As Navasky admits, "Many of our lines were in the Democratic Party . . ." More importantly, *Monocle* shared a sense of kinship with the Kennedy administration. Arthur M. Schlesinger Jr., John Kenneth Galbraith, and numerous liberal subinfluentials who worked for the Kennedy administration were reportedly *Monocle* readers. Whether or not President Kennedy himself read *Monocle* or the *Outsider's Newsletter* is uncertain, although editors Navasky and Lingeman playfully suggested in the revamped *Monocle*'s inaugural issue that they had discovered, through "exhaustive research," that *he* was their target reader. "We have decided to revise *Monocle* accordingly," Navasky and Lingeman declared tongue-in-cheek, "We hope you like us, Jack." As C. D. B. Bryan recalls, he and other *Monocle* contributors felt that Jack Kennedy was "our generation, hip, with it, funny, so satire was a way of laughing with him, we felt he got the joke." "We never refer to the President by anything but Jack," Navasky explained in a 1962 *Newsweek* interview. "It gives us a sense of community."[69]

In 1962, *New York Times* columnist Russell Baker jokingly warned Navasky, "You are wasting your time if you think America is really ready and ripe for a national magazine of political satire . . ." "On the *Times,*" Baker offered, "overt display of a sense of humor provokes the sort of suspicion a sex deviate can expect at a policeman's ball." But at the moment it appeared to Navasky "most important to have a satire magazine . . . when we have an Administration so cool and able, which dominates the press so much." "Some people say contemporary life is too grim to satirize," Navasky told *Time* magazine, "[o]thers say it is too absurd to satirize. I say it is too grim and absurd not to try." In New Frontier America, with a witty president in the White House and political satire suddenly in vogue, the prospects for commercial publication of timely, topical humor appeared far better than they had in decades. It was with considerable confidence then that Navasky and his colleagues maintained their earlier promise to the liberal readers of *Monocle* and the *Outsider's Newsletter* that they would "plow through the platitudes and batter the bromides with reckless abandon."[70]

*   *   *

During the early 1960s, the *San Francisco Chronicle*'s Arthur Hoppe contributed a series of columns titled "Just Plain Jack," which were similar in spirit to the articles C. D. B. Bryan and his colleagues published in *Monocle.* Modeled along the lines of a television soap opera, Hoppe's columns typically began in the voice of an announcer saying, "Good morning, housewives and other shut-ins. It's time for another episode of 'Just Plain Jack,' the heartwarming story of one young man's struggles to overcome the handicaps of good looks and incredible wealth." In addition to Jack, the episodes Hoppe wrote for his readers involved Teddy, Bobby, Beautiful Society Girl (the First Lady), Sister Pat and her "ne'er-do-much" playboy husband Peter (Lawford), and Portly Pierre (Salinger, Kennedy's press secretary) and invariably poked fun at the Kennedy family's nepotism as well as it's high-society background and obsessions with style.[71]

With their spoofs directed at President John Kennedy and his family, Hoppe's popular "Just Plain Jack" columns mirrored perhaps the most notable and publicized development in American political humor during the early 1960s. Although there remained some Americans, particularly social and political conservatives, who believed that the presidency of the United States was not a subject fit for humor, a large segment of the population welcomed light satire directed at "Jack." Improvisational troupes in particular were quick to capitalize on this new climate. In 1962, Compass founder David Shepherd attempted to seize the trend for Kennedy humor by installing a new Compass troupe (his last) in a hotel near the Kennedy family's Hyannisport summer retreat. Throughout July and August 1962, the Hyannisport Compass's Alan Alda impersonated President Kennedy to the delight of White House aides, Secret Service men, and reporters encamped on Cape Cod.[72]

Mock presidential news conferences proved a favorite device for America's improvisational troupes. Throughout the early sixties, the Second City regularly staged them with its performers playing the parts of President Kennedy, Press Secretary Pierre Salinger, and Soviet Premier Khrushchev and his interpreter. When fielding questions given to them by audience members, the Second City's Andrew Duncan and Eugene Troobnick (playing the role of Kennedy) were renowned for making deft jabs at the Kennedy family's wealth and nepotism.[73] On other occasions, Chicago author Nelson Algren joined Second City performers on the stage and played the role of Edgar Kennedy, the secret bastard Kennedy brother who they said ran the Merchandise Mart's janitorial service.[74]

More chummy with President Kennedy and his administration were the chic revues staged by Julius Monk and Arch Lustberg. Clearly betraying their sentiments in their opening number, members of Lustberg's Washington D.C. revue *The Uniquecorn* sang,

> Believe it or not, we like it a lot, the White House.
> We leave it a lot, but certainly not for long.
> We find it unique and terribly chic, the right house . . .[75]

With material supplied by *Monocle's* C. D. B. Bryan and several other writers, *The Uniquecorn's* performers regularly lampooned the President and First Lady. In one of their most popular routines, Lustberg depicted President Kennedy phoning Premier Khrushchev in order to inform him of the accidental launch of nuclear missiles pointed at Moscow. Not long after he has broken the bad news, the president requests that Khrushchev play the part of Santa Claus and bellow "Ho Ho Ho" for the sake of his daughter Caroline.[76]

Similar to *The Uniquecorn* in content and spirit were a host of Kennedy lampoons published or released in 1962, including *Who's in Charge Here?* (a picture-caption book done in the style of Harvey Kurtzman's *Help* and the Peter Cook's *Private Eye*), *The New Frontier Coloring Book, The JFK Coloring Book,* and, most notable of all, the hit comedy album *The First Family.* Recorded by comedian Vaughn Meader (with Earl Doud) during the Cuban Missile Crisis and released for the Christmas season, *The First Family* sold two and half million copies in four weeks, a new sales record. Although the First Lady reportedly thought Meader a "rat" for making the album, *The First Family* subjected the Kennedy family to only gentle, affectionate ribbing. In addition to the Album of the Year Award, it won the endorsement of anthropologist Margaret Mead. "This making fun of people in authority is very healthy," Mead told readers of *Life* magazine. "It is the difference between democracy and tyranny . . . When you have people who cannot laugh at people in power—that is when you're in trouble."[77]

By their nature, the type of impersonation that Vaughn Meader, Arch Lustberg, and others offered was potentially subversive since, as Plato warned and as theater historian Joel Schechter has more recently argued, comic mimicry of this kind possesses the ability to expose its subject as "a fraud or 'gross imposter.'" In the hands of America's liberal satirists, however, acts of impersonation rarely provoked new insight into the character and foibles of America's popular president. Many satiric performers simply found it too difficult to satirize a man whom they admired. "We were on Kennedy's side," the Second City's Avery Schreiber admits. "So it was really hard to come up with anything that would make fun or pick the guy apart." Vaughn Meader explained that he and his colleagues "wanted to kid the Kennedy's good-humoredly, as though they might be anybody's next-door neighbor."[78] The true effect of much of the gentle satire aimed at the Kennedys was, in fact, to reinforce a perception that they and America's mainstream media carefully fostered, namely, that they were, at heart, just a well-educated, cultured, fun-loving upper-middle-class suburban family.

It is for good reason then that President Kennedy and his administration did not resist the lampoons offered by Meader and his cohort. They undoubtedly agreed with television pop psychologist Dr. Joyce Brothers when she stated that "[s]atire like this is marvelous for Kennedy politically."[79] Acutely aware of the American media's ability to burnish their public image, receptive to new methods of melding politics and show business, the Kennedys had little objection to forms of light satire and parody that ratified, rather than questioned, their good reputation. The Kennedys embraced satirists' amiable spoofs and thereby sent a powerful and long-lasting message to American politicians: one had little to lose and everything to gain from appearing hip, self-assured, and "in on the fun." The Kennedys' lesson was not lost on anyone, not least the six politicians who largely shaped American national politics during the mid- and late 1960s: Hubert Humphrey, Lyndon Johnson, Barry Goldwater, George Wallace, Richard Nixon and Ronald Reagan.

* * *

The Premise's Theodore Flicker understood American politicians' new openness toward political satire and moved quickly to exploit it. In 1961, he began thinking of ways in which he might ingratiate his troupe with the Kennedys and Kennedy administration officials. In a letter to his former colleague George Segal, Flicker announced that he had "decided to open [The Premise] in Washington before San Francisco on the very good chance that we will receive great national publicity by becoming the White House favorite." During the early months of 1962, Flicker and his troupe became the featured entertainment at Washington's elegantly appointed Shoreham Hotel, the same venue where a young, piano-playing political satirist named Mark Russell had begun to gain an audience. In a large room decorated by flags, Doric columns, and U.S. income tax forms, the Premise performed nightly in front of an audience of two hundred. With Lady Bird Johnson serving as their unofficial hostess, Flicker and his colleagues developed a cozy relationship with congressmen, ambassadors, and government employees during their five-month engagement in the nation's capital. The four Premise members were reportedly issued VIP passes and were even slipped gossip about high-ranking officials for their improvised sets.[80]

By all accounts, catching the Premise at the Shoreham became one of Washingtonians' favorite nights out during the winter and spring seasons of 1961–62. According to *New York Times* reporter Arthur Gelb, "Washington officialdom has been heading for [The Premise] with increasing enthusiasm to listen gleefully to the demolition of its most earnest endeavors." Liberal Republican Congressman John V. Lindsay of New York likewise reported in the *Village Voice*, "The word is out around Georgetown circles, and now Washington cocktail and 'snack' parties are being put together before going to 'The Premise.' What better way to spend an evening?" Flicker recalls that while at the Shoreham, Washington's political elite "couldn't do enough for us. We really let them have it, and they loved us."[81]

At a special "VIP preview" in January, the Premise attracted a host of notable government officials including Vice President Johnson and Senators Hubert Humphrey and Barry Goldwater. All three of these men enjoyed reputations as good-natured, though in the case of Johnson and Goldwater, somewhat crude, jokers. Predictably, each claimed to have enjoyed the Premise immensely. In ads promoting the Washington, D.C., Premise ("Political Satire at its Best") Humphrey was quoted as saying, "Wonderful! Takes the stuffing out of Washington's stuffed shirts." Vice President Johnson's aide and chief joke writer Liz Carpenter was likewise so impressed that she even asked Flicker for any "left-over Goldwater gags" that he might have.[82]

Personal recollections of other satiric performers and artists active during the early sixties abound with tales of how Kennedy family members and administration officials patronized their work. As Arch Lustberg, for example, recounts, "everybody who was in the administration came to see us." The stage antics of *The Uniquecorn* were reportedly the occasional subject of conversation at Robert Kennedy's Hickory Hill estate—the same estate that was known to host guests such as Art Buchwald and David Brinkley.[83] Gerald Gardner, the author of the Kennedy spoofs *Who's in Charge Here* (1962), *Miss Caroline* (1963), and *Gerald Gardner's News-Reals* (1963) befriended the Kennedys and eventually worked as a joke writer for Robert Kennedy's 1964 Senate campaign. Julius Monk and the members of his *Struts and Frets* revue were even invited to perform at the White House in 1963.

The Kennedys were particularly smitten with the amiable young rebels in Britain's *Beyond the Fringe* and The Establishment. Aides for the President even requested a private performance of *Beyond the Fringe,* though in the end he and the First Lady were forced to catch the show in New York.

Jacqueline Kennedy became so fond of Peter Cook and his colleagues in The Fringe that she invited them (through her emissary Adlai Stevenson, another of their fans) for private visits to the White House. After being introduced to the charming Cook at a dinner given by Vice President Lyndon Johnson and his wife, she reportedly was fond of catching his Establishment Club's late show when she was in New York.[84]

The Second City theaters in Chicago and New York were also well regarded by members of the Kennedy family and even began to serve as hangouts. "The Kennedys loved us," Barbara Harris remembers, "they were always following us around." Adlai Stevenson, the man President Kennedy appointed ambassador to the United Nations, was as much a fan of Second City as he was of Mort Sahl. Remarkably, Stevenson arranged for the New York company of Second City to perform a special program for foreign (including Soviet) diplomats. In Stevenson's home state, the Democratic mayor of Chicago, Richard J. Daley, although occasionally the subject of Second City jokes, decided to honor his city's homegrown satirists in 1961 by declaring a "Second City Day." In a letter of introduction to the Lord Mayor of London the following year, Daley boasted that its brand of political and social satire, although it "carries no official sanction from my office," had been "seen and enjoyed by representatives from most of our great institutions."[85]

Given the support that Stevenson, Daley, and other prominent Democrats gave America's young satirists, it is no surprise that they began to view themselves as unofficial diplomats when they appeared overseas. When a Second City company played London's Establishment Club in late October 1962, they were forced to respond to the left-leaning audience's angry and hostile requests for scenes involving the Cuban Missile Crisis. Del Close, a Stevenson stalwart like Sahl who on the Second City stage in Chicago repeatedly took shots at the Kennedy administration's aggressive anticommunist, anti-Castro foreign policy, took charge of the situation and instructed his colleagues to defend President Kennedy from criticism. In addition to pulling a scene critical of American foreign policy, Close engaged the combative London audience with tart reminders of British failures in the Suez. "I would like to point out," Close likewise told the audience, "that you are also members of NATO and that we are in this together."[86]

When Ted Flicker and his Premise troupe appeared in London a few months earlier, they called on their connections within the Kennedy administration when they became embroiled in a highly publicized dispute with Britain's Lord Chamberlain. According to British law at the time, all theater texts had to be submitted to the Lord Chamberlain, Britain's censoring agency, to see whether they contained anything that would "deprave and corrupt those whose minds are open to such immoral influences and of a nature calculated to shock common feelings of decency in any well-regulated mind." Included within the category of "subversive" theater material were impersonations of heads of state. The Premise, therefore, was barred from performing several scenes in which it poked mild fun at President Kennedy and his family. Flicker appealed directly to President Kennedy for assistance. A short while later, the president, on the advice of Vice President Johnson and several Cabinet members, sent a cable to the Lord Chamberlain's office stating that he did not mind being lampooned by the Premise.[87]

* * *

Though a minor intervention, President John Kennedy's endorsement of the Premise did serve as an important symbolic gesture. At long last, it appeared, political humor and satire had rid themselves of their inhibitions and, with the President's blessing, were free to go after anything or anyone. Reflecting back on the numerous forms of political satire spawned during 1962—the year that marked the high water mark for Anglo-American "satire boom"—Russell Baker echoed the widely held view that it was President Kennedy and his administration who were primarily responsible for creating the necessary conditions for satire's new golden era. "One of the Kennedy Administration's brighter achievements in 1962," Baker wrote in a December "Observer" column, "has been its restoration of the sound of laughter" to the American scene. Jack Kennedy has "demonstrated a taste for the game and the talent to give as well as he gets," Baker continued. "Like the twist, wigs and bossa nova, political satire has become a national fad." America under Kennedy had come a long way, Baker argued. In fact, jokes aimed at the Presidency would have been inconceivable two years ago, for at that time, he suggested, if one joked about President Eisenhower "among strangers . . . [one] was perilously open to rebuke and, sometimes, to the suggestion that he was un-American." A year later, after President Kennedy's sudden passing, a somewhat remorseful Norman Mailer similarly argued that the fallen president's "best claim to greatness was that he made an atmosphere possible in which one could be critical of him, biting, whimsical, disrespectful, imaginative, even out of line. It was the first time in America's history that one could mock the Presidency on so high a level, and we may have to live for half a century before such a witty and promising atmosphere exists again."[88]

CHAPTER SIX

"Are There Any Groups Here I Haven't Offended Yet?"

LIBERAL SATIRE TAKES A STAND

During the height of the late-1950s and early-1960s "satire boom," political humor flourished to an extent unprecedented in the postwar period. In numerous newspaper and magazine feature articles, editorials, and advertisements, it was welcomed as a long lost child. For these sources, the popularity of topical, "new wave" comedians and the sales of their albums, the success of satirical cabarets and revues, the publication of small-circulation satirical magazines such as *Monocle,* and the high profile of satiric cartoonists signaled a long overdue break from America's recent McCarthyite past, the expansion of new social and political consciousness, and the flowering of middle-class sophistication. Reviewing the newest crop of long-playing comedy albums to appear in stores in 1960, *Playboy* magazine, one of liberal satire's biggest cheerleaders, envisioned the possibilities afforded by these new "Hip Wits Disc Hits." "Serving up Nichols and May with cocktails," *Playboy* began, "then Mort Sahl on disc for dinner, followed by Lenny Bruce with the cognac, is the latest cachet of social awareness—a sort of do-it yourself nightclub with a bill of entertainment that no single club in the country can match."[1]

The critical edge of the humor appearing on these albums during the Kennedy era did not always fulfill the hype generated by *Playboy,* liberal critics, and entertainment entrepreneurs. Moreover, accounts of satire's belated return to public life during the early 1960s betrayed a certain smugness among its college-educated, middle-class fan base. The individuals who paid to see the Premise perform in the Village, bought Mort Sahl comedy albums, or avidly followed Herblock's cartoons in the *New Re-*

public were prone to consider themselves as members on the same team. Convinced of their rectitude, some enthusiasts of early-sixties satire were willing to absorb criticism directed at people of their class, education, and outlook as a way of demonstrating their tolerance and good taste. In this sense liberal satire occasionally served as a type of chic parlor game, one working to ratify rather than disrupt the assumptions of its middle-class players.

This point was not lost on perceptive critics such as the *Village Voice*'s Nat Hentoff, who in a 1961 article titled "Satire, Schmatire" equated Mort Sahl with Bob Hope and argued that Bob Newhart made Shelley Berman seem like Eugene Debs in comparison. "Beneath the mask of a comic hipster," Hentoff later wrote in *Gent,* "is usually the attitude—and goals—of an account executive." Several other observers noted that the commercial imperatives of the Second City's and the Premise's owners, coupled with their performers' political naïveté, resulted in pulled punches and a lack of real commitment. Handicapped by the fear that they might alienate the middle-class suburbanites and tourists in their audience, the Premise and, to a lesser extent, the Second City all too often dealt "bluntly with soft targets," as one observer noted, or temporized their criticism of popular public figures and institutions. "True satire is not just poking cheerful fun at something, as they do in 'From the Second City,'" wrote a *New York Daily News* critic in 1961. "It must be wicked, cruel, destructive criticism, and these nice people from Chicago aren't up to it." "One can't help concluding," another critic offered several months later, that it is the tendency of American satiric troupes such as the Premise "to have topicality that is only topography; we rarely probe below the surface of an issue; we never hurt."[2]

In terms of its political outlook, certainly, most of the satire celebrated throughout American popular culture during the 1950s and early 1960s dovetailed with the cold war liberalism of Adlai Stevenson and John F. Kennedy. Once they began to see themselves as part of the liberal establishment, American satirists yielded their positions as critical outsiders for the sake of becoming court jesters or what sociologist David Riesman termed "inside dopesters." Yet the history of American liberal satire during the 1960s does not submit neatly to the process of cooptation that critics such as Hentoff were wont to describe. Even its toughest critics allowed that popular American satire did much more than simply ratify John Kennedy's New Frontier agenda. More than a few liberal satirists were highly conscious of the dangers of "selling out" and resolved to use humor to prod the Kennedy administration and question its foreign and domestic policies. As this and the following two chapters will demonstrate, there was a sizeable body of provocative, intelligent, and trenchant satire produced during the early 1960s that criticized the domestic and foreign policy agenda of the Kennedy administration. Whether through the stand-up routines of comedian Dick Gregory, the syndicated cartoon strips of Jules Feiffer, articles published in *Monocle* and the *Outsider's Newsletter,* performances of improvisational troupes such as the Living Premise, or the film *Dr. Strangelove,* liberal satire articulated concerns that more than a few Americans — particularly civil rights supporters and New Left students — shared over American foreign policy, domestic racial inequality, and other issues that could not be ignored.

*   *   *

One good indication of satirists' willingness to test the limits of their criticism was the estrangement several of them suffered from the liberal establishment. Despite their reputation as patrons of political satire, President John Kennedy and some of his associates had little tolerance for criticism that cut too close to the bone. This was certainly evident to Norman Mailer and Gore Vidal, two writers who had supported Kennedy in the 1960 election but who later cooled toward him when he was in office. Mailer, the self-described "court wit" who shortly before the 1960 election had painted Kennedy as an existential hero (one possessing a "good lithe wit") in *Esquire* magazine, found himself cut off from the president and his wife because of critical remarks he had directed at them in 1961 and 1962.[3] Gore Vidal, a legitimate member of the Kennedy court, likewise discovered firsthand the Kennedy family's aversion to negative criticism. While still in the president's good favor, Vidal was often called upon to perform favors for the Kennedy family. At one point in 1961, John Kennedy, recognizing Vidal's capacity for stinging wit, slyly suggested that he help deflate the reputation of ex-President Dwight Eisenhower, a man whom he believed was still too much of a sacred cow. Vidal was happy to oblige Kennedy's requests, yet over time he began "spoiling, unconsciously," as he remembers in his autobiography, "for a row of some sort in order to break the Kennedy connection." He succeeded in spectacular fashion when he published an *Esquire* article in early 1963 titled "The Best Man 1968" that belittled Bobby Kennedy and his wife Ethel. By mid-1963, Vidal too had lost all access to the Kennedys.[4]

The experience of other wits and satirists further undermined the notion that the Kennedys shared a good, healthy sense of humor. According to author Bill Adler, President Kennedy became "furious" when he learned that Adler was planning a book on "The Kennedy Wit." Still stinging from the embarrassment of the Bay of Pigs incident, Adler suggests, Kennedy moved swiftly to have Random House publisher Bennett Cerf cancel the book's publication.[5] More serious yet were the troubles Mort Sahl encountered when he began to make jokes at the Kennedys' expense. Although Sahl has never implicated John Kennedy personally, he has claimed for years that people connected to the Kennedy administration and Kennedy's father in particular were so angered by the sallies he began to direct at them in 1960 that they effectively destroyed his career. As an unofficial joke writer for the Kennedy campaign in 1960, Sahl was expected to stifle his criticism of the young candidate. Kennedy and his intimates made this clear to Sahl when they called him aboard their airplane and then questioned him about jokes he had been making about Joseph Kennedy's wealth.[6] Despite warnings that he should not bite the hand that fed him, Sahl, ever the iconoclast, announced publicly that he was beholden to no one. "It is not my ambition to become court jester to the Democratic candidates for President," Sahl told a *New York Times* reporter in 1960. "They think I agree with them. They are lucky if they agree with me."[7] In this respect, it is clear that Sahl aimed to differentiate himself from Will Rogers, the comedian with whom he was most often compared. After all, if Rogers was able to claim "I never met a man I didn't like," Sahl's motto, repeated at nearly every one of his performances during the late 1950s and early 1960s, was the question, "Are there any groups here I haven't offended yet?"

Following the 1960 election, Sahl states, "the Kennedys started ruling and I started attacking them." On his first two postelection albums, *The New Frontier* and *Mort Sahl on Relationships*—both recorded on Frank Sinatra's Reprise label—Sahl took swipes at the administration and the American press's seeming infatuation with the Kennedy family. Sahl's opening line on the former (a performance recorded at the hungry i in San Francisco) was, "Here we are on the New Frontier—Cuba." He claimed here that the Kennedy administration tried to convince him that Castro posed a considerable threat to the United States "because you can see the island." "And I used to look, and I'd say, 'I can't see it,'" Sahl continued. "And they'd say, 'Well, it's right behind the aircraft carrier.'" In addition to criticizing the Kennedys' obsession with Cuba, Sahl laced his monologue with references to Attorney General Bobby Kennedy ("now Little Brother is watching you") and the "brainwashing" that was being done in the service of the Kennedy "royal family." To his credit, Sahl understood how the flair and élan of Camelot beguiled the nation's press and therefore began blasting it for its unquestioning "idolatry" of the Kennedys. United States Information Agency chief Edward R. Murrow, Sahl joked, was so enamored with the new administration that he was preparing to airdrop scores of *Time* magazine's "Inauguration Issue" on Russia.[8]

Before long, Sahl learned through his friend Hugh Hefner that Ambassador Kennedy was "going to teach me the meaning of the word 'loyalty.'" Sahl's manager, a close associate of Peter Lawford's, repeatedly warned his client of Joseph Kennedy's threats, but these warnings only prompted Sahl to do "three times as much material" on the Kennedy family—some of it particularly hard-hitting. During a monologue on ABC-TV's short-lived "Jerry Lewis Show," for example, Sahl even jokingly referred to a connection between President Kennedy, mobster Sam Giancana, and the singer Frank Sinatra.[9] Suddenly, Sahl recalls, "the work dried up." "I went back to every club where I used to work but nothing was available at any price." The new owner of Los Angeles's Crescendo reportedly informed him, "I've been told that the White House would be offended if I hired you and I'd be audited on my income tax. I heard that you offended the President." Enrico Banducci, owner of the hungry i, claims that as a result of his failure to curb Sahl, he was audited by the Internal Revenue Service and then promptly put out of business.[10]

*   *   *

As Mort Sahl's career foundered during the early sixties, cartoonist Jules Feiffer was becoming recognized as one of the sharpest political satirists working in the United States. Feiffer had originally made his mark as a commentator on the work environment, mating habits, and private anxieties of middle-class urbanites. Throughout the mid- and late 1950s, Feiffer had flayed the "self-hypocrisy" afflicting, as he put it, "my own kind," but by 1961, as he admitted to an interviewer, he was much more interested in satirizing hypocrisy "at its most serious level—the level of authority . . ." "When one of my characters is telling lies in a social situation," he continued, "he's hurting only a few people, but when it's someone lying in a position of power, then it becomes more serious and frightening." With this sentiment, Feiffer clearly echoed Sahl, and indeed the two men resembled each other in significant respects. Each professed an admiration for the other's work. As Feiffer was beginning to gain notoriety for his social satire several years earlier, Sahl appointed himself his "West Coast publicist." "I'm glad he's in our group," Sahl confided to mutual friend Hugh Hefner in 1958, "because he seems to know all our secrets." Feiffer explained their affinity to a Harvard *Crimson* interviewer in 1959, "Our outlook is similar because we have a similar approach to many things, and because some of the same things frighten us." Indeed, both Feiffer and Sahl enjoyed targeting the self-deluding, overanalyzed neurotics populating the ranks of the educated, urban upper middle class. And like his fellow *Playboy* contributor, Feiffer was very much interested in sexual politics and the troubles men and women faced in relating to each other. As an agitated, admittedly angry liberal during the mid-1950s, Feiffer took delight in Sahl's jabs at J. Edgar Hoover and President Eisenhower. But by 1963, Feiffer was left lamenting that Sahl, "the man most responsible for the breakthrough [in satiric expression] seems to have become a victim of the New Frontier."[11]

Feiffer himself did not become a "victim of the New Frontier" for several reasons. First, he operated in the more sustainable medium of cartooning and was therefore not subject to the capricious whims of executives within the broadcast and entertainment industries.[12] He also maintained a more serious commitment to left-liberal politics—a commitment that he, unlike Sahl, never really lost—and to satire as a form of dissent. As with other liberal satirists, politics figured prominently in his consciousness. He was a raised in a home of liberal Jews who idolized Franklin Roosevelt—"the only president I ever loved," he later remembered. He suspected that his father was a "closet socialist," but it was his older sister who was the family's true political rebel. A member of various left-wing political organizations while in high school and later a member of the Communist Party and organizer for the United Electrical, Radio and Machine Workers of America, Mimi Feiffer exercised a profound influence over her younger brother. "Her opinions have been rattling around in my head all my life," Feiffer stated at her funeral in 1988. From his experience debating with his sister and through contacts he made with the Jewish liberals and radicals that populated his neighborhood, Feiffer became well acquainted with the politics and the moral passion animating New York's liberal left in the interwar years.[13]

Throughout the fifties and early sixties, Feiffer's politics stood to the left of other American satirists. A self-described "subversive and propagandist," he was more attracted to the anarcho-existentialist radicalism of Paul Goodman than the centrist, cold war liberalism of Adlai Stevenson and John Kennedy. Perhaps the greatest influence on the direction of Feiffer's politics was the probing, iconoclastic journalist I. F. Stone. As Feiffer recalls, he "generally followed the I.F. Stone party line" in his political cartoons during the late fifties and early sixties. As he gained a reputation of one of the liberal left's brightest new voices, Feiffer befriended Stone and joined a circle of prominent liberal New York intellectuals and writers, including Norman Mailer, Philip Rahv, Norman Podhoretz, Philip Roth, Alfred Kazin, and Dwight Macdonald. A frequent guest at college campuses, Feiffer throughout the late 1950s and early 1960s exhorted students to question their government and its foreign policy. If they did not, he warned Princeton students in 1958, they would soon find themselves "cannon fodder."[14]

Feiffer viewed satire as a vehicle for political dissent and was able to articulate its strengths while reckoning with its pitfalls. During the 1950s, when public dialogue about important social and political subjects was severely curtailed, humor and satire, in Feiffer's view, "became a natural outlet." "It was terrible," Feiffer remembers of the time, "you couldn't say anything critical about America, you couldn't join a rent strike without being accused of being subversive." "There was no real social criticism going on. It began with people like Mort Sahl and nightclubs. You couldn't find it in the pages of the *New Yorker* or anywhere else." Since the bulk of American humor and comedy was in Feiffer's opinion "mired in insults and gags," Feiffer saw an opportunity to use his cartoons in order to translate his irreverent, satiric perspective. Unlike other satirists who issued cagey and elusive responses to questions regarding the critical content of their work, Feiffer never shrank from defining the demands and responsibilities of the satirist. Feiffer remembers thinking as a young man that if he ever was "in a position to talk to my readers I want to be able to tell them the truth [about his intentions] because there may be people like me right now who are young and need direction out there and I'm not going to fuck with their brains." As his fame grew, he took advantage of published and televised interviews to explain that it was the role of the satirist to "go against the grain of his times" and to stake a discernible position on pressing political issues—something that Harvey Kurtzman personally admonished Feiffer against doing. For a 1962 ABC television

Close Up! documentary on America's "New Humor," Feiffer addressed the obligations of satire head-on. The role of satire, he explained to a national audience, "is primarily to be subversive" and to "attack what it sees as hypocrisy."[15]

Feiffer's first attacks against the hypocrisy of those in positions of authority were leveled against President Dwight Eisenhower since he appeared to be "getting away with murder in the media." As Feiffer remembers, "Eisenhower brought me into politics and, of course, once I was in, it was irresistible." Feiffer, like his fellow cartoonist Herblock, regarded President Eisenhower not as a well-intentioned father figure but as the "bland patron of our suffocation," a man hiding behind his empty, "deliberately bumbling" rhetoric. In several strips for the *Village Voice,* Feiffer pictured the president formulating the administration's position on civil rights or foreign policy issues in his characteristic "garbled Eisenhowerese." In an October 1958 *Village Voice* strip, for example, Feiffer depicted Eisenhower's rhetorical evenhandedness regarding the crisis surrounding desegregation in Little Rock' public schools. "I want to correct any misunderstanding on this point," Feiffer's crudely drawn caricature of Eisenhower tells the press, "because I deplore the actions of extremists on both sides—those who blow up schools and those who want to keep them open. I can't stress that too firmly!"[16] Deliberately evasive and incoherent on the pressing issue of race, President Eisenhower throughout his second term in office earned the ridicule Feiffer directed at him.

Throughout the late fifties and early sixties, Jules Feiffer's nationally syndicated strips intimated that hypocrisy lingered everywhere, from the living rooms of suburban ranch houses to the classroom and big city newsroom, spilling forth from the pronouncements of cold war policy makers, educators, public relations men, members of the press, and elected officials. With these strips, Feiffer, more than any other artist working in the United States, revived the cartoon's potential for sharp, incisive satire. Feiffer's cartoons did not comment blandly on the passing scene or poke fun at elected officials; they harnessed the narrative possibility of the strip and, at their best, provided a strikingly original vehicle for commentary. In a manner not typically allowed by single-panel cartoons, Feiffer's strips were able to interrogate cold war liberalism's ideological underpinnings and follow the course of Americans' creeping disillusionment. Few other American satirists working during this period concentrated so directly, so presciently on the Bomb, racism, and the failures of mainstream American politics—concerns then resonating within the emerging New Left. And with the exception of Mort Sahl, no other New Frontier era satirist was as willing as Feiffer to directly scrutinize the character and conduct of John F. Kennedy's administration.

Like many other intellectuals and artists who identified with the left-liberal wing of the Democratic Party, Feiffer had reservations over the candidacy of John Kennedy in 1960. During much of that election season, Feiffer counted himself a Kennedy supporter. As a member of the Arts and Letters Committee for Kennedy, Feiffer was more than happy to join Robert Osborn in donating cartoon drawings for invitations to a Kennedy campaign fund-raising dinner at New York's Waldorf-Astoria Hotel. But when Kennedy accused Vice President Nixon of being soft on Cuba during their presidential debates, Feiffer became, as he recalls, "anti-Kennedy." In a *Village Voice* cartoon published on the eve of the election, Feiffer betrayed his loss of enthusiasm for Kennedy by picturing a man from a newly independent African state assessing the state of American mainstream politics. Considering the choice between Kennedy and Nixon, "two governmental careerists," and the "increasing decline of principles of sound government," this man notes, ironically, "one serious question must be raised . . . Are the American people ready for independence?"[17]

Once Kennedy was in office, Feiffer clearly bristled at the elitist aura surrounding the New Frontier's leadership. As he remembers, he, a Bronx-born Jewish intellectual, simply "could never make it with Camelot."[18] On occasion, Feiffer targeted Kennedy and his cabinet as vain and arrogant, more committed to power than to principle, more concerned with image than substance. In a strip intended to call attention to what he and other critics believed was John Kennedy's undue attention to showmanship, Feiffer depicted the president confessing his shortcomings in a jaunty song-and-dance number: "Rhythm's rhythm. Go Along . . . Liberal program easily wreckable, unimportant—Look impeccable . . . Posture strong in any crisis, in between, melt like ices . . . Power need not corrupt, it needn't even interrupt. Be amorphous, stay in office. Doing the Frontier Drag!"[19] Feiffer used his syndicated strip on other occasions to take direct aim at John Kennedy and his brother Robert. In an October 1962 strip, for example, a little girl reads a fairy tale with reference to "a beloved ruler admired for the manner in which he sought world peace and sent troops to Asier" and, in the case of the attorney

248

general, "a legal scholar, a friend of minorities and an advocate of a wire tap bill . . ."[20]

*   *   *

Like Feiffer, a number of improvisational stage performers believed that they could harness satire as a vehicle of legitimate, hard-hitting social and political criticism. Overall, members of the Second City and the Premise were far more attuned to current events and political issues than the Compass's first commercially successful performers—Shelley Berman and Nichols and May—had been. While there certainly was no consensus within the Second City on the relative merits of addressing political issues through stage improvisations—for Bernard Sahlins and those Second City performers who retained a respect for the conventions of classical theater, the most accomplished, most affecting Second City scenes were those that addressed some truth about the "human condition"—a number of key Second City performers—particularly members of Second City's founding troupe such as Roger Bowen, Howard Alk, and Andrew Duncan—believed that they might use the stage to alert audiences to political issues marginalized by America's cold war consensus. Second City members such as Paul Sills, Alan Arkin, and Avery Schreiber were children of Jewish progressives who were politically active during the 1930s. While growing up in Chicago, Paul Sills met Studs Terkel and many members of the Popular Front, "Jewish-left art community" through his mother, Viola Spolin. "We were all left-wingers," Sills remembers fondly about his early Second City colleagues. "Oh, were we left," concurs Sills's fellow Brechtian and longtime Second City member Andrew Duncan. Although Sills and Duncan may not have wished to directly emulate the overtly political Popular Front theater of the 1930s, they were committed to addressing in some way important issues of the day.[21]

More than a few Second City and Premise members understood the potential that an off-Loop, off-Broadway cabaret-style theater had in offering intelligent, up-to-the-minute topical commentary. Theodore Flicker has remarked that the Premise initially turned to political satire in response to the appetite of its Village audience, but once forced into political satire he found that he "enjoyed [it] most of all." "For me," Flicker remembers, "that was the best." Flicker's Premise billed itself as "fresh as the day's newspaper" and a "theatre whose actors are able to improvise and comment every night on the events of the day." Not long after it

CHAPTER SEVEN

opened, it devoted its entire second act to scenes—some improvised on the spot but most prepared beforehand—dealing with current events. Barbara Harris, one of several Second City performers who later achieved stardom on Broadway, told a *Village Voice* interviewer that "you couldn't put into a play" some of the world's biggest problems such as "people starving in Vietnam [and] the Bomb . . . You can only do it at Second City." Likewise, the Premise's Joan Darling claimed that she was dissatisfied with "playing children's games" onstage and would have "left the theater" if the Premise had not come along. "The older you get," she told a reporter in 1962, "the more you get interested in the world, the more you want the opportunity to say something." Others such as the Second City's Avery Schreiber, the son of a Southside Chicago union organizer, more candidly recall how performing with the troupe led to a kind of political reawakening. Under constant pressure to create new topical scenes suggested by the audience, Schreiber remembers, Second City performers were prompted to devour a wide variety of newspapers and magazines, from the *Chicago Tribune* and *Time* to I. F. Stone's weekly newsletter.[22]

In the opinion of several Second City members, the critical acclaim and sudden fame the troupe received, together with the inevitable complications caused by personal ambitions and the commercial imperatives pursued by Second City's owner, ultimately compromised the troupe's critical intentions. Roger Bowen was a writer and performer who early on believed, more than any of his Second City colleagues, that satire could be an effective tool for social and political criticism. Yet he well understood the compromises the Second City began to make once it evolved into a popular venue of entertainment. As other liberal satirists discovered throughout the late 1950s and early 1960s, Bowen came to realize that the line separating criticism and flattery could be very thin indeed. "It's funny how people react to satire," Bowen recalled in an interview with Jeffrey Sweet. "They love to be satirized. I remember one night at Second City somebody said, 'There are Ford Motor executives out there' . . . It was, 'Oooh, satirize me again!'"[23] For Bowen, Andrew Duncan, and a few other Second City performers, the sight of well-dressed corporation executives, politicians, and high-society types howling at their tables raised troubling questions about the real efficacy of their satiric commentary. To a greater degree than some Second City performers were willing to admit, the Second City found itself cast into the role of court jester. A letter to the Second City from Chicago Mayor Richard J. Daley in November 1964 certainly helped remind them of this fact. "Last Friday night's program honoring President Johnson," Daley wrote, "was, in the opinion of the members of his staff, the greatest event of its kind ever to be staged in the United States."[24]

Ultimately, the compromises that the Second City and its management made proved too great for troupe members such as Alan Myerson. Like Jules Feiffer, Mort Sahl, Paul Sills and a number of other young liberal satirists who came of age during the 1950s, Myerson was raised in a Jewish household of left-liberal Democrats. Myerson's father, an architect, worked as a set designer in Hollywood for a few years after the war but was fired and then blacklisted for attempting to organize a studio union. Myerson's brother Michael also absorbed his parents' clearly defined political principles and became a founding member of SLATE, a student political party organized at the University of California at Berkeley in the late fifties. He later worked as a radical political activist throughout the sixties. Committed to social justice like his father and brother but lacking a clear sense of vocation, Alan Myerson decided to drop out of UCLA and move to New York City. In the late 1950s he drifted into off-Broadway theater and eventually began to direct.[25]

Based on the work he had done with an offbeat revue called *The Stewed Prunes,* Myerson was hired by the Second City in 1961 (upon the recommendation of Roger Bowen) to direct its new replacement cast in Chicago. Throughout late 1961 and 1962, he directed Second City companies in Chicago, New York, and, briefly, Shaker Heights, Ohio. Although he was satisfied with some of the work he and his colleagues did in the Second City, he lamented that there was, as he remembers, no "real solid political stance in the theatrical culture there." Testing the patience of Second City's management, Myerson, according to Del Close, picketed the Kennedy administration outside the theater during the Cuban Missile Crisis.[26] Frustrated by the Second City's lack of political commitment, its penchant for highbrow patter, and the internecine squabbles taking place between Second City performers and management, Myerson decided to move west and initiate his own improvisational troupe.[27]

In early 1963, he and his wife Irene Riordan (another Second City alumnus) began preparing an improvisational theater in San Francisco, one that would draw from the iconoclastic milieu surrounding the city's North Beach area. With funding gathered from an intriguing variety of sources including six Bay Area psychiatrists, writers such as Herbert Gold, businessmen, and several labor leaders, Myerson and Riordan constructed a new three-hundred-seat theater on the site of a former bocce ball court. In an ironic tribute to the House Committee on Un-American Activities Committee—the Congressional investigatory body that had earned the enmity of liberals and radicals like his parents since the late 1940s and that in 1960 spurred his brother and other UC Berkeley students to demonstrations in San Francisco—Myerson and his wife named it the Committee. For performers, Myerson and Riordan recruited an assortment of actors and jazz and folk musicians, many of whom had worked previously with the Compass, the Second City, and the Premise.

From the moment Myerson's troupe began performing in April 1963, it drew favorable comparisons with its improvisational predecessors. A number of critics who saw the Committee also noted its affinity with Jules Feiffer's cartoon work. As the *New York Post*'s Richard Watt put it, the Committee had "a charm, brightness, wit and a civilized young intelligence full of satirical awareness of a Jules Feiffer kind . . ."[28] Like Feiffer and many other satirists of the late 1950s and early 1960s, Myerson and his colleagues were prone to making bold pronouncements about how satire might provide cant-ridden America with some "truth" and "authenticity." In typical fashion Myerson pronounced, "We're all in the same boat and it's leaking. We're all accomplices in a hypocritical world: our job is to walk through it, pointing."[29] Myerson well understood that pointing out hypocrisy had its financial rewards as well. In 1964 he and his troupe followed the path of Nichols and May and the Second City to Broadway, where in a successful limited engagement they performed a well-rehearsed and carefully edited version of their program to audiences at the Henry Miller Theatre.

The connection between the Committee and its predecessors was most apparent in the range of subjects it chose to address onstage. Parodies of folksinging groups and modern psychological jargon and comic scenes involving sex, seduction, and surreal confrontations with mechanical people were all part of the repertoire the Committee prepared for its Broadway run. Scenes about homosexuals and effeminate (often "intellectual") males were occasionally performed by the Compass, Second City, and Premise, so it was not a surprise that the Committee included one entitled "Bar Scene" in its program. Here the Committee comically depicted what might happen when a straight businessman (Larry Hankin) accidentally wanders into a San Francisco gay bar. Once again ratifying popular satire's thoroughly masculine orientation, the Committee here comically ridiculed (much to the audience's delight) Garry Goodrow's gay character.

"Are There Any Groups Here I Haven't Offended Yet?"

29. The Committee in 1963 (clockwise from bottom): Hamilton Camp, Irene Riordan, Garry Goodrow, Larry Hankin, Ellsworth Milburn, Kathryn Ish, and Scott Beach. Courtesy of Alan Myerson.

Although Michael Smith, the theater critic for the *Village Voice,* appreciated "Bar Scene," he presciently noted that the tone of such material made the Committee seem smug and, at bottom, "all very hip on roughly the level of the *Playboy* Philosophy." Smith's criticisms mirrored those of several left-leaning critics whose expectations for hard-hitting satiric scenes were disappointed by the early Committee. One of these critics, San Francisco Beat poet Kenneth Rexroth, compared the Committee's scenes to "charades in a Quaker work camp." Yet at least one other left-liberal, Popular Front veteran could not dismiss the Committee so easily. Group Theatre founder Harold Clurman praised the Committee in the *Nation,* noting that its intentions seemed "actually more political and specifically critical than is common in some of this show's Greenwich Village counterparts."[30]

Many people familiar with the range of the Committee's work back in San Francisco—far away from the commercial constraints that were surely imposed by the Committee's producer, Arthur Cantor—concurred with Clurman's favorable assessment. The Committee, in fact, had become the darling of Bay Area writers including poet Michael McClure and *San Francisco Chronicle* columnist Ralph Gleason. Through them, word of the Committee's funny and astringent social and political satires spread quickly. By the summer of 1963, the Committee's original audience of second-generation North Beach Beats and college students (many of them from UC Berkeley in particular) had expanded to educated, urban professionals from the suburbs. Taking note of the Committee's wide and devoted following, the left-liberal journal *Ramparts* in December 1964 claimed that its "instant theater" had indeed become "a forum and a club and a warm little island for thousands of exurbanite liberals who have no town square (just drive-ins) and no viable church or political party in which to celebrate honest ideals."[31]

What won the admiration of student radicals and exurbanites alike were the Committee's satiric commentaries on the absurdity of the cold war, racism, and the hypocrisy of white, middle-class liberals, among other topics. More consistently than either the Second City or the Premise, the Committee confronted its audiences with material that was deliberately provocative. Some liberals who saw the Committee perform in New York in 1964 reportedly took offense at jokes the Committee made at the expense of Adlai Stevenson, a sacred cow among many liberals. In the scene "Failure 101," an earnest student taking an oral examination cited Stevenson as a perfect example of a failure in business, government, and religion—what his professor calls "a true Renaissance Man of failure." According to witness Nat Hentoff, the jabs at Adlai Stevenson in "Failure 101" elicited angry hisses from the liberals in the audience. More controversial yet was the Committee's commentary on convicted killer Caryl Chessman. In a scene performed in 1963 and 1964, a liberal warden, prison chaplain, and the California governor assure the death row inmate that they care deeply about his plight. Referring to his impending death in the electric chair, they tell him, "It will hurt us more than it will hurt you." When the time has come for the prisoner to receive his sentence, the current from the electric chair suddenly fails. The three men who moments before had expressed their remorse then quickly move in and pummel the defenseless prisoner to death. For a critic such as the *New York Herald Tribune*'s Walter Kerr, this scene, like so much other "doomsday comedy" in 1964 America, was "drawn down into an abyss," its exposure of hypocrisy simply too real and too dark to be funny.[32]

Like another San Francisco theater group, R. G. Davis's San Francisco Mime Troupe, the Committee also distinguished itself with its political activism at the local level. Under Alan Myerson's direction, the Committee translated its commitment to peace and social justice—the ideals underwriting its satiric performances—into political engagement. Myerson led Committee troupe members such as Garry Goodrow—a jazz musician and former performer in Julian Beck's Living Theater who had been arrested in the mid-1950s for protesting New York City air-raid drills—in sit-in demonstrations at San Francisco's Federal Building and had them perform benefits for civil rights groups such as the Congress on Racial Equality (CORE) and the Student Nonviolent Coordinating Committee (SNCC).[33]

In the summer of 1963, Peter Cook's "the Establishment" played to packed audiences at the hungry i, not far from the North Beach headquarters of the Committee. At previous engagements at the Theater Club in Washington, D.C., Second City in Chicago, and Strollers Theatre Club in New York, Cook's ensemble distinguished itself with satirical material that was at times trenchant and politically astute. In addition to taking shots at President Kennedy and the Bay of Pigs fiasco, Bobby Kennedy (in a bit that critic Judith Crist branded "tasteless") disgraced army general Edwin Walker, as well as America's involvement in Southeast Asia. The Establishment featured mock news interviews, and most novel of all, a presentation of topical film clips juxtaposed in a manner that many audiences considered wickedly funny. Throughout late 1962 and early 1963, the Establishment in fact closed its program with a film montage that was accompanied by a romantic ballad titled "Sitting Around." Interspersed with images of various heads of state and the Royal family at leisure were newsreel clips of riots and police brutality, picket lines, and world famine and, finally, exploding nuclear bombs. According to *Saturday Review* critic Henry Hewes, this film had "an undeniably effective impact," despite the fact that many found its dark irony "unpleasant." Early in 1963, the Establishment performed a parody of the film *Advise and Consent* in which British Foreign Secretary Sir Alec Douglas-Home was portrayed as a drag queen. When performed in Washington, this scene spurred one Washington newspaper correspondent in the audience to mutter appreciatively to his partner, "salacious, salacious," and it reportedly motivated McGeorge Bundy and Arthur Schlesinger Jr. to question troupe member John Bird about Douglas-Home's "masculinity."[34]

Taken as a whole, the type of material that Bird, Cook, Jeremy Geidt and their Establishment colleagues presented onstage impressed many with its satiric daring. One New York audience member who witnessed the Establishment described it as "highly bracing fare." Similarly impressed, a *Theatre Arts* critic gushed that the Establishment "provided the most freely creative experience in our lives." After witnessing the Establishment's "smartly incisive strokes," Harold Clurman questioned whether it was appropriate to criticize the "nihilistic" cultural rebellion taking root in the early 1960s. "I have begun to wonder," Clurman wrote in the *Nation,* "whether it is not foolish to be critical of the noisy or bleak mockery I sometimes find objectionable. For today, it seems, the nihilists are our only radicals."[35]

In the minds of some audience members, particularly those patrons (including politicians) who walked out of performances, the Establishment's "bleak mockery" crossed the line of propriety. According to press and critics' accounts, the Establishment did not always receive a warm, enthusiastic reception from audiences. Even though the Establishment played to sold-out crowds in San Francisco, audience reaction there was so slow that Jeremy Geidt had to explain to the *New York Times* that "the audiences haven't seemed to really know what they were coming to see." Undeterred, Geidt and his colleagues shared the aim of "making people reconsider some of the values they already have." In other interviews, Establishment members encouraged the perception that they were independent foreign observers and therefore beholden to no one, not even the president. John Bird even bragged that when President Kennedy attempted to contact a cabinet official attending an Establishment performance in Washington, he was told to wait since the troupe would not tolerate interruptions.[36]

*   *   *

Although *Monocle* and the *Outsider's Newsletter* were ostensibly edited with "Jack" Kennedy in mind, although they owed their success in large part to the improved climate for political humor that the Kennedy administration helped bring about, both publications proved quite adept at exposing the weaknesses and hypocrisies of moderate, mainstream liberals. Indeed, *Monocle* and the *Outsider's Newsletter* at times gave the impression of operating beyond the left flank of the Democratic Party. *Monocle's* politics often mirrored the type of independent radicalism kept alive during the fifties by I. F. Stone and C. Wright Mills and revived by the student New Left in the early sixties. In hindsight, Victor Navasky—since 1978 the editor of the *Nation*—has defined the political slant of *Monocle* as "progressive . . . with a socialist openness to anarcho-socialist solutions."[37] Indeed, when Navasky reprinted an article from the *New Leader* titled "What Is Socialism?" in the first issue of *Monocle,* it appeared that he was going to steer his magazine on a course further to the left than most mainstream and liberal publications.

The initial issue of the *Outsider's Newsletter* was branded the "No Dynasty Issue," and within it Navasky and his colleagues took a shot at the president's younger brother Edward. In the first of many counterfeit news stories that it would deploy to satirize the Kennedys, the *Outsider's Newsletter* here reported that John Kennedy had established a foundation "to provide other unqualified, mediocre young men the same advantages" as his youngest brother enjoyed while campaigning for the Senate in Massachusetts. In numerous pieces such as "The Ordeal of Power," Leonard Lewin's wicked parody of Arthur Schlesinger Jr. and Eisenhower speechwriter Emmett Hughes, *Monocle* and the *Outsider's Newsletter* took aim at the president's other brother, the headstrong, irascible attorney general. While criticizing Robert Kennedy's wife for her "comic skill in the role of Washington society leader," the *Outsider's Newsletter* took aim at the high social standing and elitism of Jackie Kennedy. "Americans need some pomp and glitter," it imagined the First Lady complaining, "Democracy is so drab." As C. D. B. Bryan's "Jack and Jackie: A Perfect Day for Honeyfitz" (modeled along the lines of J. D. Salinger's *Franny and Zooey*) demonstrated, *Monocle* and the *Outsider's Newsletter* showed little compunction about subjecting the president himself to satiric ridicule. Quoting a film critic who opined that actor Cliff Robertson in *PT-109* played John Kennedy with "the sense of a man doing his best to exercise unfamiliar authority with wisdom and justice," the *Outsider's Newsletter* quipped, "That's nothing—Jack's been playing it that way for the last three years."[38]

The satiric jabs *Monocle* and the *Outsider's Newsletter* directed at President John Kennedy were in large part rooted in the disappointment their editors and contributors shared over New Frontier liberalism and the administration's measured, cautious response to the civil rights movement in particular. Reflective of this frustration was contributor Dan Wakefield's satiric accounting of the "radical middle's" hold on the Kennedy administration and national politics, published in the summer of 1963. Describing the "Thunder in the Middle," Wakefield here commented critically on political moderates and their obeisance to "responsible," middle-of-the-road political solutions. Although John Kennedy initially disappointed "Radical Moderates" with the commitments he made on the campaign trail, Radical Moderates eventually realized "that his slogans are far more inflammatory than his deeds . . ." "[W]hen we 'look at the record,'" Wakefield commented, "we find that his program rests remarkably close to what might be termed 'Dead Center.'"[39]

Cartoonist Jules Feiffer had by this time also become increasingly critical of what he identified as the "disillusionment of the liberals" and President Kennedy's deliberate "radical middle" strategy—a strategy, as Feiffer understood it, by which the president aimed to cancel out opposition from the left and right through accommodations to both "extremes." His frustration with the wishy-washy tack taken by Kennedy administration officials and New Frontier liberals resulted in a series of strips, beginning in 1962, satirizing what he also labeled the "radical middle." Reminiscent of the critical spirit informing Herblock's earlier jibes at "middle-of-the-roadism," these strips staged fictional interviews with a spokesman for "The Radical Middle." Willfully blind to the contradictions of his positions, this modern-day liberal pledged to favor labor but not "the need to strike" and announced support for "a strong civil rights program" lacking "the undue haste which creates deep scars." Summarizing his cohort's out-

"Are There Any Groups Here I Haven't Offended Yet?"

look in yet another strip, this figure declares, "Bold times call for bold answers. Within reason. In a manner of speaking. More or less." An October 1963 syndicated strip again featured an interview with a spokesman for the Radical Middle Party. "The Radical Middle believes that all power once obtained, collapses toward the middle," he states. "The Radical Middle strongly favors free elections just so long as there continue to be no real differences between the parties." "Then you have no preference at all in next year's elections?" asks his interviewer, to which the spokesman replies, "We have met the candidates and they are ours."[40]

While commencing work on a book titled *Man in the Radical Middle,* Feiffer delivered speeches and wrote articles addressing liberalism's moral drift and the attendant challenges facing satire and other forms of dissent. In response to critics such as a Harvard *Crimson* writer who asked whether it should not "worry Feiffer that of all people," Arthur M. Schlesinger Jr., an avowed admirer of Feiffer's political cartoons, "should find his commentary so palatable?" Feiffer acknowledged that "the Kennedys" and their supporters "had learned how to make [satire] ineffectual by embracing it." Gone were the days when political satire was dangerous, when listening to Mort Sahl was like "singing Spanish Civil War Songs at Fort Dix, New Jersey," Feiffer maintained. "Laughing at McCarthy in those dear gone days," Feiffer wrote in the *Crimson* in March 1962, "was like laughing at God—or worse—J. Edgar Hoover." By the early 1960s, however, Sahl had contributed jokes to John Kennedy's speeches. Nichols and May had performed before the president at his Madison Square Garden birthday celebration. And "no one laughed louder" than the Kennedys, Feiffer wryly observed.[41]

While underestimating the potential for genuine, potent challenges to the liberal establishment—a potential soon realized by members of the SNCC and SDS—Feiffer's analysis of the radical middle and the process of cooptation raised important questions concerning the impact of the Kennedy-era "satire boom." With candor, Feiffer admitted to himself, to readers, and to college audiences who invited him speak that popular satire "like much of our current social criticism, is very much an accepted part of the system." In a handwritten drafts to comments he made on satire's effectiveness, Feiffer noted,

> No one gets hurt by it. No one disagrees with it. Everyone (attacker and attackee) has a wonderful time with it. The Birchite may be annoyed but no one in any position of *real* power will be. My own work is no exception. The coterie I attack is the coterie that loves me most for the attention I give them.[42]

Once the weapon of "losers," Feiffer argued, satire had now been embraced by educated, affluent "new style" liberals, publicized by *Time* magazine (in its 1959 "Sickniks" article), and peddled by entertainment entrepreneurs. "'Attack us!' came the cry from the audience across the land, 'attack our corrupt middle class values. We will laugh as long as you don't make us listen. We will applaud as long as you don't ask us to think.'" "That's why [satirists] are so popular today," he continued. "If a satirist represented even the slightest threat to our established institutions he'd be in and out of jail with the rest of the Smith Act cases. The marvel of American society about which there hasn't been nearly enough comment is our ability to swallow our critics."[43]

Feiffer's pronouncements clearly exaggerated the process of cooptation and contradicted his own stated beliefs in satire's critical potential. But Feiffer was nevertheless contributing an astute and necessary corrective to the impression, often exaggerated by the press, that popular American satire was a bold challenge to the status quo and a portent of sweeping changes in public consciousness. While its popularity during the 1950s and early 1960s evidenced a new critical awareness taking hold among educated, middle-class Americans, satire's social impact was overestimated by both its supporters and its detractors.

Feiffer's critiques had other intentions as well. By raising questions concerning liberal audiences' reception and cooptation of popular satire, Feiffer was at the same time calling his fellow satirists to task for their timidity and complacency. Feiffer took direct aim at his cohort in a brief playlet titled "You Should Have Caught Me at the White House," published in the July 1963 issue of *Holiday* magazine. Feiffer here adopted the persona of a "Satirist" who engages several other colleagues in a debate on what obligations they carry as political critics and commentators. Throughout their dialogue Feiffer exposes the Vaughn Meader and Shelley Berman–type "satirists" as sellouts who are at bottom unwilling to say anything that might alienate their audience. Several years earlier, in an interview for the *Realist,* Feiffer complained that too many American satirists during the Kennedy era had made a critical transition from the position of "I'm not kidding, things are wrong" to "I'm only kidding, things are wrong." "It's the difference in attitude between a man fired by the company telling a joke on the company," Feiffer astutely remarked, "and the man who fired him telling a joke on the company—at the company picnic, of course." Moreover, at a time when social and political satire were becoming more acceptable and marketable, the satirist had begun to "jump up and down a bit too frantically in order to get attention; to wave his flag while waiving his imagination; to do what is chic rather than what is basic." It is too easy "for an artist to feel daring and nonconformist and still stand for nothing," he added. "In a room full of deaf-mutes, the slightest, most subtle whisper will sound like an explosion of sound to the man who makes it. He often forgets that the deaf-mutes haven't heard a thing."[44] What he and his fellow satirists needed to remember, he told audiences in 1962, is that it is "important to be in constant opposition to the regime," for "subversion is the legitimate province of the satirist." Feiffer continued,

> If he's not in the business to overthrow one institution or another; if he's only in business to poke irreverent but gentle fun, to amuse without biting, to comment without caring then, in my terms, he may be a lampoonist or a parodist or a light humorist, but he's not a satirist.[45]

In the end, Feiffer still held out hope that satire could serve a vital purpose by communicating to the "silent disorganized" and "dissatisfied" Americans who "feel they are alone." In drafts and notes for speeches and writings Feiffer prepared in 1962, Feiffer reminded himself that reaching this group still made work "worthwhile."

> They feel they must operate as an underground, be quiet about the dangerous ideas whether these ideas concern the recognition of Red China or the recognition of Red Cuba . . . [then they] see a nationally distributed cartoon in rather respectable, conservative newspapers suggest that at least a few of their questions can be posed in public and nobody gets shot for it, they get to feel, I think, a little less paranoid about their sense of separation. It makes them a little more open. It helps allow the undebatable questions of a few years ago change the atmosphere enough to at least be debated if not satisfactorily answered.[46]

Much like Jules Feiffer, Mort Sahl by 1963 had grown leery of the overinflated praise liberal satire had been receiving. "There's hundreds of people running around called 'The New Comedians,'" Sahl complained in an interview, "but none of them are *saying* anything." For Sahl, the New Comedians, well paid and in awe of the Kennedys, behaved more like sycophants than satirists. "You cannot have a protective cloak over the Democrats . . . forever," Sahl maintained. "We've got to look at them and see what they are. But that means looking *completely*. That doesn't mean people saying, 'Don't you think the President's doing a wonderful job?' . . . "

With too few satirists, critics, and intellectuals holding the Kennedys and Democrats accountable for their political compromises, Sahl further argued, the New Deal liberalism of his parent's generation had regrettably succumbed to the radical middle consensus that Feiffer had described. "The administration with few exceptions is generally in agreement with the Republicans," Sahl argued. "You have to compromise to be a *Democrat,* so you might as well—you can be a Republican at the same time, you don't have to cross the road. It's two stores on one side of the street." "The Republicans will never run a Republican, any more than the Democrats will run a Democrat. That's *all over* in America." "I mean the whole thing is *ugh!*" Though frustrated by this state of affairs, Sahl was no more willing to forfeit his satiric criticism than was Feiffer. While renouncing any ties to the Democratic mainstream—"Listen," he told his interviewer, "I'm so much farther on than that"—Sahl declared that "you've got to give [the American audience] the facts; you've got to get to the people." Consonant with the messianic temperament that he had begun to manifest publicly in 1960, Sahl concluded, "That's the virtue of night clubs. *Get to that audience.*"[47]

*   *   *

For Sahl, Feiffer, and a few other of the more serious, daring, and politically minded satirists at work in the early 1960s, the threat of "selling out" or of being "coopted" loomed large. To a Chicago newspaper reporter in 1963 Feiffer confessed, "My only unhappiness is the way I find myself being accepted by the very people I'm trying to wound. They wound me by loving me to death while I'm expressing my hostility." Sahl meanwhile declared that he was "completely in favor of being accepted by the Establishment, but you have to be accepted on your own terms." British performers and critics were by and large more acutely aware of the dangers of "selling out." When Beyond the Fringe's Jonathan Miller contemplated the challenges facing Peter Cook's Establishment, he warned of the threat of "castration by adoption." Recalling the elite, establishment appeal of the Fringe, a troupe whose admirers included Queen Elizabeth and Princess Margaret, Miller stated, "Each night, before curtain-up, sleek Bentleys evacuate a glittering load into the foyer. Some of the harsh comment in the programme is greeted with shrill cries of well-bred delight which reflect a self-indulgent narcissism which takes enormous pleasure in gazing at the satiric reflection." When it was reported that the queen adored Peter Cook's impersonation of Prime Minister Harold Macmillan, Miller told reporters, "It proves we haven't done our job properly." [48]

To some London critics, the Fringe had become, in the words of the *Daily Telegraph,* little more than "court jesters to the affluent society." Former *Punch* editor Malcolm Muggeridge, a frequent advocate for satire, was one of several British critics and intellectuals who expressed skepticism about the feats of the Fringe and the Establishment. After witnessing the latter, he was struck "by the general air of affluence." "Laughter is bold as brass," Muggeridge commented. "Indeed, it is the Brass who laugh." "The lash [of modern satire] falls on willing shoulders, and evokes cries, not of pain or outrage, but of delight." "The pleasure that is taken in contemporary satire by its victims," he concluded, "necessarily raises certain doubts about it." [49]

According to the Premise's Theodore Flicker, the realization that his troupe had been coopted prompted him to initiate a new venture in improvisational satire, one which was capable of tackling the controversial and emotionally laden subject of American race relations. In interviews and in a promotional article for his new troupe, the Living Premise, Flicker described how he eventually decided to assume a more risky approach to improvisational satire. When the Premise opened in 1960, he claimed, "we felt called upon . . . to start doing political satire and improvise." By 1962, however, it appeared that nearly everyone was "doing satire." [50] Flicker describes the epiphany that altered his course:

> And then one day I realized it was all bullshit . . . The political satire part of it . . . It was political, but it was acceptable. We were playing in London, and [Prime Minister] Harold Macmillan was watching us make fun of Harold Macmillan . . . And he laughed and applauded, and I came backstage and said: 'We're doing something wrong; that man should be running from the theatre in horror, going to the Lord Chamberlain to close us down.' [51]

In effect, Flicker confesses, "we and the Second City were all giving a sort of intellectual stamp of approval to the very people we were satirizing by satirizing them very gently . . ." [52] Flicker claimed elsewhere in 1963,

> Fact is, or was, that we were the first of the safe satirists. When it was just The Premise . . . three years ago we were the only one doing political and social satire. We thought we were pretty daring and that we would be accomplishing one of the ideals of theater: to educate while entertaining; to use laughter, shock and terror as a means of social reflection. But the fact is we were deluded. The

incredible cowardice of television, perhaps, made our timid forays into social satire seem more pungent than they were.[53]

*　　*　　*

In the end, Flicker decided to close *The Premise* and, as he announced to the press, "open with a new show that would speak on the dominant issue in American life today, the race problem."[54] Retitled *The Living Premise*, Flicker's new improvisational program would attempt to represent African Americans' perspective on race relations. Joan Darling, the former Premise member whom Flicker appointed to direct the new venture, likewise recalls that *The Living Premise*'s primary aim was to use improvisational theater and humor to "find out what black people really think." Both Flicker and Darling were liberal Jews committed to the ideal of racial equality. By presenting the satiric perspective of blacks on the Premise's stage, they hoped to provide an outlet for African American expression and, at the same time, raise the consciousness of white liberals like themselves. Darling, whose husband was a member of the folk group the Weavers and one of the original Freedom Riders, believed that through *The Living Premise* she and her colleagues "could make changes" and at the very least "enlighten people." "We were carrying a banner," she remembers. "We were bright shining lights of belief."[55]

The Living Premise was not the first satiric stage production of the sixties to use black actors and prod American race relations. In late September 1961, *Purlie Victorious,* a play that slyly mocked black and white stereotypes, premiered on Broadway with an integrated cast. *Purlie Victorious* was the creation of black actor and civil rights activist Ossie Davis. By melding the African American oral tradition with the poignant Yiddish folklore he had absorbed as the stage manager for *The World of Sholom Aleichem,* Davis created in *Purlie Victorious* a play that he hoped would "laugh [racial segregation] out of existence!" Unfortunately, since white audiences were reportedly uncomfortable with the "raucous laughter" Davis' play prompted from black theatergoers, they reportedly stayed away in droves. In the end, *Purlie Victorious* managed to stay alive for seven months, largely through the patronage of black church congregations.[56]

To their credit, Flicker and Darling managed to enlist two of the best African American comic actors working in New York, both them formerly in the cast of *Purlie Victorious:* Godfrey Cambridge and Diana Sands. In addition to his role in *Purlie Victorious,* the smart, physically im-

30. Members of the Living Premise (top to bottom): Al Freeman Jr., Diana Sands, Calvin Ander, Jo Ann Le Compte, and Godfrey Cambridge. *Daniel Blum's Theatre World,* 1963.

posing method actor Cambridge had earlier distinguished himself in Jean Genet's searing off-Broadway racial drama *The Blacks,* for which he won a *Village Voice* Obie award. Sands likewise impressed critics and audiences with her performance in Lorraine Hansberry's *Raisin in the Sun.* As a member of the short-lived Hyannisport Compass, she was also one of the very few African Americans to be hired by the popular improvisational troupes.[57] Rounding out *The Living Premise*'s integrated cast were another black actor, Al Freeman Jr., and two white actors, Calvin Ander and Jo Ann Le Compte.

At their initial rehearsals, codirectors Flicker and Joan Darling had Living Premise actors engage in a type of group therapy session, where Cambridge, Sands, and Freeman revealed their experiences as African Americans living in a racist society. These three actors, whom Flicker claimed joined the Living Premise on the condition that "they could tell it like it is," apparently succeeded at first in lowering "major barriers" with their white colleagues. In an article for the *New York Herald Tribune,* Darling claimed that Living Premise rehearsals had been a "revelation" to her "as a 'white' who has had many Negro friends." By "reaching each other through honesty and through laughter," she wrote, Living Premise actors were creating a "theater of truth," a place that Darling hoped might "dispel the embarrassment that haunts us all . . . tell the truth about color . . . let the audience hear the voice of the Negro and . . . make people see the laughter in the difficult situation we now face as Americans." Flicker likewise told a *New Yorker* writer visiting rehearsals that "These kids . . . believe that this is the most important work being done by actors—especially Negro actors—in America today, this letting race relations happen publicly." "Real dramatic integration," he continued, "is actually possible only in improvisation, when all responses are quick, personal, and honest, and not the products of afterthought." After Flicker turned to Cambridge and asked whether they *were* "reacting to each other without restraint," Cambridge responded, "Not quite, but we sure are getting there . . ."[58]

When *The Living Premise* premiered on June 13, 1963, it offered audiences a mix of fast-paced scenes such as "The Emasculation of Militant Negro Organizations by White Northern Liberals" and "The Negro Sexual Myth." In the former, three black militants plot to kidnap Jackie Kennedy from a New York department store. Their plan is foiled when a white liberal lawyer ("a great friend and defender of the Negro") assumes control and instead calls Ralph Bunche to request "a study . . . of the possibility . . . of recommending a committee . . . to look into . . ." the situation. The latter satirized a liberated white woman named, appropriately, Anita O'Fay who demands of the black man she is pursuing, "Don't treat me like a white woman—let yourself go."[59] In addition to set scenes involving hypocritical white liberals and interracial love, Living Premise members improvised a question and answer session with their audience. Here Sands, Cambridge, and Freeman lampooned black militants, "Uncle Toms," and other stereotyped black characters through their impromptu replies.

Short summaries of scenes mentioned here fail to evoke the sense of moral earnestness and daring that audiences appreciated most about *The Living Premise*. If it did not live up to its claim for being "The Wildest Satire Ever!" it nevertheless impressed many with its crusading spirit. By all accounts, the Living Premise created satiric theater that was often "breathtaking" and filled with "extraordinary moments." Because of this, it remained popular throughout the summer of 1963. Numerous black entertainers reportedly visited the Living Premise regularly, including the young comedian Bill Cosby, who was then performing across the street at a venue called the Bitter End. New York theater critics for the most part shared audiences' enthusiasm. According to the *Village Voice* and the *New York Times*, Flicker's new program had an effect that was "very disturbing" and almost "paralyzing." One overwhelmed reviewer wrote that it "might well be responsible for laughing bigotry right out of the hearts of the most frightened segregationists."[60] *The Living Premise* even attracted the notice of the Paris *Presse*, which ran a picture of Le Compte and Freeman kissing above a caption reading, "L'amour impossible du Noir et de la Blanche."

Not surprisingly, conservative audiences and critics were little impressed by what they witnessed at the Living Premise. This did not matter much to Flicker or Darling since both believed firmly in the righteousness of their cause. "We did not take any prisoners," Darling remembers, "and if an audience was going to come and see this show they had to stand up to the way the world should be as far as we were concerned." Flicker was actually quite proud of the fact that he lost audience members every night. Years later he recalled his satisfaction at having offended people like his mother with a cliché-reversing scene in which a black middle-class couple kindly offer their pregnant Jewish maid an old dress to wear to the *Hadassah*. When the maid fails to express the appropriate amount of gratitude the couple complain that "you just can't be nice to those people." "Well," Flicker later related of this scene, "we offended so many people in New York with that that I knew it was serving the function."[61] More controversial yet was the scene in which the black militants plot to kidnap the First Lady, who was pregnant at the time.[62]

Among the ranks of the offended was a conservative reviewer for the *Brooklyn Eagle*. He objected to *The Living Premise*'s "aggressively interracial skits" and argued that "the cumulative effect of the evening is of a one-note joke, conceived and executed in bitterness, and played out to the fraying point." Joining him was Judith Crist, critic for the *New York Herald Tribune*. Although she lauded *The Living Premise*'s motives and complemented the quality of its satire, she maintained that it proved that "there are limits" to how much "humorous bitterness" an audience should be exposed to when considering sensitive issues such as America's race relations.[63]

Ultimately, it was not the bitterness that *The Living Premise* communicated to audiences but the ill will it eventually generated among its integrated cast that precipitated its demise. In short, what began in a spirit of honesty and openness ended in acrimony and mistrust. It is clear that the white members of the cast had difficulty accepting the true feelings and the rage black cast members displayed on and off the stage. Calvin Ander, the cast member who played the role of the white, middle-class suburbanite, was so often humiliated and intimidated by his black colleagues that he finally quit the show. Joan Darling considered herself well-informed, so she was "stunned" when Cambridge, Sands, and Freeman suggested that the Kennedy administration was not doing all that it could to support the civil rights cause.[64]

Ted Flicker was also not entirely prepared to handle the challenges of his enterprise. Before *The Living Premise* opened, he confessed to a *New York Herald Tribune* reporter, "I consider myself fairly 'hip' on most subjects ... but what I don't know about what these people feel is staggering." "Here I was," Flicker later recalled, "a middle-class Jewish guy, well-educated ... [but] I never met a Negro as an equal until I met Godfrey Cambridge." During rehearsals Cambridge challenged Flicker regularly, at one point demanding that his employer stop giving his Jewish prejudice "crap" since every time he walked down the street people still saw a white person. Flicker was easily ruffled by what he interpreted as Cambridge's ingratitude. Shortly after Flicker offered the cast a financial stake in *The Living Premise,* Cambridge reported him to Actors Equity for violating certain dressing room regulations. Eventually Cambridge and Sands suspected that Flicker was withholding profits and quit. A short time later Flicker angrily informed their replacements and the other cast members, "Listen, you sons of bitches. You turned me into Mr. Charlie, and now I'm doing what Mr. Charlie does: I'm closing the fucking show."[65]

On November 3, 1963, after 192 performances in the Village, *The Living Premise* ceased its run. Although compromised by internecine squabbles and dissention, *The Living Premise* had provided its cast members a valuable venue for acting out and commenting on issues that divided white and black Americans. At its best, *The Living Premise* validated the hope that Jules Feiffer and other liberal satirists shared over satire's critical potential. Though popular American satire, taken as a whole, was hardly the revolutionary cultural movement trumpeted by its critical and commercial advocates, it did provide writers, artists, and performers a vehicle to critically assess urgent social and political issues of the day. For Godfrey Cambridge, the opportunity to address racial prejudice through bold, honest humor did not end with *The Living Premise*'s demise. By the time Cambridge departed he had already begun to translate his satiric perspective into a successful stand-up comedy act, thus following the example set by black comedian Dick Gregory. As Cambridge, Gregory, and a number of other performers, artists, and writers well understood, satire directed at American race relations was in great demand during the peak years of the modern civil rights movement.

CHAPTER EIGHT

"Well-Aimed Ridicule"

SATIRIZING AMERICAN RACE RELATIONS

For the white and black members of the short-lived Living Premise improvisational troupe, there was no other subject more urgent, no topic more worthy of satiric criticism than the racial crisis enveloping the United States during the 1950s and early 1960s. On this, liberal satirists of all stripes could agree. While African Americans engaged in a struggle for racial justice and equal rights—the most significant mass movement in modern times—American satirists routinely assaulted the South's stubborn resistance to desegregation and the persistence throughout the United States of racial bigotry and prejudice. Occasionally, this was liberal satire at its best, holding President John Kennedy, Attorney General Robert Kennedy, and members of the administration accountable for failing to live up to their promises and exposing uncomfortable truths about white liberals' hypocrisy. Offered by black and white artists, writers and performers, this liberal satire betrayed an urgent moral motive and gave voice to the type of anger that had earlier motivated satirists to attack the ravages of domestic anticommunism.

*   *   *

The impulse behind Ted Flicker's decision to highlight race in *The Living Premise* was broadly shared by many other liberal Jewish American satirists in the 1950s and early 1960s. Sensitive to the injustice and prejudice African Americans continued to experience in the decades following

World War II—a war waged ostensibly to eliminate fascism and racial oppression—Jules Feiffer, Victor Navasky, and many other Jewish American writers, artists, and performers used their own brand of coruscating wit to register their dissent with America's ongoing racial crisis. Journalist Harry Golden, another second-generation Jewish American, deployed a more gentle, although occasionally penetrating, satiric thrust against Southern segregation. Born Herschel Lewis Goldhirsch and raised on New York's Lower East Side, Golden decided in the early 1940s to relocate to the South and begin publishing a monthly journal titled the *Carolina Israelite*. By the mid- and late 1950s, the heavily ethnic Golden, dubbed the "Jewish Will Rogers," was well-known throughout the United States for his pithy observations concerning the absurdity of segregation. In 1956, as Southern states were continuing to dig in against the 1954 *Brown v. Board of Education* Supreme Court decision, Golden famously proposed his "Vertical Negro Plan," a plan that would do away with the challenge of court-ordered desegregation by eliminating situations where blacks and whites had to sit down together. Since whites and blacks interacted peacefully while standing, Golden suggested, the solution was to simply eliminate seats from schools and other public facilities. Confirming once again the impression that Feiffer, Navasky, and other satirists increasingly shared—namely, that the absurdity of the times were beginning to outstrip satire's ability to comment upon it—the Danville Public Library in Danville, Virginia, in 1960 did in fact remove its seats in an officially designated "vertical 'get-book-get-out'" system.[1]

In strips for the *Village Voice,* the *New Republic,* and dozens of other publications, Jules Feiffer blamed President John F. Kennedy for stalling substantive action on behalf of racial justice. And for *Harper's* in June 1962 he wrote a fictional dialogue between Kennedy and an interviewer that was set in the future, some time following the South's impending secession from the United States. By having Kennedy explain how he came to appoint John Birch Society founder Joseph Welch president and how "I was doing my best to unite the Republicans behind my policies by appointing them to important administrative posts—thereby weakening their opposition," Feiffer joined other liberals and civil rights advocates who were complaining of the president's capitulation to Southern conservatives. "Then you think you may soon be a potent third force in our political life?" the interviewer poignantly presses the president at the conclusion.[2]

More than John Kennedy and his brother, it was the political tacticians helping to shape New Frontier domestic policy who served as Feiffer's primary targets. By this time, the duplicity and cynicism that tainted high-ranking government officials and establishment liberals had become a growing source of concern to Feiffer. In October 1962, Feiffer caricatured an administration official schooling a younger colleague on the virtues of consensus politics. "*I* was an idealist myself before I joined the administration," he confesses. "But then I learned *politics is the art of the possible.*" By watering down legislation sufficiently, the administration is able to retain "an issue to campaign on" while not compromising "*future* measures that we might feel *equally* strong about!" "It's easy to be principled," he drives the point home, "but it's another thing to get your program through."[3] In another strip depicting New Frontier liberals as indecisive over matters of racial integration, an establishment figure from the "fact finding trouble shooting presidential team" is "sent out to seek ways of restoring bi-racial communications in Southern cities." "Our present attitude," the man reports in familiar liberal double-talk, "is that this meaningful dialogue should be continued."[4]

In several strips dating from the early sixties, Feiffer dissected the private, hidden prejudice rooted in his white characters' resentments. One strip from this period had a burly, yet loving father tell readers about how his family wished him luck when he left the house with a baseball bat. When he reveals in the last panel that he then "drove downtown to the civil rights demonstration," readers realize that it was not a softball game that this family man was off to.[5] In other strips published during this period, Feiffer portrayed upper-middle-class whites' shameful treatment of black maids and the general hypocrisy of white liberals with stinging irony. As Bayard Rustin noted, he "was one of the very first to understand that there were complexities—and even hypocrisies—in some of the attitudes of white liberalism." In a strip appearing in the *New Republic,* Feiffer pictured a black man explaining to the reader how he alienates white liberals at parties when he justifies civil rights to them on the basis of "self-interest" rather than strictly "humanist" principles. "At their next party they had two Negroes," he continues, "just in case the first one didn't work out." In another cartoon, Feiffer pictured a tolerant white liberal who, when pressed by a black advocate for the "sit-in," confesses that "Civil rights used to be so much more tolerable before Negroes got into it."[6]

*　　*　　*

Several of the liberal cartoonists Feiffer most admired continued their caustic commentaries on segregation and America's race crisis throughout the late 1950s and early 1960s. Mauldin and Herblock in particular had both been passionate defenders of racial equality throughout their careers, so they did not hesitate to join the fray during these peak years of the civil rights movement. By deliberately avoiding the demands of the burgeoning civil rights movement, President Dwight Eisenhower and his administration were the first to invite cartoonists' satiric, sometimes angry scrutiny. Frustrated by the administration's stonewalling of court-ordered school desegregation, Herblock in August 1958 depicted a sphinx-like Eisenhower beset by cobwebs and holding a placard stating "Let's Go Slower." Given the lack of moral and political leadership from the top, the racist tactics of Southern state politicians too often went unchecked during this period. Commenting ironically on American gunboat diplomacy in the Middle East and the one notable occasion when President Eisenhower *did* act affirmatively on behalf of civil rights (the desegregation of Central High School in Little Rock, Arkansas, in 1957) Mauldin portrayed one soldier pointing to a medal anointing his uniform while informing a comrade, "No, *this* is my Lebanon ribbon. The other one is for Little Rock."[7]

Arkansas Governor Orval Faubus and his fellow Southern segregationists were often subjects of cartoonists' ridicule. In the fall of 1958 Faubus fell prey to *Pogo* cartoonist Walt Kelly. In a series of panels stretching from October through December, Kelly's strip illuminated the folly and hypocrisy behind the governor's most brazen tactic of forestalling racial desegregation—the closing of Little Rock public schools. In November, Pogo and Snavely the Snake decided to bypass the "prohibition 'gainst education" decreed in the swamp by opening a ("consegregated or de-consegregated") speakeasy schoolroom. Upon hearing of the proposed plan, Albert the Alligator, representing the bulk of Southern segregationists, exclaimed, "You open a school, next thing you know all kinds of ingnoramusses is comin' in . . . they meets yo' daughter . . . splits a orange with her, poof! They's engaged, married, an' livin in the attic." Kelly later attempted to capture the virulence of Southern racism with a gun-toting, redneck character named Wiley Catt.[8]

Herblock too was quick to assail the actions of racist Southern governors such as Alabama's George Wallace. In one of several cartoons

31. "Let that one go. He says he don't wanna be mah equal." Like other liberal cartoonists, Bill Mauldin assailed Southern segregationists throughout the early 1960s. Copyright by Bill Mauldin. Reprinted courtesy of the William Mauldin Estate.

Herblock aimed at Wallace, the cartoonist pictured the governor in his office (an office adorned with a homey wall hanging proclaiming "Alabama Uber Alles") pointing angrily to the American flag flying outside. "Ask the Un-American Activities Committee to investigate what this strange flag is doing down here," he shouts into the telephone. Several months before Herblock drew Mississippi governor Ross Barnett washing his hands in a large bowl of blood, a reference to the collective guilt of Jesus Christ's persecutors. Mauldin set his sights frequently on the abhorrent actions of the redneck racists and white mobs who lent their support to Ross Barnett and George Wallace. Against a backdrop of thugs beating a protestor with clubs, Mauldin pictured two men plotting their next move. "Let that one go," one says to the other. "He says he don't wanna be mah equal." In another cartoon, one vigilante carrying a canister of gasoline says to his dynamite-wielding partner as they are about to engage in their nocturnal misdeeds, "See you in church." [9]

To their credit, neither Mauldin nor Herblock intimated that America's racial crisis was confined to the segregationist policies of the Deep

South. A May 1963 Herblock cartoon, for example, pictured two suburbanites waiting for a train in "North Suburbia." "Those Alabama Stories
Are Sickening," one declares to the other. "Why Can't They Be Like Us
And Find Some Nice, Refined Way To Keep The Negroes Out?" At the
time of the 1963 demonstrations in Birmingham, Alabama, Mauldin pictured a white poodle informing a German shepherd (who still has the remains of a protestor's pants lodged in his teeth), "Up North we sort of nib-
ble 'em to death."[10]

As liberal supporters of John Kennedy, Mauldin and Herblock were
quick to credit his administration for its interventions on behalf of the
movement. In September 1963, Mauldin pictured President Kennedy ordering an Alabama National Guardsman "About face" so that the guardsman saluted him (and the authority of the federal government) instead of
Governor Wallace. Since John Kennedy had by then finally begun to act
forcefully against recalcitrant Southern state governments, Mauldin's
tribute was merited. But his earlier cartoons in praise of the administration's "vigorous" handling of America's racial crisis were clearly premature. As histories of the civil rights movement demonstrate, the Kennedy
administration's response to the demands of African Americans was until
1963 halting at best. On rare occasions Mauldin commented on Robert
Kennedy's foot-dragging and the frustrations experienced by African
Americans—frustrations poignantly evoked in the May 1963 cartoon of
an African American who, while reaching for "Equality" amid a jumble of
thorns, asks, "What do you mean, 'not so fast'?" Yet by and large Mauldin
and Herblock never called President John Kennedy personally to account
for these frustrations. When Mauldin did address Kennedy's leadership
directly in a June 1963 cartoon captioned "Runaway," he pictured the president as a cowboy struggling to maintain control of a wild horse labeled
"civil rights movement." By comparing the civil rights movement to a runaway horse Mauldin was commenting more on the insurgent forces within
the movement than the horsemanship (leadership) of the president.[11]

*   *   *

Victor Navasky and his colleagues at *Monocle* and *Outsider's Newsletter*
echoed Feiffer's frustration with white liberals and, more significantly, his
anger with the Kennedy administration's slow response to African Americans' demands for equality. *Monocle's* editors and contributors all shared a
deep commitment to racial equality—a commitment nurtured by their

individual life experiences and, for several of them, their legal training at Yale. Among the liberal faculty at the Yale Law School under whom Navasky and his colleagues studied in the fifties were Charles Lund Black and Fred Rodell, men who had helped write the landmark *Brown v. Board of Education* brief and who had exerted considerable personal influence over Supreme Court justices such as Earl Warren and William O. Douglas.[12] *Monocle*'s interest in pointing out the absurdity of racial segregation was manifest in its very first article, an unsigned fictional piece titled "The Innert Story." This clever story, reminiscent of George Schuyler's 1931 satiric novel *Black No More*, was told in the manner of a news report and depicted the chaos that broke out in an Alabama town after a young physics teacher there discovered that everything white on the light spectrum was really black and vice versa. Suddenly, whites painted themselves black, run-down Negro schools were ordered reconstructed, confused Ku Klux Klan members burned crosses on each other's lawns, and "Caucasian fathers were unable to tell their little children whom to hate."[13] By demonstrating how life could be radically disrupted through a sudden chromatic reordering, this ironic story questioned the color's absurd yet deeply embedded position within American racial ideology.

Subsequent satiric stories and poems ridiculed the South's resistance to desegregation. Several *Monocle* and the *Outsider's Newsletter* articles and a David Levine caricature strongly hinted at an association between the South and Nazi Germany and the "Aryan traditions" that they shared. "Berlin has many kindred souls in America," a fictional former Nazi declares in a 1959 issue of *Monocle*. "The entire South, for example." More typical were counterfeit news reports and interviews emanating from the South. In 1963, the *Outsider's Newsletter* reported, for example, commemorative events planned by a confederate veterans organization—"Son of a Reb" (SOAR)—"for the beginning of the [Civil War's] second 100 years." While SOAR members prepare to reenact the Battle of Little Rock, *Outsider's Newsletter* reported, its Ladies Auxiliary was "working on spitting and catcalls for the [restaged] Battle of New Orleans." Other *Outsider's Newsletter* stories published that tumultuous year reported a proposal made by Mississippi senator James Eastland for an extension of the poll tax and a new "Pigmentation Tax"; an All Southern Dog Show in Greenwood, Mississippi, which showcased prized canines from Birmingham that had demonstrated "excellent initiative in attacking Negroes"; and a "Calendar Reform Bill" devised by a southern state as a way of circumventing federal court desegregation orders.

"Well-Aimed Ridicule"

Monocle's satiric commentary was similar in spirit to Tom Lehrer's "Bring Me Back to Dear Old Dixie," the Second City's lampoon of "Governor Sunshine," and many other satiric jabs that liberal cartoonists and performers made at the expense of Southern governors and "redneck" racists. Although satires of this variety could sting, they were aimed at easy targets. In many instances, *Monocle's* satiric jabs merely confirmed what many white Americans living above the Mason-Dixon Line already safely assumed: that racism in America was a distinctly "Southern" problem. Yet like the best political satire of the early 1960s, *Monocle's* cartoons, articles and poems expressed genuine, justifiable anger at one of the most pressing issues of the day. At a time when Americans were repeatedly stunned by the violent clashes between African Americans and the southern white establishment, *Monocle's* editors and contributors articulated their point of view with a consistent moral clarity.[14] While proposing that federal aid to the state Mississippi ought to be halted, Navasky and his colleagues argued, "Mississippians are still as anti-American as ever. At a minimum, we should demand that they install a democratic form of government. Aiding backward, semi-feudal autocracies such as Haiti, Spain and Mississippi runs counter to our American principles and hinders us in winning the support of the uncommitted nations."[15] And in the "March on Washington" issue of the *Outsider's Newsletter,* Navasky and Lingeman offered readers an ingenious and humorous guide to which House and Senate offices were best for potential sit-ins. In early 1964, Navasky and his colleagues considered relocating to Mississippi so that they could cover the movement's Freedom Summer, thus providing further evidence of the commitment *Monocle's* staff shared toward the civil rights struggle.[16]

To their credit, the staff of *Monocle* and the *Outsider's Newsletter* joined Jules Feiffer in attacking Northern liberals' racial prejudice as well as their belief that civil rights, as contributor Calvin Trillin put it, "is mainly a matter of Really Knowing Negroes . . ." Regular features such as "I'm Not Prejudiced but . . ." in the *Outsider's Newsletter* and "Trial Balloons" in *Monocle* called attention to the more covert racism shared by liberal urbanites in the North. In the latter, Navasky and his colleagues ironically recommended the formation of an organization titled White Moderates for Militant Non-Action for procivil rights liberals and, second, the conversion of the District of Columbia into a black republic—a move that might agree with white liberals who were already fleeing the area "so they don't have to live next to Negroes." In it's "Northern Discrimination Summer Special" from 1963, the *Outsider's Newsletter* ironically noted that while white southerners proclaim, "We love ouah nigras," their counterparts in the North were quick to boast that the "Negro has made great progress" there. Additionally, this issue advertised a product every Northern neighborhood wishing to escape the "stigma of being labeled lilywhite and the nuisance of being the target of pickets [and] sit-ins . . ." must have "an emergency Negro family in a glass case." "Once integration threatens," the article continued, "and you break the glass, [the black but 'not *too* dark' father] works as an assistant letter sorter at the Post Office. This job manages to support his family but just barely, thus preventing unseemly keeping up with the Joneses." Since the family has no friends, "there is no danger of a house and yard full of Negroes over the week-end." "Act now," the advertisement ends, "[w]ith the recently accelerated demand you may wait too long and end up with a house full of uppity niggers."[17]

In a much more consistent and unequivocal manner than nearly all of the liberal satirists commenting on America's racial crisis during the early 1960s, *Monocle* and the *Outsider's Newsletter* chided President John Kennedy and his administration for not pursuing the cause of civil rights with the commitment they had earlier promised. In 1962, for example, *Monocle* drew attention to the Kennedy administration's reluctant support for desegregation by launching an "Ink for Jack" campaign. Citing Kennedy's failure to integrate publicly assisted housing with the "stroke of the presidential pen" as he had pledged, *Monocle* urged its readers to deluge the White House with bottles of ink. The *Outsider's Newsletter* in late 1962 and 1963 repeatedly targeted Robert Kennedy and the Justice Department for their cautious, politically calculated response to America's racial crisis. In counterfeit news reports and in fictional excerpts from Bobby Kennedy's personal diary, the attorney general and his spokesman were quoted as saying that the administration's "overriding concern is for law and order," that "Negro organizations [ought] to avoid 'unnecessary' and 'poorly timed' mass demonstrations which might serve to interfere with orderly action in the courts against the [civil rights] bill," and that sending federal marshals to Mississippi was risky but "public support was sufficiently aroused" so that it wouldn't hurt the administration. In a parody of *Vogue* magazine's "People Are Talking about . . ." feature, *Outsider's Newsletter* in late 1963 lauded "Bobby Kennedy's rare ability [to] passionately . . . defend a moral issue he never knew existed a few months before."[18] Undoubtedly encouraged by the Kennedy administration's new commitment to racial justice, Navasky and his colleagues were nevertheless miffed at its long, unnecessary delay.

One of the *Outsider's Newsletter's* sharpest features, "Outsider's News-real," served as an effective vehicle to humorously depict how President Kennedy and members of his administration skirted the issue of race. In one "Newsreal," the president's brother complains about his failed meeting with African American author James Baldwin. When Bobby Kennedy repeats Baldwin's demand that the president bring the "moral force of [his] office to bear against segregationists," President Kennedy retorts, "Did you tell them the theory that a President shouldn't dilute the prestige of his office by too-frequent appearances? I've already been speaking on behalf of my tax program and the prosperity it will bring." After the attorney general recommends ordering an FBI investigation into Baldwin's "effeminate" nature, the president muses, "I wish Robert Frost were still around. He'd know how to talk to these fellows." Several issues later, "Outsider's Newsreal" imagined an Oval Office discussion about how to deal with the Birmingham church bombing. "While the president is open to the idea of declaring a national day of mourning, he is still willing to hear the practical arguments against it." Arthur Schlesinger Jr. recommends issuing a press release stating the president is considering the gesture. "That way you avoid all the pitfalls of actually doing it, but you still show the Negro voters that your heart is with them," Schlesinger concludes cynically. "As a propaganda gesture, it has a definite appeal," McGeorge Bundy tells the president. "Why don't you dispatch a contingent of Negro troops to South Vietnam, to emphasize that the American Negro is basically loyal to his country and will fight for it if necessary."[19]

* * *

Improvisational troupes such as the Second City and the Committee often deployed heavy irony when targeting racial prejudice. In one of Roger Bowen's signature 1960 "Businessman" scenes, the Second City pointedly ridiculed the shallow motives and hypocrisy of Northern probusiness liberals. On its surface this scene and its predecessor, "Businessman," parodied *Superman* comics. Both featured an ace reporter for the *Kiplinger Letter* named Pierce Finner (played either by Bowen or Eugene Troobnick) who heroically transforms into Businessman in order to defend and protect American corporate interests. In Japan he speedily constructs a trade barrier. In South America he quells a revolutionary mob by reminding it that the United States is making a sacrifice, as he explains, "by bearing the guilt of your low standard of living."[20] At home in America, Business-man—in "his never-ending battle against the enemy to the profit sys-tem"—is forced to deal with racial discrimination at a Woolworth lunch counter located in the South—a reference to the Greensboro, North Car-olina, protests that prompted the founding of the SNCC in April 1960. When informed that black students cannot be served at the counters he exclaims, "Eee gads [sic], that's not only unfair, that's contrary to the stan-dard business practice of operating the Negro race at a profit." Despite the black students' pleas for immediate rectification, Businessman— a composite caricature of the business community and the Kennedy administration—counsels patience and the amelioration of injustice through the gradual progress of genetic evolution. In the meantime, he heroically replaces all lunch counters in the South with "highly-profitable vending machines." "Now you can buy your lunch in freedom," he proudly states, "and enjoy it outside in the great integrated outdoors!" After suc-cessfully battling the Klan and governor, Businessman proclaims, "Let's all shake hands to show that after centuries of slavery, lynching, torture, and discrimination, there are no hard feelings."[21]

In Bowen's "Oldtime Minstrel Show" and numerous other scenes, the Second City pinned the blame of segregation on the intransigence of "backwards" Southerners and their elected officials. In "Governor Sun-shine," for example, Severn Darden (a native of New Orleans) lampooned the governor of Louisiana, a man who in Darden's interpretation is willing to accept desegregation as long as it lasts only a week. The Premise simi-larly parodied the racist governor of Louisiana in a blackout in which he dies, goes to heaven, explains his deeds as governor, and then hears God say, "Well I'se the Lawd." Another Premise scene pictured the encounter between a German and a Southerner in Munich. While the German de-nies the existence of the Nazi Party and Adolf Hitler, the Southerner claims no knowledge of George Wallace and Ross Barnett.[22]

Fans of the Committee in San Francisco appreciated the troupe's fre-quent attacks on segregation and racial prejudice. Like members of the Second City and Premise, the Committee's liberal company reviled the segregated, racist South. To open its second act on Broadway, the Com-mittee's pianist Ellsworth Milburn softly played "The Old Rugged Cross" while images of hooded Klansman burning crosses were projected onto a large screen. To its credit, the Committee did not lay the blame of American racial prejudice solely at the feet of Klansmen or Southern rubes. On its home stage, the Committee often indicted hypocritical white liberals. In a little ditty satirizing Berkeley's failure to combat discrimination in real estate sales and rentals, the Committee's Garry Goodrow and Hamilton Camp sang,

> I'm not the least bit prejudiced . . .
> With all my colored brothers
> I get along real fine
> Why I'd even let a nigger
> Marry a sister of mine . . .
> If I had a sister . . .[23]

And in "The Party," a standard scene in its 1964 repertoire, the Committee satirized patronizing white liberals, the type of people who momentarily shower a black party guest with attention and praise—yes, they too greatly admire Ella Fitzgerald—only to showcase how enlightened and "tolerant" they are.[24] Whether by targeting the racist ramblings of a Southern segregationist or the ill-concealed prejudices of white liberals, satiric improvisational troupes such as the Committee reminded audiences routinely of the tragic absurdity of America's racial predicament.

*   *   *

The absurdity behind American race relations never escaped the notice of those who suffered directly from its ill effects—African Americans. In 1961, for example, *Ebony* magazine took delight in reminding its African American readers of the ridiculous furor recently created in the South over Garth Williams's *The Rabbit's Wedding* (1958), an illustrated children's book concerning the love shared by a white and black rabbit. With incidents like this, *Ebony* correctly pointed out, segregationists were making it all too easy to laugh. Indeed, the acknowledgment of the ridiculous lengths to which whites went to assert their authority and power inspired a tradition of assertive, impious, absurdist jokelore traded privately by African Americans since the days of slavery. Like American Jews and other ethnic groups occupying the margins of American life, African Americans had long found solace and enjoyment by laughing at whites "from the outside." "To the black world alone," W. E. B. DuBois observed in 1940, "belongs the delicious chuckle . . . . We are the supermen who sit idly by and laugh and look at civilization." Since African Americans prior to the 1960s were required to enjoy their practice of comic reversal and comic revenge in private, white Americans could little imagine or admit the extent to which they and their institutions were subjects of such hearty laughter. Ralph Ellison, author of perhaps the best comic novel of the postwar years, *Invisible Man* (1952), described in his 1986 essay "An Extravagance of Laughter" how black Americans deployed the "tarbrush of their comic imaginations" and in the privacy of their imaginary "laughing barrels" enjoyed the "coarse merriment" inspired by foolish Caucasians. By "allowing us to laugh at that which is normally unlaughable," Ellison wrote, "comedy provides an otherwise unavailable clarification of vision that calms the clammy trembling which ensues whenever we pierce the veil of conventions that guard us from the basic absurdity of the human condition."[25]

The tragicomic nature of American race relations was very much evident to poet Langston Hughes, particularly when he traveled throughout the American South. Recalling his encounters with segregation and prejudice in a 1944 essay titled "White Folks Do the Funniest Things," Hughes related that senseless "incidents of Jim Crowism" inspired more amusement than anger within him. For a number of other African Americans, Hughes noted, white prejudice spurred jokes of a discernibly aggressive and macabre quality. Written at a time when African Americans were newly determined to rekindle their struggle for freedom within the United States, Hughes' wartime observation signaled a taste for jokes in which whites were the butt or victim. "Everybody," Hughes noted, "enjoys seeing a devil get his due." A year later, when writing the introduction to a *Negro Digest* anthology of African American humor, Hughes issued a call for "some social satire and fun at the expense of the Rankins, Dies, Bilbos, Smiths, and K.K.K." "Since we haven't been able to write them out of existence with heated editorials," Hughes argued, "maybe we could laugh them to death with well-aimed ridicule."[26]

By 1945 Hughes had already begun to inject a little "well-aimed ridicule" into the pithy musings of Jesse B. Semple, a comic everyman character he created for his *Chicago Defender* column. Semple had become such a popular figure among African Americans that Hughes began toying with the notion of revolving a comic strip around him or, at the suggestion of *Ebony* publisher John H. Johnson, featuring him in pocket-sized volumes with illustrations provided by his friend and fellow Popular Front veteran Ollie Harrington.[27] In the end, the proposed collaboration between Hughes and Harrington never transpired. Hughes went on to write his Semple column—which he continued until 1965—while Harrington, fearing the possibility of legal hearings and a jail sentence because of his past political affiliations, fled the United States for Paris.

While living in Europe, Harrington on occasion conceived and drew angry, ironic commentaries on racial injustice within the United States. Published in the *Pittsburgh Courier*, these satirical drawings were informed by news reports he received from the United States. Some were inspired by his own painful experience growing up in New York. The son of a mixed-race couple (his mother was a Jewish immigrant from Hungary), Harrington first came into contact with racism when his family moved to the South Bronx. There, in the sixth grade at P.S. 35, he was humiliated by his teacher when she announced to his class that he and a fellow black classmate "belong in a waste basket." As a result of this crushing insult, Harrington later recalled, he "began to build up a kind of rage against her"—a rage relieved only by drawing vicious caricatures of her in his notebook. To Harrington, these caricatures were "an opening to a source of pleasure which has remained and sustained me; the art of what we might call, loosely, cartoons." "I began to dream of becoming a cartoonist."[28] After receiving formal art training at Yale and the National Academy of Design, Harrington began fulfilling his dream by producing a panel cartoon for African American newspapers such as the *Pittsburgh Courier* and *Chicago Defender*.

Many of Harrington's single-panel cartoons featured an urban everyman character named Bootsie and poked fun at the foibles, the misapprehensions, and the predicaments of African Americans living in the 1950s. As such, they reflected what his friend and early benefactor Langston Hughes identified as "the quality of the blues." In 1958, Hughes, whose Jesse B. Semple resembled Bootsie in significant respects, identified a sadness of the "When you see me laughin', I'm laughin' to keep from cryin'" variety behind Harrington's irony.[29] Yet there was also an angry core to many of Harrington's cartoons from the late 1950s and early 1960s. When a white faculty member pats a black colleague on the back in one of Harrington's panel cartoons and then asks, "Doctor Jenkins, before you read us your paper on inter-stellar gravitational tensions in thermonuclear propulsion, would you sing us a good old spiritual?" Harrington is commenting caustically on the harmful stereotypes that even highly educated whites maintain.[30]

More typical of the irony Harrington deployed on occasion are his cartoon commentaries on the segregated South and, specifically, the school crises sweeping Little Rock, Arkansas, and other communities in the late

32. "... after havin' courageously held your position in the face of a suicidal charge by several frenzied niggra children tryin' to enter the General Lee Elementary School, our great governor bestowes Dixie's noblest medal for gallantry in action!" Expatriate cartoonist Ollie Harrington comments on the showdown over school desegregation at Little Rock, Arkansas. By permission of Helma Harrington.

1950s. In one of these cartoons, a small black schoolboy sits on a stool in the foreground while National Guard commanders plot a strategy for ushering him to class. "General Blotchit," one of the commanders barks out, "you take your tanks and feint at Lynchville. General Pannick, you move into the county seat. And then in the confusion, my infantry will try to

"Well-Aimed Ridicule"

take little Luther to school!" In another cartoon a Southern state official informs a buck-toothed private in the National Guard that he is being awarded "Dixie's noblest medal for gallantry in action" for "havin'
courageously held [his] position in the face of a suicidal charge by several frenzied niggra children tryin' to enter the General Lee Elementary
School."[31] White Southerners in these cartoons were caricatured as mali-
cious, slightly grotesque figures, leaving little doubt about Harrington's
justifiable rage.

"I believe, as Langston Hughes did," Harrington later commented,
"that satire and humor can often make dents where sawed-off billiard
sticks can't."[32] In one drawing in particular, the frontispiece illustration
for Dora Teitelboim's *Ballade von Little Rock,* published in Berlin in 1961,
Harrington's depiction of Southern whites assumed a uniquely harrowing,
taunting quality unmatched by the work of any African American artist at
the time. Unfortunately, African Americans had little opportunity to appreciate this and other satiric drawings and cartoons produced during the
mid-1960s. When the *Chicago Defender* ceased publishing Harrington's
cartoon in 1963, his only remaining outlet for work came from publishers
within Eastern Europe and the Soviet Union. By this time, Harrington
had settled in the Eastern Bloc. A resident of East Berlin by necessity
rather than by choice (he was trapped in East Berlin without a visa when
the wall separating East and West Berlin was erected) he lived the remainder of his life in exile, far removed from the movement he had long
hoped might come to fruition.[33]

As the modern civil rights movement intensified in the late 1950s and
early 1960s, the type of satiric expression championed by Hughes found
outlet not only in the musings of Jesse B. Semple and the cartoons of Ollie Harrington, but in the jokes commonly traded within African Americans communities throughout the United States. Historians, sociologists,
and folklorists who have studied African American vernacular humor
have documented an increased circulation of jokes ridiculing segregation
and racial prejudice following the *Brown v. Board of Education* Supreme
Court decision of 1954. Observing joking patterns among African Americans while living in a working-class area of Washington, D.C., a doctoral
student at the New School for Social Research concluded in 1960 that in
"Negro humor we have a surreptitious form of protest which contains
within itself much aggression and hostility that cannot find socially acceptable outlets in the power structure of White society." Within the civil
rights movement itself, defiant, biting satiric humor directed at the most

despised representatives of the white power structure—Alabama governor George Wallace and Sheriff Jim Clark of Selma, to name a few—was enjoyed by those who were bravely demonstrating for racial justice. "Invariably," *Ebony* reported in 1965, "the brunt of the race humor is aimed at Mr. Charlie, alias Whitey, alias Chuck, whose obvious shortcomings regarding his racial attitudes are blasted, parodied and analyzed." In the end, *Ebony* concluded, "race humor" had proved to be an "effective morale booster for civil rights workers in the Dixie badlands . . ." Indeed, as historian Joseph Boskin has observed of the humor of the movement, "Laughter reverberated throughout the meetings and marches, taking the edge off the anxieties by belittling and demeaning the opposition."[34]

*　　*　　*

As a result of the civil rights movement and African Americans' appreciation for "race humor," a cadre of smart, assertive, professional black comedians satirized segregation and racial prejudice in their stage acts in the 1950s and early 1960s. Appearing in Theater Owners Booking Association (TOBA) and black chitlin' circuit showplaces in New York, Chicago, Detroit, St. Louis, and other cities, Jackie Mabley, Redd Foxx, Slappy White, and Nipsey Russell leveled jokes at white bigotry that left their all-black audiences in stitches. Although their jokes were not always as bold as those traded on the streets, even the most seemingly innocuous member of this group, 63-year-old TOBA veteran "Moms" Mabley, a comedienne who disguised herself as a frumpy, toothless, yet lusty grandmother, was capable of regaling audiences with an impudent yarn concerning a fictional encounter with John Foster Dulles on the lawn of the White House. To black and later mixed audiences, Mabley would croon, "I ain't Alabamy bound" and then protest, "I'm not going to let the Greyhound take me down there and the bloodhounds run me back! You know Moms is too hip for that." While Slappy White helped break the color barrier, performing before white audiences in cities such as Miami and Las Vegas, Nipsey Russell, quick-witted and college-educated, occasionally traded barbs on segregation and racism. Of Russell, African American humor scholar Mel Watkins concludes, "Bristling, challenging, defiantly confident, Russell pushed black comedians a step closer to popular acceptance by reclothing the impious vernacular of the streets in proper, middle-class language."[35]

Despite his skill and intelligence, Russell found little work in white-owned clubs and instead established himself as a headliner at the Baby

Grand in Harlem. Warned against using material that was either too "smart" or topical, Russell, like Mabley and Foxx, decided to focus much of his act on sex jokes—jokes marked, as Beyond the Fringe's Jonathan Miller observed firsthand, by "breathtaking obscenity." Unfortunately, once typecast as "smutty" comics, Mabley, Foxx, and Russell found it even more difficult to perform for white, mainstream audiences. Each of them discovered that until 1961 it was nearly impossible to get on a network television program such as *The Ed Sullivan Show*. Sullivan admitted that Mabley was the cleverest comedienne he knew but that her material was as "blue as the Danube"—a charge to which Mabley keenly responded, "It's you and others in your position who keep me working where I have to use that kind of material." When Foxx and Russell auditioned for Sullivan, they were explicitly warned against performing topical or political satire. Even before Foxx began his routine in front of Sullivan and his talent coordinators, he told an interviewer in 1961, "they told me to stay off the South, white women, the Congo and the President. I asked them if I could do *The Lord's Prayer*." [36]

Of all the African American comedians who emerged in the wake of the civil rights movement, it was a relative newcomer, Dick Gregory, rather than veterans such as Mabley or Foxx, who first brought the type of biting satiric expression envisioned by Langston Hughes to mass audiences. Gregory was born in St. Louis during the Depression, the second eldest of six children. As he later recounted in his rags-to-riches memoirs, *Nigger* (1964) and *Callus on My Soul* (2000), he endured a childhood marked by desperate poverty and humiliation. As a child, Gregory experienced the brutal racism of whites and the humiliation of being the poor son of an absent father. Like Ollie Harrington, Gregory learned to use biting humor as a way to cope with the indignities that he suffered as a child. Following his mother's dictum that "there is freedom in laughter," Gregory developed an agile comic mind that he freely deployed against his boyhood foes. Determined to succeed, he entered Southern Illinois University on a track scholarship. In addition to being a standout half-miler, he distinguished himself on campus with his ability to tell jokes and make people laugh. To help counter the personal pain racism and segregation brought him, he later wrote, he became "Happy-go-lucky Greg. Personality Kid. Funny man. Always laughing." For an all-fraternity variety show, he stood up onstage and, as he later wrote, "started doing some satire . . . [although] I didn't know it was satire." He began performing satiric monologues regularly during the mid-1950s while serving in the army. Military service sat no better with Gregory than it did Jules Feiffer or Mort Sahl, so a stage act was more than likely a good outlet for his comic inclinations. In 1955 he qualified for the All-Army Show at Fort Dix and almost earned an appearance on *The Ed Sullivan Show.*[37]

Shortly after returning to civilian life, Gregory moved to Chicago. It was there, as a weekend emcee in a South Side, black, working-class nightclub called the Esquire Show Lounge, that he honed his skills as a stand-up comic. To help prepare himself for gigs, he absorbed all the comic material he could get his hands on: comedy records, jokebooks, even the public library's "musty old books on humor." As his technique developed and his confidence rose, Gregory began to gravitate toward material that was fresh and topical. To ensure that he had a venue for his act, Gregory even briefly operated a nightclub of his own in the Chicago suburb of Robbins. After his Apex Club was forced to close in 1959, he hustled and begged agents and nightclub owners for work. He eventually landed a spot at Roberts Show Club, one of the largest African American nightclubs in the country.[38] In September 1960, the ABC documentary series *Bell & Howell Close Up!* televised a portion of Gregory's "immediate and edged" performance at the Roberts Show Club. In front of a mixed audience, Gregory wryly observed about the situation facing African Americans in cities like Chicago,

> Lot of people say 'come up North where you don't worry about racial problems.' That's a lie. I had better advantages back home on the farm than I had up here. You stand on the corner three hours waitin' on a bus and wondering where you gonna sit. Back home we *know* where we are going to sit.[39]

By the fall and winter of 1960, Gregory had found work at the Fickle Pickle, a beatnik coffeehouse on Rush Street, and several all-white clubs in Indiana and Ohio. While playing to white audiences at a supper club in Akron, Gregory learned how to handle the unique challenges that confronted a black comedian performing before a white audience. In addition to passing up on the opportunity to comment on a woman making her way to the restroom (an occasion white comics were almost expected to exploit), Gregory withstood racist taunts and epithets with steely resolve. After a month-long gig "with those White boys" in Akron, Gregory remembers, "believe me, I was prepared for the big time."[40]

Gregory's big break came on January 13, 1961, when he was asked to substitute for the ailing Irwin Corey on the stage of the Chicago Playboy Club's Penthouse Room. The Playboy Club's white management was understandably nervous about presenting Gregory onstage since the audience that night was composed almost entirely of frozen food executives from the South who were there attending a convention. Gregory, however, was undeterred. "I told [the room manager] I didn't care if he had a lynch mob in that room," Gregory later recalled, "I was going on . . ." Onstage, Gregory began his routine, "Good evening, ladies and gentlemen. I understand there are a good many Southerners in the room tonight. I know the South very well. I spent twenty years there one night . . ."[41] Drawing from a body of vernacular humor known mainly to African Americans, Gregory continued,

> Last time I was down South, I walked into this restaurant. This white waitress came up to me and said, 'We don't serve colored people here.' I said, 'That's all right, I don't eat colored people, no way! Bring me a whole fried chicken.' About that time, these three cousins came in. You know the ones I mean—Ku, Klux, and Klan. They said, 'Boy, we're givin' you fair warnin'. Anything you do to that chicken, we're gonna do to you.' About then, the waitress brought me my whole chicken and the cousins said, 'Remember, boy, anything you do to that chicken, we're gonna do to you.' So I put down my knife and fork, picked up that chicken, and kissed it![42]

At first, Gregory later wrote, the Playboy Club's audience "fought me with dirty, little, insulting statements, but I was faster, and I was funny, and when that room broke it was like the storm was over." By the time the night was through, Hugh Hefner had signed Gregory for a six-week stint at his club. Within weeks, Gregory was offered work at well-known "sophisticated" nightclubs such as New York's Blue Angel, San Francisco's hungry i, and Chicago's Mister Kelly's and was described by *Time* magazine as a performer who was "just getting started on what may be one of the more significant careers in American show business." Before long, white and black audiences around the country were thoroughly familiar with Gregory and his new style of racial satire. Whether through newspaper columnists' appropriation of his witty quips, his groundbreaking guest appearances on *The Jack Paar Show,* or the monologues he recorded for Colpix and Vee-Jay Records, Gregory became one of the most highly visible satirists and black entertainers in America. By 1962 he had good reason to marvel, "When I left St. Louis, I was making five dollars a night. Now I'm getting $5000 a week—for saying the same things out loud I used to say under my breath."[43]

33. Shortly after bursting onto the scene in 1961, Dick Gregory was one of the most important and controversial satirists in the United States. Library of Congress, Prints & Photographs Division, *Look* Magazine Photograph Collection.

Several factors help explain why Dick Gregory emerged so quickly in the front ranks of American comedians in the early 1960s. To begin, the progress of the modern civil rights movement itself had by then opened the possibility of satirizing racial issues in front of a liberal, interracial audience. During the early 1960s, the courage of black activists in the South and the eloquent oratory of Dr. Martin Luther King Jr. had awakened white Americans to the urgency of the country's racial crisis. For white liberals sympathetic to the civil rights movement, the idea of a black man such as Gregory using humor to address America's racial predicament had considerable appeal. Whether motivated by a genuine respect for tolerance or, as it was suggested at the time, by feelings of guilt, a growing number of white Americans by 1961 were receptive to Gregory's irreverent take on race relations. Gregory's big-stage debut took place one week before the inauguration of President John F. Kennedy, a politician who had successfully convinced white and black Americans that he would be more committed than his predecessor to tackling segregation and racial discrimination. Early 1961 was also the apex of the vaunted "satire boom." The American public by this time had already been exposed to the work of Nichols and May, Mort Sahl, Bob Newhart, and other liberal, "cerebral" satirists who had broken the mold of old vaudeville-style stand-up comedy. Media outlets prone to self-congratulatory analyses of new trends in American popular culture seized on the occasion of Gregory's debut as further proof of the "new humor's" social significance. In the opinion of a *New York Times* critic who caught Gregory's debut at the Blue Angel in New York, Gregory deserved notice since he was "the only member of his race thus far to join with and hold his own in the ranks of the bright, young, intellectually oriented, wittily topical, stand-up comics."[44]

The assistance that *Playboy* publisher Hugh Hefner provided during the early months of 1961 also worked to Gregory's advantage. For Hefner, Gregory, like Harvey Kurtzman, Jules Feiffer, Lenny Bruce, and Mort Sahl, signaled the arrival of a new, irreverent liberal voice on the American scene—a voice capable of promoting tolerance and cultural freedom. "The ability to poke humor at the sacred cows of our society is a healthy thing," Hefner told *Ebony* magazine in May 1961. "Dick is saying the right thing at the right time."[45] Hefner not only provided the venue for Gregory's big-time debut, he brought his fellow Chicagoan to the attention of press agents and newspaper and magazine reviewers, many of whom were more than willing to publicize Gregory as the "Jackie Robinson of stand-up comedy" and the "Negro Mort Sahl." He also brought Gregory attention through articles and interviews published in *Playboy* and his short-lived *Show Business Illustrated*. Hefner even contributed the introduction to Gregory's first published collection of jokes, *From the Back of the Bus* (1962).

Gregory's cautious, moderate approach to performing also proved a key ingredient in his initial success. Gregory was well aware that no matter how open educated, liberal whites may have been to the idea of listening to him perform onstage, there were limits to the amount of aggression—often read as "hostility" or "bitterness"—they were willing to accept in his comic monologues. Before he hit it big, Gregory received numerous lessons about the caution he would need to exercise if he wanted to perform in front of white audiences. In 1960, bandleader Count Basie took Gregory off the bill he and his band were scheduled to share for a Chicago show because he feared that the unknown comic might antagonize whites in the audience. Gregory had also observed how veteran black comics such as Moms Mabley, Nipsey Russell, Timmie Rogers, and Redd Foxx struggled against the restrictions imposed on them by white nightclub owners. The lessons Gregory drew from the experience of these comedians helped shaped the content and style of his comic routine significantly. Most importantly, Gregory learned that in order to enhance his appeal among middle-class whites, he first needed to eschew risqué sexual humor. "If you use blue material only," he recognized, "you slip back into being that Negro stereotype comic." Looking back on his early years as a comedian, Gregory remembers determining that in the end he had to "go up there [onstage] as an individual first, a Negro second." "I've got to be a colored funny man," he resolved, "not a funny colored man." Early on, Gregory also determined to expand his repertoire beyond jokes concerning race. With the assistance of Robert Orben, a gag writer whose joke book *30,000 Laughs* was advertised in the early 1960s as one of the largest professional resources for comics in show business, Gregory by 1962 was routinely directing jokes at subjects such as the space race, Soviet Premier Nikita Khrushchev, and Cuba.[46]

Unfortunately, because Gregory often relied on other writers for his topical material, a significant portion of his comic repertoire was, as the astute critic Nat Hentoff noted, "awkward and obvious." Worse yet were jokes Gregory made at the expense of his mother-in-law and wife. To a Maryland audience, for example, he complained, "My wife can't cook. How do you burn Kool-Aid?" With gags like these, Gregory harkened back to the repertoire of old-school comics such as Bob Hope—a comedian Gregory had long admired but from whom many other members of the new generation of liberal satirists were eager to distance themselves. Gregory's reliance on stock gags, tepid topical material, and self-deprecating humor may have compromised somewhat his status as a "new wave" satirist, but Gregory viewed it as a necessity. "I've got to make jokes about myself," Gregory told himself, "before I can make jokes about them and their society—that way they can't hate me." Looking back on his early years as a comedian breaking into the limelight, Gre-gory recalled that he desperately "wanted to make it standing up in a white club." "It took me until 1960 to realize," he continued, "that I needed eighty percent *white* material—you know, mother-in-law jokes and Khrushchev. I bought white man's joke books to figure out what Whitey was laughing at."[47]

White, educated, middle-class Americans living in urban areas in the North and on the East and West Coasts could be counted on to laugh at jokes ridiculing the racist South during the 1950s and early 1960s. These were jokes in which Gregory, more than any other liberal satirist, specialized. Throughout the early sixties, Gregory repeatedly convulsed audiences with jabs directed at the KKK ("It's the heads that are pointed . . . "), Southern judges ("they just light their cross and you know court's in session"), the Southern moderate (a "cat who will lynch you from a low tree"), and the "redneck" racists proliferating in the South. To patrons of Chicago's Playboy Club he quipped, "I need to take my act to Mobile like Custer needed more Indians. I don't even work the southern part of this nightclub." Gregory likewise delighted crowds at San Francisco's hungry i in 1961 when he suggested that he would turn the South into an "H-bomb testing area" if he were elected.[48]

The caustic jokes Gregory made at the expense of easy targets such as the KKK and Governor Faubus were legitimate expressions of the anger and frustration that Gregory experienced since boyhood. As such, they were in line with the caustic, satiric humor that African Americans had long traded among themselves. In front of Northern liberals, however, jokes directed at Southern racists often worked as subtle forms of flattery. At times Gregory's scathing put-downs of racial prejudice appeared to do little more than confirm the sense of moral and intellectual superiority that patrons of hip urban nightclubs such as the Playboy Club and hungry i felt. Many of these patrons undoubtedly viewed racism as a distinctly "Southern" problem. Robert Lipsyte, a close observer of Gregory and the coauthor of his autobiography, noted that when the comedian received, onstage, the Scotch and soda that he had ordered from a nearby white waiter, he would typically shake his head and say, "Damn, Governor Barnett should see this." When nightclub audiences subsequently broke up over this remark, they in effect ratified "the subtle compliment [Gregory] had paid to the liberality of their city."[49]

The calculated cautiousness of much of Gregory's comic material was enhanced by his humble, low-key presence onstage. By perching himself on a stool and delivering his monologue with a lit cigarette in his hand, Gregory's approach resembled that of fellow Chicago stand-up satirists

Shelley Berman and Bob Newhart. Unlike Berman, Newhart, and other satirists, however, Gregory in his early stage career was not prone to bursts of animated intensity. Onstage, Gregory, dressed in a Brooks Brothers suit, appeared cool and relaxed. The language he used onstage was rooted in the black vernacular; it borrowed little from the sociological and psychoanalytic lexicon that Sahl and others used onstage. In sum, there was little about Gregory's onstage persona that either threatened or intimidated white audience members. Neither outwardly aggressive nor passive, he conveyed a manner that was warm and self-effacing. "You don't see any bitterness in me," Gregory told a *New York Times* reporter in 1961. "Anyone catches my eye can tell. Nothing bitter, mean or aggravated." Indeed, in the eyes of his promoters, it was exactly this ability to avoid appearing angry or bitter that made his act palatable to whites. For Hugh Hefner, *Time* magazine columnist Robert Ruark, and ABC-TV commentator Alex Drier, for example, what made Gregory's humor worth listening to was its "level view," its lack of indignation, its avoidance of "the biting edge and the too-sharp point." As Drier argued in the liner notes for *Dick Gregory in Living Black & White* (1961), Gregory was "no knight on a white charger, jousting with segregation windmills . . . He doesn't preach or teach . . . [His] humor is not 'negro humor' in the traditional sense. Nor is it 'shock' type humor. It does not jar you, nor does it 'shake you up' . . . It isn't bitter, and yet, there often creeps in a rueful quality, but it never offends."[50]

If Gregory's technique at first departed from that of Mort Sahl and other, more assertive comedians, Gregory shared his cohort's skill at relating intimately with audience members. Unlike other satirists, Gregory never forgot that comedy, performed onstage in front of an audience, is "friendly relations."[51] Gregory initially presented himself to white audiences as a weary, detached ironist, an innocent who was, as he often said, "confused and mixed up" by the world in which he lived. By muting his anger and, at the same time, distancing himself from the demeaning, happy-go-lucky manner long associated with black comics, Gregory was able to address middle-class whites as peers. Even if white audience members were still unprepared to accept Gregory as a social equal, they were at least able to sympathize with his bemused, though hopeful, perspective on the world. Gregory defused the urgency of the issues he addressed onstage by reminding audiences that "we all have problems" and by asking, "Why do we worry so much?" Equally reassuring for audiences were his reminders that everything would be all right in the end as long as we "just think things through."

What is perhaps most notable about the likeable stage persona Gregory developed for the stage is the license it ultimately provided him to render subtle yet penetrating satiric remarks about race. Beneath Gregory's cool, self-effacing onstage persona, there lurked an angry moralist bent on awakening white America to racism's appalling hold on private and public affairs. Gregory desired the approval of white liberals, yet like many other satiric artists and performers at work in the early 1960s, he was not always willing to let them off the hook. Once he gained their attention through easy comic banter and self-deprecating humor, he could, as he figured it, "blow a cloud of smoke at [them] and say: 'Wouldn't it be a hell of a thing if all this was burnt cork and you people were being tolerant for nothing?'"[52] Wry, indirect comments such as this were characteristic of a long tradition of African American comic expression, a tradition from which Gregory and his chief writer James Sanders borrowed liberally.[53] Delivered by Gregory in a quick and unexpected manner, these sly jabs and brilliant, sudden comic reversals often caught audiences off guard. Quick timing, Gregory realized, was essential. Early in his career he resolved to "hit [white audiences] fast, before they can think . . ."[54]

In addition to their good timing, Gregory's jokes about race in America were often marked by poignant irony. When he explained to patrons of the Playboy Club how African Americans were able to purchase Cadillacs, for example, he credited racial segregation since it prevented them from paying for quality medical care and vacations to Florida. At Mister Kelly's in Chicago, Gregory told patrons to "treat me right, because with Kennedy's new housing bill I might be your new neighbor." And to other audiences in 1961 he observed, "In the South they don't care how close I get as long as I don't get too big, and in the North they don't care how big I get as long as I don't get too close." The critic Gilbert Millstein observed that there was "something a trifle eerie" about Gregory's use of such irony in his routine, "considering that what [Gregory] is actually doing is a . . . reading of indictments." "The sterner the indictment," Millstein continued, "the more convulsed are his listeners."[55] It is difficult to assess exactly what prompted white audiences to laugh at Gregory's ironic jabs, but based on the few recordings of Gregory's performances from the early 1960s, it seems clear that the laughter emanated partly from a shock of recognition—Gregory's delivery of unexpected, unspoken truths about race often caught audiences off guard—and was aided by a palpable nervous edge that permeated the venue.

* * *

Whether motivated by the sudden recognition of truth, embarrassment, or some other intellectual or nervous reaction, the laughter Gregory received from mixed or white audiences was copious throughout 1961 and 1962. During this period of peak popularity, Gregory was in constant demand on the nightclub circuit and was a frequent guest on late-night network television programs. As the first African American comedian to escape the demeaning, retrograde style of Mantan Moreland and other old-school comics and successfully cross over to white audiences, Gregory became one of the most visible and highly paid black entertainers in the United States. As such, he opened a door that had been long closed to African American comedians. Recognizing the sudden commercial potential for "integrated humor," nightclub owners and record and television producers signed Nipsey Russell, Jackie Mabley, and Bill Cosby to new bookings, recording contracts, and guest appearances on *The Jack Paar Show*.

By far the sharpest and most talented black satirist to follow in Gregory's footsteps was the former Living Premise actor Godfrey Cambridge. After quitting the Living Premise, Cambridge began honing a stand-up comedy act that he had been developing and performing for several years. "Before Dick [Gregory] came on a Negro comedian couldn't get arrested," he observed in an *Esquire* interview. Now, in Gregory's wake, Cambridge was able to find work at the Blue Angel and Village Vanguard in New York and on college campuses. Still, Cambridge was unable to break through to network television because of his highly sensitive racial material. In early 1964, however, Jack Paar presented taped excerpts from a performance Cambridge had given at Morgan State College. The response was so favorable that Cambridge soon found himself in great demand. His first recorded comedy album *Ready or Not, Here's Godfrey Cambridge,* taken from a performance before a mainly black audience, showcased his considerable skill at lampooning racial stereotypes. Mining his own personal struggles within the entertainment industry, Cambridge presented a poignant, funny monologue about a theatrical Uncle Tom (a bit he developed earlier for *The Living Premise*) and a series of devastating riffs—deemed "too uncomfortable for café consumption" by a *Variety* reviewer—on the continuation of racist typecasting in Hollywood. Best of all were Cambridge's pithy observations on de facto job and housing segregation in the North. In a bit on "Block Busting," he observed, "I keep telling all my white actor friends 'Go on, fool, keep tanning. You'll tan yourself out of a job.' And I have a whole lot of experience to prove it." Nothing worries middle-class, suburban whites more, he continued, "than the sight of a Negro couple walking down his street carrying the real estate section of the *New York Times.*" And in a bit reminiscent of a Feiffer cartoon, Cambridge related how his liberal white friends were so "bugged" by his unwillingness to play the role of "token Negro" at parties that they began to invite a second African American "in case the first did not work out." [56]

Ironically, as the opportunities for exploiting the absurdities of American race relations expanded for Cambridge and other black comedians, Dick Gregory began to question whether satire was truly a legitimate and effective weapon against racial oppression. Beginning in 1963, Gregory began to forsake his role as detached stage satirist in the interest of committing himself to the one cause that really mattered—the civil rights movement. Gregory's interest in taking direct action on behalf of equal rights actually dated back to the early fifties when, at the age of nineteen, he protested the discrimination that African American runners faced in St. Louis–area high school athletic programs. Several years later, as a college student in the small southern Illinois town of Carbondale, he bucked the system of segregated seating operated by the local movie theater. During the late 1950s and early 1960s, Gregory invested so much of himself into his evolving career that he remained on the margins of the civil rights struggle. Yet as he began to achieve success as an entertainer, he found it more difficult to contain his sense of moral indignation—what he called the "old monster"—over America's racial crisis.

In November 1962 Gregory was approached by civil rights activist Medgar Evers and asked to speak at a voter registration rally being held in Jackson, Mississippi. Gregory's emotional encounter with defiant Mississippi African Americans and dedicated civil rights activists marked a turning point in his personal life and career. He later remembered of his experience there,

> For the first time, I was involved. There was a battle going on, there was a war shaping up, and somehow writing checks and giving speeches didn't seem

enough . . . Sure I could stay in the night clubs and say clever things. But if America goes to war tomorrow would I stay at home and satirize it at the Blue Angel? . . . I wanted a piece of the action now, I wanted to get in this thing.[57]

Five months later Gregory traveled to Greenwood, Mississippi, at the request of SNCC activists in the hopes that he would help focus media attention on the repressive tactics of the local government and police. Dressed in an expensive, Italian-cut silk suit, Gregory reveled in his role as the "uppity" provocateur. With reporters looking on, Gregory began taunting white police officers with humorous jibes and angry epithets. Gregory reportedly called local police "dirty dogs" and even told one officer that his mother was a "nigger." Gregory displayed similar bravado six months later when he traveled to Selma, Alabama. Addressing a crowded church meeting attended by local blacks and a handful of white town officials, Gregory launched into a fiery two-hour speech that was only occasionally punctuated by humor. As Howard Zinn recounted, Gregory's performance in Selma was in many ways remarkable. "Never in the history of this area had a black man stood like this on a public platform, ridiculing and denouncing white officials to their faces," Zinn wrote. "It was . . . something of a miracle that Gregory was able to leave town alive."[58]

As his commitment to the movement grew, Gregory resolved to use his celebrity to advance the cause of equal rights. He began to insist that nightclubs where he performed hire black employees, and he routinely performed benefit shows on behalf of organizations such as CORE and the NAACP. Onstage, Gregory began to challenge his audiences with material that was more angry and confrontational. "The integration material is even sharper now and cuts deeper," a *New York Times* critic noted of Gregory's act in September 1963. "I kept pushing my material further," Gregory later recalled, "more topical, more racial, more digging into a system I was beginning to understand better and attack more intelligently." Adapting Mort Sahl's motto for his own use onstage, Gregory began to inform audiences, "If I've said anything to upset you, maybe it's what I'm here for." For some white audience members, Gregory's ironic observation that Northern whites don't lynch African Americans, "they just pay you $1 an hour and let you starve to death," was a little much to swallow. For other white liberals such as *New York Post* columnist James Wechsler, however, Gregory's transformation into satirist-cum-activist was thrilling to behold. Writing in May 1963, Wechsler observed that Gregory "has the passion of James Baldwin, but his weapon is ridicule, and it is deadly."

"Well-Aimed Ridicule"

"[H]e is perhaps the most serious threat to the segregationist system to emerge in recent years," Wechsler added, "[and] his will be the last laugh, echoing through the history books."[59] In the opinion of Wechsler, certainly, Gregory, more than any other liberal satirist in America, was bringing to fruition the type of "well-aimed ridicule" envisioned earlier by Langston Hughes.

Mocking Dr. Strangelove, or

HOW AMERICAN SATIRISTS FLAYED THE COLD WAR, THE BOMB, AND AMERICAN FOREIGN POLICY IN SOUTHEAST ASIA

A sense of the absurd not only inspired the jokes Godfrey Cambridge, Dick Gregory, Jules Feiffer, and other satiric performers and artists directed at race relations during the early 1960s, it served as a wellspring for darkly comic perspectives on the cold war and nuclear weaponry. On their surface, of course, the cold war and the bomb were hardly laughing matters. Indeed, aside from the crisis in race relations, no greater, graver challenge faced the United States in the late 1950s and early 1960s than maintaining its stance against the Soviet Union and the spread of communism. During this particularly intense period of the cold war, the threat of communism and the policy of containment that was formulated to respond to it set the parameters of American foreign policy and helped direct the priorities of both major political parties on the domestic front. Policy makers' resolve to augment American hegemony abroad spurred the development of a substantial nuclear arsenal—particularly during the Kennedy years—for which the atomic and hydrogen bombs stood as inescapable, central facts in postwar life. Yet as deadly serious as the intensifying cold war was at the time, it also spawned a variety of absurdist, subversive black humor.

Surveying the growth of literary "black humor" during the early 1960s, literary scholar Morris Dickstein concludes that novels such as Joseph Heller's *Catch-22* (1961) caught on "in apparent contradiction to the idealism, optimism, and high style that we still like to attribute to that period." Black humor novels such as *Catch-22* are "like a secret history of the Kennedy years," Dickstein explains, "when the terrifying specter of thermonuclear war flared garishly one last time before beginning to dim . . . when a President's civilized, cosmopolitan vision helped conceal the expansion of our imperial role." Historian Margot Henriksen similarly identifies *Catch-22* as well as Stanley Kubrick's 1963 film *Dr. Strangelove, or: How I Learned to Stop Worrying and Love the Bomb* as prime examples of the early-sixties "culture of dissent" spurred by America's far-ranging cold war commitments. Both choices are apt, for they stand out as two of the period's most brilliant comic assaults on bureaucratic authority within the military, the absurdity of the cold war, and the corruption of ethics resulting from what Heller identified as America's "regimented business society." What is missing in the appreciations Henriksen, Dickstein, and other cultural historians have written for *Catch-22* and *Dr. Strangelove,* however, are their vital links to a wider stream of liberal satiric criticism aimed at the bomb and the military. Indeed, dark, grotesque, pointed comic assaults on the bomb, the military establishment, and American cold war foreign policy were far more sustained during the late 1950s and early 1960s than cultural historians have allowed. Before *Dr. Strangelove* provoked the nervous laughter of American audiences in early 1964, a number of satirists had consistently aimed their barbs at the bomb, civil defense, the U.S. military, the dictates of the cold war, and even the escalating conflict in Southeast Asia—a conflict that would soon develop into the type of tragically absurd war that even Joseph Heller's *Catch-22* could not have foretold.[1]

*   *   *

In *By the Bomb's Early Light* historian Paul Boyer describes a "mood of diminished awareness and acquiescence in the developing nuclear arms race" in the United States during the early 1950s. This mood was soon disturbed, however, by the series of atmospheric tests of multimegaton thermonuclear bombs that both superpowers began running in 1952.[2] Responding to the heightened danger of the new hydrogen bomb and atmospheric testing, mathematician Tom Lehrer composed a song titled "The Wild West Is Where I Want to Be." Although intended primarily as a "jokey kind of send-up" of songs such as "Home on the Range," "Wild West" was partly inspired by Lehrer's experience as a researcher at the Los Alamos Scientific Laboratory in 1952. To the accompaniment of his perfectly pitched piano playing, Lehrer sang in the late 1953 recording,

Along the trail you'll find me lopin'
Where the spaces are wide open
In the land of the old A.E.C. (yahoo!)
Where the scenery's attractive
And the air is radioactive
Oh, the Wild West is where I wanna be . . .

Mid the sagebrush and the cactus
I'll watch the fellas practice
Droppin' *bombs* through the clean desert breeze . . .[3]

This grim little ditty, like much of the dark humor that would follow in the same vein, gave voice to the concerns some Americans had over the atmospheric testing of thermonuclear weapons in the American West. Six years later, Lehrer returned to the subject of the bomb and struck at the cosmic absurdity of the escalating arms race through an apocalyptic "survival hymn" titled "We Will All Go Together When We Go." By this time, the audience for dark, satiric reflections on the menace of nuclear weaponry and radioactive fallout had grown appreciably. Increasing numbers of Americans had begun to feel uneasy with the escalation of nuclear arms and were even beginning to question the reassurances of the Atomic Energy Commission (AEC). In 1956, some of these concerned citizens agreed with Democratic presidential candidate Adlai Stevenson when he proposed to halt the testing of the hydrogen bomb. A year later, they helped form The Committee for Sane Nuclear Policy (SANE). By 1959 then, Lehrer's discordant, irreverent singing in "We Will All Go Together When We Go" was only part of a growing chorus of voices interrogating the sanity of nuclear diplomacy.[4] Lehrer sang,

We will all go together when we go.
All suffused with an incandescent glow.
No one will have the endurance
To collect on his insurance,
Lloyd's of London will be loaded when they go.

We will all fry together when we fry.
We'll be French fried potatoes by and by.
There will be no more misery
When the world is our rotisserie,
Yes, we all will fry together when we fry.[5]

Lehrer insists that he had no overt political intentions with "Wild West," but he also admits that he had been uncomfortable with how his

Mocking Dr. Strangelove

AEC colleagues at Los Alamos "talk[ed] about . . . taking out a city or something like that." Cartoonist Jules Feiffer, whose antipathy toward the bomb and U.S. foreign policy during the cold war inspired a sizeable output of work during the late 1950s and early 1960s, disavows nothing about his satiric intentions. It was the Eisenhower administration's advocacy of a nuclear deterrent in the cold war, in fact, that first inspired Feiffer to translate his ire into cartoons. Feiffer's mistrust of the Eisenhower administration, the U.S. military, and the manner in which they helped escalate the cold war was rooted in his left-liberal political worldview and his moral opposition to violence. They also stemmed in part from Feiffer's personal experience in the U.S. Army. During the early 1950s, Feiffer served in the Army Signal Corps Photo Center on Long Island. When the army transferred him to signal training at Georgia's Camp Gordon (an inevitable step toward duty in the Korean War), Feiffer objected. "That was my first outright rebellion in my life," he recalls. Like Bill Mauldin and Mort Sahl, Feiffer bristled at army discipline and resented the way "grunts" were treated by their officers.[6]

The letters Feiffer wrote family members in 1951 reveal the depth of his bitterness toward military authority. "I would not be able to stand this dump without the hope of getting out," he despaired in correspondence to his parents. Feiffer's older sister sent letters back to her brother offering moral support, Marxist class analysis, *Pogo* strips clipped from the newspaper, and some pragmatic counsel. If "you dare to act on any of the bitterness and anger you feel at this shit-hole you're in," she warned her brother in August 1951, "you're a dead duck." The idea of playing the role of the "good soldier" and thereby submitting himself to his commanders' authority did not sit well with the young Feiffer. "The standard of 'if he can take it, why can't you' is a slogan I learned to distrust at the age of five when it was first used on me," he wrote his dismayed parents. "I can't write a happy cheerful letter because I have no patience to lie and I only write this many letters in so short a time to help get this dung heap out of my system." In retrospect, Feiffer maintains that the army provided his "first direct contact with open fascism." The army "really changed my entire direction" and "propelled me into the world of satire as a way of expiating my grief and rage." "While I felt totally miserable, I felt more justified and more in the right than I had ever felt before. It was a period when I could really allow myself the luxury of hate—pure and blissful hate." "I owe everything I am to the Army." In the end, because the military "displayed every rule of illogic and contempt for the individual and mindless exercise of power," it became Feiffer's first object of ridicule, his first target of satire.[7]

While still in the Army Signal Corps, Feiffer wrote an extended strip titled *Munro*. Created "in fury," as Feiffer later related, "so I wouldn't go crazy," *Munro* told the story of an innocent five-year-old boy who is accidentally drafted into the army. At the outset, Munro attempts to bring the error of his conscription to the army's attention. Fearing that, as the narrator explains, "someone might call him unpatriotic," however, Munro decides to submit to the system and join along with everyone else. When he is inducted, he listens to a dignitary explain the world situation and issue his country's holy call to duty. "The man used very simple words," the narrator comments, "[E]ven Munro could understand." When the absurdity of his situation finally overwhelms him, Munro begins to cry. Seeing this, his commanders suddenly realize that he is only a boy, and they consequently release him.[8]

Upon his own discharge in 1953, Feiffer finished *Munro* and then attempted to sell it to various publishers in New York. Not surprisingly, Feiffer failed to find a buyer. In the mid-1950s, caustic commentaries on the mindless regimentation of bureaucracies and the hollow cant of cold war military leaders had little appeal for cautious publishers. Although discouraged by the results, Feiffer nevertheless felt compelled to write and illustrate some "straight-out satiric work against the cold war and the cold war machine and the bomb."[9] He accomplished just that in an extended cartoon strip titled *Boom*. Eventually published (along with other previously rejected pieces) in *Passionella and Other Stories* (1959), *Boom* addressed what Feiffer understood as the "conditioning of public attitudes" toward the acceptance of radioactive fallout. Written and drawn "in fury," as Feiffer remembers, *Boom* told of an enormous, worldwide escalation of nuclear arms and the American government's attempts at assuaging the public's fear of them. "Once the surface of the earth looked like this," *Boom* begins with Feiffer's depiction of an urban terrain pockmarked with craters, "and it was, of course, all due to the Bomb tests." With more tests, the bombs got better. "This is last year's bomb," one military authority says of one very large bomb. "We thought it was pretty ultimate. Remember?" "Boy were we naïve!" responds his colleague. Although the skies darken with radioactive pollution, the American public says, "I guess the government must have its sound reasons" and goes about its business. Not taking any chances with popular discontent, however, the authorities hire a public relations firm to declare "Big Black Floating Specks Are Very

Pretty!" in billboard campaigns. Better yet, they sell the public big black floating speck–proof eyeglasses and tranquilizers. Eventually military planners devise the ultimate "deterrent for peace," a bomb that will "blow up the whole works!" Again the government masks the new bomb's dangers, the public offers its tacit consent to the bomb's testing, and, in the last, full-page panel, the planet is annihilated. When Feiffer presented *Boom* as a slide show to an audience of Harvard students and faculty in 1962, it is easy to see why, as the *Boston Globe* reported, "laughter left the audience at [its] conclusion."[10]

Boom's dark satire was informed by Feiffer's deep mistrust of the defense establishment and the AEC. As a regular reader of journalist and cold war critic I. F. Stone during the 1950s, Feiffer was convinced that the AEC had been deliberately and routinely deceiving the American public about the effects of nuclear testing. By the late 1950s and early 1960s, concerns over the credibility of the AEC, the adequacy of America's civil defense program, the harmful effects of radioactive fallout from nuclear testing, and the proliferation of annihilating nuclear weapons grew significantly and reached well beyond Feiffer and his readers. Atomic-age anxieties multiplied after the election of John F. Kennedy in 1960. An aggressive cold warrior who had campaigned on the false issue of a "missile gap" with the Soviets, President Kennedy prompted grave worries among Feiffer and other liberals attuned to the dangers and moral compromises inherent in America's new militarism. In 1961, President John Kennedy greatly raised the stakes of the cold war by authorizing the disastrous Bay of Pigs invasion and by sternly countering Premier Nikita Khrushchev at Berlin. Kennedy approved a substantial buildup of nuclear weaponry and then, in a move that surely portended apocalyptic peril, urged American families to construct private fallout shelters.

In strips he contributed to the *Village Voice,* the *New Republic* and other newspapers and magazines during this period, Feiffer responded to growing nuclear peril by returning repeatedly to the satiric themes he struck with *Boom:* the social and psychological fallout from the Bomb's stupefying irrationality, the deleterious effects of public apathy, and the chronic distribution of misinformation by duplicitous experts and government officials. In a *Village Voice* cartoon from March 1958, Feiffer pictured a child relating the history of a nation (the United States) that solved its unemployment problem by initiating an "accidental bomb dropping program." By requiring massive cleanup efforts after the bombs' detonations, the nation achieved a full-employment economy. "You mean some people didn't complain?" the child's companion inquires, referencing conservatives' long-standing antipathy toward government programs aiding the unemployed. "*Nobody* complains about national defense, dopey," his friend replies. Two years later Feiffer again focused on the cold war's stupefying irrationality by depicting a conversation between two men at their workplace. Relaying a dream he had had the night before, a man tells his colleague how the Soviet Union had suddenly decided to dismantle its nuclear arsenal. Catching its enemies off guard, this rash move causes wide-scale panic and, eventually, the collapse of the West. Failing to recognize that the man's dream describes, albeit in fantastic, exaggerated detail, the illogical behavior and perverted psychology unleashed by the cold war, the second man responds, "It's a good thing we have people in power who can handle the situation." [11]

In other syndicated strips, Feiffer commented trenchantly on the moral compromise and conformity bred by the cold war. In one memorable strip reprinted in *Boy, Girl, Boy, Girl* (1963), two men having drinks discuss the sacrifice societies must make during periods of crisis. "When a country is involved in a life and death struggle it *can't* be all that liberals would *like* it to be," the first asserts. The second man agrees and in a subsequent panel assents to the proposition that a "*perfectly* free press" can only be guaranteed "when you're more or less *secure.*" "When the enemy is all *around* you," the first man continues, "*true* democracy just *isn't* always feasible!" "*Precisely!*" responds the second, "and *that's* why I say our criticism of *Cuba* is unfair and unrealistic!" "*Cuba!*" the first retorts, startled. "I thought we were talking about the *United States.*" Stunned, the two men stare at each other and then, in the last panel, scream for the waiter to deliver the check. [12] In a similar vein, Feiffer in 1958 pictured an establishment figure at a desk discoursing on the importance of debate in democratic societies,

> Debate, I say to you, is the most priceless heritage of [a free society]! . . . Except in times of emergency . . . At such times, I say, it is incumbent upon each of us to put aside the conceit of *partisanship* and shoulder, manfully, the burden of our mutual ordeal! . . . We must, I say to you, *march unquarreling, uncompromisingly, forward toward the preservation of our ideals!* . . . Then when the crisis is over, we can resume the debate. [13]

In cold war America, Feiffer's strips intimated, cynicism knew no bounds, its corrosive effects seeping beyond the establishment into the ranks of the middle and upper-middle classes. Pondering the unjustified "hostility"

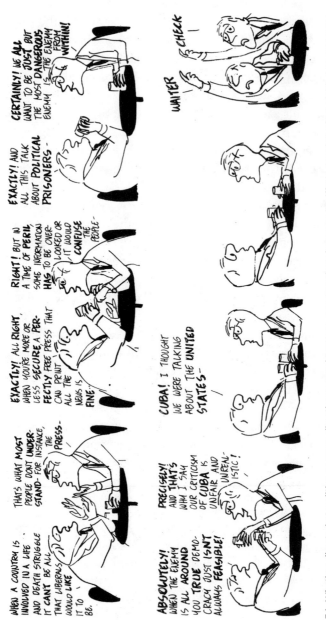

34. Whether directed at politics or more directly personal matters, conversations between "Feiffer's people" often yielded to misunderstanding and confusion. © Jules Feiffer. Used by permission.

of Cuban revolutionaries toward America's middle class, two Feiffer characters plot a "prerevolt" campaign in emerging countries that revolves around a "quality family [television] series"—"a Cuban Andy Hardy series" complete with "a house in the suburbs, two cars in the garage, and a wacky kid brother who looks like Raul Castro!" "Once we couple the innocent zeal for independence with the more sophisticated zeal for installment buying," muses one of them, "our friendship with the have-not nations is guaranteed."[14]

For Feiffer, as for many satiric artists and performers working in the early sixties, the promotion of the bomb shelter and civil defense programs represented the height of atomic culture's lunacy. In a December 1961 strip, a mother chastises her son for using the family's expensive fallout shelter as a place to read his "Yahoo World War III Hooray Comics," thus revealing that she is in no way conscious of the conditions compelling her family to erect its flimsy barrier to fear. In May 1960, the moment when New York's Civil Defense Protest Committee had organized a protest against civil defense drills, the *Village Voice* devoted its entire front page to a Feiffer strip satirizing civil defense programs and the survivalist mentality they encouraged. Feiffer here probed the mind of a law-abiding citizen who took shelter during an air raid drill and through his appeals to cold war "logic" manages to convince his fellow shelter dwellers to remain underground. "We took shelter because the law told us to," he told them. "If we leave our shelter before the law tells us to, we're as bad as those people sitting out in the park who insist this whole business is insane." Three days later, he is wilting, but he remains prepared to use the force of his logic once more against those who are beginning to stir. "Without proper respect for the law," he states ironically at the end, "society must crumble."[15]

A well-equipped bomb shelter provided one of the focal points to Feiffer's one-act play *Crawling Arnold,* a scattershot assault on the dysfunctional attitudes and anxieties inhibiting the upper-middle class in New Frontier America. First performed at Gian-Carlo Menotti's Festival of Two Worlds at Spoleto in Italy and subsequently published in *Horizon* in 1961, *Crawling Arnold* broadly lampooned the comfort Americans took in their civil defense program. Barry and Grace Enterprise are proud of their shelter and have even spent "many happy weeks" in it in preparation for a future nuclear attack. Indignant over their black maid's objection to the family's plans for "separate but equal air-raid shelters," they become incensed when their adult son Arnold, who has regressed to a toddler, balks

Mocking Dr. Strangelove

at fleeing to the shelter when the siren sounds. Miss Sympathy, a sexy psychiatric social worker whom the Enterprises have hired to straighten their son out, patiently explains to Arnold, "I, as do you, question the sense of such a drill, but objecting to this law by defying it robs *all* laws of their meaning." Arnold's seduction of Miss Sympathy, successfully launched under the threat of nuclear attack, together with Feiffer's irreverent outlook on America's civil defense program, struck a chord with young Americans sympathetic to SANE and other peace movements. Throughout the early 1960s, Feiffer was contacted by dozens of amateur and college performing troupes around the United States who wished to stage their own production of *Crawling Arnold.* Predictably, Feiffer's commentary proved too much for cold war conservatives, including a Canadian MP who charged that the Canadian Broadcasting Company's decision to broadcast *Crawling Arnold* was proof that the network had been taken over by "apparently degenerate minds."[16]

Beaten down, fad obsessed, psychoanalyzed, and tragically unaware of the circumstances under which their lives have become constrained, the muddle-headed Americans like the Enterprises whom Feiffer satirized throughout the late fifties and early sixties ultimately fell prey to what Feiffer resented and feared most: withdrawal and apathy. In a September 1958 strip two men, paralyzed flat on the ground, discuss why they are no longer aroused by the threats of MISSILE MADNESS! and ATOMIC HOLOCAUST! "Do you think we've turned apathetic?" the second man asks the first. "Apathy is such a *bad* word," he responds. "I'd hate to think its apathy we suffer from. Let's just call it faith." Several years later Feiffer depicted these same two men contemplating the neutron bomb—a sinister "enhanced-radiation weapon" that promised to deliver increased levels of deadly fallout with a smaller blast. "It only kills people. It doesn't harm property or machines," says the first. "Doesn't harm machines, eh?" responds the second. "Very encouraging." "How so?" asks the first. "Then most of us will be safe." In a similar fashion another Feiffer character comforts himself with the idea that someday, during World War III, differences of opinion will finally be laid to rest and everyone will share "*one* universal consolation"—"At the moment before the bomb drops—every person in the world will have the satisfaction of knowing *his* side was right."[17]

In more than a few of these strips satirizing the Bomb and the cold war, Feiffer reiterated the type of mass culture critique put forward by liberal intellectuals such as David Riesman, William Whyte, and John Kenneth

Galbraith—a critique that at times denigrated middle-class Americans as unthinking, tasteless conformists. Yet the politically astute Feiffer never lost sight of the structures of power operating behind the cold war and therefore never failed to indict those who abused their authority. Feiffer, more consistently than perhaps any other American satirist during the early sixties, placed the blame for America's atomic-age paranoia and irrationality where it rightly belonged—on the military and corporate elites that shaped cold war domestic and foreign policy. More effectively than his cohorts, Feiffer used his satiric strips to question the way in which the government and the AEC in particular sanitized information about America's nuclear policy. In one memorable Feiffer strip from late 1956, an advertising executive working for the military directs his staff to devise a "'Fallout Is Good For You' saturation campaign" complete with catchy "I Like Fallout" and "Your Government Knows Best" decals. Another Feiffer strip from July 1957 pictured a technocrat from the AEC explaining to an adoring crowd how scientists had reduced the level of fallout on each new bomb they manufactured. "And *now* at *last*," he explains, "we have built one *so* big it will blow up *everything!* . . . And its 100% *clean!* . . . We feel our progress has been amazing." In March 1960 Feiffer depicted physicist Edward Teller discussing ways to make the American public more accepting of his son, the big Bomb. "If a father can't testify to the behavior of his own son—who can? . . . There is no such thing as a really *bad* bomb." "Right!" responds a government official. "Now if we could get people to *accept* that—maybe show that we only want to test him for *peaceful* purposes" "Yes!" says Teller. "Sonny must be tested so he can *teach us!*" "Great!" replies the official. "I'll pick out a test site and we'll ready the press releases."[18]

As a guest columnist for the *New York Herald Tribune* in 1959, Feiffer playfully but pointedly mused on the utility of satire in the nuclear age. How could a satirist top the lunacy of the AEC convening experts into a "Sunshine Group" to study the effects of nuclear radiation or humorously exaggerate the futility of attempting to survive a nuclear blast that promised to bring massive, unimaginable carnage? "The satirist has been made unemployable by the very facts around him," he concluded. In the minds of many liberal readers, Feiffer fortunately never actually succumbed to the competition cold war realities posed. Instead, he repeatedly took advantage of cold war America's abundant ironies to condemn the duplicity of experts and government officials, the hubris of diplomats, and the greed of the weapons industry. On multiple occasions Feiffer derided the support America's "free press" lent to the cold war. One syndicated strip in 1961 featured a man, clearly a surrogate for Feiffer himself, who explains that American newspapers publish only "All the news that's safe to print." The function of America's free press, he explains, "is to publish free press releases." "Free press?" he concludes. "We're a nation of trade journals."[19]

Anticipating concerns the student New Left would convey over American universities' complicity in the cold war, Feiffer in 1958 satirized an American humanities professor invited by a university's administration ("all these other generals") to deliver the school's annual graduation address. "Do we dare allow ideas to remain unmobilized?" he asks his audience, twisting the educational imperative that resounded throughout post-Sputnik America. "Let us prove for all time that the humanities do have a place in the defense program." Several years later Feiffer depicted two university professors—presumably Ivy League theorists with some political clout—gloating over their success over having re-educated the American public about the dangers of nuclear war. "The lay public no longer feels that all of us would be destroyed," the first asserts. "Quite true, Professor," responds the second. "The lay public now feels that only *most* of us would be destroyed." Surveying their future prospects, the first envisions a limited nuclear war restricted to each superpower's missile bases. "Quite *neater* than rival forms of war, really," remarks the second. "And what a boon to full employment!" "Happy wars, Professor," the first toasts their ingenuity. "Let's all join hands and push."[20]

In Feiffer's view, cynicism and opportunism were hallmarks of the Kennedy administration's foreign policy. In a July 1961 cartoon, a bow-tied liberal intellectual akin to Arthur Schlesinger Jr. discusses the possibility of pursing new peace initiatives with our cold war enemies, as long as these initiatives are made "behind the scenes." "To avoid too open a break with previous policy," he explains, "Kennedy will continue our series of Latin American invasions and be photographed with all Republican leaders." "With the discreet manipulation of home opinion," he concludes in the last panel, "who knows but within three or four years after the cold war *ends* the American people may be ready to hear about it."[21] Several weeks later, Feiffer pictured a man formulating a novel brand of *realpolitik* as he attempts to seduce a woman over cocktails. "To win the cold war we must *return* to the concept of *revolutionary* change," he tells her. If we could only use our corporate wealth for "trading purposes with our adversaries," we might "swing a deal where *we* offer our enemies *Laos, Vietnam* and *Formosa*" on the condition that they also "take over all our fruit, oil, sugar, mining, telephone and soft drink interests." "*Then* when Latin America rebels it will be against *them*—not *us!*" "By exchanging areas of exploitation," he concludes, "we may *yet* be able to build the cold war to a standstill." Impressed with his peculiar logic, his female companion gushes, "If President Kennedy could hear you now—I *swear* Marvin, there'd *be* no Arthur Schlesinger."[22]

In a March 1962 strip, Feiffer took aim at the administration's diplomatic and foreign policy failures—Feiffer, like Norman Mailer and other left-liberal intellectuals, was greatly disturbed by the previous year's disastrous Cuban invasion—by depicting a cabinet meeting over the rivalry between the CIA and the State Department. When Kennedy relates that the State Department "finds it increasingly frustrating to recognize a *new* government in the *morning* only to have *C.I.A.* try to overthrow it in the afternoon," Walt Rostow recommends that the two agencies should, "on occasion," share the same foreign policy. "I'll buy that, Walt," Kennedy responds. "Type up a classified memo and leak it to the press. Now after lunch I want to discuss possible sites for a future series of atmospheric tests. I understand that somebody suggested Havana."[23] Feiffer well understood Kennedy's penchant for aggressive, heroic posturing and took the opportunity to portray the president as a gun-slinging cowboy, one who was engaged in a showdown with his arch nemesis, "Nicki Boy."

With their frustration over the moral compromise and narrow vision constraining cold war liberalism, Feiffer's early-sixties cartoons at times evinced the outlook taking shape within the student New Left. In an April 1962 strip, Feiffer sympathized with young peace advocates who suffered the opprobrium of liberal officials and other self-professed "realists" who tolerate protest as long as it is "responsible." "Don't get me wrong," a striped-pants official tells a young protester repeatedly, "I *favor* full debate of our global policies, but won't we *harm* ourselves by seeming divided in the eyes of the rest of the world?"[24] For Harvard student and future SDS president Todd Gitlin, Feiffer's hard look at the liberal establishment's penchant for equivocation rang hilariously true. Gitlin wrote Feiffer in a fan letter,

> I was tickled pink (almost Red) to see your cunning strip . . . Having spent about three-and-a-half months organizing last month's demonstration in Washington, I was overjoyed—in my brain and in my gut—to see that someone with two eyes in his head had finally exposed the attitudes of the quasi-Antis in the light of day. In the first frame, the diplomat type is a State Department hack we encountered on February 16; in the second, he is McGeorge Bundy; in

Mocking Dr. Strangelove

the third, Arthur Schlesinger, Jr.; in the fourth, many parents and the *New York Times*. Brings back poignant memories. Congratulations on your perspicacity.[25]

*   *   *

Other liberal satiric cartoonists likewise registered their dissent over the looming threat of nuclear annihilation. Indeed, on the topics of cold war diplomacy and the dangerous buildup of nuclear weapons, Herblock, Bill Mauldin, and Robert Osborn contributed some of the sharpest and most poignant work of their careers. In his skull-shaped drawing of the mushroom cloud for *War Is No Damn Good* (1945), Osborn effectively rendered the deadly force unleashed by the atom bomb. This harrowing depiction of the bomb's annihilating capacity proved influential, eventually finding its way into the work of Herblock and other cartoonists. Herblock's own unique contribution to the negative imagery of the bomb was a figure he named "Mr. Atom." Throughout the late 1940s and 1950s Herblock drew his well-known and much imitated personification of atomic weaponry as a thoughtless and arrogant figure, a hirsute thug who wore a five-o'clock shadow (like the caricatures of McCarthy and Nixon) and a Spartan helmet.[26]

Herblock's crude yet ominous portrayal reflected anxieties Americans had harbored since the dawn of the atomic age about nuclear weapons' enormous destructive potential. In reference to the Eisenhower administration's "New Look" defense posture—a posture that relied on the threat of massive nuclear retaliation and a corresponding buildup of atomic weaponry—Herblock pictured Mr. Atom in a July 1956 cartoon informing Secretary Wilson and the chairman of the Joint Chiefs of Staff, Admiral Arthur Radford (both of whom are seated in front of the national budget ledger and at work on "Preparedness For Possible Limited Wars"), "I Can Do It For You Wholesale." In other cartoons Herblock took aim at AEC chairman Lewis Strauss and other officials within the American defense establishment for their silence and deception. In response to what the AEC and Eisenhower touted as a "clean bomb," Herblock pictured Mr. Atom in June 1957 scrubbing himself with "AEC Soft Soap" and singing merrily, "It Makes Me Feel So Deliciously Clean." In other cartoons Herblock echoed the other concerns raised by SANE and other grassroots peace organizations, particularly concerns over the harmful effects of fallout from nuclear weapons testing. In a 1957 cartoon Herblock pictured an administration official rocking "The Next Generation" in a cradle high atop a tree branch. As nuclear fallout rains down on the cradle the official blithely sings, "Rock-A-Bye Baby, In The Tree Top—Let's Make Believe The Fallout Will Stop."[27]

During the early 1960s, when the Kennedy administration oversaw a dramatic escalation in military spending and nuclear weapons development and when the United States and the Soviet Union came within a hairsbreadth of nuclear confrontation, Herblock, Mauldin, and Osborn were eager to issue their foreboding satiric commentary on the bomb and its repercussions. An August 1961 Mauldin cartoon, for example, pictured two men emerging from the smoldering ruins of a city destroyed by a nuclear bomb. "We won!" calls out one of the men. Osborn's admonitions in the *New Republic* took the shape of a skeleton poised to drop an atomic bomb—a cover illustration for an article titled "Peaceful Use of Terror"—and a drawing of two snarling, muscular beasts poised on both ends of a teetering plank, titled "The Balance of Terror." And throughout this period of heightened tensions, Osborn and his colleagues continued to register their complaints against the internal security apparatus and its deleterious effects on Americans' civil liberties. Mauldin, for example, pictured a cold war "Realist" outfitting Lady Liberty with a gun. "It looks great on you, kid," he declares. And with reference to her torch, he then asks, "Now why not drop that other junk?" And in May 1961 Mauldin illustrated a cartoon of a cat with hammer-and-sickle eyes stalking a man labeled "hysteria." Panicked, the man exhorts Lady Liberty while pointing to her torch, "Maybe it'll go away if we put out the light."[28]

Given Robert Osborn's facility with depicting interior states of being, several of his best drawings of the period attempted to render the psychic toll thermonuclear testing and cold war diplomacy wrought on Americans. In a brilliant series of cartoon illustrations for a January 1962 *New Republic* article titled "Shelters and Survival," Osborn pictured a nervous man caught in a rain of nuclear fallout desperately clutching a badly tattered umbrella. A second cartoon depicted a family of four crouching within a bomb shelter underneath a grassy knoll marked by four tombstones. Best of all was Osborn's ironic tribute to the "Progress of Mankind." In a sequence stretching across a straight line, Osborn here ironically illustrated the progress of mankind as it advanced from the age of prehistoric caves to that of the pyramids, cathedrals, and skyscrapers and then to the modern age when man has regressed back to the cave—the contemporary family bomb shelter. Bill Mauldin likewise captured the comic pathos of Americans' nuclear-age predicament. In "April showers"

Mocking Dr. Strangelove

Mauldin pictured a family standing under a lead umbrella attempting to protect themselves from nuclear fallout. Several days before Christmas 1962 he pictured Santa Claus flying through the air with a sled full of toys while testing the air—with the help of a Geiger counter—for fallout radiation. In yet another Mauldin cartoon, a man sits with his girlfriend in a convertible, peers into the nighttime sky, and declares aloud, "Wow! Look at the shooting star . . . I hope."[29]

Other cartoons drawn by Herblock, Mauldin, and Osborn aimed beyond atomic-age anxieties to the military authorities and government officials responsible for escalating tensions between the two superpowers. Osborn did not target defense officials within the Kennedy administration as he once had John Foster Dulles during the 1950s, but on one notable occasion he condemned the influence scientific think tanks had on the Defense Department and its military planning. In a 1962 issue of the *New Republic* exploring the role of strategic theorist Herman Kahn and "Think Factories" such as the RAND Corporation, Osborn provided a single-page cartoon drawing of white-coated scientists at the helm of a large computer control panel. While recording data on their clipboards, these detached foot soldiers for the defense establishment observe scores of numbers, bodies and, further in the distance, grave markers that spill out of the computers' data bank towers. Physicist Edward Teller, an influential advocate for the development of the hydrogen bomb, was the object of several Mauldin critiques, including a 1963 cartoon in which he is pictured hugging an H-bomb like a child as he entreaties the reader, "Don't fence my baby in." On the subject of arms control and a nuclear test ban treaty, Mauldin, Osborn, and Herblock were likewise eager to comment. Before the U.S. Senate ratified the treaty in September 1963, Herblock proffered dire warnings of the consequences of not securing a mechanism for controlling nuclear waste. Mauldin more directly commented on the role that President John Kennedy and Soviet Premier Nikita Khrushchev would personally have to play in the treaty negotiations and, more importantly, in avoiding future nuclear conflict. Mauldin depicted Kennedy and Khrushchev as petulant schoolyard antagonists, and in one cartoon the two leaders stand face-to-face with their fists clenched. As they each warn "I'll bury you," they are in reality both sinking in quicksand. In a March 1962 cartoon captioned "We've got time for one more hand," Kennedy and Khrushchev sit at a card table while death, represented by a skeleton, sits between them while glancing impatiently at his watch.[30]

On the Kennedy administration and the CIA's handling of cold war hot spots such as Cuba and Vietnam, Mauldin and Herblock were capable of producing biting satiric criticism. For their part in bungling the ill-advised Bay of Pigs invasion, the Joint Chiefs of Staff and CIA earned Mauldin's caustic rebuke. Commenting on the type of support the United States was lending South Vietnam in 1961, Mauldin pictured large artillery ("Compliments of USA") in the center of a Vietnamese village. "It's beautiful," a Vietnamese peasant tells his American benefactor, "but we were sort of hoping for a plow." A year later, Mauldin drew a belt-fed machine gun labeled "Vietnam." In place of bullets is a line of U.S. soldiers—"Live ammunition," as the caption reads. Despite these and other notable examples, however, Mauldin and Herblock often pulled their punches when they addressed New Frontier foreign policy. While Herblock was admittedly slightly hawkish on America's involvement in Vietnam during the early sixties, Mauldin betrayed ambivalence. Above all, Mauldin appeared reluctant to criticize Kennedy administration officials and John Kennedy personally for their role in escalating cold war tensions. Soon after Kennedy took office, Mauldin was wont to portray the president as victim of circumstances, as a man made vulnerable to the foreign policy errors Republicans had previously committed. Whether he slipped on a "Cuba" banana peel carelessly left by Dwight Eisenhower or was pulled along by a seeing-eye dog in hot pursuit of a communist skunk, Mauldin's John Kennedy was only partly culpable for his foreign policy missteps. In Mauldin's view, President Kennedy was beset by enormous foreign policy challenges and therefore deserved as much sympathy as satire. In a characteristic cartoon from 1961, Mauldin depicted John Kennedy as the pilot of a canoe careening down a river gorge between hazards such as "Laos Falls" and "Berlin Boil."[31]

*   *   *

The bomb and the American defense establishment became subjects of sustained, often very witty satiric commentary in Victor Navasky's *Monocle* and the *Outsider's Newsletter*. In fact, from their inception, these two publications targeted the atomic bomb, cold war diplomacy, and overseas military activity more consistently and sharply than any other contemporary outlet for satire. In its first two issues, *Monocle* published ironic commentaries ("Sitting on Defense, Watching All the Bombs Go By" and "Hallelujah I'm a Bomb or Singing in the Bathtub") that struck at the

Mocking Dr. Strangelove

heart of America's civil defense system and called into question the Eisenhower administration's plans for developing a "clean bomb." In the latter article, a Yale University English instructor named Bob Bone opined that the idea of a "clean bomb" emanated from a combination of America's peculiar obsession with cleanliness and its propensity for value-free, "technical know-how." "Slowly but surely," Bone wrote, "American ingenuity is taking the horror out of war." "Painless dentistry will seem a puny achievement indeed, compared with the painless extermination of which the human race will soon be capable." Navasky and his colleagues betrayed a similarly dark, absurdly comic perspective on the cold war in subsequent stories about a top-secret "Pleasure Principle" developed at high levels of the security apparatus, an ozone leak caused by hydrogen bomb tests in the atmosphere ("There will be plenty of air for all," an AEC spokesman allegedly reports, "just as long as people don't make pigs of themselves breathing . . ."), embarrassing missile surpluses, and a program guide to a proposed National Defense Television station, which featured such fare as "Your Good Health" (in which "first aid for radiation burns is discussed") and "Evening Devotions" ("Famous wartime prayers for the annihilation of the enemy"). For *Monocle's* 1958 "special H-bomb issue," contributor Allan Danzig penned satiric verse on the dangers strontium 90 posed to the nation's milk supply. "All her bones had turned to water an' they wuzn't any doubt," Danzig's poem read, "That the strontium had got 'er 'Cause she Didn't Watch Out!" Danzig's grim verse reflected the same concern and anger that simultaneously prompted citizens and scientist activists in St. Louis to launch a study of baby teeth to help document the spread of strontium 90's radioactive poisoning.[32]

In many instances the *Outsider's Newsletter* and *Monocle* anticipated the dark irony and sharp criticism behind Stanley Kubrick's film *Dr. Strangelove*. Navasky and his colleagues were particularly adept at burlesquing missile engineer Wernher von Braun, nuclear strategist Herman Kahn, and the military leaders who cooperated with them. A cartoon depiction of a statue of von Braun clutching a missile ("I Aim At The Stars") made the point that the engineer who had helped develop the V-2 rocket for the Nazis had switched his allegiance from "The Master Race" to "The Space Race." Herman Kahn was a frequent target in the pages of the *Outsider's Newsletter*, most notably in the superhero comic strip *Superkahn, Government Contractor*, drawn by Ed Koren. "Swifter than 100 TFXs, fasterthinking than one hundred IBM data processing systems," Superkahn was "the only superhero under contract to the U.S. government to solve the complex range of political, social, diplomatic, economic and military problems exclusively by force." Sharper yet was a fictional *Monocle* interview with Dr. Heinz Grubble, director of a think tank called the Boston Institute of Advanced Studies [BIAS], and a man who advised the Kennedy administration to drop ten hydrogen bombs on Cambodia as a "precautionary deterrence" while allowing Russian bombs to rain on Harlem as a way of decreasing New York's African American population. Echoing the dangerously objective, value-free mind-set of America's nuclear strategists, Grubble justifies his aggressive strategy: "We are scholars and thinkers here at BIAS. We leave rights and wrongs to politicians and theologians and journalists like yourself." A recurring *Outsider's Newsletter* column by Colonel C. C. Chesnut, a military man and the public relations director of the Rande Corporation, similarly satirized the nuclear establishment's technical expertise and the type of advice it doled out to the American public. Inspired by "the well-known American philosopher, Herman Kahn" and "atomic behavioral scientists" at Rande, Chesnut blathered that "[t]hinking the unthinkable is one of the primary duties of the American citizen" and that "[p]arents should emphasize the positive aspects of a nuclear war."[33]

During the early 1960s, *Monocle* and the *Outsider's Newsletter* joined a number of satiric writers, performers, and cartoonists in ridiculing the promotion of fallout shelters as protection devices against the ravages of thermonuclear war. In addition to issuing a special "Emergency Bulletin" that featured "hilarious fallout shelter designs," *Monocle* published a counterfeit internal memorandum prepared by the Public Relations Department of the National Association of Fallout Shelter Manufacturers (NAFSM). Contributed to *Monocle* in 1963 by Karla Kuskin and Kurt Vonnegut Jr., the author of the apocalyptic black humor novel *Cat's Cradle* (1963), the memo begins by citing NAFSM's conviction—backed by its motivational research department—"that with proper exploitation, the market for shelters, and by implication, a magazine for shelter owners, is a vast one." To further NAFSM's chances of overcoming "the negative image" of death and thus "customer resistance to building fallout shelters," the memo recommends marketing a new magazine titled *Hole Beautiful,* "the magazine of gracious survival." "The motivational research people tell us," the memo relates, "that this name has positive connotations wombwise." In an Orwellian vein, the memo's copy continues, "The magazine will, for obvious reasons, be pro-bomb; although, because of the negative connotations of 'bomb,' that word will never be used and instead

Mocking Dr. Strangelove

it will be referred to as 'the Big Fella.'" To promote the new magazine, the public relations department recommends a "small but dirty nuclear explosion in a desert area," the creation of radio station HOLE (operating on privatized CONELRAD radio frequencies), and the launch of tie-in products such as Shelter Hopping Kits. With editorial articles such as "Unilateral Disarmament by the Russians—Does It Violate the American Sense of Fair Play?" and drama reviews focusing on theaters' safety hazards, the memo boasts, "Advertisers will find [*Hole Beautiful*] an excellent vehicle for reaching a prosperous, self-reliant, anxious group of consumers."[34]

Closely linked to *Monocle*'s satiric scrutiny of the bomb were its critical, at times incisive glimpses into United States foreign policy. At first, Navasky and his colleagues satirized incompetence within the ranks of the civil service, the techniques of the Voice of America, "strategic slogan mouthing" by the State Department, and the military assistance and financial aid of the United States to Latin American and third world countries. Although uneven in quality, the best of these succeeded in questioning the sagacity of cold war diplomacy and the legitimacy of American hegemony overseas. *Monocle* and the *Outsider's Newsletter* did not hesitate to implicate the Eisenhower and Kennedy administrations for their military adventurism. In response to objections raised to President Eisenhower's decision to mobilize 5,000 U.S. troops to Lebanon in 1958, *Monocle* quipped that it was merely an "itsy-bitsy violation of international law" and that Eisenhower was merely following precedents in U.S. foreign policy—"[a]sk Nicaragua, and the Dominican Republic, and Cuba and Haiti." In the 1963 piece "Cold War Cut-Outs," *Monocle*'s Edward Sorel and Seymour Chwast provided readers the opportunity to dress President Kennedy (pictured in boxer shorts and tee shirt) in the type of outfit that best fit his accompanying cold war rhetoric (cowboy, boy scout leader, etc.). In that same issue, frequent *Monocle* contributor C. D. B. Bryan used a parody of William Golding's 1954 novel *Lord of the Flies* to depict top officials within the Kennedy administration as dangerous war hawks. Set on a remote island and taking place after nuclear Armageddon, this postapocalyptic fantasy pictured National Security Advisor McGeorge Bundy and Secretary of Defense Robert McNamara as bellicose bullies intent on turning their fair-haired leader "Jack" as well as "Bobby 'n' Teddy," "Porky Pierre [Salinger], Lyndon, and all the other boys stranded on the island against a thoughtful, though effeminate, pacifist named Adlai [Stevenson]." In the final scene, set on the shore by the Bay of the Pig,

35. Edward Sorel's illustration for *Monocle*'s "Lord of the Hawks" parody. Pictured clockwise from top left: Chester Bowles, John F. Kennedy, Adlai Stevenson, Barry Goldwater, Robert McNamara, McGeorge Bundy, Robert Kennedy, Pierre Salinger, and Lyndon B. Johnson. By permission of Ed Sorel and Victor Navasky.

McGeorge gleefully detonates bombs that had washed ashore and then leads the other boys in a "red beast" hunt. After Adlai cries out "something about moral leadership, a clearing in the jungle where all could talk," he is pummeled by the boys and left "limp and still and white . . . like a drowned dove."[35]

Shortly before *Monocle* published "The Lord of the Hawks," the *Outsider's Newsletter* deployed its favorite satiric device, the counterfeit news report, to unveil Kennedy administration plans for invading a second Bay of Pigs, this one located in a marshy inlet adjacent to Secaucus, New Jersey. The Cuban exiles hired for the job, the *Outsider's Newsletter* reported, "feel they must act fast—before Bobby Kennedy lures all the exile troops into the U.S. Army to help liberate Laos . . ." Significantly, this reference to U.S. Army interventions in Laos was far from the only satiric allusion the *Outsider's Newsletter* made to Southeast Asia in 1963. Navasky and his colleagues hinted darkly at the growing turmoil within South Vietnam through counterfeit news reports concerning the grand opening of the Bien Phu Hotel (with deluxe accommodations and rooms "overlook[ing] the Temple compound and schools where daily beatings and arrests take place," it was already "jam-packed" with 25,000 U.S. military advisors) and the self-immolation of a *Time* correspondent who had been fired by the "Luce regime" for "failing to report the truth about the situation in South Vietnam as his New York editor saw it." By quoting fictitious entries from the diary of Madame Nhu, the sister-in-law of South Vietnamese leader Ngo Dinh Diem, the *Outsider's Newsletter* took pleasure in mocking the "Dragon Lady's" outrageous insensitivity (a convert to Catholicism, she admits that her favorite historical periods "are the Crusades and the Inquisition") and her Machiavellian political instincts. "The Kennedys have turned against us," she reportedly tells her diary. "Thank God for [CIA director John] McCone." McCone was himself the subject of an "Outsider's Newsreal" satirical fantasy set at CIA headquarters in Langley, Virginia. "I think the best way to proceed," McCone tells his aide, "is first to decide whom we're going to support there." "By 'we,' John," the aide asks, "do you mean the CIA or the United States?" In obeisance to the president's "wistful desire" to overthrow the Diem government, McCone plots a coup that will hinge in part on the organization of American Zen Buddhists into a "sort of Abraham Lincoln Brigade."[36] In a final, tragic premonition of the trouble that would soon unfold in South Vietnam, the *Outsider's Newsletter* adapted Frank Sinatra's hit "I've Got You under My Skin" for President John Kennedy, whom it imagined singing,

the Outsider's Newsletter

"All We Know Is What We Don't Read in the Papers"

Vol. 1, No. 2   **A Monocle Publication**   **Price: 25¢**

Myths and Realities About Cuba!
True Facts Bared: No Holds Barred

36. Like other left-liberal critics of President John F. Kennedy, the staff of the *Outsider's Newsletter* were not pleased with the 1961 debacle at the Bay of Pigs. Of course, cartoonist David Levine could not imagine how eerie his caricature of the president would later seem. By permission of David Levine and Victor Navasky.

You've got me under Ngo Dinh
You've got me in deeper than I want to be,
So deep that I feel it's really not smart of me . . .

Despite the warning voices Left and Right
That repeat and repeat on the Hill-
'Don't you know, little Jack, you never can win

Mocking Dr. Strangelove

'You'll lose your plurality
'Remember political realities'[37]

Perhaps the most effective issue of *Monocle* to deal with U.S. foreign policy was its "Special CIA Issue," published in late 1963. Within this issue, evidence of *Monocle*'s inspired sense of mischief was provided by a comic strip written and drawn by Chuck Alverson and Robert Grossman involving the adventures of "Roger Ruthless of the CIA" and, in the vein of Kurt Vonnegut's satiric look at bomb shelters, a counterfeit interoffice memo addressed by the Creative Director of the CIA's Public Relations Department. "I think it's pretty clear to all of us by now just what kind of trouble we at CIA are in, imagewise," Dan Greenburg, the memo's author began. "The three little words that kind of bring it home to me, personally, are: South Viet Nam." Astutely drawing from the postwar trend in which the citizen was increasingly identified as a consumer and politics as entertainment, Greenburg had his CIA PR man insist to his colleagues that they capitalize on "youth, fitness and fun." "Let's face it kids," he states parenthetically, "we ain't going to survive another Bay of Pigs unless we *are* the Fun Intelligence Agency."[38]

Some of the best portions of *Monocle*'s "Special CIA Issue" were contained within Richard Lingeman's parody of a CIA in-house weekly titled *For Your Eyes Only*. This house organ featured recent news of John Furzer "(Assassinations, Middle East Desk)," a colleague who, according to his wife, is on "assignment in South Vietnam, where he has been awaiting orders for the past six weeks on whether to lead a coup against President Diem or his brother, Ngo Dinh Nhu, or both." In its "Personnel Briefs" column it announced a nighttime meeting of the CIA Sport Parachute Club at Attorney General Robert Kennedy's Hickory Hill estate. After a staged battle with "Red" forces (Kennedy's children) "MRS. KENNEDY," the column continued, "will preside at a Vietnamese-style barbecue around the swimming pool . . ." *For Your Eyes Only* also contained small ads for a hand-held communist detector, personal disguises, and lethal weapons. Also included were a sampling of classified ads that might appear in such a publication:

> *Commemorative Photos.* Personnel involved in the Bay of Pigs invasion—I have the class pictures we took at the training camp in Guatemala . . .
> *Information Wanted.* I would be interested in any and all information pertaining to CIA policies, past and present, in South Vietnam. Strictly confidential. Dean Rusk, Dept. of State, Washington 25, D.C . . .

37. The cover for *Monocle*'s 1963 "Special CIA Issue." Illustration by Paul Davis. By permission of Victor Navasky.

Author's Query. For a book I am writing, I would like to get hold of an alleged note reading 'Dear Bobby, Don't forget air cover at Bay of Pigs. (Signed) Jack.' Or is this just an old joke? (If it is, it's not funny.) Allen Dulles.[39]

*　　*　　*

The Second City, the Premise, the Committee, and other improvisational stage troupes and revues of the early 1960s often performed scenes that challenged cold war orthodoxy and questioned American foreign policy. In a *MAD* magazine–inspired ad parody titled "A Word from Our Sponsors," Julius Monk's 1961 stage revue demonstrated how U.S. propaganda agencies might soon tout new, "clean" nuclear bombs. From the Los Alamos testing site, an exuberant announcer points out to a housewife the results of their comparison test: "Let's see whose you picked . . . the U.S. or the U.S.S.R. The U.S.! Less radioactive! *Proof* that U.S. bombs are cleaner by far—even *cleaner* than clean!"[40] Chicago's Second City struck at the subject of nuclear diplomacy and cold war politics more consistently and deeply, deploying the type of irony that suggested a lunatic mentality shared by American political and military elites. As caricatured by the Second City, President John Kennedy appeased peace activist Linus Pauling with the assurance that "for every [nuclear] weapon we detonate, we deplete our supply by one."[41]

More common yet were jibes made at the expense of America's military leadership. Throughout the early sixties, the Second City's Del Close played a double-talking army general named John C. Clevis. Interviewed by an NBC newsman named Ned Polsky—an in-joke reference to the well-known University of Chicago sociologist—Clevis unleashes a torrent of cold war clichés extolling America's heroic mission overseas. After elucidating how the "communist menace" threatened the "corridor of freedom"—that "tender underbelly of the democratic allies"—Close's slightly delusional general describes how his training school helps American soldiers resist the "terrible communist threat of brainwashing." With his rambling interrupted only by his nervous tic, Clevis declares with typical Second City–style irony that "the best and only defense against brainwashing is an unswerving, unshakable faith in the American way of life." "We use the very finest audio-visual tools," he explains. "We drill it into them, day after day, after day, after day."[42]

Close's Clevis character and the subject of nuclear weapons were the centerpieces of the only extended performance the Second City staged during the early sixties. Running in Chicago during the summer of 1962, "My Friend Art Is Dead" featured Clevis as a Pentagon general with close ties to a weapons manufacturer and to *Playboy* publisher Hugh Hefner. Preparing himself for a television panel show debate on the arms race with stripper Lili St. Cyr, Clevis rehearses the military establishment's position on the arms race ("we simply regard war as a military alternative to peace") and his positive evaluations of nuclear fallout. "We learn a great deal from the radioactive byproducts of nuclear explosions," Clevis states. Were it not for the presence of strontium 90 in American milk, the AEC would not have the data it needs to "raise human tolerance limits." In a later parody of the NBC-TV *Meet the Press* program, Close's General Clevis character argues that he supports the AEC's decision to change the name of radiation emitted from strontium 90 to "sunshine units" and then explains that the Defense Department's consideration of the neutron bomb "goes along with the ideal of the preservation of the home."[43]

Performances staged and improvised by Second City members and their cohort during the early 1960s were studded with dark references to the possibility of a nuclear catastrophe. While the Establishment in New York closed out its program with Carole Simpson singing "Sitting in the Sun" to the accompaniment of newsreel footage of exploding nuclear bombs projected onto a screen, the Premise concluded its performances with a macabre scene titled "The Button Room." Here, a dim-witted private in a top-secret U.S. Army command room was shown obsessing neurotically about "the button" he would be called to hit during a nuclear war. As he begins to meditate on the immense power his position commands, he begins practicing his technique and then mutters, "Button, button, who has the button. I've got the button." As the remaining cast sings "He's Got the Whole World in His Hands" in the wings, the stage lights fade. According to critic Nat Hentoff, a demanding critic not often taken in by hokey material, the effect of this dark piece was nothing less than "chilling."[44]

One of the most popular and talked-about scenes performed by the British troupe Beyond the Fringe while it was in residence in New York City was "Civil Defense Commission," a wry look at the absurd logic undergirding the Anglo-American civil defense strategy. Staged to great effect, according to a *New York Times* reviewer, during the Cuban Missile Crisis and to a national audience in early 1963 on *The Jack Paar Show,* this scene parodied the type of recommendations civil defense officials commonly issued to the public. If you are in the target area during a nuclear

Mocking Dr. Strangelove

area, Peter Cook's character proclaims, "you are *really* in it." However, once an attack is launched, they maintain, civilians have four minutes to evacuate the target area since some individuals (a reference to British track star Roger Bannister) can run up to a mile in that time. "If we are fortunate enough . . . to be the aggressor," Jonathan Miller's character announces, "we are in a position to strike a blow of 20, 30 or even 40 mega deaths, or . . . 40 million lifeless forms strewn about here and there." When Dudley Moore, seated in the audience, asks the panel how long it will take for "normal public services" to be resumed after Armageddon, Miller responds that it would not be long before a "skeleton service" was available. In the event of heavy radioactive fallout, Cook recommends donning a large paper bag and then locating a civil defense official who will "tell you *exactly* where you can go."[45]

Less maudlin and perhaps more funny were the scenes the Second City and the Premise devoted to the early-sixties fallout shelter craze. Performed throughout the early 1960s, these scenes in significant respects mirrored the escalating cultural debate surrounding the ethics of civil defense programs and fallout shelters within the United States. In "Fallout Shelter Salesman," a popular Second City scene performed throughout 1962 and 1963, a representative of the Acme Fallout Shelter Company attempts to train three aspiring shelter salesmen in a hotel room. As this scene develops, it becomes clear that one of the three hucksters will be particularly adept at his job since he is prepared to use a full-color brochure containing pictures of "blast victims from Hiroshima and Nagasaki." In a reference to press reports about shelter owners arming themselves in order to protect their underground investments, the salesman declares that he is willing to throw in a free machine gun to use on panic-stricken neighbors who try to invade their safety zones. He even offers a money-back guarantee in case, in the event of a thermonuclear attack, the shelter fails to provide adequate protection.[46]

Not far from the Second City, at the headquarters of *Playboy* magazine, Hugh Hefner and his staff imagined how Madison Avenue advertising agencies ("wherein such soothing concepts as reposeful shelters are hatched") might market private fallout shelters to the American public. In a parody of a popular religious maxim from the 1950s, *Playboy* envisioned an advertising executive pitch: "The family that burrows together stays together." Several years earlier, Hefner and his colleagues editorialized strongly against the "conspiracy of silence" surrounding the radioactive effects of strontium 90. Now, in February 1962, they explained that they were moved to satirize fallout shelters because they could not "erase from our mind [the picture] of a young family snugly ensconced in the buoyant relaxation of its Family-Library-Music room shelter, sipping the bubbly and watching the true-life adventures of *Nikki, Wild Dog of the North*— while above them civilization dissolves into radioactive dust." The next issue of *Playboy* returned to the absurdity of private fallout shelters in a two-page satirical spread on "How to Stop Worrying about the Bomb," authored and drawn by *Monocle* contributors Seymour Chwast and Ed Sorel. Here Chwast and Sorel offered prescriptions for "bomb worriers" (hallucinogenic mushrooms) and advised that, following nuclear blasts, Americans "find a Zen master quickly" and don asbestos-lined, ankle-length coats.[47]

Without question, the hardest-hitting and most prescient satiric scenes that the Second City and the Premise developed in response to the cold war and American foreign policy were those that addressed America's escalating presence in Southeast Asia. As early as 1961, the Premise routinely presented a scene in which a Soviet and American official each attempt to persuade a Laotian rice farmer why their aid would benefit him most. After the two officials begin to scuffle, they declare "total war" on each other and then proceed to deal a mortal blow to the bewildered farmer. In that same year, the Second City presented "How to Avoid the Draft," a scene that a *Variety* reviewer considered "a prime gaffe in the midst of the current mobilization." Shortly later it performed "Technical Assistance in Vietnam," a piece in which Del Close again played his General Clevis character. This time Clevis is interviewed in Vietnam by a reporter from *Life* magazine who is doing a cover story, "*Life* Goes to a Limited War." When asked about the five thousand troops under his command, Clevis is quick to insist that they are "fully-armed technical advisors," not soldiers. Suddenly he yells to his sergeant to "get those gooks out of the field. I am trying to give those photographers from *Life* a true image of what is going on in Vietnam." Clevis explains that his biggest problem is having an army of pacifists under his command. "They're Buddhists," he explains, "and from a military standpoint it's tricky." With a note of irony that many in the Second City audience apparently failed to appreciate, Clevis says that he is hopeful that the Vietnamese will learn to kill since "Christianity is catching on."[48]

The escalating crisis in Southeast Asia did not escape the notice of Peter Cook's Establishment troupe. Throughout 1963 and early 1964, the Establishment hit hard at the American-supported regime in South Vietnam and Madame Nhu in particular. In reference to the Dragon Lady's cold dismissal of Buddhist demonstrations in Saigon, the Establishment's Alexandra Berlin caricatured her in mock interviews complaining, "How can you talk to me of the burning of monks when only last week Edith Piaf died in Paris?" and explaining that the burning of monks would be suspended with the arrival of the monsoon season. In late 1963, Cook included newsreel footage—"wild with double entendres," according to *New York Herald Tribune* critic Judith Crist—of a press conference given by Madame Nhu. Better yet was an Establishment scene in which John Bird, playing an American "expert" on Southeast Asia, fumbles through a confusing list of leaders propped up by the United States government. Bird's rambling explanation was immediately followed by a newsreel clip of President Kennedy at a press conference explaining the leadership situation in Laos with disturbingly similar double-talk.[49]

*   *   *

Although dark, satirical treatments of the bomb and nuclear diplomacy appeared on independent label recordings and in newspaper cartoons, small-circulation periodicals, and the performances of improvisational troupes, they seldom entered mainstream popular culture. Ever mindful of the cautiousness of its advertisers, commercial television and radio broadcasters had little stomach for such fare. The controversy surrounding the 1957 premiere of *The Stan Freberg Show* on the CBS radio network was certainly proof of that. The most notable segment of this relatively tame program was its longest, a twenty-minute satiric piece titled "Incident at Los Voraces." This "Freberg Fable" was a thinly veiled attack on Las Vegas, a city the Baptist-raised Freberg considered overrun with greed and sin. Set in the future, "Incident at Los Voraces" recalls the events of 1960 when the rival casino-hotels El Sodom and Rancho Gomorah begin attempting to drive each other out of business by staging magnificent entertainment spectacles. After the Rancho Gomorah is able to book the 1960 presidential inauguration (twice a night for two weeks), the El Sodom retaliates by reassembling the Gaza war in its new Suez Room (capacity, 750,000). In a final gesture meant to reap huge profits and drive its competitor out of business once and for all, the Rancho Gomorah books and sells out a million-seat, one night only presentation of "The Hydrogen Bomb."[50]

Judging by the nervous laughter and periods of silence accompanying

Freberg's satiric parable, the staging of nuclear annihilation caught many in the studio audience off guard. According to Freberg, CBS itself "went into shock. What kind of comedian was this? They seemed to forget that they had hired a satirist, if indeed they had ever known it. It was like they were expecting maybe Henny Youngman and got Jonathan Swift."[51] Network officials in CBS's New York office at first demanded that Freberg drop the "Incident at Los Voraces" segment before the program was scheduled to air on the West Coast, but Freberg managed to revise it in time so that only the references to the Gaza strip and nuclear catastrophe were deleted. Reviewers of the premiere, most of whom responded to it with praise, were unaware of the problems Freberg encountered. *Time* magazine did mention the last minute editing and quoted Freberg complaining about the "tapioca curtain" that "panicky network people and panicky sponsors" erect between the public and the comedian. Reflecting on his experience with network "censorship" Freberg remarked, "Now I know what killed Fred Allen!"[52]

Over the next six years, a period that witnessed significant social and political change, critical evaluations of the bomb and the cold war began to slowly seep into mainstream commercial culture. By the early 1960s, episodes of Rod Serling's CBS television program *The Twilight Zone* addressed the consequences of thermonuclear war in a veiled though compelling manner. Hollywood studios, which by the late fifties had demonstrated a willingness to take risks in order to compete against television, began producing movies that poked gentle fun at the military—most notably *No Time for Sergeants* (1958), *The Perfect Furlough* (1959), and *Don't Go Near the Water* (1957). Billy Wilder's cold war comedy *One, Two, Three* (1961) featured a Coca-Cola executive (James Cagney) who serves the objectives of corporate headquarters—the conquest of the soft drink market behind the Iron Curtain—from his outpost in West Berlin. Amid the wild plot that develops around his daughter's affair with an unrepentant East German Communist are scattered numerous satiric jokes made at the expense of Coca-Cola colonialism, American popular culture, cold war diplomacy, and the rehabilitation of German Nazis. And in one of the most interesting films of the early 1960s, John Frankenheimer's dark thriller *Manchurian Candidate* (1962), "simplistic modes of cold war logic," as Margot Henriksen has argued, came under comedic assault.[53]

That there was a growing audience for sharp-edged political humor, particularly among Americans dismayed over the cold war's malevolent influence, is nowhere more evident than with the commercial success and popularity of the film *Dr. Strangelove, or: How I Learned to Stop Worrying and Love the Bomb,* released in early 1964. Director Stanley Kubrick, the artist mainly responsible for *Dr. Strangelove,* was regarded by influential critics during the late 1950s as one of the most promising talents working in the film industry, in large part because of his willingness to tackle socially significant, controversial subject matter. In 1957, Kubrick had translated his concern with the callousness of the military and the insidiousness of warfare into the drama *Paths of Glory.* As a moralist deeply concerned with mankind's inability to keep pace with scientific progress, Kubrick was understandably perturbed by the escalating arms race. Like many other Americans who had lived through the 1961 Berlin crisis and the Bay of Pigs fiasco, he worried over the global escalation of nuclear arms and the dreadful possibility of nuclear war it portended.

Kubrick's concerns grew into an obsession, and he soon engaged in a fevered pursuit of information regarding cold war nuclear strategy. He read a vast quantity of literature addressing the technical aspects of modern warfare, including articles in the *Bulletin of the Atomic Scientists* (to which he subscribed) and, most importantly, Herman Kahn's seminal treatises *On Thermonuclear War* (1960) and *Thinking the Unthinkable* (1962). Kubrick was fascinated with nuclear strategists such as Kahn and Thomas Schelling and engaged them in conversation. Once he began to consider the possibility of framing a film around the subject of nuclear war, he purchased the rights to *Two Hours to Doom,* retired Royal Air Force pilot Peter George's suspense thriller about a nuclear defense system that goes tragically wrong.[54]

The idea of translating George's book to the screen posed significant challenges—challenges that even the world's best directors seemed unwilling or incapable of accepting. When *Show Magazine* in June 1962 polled Louis Malle, Carol Reed, Ingmar Bergman, Elia Kazan, François Truffaut, and other prominent film directors about how they would create a film "about the Bomb and its effects on modern man," Bergman, Kazan, and Truffaut were unable to offer suggestions. Malle and Carol Reed, on the other hand, recommended approaching the bomb through comedy. "For nothing in the world would I make a film about the H-bomb," Malle responded, "except perhaps a very gross farce . . ."[55]

At some point it dawned on Kubrick also that a comedic and, more specifically, a satiric approach was perhaps best suited for this grim subject. "As I kept trying to imagine the way in which things would really happen," Kubrick remembered, "ideas kept coming to me which I would discard because they were so ludicrous. I kept saying to myself: 'I can't do this. People will laugh.' But after a month or so I began to realize that all the things I was throwing out were the things which were most truthful." "Why should the bomb be approached with reverence?" Kubrick asked. "Reverence can be a paralyzing state of mind." Echoing the sentiment shared by Tom Lehrer, Jules Feiffer, and the other liberal satirists who had addressed the bomb throughout the 1950s and early 1960s, Kubrick believed that "the comic sense is the most eminently human reaction to the mysteries and the paradoxes of life." Realizing that "the only way to tell the story was as a black comedy, or better, a nightmare comedy, where the things you laugh at most are really the heart of the paradoxical postures that make a nuclear war possible," Kubrick called his collaborator James B. Harris and declared, "The only way this thing really works for me is as a satire."[56]

Kubrick had evidenced an attraction to the genre of satire earlier, when he adapted Vladimir Nabokov's novel *Lolita* for the screen. Although *Lolita* (released in late 1962) failed to provoke the Legion of Decency and the Motion Picture Association of America as much as many liberal critics hoped it might, it demonstrated that its director possessed a keen, satiric insight into the social landscape and sexual hang-ups of cold war America. Further proof of Kubrick's affinity with liberal satire is manifest in his choices for collaborators. Kubrick had once approached comedian Lenny Bruce with the idea of working together on a film, and in the early stages of *Dr. Strangelove's* development he turned to his fellow Bronx native Jules Feiffer for assistance. Kubrick had been attempting to collaborate with Feiffer on a film project for several years before he approached him about *Dr. Strangelove*. In 1959, he had invited Feiffer to move out to Beverly Hills so that they could work on a screenplay titled *Sick, Sick, Sick.*[57]

Although Feiffer in the end declined Kubrick's invitations, *Dr. Strangelove* would owe some of its attitude and outlook to his influence. Like Feiffer and the other liberal satirists who critiqued the cold war, Kubrick was appalled by the deception and chilling logic practiced by the U.S. military and by the passive resignation of those Americans who believed that nuclear annihilation was inevitable. Together with Jules Feiffer, Joseph Heller, and their cohort, Kubrick was attuned to the way the military establishment manipulated language in order to validate its objectives. In an interview he gave while he was editing *Dr. Strangelove*, Kubrick spoke indignantly about the way defense authorities had trans-

38. Director Stanley Kubrick on the Shepperton Studios set of *Dr. Strangelove, or: How I Learned to Stop Worrying and Love the Bomb.* Columbia Pictures/Hulton Archive/Getty Images.

mogrified the concept of a nuclear attack into a "preemptive strike" or "defensive" maneuver. In this context, Kubrick pointed out, the H-bomb was no longer a bomb but a "nuclear device." Kubrick likewise bristled at the AEC's attempt to get a fix on a nuclear bomb's "probable biological effects"—a disturbing calculation, Kubrick ironically noted, "in which they figure out with this little computer how much flying glass will gouge one centimeter deep into soft tissue and kill how many people. Soft tissue! They don't even say flesh! Isn't it great? Isn't it one long laugh?" As it was with Feiffer and other liberal satirists, laughter for Stanley Kubrick was not merely an escape from reality but a direct engagement with it. "The most realistic things are the funniest," Kubrick professed. "Laughter can only make people a little more thoughtful."[58]

* * *

In the end the assignment of converting *Dr. Strangelove* into a "nightmare comedy" fell upon the willing shoulders of writer Terry Southern. Southern came to Kubrick's attention through Beyond the Fringe's Jonathan Miller and the British comic actor Peter Sellers, both of whom were great admirers of Southern's picaresque satire *Magic Christian* (1960). Kubrick found in Southern a wildly iconoclastic temperament, the perfect muse for what would become *Dr. Strangelove's* inspired satiric onslaughts. At the creative peak of his career in the early 1960s, Southern was contributing articles to the *Paris Review, Olympia,* and *Esquire.* He proved himself well suited to Kubrick's satiric outlook not only through his comic novels but through the critical praise he made of "dark laughter" and "existentialist humor" in an April 1960 review article in the *Nation.* Reviewing Kurt Vonnegut's *Cat's Cradle* later for the *New York Times,* Southern confirmed his predilection for treating grave subjects with humor. Southern here praised Vonnegut's satiric fantasy "concerning the playful irresponsibility of nuclear scientists" as a "far more engaging and meaningful order than the melodramatic tripe which most critics seem to consider 'serious.'" Welcoming the opportunity to translate his own irreverent, antiauthoritarian perspective to motion pictures, Southern traveled to England, the faraway location where Kubrick had chosen to film *Dr. Strangelove.* Beginning in November 1962, Kubrick and Southern reworked *Dr. Strangelove's* script every morning in the back seat of a Bentley while on their predawn commute to Shepperton studios.[59]

Inspired, no doubt, by the tense atmosphere left in the wake of the recent Cuban Missile Crisis, Kubrick and Southern succeeded in completing a script that was suspenseful as well as outrageously satirical. Their plot roughly followed the form of a 1950s science fiction horror film. General Jack D. Ripper (Sterling Hayden), Strategic Air Command base commander at Burpleson Air Force Base, loses command of his senses and orders a thermonuclear air strike against the USSR in retaliation for what he believes is a "commie conspiracy" to deprive Americans of their "precious bodily fluids." Much to the horror of his assistant, British Royal Air Force Captain Mandrake (Peter Sellers), Ripper then puts Burpleson Air Base on "condition red." Later, underneath billboards proclaiming "Peace Is Our Profession," Ripper's men obediently defend their base against American troops who are sent in to foil Ripper's messianic mission. After obtaining Ripper's strike code, Major "King" Kong (Slim Pickens) and his crew aboard a patrolling B-52 bomber prepare for, as Kong exclaims excitedly, "nuclear combat, toe to toe with the Russkies." Meanwhile, President Merkin Muffley (Peter Sellers) has gathered his Joint Chiefs and military advisors around a large circular table within the War

Room, an eerily dark chamber located deep within the Pentagon's belly. With the smoke of their cigars wafting up to the overhead lights, Muffley and his advisors are seated as if they were players at a very high-stakes poker game. When President Muffley expresses his exasperation at their predicament and the flawed system that allowed it, General Buck Turgidson (George C. Scott), recently arrived from a tryst with his bikini-clad secretary, counters, "I don't think it's quite fair to condemn a whole program because of a single slip-up." Turgidson argues that the most sensible plan for the Joint Chiefs to follow would be to launch an all-out attack, thus preempting a Soviet retaliation. When the horrified president accuses the general of advocating "mass murder," General Turgidson argues, "Mister President, I'm not saying we wouldn't get our hair mussed, but I do say not more than ten to twenty million killed, tops, depending on the breaks."[60]

The Russian ambassador (Peter Bull) is allowed entry into the War Room, over General Turgidson's strenuous objections to this "serious breach of security," in order to help President Muffley contact the Soviet's soused leader, Premier Dimitri Kissof. In a manner very reminiscent of Bob Newhart's solo phone conversations, Muffley attempts to explain the fail-safe system's glitch.[61] "Now, Dimitri," President Muffley addresses the Soviet leader in the voice (according to the script) "of a progressive school teacher," "you know how we've always talked about the possibility of something going wrong with the bomb . . . the *bomb*, Dimitri, the *hydrogen bomb* . . ." At the conclusion of their brief exchange — an exchange that resembles a lovers' quarrel — Premier Kissof reveals that the Americans' attack will trigger something called the Doomsday machine, a device "which will destroy all human and animal life for one hundred years." Meanwhile, Burpleson Air Base and General Ripper's troops are finally seized by Colonel "Bat" Guano. Although convinced that Colonel Mandrake is "some kind of deviated prevert," Colonel Guano grudgingly assists him in relaying the recall code back to the Pentagon. An all-out assault is thus averted, but it is soon discovered that Major Kong's loaded B-52 is still hurtling toward its target. Facing the increasingly grim reality of thermonuclear catastrophe, President Muffley consults his chief nuclear weapons technician, a wheelchair-bound German emigré named Dr. Strangelove (Peter Sellers). Reverting back to his Nazi past, Strangelove proceeds to inform President Muffley of the possibility of preserving "a small nucleus of human specimens" within a mineshaft. Strangelove suggests that members of this surviving elite be composed of "top government and military men" as well as a few women selected for their fertility and, much to General Turgidson's amusement, for "sexual characteristics which will have to be of a highly stimulating order!" Shortly after concluding his presentation on behalf of his postapocalyptic playboys' paradise, Dr. Strangelove's spastic bionic arm thrusts him onto his gnarled limbs and into the direction of the president. "Mein Führer," Dr. Strangelove shouts, "I can walk!" The film then quickly cuts to the final scene: a jarring juxtaposition of Vera Lynn's sentimental ballad "We'll Meet Again" and the image of multiple atomic bombs exploding.[62]

*   *   *

The comic genius Kubrick and Southern attained in *Dr. Strangelove* stands by itself, yet a previously unacknowledged debt is clearly owed to the liberal satiric artists, writers, and performers who had been active during the fifties and early sixties. If it is true, as historian Elaine Tyler May suggests, that *Dr. Strangelove*'s attacks "against the sanctity of the postwar domestic ideology and the politics of the cold war would have been risky endeavors ten years earlier" and that Kubrick and his collaborators would have been "called before the House Un-American Activities Committee,"[63] it is fair to speculate that Kubrick's path was made easier by the commercial and critical success Mort Sahl, the Second City, Jules Feiffer, Nichols and May, and others had achieved earlier. From its title and opening sequence to its cataclysmic conclusion, *Dr. Strangelove* drew from the same brand of edgy, smart irony that underwrote Jules Feiffer's cartoons, the *Outsider's Newsletter*'s counterfeit news stories, and the Second City's best stage scenes. By highlighting the insane logic behind mutual deterrence theory, John Kennedy's cynical political ploy of decrying a missile gap with the Soviets, the incompetence of military authorities, and the ways in which aggressive masculinity might be spurred on by psychosexual dysfunction, *Dr. Strangelove* harkened back to the irreverent ideas Feiffer conveyed in his cartoons throughout the late fifties and early sixties. While its hilarious references to interservice rivalry within the U.S. military recalled the ranting of Del Close's General Clevis, its reference to the alcoholic appetite of the Soviet premier mirrored the *Outsider's Newsletter* caricature of Khrushchev drinking beer and watching television "in what Marxist-Leninist terminology calls 'the rumpus room.'" While its dark imagery of exploding nuclear bombs revisited the work of Stan Freberg and the Establishment, its focus on the absurdity of warfare and military bureaucracy was akin to Joseph Heller's *Catch-22*. *Dr. Strangelove's* rich use of visual gags ("Hi John" read an inscription scrawled on one of the H-bombs) would have been at home in the pages of *MAD*, and its scene involving General Turgidson's telephone conversation with his secretary ("Of course it isn't purely physical, I deeply respect you as a human being") is reminiscent of seduction routines developed by Nichols and May. The inspired performance of Peter Sellers in particular benefited enormously from the same type of improvisational freedom enjoyed by members of Second City and their cohort.[64]

As consistent as it was with late-fifties/early-sixties satiric art and performance, however, Kubrick's film distinguished itself with its intelligence, humor, and striking verisimilitude. Without question, *Dr. Strangelove* stands out as one of the major achievements of the early-sixties "satire boom." Few other examples of American humor and comedy dating from this period had a sharper point of view or have had a more enduring significance. No other work of early-sixties American satire, certainly, had a wider range of targets. At various points throughout *Dr. Strangelove's* ninety-four-minute running time, fifties war movies, religion, American patriotism, right-wing anticommunists, John Birch Society–style cold war paranoia, Stevensonian liberals, sexual neuroses, and the Russians all received their share of rough treatment. Most significantly, *Dr. Strangelove* raised significant questions about the sanity, morality, and intelligence of America's military establishment. The names of the clowns running Burpleson Air Base, the B-52 bomber, and the War Room (General Jack D. Ripper, Colonel "Bat" Guano, Major "King" Kong, and General Buck Turgidson) called attention to the machismo, psychopathic violence, and rigid thinking afflicting the military's top ranks. With General Ripper's character in particular, Kubrick clearly had Air Force Chief of Staff General Curtis LeMay in mind. As head of the Strategic Air Command in 1957 LeMay told members of the Gaither Commission that if a Soviet attack ever seemed likely he would launch a preemptive strike and "knock the shit out of [Soviet bombers] before they got off the ground." With Turgidson's wild ranting about "doomsday gaps" and "mineshaft gaps," Kubrick and Southern's hyperbolic warnings issued from military officials and John Kennedy himself were dead-on. The name of President Merkin Muffley, meanwhile, hinted at the "egghead" effeminacy of Adlai Stevenson as well as the ineffectualness of rational, cold war liberals in the face of apocalyptic scenarios bereft of rationality.[65]

39. Peter Sellers (center), George C. Scott (right), Stanley Kubrick (left, facing forward), and their colleagues share a laugh on the "war room" set of *Dr. Strangelove.* Courtesy of the Wisconsin Center for Film and Theater Research

Inspired, no doubt, by the vogue of Freudian psychology, Kubrick and Southern suggested that the irrationality driving military authorities was in part a product of their aggressive masculinity and libidinous obsessions. Phallic imagery and the conflation of sex and violence are manifest throughout *Dr. Strangelove,* from the opening shot of B-52s gently refueling over the Arctic (to the tune of "Try a Little Tenderness") to the visual gag of the *Playboy* centerfold whose derrière is concealed by an issue of *Foreign Affairs* and to the scene late in the film when Major Kong straddles a hydrogen bomb and rides it to its cataclysmic explosion on earth. While displaced sexual frustration pushes the cigar-chomping General Jack D. Ripper toward insane paranoia and prompts his decision to initiate World War III, it is the contemplation of free sex in the mineshaft that miraculously lifts Dr. Strangelove erect from his wheelchair in the film's closing moments.[66] Taken together, *Dr. Strangelove*'s satiric caricatures of the psychosexual hang-ups, blinding hubris, and personal weaknesses of those in command rendered the possibility of accidental, irreversible war more imminent. At the very least, they raised momentary doubts about whether military and governmental authorities overseeing the cold war deserved the unquestioning respect of the people they served.

Aside from members of the political and military establishments, it was the irrational logic of the cold war itself that most inspired *Dr. Strangelove*'s broad satiric assaults. Only an ideology that was deeply and dangerously irrational would encourage a massive buildup of nuclear weaponry, permit the shameless appropriation of technical expertise (regardless of its source), deny the fallibility of human or technological "fail-safe" systems, or, most illogical of all, entertain the idea of a tactical, limited nuclear attack. The amoral scientific rationalism and absurdity underwriting cold war strategists' outlook on deterrence and postwar survival was personified in the grotesquely mechanical (and therefore hilarious) character of Dr. Strangelove. Brilliantly improvised by Peter Sellers, Strangelove was a composite of emigré scientists and intellectuals who had helped shape America's cold war policies throughout the 1950s and early 1960s: Hungarian physicist Edward Teller, former Nazi rocket scientist Werner von Braun, and Harvard University political scientist Henry Kissinger. To the most well-informed audience members, Dr. Strangelove bore a striking, if not somewhat unsettling resemblance to Herman Kahn, the RAND Corporation and Hudson Institute nuclear strategist who in his seminal study *On Thermonuclear War* (1960) — a book Kubrick had read several times — pondered automated response systems and even charted "Tragic but Distinguishable Postwar States." Taken together, the cold war scenarios formulated by Strangelove and the cast of military officials assembled in the War Room pegged their targets with disarming accuracy. Indeed, after RAND analyst and Defense Department consultant Daniel Ellsberg and a midlevel official saw *Dr. Strangelove* one afternoon in 1964, Ellsberg turned to his colleague and reportedly said, "That was a documentary!" [67]

*   *   *

Given the provocative challenges *Dr. Strangelove* posed to cold war orthodoxy, it surprised many motion picture insiders and critics that Kubrick was able to get his film produced and released. Indeed, Kubrick's film encountered obstacles from the early stages of its development. In early 1963, the president of the Motion Picture Association of America read

Kubrick's script and expressed concern over its portrayal of the American president as well as its numerous sexually explicit references. Mo Rothman, an executive at Columbia Pictures, the studio for which Kubrick was working, reportedly grew concerned about the trajectory of his "nightmare comedy" and sent him word, through the emissary Terry Southern, that "New York does *not* see anything *funny* about the end of the world!" Southern has claimed that Rothman and other Columbia Pictures executives even employed spies to report back on what Kubrick was doing on his set in England. When Kubrick finished his film in late 1963, Columbia's vice president in charge of production declared that it was a "disgrace" to the studio. In an effort to distance itself from Kubrick's final product, Columbia Pictures described it as "just a zany novelty flick which did not reflect the views of the corporation in any way." Columbia's decision to distribute pocket Nuclear Bomb Effects Computers—like the kind Dr. Strangelove himself uses in the film—as "sensational giveaways to VIP's—editors, critics, radio and TV personalities" certainly was intended to help reinforce the impression.[68]

The fact that Kubrick and his collaborators were touching a raw nerve was evident not only in their struggle with their studio but by the critical fallout that followed their film's release. Although the signing of the Limited Test Ban Treaty among the United States, the USSR, and Britain in the summer of 1963 gave hope that the cold war might be thawing somewhat, the memory of the Cuban Missile Crisis and anxiety over the use of nuclear weapons still lingered when *Dr. Strangelove* arrived in theaters the following January. It was this anxiety that perhaps explains the reactions *Dr. Strangelove* received from several left-liberal critics and intellectuals. For a few of them, *Dr. Strangelove* appeared to signal a distressing accommodation to the possibility of nuclear disaster. Along with a critic for Britain's *New Left Review* and *Commentary*'s Midge Decter, Susan Sontag in the *Partisan Review* objected to what she identified as *Dr. Strangelove*'s nihilism. Sontag claimed that Kubrick had actually created a cheerful, reassuring film since, she argued, nihilism by the early sixties had become "*our* contemporary form of moral uplift."[69]

Moira Walsh, writing in the Jesuit journal *America,* argued against "Mr. Kubrick's loud declaration of 'a plague on both your houses'" but claimed that it was "silly" to argue against it since "the vast bulk of American moviegoers" would not be able to "filter out" its "serious and disturbing overtones." Few critics followed Walsh's condescending reasoning. In fact, many worried greatly about *Dr. Strangelove*'s impact on the minds of

Americans and foreigners. This was certainly the case with *Commonweal's* Philip T. Hartung, who objected to what he identified as the film's "extreme tastelessness." In the minds of opponents such as Hartung, *Dr. Strangelove* was not only lacking in taste, it was socially and politically irresponsible. Its greatest danger, its detractors believed, was in its capacity to undermine America's high-tech security blanket and, as a result, rekindle public anxiety. Shortly after it opened, a columnist for the *Washington Post* claimed it could "cause as much harm as many a coup or revolution." "No Communist could dream of a more effective anti-American film to spread abroad than this one," he concluded.[70]

Bosley Crowther, veteran film critic for the *New York Times*, likewise entertained the possibility that foreigners might consider the film as a "shocking exposure of the sort of people Americans are . . ." In his initial review of *Dr. Strangelove*, Crowther wrote that he was "troubled by the feeling, which runs all through the film of discredit and even contempt for our whole defense establishment, up to and even including the hypothetical Commander in Chief." Kubrick's satire proved so troubling that Crowther called it "malefic and sick," "the most shattering sick joke I've ever come across." Several weeks later, as the controversy over *Dr. Strangelove* intensified, Crowther felt compelled to readdress the movie and detail exactly where Kubrick's satire had crossed the line. To poke fun at "military minds" is one thing, he wrote, but Kubrick was "saying that the top-level scientists with their computers and their mechanical brains, the diplomats, the experts, the prime ministers and even the President of the United States are all fuddy-duds or maniac monsters who are completely unable to control the bomb." "To make a terrible joke of this matter is not only defeatist and destructive to morale," he concluded. "It is to invite a kind of laughter that is only foolish and hysterical."[71]

By branding *Dr. Strangelove* "malefic and sick," Bosley Crowther deployed terminology that American critics had used against forms of popular satire since the early fifties. Whereas Crowther's stern judgments would have found wide acceptance in the fifties, however, by 1964 they appeared stodgy and dated. Judging by the responses he provoked among some *New York Times* readers and the positive, often ecstatic reviews *Dr. Strangelove* received in *Time*, the *Nation, Newsweek, Life*, the *New York Herald Tribune, Show*, and other mainstream publications, it was Crowther who was the "fuddy-dud." One particularly eloquent response to Crowther came from the liberal social critic and writer Lewis Mumford. Mumford, like Kubrick in important respects, was a perceptive critic of technology and of mankind's growing dependence on machines. In an essay titled "The Human Prospect," Mumford in 1962 summarized his long-standing reservations concerning technology's eclipse of humanity:

> The threat of wholesale nuclear extermination, on a scale that might permanently mutilate even that part of the human race which escaped immediate destruction, is only the most spectacular example of the negative results produced by science and technics when they are divorced from any other human purpose than their own propensity to increase knowledge and power, and expand the use of their own special products in a fashion profitable to the producer.[72]

Mumford was a longtime advocate of satire who in 1923 had voiced hope that Americans might "outflank" the "practices of the business community" with scabrous laughter. Forty-one years later, writing in the *New York Times,* Mumford saluted Kubrick for "having successfully utilized the only method capable of evading our national censor—relentless but hilarious satire." "It is not this film that is sick," Mumford argued. "[W]hat is sick is our supposedly moral, democratic country which allowed [nuclear gamesmanship] to be formulated and implemented without even the pretense of open public debate."[73]

Other liberal and left-liberal critics and intellectuals from Mumford's generation were quick to defend *Dr. Strangelove.* Gilbert Seldes, for example, used the letters column of the *New York Times* to refute the suggestion, prompted by the director of the University of Pennsylvania's Foreign Policy Research Institute, that the film might drive a wedge between the American people and their government and lower the morale of American troops abroad. Veteran iconoclast Dwight Macdonald, who as editor of the anarchist journal *politics* in the 1940s demonstrated a keen sensitivity to the psychic costs of technology, used his position as *Esquire's* film critic to endorse *Dr. Strangelove* as the "funniest and most serious American movie in a long time . . . a lafforama that leaves one with a painful grin on the face and a brassy taste in the mouth." In *Dr. Strangelove,* Macdonald sang, "every sacred *idée reçue* of the cold war . . . is methodically raked over with a barrage of satire."[74]

Younger liberal critics such as the *New Republic's* Stanley Kauffmann and Robert Brustein were no less enthusiastic about *Dr. Strangelove.* Kauffmann described it as "absolutely unflinching" and praised it as the best American film to appear in a generation. Writing in the *New York Review of Books,* Kauffman's colleague Brustein claimed that *Dr. Strangelove*

342

was the "first American movie to speak truly for our generation." Never one to restrain his enthusiasm for liberal satire, Brustein labeled it "the most courageous movie ever made." For Brustein, *Dr. Strangelove* was a glorious "cinematic sick joke," an extension, really, of the exciting work stand-up performers and satiric revues had been doing the past several years in America's satiric underground. With *Dr. Strangelove*, Brustein argued, "a subterranean vibration" had suddenly become "a series of earthquakes, shattering cultural platitudes, political pieties, and patriotic ideals with fierce, joyous shocks." "If the picture manages to remain open," he pronounced, "it will knock the block off every ideologue in the country . . ."[75]

Dr. Strangelove did not "knock the block off every ideologue," but it made a sizeable impact on the many Americans who paid to see it. By all accounts, it did surprisingly well at the box office. Although not as successful as the other major film comedy of the season, Stanley Kramer's *It's a Mad, Mad, Mad, Mad World,* nor any of the other top twelve grossing films of 1964, it was, according to *Variety,* "boffola" in major cities such as New York, Cincinnati, Chicago, and Minneapolis. *Dr. Strangelove* undoubtedly made its strongest impression on Americans who harbored misgivings about the conduct of the cold war. Many of these moviegoers saw *Dr. Strangelove* and then, like the writer Nora Sayre, left the theater feeling "oddly elated by a sense of possibility: a movie that defied the traditions of taste and subverted our institutions implied that the Fifties were finally fading." *Dr. Strangelove,* Sayre has written, "suggested that we owed reverence to no fixed authority—and that authority could even be disputed." Because *Dr. Strangelove* reached a large national audience and because it raised fundamental questions about the sanity of the cold war, it was a milestone in early-sixties American satire and American culture in general. As Lewis Mumford had hoped, *Dr. Strangelove* represented one of the first breaks "in the catatonic cold war trance that ha[d] so long held our country in its rigid grip."[76]

CHAPTER NINE

PART FOUR

THE LIMITS OF IRREVERENCE

CHAPTER TEN

"Sophisticated Daring" and Political Cowardice

TELEVISION SATIRE AND NBC'S
THAT WAS THE WEEK THAT WAS

In 1950, theologian Reinhold Niebuhr spoke for more than a few liberal intellectuals when he complained that the "comedy currently popular on television is almost completely bereft of any genuine wit or humor."[1] As we have seen, Sid Caesar, Ernie Kovacs, and a few other television comedians soon refuted Niebuhr's impression when, during the early 1950s, they provided viewers a mix of skillful parodies and comic mischief. Nevertheless, the type of social and political satire that intellectuals and critics often equated with "genuine wit" was indisputably a rare commodity on network television during the 1950s. Given the popularity and profitability of safe, predictable domestic sitcoms, American television networks had little incentive to experiment with spontaneous, presentational, satiric comedy. With its revenues increasing at a staggering rate, the television industry did not want to risk advertising revenue, public opprobrium, or the onset of regulatory oversight with programming that might be considered offensive or controversial. In the mid-1950s, certainly, the nation's most important communications medium was in many ways its most conservative. By the late 1950s and early 1960s, however, the situation had changed. Recognizing the critical favor won by performers such as Nichols and May, Bob Newhart, and Mort Sahl as well as the appeal they garnered among young, educated, affluent viewers, network television executives were attracted to the mode of liberal satire. When they began opening space for these performers on the nation's airwaves, American liberal satire achieved wide exposure and popular acclaim. Yet television's embrace of liberal satire was always very cautious. Nowhere was this more evident than with NBC-TV's largely forgotten, live-broadcast topical comedy program *That Was the Week That Was.* Conceived and launched at the height of the Kennedy-era "satire boom," "*TW3*" briefly pursued a type of satiric daring very rare in the history of American network broadcasting.

* * *

Television's timidity during the early and mid-1950s is easily explained by the influence McCarthyism had on the American broadcast industry and the extreme aversion networks, advertisers, and television industry groups had for controversy of any kind. Following the early-fifties censorship battles over vaudeville-style comedy and variety programming, the National Association of Radio and Television Broadcasters issued a code, finalized in 1952, that effectively prevented television humor from broaching subjects in a manner that might be construed as "insensitive" or "irresponsible." Coupled with the significant changes in the ways networks handled their production, technology, and business operations, the television industry's hypersensitivity encouraged the adaptation of the sitcom format. As television historian Lynn Spigel has argued, the sitcom's "preplanned storylines . . . mitigated against the [television variety] comics' spontaneous displays of 'adult' humor and ethnic injokes . . ." By the midfifties, CBS, NBC, and the fledgling ABC network were churning out a host of sterile "domesticoms," which were set in television's all-white, middle-class suburban arcadia. With *Father Knows Best, The Adventures of Ozzie and Harriet,* and their ilk, American network television in the Eisenhower age profited by presenting American viewers with didactic narratives legitimating the nuclear family, paternal authority, and, with the aid of sponsors' commercials, domestic consumerism.[2]

Although situation comedies such as *Father Knows Best* had their devoted followings, the *comedy* in such programs inevitably suffered because it was yoked to a set of common ideological themes, was bound to follow variations on the same setup-punchline scheme, and was forced to revisit the structurally and thematically restricted terrain of the resolvable "situation." Comic reality that was confined to suburban homes populated by middle-class organization men, their obsequious, dowdy wives, and their innocently mischievous children was bound to disappoint critics and untold numbers of American viewers. Critics in particular found sitcoms condescending, lifeless, and unforgivably unrealistic. Hugh G. Foster, for example, acidly remarked in 1960 that the sitcoms emanating from "Desiluland" churned out nothing but endless tales "about Mother, bless her conniving little heart; Father, skunked again; and their insolent young." Even some of the writers responsible for creating the sitcoms could not ignore the format's creative and aesthetic poverty and came to resent the ways these comedies squandered their talents. Mel Diamond, a writer for a number of comedy programs including *Bachelor Father,* was one of many former variety-comedy writers who regretted having to quit writing "funny monologues" and "funny sketches" because, as he recalled bitterly, he was forced to "learn to write some inane fucking sitcom." Another writer confessed that his comedic instincts were continually inhibited by the fact that "in television every time you say something, somebody worries that you said too much." In order to protect themselves, this writer claimed, networks and their sponsors compelled comedy writers to devise "treacle," "a little Sunday School lesson at the end of the show—a sermon against beating dogs or talking back to parents."[3]

By the mid-1950s, with the profitable sitcom ascendant, advertisers' and networks' interest in producing costly, big-name comedy variety programs had dissipated. Comedians who excelled in presentational comic delivery and blackout sketches and who were once the networks' breadwinners suddenly faced extinction if they could not adapt to the safe, domesticated sitcom format. With television comedy slanted toward slick, Hollywood-produced sitcoms, there was little room in network programming for the type of satire once written and performed by comedians such as Fred Allen, Henry Morgan, Bob and Ray, and Stan Freberg. In between his failed stint on NBC's *Colgate Comedy Hour* and his death in 1955, Fred Allen could only find work in television as a host or guest panelist on a series of prime-time quiz and parlor game programs such as *What's My Line?* produced by Mark Goodson and Bill Todman. In the opinion of *New York Times* critic Jack Gould, Allen's final work in television—as a "water boy on the team of Goodson and Todman"—was further proof that what sponsors and network producers feared most was "spontaneity that isn't rehearsed." Gilbert Seldes similarly remarked that Allen served as a "symbol of conspicuous waste." With his failure in television, Seldes observed, "it became progressively harder for lesser satirists to make their way."[4] Henry Morgan was also relegated brief and intermittent roles as a "personality" on quiz and chat shows. On the popular Goodson-Todman production *I've Got a Secret,* for example, Morgan assumed the role of the celebrity panel's resident comic oddball. The fate of Bob and Ray was much the same. By 1955, the only work the pair was able to find in television was for yet another Goodson-Todman game show, ABC's *The Name's the Same.* Following the demise of his CBS radio program in 1957, Stan Freberg made arrangements with CBS television to broadcast a pilot titled *Frebergland*—a madcap, visually surrealistic excursion in which he intended to point his "satiric guns on the medium of television itself, politics, and advertising." CBS executives complained that his ideas were too unpredictable and "esoteric," forbade him from "playing around with the corporate logo," and in the end, according to Freberg, suggested that he do something along the lines of *An Evening with Bea Lilly.* As Freberg relates, all hopes for broadcasting his pilot disappeared when one of the CBS executives disdainfully tossed its script aside onto the meeting room floor.[5] At the same time as Freberg's confrontation with CBS, the television careers of Ernie Kovacs and Sid Caesar were likewise taking a turn for the worse.

The sad prospects for these television comedians did not escape the notice of Groucho Marx, whose popular *You Bet Your Life* radio program made the transition to NBC-TV in 1950 and remained a fixture in prime time throughout the Eisenhower era. The dictates of commercial television had forced Marx to trade the aggressive, iconoclastic comic persona he used in 1930s films such as *Duck Soup* for a more self-deprecating and kindly host. Fans and friends of Groucho mourned the metamorphosis, but Marx viewed it as a necessary adjustment to the conditions created by the lingering effects of McCarthyism. Because of McCarthy, Marx argued in 1958, everybody "became afraid to say what they were thinking." Expanding his explanation into other areas of American culture, Marx told reporters, "There are no more Marx Brothers movies because we did satire, and satire is verboten today. The restrictions—political, religious, and every other kind have killed satire. If Will Rogers were to come back today, he couldn't make a living. They'd throw him in the clink for being subversive."[6]

Liberal critics and intellectuals, many of them fans of Sid Caesar, Fred Allen, and other performers who had disappeared from television by the mid-1950s, often echoed Marx's complaints. For novelist Philip Roth, the demise of *Caesar's Hour* in 1957 portended the general loss of satiric comedy from network television. "Woe unto the satirist, then, who passes judgment," Roth wrote in the *New Republic,* "for he is apt to find the bulk of his viewers divided into two groups: the unamused, who recognize the subject but don't get the point of it; and, what is more expensive to the comic's sponsor, the people who get offended."[7] Jack Gould, arguably one of the most influential television critics of the 1950s, maintained in 1956 that television comedy "desperately" needed "more mature spoofing of the contemporary social scene that in so many areas desperately needs a little healthy kidding." "There is a crying need," Gould argued, "for infinitely more subtlety and wit in television comedy." "All too often," he concluded, "comedy on television sinks to the level of a prefabricated commodity intended only for the toothless moron who sits transfixed in front of his hypnotic watching box." By 1956, critics such as Gould found it difficult to disagree with Steve Allen's pessimistic judgment that for some "unidentified reason" television had become "the first medium in history not only to put a low price on critical humor but practically to exclude it altogether." In a 1963 article for *Esquire* in which he asked "Can TV Be Saved?" cartoonist Al Capp assailed the logic governing network programming decisions, arguing that since television comedy writers are forbidden to use "any controversial public issue . . . public person . . . [or] publicly sold product," they may "never try to be funny about any real subject of any real interest in all the real world." "The successful TV comedy writer today," Capp ruefully concluded, "must be funny about nothing at all . . ."[8]

Al Capp's criticism was only part of a much broader chorus of complaints lodged by liberal critics, intellectuals, and affluent, educated middle-class viewers against the television and advertising industries during the late 1950s and early 1960s. As James L. Baughman, Michael Curtin, William Boddy, J. Fred MacDonald, and other broadcast historians have demonstrated, these critics and viewers lamented the disappearance of live, New York–based dramatic anthology broadcasts, fretted over the ethical transgressions revealed by the 1959 quiz show scandals, protested incidents of sponsor censorship, and in general concurred with Federal Communications Commission (FCC) chair Newton Minow when in 1961 he famously declared to a convention of the National Association of Broadcasters that America's broadcast networks had turned television into "a vast wasteland." Network and television industry executives responded to the widespread complaints by reminding critics in particular that television was "selling soap, not a course in the humanities" and, in the words of an industry publication, was "a medium for the masses, not for that minority of superior gentry with spherical crania who dwell in ivory towers of pseudo-intellectualism."[9] Assuming a more conciliatory approach, the industry began wooing viewers and critics by initiating public-service documentaries and broadcasting mature, socially conscious dramatic series. In the less restrictive cultural climate of the late 1950s and early 1960s, America's television networks even began to consider ways they might use less conventional comedy programming to win over viewers and critics.

*   *   *

The networks' new programming strategy coincided with the emergence of marketing data that suggested that networks could operate more profitably if they partially abandoned their traditional "mass-mass" audience and instead began targeting distinct demographic and taste categories. As CBS's *Route 66* (1960–64), ABC's *Patty Duke Show* (1963–66), and a host of other programs demonstrate, the networks began pursuing more narrow audience segments—the affluent "hip bachelors," the "young females"—in the early 1960s. Young, middle-class viewers with large disposable incomes were natural targets for networks and advertisers, and throughout the early and mid-1960s programming began to shift in their favor. More surprising was the networks' courtship of the "quality" or, to use the parlance of the television industry, the "egghead" audience. As a group, educated, middle- and upper-middle-class viewers—those most prone to consider television an unredeemable "wasteland"—exerted an influence disproportionate to their viewing habits. In March 1961, *Variety* reported a "growing concern among some top TV thinkers that the medium has lost a vital segment of its audience—the professional class of doctors, lawyers, teachers and business leaders." At a time when the television industry was suffering a crisis of legitimacy, a number of network executives viewed educated professionals as potential allies and yearned to win their favor. By the early 1960s, even *TV Guide* was exhorting that it was "time for all good eggheads to come to the aid of their programs." Networks also viewed the "egghead" or "class" audience as a bellwether for the general audience's evolving tastes. Numerous analysts and media studies suggested that the Kennedy-era "cultural revolution" had rubbed off on average middle-class viewers to the extent that they were even beginning to emulate the more "sophisticated" viewer's tastes. As opposed to the working-class viewer who lacked confidence "about exercising self-control in relation to television," one industry publication pronounced with characteristic condescension, the middle-class viewer was becoming more discriminating, more receptive toward new formats, more accepting of programs "which seemed more spontaneous and more alive," and more capable of handling "complicated plot structures and dramatic presentations with more personal reward."[10]

In keeping with their new, more nuanced targeting of segmented markets, network programmers and advertising executives were convinced that something new and exciting was needed in the standard mix of comedy series. One confidential audience survey compiled for a media consultant firm in 1963 affirmed for many industry insiders the necessity of varying the old family sitcom formula. "The plainest distinguishing feature now," the survey concluded, "is an upper-middle-class complaint about sameness and tiredness in some of the family situation comedies."[11] In response to the domesticoms' "sameness and tiredness," networks and the Hollywood production studios they contracted experimented with a variety of unusual comic formats. NBC in 1961 began a new Nat Hiken comedy series titled *Car 54, Where Are You?* which was shot in New York City. *Car 54* revolved around the exploits of professional police officers and, in keeping with Hiken's progressive social outlook, regularly featured black actors such as Nipsey Russell and Ossie Davis. CBS struck ratings gold between 1960 and 1963 with a run of unconventional comedies including *The Dick Van Dyke Show, The Andy Griffith Show, Mr. Ed, My Favorite Martian,* and *The Beverly Hillbillies.* The phenomenal success of *The Beverly Hillbillies* shook the industry and spurred the "big three" networks to create sitcoms that transcended the familiar domestic formula. Although early-1960s comedy programs, particularly those coproduced by Danny Thomas and Sheldon Leonard (*The Danny Thomas Show* and *The Andy Griffith Show*), did not shy away from easy resolutions and overt didacticism, they differed, occasionally significantly, from sitcoms that were prevalent during the previous decade. Lynn Spigel has cleverly demonstrated how the new breed of the fantastic sitcom represented by *Mr. Ed* and *Bewitched* poked fun at the narrative conventions of the traditional sitcom and even "engaged viewers in a popular dialogue through which they might reconsider social ideals."[12] *The Beverly Hillbillies* often elicited savage reviews from critics because of its decidedly lowbrow humor, but its supporters were quick to identify its sly, albeit muted satire of upper-class cultural pretensions.

More importantly, local and network broadcasters by the late 1950s and early 1960s began appealing to the growing audience of educated, middle-class viewers by including satire and parody within their mix of comedy programming. Beginning in 1958, a number of satiric performers who some feared would never broadcast again made brief, intermittent television appearances. Early in 1958, Sid Caesar performed a series of specials for ABC titled *Sid Caesar Invites You*. Later that year he collaborated with Art Carney and Shirley MacLaine in an NBC *Chevy Show* cowritten by Larry Gelbart and Woody Allen. Throughout this hour-long special, Caesar and the cast parodied novice political speechmaking, *Playhouse 90*–style drama, Tennessee Williams, and Dick Clark. More significant were the returns of Henry Morgan, Ernie Kovacs, and Stan Freberg. Although Morgan continued to find no work in network television outside of *I've Got a Secret,* he conducted his own live talk show in 1959 on New York's independent station WNTA-TV. A year later he initiated a late-night television version of *Here's Morgan* on Los Angeles station KCOP. Ernie Kovacs returned to television in 1959 with a prime-time network game show, ABC's *Take a Good Look* (1959–61). With its quirky mixture of comic playacting and its lampooning of other quiz shows, *Take a Good Look* was hardly typical of programs in its genre. Better yet were a string of seven offbeat specials Kovacs taped for Dutch Masters Cigars and ABC in 1961. These specials—the last programs Kovacs produced before his untimely death—yielded memorable skits including a bizarre panel show lampoon titled *Whom Dunnit?* Finally, Stan Freberg appeared on Dinah Shore's *Chevy Show* five times in 1958. Using a Martian hand puppet named Orville, Freberg was able to make veiled satiric references to segregation and other odd practices permitted on Planet Earth. In February 1962, he presented a *Chinese New Year's Eve* special on ABC. In addition to lampooning David Susskind's *Open End* and *Sing Along with Mitch,* Freberg smartly critiqued networks' creative control as well as the artifice and vapidity behind programming schedules, commercial lead-ins, and laugh tracks.[13]

In 1959 several of Freberg's associates and former colleagues joined Jay Ward in putting together a novel daytime animated cartoon series for ABC titled *Rocky and His Friends*. Ward, a shrewd California real estate salesman and Harvard MBA who had first tried his hand at animated cartoons in the late 1940s, was assisted primarily by a talented writer-actor named Bill Scott. Scott had previously worked with Freberg on *Bedtime for Beany* and together with fellow Disney Studio exiles Phil Eastman and John Hubley ran the Popular Front cartoon production company United Productions of America (UPA). Under pressure from HUAC's investigations into left-wing political influence within Hollywood, Scott had been fired from UPA in 1952. Now, with partner Jay Ward, Scott was able to use *Rocky and His Friends* and its NBC prime-time successor *The Bullwinkle Show* (1961–64) to farcically send up everything from the cold war superpower struggle to the space race, Walt Disney, newsmen, fairy tales, Red Skelton, Nazis, college athletics, and show business.[14]

Although *Rocky and His Friends* and *The Bullwinkle Show* were ostensibly children's programs, adults (the program's most loyal viewers) savored the campy cultural references, puns, comic one-liners, and the sly, self-referential asides that punctuated *The Bullwinkle Show*'s slapstick action and silly plotlines. On occasion, Scott inserted jokes into the programs that were both sharp and topical. In one episode of the program's recurring "Peabody's Improbable History" segment, for example, the conquistador Francisco Pizarro answers the native Incan Indians' charge that he is a hostile invader by claiming, "No! I'm only an advisor from the U.N." As a *Variety* reviewer noted, even its commercials for General Mills had a satiric edge. In a spot for Cheerios cereal, for example, Ward and Scott created a live-action parody of David Susskind's *Open End* panel program. When *The Bullwinkle Show* peaked during the 1961 and 1962 seasons, it was widely praised for its intelligence and wit. *Newsweek* spoke for many when it judged *The Bullwinkle Show* in 1961 as "the most courageous program on the air." Jules Feiffer, who had long admired Bill Scott's work at UPA, wrote in praise of *Bullwinkle* in Hugh Hefner's *Show Business Illustrated*. Feiffer here labeled *Bullwinkle* as the "Genêt of television" and singled out its skillful use of "social comment."[15]

Unfortunately for Scott and Ward, *Rocky and His Friends* and *The Bullwinkle Show* claimed few admirers among the executive staffs at ABC and NBC. Ward and Scott reportedly prompted confrontations with officials at both networks over material that the networks deemed objectionable. After NBC succeeded in cutting a *Bullwinkle* episode involving cannibalism, Ward and Scott had Rocky the Squirrel make a cutting reference to the network's "standards and practices." Much more offensive from NBC's point of view were the outrageous publicity stunts Ward and Scott staged on behalf of the program. In addition to organizing a parade down Madison Avenue and irreverent letter-writing campaigns directed at prominent television, advertising, and government officials, Ward and Scott distributed lyrics for a "Sing Along with Bullwinkle" in which they ridiculed NBC for falling behind in the Nielsen ratings. Ward and Scott may have been what *TV Guide* called "official 'inside' jokesters of the industry," but NBC was clearly not amused. Relations between NBC and Jay Ward Productions had reportedly grown so chilly by 1962 that the network decided to withdraw *The Bullwinkle Show* from prime time.[16]

*　　*　　*

Although executives at NBC and ABC were clearly nervous about the potential hazards of bringing satiric comedy to the airwaves, they were nevertheless determined to capitalize on the late-fifties and early-sixties "satire boom." A number of television and advertising industry analysts at this time foresaw a large, untapped market for hip, "new wave" satire among affluent, educated middle-class viewers. *Television Magazine,* a publication committed to spotting the latest trends for its television and advertising industry readers, brought attention to the "new humor" in 1961 and declared, "Gimmicks are OUT, satire is IN . . ." Referring to "sicknik" comedians such as Mort Sahl (the "angry young comedian"), Shelley Berman, Dick Gregory, and Nichols and May, *Television Magazine* argued in 1961 that the new humor had brought "new TV sophistication and a new sociopolitical commentary, a comedy that bites at life and picks at mores . . . [T]he effect is at once shattering and, to those who dig, hilarious." Two years later *Television Magazine* reported that new audience surveys suggested that viewers, "particularly in the younger, upper-class group," hungered for more of "the Shelley Bermans, Bob Newharts, Mort Sahls and Mike Nichols and Elaine Mays . . ."[17]

By the late fifties, these satirists began achieving wider public exposure through guest appearances on variety and late-night talk shows. NBC was particularly vigilant in booking this cohort for programs such as Perry Como's *Kraft Music Hall, The Steve Allen Show, Today,* and Jack Paar's *Tonight Show.* Paar's hip, controversial late-night program was by far the most popular venue for Sahl and his fellow satirists. Between 1958 and 1962, Sahl made four appearances on the *Tonight Show* and even substituted for Paar as a host. During the same period, Paar and his producers booked Nichols and May on five occasions, Gregory on twelve, and Berman on over two dozen.[18]

Throughout the early 1960s, local and network television provided viewers with a glimpse of the type of satirical comedy improvisational troupes were performing in Chicago, San Francisco, and New York. Between 1962 and 1964, Beyond the Fringe, the Committee, and the Premise each made appearances on Jack Paar's *Tonight Show;* the Establishment, the Premise, and the Second City were given airtime on New York's WNEW; and Chicago's WBKB ran *Second City Reports,* a special presentation of the hometown Second City performers directed by William Friedkin. Perhaps the most provocative of these performances was the Premise Players' cruel parody of a racist Southern governor, broadcast on NBC's *Today Show* in February 1963. Among the Southerners not amused by the Premise's irreverent jab at segregation and "Rankin Faubus Barnett" was Senator James Eastland of Mississippi. Eastland initiated an FCC inquiry into the performance but was stymied by executives at NBC who argued that the Premise's satire was "wholly consistent with television's right and obligation to encourage free discussion of current issues and affairs and certainly in keeping with our nation's democratic tradition."[19]

*   *   *

When NBC began looking for someone to host a new satiric variety program during the early 1960s, it approached Bob Newhart, the gentle "everyman" nightclub satirist whose *Button-Down Mind* albums were phenomenal hits in 1960 and 1961. Newhart had been offered opportunities to work in sitcoms series at ABC and CBS, but he turned them down. "That would have been death for me," Newhart told *TV Guide.* "To do the same character week in and week out would have been boring for me and the audiences." When Newhart finally made a deal with NBC, he demanded and was granted a free hand in the production of his program. To assist Newhart with the writing of the nonmonologue material, namely, the guest star sketches, NBC hired former *Fred Allen Show* writer Roland Kibbee. When one of the MCA agents arranging the deal with NBC introduced Kibbee to Newhart at San Francisco's hungry i, Kibbee began to anticipate great things for the program. "I thought, here is a man who can do satire and not be heavy-handed about it," he later remembered. "I'd waited a long time since Fred Allen."[20]

When *The Bob Newhart Show* premiered on October 11, 1961, Kibbee sent FCC chairman Newton Minow a telegram inviting him to tune in. "We believe it to be adult, enlightened social satire," Kibbee wrote, "unprecedented on TV." The amount of "adult, enlightened social satire" *The Bob Newhart Show* actually delivered was a matter of some disagreement among viewers and critics. In the mind of its supporters, Newhart's program deserved praise because it respected the intelligence of its audience.

In interviews with the press, Newhart vowed that he would eschew the traditional targeting of the "lowest common denominator" and aim high. "What the TV biggies don't know is that people like entertainment with bite," Newhart told the *Saturday Evening Post,* "They want satire." Satire, he predicted, "could be the next TV trend." Newhart vowed that he would not allow NBC to "pour soothing syrup into my TV stuff," and indeed *The Bob Newhart Show* was unlike any television comedy on the air.[21]

The strength of the program was in its exploration of those areas, as Newhart explained it, "outside show business" such as the "situations people get into trying to cope with bureaucracy and the 9-to-5 mind." In both monologues and sketches Newhart revisited subjects that he successfully addressed in his comedy albums, namely, the scourge of bureaucratic incompetence and the hazards of white-collar conformity. He also aimed jokes at right-wing extremists, the Kennedy administration, fallout shelters, and a host of other targets at which early-sixties liberal satirists regularly took aim. One trademark sketch had Newhart playing Thomas Jefferson in an Ivy League suit and demonstrating what a group of Madison Avenue admen might have done to the Declaration of Independence if they drafted it over a martini lunch. Such antics delighted critics who had been continually disappointed by television comedy. The critic for *Show Magazine,* for example, singled out *The Bob Newhart Show* for praise and remarked presciently, "I don't know how Mr. Newhart managed to slip past the screening committee, but they are surely not going to let him stay around very much longer."[22] Perhaps the best gauge of the program's popularity was the rewards it received from the industry: in 1962 it won a Peabody Award for the best entertainment in television and an Emmy Award for the most outstanding comedy program.

Acclaim for *The Bob Newhart Show* was not universal. A number of critics and viewers felt that Newhart failed to deliver the satire he promised. A critic for the *Village Voice,* for example, dismissed Newhart as a "Middlebrow Sickcomic" and argued that there were "sketches on the Perry Como show which cut a lot deeper and with a lot less pretentiousness" than Newhart's sketches. In the opinion of his detractors, Newhart's failings were linked to his lack of politics. When he told the *New York Times* in April 1962 that he was satisfied with "presenting the absurdity of the situation [in this case the intransigence of racist extremists] without commenting on it," Newhart betrayed the sense of caution that often mitigated satire's critical potential. In the end, Newhart's failure of nerve eventually led to the defection of Kibbee and another writer named Bob Kaufman. "I kept fighting to do satirical comedy and hitting sacred cows," Kaufman later explained, "and Newhart didn't want satire on the show."[23]

The internal strife between Newhart and his colleagues mattered little in the end since his sponsor, Sealtest, and NBC decided to cancel *The Bob Newhart Show* after its first season. In statements to the press, Newhart appeared relieved that his tenure as a television comedian had ended. "I began to feel," he explained to *TV Guide,* "I'm not a comedian, I'm a corporation. And then—you die a little every week." Fans of the program found little comfort in Newhart's remarks. For them, the cancellation of *The Bob Newhart Show* confirmed every ugly truth about the television industry, particularly its shameful lack of guts. NBC was belittled in the press and barraged by angry fan letters, but it did little except hope that the minor controversy surrounding the program would blow over.[24]

*   *   *

For NBC and the other two major television networks, the controversy surrounding the cancellation of *The Bob Newhart Show* illustrated the risks of jumping on the satire bandwagon prematurely. In fact, while attempting to demonstrate their openness to daring and intelligent comedy, CBS, NBC, and ABC often ended up confirming critics' worst suspicions. All three networks suffered bad publicity during the early 1960s when they clamped down on comedy that they and their corporate advertisers deemed inappropriate for the airwaves. CBS in 1963 drew criticism when it forced Allen Funt to drop a six-minute parody of Proctor & Gamble household detergents on his *Candid Camera* program. Three years earlier, NBC set off a small firestorm of debate when it censored a joke that Jack Paar had made on his popular *Tonight Show.* The program's petulant host resigned over the episode but was soon coaxed back by NBC president Robert Kintner. In 1961 NBC again received bad press when it ordered an eight-minute sketch about President-Elect Kennedy and his wife to be deleted from *The Art Carney Show.* An NBC spokesman explained the network's actions: "We have never shied away from spoofing political figures, but we thought it would have been improper to have performers actually portraying the President and his wife. Our decision was based on a matter of good taste." The matter of "good taste" surrounding President Kennedy was again the issue in 1963 when ABC decided to delete Mort

Sahl's jibe about John Kennedy's connections to Sam Giancana from its West Coast transmission of the *Jerry Lewis Show*.[25]

*   *   *

Throughout the early sixties, the best opportunities liberal satirists had for reaching audiences came through syndicated, pay, or foreign television, not the big three networks. By 1962, the Second City had performances broadcast by the pay TV operation Telemeter. Sahl appeared in a special Canadian broadcast in 1962 and a year earlier performed *The Mort Sahl Show* for the BBC, Great Britain's state-owned broadcast network. The BBC, in fact, was one television network that appeared willing to risk its reputation by broadcasting political satire. In 1962, while under the leadership of Hugh Carleton Greene, it attempted to shed its stodgy "Auntie BBC" image by initiating a hip satirical news program titled *That Was the Week That Was*. *TW3*, as the program was commonly called, drew its inspiration and most of its personnel from the same youthful, anti-establishment satiric underground that spawned the Establishment, Beyond the Fringe, and *Private Eye*. At the time that the BBC commissioned *TW3*, British satire, like its American counterpart, was peaking in popularity. The two young men credited for establishing the idea for *TW3* and then setting it in motion were producer Nat Sherrin and an ambitious comic performer named David Frost. Frost, like Peter Cook and nearly all the young turks in the Establishment and Beyond the Fringe, had begun performing comedy as a member of Cambridge University's Footlights Society. As coeditor and lead performer, he was primarily responsible for establishing the tone and defining the style of the BBC's *TW3*. The ironic catchphrase he directed at government officials—"But seriously, you're doing a grand job"—typified the brand of brash, youthful insolence that appealed to a growing number of Britons. In the minds of many British television viewers, Frost and *TW3* appeared to be marching on the same path as playwright John Osborne and the other angry young men dissenting from the staid British establishment. As Frost has explained in his autobiography, he and his fellow performers and writers at *TW3* were "Exasperated Young Men—exasperated by Britain's recurring failures, by hypocrisy and complacency and by the shabbiness of its politics." In certain respects, Frost was the perfect ambassador for satire on the BBC. Although impudent and mocking, Frost was also well-heeled, amiable, and dedicated to the sensible proposition that *TW3* should "lift public satirical commentary," as he explained it at the time, "on to the plane of intelligent adult private conversation."[26]

Not long after it premiered, the BBC's *TW3* became enormously controversial. In mock news segments, interviews, and song, it shocked viewers with its relentless attacks on the royal family, religion, the hypocrisy of the ruling class, and the aloofness of Prime Minister Macmillan's Tory government. On occasion, it was sharp and intelligent, and it prompted Ken Tynan and other influential British critics to wax rhapsodic about the social and cultural virtues of satire. In the eyes of its detractors, however, *TW3* was more often crude, profane, and even sacrilegious. In one celebrated sketch, David Frost imitated a stuffy BBC announcer describing for viewers the sinking of the queen's royal barge in the Thames River. As the royal band plays "God Save the Queen" Frost narrates, "And now the Queen, smiling radiantly, is swimming for her life. Her majesty is wearing a silk ensemble in canary yellow." *TW3* also suggested, jokingly, that Pope Pius XII had been a Nazi sympathizer, and on another occasion it broadcast an inflammatory "Consumers' Guide to Religion." Frost and his colleagues did not pass up the opportunity to comment on the American scene as well. In May 1963, *TW3*'s Millicent Martin and a blackface chorus performed a pointed mock minstrel ditty about the slaying of civil rights activists in the American South, "Where the Mississippi mud / Mingles with the blood / Of niggers hanging from the branches of the trees."[27]

By the end of its first season, *TW3*'s live broadcasts had attracted a weekly audience of nearly thirteen million Britons. It had also generated a host of Parliamentary squabbles and spurred nearly a dozen libel suits. To BBC officials, it had become clear during *TW3*'s second season that the program was more trouble than it was worth; its mockery of religion, royalty, and conservative political personalities, they believed, simply could not be contained. In November 1963, the BBC's *TW3* was abruptly canceled, ostensibly because of an upcoming general election.

On the other side of the Atlantic, *TW3*'s travails were extensively reported by the American press. Throughout its run, in fact, *TW3* became the subject of some intrigue, particularly among liberal American critics and writers despondent over the poor state of early-sixties television comedy. Those who had the opportunity to view it in Great Britain were often impressed by its irreverence. Novelist Angus Wilson, for example, claimed in *Show* magazine that it was "one of the best things that has happened in mass entertainment anywhere." *New York Herald Tribune* critic John Crosby likewise praised it for "scotch[ing] . . . forever the idea that the mass audience likes pablum rather than strong meat." *TW3,* Crosby argued, "powerfully advanced the argument that television should be important, not trivial" and created an environment where "every one's a little freer to speak up."[28]

*　　*　　*

In May 1963, WNEW-TV, New York's independent Channel 5, attempted to replicate the success of *TW3* in a syndicated pilot titled *What's Going On Here?: A Shrewd and Somewhat Rude Look at the News. What's Going On Here?* was the brainchild of former *Esquire* editor Clay Felker and Jean van-den Heuvel, the onetime *Paris Review* editor who was married to prominent New York attorney and Robert Kennedy assistant William vanden Heuvel. With characteristic aplomb, Felker announced that this venture in broadcast satire would "perform a standard journalistic function" by "keeping people in power in line." To fulfill this promise, Felker and van-den Heuvel solicited the participation of the Second City's Roger Bowen and MacIntyre Dixon, Jonathan Miller of Beyond the Fringe, the Establishment's Peter Cook and John Bird, and journalists such as Richard Rovere and Calvin Trillin. The hour-long pilot that this diverse collaborative team eventually put together offered American viewers a good idea of what they could expect from *TW3*-style topical satire: news bulletins interspersed with short sketches and interviews, all offering varying levels of comic commentary.

Critics who reviewed *What's Going On Here?* disliked the British performers' penchant for one-liners and their use of "macabre" film clips, but they were favorably impressed by several of the program's segments. The first, contributed by Bowen and Dixon, savaged the American Medical Association's opposition to public health proposals and called attention to the greed and callous self-interest of physicians. In a mock interview, Dr. Hernando Gatty, the president of the AMA (Anti-Medicare Association) reveals his disgust with the sick and the elderly. When asked if the AMA would oppose the Savior when he returns to Earth Gatty (played by Dixon) responds, "Of course not, no one would oppose him, but I think someone would have to take him aside and make it perfectly clear that America has no time for 'creeping socialism.'" Another favorably reviewed segment offered a "Focus on Chaos," a comic revelation of the confusion inhabiting Southeast Asia and, more ominously, the presence there of dangerously gung ho and inept American military advisors.[29]

Segments such as these prompted *New York Times* critic Jack Gould to claim that *What's Going On Here?* marked "a breakthrough in the use of sauce and sass as instruments of comment on the passing scene." Even British critics, many of whom had grown weary of the smug and self-congratulatory air surrounding *TW3,* complimented its fresh approach. The *Times of London,* for example, lauded *What's Going On Here* for its commitment "to social ends rather than to a general display of scorn" and described its satire as "firmly based in an essential social morality . . ." Despite the enthusiasm of critics such as Gould and the endorsement of President Kennedy (*Time* magazine reported that Kennedy "laughed and stayed with the show to the end"), plans for syndicating *What's Going On Here?* apparently fizzled during the summer of 1963.[30]

What's Going On Here? would have remained a dead concept if it had not been resuscitated by CBS's *Ed Sullivan Show* several months later. CBS and Sullivan were both latecomers to the satire vogue. In 1962, CBS touted the premiere of a "satirical" variety show hosted by Jackie Gleason. Despite its billing as "satire," *Gleason's American Scene Magazine* devoted itself to slapstick sketches of little substance. Few observers would have predicted that Sullivan, a showman who evinced a preference for safe acts, would follow in Gleason's footsteps and attempt to incorporate topical satire into his popular weekly variety program. Yet as Sullivan's celebrated showcasing of Elvis Presley and, later, the Beatles demonstrated, Sullivan was occasionally willing to harness "hot" or risky acts for the sake of boosting his ratings. Since "satire" had become a widely publicized cultural phenomenon by the early 1960s, Sullivan no doubt believed that he could safely package it to the masses.

By all accounts, Sullivan was extremely uncomfortable with the concept of broadcasting topical satire. According to Calvin Trillin, one of the *What's Going On Here?* writers, he was visibly agitated about the nature of the proposed satiric material. To his credit, however, Sullivan ultimately approved the construction of an elaborate news set, hired the comic team of Bob Elliott and Ray Goulding to serve as mock news anchors, and broadcast two *What's Going On Here?* segments over two consecutive weeks in October 1963. By and large, the comic material Bob and Ray presided over was quirky and, in the case of Peter Cook's impersonations of a Scotland Yard investigator and a Foreign Office observer on Quemoy, delightfully absurd. One scene involved an African American man (played by Godfrey Cambridge) and a white liberal (the Second City's Eugene Troobnick) who awkwardly attempt to negotiate the space they share within an elevator compartment. It is difficult to see how this relatively tame comment on clichés surrounding racial relations might have raised objections, but Sullivan nearly blocked it from his program because he considered it "crazed" and "too racially charged."[31]

Given Sullivan's skittishness, it is not surprising that the CBS version of *What's Going On Here?* steered clear of incisive comic commentary. The only exceptions were a "sports item" that made a pointed comparison between the racial intolerance of the American South and South African apartheid and a mock interview with a British observer named "Sir George" concerning the political chaos engulfing Southeast Asia. In the latter sketch, Sir George, a man who is "closely" tracking developments in the region from his cottage in Devonshire, issues a torrent of confusing gibberish in his desperate attempt to explain the rapid succession of ruling elites and the way in which "America is defending the Western way of life" there. A quick cut then took viewers from the interview to a presidential news conference newsreel clip in which President Kennedy likewise fumbled (painfully) over his explanation of the situation. The juxtaposition of "Sir George" and President Kennedy was poignant, perhaps too poignant for Sullivan and CBS. Immediately following this segment Sullivan attempted to defuse the sketch's message by explaining to viewers at home that Kennedy and the good sports at the White House were willing accomplices in the fun. Shortly thereafter, Sullivan and CBS decided to opt out of the final two scheduled installments of *What's Going On Here?* and end their brief flirtation with *TW3*-style satire.[32]

*   *   *

In the end, it took another patron, Broadway producer Leland Hayward, and another television network, NBC, to successfully package the *TW3* concept for the American viewing public. Given NBC's problematic handling of *The Bob Newhart Show* and *The Bullwinkle Show,* few would have guessed that the network was prepared or truly willing to usher hip, cutting-edge satire into the prime-time schedule. Equally unforeseen was the idea of having Hayward—a Broadway and Hollywood producer best known for presenting middlebrow musicals such as *South Pacific* and *The Sound of Music*—at the helm of *TW3*. Prior to 1960 Hayward had had no experience with satire and relatively little exposure to avant-garde culture in general. In other ways, however, Hayward's involvement was not a surprise. Few other figures in the world of postwar popular entertainment, in fact, possessed the clout and the savvy necessary to market "satire" to network television. For nervous network and advertising executives in particular, it was essential to have someone of Hayward's stature to assume control over a program as potentially unpredictable as *TW3*.[33]

By the early 1960s Hayward had enjoyed success in film, television, and the theater. He had also become the ultimate insider, friend to the famous, powerful, and the wealthy. Through the marriage to his third wife, Pamela Digby Churchill, he gained affiliation with English aristocracy and solidified his ties to the American political elite, particularly the Kennedys and other members of the Democratic establishment. Yet despite all these signs of prestige and achievement, it was apparent to many show business insiders in the early sixties that Hayward's star was beginning to wane. As a Broadway producer during this period, he seemed out of touch with theatergoers' changing tastes.[34] Desperate to elude failure, halt his declining prestige, and once again make some money, he saw his chance to bring "sophisticated" entertainment to American television, an industry thirsty for critical respect. When he viewed *TW3* in England, he was thrilled with its immediacy and intelligence. He was convinced that done properly, it might succeed on American television just as his widely praised 1960 *The Fabulous Fifties* television special had. To a man who had always taken pride in his sense of style, his refined taste, and his instinct for all things "chic" and fashionable, *TW3* seemed an emblem of sophisticated daring, a mark of things to come, a surefire success.

During the summer of 1963 Hayward acquired the rights to the BBC's *TW3*. Almost immediately he began to staff a new *TW3* unit of his New York–based production company, Leland Hayward Productions, with men who shared his commitment to intelligent, "sophisticated" entertainment. Marshall Jamison, a member of Hayward's original *Mr. Roberts* cast and key collaborator on *The Fabulous Fifties* reluctantly accepted the daunting challenge of heading *TW3*'s production team. Fortunately for Jamison, locating writers and performers willing to work on *TW3* was not difficult given the enthusiasm the project was generating among talent agents. So great was the interest in staging an American version of *TW3* that even people with little or no experience in show business—a U.S. Senate staffer, for example—volunteered their special insight and writing talent. Careful to distinguish *TW3* from existing comedy-variety programs and sitcoms, Hayward and Jamison insisted that their writers would "not be gag writers in the usual television manner" and would "be cast with infinite care . . ."[35] Eventually Hayward and Jamison secured commitments from a group of young comedy writers (Roger Price, Woody Allen, and Buck Henry), Kennedy impressionist Vaughn Meader, and Gerald Gardner, a young man who had parlayed his experience at Kurtzman's *Help!* into a line of popular photo-caption books that mildly and somewhat affectionately jabbed at politicians—the First Family in particular.[36] To anchor their team of writers, Hayward and Jamison settled on Robert Emmett, a young man who, like all of the key players on the production staff, was schooled in theater and live television but who had no experience in producing or performing satire.

When Hayward and Jamison pitched *TW3* to network executives at NBC during the summer of 1963, they exercised considerable caution. In a series of "mock-up" presentations, Hayward, Jamison, and Emmett carefully demonstrated how topical satire could be fresh, irreverent, and thoughtful, yet not inflammatory. As Emmett recalls, these mock-up presentations were intended "to show [NBC executives] that we could take anything and make fun of it and not be tasteless . . . [or] 'yocky.' The main point of view was that it should be sophisticated, that it should be tastefully daring, over the edge a little but not so that you offended people." In written proposals, Emmett and his colleagues emphasized the enormous appeal topical humor was enjoying during the Kennedy era and delineated satire's role in a healthy, democratic society. An early draft of one proposal explained that *TW3*'s goal was to "*establish a point of view that stimulates laughter and at the same time provides provocative thought.*" "It must be emphasized," the proposal continued, "that our first thought is to entertain, to puncture the pretentious, and to poke fun at the mores of our time." With *TW3,* NBC's viewers would be "invited to join a group of varied performers who, with impudence and humor, will turn the week upside down and take it to pieces, investigating, commenting and laughing at the foibles of American life . . . For it is true that our countrymen have always had the healthy capacity to laugh at themselves." In private correspondence to Hayward, Jamison suggested staging a show capable of creating "tremendous excitement by nature of its impudence and lack of respect for establishment mores, sponsors and network."[37] His boss Leland Hayward was clearly more cautious. Indeed, by framing *TW3* as an "entertainment," by inviting audience members to "join" a group of amiable wits as they laughed at America's "foibles," Hayward gave the impression that he intended his program to be more like a hip parlor game than a venue for provocative moral and political commentary.

Hayward's ambitions for *TW3* were shared to a great extent by executives at NBC, particularly network president Robert Kintner.[38] Like Hayward, Kintner took a special interest in the smart, timely comedy *TW3* promised to deliver. He and his fellow NBC executives were well aware of the risks attendant with the live broadcast of topical satire, but they also knew that presenting *TW3* would undoubtedly win their network the approval of critics and the small but important "egghead" audience. In the summer of 1963, a time when networks were intent on "redeeming the wasteland" but were still open to charges of cowardice and repetition in their programming, the idea of broadcasting an exciting and intelligent program such as *TW3* had considerable appeal. With this in mind, NBC finally decided to give Hayward and his staff the opportunity to air a pilot episode in November. If the pilot provided NBC with enough critical approval and commercial success, Kintner and his colleagues promised Hayward they would option *TW3* as a series.

As the broadcast date of the November *TW3* pilot neared, NBC began marketing it aggressively. In press releases and promotional brochures aimed at potential advertisers the network predicted that the *TW3* pilot would reach 8.6 million homes with the "booming" lead-in of *Bonanza*. In order to reassure advertisers, NBC made a special effort to tag Hayward's name to the project. Hayward, an NBC brochure stated, "knows a hot property when he sees one . . . and is determined to come up with an equally bright and bold American counterpart" to the successful BBC *TW3*. While intent on proving that Hayward would lend his "distinguished professional stamp," NBC was also careful not to downplay the components that would mark *TW3* as innovative and brave. Its promotional brochure described *TW3* as a "topical Hellzapoppin" that will "comment on practically anything and anybody currently in the news." Viewers "are warned," it declared, "not to watch unless they're interested in seeing something new and radically different on the home screen . . . No one will be safe from . . . the program's performers and their mercilessly satiric approach. Not even NBC top brass."[39]

In his comments to the press, Hayward demonstrated a penchant for both caution and daring. While declaring that he and his staff would "make comment," "get into the area of politics," and not "pull back," he conceded that "there are limits" and promised "that good taste will be maintained."[40] Hayward's reference to "good taste" betrayed his cautious bent and therefore signaled something of the contradiction at the heart of the *TW3* enterprise. By promising pointed commentary and, at the same time, judicious restraint, Hayward was exercising, as could be expected, expert promotional skills. Yet as time would prove, Hayward's remarks were indicative of a fundamental and, ultimately, debilitating ambivalence that he shared with NBC over the goals of *TW3*'s satire. On the one hand Hayward promised and even encouraged a variety of comedy that was fresh, daring, and provocative, yet on the other hand he counseled caution and restraint in order to protect his investment. Whether or not it was possible to present satire to American audiences that was provocative yet inoffensive remained to be seen.

* * *

After several months of intense preparation, Hayward, Jamison, and their staff aired the *TW3* pilot on November 11, 1963. From its opening cut, it promised to be unlike any program currently inhabiting the safe confines of pretaped, prime-time network television. After announcing that it was "LIVE from Radio City," *TW3* rapidly cut to a member of Billy Taylor's jazz band playing bongo drums, a picture of French President Charles de Gaulle, and then newsreel footage of an exploding atomic bomb. It immediately demonstrated a willingness to jab at politicians, particularly Republicans. During the opening theme song segment, when Richard Nixon was mentioned as a potential presidential candidate, Jamison and his director Hal Gurnee quickly shot to the interracial folk quartet The Tarriers who proceeded to sing, "Happy Days are here again / Let's all get out and smear again." In other "conservative folk songs" performed later in the program, The Tarriers jibed oil tycoon John Paul Getty and arch-conservative General Edwin A. Walker. In a sketch authored by Gerald Gardner, the actress Doro Merande played a frail eighty-three-year-old Senate Office Building cleaning woman who, despite her advanced age and the benefits she might derive from social welfare programs, was a staunch supporter of conservative Republican Barry Goldwater. When asked by a newsman why she supported Goldwater, she states that she admires his affinity for the elderly and his belief that "the government ought to be run by people of the middle ages." Another scene had satirist Henry Morgan play a CIA official who displayed a talent for meaningless double-talk and who, as the punch line declares, used to be a speechwriter for President Eisenhower.[41]

Other scenes performed in the pilot reflected Hayward's conservative cultural outlook and addressed the reputed decline of American morality. While onetime Premise performer Gene Hackman played a clergymen whose preoccupation with bingo (expressed in his motto "church lovers who pray together play together") distracted him from the tenets of his faith, actor Henry Fonda, a friend and longtime client of Hayward's who agreed to anchor the program, played the role of a despicable author of "dirty books." A third scene, the runaway success of the entire program, was performed by Mike Nichols and Elaine May and was inspired by the publication of Jessica Mitford's *American Way of Death* (1963). In it, Nichols, a grieving brother of a deceased man, and May, a funeral home director, depicted the avarice and greed infecting the funeral business with great comic effect.[42]

In the days following the pilot's broadcast, television critics, gossip columnists, and industry insiders responded to it in glowing, almost rhapsodic terms. While the *New York Herald Tribune*'s John Horn praised *TW3* for "cut[ting] through cant like a knife through cheese," New York *Newsday*'s Barbara Delatiner deemed it a sign that "Maybe the revolution is coming." Unlike the "bumbling . . . English civil servants" representing the British wing of satire, Delatiner argued in reference to Beyond the Fringe, *TW3*'s performers were thoroughly American and "not necessarily effeminate." Syndicated critic Harriet Van Horne was amazed that NBC aired *TW3* and like other critics was convinced that *TW3* had reached the apogee of "hip." "If you missed this show," Van Horne wrote, "you might as well crawl under the table today. Conversationally, you'll be in what sociologists call 'the outgroup.'" For Van Horne as for many other admirers of liberal satire, certainly, watching *TW3* and laughing at its jokes conferred membership in an elite tribe of knowing sophisticates. This faddish element behind *TW3*'s appeal did not escape the attention of *New York Times* television critic Jack Gould. Exercising characteristic restraint, Gould argued that *TW3*'s satire was "intermittent" and "derivative" and that the program as a whole was "too content to settle for irreverence and nonconformity as ends in themselves . . ." He reminded New Yorkers that the pilot "could not hold a candle to the maiden presentation of 'Second City'" made on Channel 5 the year before. Unlike many other critics, Gould astutely noted that *TW3* was plugging into the "satire" craze when it was in its terminal phase. On a "first seeing" of this type of "satire," he observed, "the impact is quite overwhelming; of the fourth or fifth, there is a realization that the modern school of satire might be teetering on the edge of its own rut." Still, even Gould was eventually forced to admit that *TW3* was "immensely refreshing" and represented an "important turning point for network TV."[43]

American viewers who tuned into the *TW3* pilot were no less impressed than the critics. After it aired, NBC was reportedly besieged by more than 12,000 telegrams, letters, and phone calls. Anticipating heavy viewer response, NBC added twenty additional telephone operators to its staff. Over 1,200 viewers eventually contacted NBC by phone, the heaviest response to any network program in ten years. A number of these viewers criticized Hayward and NBC for joking about the president (referred to with easy familiarity in *TW3*'s opening song as "Jack") and religion. One quick joke in which Soviet Premier Khrushchev asks who is running America and is answered by an African American actor who says, "We are," received numerous complaints from white Americans.[44] Aside from these objections, viewers were overwhelmingly supportive. Of the 1,200 viewers who called NBC, 830 made "favorable" reactions and 430 reportedly described *TW3* as "new and brilliant." According to NBC's internal records, nearly ninety-four percent of the 10,516 letters it received were "in favor" of the pilot.[45]

Many viewers who enjoyed *TW3* expressed their appreciation directly to Leland Hayward and his staff. In one of many letters sent to Hayward gauging the impact of the pilot, the news director for NBC's affiliate in Honolulu reported that people had been stopping his staff in the streets to express their admiration of *TW3*. Most viewers writing Hayward expressed their appreciation for what they termed *TW3*'s "intelligent" and "adult" approach to humor. "Down with Jackie Gleason! Up with sophisticated entertainment!" a Detroit woman wrote Hayward. "Americans are adult enough (I hope) to appreciate topical satire on politicians, businessmen and clergymen," this woman declared. "After ten years of [sitcoms'] death-grip on TV humor, it's about time someone did do an adult, timely show of satire." An Alabama citizen similarly argued that *TW3* was a refreshing break from the "stupid, asinine, silly, commercial stuff" that "is making us all into a nation of idiots."[46]

A large proportion of such comments were voiced by educated Americans, particularly students, academicians, teachers, and other professionals. "Congratulations for the courage to put on this wonderful satire," wrote a Smith College professor of philosophy. "'The Week That Was' *now!* 'The Beverly Hillbillies' *never."* An English professor at the University of Michigan likewise praised Hayward for providing "something new for Americans—clever, witty, sophisticated satire—the best thing of its kind since the early satirical sketches of Sid Caesar and . . . Ernie Kovacs." Like many other correspondents, one professor of history at a Texas college addressed the virtues of satire in early-1960s America. This program, he wrote, is "precisely the kind of thing we need if we as a people and a nation are not to sink into a morass of 'decency,' propriety, and conformity."[47]

Hayward and his staff were quick to publicize the outpouring of critical and popular approval the *TW3* pilot received. To help persuade NBC to exercise its option, Hayward made a special point of highlighting comments viewers made praising the "bravery" of the pilot's sponsors—Contac, Clairol, and L&M cigarettes. Hayward and his staff ceased all efforts to extend *TW3* into a series, however, on November 22, the day President Kennedy was assassinated. The assassination had a devastating impact on the *TW3* production team (as well as many liberal satirists) and immediately threw into question whether topical humor in America, particularly satire directed at the White House, was appropriate. Suddenly, it appeared to many, the Kennedy-era "satire boom" was over. While the assassination left Robert Osborn unable to draw and cast a lasting pall on the fortunes of *Monocle* and the *Outsider's Newsletter,* it convinced some Second City performers to suspend political satire altogether.[48] Fortunately for Hayward, NBC rebroadcast a critically acclaimed, reverential Kennedy tribute made by the British *TW3*. On December 4, 1963, the day Senator Hubert Humphrey motioned to enter a transcript of the BBC *TW3* tribute into the *Congressional Record,* newspapers reported that NBC had decided to air its American cousin on Friday evenings, beginning on January 10.

Speculation over how NBC would manage both *TW3* and its commercial sponsors began immediately. Colgate-Palmolive, the company paying for the program *TW3* was replacing, and its agency, Ted Bates & Company, believed *TW3* was "too controversial" and therefore refused to sponsor it. Few observers within the advertising and television industries were surprised at Colgate-Palmolive's reticence. According to prevailing wisdom within the television industry, no American corporation would bankroll a controversial program such as *TW3* when, as *Variety's* George Rosen observed, "innumerable Senators and Congressmen . . . highly al-

lergic to satire and lampooning, can instigate a Congressional investigation whose publicity . . . could backfire against the sponsor's sales and
public image posture." When it appeared that other companies would
follow in Colgate-Palmolive's footsteps, NBC bravely announced that it
would assume "full responsibility" for *TW3* and broadcast it even before
it had secured sponsorship.[49]

On its surface, NBC's decision to forego sponsorship appeared highly
unorthodox and risky. Yet as ad industry analysts who studied this situation closely concluded, NBC was losing nothing in this arrangement.
NBC executives were well aware that the excitement stirred by the pilot
had attracted the interest of a number of other companies such as Speidel, Clairol, Consolidated Cigar, and others willing to pay for ad time.
While assuming total control over the program, NBC could simultaneously take steps to minimize its own risks with the venture. By subcon-
tracting *TW3* through Leland Hayward, by requiring that he provide
"errors and omissions" (professional broadcasters liability) insurance, by
securing merchandising and distribution rights, by stipulating approval of
"all key elements," by subjecting Hayward's choice of writers to network
"approval," by reserving the right "to require shows be prerecorded," and
by assigning Ed Friendly, the man once responsible for handling Walter
Winchell on radio, to oversee the program's development, NBC established a series of mechanisms it believed *TW3* required in order to become a safe and profitable enterprise.[50]

After receiving word from NBC that *TW3* would begin midway
through the current television season, Hayward, Jamison, and their production staff hurriedly prepared themselves. In order to meet the heavy
demand of staging a weekly, live broadcast television program, Hayward
and his staff hired additional writers such as Tom Meehan, a freelance
comic writer for *Esquire,* the *New Yorker* and the *New York Times Magazine;*
Saul Turteltaub, a self-described "Catskills comedy writer" who had previously worked for puppeteer Shari Lewis and for *Candid Camera;* and
Tony Webster, an incisive comic writer who had earlier collaborated with
Nat Hiken, Sid Caesar, Bob and Ray, and Phil Silvers. For performers,
Hayward employed Stanley Grover, Henry Morgan, and Doro Merande,
all of whom had performed well in the pilot; Sandy Baron, a former member of the Second City and Premise Players; Elliott Reid, a veteran
straight man and satiric mimic who won attention in the early 1960s with
his pre–Vaughn Meader Kennedy impersonations; and, newly freed from
his duties of hosting the British *TW3* when it was canceled, David Frost.

Throughout its first season, Hayward and Jamison also arranged for guest appearances by Woody Allen, Mel Brooks, Allan Sherman, Bill Cosby, and a number of performers affiliated with the Second City. NBC strongly urged Hayward to contract Bob Newhart, Mike Nichols, and Elaine May, but his budget prevented him from employing such expensive talent. Finally, to ensure that *TW3* had at least some "sex appeal," NBC contractually obligated Hayward to use a peppy, attractive female folk singer named Nancy Ames.

*   *   *

During its premiere and throughout its initial season, *TW3* fine-tuned the general style, pace, and irreverent attitude it had established in its pilot. Viewers tuning in to *TW3* Friday nights were transported to NBC Studios 6A and 8H in New York City where the tension was palpable, action slightly unpolished, and the chances that something would go awry or, worse yet, jokes would fail were very real. By the standards of modern television, the set for *TW3* was relatively sparse, inhabited only by a news desk, a large "That Was The Week That Was" sign, and various props. During the opening "That Was the Week That Was" theme song, Nancy Ames ("The *TW3* Girl") made rhymed references to events in the previous week's news. On occasion, a lyric line might spur a cut to a news item delivered by the *TW3* anchors, David Frost and Elliott Reid, or a quick blackout sketch. Other news items ("Newsflashes") served as introductions to songs (usually performed by Stanley Grover or, later, Phyllis Newman), a monologue written and performed by Frost, and several short sketches, typically involving the week's special guest. By the time Ames repeated the theme song at the end of the program's thirty minutes, Hayward and Jamison and their staff typically managed to fit in two songs, three or four sketches, two commercial breaks, and a miscellaneous monologue or editorial comment.

In addition to continuing many of its stylistic elements, *TW3* also followed up on many of the satiric themes it struck in the pilot. At the behest of Hayward, it routinely used Doro Merande (in the character of Mrs. Rhineburger Havershaw, fictional friend of the Philadelphia Wanamaker family) and later Phyllis Newman (as gossip columnist "Latrivia Montague") to lampoon high fashion and high-society women. In assorted gag lines and songs, *TW3* repeated the conservative, elitist cultural stance Hayward and his colleagues made in the pilot, targeting teens and

40. Members of the cast and production staff for the first season of NBC's *That Was the Week That Was:* (left to right) Leland Hayward, Billy Taylor, Patricia Englund, Bob Emmett, Gerald Gardner, Marshall Jamison, Hal Gurney. On the ladder are George Hall and Charlie Manna. By permission of Sean Emmett.

youth culture, "smutty" books in the news (*Fanny Hill* and Helen Gurley Brown's *Sex and the Office*), and America's changing sexual mores.[51] To the great satisfaction of its fans, *TW3* lambasted television and the "blight" of network programming.

On occasion *TW3* performers delivered short, pithy, morally indignant editorials. As a guest on *TW3*'s January 24 broadcast, the actress Kim Hunter (the wife of head writer Robert Emmett) read portions of a withering speech critic Marya Mannes had earlier delivered to the Women's Press Club regarding Congressional venality and special privilege. Likewise, segments in subsequent broadcasts issued vitriolic commentary on rising crime, America's desensitization to violence, and the country's dangerous romance with guns and weaponry.[52] In one of its sharpest early scenes, *TW3* critiqued *Time* magazine—small payback, perhaps, for *Time*'s negative review of the series premiere. Set in the magazine's editorial office, Henry Morgan (an actor who, like Kim Hunter, had been blacklisted a decade earlier) caricatured *Time*'s brusque editor-in-chief, a man who confesses "slanting stories [and] ruining reputations" and who encourages his religion editor to give his stories "a real anti-liberal, anti-labor, anti-intellectual, anti-Democratic twist."[53]

As Morgan's jab at *Time* demonstrates, *TW3* during its first season was generally sympathetic to the political outlook of early-sixties, Great Society liberalism. On domestic political issues, particularly America's civil rights crisis, *TW3* performed sketches and delivered punch lines with astringent irony. Reminiscent of liberal cartoonists' work, multiple *TW3* jokes and sketches took aim at the racial intolerance of Southern Senators, the John Birch Society, the KKK, and other conservative organizations. While the Civil Rights Bill was being filibustered by Southern

41. *That Was the Week That Was* cast members (from right to left) Elliott Reid, Henry Morgan, David Frost and Nancy Ames send up the events of the day during the program's opening segment. Courtesy of NBC/Globe Photos.

"Sophisticated Daring" and Political Cowardice

Senators in March 1964, African American comedian Bill Cosby (a frequent guest star) introduced a segment intended to alert *TW3*'s estimated twenty million viewers to the remarks of pro–civil rights Democratic senator Joseph Clark of Pennsylvania. As the Freedom Summer of 1964 progressed, *TW3* performers made stinging references to Mississippi ("Murder isn't considered a crime in Mississippi") and the civil rights activists slain there. On the program broadcast on June 21, Nancy Ames sang "Good Ole Summertime" while photographs depicting violent confrontations between civil rights workers and white Southerners (particularly the citizens of St. Augustine, Florida) flashed on the screen. The ironic juxtaposition of the jaunty song and the disturbing images amused few Southerners. An internal NBC report claimed that one photograph used during this segment, that of the burnt-out automobile of missing Mississippi civil rights workers, "received heavy adverse comment." More seriously, a number of NBC affiliates based in the South were prompted by such segments to drop *TW3* from their programming schedules.[54]

To their credit, *TW3* writers and cast members were hardly blind to the racial hypocrisy of fellow white liberals. In one sketch dating from the same February 21 broadcast, African American actor Roscoe Lee Brown played a man applying for an entry-level, white-collar job. The personnel manager (played by Henry Morgan) interviewing him trumpets his racial tolerance, claiming that he and his wife own Ella Fitzgerald records, watched the March on Washington on TV, and are even members of the Urban League. As their conversation continues, the personnel manager trips on his hidden prejudice when he blurts out, "It's terrible, after all these years to have prejudice against inferior minorities." Upon learning that the black applicant has an MBA degree, aspires to become a personnel manager, and, worse yet, intends to live in his neighborhood, he slyly denies him further consideration. "I'm in your corner, boy," the personnel manager says while whisking the applicant from the office. "Oh, I can see that," the interviewee retorts. "And may I say, it's damn white of you." Immediately following this sketch, *TW3* cut to Stanley Grover who then sang Tom Lehrer's ironic commentary on efforts to promote racial tolerance, "National Brotherhood Week." When Brown joined Grover for the final chorus, the studio audience—typically sympathetic to *TW3*'s liberal political and social outlook—erupted in enthusiastic applause.[55]

When treating the subject of international affairs, *TW3* continued to jab French president de Gaulle and initiated a series of cruel jokes—usually delivered by David Frost, the program's resident "firebrand satirist"—implicating the continuing presence of Nazis in West Germany. As befitted its liberal anticommunist bent, *TW3* routinely made jokes at the expense of China, the Soviet Union, and Cuba.[56] On occasion, *TW3* departed from its cold war liberal outlook and revealed a sympathetic stance toward early-1960s antiwar and peace movements. When the *"That Was the Week That Was* Newsreel" mentioned on the April 17 broadcast that Air Force General Curtis LeMay was advocating a new one hundred-megaton nuclear bomb, a *TW3* newsman cracked, "That's what we like about our military men; they're always looking for new ways to beat the population explosion." During the January 25 broadcast, David Frost conducted a symphony for 1964 in which his baton elicited bomb explosions, air-raid sirens, and machine-gun fire. For critic Jack Gould, Frost's slightly surrealistic piece registered "a vivid protest against war." "The reservation of a final shot for a chirping sparrow, the last living thing on earth," Gould continued, "was a moving climax."[57]

Frost's "symphony," like the "Good Old Summertime" segment, effectively contrasted visual imagery with sound to make its point. Two other film montage sequences aired on *TW3* during its first season were similarly striking. Originally created for the BBC *TW3* by Geoffrey Martin and run during the American version's January 24 and February 21 broadcasts, these sequences provided American viewers with some of the most innovative and startling uses of visual imagery to appear on nondocumentary television in the early 1960s. In the latter segment, coinciding with news regarding the 1964 Cassius Clay–Sonny Liston boxing match, *TW3* juxtaposed the lilting love ballad "You Go to My Head" with a rapid succession of photographs depicting bloodthirsty fans, greedy agents, and boxers disfigured by injuries they acquired in the ring. The other Martin montage, a commentary on the recently released surgeon general's report on cigarette smoking, contrasted Jerome Kern's "Smoke Gets in Your Eyes" with flashed images of advertising slogans ("More satisfaction"), young smokers, and, amazingly, graphic photos of lung surgery, a deceased woman, and her scarred, cancerous lung.[58]

*　　*　　*

Although *TW3* devoted attention to a wide range of issues, its primary targets throughout the election year of 1964 were politicians (particularly

Republicans) vying for public office. In a multitude of quick quips, gag lines, song lyrics, and short sketches, *TW3* often took aim at Republican contenders Richard Nixon, Nelson Rockefeller, and Barry Goldwater. Jokes directed at these politicians were neither trenchant nor original, focusing in large part on their wealth, their disreputable pasts, and—from a liberal's perspective—their fundamental lack of appeal. Goldwater's rise to prominence within the Republican Party irked all liberal satirists, and throughout 1964 his hard-line, antistatist, anticommunist conservatism elicited their unsparing criticism. In characteristic style, Frost referred to the Arizona senator as "a great eighteenth-century American" who during the summer of 1964 "will announce that being a Negro is unconstitutional." With Goldwater, Frost quipped, Republicans claimed that the GOP is "on the way back. And who knows, one day it may even go forward."[59]

The jokes and gags *TW3* aimed at politicians were not made at the sole expense of Republicans. In a number of sketches focusing on Congressional obstructionism, overspending, and hypocrisy, Democrats and liberals were on the receiving end of *TW3*'s satiric scrutiny. *TW3*'s targeting of both Democrats and Republicans was carefully calculated. From the beginning Hayward and his staff knew they would have to appear nonpartisan and, in the name of "fairness," evenhanded in order to avoid alienating NBC and its audience. What surprised many, however, was the consistency with which the liberal-slanted *TW3* went after President Lyndon Johnson. Following the assassination of President Kennedy, Hayward and his production staff predicted that the American audience would have little appetite for jokes involving the presidency. Hayward even instructed his writers that they should not "hurt" Johnson because the situation he faced was so difficult. Throughout its first season, however, *TW3* repeatedly poked at the notoriously thin-skinned Johnson with references to his vacillating leadership and chameleon-like personal traits ("Everybody likes L.B.J.," sang guest star Audrey Meadows during the January 10 premiere, "General Motors, General Taylor, Norman Thomas, Norman Mailer . . . People for segregation . . . people for miscegenation like Lyndon"), his Austin television station and other financial assets, his family and pet beagle, and his administration's duplicity (Henry Morgan on the "LBJ sweater": "you get such a warm, comfortable feeling as they pull the wool over your eyes."). Jokes about Johnson's ignominious connection to Bobby Baker, the unscrupulous former Senate majority secretary investigated by the Senate Rules Committee during the winter of 1964, were legion.[60]

Over time, *TW3* even began to implicate the Johnson administration's foreign policy. On occasion, these satires made incisive commentary. In addition to offering viewers a "primer" on dollar diplomacy in Latin America, *TW3* performed a mock interview with a bumbling State Department representative (played once again by Henry Morgan) who agrees with the *TW3* correspondent's suggestion that U.S. foreign policy is "fraught with contradictions and hypocrisy" and concedes that "We sell wheat [to the Soviet Union] so we can build more missiles." When asked what happens when the Soviets cannot pay for the wheat, the representative ironically replies, "Then, of course, we'll know they can't be trusted and it will prove we were right in selling them the wheat [and building the missiles]."[61]

TW3 extended its satiric thrusts forebodingly when it addressed the Johnson administration's Southeast Asia policy. The subject of Vietnam was not approached in the pilot, much to the relief of some viewers who believed it to be too sensitive for television.[62] Not far into its initial season, however, *TW3* began commenting on the trouble brewing there. Several weeks after *TW3* premiered, in fact, Sandy Baron and guest star Paul Sand revived a Second City sketch in which an American sergeant (Baron) teaches a Vietnamese peasant (Sand) how to use an M1 rifle. Blustering and boorish, the sergeant informs the peasant that the rifles were "kindly" provided by the beneficent United States government. When the peasant begins to use the rifle's bayonet as a hoe, the sergeant berates the "stupid savage" and informs him that it is intended to "stick in PEOPLE." Driven to violence when made to practice on a Vietcong dummy, the peasant suddenly turns to the sergeant, stabs him dead, and then returns to his weaving. Other *TW3* sketches painted Ambassador Henry Cabot Lodge and Secretary of Defense Robert McNamara as untrustworthy. On April 10, 1964, for example, *TW3* featured a sketch titled "Lodge and the Lie Detector" in which Ambassador Lodge (Elliott Reid) is subjected to verification testing in his Saigon office. When asked how the "war is going in Vietnam," Lodge answers, "very well," and the detector shrieks loudly. For a sketch titled "Memorial Day," a uniformed soldier named Charlie (Sandy Baron) is back from Vietnam and seated at a bar, where he is approached by a veteran named Fred (Tom Bosley). When Fred tells Charlie about the funny U.S.O. acts he saw while on duty overseas, Charlie replies that he

42. Second City members (left to right) Andrew Duncan, Alan Arkin and Anthony Holland illustrate the barriers in communication between U.S. military advisors and Southeast Asian peasants. Courtesy of the Wisconsin Center for Film and Theater Research

and his fellow soldiers in Vietnam were only treated to McNamara and Secretary of State Dean Rusk. As Fred departs singing, Fred mutters, "Well, we used to sing, too . . . 'What Kind of Fool Am I?'"[63]

On the subject of Vietnam, *TW3* aimed its satire at the military, diplomatic, and administration officials formulating America's policy, but it did not exclude the chief executive altogether. In a song titled "I Made 'Em Laugh," news footage of President Johnson giving a funny speech to a group of Chamber of Commerce businessmen was juxtaposed with prescient lyrics:

> When they asked about my policy
> On fighting in Vietnam
> I made em laugh
> I made em laugh.
> They said about the war the folks at home
> Don't really give a damn
> I made em laugh
> Let's make the war more popular

With Junior and with Granny
Let's call it what it really is
A shootin "Hootennany." [64]

The satirical critiques *TW3* made of America's racial dilemmas and its involvement in Vietnam often lacked subtlety and real bite, particularly when juxtaposed with the critiques rendered by left-liberal American intellectuals and African American civil rights activists. Yet considering the dearth of critical commentary directed at America's policy in Vietnam during the spring and summer of 1964, *TW3*'s critiques were, much to the credit of Jamison and his writers, quite telling. When judged against the standard of most mainstream commercial entertainment produced during the early 1960s, certainly, *TW3* stood out as a bold, intelligent, and courageous program. Particularly during February and March 1964, when *TW3* appeared to be gaining momentum, a number of critics and newspaper columnists cited it as the most exciting program on television. "This sort of sardonic fun is long overdue," one critic opined, "never has a civilization been more ripe for it." Harriet Van Horne concurred with other critics writing about *TW3* in February 1964 when she stated that it was "all that a topical, satirical revue ought to be": "gimlet-eyed, adder tongued, shark-cunning . . . totally irreverent, sweetly disrespectful and ingenuously shrewd." [65] In the opinion of many other commentators, *TW3* succeeded in providing a significant audience—it attracted between ten and twenty million viewers a week in early 1964—with a brand of topical, hip satire that was unavailable outside the small nightclubs and improv cafes populating New York City, Chicago, and San Francisco.

*   *   *

The topical satire *TW3* offered was at times sharp, innovative, and unique, but it was also noticeably uneven. While *TW3* produced flashes of wit and biting commentary, it often pulled its punches and delivered its jokes with a wink. With increasingly regularity, an air of smug complacency began to compromise the moral urgency that originally lent *TW3* its distinctive touch. Particularly by the latter half of the season, incisive satiric commentary was often subsumed by the demands of producing funny one-liners and thin, clichéd political references. In the monologues of David Frost in particular, the sour notes of bad puns and quick gags proved distracting, even painful. Of course, these faults hardly escaped the notice of critics. Given the hype that Hayward and NBC drummed up over their satiric venture, critics expected much, perhaps too much, from *TW3*. Many were inevitably disappointed. That conservative critics found *TW3* disrespectful and distasteful was not surprising, but few people affiliated with *TW3* could have anticipated the complaints of liberal critics, the self-professed fans of "satire" who Hayward and NBC were counting on for support. According to John Horn, *TW3* by June was suffering from "juvenile" material and witless "one-line gags." *TW3*'s biggest sin, Horn argued, was that it "doesn't really care about the issues and personalities it is supposed to be satirizing." Even Jack Gould was prepared to admit by midseason that *TW3* had veered away from satire toward "one-line gags," "pretentious liberalism and [a] tiresome reliance on 'shock' . . ."[66]

That *TW3* was criticized for being trite and silly on the one hand and overly serious and didactic on the other illustrates the precarious position a program of satire—one that promises entertainment *and* commentary, high ratings *and* critical acceptance—occupies within mainstream commercial media. *TW3*'s inconsistency also may have been a symptom of the fatigue afflicting its writing and production staff. The task of producing material every week for a live, informed, satirical program was certainly very difficult, and Jamison and his writers were evidently under great strain. Strapped by his low budget, Hayward was incapable of infusing his staff with fresh writing talent. As a result, head writer Robert Emmett remembers, *TW3* became "too hurried . . . [and] settled for less."[67]

Jamison and his writers were not, however, solely accountable for *TW3*'s weaknesses. While not directly responsible for *TW3*'s poor writing, executive producer Leland Hayward was culpable for many of the contradictions and the ambivalence that would terminally wound the program's prospects. To fulfill the difficult task of pleasing NBC, American viewers, critics, and advertisers, *TW3* required an executive producer in touch with the times, a man with conviction, a steady hand, and patience—someone, in other words, other than Leland Hayward. Marshall Jamison remembers that Hayward was never "very clear about what he wanted." In panicked memos to Marshall Jamison, Hayward began to echo critics' complaints but offered few ideas for remedying the program's problems. With a sense of doom and foreboding that infused nearly all of Hayward's correspondence with Jamison, Hayward warned that "time is running out very-very fast."[68]

Lacking a firm sense of what *TW3* ought to be, Hayward proved susceptible to the dubious advice proffered by associates and well-wishers.

Frank Gibney, an expert on popular entertainment and the publisher of *Show* magazine, recommended that Hayward spend less time on politics ("casting jibes at Republican politicians") and devote more attention to subjects such as "the topless bathing suit and the bottomless bath, the Shakespeare craze . . . ad agencies, executive proxy fights, etc." For performers, Gibney recommended "a good low-brow type [who] would help universalize the tone of the show which is very much highbrow, or aspiring highbrow." In a similar vein, screenwriter Howard Estabrook advised Hayward to make *TW3* into "THE GRIDIRON CLUB OF THE AIR . . ." (a reference to the clubby Washington press corps whose annual roast of politicos "singes, but never burns") rather than the "outright political propaganda medium" it had become. The humor of comedian Vaughn Meader, Estabrook reminded his friend, was "unassailable . . . devoid of bias . . . nothing demagogic or offensive—and the financial returns . . . were amazing."[69]

It is difficult to gauge exactly how such advice might have swayed Hayward. What appears clear, however, is that the concerns of advertisers—the people still responsible for underwriting *TW3* financially—carried considerable weight with him. Usually these concerns were directed to Hayward through NBC. On one occasion, however, an official at the Speidel company (a steady advertiser during *TW3*'s Friday night slot) contacted Hayward directly in order to voice his concern over the direction *TW3* was taking. In his letter, the Speidel official congratulated Hayward for appealing to "highly intellectualized audience[s]" residing in large urban markets. At the same time, however, he worried that the program's rating was "pulled down tremendously because there is an apparent lack of appeal to the mass of people in small cities." "I feel that the show should have a greater variety of subjects dealing with matters close to the heart of all of the people of the TV audience rather than the more intellectual and sophisticated," he continued, matters "covering many of the homier facets of life . . . social security benefits, red tape, housing cost, interest rate on credit, automobile traffic problems throughout the country, toll charges and hundreds of other such subjects that people have gripes about and would like to see expressed in a manner that they never would be able to do."[70]

Hayward apparently took such advice to heart. By mid-March he attempted to woo the recently departed star David Frost back to *TW3* by promising "a lot of changes, and hopefully improvements" "in the next few weeks." "The further away we get from New York," Hayward now told

Frost, "the less good the rating." Several weeks later, Hayward openly declared his plans to popularize *TW3*. To one reporter he claimed, "Nobody ever said we'd have a 30-minute satire show every week . . . all satire—never." Echoing the complaints of Speidel's official almost word for word, Hayward claimed that the problem *TW3* faced was in "cutting across interest lines and hitting subjects about which everybody is interested."[71]

Hayward's plans for expanding the demographic base of *TW3*'s audience included explicit appeals to female viewers. Judging from the prominent role Clairol played as a participating sponsor and the large number of letters Hayward and *TW3* received from women, female viewers were indeed an important constituency. At the same time that Hayward began fielding advice about how to popularize *TW3*, he complained to Jamison that *TW3* had "no girl—and really no material aimed for a girl." In one memo sent to Jamison in mid-March, Hayward stressed, "I am positive we must get women and sex on the program." By late April, Hayward's desire for material aimed at women and involving what he termed "He-She" subjects translated into a new weekly series of "Francis and Frances" sketches. Authored by veteran gagman Goodman Ace, "Francis and Frances" featured a husband and his flighty wife (played by former Compass Players and Second City performers Alan Alda and Pat Englund) spatting over the year's political candidates. These domestic segments were sorely out of place with the rest of *TW3* and reminiscent more of the *Easy Aces* radio comedy of the 1940s than the smart early-sixties satire that Ace publicly advocated. In addition to initiating "Francis and Frances," Hayward hired a Broadway singer/actress and panelist on CBS's *To Tell The Truth* named Phyllis Newman. Although Newman admitted that she thought of herself as nothing "more than a bathroom satirist," Hayward and NBC anticipated that she would become the favorite of young, intelligent housewives all across America. This was exactly the audience Hayward believed would appreciate Newman's ditty on the travails of modern-day motherhood, delivered in the key of Betty Friedan's 1963 bombshell, *The Feminine Mystique:*

> There's nothing like being a housewife
> Such a marvelous life
> If you have kiddies what joy, what fun.
> Washing their dresses . . .
> Hooray for my college degree.

Every day's just like the other . . .
I'm in isolation, I'll never be free.
It's starting to hurt psychologically . . .
I'm tired of being a housewife.[72]

The hiring of Newman signaled the start of several key personnel changes that would alter the style and the substance of *TW3* significantly. Throughout the month of March, Hayward appeared determined to liquidate what he privately called the "superficial and thin" and the "fat and ugly" from *TW3*'s "old dreary cast." Ever conscious of style and beauty, Hayward was convinced midway through the first season that *TW3* must showcase young and attractive performers such as Frost and Newman, not the "hideous-unattractive-middle-aged people" who actually had greater experience with comic acting. Perhaps the biggest lost to *TW3* during April was Henry Morgan, the experienced satirical radio performer whom Hayward dismissed as an "unpleasant personality." Morgan, a man who proclaimed that if *he* "ran the show, it would be on for a half hour, *one* time," was an undeniably strong influence on *TW3* during its first three—and, in retrospect, strongest—months on the air. In a revealing behind-the-scenes report on the production of *TW3* for *TV Guide,* Peter Bogdanovich demonstrated the ways in which Morgan collaborated with writers on a racial integration sketch. Evidently proud of his involvement with *TW3,* Morgan told Bogdanovich that it was "the only show on TV where everyone is a writer."[73]

Morgan was not the only contributor who mysteriously departed from *TW3* during its fourth month. Tony Webster, an intelligent, witty writer also ended his affiliation with the program at the end of April. Just as Phyllis Newman filled the spot left vacant by Morgan, a young comic writer named Larry Siegel (a frequent contributor to *Playboy* and *MAD*) was hired to replace Webster. By late April then, Hayward and his staff were sending clear signals that *TW3* was turning toward younger writers and performers. "We're trying for a younger image," associate producer Willard Levitas told the press on April 23. "Everybody knows about angry old men, so to speak. We are trying for angry young men who have something to say."[74]

If one person could be held responsible for mandating the changes in *TW3* that ultimately compromised its satirical content, it is Hayward. Yet it is also clear that many of the key decisions he made were strongly encouraged and, in some cases, pressured by NBC. The commitment NBC and its programming executives made toward *TW3* and televised satire appeared to wane only weeks after it premiered. Like the BBC, NBC began to balk when it discovered what the stakes for broadcasting satire actually were. Particularly when Jamison and his writers displayed an interest in addressing subjects such as race and American foreign policy, NBC became noticeably agitated. Ed Friendly, the NBC executive overseeing *TW3,* recalls that the network's management and legal department were "nervous as hell" and "worried to death" about the program. Rehearsals held prior to the Friday evening broadcast were attended by a small band of attorneys representing NBC, the insurance companies underwriting the program, and Leland Hayward Productions. Although advertisers sponsoring *TW3* were not allowed to "censor" material, the presence of their representatives at rehearsals undoubtedly had its effects. NBC's Continuity Acceptance Department also attempted to keep a tight rein on the program content. Littered throughout draft copies of the *TW3* scripts are reminders of the NBC's "right of approval" and comments such as "let's discuss." By the time *TW3* was ready to be aired, the final draft of the script was "locked." No improvisations or deviations from the final draft were allowed, though the mischievous Frost frequently transgressed this provision.[75]

NBC advertised that it would not censor *TW3,* but there is little doubt that it managed to intervene surreptitiously. As Friendly has remarked, he and NBC found ways to "cajole" Hayward and "keep things from being done . . ." Friendly and NBC president Robert Kintner reminded Hayward of his program's precarious situation by forwarding ratings statistics and letters of complaint addressed to the network. Not all of NBC's efforts to control *TW3* were quite so subtle. Several weeks into *TW3*'s initial season, in fact, evidence of coercion and de facto censorship were not hard to find. By this time, television magazines such as *TV Time* and *TV Guide* reported that Hayward was being compelled to put his "thumbs down" on material "that smacks in the least of the Angry Young Men or those who make satire bright." *TV Guide* quoted an "insider" who claimed that *TW3*'s "writers and production staff are running scared. They're watering down the material before it even gets to the level where anyone might object." Several months later, Nancy Ames stirred further controversy when she claimed in a *Daily Variety* interview that she and the cast had been told to mind their own business and forget "more biting things."[76]

*   *   *

After only several months into *TW3*'s first season, NBC showed signs that it was effectively forfeiting the idea of broadcasting the program as it was originally conceived. As reported in *Variety* in March and April, NBC decided to suspend production of *TW3* during the upcoming Democratic and Republican political conventions. When *TW3* returned to the air the following fall, it would relinquish its Friday night slot to Jack Benny and assume another position on Tuesday evening, opposite CBS's smash hit, *Petticoat Junction,* and ABC's promising prime-time soap opera, *Peyton Place.* It is difficult to fathom exactly what NBC's strategy might have been by removing *TW3* from its crucial Friday night slot and instead pitting it against these programs.[77] Since *TW3* was premised on the idea that it would use the news of the week as its primary source material, the move to Tuesday was nothing less than a kiss of death. As Ed Friendly admits, pulling *TW3* from its Friday evening slot was "NBC's way of saying 'We give up.'"[78] Shortly after announcing its schedule change, NBC decided to preempt an installment of *TW3* with a program titled *Inside the Movie Kingdom.* To the writers and performers on the staff at *TW3* NBC's decision to move and preempt *TW3,* coming at a time when they were producing some of their best programs, was a bad omen.

As *Variety* observed, both the preemption and the rescheduling came at a time when *TW3* was achieving a level of success that few would have anticipated. Throughout its initial two months on the air, in fact, *TW3* either beat or placed close behind its CBS competitor, *The Twilight Zone.* With a strong thirty-five percent share in urban markets and a low advertising cost of $36,000 a minute, NBC had no trouble selling *TW3*'s advertising time to Clairol, Speidel, Mennen, and Brown & Williamson. Judging by the response of studio audience members and the letters of viewers who bothered to write Leland Hayward and NBC, fans of *TW3* were generally approving of its "adult" perspective and liberal point of view. In contrast to some television and media critics, many of these fans believed *TW3* was one of the few programs on the air that did not insult their intelligence. Devoted Jewish viewers wrote in to complain that *TW3* was interfering with their Sabbath. Since many Americans believed *TW3* was best viewed in groups of like-minded, liberal citizens, *TW3* parties became a brief, minor fad. Because Hayward and Jamison explicitly targeted a "quality audience" comprised of middle- and upper-middle-class viewers, it was no surprise that, as Nielsen reports indicated, *TW3* consistently ranked among the top fifteen programs tuned in by viewers belonging to "upper income and college-educated audience segments." The only audience disappointed with *TW3*, *Variety* reported in April 1964, were the true "cognizanti"—the intellectuals. *Variety* then asked,

> But who in his right mind would expect a show surrounded by the pressures of affiliates, advertisers and a network with 50 veepees to come off week after week like "The Establishment," "Second City," "Beyond the Fringe" or the nitery comedians of political-social bent? "TW3" still has comedic aims— and potential—that could outstrip the situation-comedy grind and village-bumpkin norm of primetime by a country mile. In its way, it is every bit as important a flicker in the night as a "CBS Reports."[79]

Not long after *Variety* gave Hayward and his staff this vote of confidence, NBC began taking steps to remind them of its authority over *TW3*'s production. In a terse letter written to Thomas Ryan, Hayward Production's legal counsel, at the end of May, NBC Director of Talent and Program Administration Robert Dunne reiterated that his network had "a right of approval over the key elements in each [*TW3*] show" and that it wanted "the full opportunity to exercise this right of approval." A week later, Hayward and Ryan were called to the network's offices for a meeting with Friendly and other NBC executives and talent agent Lester Gottlieb. According to notes taken by Ryan at that meeting, Friendly demanded that "all performers, producers, directors, etc. must be cleared through his office before they are hired." Friendly also insisted on a new production team and suggested that Hayward hire Gottlieb's client, Herb Sargent, a comedy writer who had previously worked for Steve Allen and Perry Como. Friendly apparently made no mention of the program's satiric objective, but he did suggest that Hayward make Nancy Ames "more sexy" by outfitting her with "a tight sweater and skirt for [the] next week's show."[80]

Two weeks later, Marshall Jamison was pressured to resign as *TW3*'s producer and editor. Although many people speculated that he was being nudged out, his departure in June was precipitated by an angry encounter with NBC president Robert Kintner. In addition to his powerful connections within media corporations, Kintner maintained close ties to the Democratic Party. He was a godfather to Adlai Stevenson's son, and he remained a good friend and ardent supporter of Lyndon Johnson. Kintner's wife, in fact, served on President Johnson's 1964 reelection campaign, and in 1966 Kintner himself would serve as a special assistant in Johnson's cabinet. It is perhaps understandable, therefore, that his tolerance for jokes regarding Johnson, a man he once hailed as "America's greatest patriot," was limited.[81]

Throughout *TW3*'s short lifespan, numerous rumors alleged that Kintner acted on Johnson's behalf and issued orders to go soft on his administration. In a 1965 interview published in the *Newark Evening News,* an anonymous member of Hayward's staff claimed that because of communication between NBC and the White House, "cracks about LBJ himself were strictly forbidden." "We could hit Goldwater with a sledge hammer," this source continued, "but if we took just a gentle dig at Johnson, the telephones would ring." Even Jamison, a man who has been reticent to comment on Lyndon Johnson's involvement, has admitted, "Orders came down [from Washington] to be soft on Johnson, but it was generally not known." When Jamison met with Kintner and Hayward in June, Kintner mandated that Jamison and *TW3* refrain from all Johnson jokes. As Hayward remained silent, "I raised my voice," Jamison remembers, and argued, "If we can't hit Johnson, we can't have a program." Pushed into a corner by Kintner and, worse yet, betrayed by Hayward, Jamison maintains that resignation became his only option.[82]

On June 16, New York newspapers officially reported that Jamison was being replaced by Herb Sargent. In interviews Jamison and Hayward naturally made no mention of Kintner and only cited "editorial differences of opinion." Hayward claimed that he had "asked for certain changes in material and approach" and that NBC "enthusiastically endorsed" Jamison's replacement. As *Variety* reported, Hayward's statement was a sure sign that NBC was beginning to play "an active role in the series." Jamison elaborated his grievances: "I have always disagreed with Leland on the basic concept of the show. 'TW3' has a strong, limited appeal and it should not be made a popular, mass-appeal network show. I don't believe that this show produced for the mass will get any kind of an audience."[83]

*   *   *

Prior to *TW3*'s second-season premiere, Hayward and NBC recruited an almost entirely new crew of writers and performers. After Herb Sargent assumed the role of head writer and editor at the end of *TW3*'s initial season, Robert Emmett and a few other key *TW3* staff members originally recruited by Jamison—those whom Friendly labeled as "too esoteric"—

grew disillusioned and decided not to return. To replace Emmett and Turteltaub, Hayward recruited a fresh group of writers including Calvin Trillin, James Stevenson, Dee Caruso, William F. Brown, Peter Myerson, Buck Henry, and Gloria Steinem. To anchor *TW3*'s cast, Hayward settled on Frost, Newman, Ames, and Henry. The new, smaller cast was composed solely of young, likeable, "star" talent. In addition to hiring new writers and performers, Hayward and his staff vowed to broaden *TW3*'s appeal by cutting the length of sketches to three minutes. They also pledged to renew their program's "impartial" stance. In an interview with the *New York Times,* Hayward announced that when *TW3* returned, all of its political observations would be confined to the "equal time department." "We've got to be very careful," Hayward claimed, "one slip and we could lose our heads." "We've got nothing to fear," he ironically added, "but satire itself."[84]

By sounding such notes of caution, Hayward appeared quite desperate to do anything in order to keep *TW3* alive. Unfortunately, his sense of determination was not matched by anyone at NBC. Executives at the network decided to air *TW3* for another season because it retained a respectable audience share and, more importantly, because it demonstrated that their network was still a dynamic, innovative force within the industry. Although Kintner, Friendly, and other executives took measures to broaden *TW3*'s appeal, they had no real expectations that *TW3* would steal viewers away from *Petticoat Junction* and *Peyton Place,* two of the most popular and promising programs on the network schedule. As long as Hayward and his staff were willing and able to contain the risks involved with broadcasting topical comedy, NBC would allow *TW3* to die a slow, natural death.

CHAPTER ELEVEN

Satire That Would "Gag a Goat"

CROSSING THE LINE WITH
PAUL KRASSNER AND LENNY BRUCE

During the second season of *That Was the Week That Was* instances of network censorship only multiplied. After *TW3* guest star Alan Alda made a joke about ordained priests "going steady," the program's principal sponsors demanded that producer Leland Hayward issue a public apology. Shortly thereafter, NBC's executive in charge of programming, Mort Werner, summoned Hayward and his production staff to a meeting in which he declared that the network was asserting final authority "with regard to what goes on the air whenever [it] feel[s] there is a question of taste involved." As a result, program writers such as Gloria Steinem began to observe NBC continuity acceptance staff vigilantly expurgate material from rehearsal scripts. Likewise, Tom Lehrer, who had been coaxed out of retirement in order to contribute to the program, was chagrined by the network's habit of cutting and diluting the pithy ditties he wrote criticizing cold war nuclear diplomacy ("Who's Next?" and "So Long, Mom [a Song for World War III]") and other timely subjects. Lehrer did not even bother to submit "The Vatican Rag," a song recommending a new form of liturgical music for the Roman Catholic Church after Vatican II.[1]

The troubles Lehrer and other *TW3* contributors encountered with their material were exacerbated by the institutional conservatism of network television, but they were hardly new to liberal satirists working in the fifties and early sixties. Nearly all liberal satirists at one time or another tested the limits of irreverence. During the conservative 1950s, a time when even the Christmas holiday was deemed off limits to jokes, liberal satirists invited charges of "going too far" or "crossing the line" when they commented caustically on conservative politicians and their anti-communist demagoguery, the failure of American race relations, and the threat of the bomb.[2] Yet no matter how offensive these satirists may have appeared to their opponents, it was not until they uttered obscenities and addressed the subjects of sex and religion onstage that they encountered truly bitter and angry resistance. This was particularly the case for *Realist* publisher Paul Krassner and comedian Lenny Bruce, both of whom used satire as a vehicle for testing the boundaries of acceptable speech and for confronting religious and sexual orthodoxy. Because these two men provocatively challenged the limits of what was considered appropriate comic territory, they met stern disapproval and, in the case of Bruce, debilitating legal action.

*   *   *

When cartoonist Bill Mauldin in 1961 labeled Spain's fascist autocrat Francisco Franco a "Defender of the Faith," American Roman Catholics were quick to complain. "This is the type of poison that this man is trying to inject into the blood stream of America," one irate reader wrote J. Edgar Hoover. "I am fully aware that we have a free press and free speech, but this man is going far beyond the realms of decency and propriety." Not far from Mauldin's office at the *Chicago Sun-Times,* members of the Second City alienated even the liberals in their audience when they performed their "Homosexual Priests" blackout and a scene titled "The Faith Healer." In the latter, the Second City's John Brent or Jack Burns played a preacher from Tulsa, Oklahoma (a reference to evangelist Oral Roberts), named Reverend Moly who promulgates "faith healing and [a] Christian crusade against Communism" in his *The Word of Truth* television program. After soliciting donations for his Kill a Commie for Christ campaign, he attempts to heal several ill members of the studio audience. When he fails to cure a man's thumb, however, he explains that the man was from "Godless Cuba." "This spic comes up here and wants God to cure him?" he asks the audience. "My friends, God will not cure those spics." When presented a homosexual, he asks the Lord to "make him a [straight and] tall Christian in Your army." Unexpectedly, Reverend Moly's divine injunction succeeds. "Reverend Moly," the jubilant man exclaims, "look! You did it! You cured me! I'm straight!" "Are you bullshitting me?" the incredulous Reverend Moly asks. "No," the man responds. "Jesus Christ," Reverend Moly concludes, "it's a miracle."[3]

Outrage at satire's provocations was not confined to the nation's heart-land. In San Francisco, the Committee raised the ire of some audience members with "Summer Vacation," a scene in which two female friends from high school (Irene Riordan and Kathyrn Ish) compare notes on what they each experienced during their first year of college. The subject of their conversation turns to sex and how one of the women had lost her virginity. Some audience members were so appalled by the sight of women discussing sex and orgasms on the stage that they beat a hasty retreat to the theater's exit. On the East Coast, meanwhile, Peter Cook's Establishment invited charges of blasphemy with a scene depicting the crucifixion of Christ. Cook, who reportedly was disappointed if at least some members of his audience did not "have their self-righteousness so offended that they get up and walk out during the show," had previously offered a consumer's guide to the "big three" religions. In addition to making disparaging comments about the pope, the Establishment here illustrated Judaism by flashing a slide of an empty cross with a sign reading "Watch This Space!" posted on it. In its crucifixion scene, Jesus Christ, dying on a cross, engages in a conversation on class privilege with the two working-class Cockneys who flank him. Although this scene's humor was based, like other Establishment material, on a peculiarly British preoccupation with class, it was irreverent enough to spur New York license commissioner Bernard J. O'Connell—invoking an old and no longer enforced 1911 law outlawing depictions of the deity onstage—to enjoin Cook and his American partner John Krimsky from performing it again in Manhattan. Together with other commentaries on sex, religion, abortion, and language taboos, the crucifixion scene confirmed for more than a few critics that Establishment satire "border[ed] dangerously on the smutty side" and was "vulgar," "bluntly sacrilegious," "resolutely indecent," and in "poor taste."[4]

Judgments of "poor taste" were more consistently rendered against Paul Krassner and his satirical magazine the *Realist*. As a boy growing in Queens during the 1930s, the progeny, like many other future satirists, of Jewish parents, Krassner was introduced to what he claims was his only religion, humor, by listening to comedians such as Fred Allen on the radio. While performing on the violin on the stage of Carnegie Hall at the age of six, he inadvertently triggered giggles from his audience and thus realized immediately, as he recalls in his autobiography, that he was "hooked" on the idea of making people laugh. Years later, as a young man, he assumed the stage name of Paul Maul and with his violin in hand initiated a brief career as a stand-up comedian, the highlight of which was the commotion he caused by "satirizing Senator Joe McCarthy's anti-Communist crusade" and by joking about the Virgin Mary's menstrual cycle. At the same time, Krassner had managed to escape military duty in Korea, a fortuitous event since he, like Jules Feiffer, harbored a "pathological resistance to authority" and was planning, with the aid of the American Civil Liberties Union, to challenge the constitutionality of the army's loyalty program. Once he was rejected from the army, Krassner was able to continue the apprenticeship that he had begun under publisher Lyle Stuart while he was still studying journalism and psychology at the City College of New York. In 1954, Stuart hired Krassner as the managing editor of his iconoclastic, muckraking publication the *Independent.* Working next door to the offices of *MAD* (where Stuart served as Bill Gaines's business manager), Krassner brought his interest in humor and satire to the *Independent* in his "Freedom of Wit" column and various other writings.[5]

In 1958, Stuart proposed that Krassner initiate a new magazine using the subscription list that William and Helen McCarthy, founders of the United Secularists of America, had used for their *Progressive World* magazine. Krassner seized the opportunity of editing his own satirical magazine, which he named the *Realist.*[6] With a masthead bearing the slogan "social-political-religious criticism and satire," Krassner's new magazine made its debut in the summer of 1958. In the premiere issue's lead editorial, "An Angry Young Magazine . . . ," Krassner declared that the *Realist* would be devoted to the "reporting and analysis of timely and significant conflicts that are ignored or treated only superficially by the general press" and would keep a close watch over the "political activities of organized religion" in particular. Krassner continued, "The second purpose of the *Realist*—not really unrelated to the first—is to provide satirical commentary on the tragicomic currents of our time." In subsequent issues the *Realist* declared itself a magazine of "freethought criticism and satire," while Krassner reiterated his intention to "criticize, via satirical comment, some of the utterly ridiculous goings-on in the world." "For us," Krassner wrote in the *Realist's* fifth issue, "laughter encompasses a positive attitude toward life."[7]

Throughout its first six and a half years, the *Realist's* orientation reflected a loose allegiance to segments of America's (particularly New York City's) bohemian, anarchist, pacifist left. Though issued partly tongue-in-cheek, Krassner's call for a "United Nonjoiners for the Use of Creative Kinetic Energy to Resist the System" indicates something of his identification with radical individualism, rational humanism, and anarchism. In general, the fifty-five issues of the *Realist* that spanned this period advocated racial equality, academic freedom, a free press, the protection of civil liberties (particularly the freedom of speech), and causes such as the Fair Play for Cuba.[8] Because Krassner used the *Realist* to strike out against provincialism, commercialism, and nuclear weapons, as well as any "organized superstition" or religious orthodoxy, its tone could at times be heavy, portentous, and vitriolic. In order to lend his magazine a light, irreverent spirit, therefore, Krassner needed to offset the *Realist's* journalism and commentary—and Robert Anton Wilson's ranting "Negative Thinking" column in particular—with a steady supply of ironic, bemused observations concerning the absurdities and paradoxes thriving in contemporary cold war America. Aided, no doubt, by clippings and samples *Realist* readers sent to him in New York, Krassner quoted verbatim items such as an advertisement in *Salesman's Opportunity* extolling the marketing opportunities for fallout shelters. Regular features such as "As the Realist Sees It," "The Department of Satirical Prophecy," and Bob Abel's "Quarterly Report on Some of the Crap That's Been Going On . . ." offered much of the same type of ironic commentary on the "unreal" and "surreal" events of the day. In addition, Krassner dispersed sardonic announcements throughout the *Realist's* pages, advocated mischievous hoaxes and public rumors, and in "Diabolic Dialogues" regularly featured fictitious conversations between public figures such as John Foster Dulles and Bertrand Russell.[9]

As with other venues for liberal satire during the 1950s and early 1960s, the *Realist* provided an opportunity to target, at times very poignantly, America's advertising and media industries, political personalities such as Richard Nixon and Barry Goldwater, and issues such as the bomb and racial segregation. What distinguished Krassner from his peers, however, was his highly irreverent attitude toward taboo subjects, particularly religion and sex. The *Realist's* periodic revelations about President John Kennedy's private life provide a good example of Krassner's willingness to go beyond the acceptable bounds of journalism and commentary. Whereas improvisational troupes such as the Premise stopped short of addressing Kennedy's sexual dalliances, the *Realist* brought them into full view. In September 1961, Krassner reported "rumors" surrounding the president's sexual affairs. "He is a real ladies' man," Krassner stated. "Sweet young models are at his beck and call . . . because the President is a busy man and has no time for foreplay." Several years later, the *Realist* provoked a stir when it alluded to other Kennedy affairs by slyly asking, "What is the story behind Pat Newcomb, the late Marilyn Monroe's press agent, now working for the U.S. Information Agency? What has been actress Angie Dickinson's greatest supporting role?"[10]

In many other *Realist* articles and cartoons, Krassner reinforced what he and his male colleagues considered "healthy" perspectives on premarital sex and sexual liberation.[11] Although *Realist* readers appreciated Krassner's frank discussions of sex, there were those who voiced objections to his decision to publish a discussion concerning the caloric content of semen and his self-indulgent recollections of time spent with a Cuban prostitute. What bothered many more readers, however, was Krassner's endless needling of religion. Throughout the *Realist's* first several years of publication, organized religion and the Catholic Church in particular served as Krassner's principal bugbear. Jokes, cartoons, and other comic features provided Krassner and his colleagues with a vehicle through which they could impugn religious figures. In "A Fable for Our Time: The Second Coming," for example, Krassner related how Jesus Christ might return to Earth as a panelist on the *What's My Line* television game show, land his own network program, *Savior Time,* but then succumb to the bane of many other "entertainers"—overexposure. In his "Rumor of the Month" feature, Krassner quipped that "'flying saucers' are actually diaphragms being dropped by nuns on their way to Heaven." In an advertising parody he juxtaposed a picture of the Virgin Mary with the famous Clairol ad copy, "Does she . . . or doesn't she?"[12]

It is clear that the *Realist's* irreverent stance toward sex and religion alienated a good number of the magazine's liberal readers. In response to Terry Southern's September 1963 interview with a "Faggot Male Nurse," a San Diego man complained that "publishing such pointless and tasteless articles" would ultimately jeopardize the *Realist.* "Damn it, man!" he continued. "Whether you like it or not, you've got a *mission.* Don't betray it." Another reader criticized a *Realist* gag that, he rightly claimed, had "no social criticism in it, no meaning; it's just sort of wanton hitting where there's nothing to hit, except people's feelings." One astute subscriber pointed out to Krassner that readers of the *Realist* "do not have to be convinced about the pointlessness or hypocrisy of religion," a point reiterated by a New York man who complained in 1960 that the *Realist* had become "a harangue against religion." This reader recommended that Krassner ease up on religion and instead "rip into business." Even Mort Sahl, who

43. "It's his turn now and then me again . . ." Richard Guindon's cover illustration for the November 1962 issue of the *Realist* exemplifies Paul Krassner's more provocative and (in the minds of his detractors) sophomoric approach to satirizing the cold war. By permission of Paul Krassner.

called the *Realist* "probably the most vital publication in the United States," accused Krassner of confusing "Puritanism and morality" and chastised him for "evading responsibility by making out that the whole world is a hoax—the whole world is a put-on, morality is a put-on . . ." "Whatever you do," Sahl reminded Krassner, "whether it's a rebellion or anything creative, has to be done within a framework. There has to be a frame of reference, and if we're not within the frame, then there is no *sanity*."[13]

Krassner attempted to fend off complaints regarding the "bad taste" of the *Realist*'s satire by claiming that "[t]here are absolutely no absolute standards of taste." "I happen to find the missile race *extremely* offensive," Krassner wrote in 1961. "I think nuclear warheads are in *terrible* taste. They frighten me much more than four-letter words." Predictably, Krassner's case for the relativity of aesthetic and moral judgments made few converts among his detractors. While *Time* magazine dismissed the *Realist* as a "shabby Greenwich Village periodical," the *Chicago Daily News* called it a "magazine the Reds would like." The *Daily News* accused Krassner of "making a dirty joke out of everything up to and including the

Creator." "While there are some magazines you wouldn't want your children to read," it continued, "this particular magazine is so filthy you wouldn't want your father to see it. It is truly obscene by almost anybody's standards." Krassner's opponents succeeded in ridding the *Realist* from newsstands, including those located in the bookstores of Adelphi University, New York University, and Stanford University. At times, even liberal and avant-garde publications such as the *Progressive,* the *Village Voice,* and *Evergreen Review* refused to carry Krassner's advertisements in its pages.[14]

Despite these challenges, the *Realist's* readership grew markedly between 1958 and 1964. Though its circulation paled in comparison to that of *MAD* magazine, the *Realist* claimed a readership of around 40,000 by late 1964. By this time, word of the *Realist's* outrageous cartoons as well as its infamous "Fuck Communism!" poster had begun to spread beyond its core audience. Krassner's brand of outlaw satire appealed to a growing group of liberal Americans, particularly male readers, who were frustrated by the hypocrisy and sanctimony poisoning American life and disillusioned with the cautious moderation of cold war liberalism. As one Montana man wrote Krassner approvingly, his magazine's "policy of tweaking the nose" of conventional liberal journalists by headlining issues such as "'Contraceptives,' 'Promiscuity' etc. is refreshing." "You point up hypocrisy in religion, sex, laws; anything that will make John Doe do a double-take and say, 'Kee-rist, who'd dare to write about anything like that' . . ." As with tamer varieties of liberal satire, the *Realist* became a source of inspiration for people who were experiencing a sense of isolation. As Krassner recognized, "One of the most common themes in the letters I get at the *Realist* is: 'I'm glad to know I'm not alone'—meaning, in terms of their outlook on life."[15]

With its daring, irreverent, and uncompromising stance on sex, religion, and politics, the *Realist* found enthusiastic support among a wide array of liberal and left-liberal writers, critics, artists, and performers. The *Realist* reportedly counted among its readers Nelson Algren, Norman Mailer, Steve Allen, and Tom Lehrer. Joseph Heller flattered Krassner when he declared that his magazine practically rewrote *Catch-22* every issue. Eager to draw attention to the liberal satirists he himself most admired, Krassner regularly featured *Monocle* writer Marvin Kitman and *MAD* magazine art director John Francis Putnam ("the *Realist's* latter-day Jonathan Swift"), published contributions from Jean Shepherd, Terry Southern, and Jules Feiffer, and, in a series of "Impolite Interviews," discussed the art of humor and satire with Mort Sahl, Jules Feiffer, Henry Morgan, Dick Gregory, Jean Shepherd, and Terry Southern.

*   *   *

By far the biggest influence on Paul Krassner and the shape of the *Realist's* satire was comedian Lenny Bruce. Krassner idolized Bruce, and he used his magazine to publish his writings and keep readers abreast of developments in his many legal battles. Krassner even sold Lenny Bruce merchandise and took advance orders for *How to Talk Dirty and Influence People,* the autobiography of Bruce that Krassner had helped prepare for *Playboy.* For Krassner, as for many other American satirists working in the fifties and early sixties, Bruce was the "real deal," the one satirist who really dared tackle the most sensitive issues extant in contemporary American life. The Second City's Paul Sills speaks for many of his cohort when he states that Bruce was "the only guy I really went out of my way to see." Pat Englund, a performer with the Second City and *TW3,* remembers that when she saw Bruce perform "it was one of the most memorable nights of my life." Bruce's impact was "radical," according to Englund and others, because he addressed "things you only talked about to friends . . . He made everything different."[16]

Because of his impact on American culture and comedy and the romantic aura surrounding his troubled career, Bruce has been the subject of more critical attention than any other American satirist active during the 1950s and early 1960s. The story of his evolution into America's "most dangerous" satirist, his drug addiction, and his legal travails has been rehearsed many times since the mid- and late sixties. Born Leonard Schneider, he grew up on Long Island during the 1930s while being shuttled back and forth in what he later remembered as an "endless exodus" between his divorced parents and their relatives. He was a student at six public schools, yet he never got beyond the fifth grade. Although he may have lacked a formal education, he was a keen observer of his environment and of American popular culture in particular. As a student at "Hollywood High," he recalled in his autobiography, Schneider watched and absorbed countless Hollywood movies. Accompanied by his mother and pal Sadie Kitchenberg, he also made frequent weekend field trips to Times Square, where he would catch burlesque shows and observe Professor Roy Heckler's Flea Circus at Huberts Museum. After running away from home to

398

work on a family farm, he volunteered for the U.S. Navy at the age of sixteen. As a shell passer aboard the cruiser USS *Brooklyn,* he saw action during several wartime invasions in the Mediterranean. Like many other future satirists, he grew restless in the service. By posing as a cross-dressing "Lady Macbeth" he was able to gain an honorable discharge in 1946.[17]

Upon returning to civilian life, Schneider drifted for several years, working various factory jobs and serving several stints with the Merchant Marines. In the late 1940s, he followed the example of his mother and broke into the world of amateur show business. At first he copied Sid Caesar routines and other material he had memorized while working as an usher at the Roxy in New York, but he eventually began developing his own act of impressions. After receiving his first laughs in little Saturday night joints in Brooklyn and Coney Island, he was hooked on show business. "It was like the flash that I have heard morphine addicts describe," he later remembered of the first approval he won from an audience, "a warm sensual blanket that comes after a cold, sick rejection."[18] Schneider then secured an agent, changed his name to Lenny Bruce, and eventually made a winning appearance (through his impressions of a Bavarian Humphrey Bogart and Peter Lorre) on *Arthur Godfrey's Talent Scouts.* Bruce's performance on the Godfrey show in 1950 helped land him work at Catskills resorts and better venues such as the Strand on Broadway, but his initial show business success proved short-lived. With his new bride Honey Harlowe, a professional stripper, Bruce fled to Southern California and the Hollywood dream factories that had held his imagination since youth.

As soon as Bruce immersed himself in Los Angeles's seedy nightlife and jazz underground, he began adopting the performing style, speech, attitude, and personal habits of the hipster.[19] Two key influences in Bruce's transformation on the West Coast were his friend Joe Maini and the comedian Lord Richard Buckley. Maini, a saxophone player who emulated Charlie Parker, encouraged Bruce to improvise onstage. He also introduced him to the jazz world's drug scene and turned him on to heroin. Bruce first met Buckley, the "Hip Messiah," when they shared a bill at Strip City, a Los Angeles burlesque club located in a "black and tan" neighborhood surrounding the intersection of Pico and Western streets. Buckley was a veteran performer who had worked gangster speakeasies in the thirties and later toured military bases with Ed Sullivan during the war. By the late forties and early fifties he had become a legend among working comedians and a favorite of bebop jazz musicians. Onstage Buckley was a one-of-a-kind performer who combined the manner of an English patrician with the imagination and spontaneity of a surrealist artist (he wore a distinctive Salvador Dali mustache) and the irreverent, outlaw attitude of a hipster from the streets (he earned a reputation for smoking marijuana onstage). Buckley was most famous for appropriating the patois of urban African Americans (which he believed possessed great "power, purity and beauty") and then rapping in his "Hipsomatic" dialect free form, parodies of the Gettysburg Address ("Four big hits and seven licks ago, our before daddies swung forth upon this sweet, groovy land, a swingin', stompin', jumpin', blowin', wailin' new nation, hip to the cool groove of liberty . . ."), Edgar Allan Poe's "The Raven," and, most notoriously, the lives of Mahatma Gandhi ("The Hip Gahn") and Jesus ("The Nazz").[20] Overall, Buckley's unique characterizations and free-form improvisations made a lasting impression on Bruce, particularly at a time when he was struggling to forge his own technique.

While struggling as a writer for B-grade Hollywood movies, Bruce found steady work as an emcee at Los Angeles burlesque clubs. Encouraged by the jazz musicians with whom he worked as well as the bartenders, strippers, struggling entertainers, and other night people who attended his late-night sets, Bruce began experimenting with a range of material onstage, much of it informed by the shattered illusions he had experienced since childhood. Many of Bruce's early bits focused on the hollow mythologies created by the American motion picture industry, what he called "the strongest environmental factor in molding the children of my day." In a manner consistent with that deployed by Ernie Kovacs, Harvey Kurtzman, and the Jewish American writers and artists at *MAD*, Bruce used parodies to take comic revenge on the shallow lies perpetrated by American popular culture. In "Father Flotsky's Triumph," for example, Bruce used his uncanny memory of movies and actors' names and his skills as an impressionist to send up trite, sentimental prison riot pictures. Bruce's "Masked Man" routine, a parody of the *Lone Ranger,* which brazenly refutes the possibility of a selfless hero who does not even expect a "thank you" in return for his services, closely mirrored the spirit of the parodies that Kurtzman produced throughout the 1950s. Other early bits, many of them featured on Bruce's first two albums, *Interviews of Our Times* and *The Sick Humor of Lenny Bruce,* similarly paralleled *MAD* with their sinister or "sicko" twists—Tarzan's Jane has an affair with

Cheetah, a drunk airline pilot plots the disposal of passengers from his ailing plane, a television commercial in which a redneck used car salesman touts a Jeep once used to ferry bodies to the furnaces.[21]

As biographer Albert Goldman has observed, the world of show business was in Bruce's early career the predominant metaphor for the scams, hustles, and lies that he believed were underwriting modern American life. What Bruce saw, Goldman writes, "simple, true and terribly funny— was this: the great world of social, political and religious power, authority and dignity is nothing but a gigantic racket run by petty hustlers and Broadway agents." This cynical point of view is well illustrated by two of Bruce's most admired early routines: "Adolph Hitler and M.C.A." and "Religions Incorporated." The latter proceeded from Bruce's observation that religious advertising had overtaken entertainment advertising in the weekend papers. Set in the Madison Avenue headquarters for Religions Inc., Bruce's scenario imagined how Billy Graham, Oral Roberts, Rabbi Wise, and other prominent religious leaders chart their "grosses" with America's religious consumers. In its climax, Roberts puts in a call to the pope in Rome. Roberts bellows, "Hello Johnny! What's shakin baby . . . How's your old lady?" and then begins to complain about the pressure he and his fellow showmen are receiving from integrationists. "No they donwannay quaotations from the Bahble," Roberts explains. "They wannus to come out an *say* things." Roberts ends his conversation with the pope with the assurance, "No, nobody knows you're Jewish."[22]

Recordings of Bruce's early performances at clubs such as the Peacock Lane in Los Angeles reveal that he strung his bits and longer scenarios together very loosely, darting back and forth extemporaneously and, occasionally, groping for a coherent structure for his ideas. "I have a thousand brilliant things in my mind," he told a distracted Peacock Lane crowd in January 1958, "but they just won't jell." In these same performances Bruce resorted to risqué material, and he assumed an antagonistic posture toward patrons, particularly female patrons who did not appear to "dig" him. "Talk to me, you Avon lady reject," he taunted one female audience member, "talk dirty to me." "Look at me, you, you, you." An inebriated woman in a San Francisco club who heckled him for mentioning diaphragms onstage received Bruce's sympathy and then, much to the delight of the male patrons, his lewd, mocking come-on. "You look pretty wild," Bruce told her, "but you can't talk while we're balling."[23]

Word of Bruce's hip, provocative comic delivery spread among Los Angeles show business people, comedy writers, and comedians, particularly after Bruce began appearing as a warm-up act for Mort Sahl at the Crescendo Club. Bruce's celebrity grew further when in 1958 he began performing at Ann's 440 in San Francisco's North Beach district. Writing Bruce's first notice in *Variety,* the influential syndicated jazz critic Ralph Gleason opined approvingly that "his humor is right out of a road band sideman's perspective and delivered in a heterogeneous mixture of underworld argot, hipster's slang, and show business patter . . ."[24] Bruce, Gleason added, was "farther out than Mort Sahl and devastating in [his] attacks on the pompous, the pious, and the phoney in America culture." Over the next seven years, Gleason served as one of Bruce's most staunch and eloquent champions. Gleason testified to Bruce's vital connections to jazz in his columns for the *San Francisco Chronicle, Down Beat,* and *Jazz* and in his liner notes for Bruce's early albums with San Francisco–based Fantasy Records. On the cover of *Sick Humor of Lenny Bruce,* Gleason wrote,

> Like the jazz musician's view, Bruce's comedy is a dissent from a world gone mad. To him nothing is sacred except the ultimate truths of love and beauty and moral goodness—all equating honesty. And like a jazz musician he expects to see these things about him in the world in a pure form. He takes people literally and what they say literally and by the use of his searing imagination and tongue of fire, he contrasts what they say with what they do. And he does this with the sardonic shoulder-shrug of the jazz man. He is colossally irreverent—like a jazz musician . . . His is a moral outrage and has about it the air of a jazz man. It is strong stuff—like jazz, and it is akin to the point of view of Nelson Algren and Lawrence Ferlinghetti as well as to Charlie Parker and Lester Young.[25]

Numerous other critics such as Nat Hentoff, Gilbert Millstein, Charles Marowitz, and Jonathan Miller repeated the connection Gleason made between Bruce and the spontaneous arts flourishing in postwar America. In addition to associating a Bruce performance with the freewheeling prose of Jack Kerouac's *On the Road* and jump-cut discontinuity of William Burroughs's *Naked Lunch,* these critics interpreted it in the light of Zen philosophy, abstract expressionist painting, and the theater of Jean Genet. Miller, in an admiring portrait for *Partisan Review* titled "Sick White Negro," described Bruce as a "Beat magician" and "collagist" who assembled "the fragments of urban consciousness without much regard for conventions or taboo." "He is almost a verbal Pop artist," Miller continued, "pasting together the thousand sordid images of the urban American imagination."[26]

Bruce, who would jokingly admit to being a "culture snob," professed a

44. In addition to thrilling audiences with his keen satiric insight, Lenny Bruce at his peak left a lasting impression with his spontaneous, jazz-inflected delivery and remarkable on-stage allure. "I don't come [to his performances] to laugh," one appreciative critic wrote of him. "I just want to be in his presence." Julian Wasser/Pix Inc./Time & Life Pictures/Getty Images.

strong attraction to modern art and the avant-garde. But it was the example of improvisational jazz that most inspired Bruce's performing style onstage. Bruce saw himself as an oral jazzman and a disciple of "abstraction." To audiences and interviewers he often described how he was "the only comic with a hangup about performing set pieces over and over" and how, if he was "extremely fertile," he could create up to ten or fifteen minutes of new material during an hour-long performance. With his willingness to experiment off-the-cuff, coupled with his superb sense of comic timing, his innate feel for rhythm, and his skills in vocal mimicry and voice modulation, Bruce created performances of stunning virtuosity.[27]

Through a combination of his exciting, spontaneous stage presence and his growing reputation for outrageousness, Lenny Bruce by the early years of the New Frontier had become one of the most talked about and admired figures inhabiting America's satiric underground. Following his

breakthrough stint at Ann's 440, Bruce had no trouble obtaining bookings at clubs such as the hungry i, the Cloisters and Mister Kelly's in
Chicago, and the Den in the Duane, Blue Angel, and Village Vanguard in
New York. In 1961, when Bruce was at the height of his career, he was, as
Max Gordon, the owner of the Blue Angel and Village Vanguard remem-
bers, "money in the bank." Even nightclubs in St. Louis, Minneapolis,
and Pennsauken, New Jersey, were filled to capacity when Bruce played
them.[28] At the end of 1960, the three albums he had recorded for Fantasy
Records had sold more than 190,000 copies, surpassing sales of Mort
Sahl's Verve label albums.

*   *   *

What many people who caught Bruce's act or purchased his albums
prized most about him was the provocative manner in which he satirized
significant political and social issues. Unlike Mort Sahl or liberal cartoonists such as Herblock, Bruce had little interest in satirizing American politics directly. "I can't get worked up about politics," he once told an audience. "I grew up in New York, and I was hip as a kid that I was corrupt and
that the mayor was corrupt. I have no illusions." From Bruce's jaded perspective, politicians were shameless opportunists who would do anything
to get elected. "If you were to follow Stevenson from New York to Alabama," he observed of the perennial Democratic presidential nominee,
"you would shit from the changes." Still, not all politicians were alike in
Bruce's mind. When forced to choose between Republican Richard
Nixon and Democrat John Kennedy for president in 1960, Bruce predictably sided with the latter. Like Norman Mailer, Bruce judged Kennedy superior because he was young, healthy, and "real" and, not least,
because he had an attractive wife—a definite "plus factor," as Bruce put
it. Among Nixon's faults, Bruce related, was his long association with
Dwight D. Eisenhower—in Bruce's view, a dim-witted, slick-talking politician who was willing to do anything to divert the public's attention from
his administration's wrongdoing.[29]

Although generally cynical about politics, Bruce was occasionally
moved to address the contradictions of the cold war. "I usually don't get
political," Bruce told a Los Angeles audience in late 1960, "but I love this
country. It's been good to me." "You don't yell at Cuba," he went on to tell
them, "not if you're Christians." "Alright Castro," he began to imitate a

tough-talking cold warrior, "'We're going to take away $90 million worth of sugar. How do you like that?' How does he like it? Russia will give him $350 billion of saccharine." Reflecting on America's long-standing reliance on realpolitik, Bruce in 1961 related how "we [white Americans] did all of the Indians in" by taking their land. "Get out of here and go to the swamps," Bruce said in the voice of a land-grabbing American settler. "Get out of here. What do you mean 'your land.' What do you got to show me is yours, man.'" In the end, Bruce saw no reason why the United States should insist on capitalism as the universal model for the world's economy. "Capitalism is the best," he would argue. "But I'm not going to buy any time for Radio Free Europe. Freak that . . . If communism cooks for you, solid man. I'm not going to free anybody. Not when the Governor of Georgia closes the schools."[30]

Bruce's reference to the hypocrisy of the white South grew from his liberal concern over America's unresolved racial crisis. In an interview with Studs Terkel in February 1959, Bruce explained that racial integration was one of the "only things that I feel very strongly about . . ." As such, he vowed to "attack [it] through satire." Characteristic of the approach Bruce's satire took toward the subject of race was a routine in which he imagined offering a Ku Klux Klan member the choice between spending fifteen years "kissing and hugging and sleeping real close on hot nights" with a "black, black woman . . . or . . . a white, white woman . . . The white woman is Kate Smith . . . and the black woman is Lena Horne! So you're not concerned with black or white any more, are you?" Bruce did not pin the blame of America's racial crisis only on Southern Klansmen and "rednecks." By 1960, in fact, Bruce was excoriating what he called "first-plateau" Northern liberals. "It's very easy to criticize the South with their obvious Anti-Christ: '*Shlepp* them away from the lunch counters, don't let them use the toilet,'" Bruce said that year. "Now I know that Philly is worse than Little Rock and New York is more twisted than Atlanta ever will be."[31]

In his most famous routine from this period, Bruce portrayed a first-plateau liberal who, during the course of a party hosted by some suburbanites, decides to strike up a conversation with the black musician hired for the evening. With the aid of a few cocktails, this Northern liberal reveals the true extent of his tolerance toward and understanding of African Americans. Before long, the white man attempts to find some common ground by remarking, "That Joe Louis is a hell of a fighter." He then ap-

45. With eye for the absurd, Lenny Bruce targeted American race relations for the cover of his 1960 album *I Am Not a Nut, Elect Me!* (Fantasy 7007) Licensed by Concord Music Group, Inc. All rights reserved.

peals to what he hopes will be their shared prejudice against Jews. Speaking of the hosts, he says, "I don't know if they're ah . . . I think they're Hebes. You're not Jewish are you?" Returning to the subject of the musician's race, the white man blurts, "The way I figure it is . . . no matter what the hell a guy is, if he stays in his place he's all right . . . Joe Louis was a guy who, the way I figure it he was a guy who just knew when to get in there and get outta there, which is a lot more than I can say for a lot of you niggers. No offense. I had a few [drinks] on the way over here." He closes by saying that he wants to have the musician over to the house (after it gets dark) but that he has a problem—his sister. "And I hear that you guys . . . you know it's my sister and well, I'll put it to you a different way. You

Satire That Would "Gag a Goat"

wouldn't want no Jew doing it to your sister would you? . . . I don't want no coon doing it to my sister. No offense, you know what I mean . . ."[32]

*　　*　　*

Many of Bruce's satiric comments about racial prejudice were motivated by, as he admitted in 1959, a "religious standpoint." Echoing the beliefs of Dr. Martin Luther King and many white and black Americans involved in the civil rights movement, Bruce argued that Judeo-Christian ethics provided the "most important and usually the most powerful argument" against racial segregation. "If you are a Christian or a Jew and you believe in the Bible, in its principles," Bruce told Studs Terkel in 1959, "you cannot really call yourself a good Christian or a good Jew and not wholeheartedly believe in integration." "If you can tell me Christ or Moses . . . would say to some kid, 'Hey, kid, that's a *white* fountain, you can't drink out of there,'" Bruce pointed out onstage, "you're out of your skull. No one can tell me Christ or Moses would do *that*."[33]

For Bruce, the failure of American Jews and Christians around the country to recognize the rights of African Americans or to urge a more aggressive path toward racial reconciliation was symptomatic of the glaring contradictions and moral failures plaguing modern-day religion. Throughout the late fifties and early sixties, in fact, Bruce called into question not only churches' silence over race, but their aloofness toward sex, birth control, capital punishment, and a number of other vital contemporary issues. In general, Bruce believed that a large gulf had grown between "true" and organized religion—a gulf so large, he liked to quip, that people were "straying from the church and going for religion."[34]

Beginning with his "Religions, Inc." routine—one that, as Ralph Gleason reported in 1960, "frequently cause[d] gasps of horror from the expense-account crowd in a club like San Francisco's hungry i or New York's Blue Angel"—Bruce's satiric attacks on organized religion became one of the most controversial parts of his act. The theme running through this and other satiric routines was that the "big three" (Judaism, Catholicism and Protestantism) were corrupt and hopelessly out of touch with present-day reality. This situation, Bruce claimed, stemmed in large part from the hypocrisy of America's religious leaders, people whom he regarded no better than politicians.[35] Much like his fellow satirist, friend, and collaborator, Paul Krassner, Bruce took particular aim at the leaders of the Catholic Church. Comparing the Catholic Church to the Howard

Johnson restaurant chain, Bruce argued that its leaders had become isolated from its customers. The pope is a good man, Bruce argued from the
stage of Los Angeles's Crescendo club in 1960, but he "can't run his business six hundred miles away." "To help you," Bruce continued, "he has to
know you."[36]

Bruce took particular delight in harpooning two of the most powerful
men in the American Catholic hierarchy: Francis Cardinal Spellman and
Bishop Fulton Sheen. In one of the most solidly constructed, pointed,
and, in the opinion of some American Catholics, most patently blasphemous satiric routines he ever developed, Bruce imagined what would
happen if Christ and Moses descended from heaven in order to assess
firsthand the spiritual condition of American Jews and Catholics. After
witnessing reformed rabbis ("so reformed they're ashamed they're Jewish") "perform" in a West Coast schul, Christ and Moses head to Saint
Patrick's Cathedral in New York where they catch Spellman and Sheen, "a
good double bill." "Cardinal Spellman would be relating love and giving
and forgiveness to the people," Bruce imagined the scene in his celebrated
Carnegie Hall midnight concert of February 1961. "And Christ would be
confused, because their route took them through Spanish Harlem. And
[Christ and Moses] would wonder what forty Puerto Ricans were doing
living in one room when this guy had a ring worth eight grand." After
Bishop Sheen and Cardinal Spellman spot Christ and Moses at the rear of
the church ("I've only seen them in pictures," Sheen tells Spellman, "but
I'm pretty sure its them"), they decide to call the pope for help. Increasingly panicked by the sight of lepers entering the front door, Spellman im-
plores the pope over the telephone, "Put them up at *your* place. What are
we paying protection for?" In the final punch line, Spellman answers the
pope's imagined query: "Of course they're white."[37]

The attention that Bruce paid to the shortcomings of modern religion
stemmed from his interest in Judeo-Christian ethics and his evolving
identity as prophetic moralist. Bruce developed a fascination with religion only during the latter stages of his career. Until 1959 or 1960, in fact,
Bruce left little hint that he had inherited religious and moral principles
from his Jewish upbringing. But he later embraced his Jewishness, and
more than any of the other Jewish American satirists of the 1950s and
early 1960s he was eager to invoke ethical and prophetic traditions of Judaism as well as discuss anti-Semitism and the secrets of what he called
"the tribe." Unlike the vast majority of successful mainstream Jewish
American comedians and entertainers working during the 1950s, Bruce

did not dissociate himself from the culture of working- and lower-middle-class Jewish Americans or the Yiddish gutter slang of his youth. Throughout his career, in fact, Bruce made heavy use of the colorful and wonderfully expressive Yiddish vernacular, often confounding the non-Jews in his audience. Being Jewish provided Bruce not only with a new, more authentic way of communicating, it provided access to a unique critical consciousness. Jewishness for Bruce was more a state of mind than an inherited identity, a state of mind that afforded him the vantage point of the marginal, the alienated, and the hip.[38]

Evidence of Bruce's gradual metamorphosis from comedian to teacher-prophet-satirist was manifest not only in his preoccupation with Moses and Christ, but in his change in appearance, his performing style, and his own descriptions of his art.[39] Onstage, Bruce no longer wore a suit and tie but instead donned a long black alpaca Nehru jacket, what he called his "Chinese rabbi suit." By the early 1960s he had also begun to deploy "macabre charades" and theatrical techniques—reminiscent of avantgarde French playwright Jean Genet in particular—which tempted Albert Goldman to compare him with a medicine man or shaman. Whether critics labeled Bruce a shaman, oral jazzman, performing analysand, stage provocateur, or preacher, it is clear that his performing style at the peak of his career was vastly different from that of mainstream American comedians. By 1961, Bruce even resisted the idea of rerunning old but still popular routines. "It's obvious that I won't do bits any more," he announced during his three-hour performance at San Francisco's Curran Theater in November 1961, "from now on I just want to cook and freeform it all the way." Like other liberal satirists, Bruce was eager to distance himself from what he called the trite, "whoopee cushion" humor of Joe E. Lewis, Joey Bishop, and the old-school comics. As opposed to them, Bruce offered audiences what he commonly described as "satire." "I satirize many subjects that are particular sacred cows," he told audiences in the early sixties. "In other words, I am a satirist basically. I am irreverent politically, religiously, or any things that I think need discussing and satirizing." To Paul Krassner Bruce confessed in the autumn of 1960, "I'm not a comedian. I'm Lenny Bruce." Several years later Bruce told the Australian press that the "world is sick and I'm the doctor. I'm a surgeon with a scalpel for false values. I don't have an act. I just talk. I'm just Lenny Bruce."[40]

*　　*　　*

Bruce's conviction that he was helping "direct the course of human conduct in the areas of religion, politics, and social action" was in part a result
of the exaggerated sense of heroism that Dick Gregory, Mort Sahl, and
other male liberal satirists experienced at the height of their careers. To be
sure, Bruce's ego was also fed by the voluminous, overembellished praise
that his benefactors showered on him. Throughout the early 1960s Bruce
was hailed as one of the most important critical voices of his generation.
In his introduction to Bruce's February 1961 appearance at Carnegie Hall,
producer Don Friedman repeated what many commentators were saying
about Bruce and his "sick" comedy. "[I]t is not that Lenny Bruce *per se* is a
sick comedian," Friedman explained to the audience, "but that Lenny
Bruce comments, reflects, holds up the mirror, so to speak, to the sick
elements in our society that *should* be reflected upon and that *should* be
spoken about." Friedman's judgment found many echoes in the writings
of newspaper columnists, critics, and essayists. "They call Lenny Bruce a
sick comic—and sick he is," rhapsodized *San Francisco Chronicle* columnist
Herb Caen. "Sick of the pretentious phoniness of a generation that makes
his vicious humor meaningful. He is a rebel, but not without a cause, for
there are shirts that need unstuffing, egos that need deflating, and precious few people to do the sticky job with talent and style." "If Mr. Bruce
is 'sick,' as the label says," argued the New York *World-Telegram*'s Arthur
Alpert, "then rape, murder, and war are 'healthy.'"[41]

In the pages of the *New York Post* and *Village Voice*, critic Jerry Tallmer
raved about Bruce, at one time claiming, "He is a truthteller, a kind of
prophet, the kind that goes right back to Ezekiel and the wheel." "No one
on any stage or screen today, or in any book, slices so frequently close to
the marrow of Known Truth—and makes us see it, know it, admit that it
is there." After seeing Bruce for the first time, Tallmer told his *Village Voice*
readers in the spring of 1960, "I suddenly found myself coming into full
health for the first time in eight or ten years . . . For I, like all of you, have
been nursing a king-sized abscess of the soul ever since the onset of the
Great Unlaughter, and if a few here and there (Mort Sahl, Jules Feiffer, Bill
Manville, maybe Ionesco) have poked and probed at it to let off some of
the pus, it is only Lenny Bruce who, with one free wild slash, has enabled
it to gush away entirely . . ." For jazz critic Nat Hentoff, Tallmer's partner
at the *Village Voice*, Bruce was the only performer truly worthy of the title
satirist. Hentoff complained in early 1963 that while the "quicksand sympathy of the softly hip ha[d] swallowed Sahl, Nichols and May, the Premise, and parts of Second City and 'Beyond the Fringe,'" Bruce had "re-

mained free because his way of getting 'acceptance' from his audience is to scourge them into at least recognizing his own values." Bruce followed Hentoff's injunction to "Do Something Wrong, Baby," and in return he received the critic's highest praise. "It is Lenny Bruce—and only in him," Hentoff wrote, "that there has emerged a cohesively 'new' comedy of nakedly honest moral rage at the deceptions all down the line in our society."[42]

Nowhere was the chorus of critical approval aimed at Bruce louder than in England. During a three-week stint at Peter Cook's Establishment Club in April 1962, Bruce thoroughly stunned and consequently divided London audiences with his act. According to the *Observer*'s Kenneth Tynan, Bruce during his opening night "crashed through frontiers of language and feeling that I had hitherto thought impregnable." Tynan became a vociferous proponent of Bruce, as he was of Mort Sahl and other American satirists. Although Tynan wished that Bruce "had broadened his viewpoint by a little selective reading of Marx," he praised him for having "the heart of an unfrocked evangelist." "Other [comedians] josh, snipe and rib," Tynan wrote of Bruce, "only Bruce demolishes. He breaks through the barrier of laughter to the horizon beyond, where truth has its sanctuary." Beyond the Fringe's Jonathan Miller, who, according to Tynan, watched Bruce "in something like awe," agreed with Tynan that "if 'Beyond the Fringe' was a pinprick, Mr. Bruce was a bloodbath." "Until Lenny Bruce," Miller recounted in *Partisan Review*, "we had known America through the Coca-colonial accents of Bob Hope and Jerry Lewis . . . tailfins, juke boxes and Palm Beach shirts." After seeing him perform nearly every night of his London engagement, Miller was moved to write that Bruce was a "Yiddish Ariel whose hesitant . . . technique, full of breaks and riffs, untunes the ear of the conventional night-club audience who are used to getting their entertainment in a smooth flow of glossy chatter." George Melly, critic for the *New Statesman*, was likewise much impressed with Bruce's style as with his satire. Bruce, Melly claimed, "swings like a negro preacher." The sum total of what Bruce did onstage, he wrote, was "beautiful, true and moving." Bruce, Melly concluded, "is the evangelist of the new morality, ousting all other favoured contenders."[43]

Becoming an "evangelist of the new morality" was a heavy burden for Bruce to bear. At times, in fact, he appeared eager to rid himself of the moralist's mantel, insisting that he was, in essence, as corrupt as everyone else. "You might assume," he wrote in an unpublished essay, "that I am an extremely moral individual, suffering pangs of conscience in an unjust so-

ciety, but I am not. I am a hustler like everyone else, and will continue taking the money as long as this mass madness continues. Sometimes . . . I see
myself as a profound, incisive wit, concerned with man's inhumanity to
man," Bruce once confessed to his audience. "Then I stroll to the next
mirror and I see a pompous, subjective ass whose humor is hardly spiritual. I see traces of Mephistopheles."[44]

In Bruce's mind, the key difference between himself and the everyday
sinner was that, as he put it, "I know I am doing wrong and don't stop."
For Bruce then honesty and consistency mattered much more than abstract, divinely inspired or socially sanctioned moral codes. Realizing this
essential point about Bruce's moral calculus not only makes it easier to understand his ethical inconsistencies and the relativism underpinning his
outlook, it highlights his obsession with honesty and truth.[45] Like Harvey
Kurtzman and other members of his cohort, the foundation of Bruce's
satiric outlook rested on the bedrock of authenticity. When Bruce was interested in truth, he said, "it's really a *truth* truth, one hundred per cent.
And that's a terrible kind of truth to be interested in." To a San Francisco
audience in late 1961 Bruce attempted to explain his obsession with the
brutal truth: "I have a need to . . . My father must have instilled in me
'there's nothing worse than a lie' . . . So apparently my father rapped [the
importance of truth] in solider than other people. So when I see the lie, I
don't want it to be that way . . ."[46] Bruce liked to explain his devotion to
comedy by claiming that it was the "only honest art form" and the best
means to destroy hypocrisy and "the paradox." Referring to the notion
that sex is "dirty," for example, Bruce responded, "Well I can't buy that
man. Because that's a paradox. That's what I'm here for, to recreate." To a
Los Angeles audience in 1960 Bruce pointed out the paradox of Milltown
users and heavy martini drinkers condemning drug addicts. The fact that
American society was prepared to "kill" jazz singer Billie Holliday yet
eulogize raconteur Alexander King (whom he called "the junkie Mark
Twain") appalled Bruce. "Just be *consistent,*" Bruce concluded disgustedly.[47]
Until Americans renounced their *zug gornischt* ("say nothing"), make-
believe culture and began facing *what is,* Bruce argued, they would continue suffering a wide range of social ills. "We're all taught a what-should-
be culture," Bruce told audiences. "Which means a lot of *bull*shit. *Emmis.*
Because instead of being taught, *This is what is*—that's a beautiful truth,
what man always has been—we're taught the fantasy, man. But if we were
taught This Is What Is, I think we'd be less screwed up."[48]

For Bruce, as for fellow satirist Paul Krassner, Beat poets such as Allen

Ginsberg, intellectuals Norman Mailer and Herbert Marcuse, *Playboy* magazine, and a growing number of young Americans, some of the most harmful paradoxes at large in New Frontier America involved sex and the codes of "respectability" that policed it. In Bruce's formulation, respectability sanctioned the Big Lie, encouraged silence, and hence impeded Americans' emotional and spiritual well-being. Running throughout several Bruce monologues from the early sixties—including his notorious "Tits and Ass" routine—was the idea that Americans' squeamishness over sex was hypocritical, silly, and quite possibly dangerous.[49] Sex, Bruce insisted, was beautiful, natural, honest. And the fact that Americans tolerated violent entertainment yet balked at anything remotely sexually risqué was for Bruce another sign of America's schizophrenic sense of values. "You can do only one thing [to the body] to make it dirty: kill it," Bruce said onstage. "Hiroshima was dirty. [Caryl Chessman's execution] was dirty."[50]

Bruce derived much of his perspective on the concept of obscenity and other related effects of sexual repression from mainstream Freudian psychology. Indeed, popular tenets of Freudian psychology saturated Bruce's monologues during the early sixties. It was Bruce's passing knowledge of Freud, for example, which motivated him to observe that Americans were suffering too many guilt feelings about toilets. "Many of our problems stem from toilet training," Bruce told a San Francisco audience in 1959. To help liberate audiences from their hang-ups, Bruce celebrated, in true Rabelaisian fashion, a full range of bodily functions and animal urges. Foremost among these urges were, of course, sexual urges. Whether discoursing on the natural beauty of the female body, oral sex, dating, or men's irrepressible sexual drive or even bragging about his own sexual conquests, Bruce was forcing his audiences to confront their sexual inhibitions—inhibitions that he traced all the way back to Saint Paul's renunciation of sex. Indeed, in many respects Bruce was attempting to enact what one British critic called the "outing of the communal Id." Or as another writer has observed, "Lenny was dragging his audiences into dark psychic byways they shrank from entering, then flicking on a light switch to show there was nothing to be afraid of."[51]

To be sure, Bruce's ideas about sexual freedom, as well as his protests against "momism" and the "drooling sentimentality" of commercial culture, were thoroughly masculine in character. Bruce's promotion of sexual liberation grew from his understanding of the prerogatives of the modern American male. When he legitimated the idea that guys would "*schtup* anything," doled out advice on what not to confess to your wife, reminded audiences of women's wily powers ("chicks are boss"), and professed that a woman who sleeps with a different man every week is a better Christian than a virgin is, Bruce betrayed a line of thinking that was remarkably similar to Hugh Hefner's *Playboy* philosophy. Given the affinity between Bruce and Hefner, in fact, it is no surprise that *Playboy's* publisher gave Bruce's career several big boosts. Aggressive, irreverent, hip, sexually liberated and financially successful (though unconventionally so), Lenny Bruce embodied many of the attitudes and values that Hefner held most dear. Throughout the early and mid-1960s, Hefner featured Bruce prominently in *Playboy* and on his syndicated television program, *Playboy's Penthouse.*[52]

* * *

Among the male readers of *Playboy,* Bruce's brutal honesty about sex and religion no doubt found much support. But because Bruce transgressed the boundaries that even Hugh Hefner observed when commenting on these subjects, because he used obscenities rarely heard onstage, he became the object of intense disapproval. Without question, Lenny Bruce provoked more bitter and angry responses than any other liberal satirist active during the fifties and early sixties. In the British and American press, critics took great delight in denouncing Bruce as "the man from outer taste." While Walter Winchell labeled Bruce "America's No. 1 Vomic," the *London Sunday Telegraph,* for example, described him as a "small, swarthy, panderous pandit" and a "household pet gone berserk." Robert Ruark told readers of the *Saturday Evening Post* that "Bruce puts on an act that would gag a goat." Numerous accounts of adverse audience reaction to Bruce indicate that newspaper critics were hardly alone with their disapproval. Audience members often made vocal protests and hasty departures. On occasion, audience members hurled objects, made threats, and even assaulted Bruce onstage.[53]

The negative reactions Bruce received from religious and cultural conservatives were to be expected. Yet as he increasingly pushed the limits of his audience's acceptance, Bruce encountered the disapproval of liberals as well. Bruce had to some extent always harbored ambivalent feelings toward liberal audience members. On the one hand he enjoyed the attention these adoring fans as well as liberal critics and intellectuals gave him. Bruce wore the badge of *satirist* proudly. Yet at the same time, he was clearly somewhat uneasy with the hype that surrounded him. To his credit, Bruce well understood that his act provided many paying middle-class customers of the Blue Angel and Crescendo with little more than a fleeting thrill, a brief walk on the wild side. As controversies surrounding his act grew, he appeared more determined to up the ante with his audiences, to separate out his true supporters from the squares.

Expanding his use of obscene and scatological language was one way in which Bruce tested his audience's tolerance. Whereas he formerly used profanity mainly in the service of his deft theatrical characterizations, Bruce by 1962 and 1963 had begun trading obscenities and explicit sexual references freely. Bruce claimed that he traded obscenities in order to liberate audiences from their hang-ups with "dirty" words—just as he forced them to confront buried feelings they harbored on sex and modern-day morality—yet even his supporters began to suspect that he was merely deriving satisfaction out of shocking the "upper bohemians" and liberals who paid to see him onstage. Indeed, it became more difficult to find the satiric intention, much less the joke behind his bit on "pissing in the sink" or, more to the point, his mock threat to urinate on the audience itself. Bruce's on-stage provocations were more than even veteran liberal comedians and satirists such as Groucho Marx and Henry Morgan could take. Morgan walked out of a Bruce performance and later told Paul Krassner in an interview for the *Realist* that he considered the young performer "terrible, untalented, [and] revolting."[54] In 1960, critic Nat Hentoff mused over "how far Bruce will go in . . . exposing his most enthusiastic audiences—the very same 'first plateau liberals' he denounces—to themselves." Several years later, he reported that the "new" Lenny Bruce was allowing such liberals "no room for self-soothing, self blurring sympathy." "Sooner or later," Hentoff remarked, Bruce "uncovers one of your own evasions or carefully bandaged confusions; and at those points your laughter too becomes as strangled as that of the squares from the ad agencies at the next table."[55]

As disturbing as Bruce's revelations about middle-class liberals' psychological "evasions" might have been, what perplexed liberals and intellectuals most during the early sixties were his sympathetic identifications with German war criminal Adolph Eichmann, the Ku Klux Klan, the American Nazi George Lincoln Rockwell, and racist Southerners. As Bruce began speaking about the teachings of Jesus and the importance of empathy and *simpatico,* he called on audience members to never compromise liberalism's spirit of tolerance. "Here's the trend," Bruce wrote in an unpublished essay titled "The Violent Liberals": "It's been chic for a long time for liberals to identify with Stevenson and hate Nixon . . . But how liberal are they if they cannot be liberal with Nixon?" Elsewhere, Bruce remarked that "the liberals are so liberal they can't understand the bigots." A true liberal, reared in the teachings of Judeo-Christian religion, Bruce claimed speciously, would not persecute a Nazi war criminal like Eichmann since he was only following orders. "Eichmann," Bruce told a perplexed San Francisco crowd in late 1961, "*rachmunous,* gotta have simpatico for him. Can't do him in. Not eye for eye. That's a lot of crap, man. Dig this cat, *schlepped* out . . . and on trial." Likewise, Bruce sympathized with a persecuted KKK leader since he was a "poor dude" who truly wasn't aware of what he was doing. The real people at fault for the KKK, Bruce claimed, were Northern liberals since they had done so little to change the economic conditions of the South. "We forgave the Japanese once, the Germans twice, but the White Southerner we've kicked in the ass since Fort Sumter," Bruce reasoned.[56]

In 1961, Bruce claimed that he was no longer interested in doing bits on integration. "I was off that six, eight months ago," Bruce told his audience at the Curran Theatre late that year. "Because the battle's won . . . So then I got on some *simpatico* with the white Southerner." Bruce noted elsewhere that he had not "seen one newspaper report that understood anything about those people [Southerners], it's just *rank rank rank rank rank.*" Bruce even began to amend his well-loved "How to Relax Colored Friends" routine with a sympathetic observation about the bigot he has just satirized. "The guy in this bit," Bruce began, "we assume—see, that's the funny thing about indictment—we assume that this cat is all bad, then, and we destroy him. But you can't man. He's bad in this sense, cause he has not matured, he has not been in the proper environment, cause if he were, to learn and to listen, he would swing, cause there are sensitive parts to him also, man."[57]

*   *   *

By arguing that "you *can* teach an old dog new tricks" through education and improvements in living conditions, Bruce betrayed his affinity with early-sixties liberalism. For their part, more than a few American liberals and liberal intellectuals seemed willing to excuse Bruce's rhetorical excesses if only to support his right to express himself freely onstage. No matter how frustrated or offended they may have been with Bruce, many came to his defense when he was hounded by America's legal establishment. During the early sixties, when he was at the peak of his career, Bruce became embroiled in numerous, costly legal battles. By 1962, these battles, particularly those stemming from his obscenity arrests, subsumed his career and began to inform nearly all elements of his satiric routines, from his interest in language and hypocrisy to his commitment to tolerance and sympathy.

Although Lenny Bruce had been arrested once during the fifties (for vagrancy), his trouble with the law did not really begin until 1960. Late that year, Paul Krassner, an acolyte and friend of Bruce's who devoted himself to the cause of free speech, began reporting on Bruce's confrontations with the "bluenoses" in the *Realist*. To his readers, Krassner described how three plainclothes Milwaukee policemen "told Lenny that he was not to talk about politics or religion or sex, or they'd yank him right off the stage." In his November 1960 profile of Bruce for *Esquire*, writer Arthur Steuer likewise related how Bruce was forced to censor "every conceivably objectionable 'obscenity'" when he performed at New York's Blue Angel. Spotting several policemen with tape recorders seated in the audience, Steuer reported, Bruce decided to "cool it" even though he believed doing so was not "natural . . . [and] not honest."[58]

According to most accounts, Bruce's legal hassles accelerated rapidly after he was arrested in Philadelphia in September 1961 for the possession of narcotics. Precipitated, as many have conjectured, by Bruce's onstage performance of "Religions Inc.," the Philadelphia bust initiated a chain of arrests that would beleaguer Bruce for the remainder of his life. Not least, Bruce's arrest in Philadelphia confirmed in the minds of many powerful public authorities that America's most outrageous "sick" comedian was a "deviant" and, quite possibly, a public menace.[59] On October 4, 1961, while performing at the Jazz Workshop in San Francisco's hip North Beach area, Bruce was arrested for uttering "obscene" language onstage. According to Ralph Gleason, an eyewitness to the arrest, the sergeant who booked Bruce "took offense" to his use of the word "cocksucker"—an epithet Bruce employed in the voice of a bigoted talent agent whom he had heard denigrate the homosexual clientele of another San Francisco nightclub. "We've tried to elevate this street," the arresting officer reportedly told Bruce. "I mean it, I can't see any right, any way you can break this word down, our society is not geared to it." Bruce responded characteristically that you "break it down by talking about it," but the sergeant refused to follow his logic. When Bruce's case went to trial in March 1962, Bruce's defense attorney Albert Bendich recruited a number of Bay Area intellectuals and writers who corroborated his view that Bruce's performance was "in the great tradition of social satire, related intimately to the kind of social satire to be found in the works of such great authors as Aristophanes, Jonathan Swift . . ." The jury chosen for Bruce's trial was not convinced by this line of argument, but it nevertheless voted to acquit. Emerging from the courthouse, the ebullient Bruce declared to reporters that the verdict was the "coming of a delightful renaissance," which would send him "off on an even greater mission." "I'm going to thwart pseudo-Christians," Bruce stated, "and make them live in their religion or back down."[60]

Bruce's defiance was short-lived. Five months after Bruce was acquitted in San Francisco, city officials in Vancouver barred Bruce from performing in their city. One month later, Bruce was driven out of Sydney, Australia because, according to press reports, he had stunned patrons of a nightclub there with a "blasphemous account of the Crucifixion" and a "steady stream of dirty words"—including "the key 'Lady Chatterley' word." Between October 1962 and February 1963, Bruce was arrested three times in Hollywood for delivering "obscene" performances at the Troubadour and Unicorn theaters. The fact that the first of these arrests—all charges were eventually dropped—was made by a Jewish undercover agent who had been assigned to monitor Bruce's use of vulgar Yiddish vernacular contributed to the impression that Bruce's obscenity arrests had become a sad farce.[61]

Events took a far more serious turn when Bruce was arrested for obscenity at Chicago's Gate of Horn nightclub in December. According to tapes that were recorded by *Playboy,* Bruce held up a picture of a nude calendar model and challenged patrons' notions about "indecent" photographs and sex in general. "It's God," Bruce then told them, "your filthy Jesus Christ, made these tits, that's all. Now you've got to make up your mind, you've got to stand up to Jesus, and you've got to say, 'Look, I admit that *doing it* is filthy, I will stop doing it.' And, believe me, if you'll set the rules, I will obey them. But . . . stop living the paradox." With this bit and with subsequent pokes at the church, Bruce clearly transgressed the limits of what many policemen and people living in Chicago—a city with the largest concentration of Roman Catholics in the United States—considered appropriate comic territory. Indeed, according to the official arrest report, Bruce's blasphemous "mockery of the Catholic Church and other religious organizations . . ." was a primary motivation behind Bruce's arrest.[62]

In Chicago, Lenny Bruce for the first time faced the real possibility that his satirical remarks on sex and religion might land him in prison. The manner in which Mayor Richard Daley and the city proceeded against Bruce and the Gate of Horn made *Variety*'s speculation that "Bruce's comments on the Catholic church have hit sensitive nerves in Chicago's Catholic-oriented administration and police department" appear plausible. The fact that the judge, prosecutors, and all twelve jurors involved with Bruce's trial were Catholic did not aid his prospects for an acquittal. Neither did Bruce's ill-considered decision to dismiss his attorney and act as his own counsel. When the Chicago jury rendered its guilty verdict in March 1963, Lenny Bruce was clearly shaken. His immediate reaction to the press was "Kafka!" As Albert Goldman observed, the Chicago conviction ultimately "galvanized Lenny Bruce. For the first time in his life he was a wanted man."[63]

As a result of his conviction in Chicago and his earlier arrests in California, Lenny Bruce's prospects for resuming his career onstage diminished rapidly. In April 1963 he was barred from making a return engagement at the Establishment Club in London. After attempting to enter England via Northern Ireland, Bruce was detained and then deported. Since club owners were reluctant to hire him after what happened to the Gate of Horn, he began to spend nearly all of his time and money fighting for what he believed were his Constitutional rights to free speech. Nearly bankrupt and increasingly paranoid about "police harassment," Bruce implored friends and scores of liberal attorneys to provide him a way to "keep those brothers clothed in love," as he wrote lawyer John Brogan in February 1964, "from killing me in the interest of Justice."[64]

Bruce's next arrest for obscenity came on March 13, 1964, while he was appearing at the Trolly-Ho in Los Angeles. When the judge and the young deputy city attorney assigned to Bruce's case listened to the evidence that had been secretly recorded by Los Angeles policemen, they were deeply offended by two routines. Both, according to the city attorney, Johnnie Cochran Jr., were "liberally laced with vulgarities [and] involved political personalities." The first, a satiric encounter between President Lyndon Johnson and a group of jive-talking Negroes ("Hey, motherfucker, you're something else, Jim!") was intended to point out the lamentable gulf in understanding between contemporary African Americans and white authority figures. It failed to impress Cochran, an African American, as did Bruce's routine on Jackie Kennedy "hauling [her] ass to save [her] ass." The routine was precipitated by a *Time* magazine photo spread of the

Kennedy assassination that claimed the First Lady heroically retreated to the rear of the president's car after the shots were fired in order to solicit help from Secret Service agents. "That's a *lie* they keep telling people," Bruce complained in his routine, "to keep living up to bullshit that never did exist. Because the people who believe that bullshit are foremen of the juries that put you away. And indict . . ." After hearing this, the judge, a Democrat, "began to sputter," Cochran recalls, "and his face turned a shade of crimson so virulent that I wondered if he could stave off a stroke long enough to give me a conviction." Unfortunately for the ambitious deputy city attorney, "fate and the First Amendment were against [him] this time" and the judge dismissed his case on the grounds that Bruce's performance constituted Constitutionally protected free speech.[65]

Even though Bruce emerged victorious from his second obscenity trial in Los Angeles, the stigma of his obscenity and narcotics arrests rendered him virtually unemployable by early 1964. Indeed, as Albert Goldman has observed, Bruce by this time "had become the victim of a nationwide lockout." In New York City, one of the few major metropolitan areas in which Bruce had not been arrested for obscenity, the owner of a new Village nightspot called the Cafe Au Go Go decided to take a chance on hiring Bruce for a stint in late March and early April. Since he had lost his cabaret card in New York, Bruce had no choice but to play liquor-free venues. In the eyes of industry observers, Bruce's engagement at the Cafe Au Go Go was particularly significant since it promised future employment for other performers—jazz musicians in particular—who were denied cabaret cards.[66] All hopes were dashed, however, when members of New York's Public Morals Squad arrested Bruce twice for obscenity during the first week of April.

Members of New York's avant-garde arts and literary communities reacted swiftly to Bruce's arrests. On the day after his second arrest, members of the Emergency Committee against the Harassment of Lenny Bruce—modeled after the Citizens Emergency Committee that was organized in 1960 to protest police harassment of Lord Buckley—picketed the precinct where he had been detained.[67] Later that month, Living Theatre founder Julian Beck, an artist who also faced numerous high-profile legal battles in 1963 and 1964, and Beat poet Diane di Prima cited Bruce's arrest in their protest march on behalf of the Committee for Freedom of the Arts. For Beck, di Prima, and many other avant-garde performers, filmmakers, writers, and artists based in New York, Bruce's arrest represented just another step in the city's ongoing campaign to rid itself—in time of the upcoming New York World's Fair—of "dirty" movies, theater, and books.[68] By June, Bruce's arrests had become the rallying point behind the formation of Allen Ginsberg's new Committee on Poetry. In a petition to New York City mayor Robert Wagner, distributed to every news outlet in the city, Ginsberg (whose poem "Howl" had been at the center of an obscenity trial a decade earlier) defended Bruce in the name of "social satire in the tradition of Swift, Rabelais and Twain." "Although Bruce makes use of the vernacular in his nightclub performances," Ginsberg continued, "he does so within the context of his satirical intent and not to arouse the prurient interests of his listeners. It is up to the audience to determine what is offensive to them; it is not a function for the police department of New York or any other city to decide what adult private citizens may or may not hear."[69]

More dramatically than perhaps any obscenity trial of the 1960s, *The People of the State of New York v. Lenny Bruce* tested the parameters of free speech and artistic freedom in the United States and, equally important, defined the limits of American liberal satire. Given the intensity of feelings shared by Bruce's supporters and opponents, it is no surprise that this would become one of the most bitterly contested and highly politicized, not to mention most prolonged and expensive obscenity trials in American history. In significant respects, it foreshadowed subsequent battles in the "culture wars" of the 1980s and 1990s—battles that would pit social conservatives and avant-garde artists in difficult, often fruitless debates about censorship and the limits on free expression. By the time the trial commenced at the Criminal Courts Building in Manhattan in mid-June, the line separating those supporting and opposing Bruce was clearly and rather predictably drawn. On Bruce's side were those artists and intellectuals marshaled by Ginsberg, businessmen in the entertainment industry who resented further government control over their operations, and the political and social liberals and fans of satire who feared the resurgence of what they perceived as subtle forms of McCarthyism. Gathered in opposition were those who believed Bruce had gone too far in his lampoons of religious figures and political figures, people who resented the arrival of beatniks, sickniks, and peaceniks and who generally viewed the rapid pace of social change during the late fifties and early sixties with alarm.

The latter group was well represented by Frank S. Hogan, the longtime and enormously influential district attorney of New York. An eminent Catholic layman who enjoyed close ties with Francis Cardinal Spellman, Hogan took an unusually active role in Bruce's arrest and arraignment.

Hogan's assistant district attorney, Richard Kuh, assumed the task of prosecuting Bruce with noticeable zeal. Reflecting perfectly the attitudes of the social conservatives whom he represented, Kuh later would observe that his prosecution of Bruce was "simply an inevitable reflex at what seemed to be a sudden effort to push too far too fast." From the opening of the trial, Kuh proved himself a tenacious and resourceful prosecuting attorney. With the aid of his chief witness, License Inspector Herbert Ruhe, a former CIA man in Vietnam, Kuh was able to reconstruct portions of Bruce's routines in a manner that depicted Bruce as a scatological clown devoid of either a point of view or a cohesive thematic structure to his performance. The fact that Ruhe described some of Bruce's reflections on social and political topics in his notes as "some philosophical claptrap about human nature" should have discredited him as a witness, but Kuh nevertheless managed to use his testimony to convince the three-judge panel that Bruce had made a mock masturbation gesture and used "meandering" bits to comment distastefully on Jackie Kennedy "hauling ass," Eleanor Roosevelt's "tits," Saint Paul giving up "fucking," "sexual intimacy with a chicken," and other profane subjects. Overall, Kuh argued to the court, Bruce's performance represented little more than the rambling of a lunatic, "an anthology of filth," as he put it. As with Bruce's previous obscenity arrests, it was Bruce's material on religion and liberal icons Eleanor Roosevelt and Jackie Kennedy that caused greatest offense. At least that is the way that many Bruce supporters and Bruce himself interpreted his arrest. "The reason I got busted—arrested—is I picked on the wrong god," Bruce later told an audience. "I picked on the Western god—the cute god, the In-god, the Kennedy-god—and that's where I screwed up." [70]

Bruce was ably defended by Ephraim London, one of the best First Amendment appellate attorneys in America. Over the course of his distinguished career, London had handled over two hundred obscenity cases. With his younger partner Martin Garbus, London argued the landmark obscenity case *Jacobellis v. Ohio* before the Supreme Court in April. [71] As they had in previous obscenity trials, London and Garbus called on expert testimony to support their defense. In Bruce's case, they used expert witnesses to support their contention that Bruce's satire had "redeeming social importance," one of the tests used in courts of law to distinguish whether or not expression was "obscene." Over the period of several weeks, London and Garbus brought *Newsweek* drama critic Richard Gilman, jazz critic and journalist Nat Hentoff, Columbia University English professor Daniel Dodson, *Ebony* editor Alan Morrison, sociologist Herbert Gans, and two ministers to the stand. When London and Garbus searched for an eminent practicing liberal satirist to testify on Bruce's behalf, the cartoonist Jules Feiffer generously offered himself as a witness. Under Garbus's examination, Feiffer called Bruce "brilliant" and argued that he went "beyond social comment" into "an area I would think of as metaphysical . . ." "He's not doing cute parodies about our pet peeves or showing how funny or disagreeable people are in this society," Feiffer continued. "He's going to the very core of what the American experience is today, in terms of my generation." Feiffer added that when Bruce was "on, there's nothing like him" and that after witnessing Bruce's "personal kind of theater" he left the nightclub "thinking I don't hit hard enough."[72]

More unexpected than the assessments Feiffer, Gilman, and Hentoff gave was the testimony rendered by Dorothy Killgallen, the longtime Hearst columnist and *What's My Line?* celebrity panelist. Although Killgallen maintained a strong allegiance to the Catholic Church and Cardinal Spellman, she had been a devoted fan of Lenny Bruce since the late 1950s. In court, she described Bruce as a "near genius" and "brilliant satirist, perhaps the most brilliant that I have even seen . . ." Killgallen disagreed with Bruce's perspective on Jackie Kennedy "hauling ass" and qualified her support of free speech, but she forcefully argued that Bruce was an "extremely moral man . . . trying to make his audiences think" and, moreover, that "there is always a thread and a unity" to his monologues.[73]

After a two-week recess, Bruce's trial resumed with the expert testimony of five witnesses hastily recruited by prosecutor Kuh: the Reverend Daniel Potter, executive director of the Protestant Council of America; *Harper's* magazine editor-in-chief John Fischer; *New York Daily News* columnist Robert Sylvester; conservative New School sociologist Ernest Van den Haag; and the critic Marya Mannes. Of all the witnesses to deny the social importance of Bruce's work, it was Mannes who proved most damaging. In some respects, she was an unlikely person to testify against Bruce. A decade earlier she had written a series of parodic personality profiles and several hard-hitting satiric poems (written under the pseudonym of "Sec.") on McCarthyism for the liberal journal the *Reporter.* Throughout the fifties and early sixties she had established a reputation as a female gadfly, one who was quick to criticize American womens' low social status and, as she explained in her 1958 anthology *More in Anger,* the "progressive blurring of American values." Like Robert Osborn, Herblock, Harvey Kurtzman, and many other liberal American satirists, Mannes abhorred the onset of social conformity and the profusion of "soft lies" in "the Never-Never Land of the 1950s." Although she declared it a "wonderful thing to exercise the voice of dissent and the muscles of rebellion," she remained wary of avant-garde artists and intellectuals. In a controversial 1960 *New York Times Magazine* article titled "Plea for Fairer Ladies," for example, she protested the psychological obsessions and "fascination with depravity" in which she believed postwar playwrights such as Tennessee Williams were indulging. When asked to deliver her opinion on Lenny Bruce's performances then, Mannes did not hesitate to state her reservations.[74]

Mannes's decision to testify against Bruce emanated from her personal dislike of the cultural avant-garde, yet it also reflects some ill feeling that existed between Bruce and his liberal supporters. Although Bruce clearly enjoyed the respect and attention he won from liberals, he, more than any other American satirist at work during the 1950s and early 1960s, was willing to risk alienating that audience. No other satirist, certainly, so consistently and effectively forced liberals to face their own hypocrisy. Whether due to his uncompromising moral righteousness, his allegiance to the code of "hip," or, perhaps, his notorious self-destructiveness, Bruce was bent on shocking, offending, and, inevitably, losing many of his liberal supporters. "Every time [Bruce] was accepted," Jules Feiffer reflects back on his comrade-in-arms, "he made himself unacceptable." "He detested the liberals who were his allies." Whatever reservations Bruce and his liberal supporters shared toward each other prior to Bruce's arrest only grew as his trial progressed. As word spread of what Bruce had said about Jackie Kennedy, Eleanor Roosevelt, and other subjects, liberals' sympathy toward his plight cooled. The liberal artists and intellectuals who signed Ginsberg's petition did not scramble to testify on Bruce's behalf when the trial went to court. Several even expressed regret for becoming involved. When Bruce's lawyers approached Mort Sahl for help, he, remarkably, turned them down. Albert Goldman, a Lenny Bruce acolyte like Paul Krassner and the young comedian George Carlin as well as a writer who had extolled Bruce's virtues in *Commentary* and the *New Leader* told acquaintances that Bruce was guilty as charged![75]

More immediately relevant to the conduct of Bruce's defense was the growing estrangement between Bruce and his liberal attorneys. Bruce's head counsel Ephraim London, the descendant of a long line of distinguished German Jews, bore an elder patrician's manner and conducted his client's defense with precision and poise. Careful not to jeopardize their chances in a future appeal, London and Garbus denied Bruce the opportunity to present his own evidence and testimony. Both men were clearly annoyed that Bruce, a man who was, as Garbus has recently put it, "innocent of [the law's] nuance" deemed "himself something of an authority on the subject of obscenity." Bruce, in turn, confided to associates that he could not talk to London because he reminded him of his father. Moreover, Bruce resented London's patronizing attitude (London reportedly told Bruce that he was too "inarticulate" to testify) and disagreed with his legal strategy. As Ralph Gleason and Nat Hentoff have remarked, Bruce was not willing to moderate his stance for the sake of winning a future appeal. Because Bruce knew that a lower-court conviction would essentially end his career on the East Coast, what he sought was absolute vindication.[76] When the trial proceedings finally came to a close in July, hopes for vindication appeared very slim indeed.

Liberal Satire's Last Laughs

Lenny Bruce's New York obscenity trial concluded at the height of the 1964 campaign season and what would prove to be postwar liberal satire's Indian summer. In response to the rise of conservative Arizona senator Barry Goldwater and his New Right constituency, liberal satirists unleashed a spirited comic assault—one that made their forays against Richard Nixon in 1960 seem mild in comparison. Throughout the early 1960s, liberal satirists of all stripes had assailed the prominence of aggressive cold warriors in America's foreign policy apparatus, the recalcitrance of Southern white segregationists, and the rise of the conservative grassroots organizations such as the Young Americans for Freedom and the John Birch Society. With the ascension of Goldwater to the front ranks of the Republican Party, liberal satirists now concentrated their focus on one large and, admittedly, rather easy target. While young Democrats had fun parodying Goldwater's slogan "In your heart you know he's right" ("In your guts you know he's nuts!"), Vice President Hubert Humphrey quipped that Goldwater was so handsome he had been offered "a movie contract by 18th-Century Fox."[1] Godfrey Cambridge added to the substantial body of jokes aimed at what was perceived as Goldwater's retrograde political outlook, particularly on American race relations, by observing that he had "come flat out against slavery . . . in principle." In addition to calling on Americans to support the Missouri Compromise, Cambridge jibed, Senator Goldwater was revising "If I Had a Hammer" for his campaign song. "If I had a Negro," Cambridge sang the refrain, "I'd whip him in the morning."[2]

Liberal cartoonists focused most of their efforts addressing what they believed was Goldwater's trigger-happy nuclear policy. Indeed, for Bill Mauldin, Robert Osborn, and Herblock as for other liberal satirists, Barry Goldwater was a real-life Dr. Strangelove. In late May 1964, Mauldin pictured a reporter asking Goldwater how he described his domestic policy. Deaf to the question posed to him, Goldwater walks a tightrope while balancing an H-bomb on his chin and juggling a bevy of atom bombs in his hands. Osborn, in addition to caricaturing Goldwater in the *New Republic* as a captive to reactionaries and cross-burning racists, illustrated an ad for the Council for a Livable World in which he pictured the senator leaning over a precipice with hydrogen bombs in each of his outstretched arms. Herblock's animus against Goldwater found an outlet in a steady stream of cartoons and, for his 1964 anthology *Straight Herblock,* a satirical pitch for a new "This Is Never-Was Land" section of Disneyland named "Goldwaterland." "As you buckle on the belt" of "Goldwaterland's" top ride, "The No-Matterhorn," Herblock wrote, Goldwater (the ride operator) "drapes the flag over your shoulders like a Superman cape, places [a small nuclear bomb] in your arms, points to the horizon and says, 'Eastward lies the enemy.'" An adjoining cartoon, originally published in August, pictured the living, erect skeletal remains of Goldwater declaring amid the destruction wrought by nuclear Armageddon, "As I was saying, a Test Ban Agreement might have resulted in a fatal gap."[3]

The 1964 campaign season witnessed not only a flurry of cartoons but the release of numerous satirical folk songs poking fun at Barry Goldwater and his grassroots supporters. The trend had actually begun in 1963, during the peak of the Kennedy-era "satire boom." While Bob Dylan that year jibed the John Birch Society in "Talkin' John Birch Blues," the Chad Mitchell Trio reprised "The John Birch Society"—a song originally performed by a Julius Monk revue and whose most memorable line ran, "If mommy is a Commie then you gotta turn her in." For the December 1963 issue of *Esquire,* Noel E. Parmentel, Jr., a self-described "Fellow Traveler on the New American Right," offered a fresh batch of "Folk Songs for Conservatives." Expanded into a book (with illustrations provided by former *Monocle* caricaturist David Levine) for the 1964 campaign season, Parmentel's song parodies took aim at Goldwater's position on New Deal social programs ("Red River Valley [T.V.A.]") and nuclear weapons testing ("Let's Test Again"), among other subjects.[4] The release of recorded satirical folk songs followed on the heels of Parmentel's anthology. By the summer of 1964, disc jockeys on New York radio stations were spinning the

46. In 1964, the prospect of a Goldwater presidency sent liberal cartoonists like Robert Osborn to the drawing board. This two-page cartoon ran in the *New Republic* and *Portrait of Goldwater: The Contradictions of a Conservative.* By permission of the Osborn family.

Chad Mitchell Trio's "Barry's Boys" and other satirical ditties such as "Hot and Cold Running Goldwater" and "Won't You Stay Home Bill Buckley."[5]

Satirical jabs at Barry Goldwater did not go unimpeded. After receiving flak for airing songs from the Art D'Lugoff–produced LP *I'd Rather Be Far Right Than President,* liberal New York radio station WNEW pulled the plug on political satire because it seemed "inappropriate," as the station manager explained, "in these days of political heat and social unrest." WNEW's July 1964 decision, coming a year after CBS barred Bob Dylan from performing "Talkin' John Birch Blues" on *The Ed Sullivan Show,* divided New York–area radio stations on the question of whether or not it was appropriate to broadcast political satire in the midst of a heated campaign season.[6]

Newspapers around the country that carried Jules Feiffer's syndicated strip faced the same dilemma. Several months following the assassination of John Kennedy, Jules Feiffer had been roused from his state of "deep depression," as he describes it, in order to set himself to the task of lambasting Goldwater and his aggressive stance on nuclear diplomacy. By late July 1964, his wife related to Feiffer's mother, he had "batt[ed] out a host of Goldwater cartoons" for his syndicated strip, as well as a body of "straight boy-girl type stuff" since client newspapers, she predicted,

Liberal Satire's Last Laughs

"probably won't print them." When newspapers did publish Feiffer's commentary on Goldwater's reckless extremism, "The Dare Devil Adventures of Bang-Bang Barry," several were forced to issues apologies. The *San Francisco Examiner,* in its mea culpa, for example, described Feiffer's satire as "venomous" and "unwarranted." "It is extremism," it concluded, "in bad taste."[7]

Liberal New York radio station WBAI-FM, let caution fly to the wind when it decided to broadcast a sharply satirical news parody during the Republican National Convention in San Francisco. The brainchild of Richard Neuweiler, a contributor to *Monocle* and a former performer with the Second City, *The Big Tune Out* was broadcast nightly from "Poverty Central" at 12:30 A.M. Those who listened to the one-hour, live, improvised broadcast heard Neuweiler, Taylor Mead, and a number of liberal satirists including Elaine May, the Second City's Barbara Harris, Severn Darden, and Bill Alton, and *Help's* Gloria Steinem stage fake (and in the opinion of a *New York Times* critic "frequently hilarious") interviews with polltakers, campaign managers, social directors for the John Birch Society, Goldwater's mother and psychoanalyst, and a host of crazed Goldwater supporters. Referring to *The Big Tune Out's* counterfeit conversations with Arthur MacArthur (who was busy cruising Republican delegates in the Cow Palace), the sounds of "Seig Heil" dubbed into background noise from the convention floor, and the final spliced Goldwater speech in which the candidate declares his desire to launch a nuclear strike against "the Soviet heartland," Neuweiler confesses, "How we got away with all of this, I don't know."[8]

*   *   *

Neuweiler's satiric antics were matched only by Victor Navasky, Richard Lingeman, and contributors to their *Monocle* and *Outsider's Newsletter.* Throughout the first half of 1964, they flayed Goldwater repeatedly, painting him as a politician who was poised to sell the Panama Canal to the United Fruit Company and launch "low-yield nuclear weapons" in the War on Poverty. Characteristic of the type of material Navasky, Lingeman, and other liberal satirists used against the eventual Republican nominee was the counterfeit obituary prepared for the March 20 issue of the *Outsider's Newsletter.* "[Goldwater's] death came as no surprise to his associates," the notice ran, "who said he had been semi-somnolent for some time. During the last six months of his life, his behavior had become increasingly eccentric, and he had taken to muttering strange things in large crowds about 'turning the water on in Cuba,' 'sending U2's over Russia' (he was apparently unaware that this country replaced U2's with reconnaissance satellites years ago), and making Social Security 'voluntary.'" For *Monocle's* summer 1964 issue, Michael Harrington, the socialist intellectual who awakened Americans to the plight of the poor in *The Other America* (1962), together with his wife Stephanie proposed a mock "Poverty Pavilion" for the 1964 World's Fair in New York City. The Harringtons here sketched plans for converting a United Mine Workers union hall into an auditorium where authentic recreations of a Harlem neighborhood and Appalachian town would provide fairgoers with a "clear demonstration of the conditions in which free enterprise flourishes." Those wishing to take a field trip to the Harlem site would be issued a slum survival kit, complete with "rat-bite antidotes, a thermos of clean water, a flashlight, and a free copy of [Senator Goldwater's] *The Conscience of a Conservative.*" Also on display would be a Hall of Aspirations of the American Poor, an exhibit sponsored by Goldwater and the editors of the *National Review* and featuring "unwed mothers on relief flagellating each other for their shame."[9]

Monocle's most intriguing attempt to discredit Senator Goldwater took the form of a mock presidential campaign, conducted on behalf of its news managing editor, Marvin Kitman. Kitman, a registered Republican who somewhat resembled his friend Art Buchwald, was an advocate of what he has called "action satire." For *Monocle* and the *Outsider's Newsletter* as well as the *New Leader* and *Saturday Evening Post,* Kitman throughout the early 1960s pulled elaborate pranks to make a point about the workings of private industry and the United States government. In *Monocle's* coeditors Victor Navasky and Richard Lingeman, Kitman found two men of considerably different background and political persuasion (Kitman was neither educated in the Ivy League nor sympathetic to the liberal left) who were yet both favorably disposed toward stirring some satiric mischief. When Kitman devised his mock presidential campaign in his *Monocle's* office on Fifth Avenue in early 1964, Navasky committed himself as his campaign manager and Lingeman signed on as his "Holy Ghost" writer. Columbia University historian James Shenton volunteered to serve as the "Staff Arthur Schlesinger Jr." In San Francisco, adman Howard Gossage enlisted the support of two of his clients, Eagle shirt makers and

Land Rover, and began to incorporate news of Kitman's campaign into their tongue-in-cheek ad copy.[10]

The idea of running a mock presidential campaign was not new, of course. In 1928 Will Rogers ran on behalf of the Anti Bunk Party, and Walt Kelly later attracted wide attention with his grassroots "I Go Pogo" campaigns. Kitman's campaign, though less noticed, was a more elaborate and directly satiric affair. In his first official press release, dated November 20, 1963, Kitman criticized Barry Goldwater for being a McKinley Republican while declaring himself a Lincoln Republican, "the only true reactionary in the race." Alluding, ironically, to Republicans' weak support for civil rights, Kitman declared, "I will be running on the Republican Party's platform of 1864, so many of whose promises to the voters have yet to be fulfilled." In order to outdo Goldwater's hawkish stance toward foreign affairs, Kitman proposed making actor John Wayne his secretary of defense. Kitman also proudly proclaimed that he was "twice as Jewish" as Goldwater and that his wife owned a cloth coat—a reference to Richard Nixon's famous "Checkers Speech."[11]

While on the campaign trail, "Honest Marvin" and *Monocle* made subtle digs at Richard Nixon and other prominent figures within the GOP, Young Republicans, and various aspects of modern-day politics. In addition to securing a delegate, Kitman received 725 votes in the New Hampshire primary. Kitman thereafter remained out of sight (a sly reference to the success Ambassador Henry Lodge achieved in New Hampshire) until the July convention in San Francisco. There, at a big rally organized by members of the San Francisco–based satiric troupe the Committee, Kitman proudly announced the endorsement of Lenny Bruce and then blasted the Republican platform committee for rejecting the basic principles on which the Republican Party was built. On the convention floor, Kitman circulated among the delegates attempting to confront those responsible for the "Stop-Kitman" movement. Finally, the Committee's Larry Hankin, posing as a delegate from the Virgin Islands, began to read Kitman's nominating speech over the public address system. He was soon seized by Cow Palace security officers and ejected from the building.[12]

*　　*　　*

In 1964 it was more difficult for liberal satirists to agree on the merits of Lyndon Johnson and his administration's policies than on the necessity of preventing a Goldwater presidency. For several months following John Kennedy's assassination, liberal satirists appeared reluctant to make jokes at the expense of Johnson. Cartoonists remained generally sympathetic toward Johnson, though Bill Mauldin evinced concern over developments in Southeast Asia. Even Jules Feiffer was willing to give Johnson the benefit of the doubt. Feiffer deeply appreciated Johnson's support for the Civil Rights Act and his Great Society legislative proposals—all of "which made him," Feiffer confesses, "so good that he was a lousy subject." "It was only after he ran as a peace candidate and became a war criminal that I went to work on him."[13] Johnson's immunity did not last as long with other liberal satirists, however. In May 1964, Elaine May returned to improvisational satire with a program titled *The Third Ear,* a reference to psychoanalyst Theodor Reik's book on creative intuition. With a cast that included Louise Lasser, Renée Taylor, Reni Santoni, Peter Boyle, and Mark Gordon, May presented *The Third Ear* in Ted Flicker's former Premise Theater. This partially improvised program on occasion deftly satirized the Johnson administration, particularly its War on Poverty program and its growing involvement in Vietnam.[14]

By the spring of 1964, *Monocle* and the *Outsider's Newsletter* had also begun to satirize Johnson and his administration's support for the escalating war in Southeast Asia.[15] In addition to recalling Johnson's association with former Senate aide Bobby Baker, the *Outsider's Newsletter* solicited anecdotes and quotes that demonstrated the new president's "attempt to the coat the news with Johnson's wax." Responding to the Johnson administration's effort at promoting American intervention in Vietnam, the *Outsider's Newsletter* in April imagined how a Madison Avenue advertising firm might handle the "coveted" war effort account. While recognizing that the war was "not the kind of product you can exactly shout from the roof tops," the upbeat admen dream up a television commercial in which Lynda Bird and Lucy Baines (dressed in pjs and bunny slippers) ponder how the war might be pitched to young men of their generation as an experience "not to be missed." More prescient yet were mock interviews the *Outsider's Newsletter* conducted with Secretary of Defense Robert McNamara and an unnamed State Department official. While McNamara insists that the United States is "engaged in an all-out limited war" that would last five or ten years or "even longer," the official declares that the administration's policy in Laos is "Say nothing, but carry a big stick." "I left full of admiration for our planning brains in the State Department," the interviewer concludes after his visit there. "They were ready for all

Nixon Declares U.S. Has Lost Respect in Asia

47. Toward the end of its run in the fall of 1964, *Monocle* issued grave warnings, like this cartoon by Lou Myers, of American military interventions abroad. By permission of Victor Navasky.

public relations contingencies. All the lessons in fighting a guerilla war we had learned in Vietnam were applied. Now it only remained for Secretary McNamara to state that while the situation in Laos is serious, the war there can be won."[16]

With this observation, the *Outsider's Newsletter* ceased publication, just weeks before the Republicans nominated Barry Goldwater in San Francisco. With the demise of the *Outsider's Newsletter* and impending collapse of *Monocle,* the task of satirizing Lyndon Johnson and his fellow Democrats meeting in Atlantic City fell principally on the shoulders of Richard Neuweiler and his *Big Tune Out* crew on WBAI-FM. Deeply disturbed by the escalating hostilities in Vietnam, Neuweiler convinced Elaine May to assume the role of Lady Bird Johnson and explain, in an improvised mock interview, why her husband had persuaded Congress to pass the Gulf of Tonkin Resolution on August 10. Equally critical of the way the Johnson administration was attempting to neutralize the challenge of the Mississippi Freedom Democratic Party, Neuweiler closed *The Big Tune Out* broadcasts at the end of the convention by juxtaposing Lyndon Johnson's lofty rhetoric in praise of African Americans' push toward freedom against the angry, tearful remarks SNCC member David Dennis delivered at the funeral of murdered Mississippi civil rights worker James Chaney.[17]

*   *   *

As election day approached, liberal satirists' attacks on Barry Goldwater continued apace. The Chad Mitchell Trio—described by the *New York Times* as "social critics of the most courageous stripe"—packed venues such as New York's Carnegie Hall and delighted audiences with satiric folk songs aimed at the Republican candidate, whom they labeled "The fascist gun in the West." Meanwhile, Richard Neuweiler, Peter Boyle, and Gloria Steinem traveled important swing states with the "The Young Dem Bandwagon," performing material from the previous summer's *Big Tune Out.*[18]

The writers and performers of NBC's *That Was the Week That Was* were eager to join the fray. Toward the end of its first season, *TW3* hit at Goldwater often. Previewing the GOP convention in its June 5 broadcast, *TW3* parodied a movie preview—for a western titled *Showdown at Cow Palace*—to make its point: "*See* . . . the most terrifying scene in motion picture history . . . The invasion of Goldwater . . . Thrill to the repeal of Social Security. Weep at the sale of TVA. Cringe at the destruction of the U.N." Frost delivered perhaps one of the most effective jabs at Goldwater when on the May 8, 1964, broadcast he recited a number of the outrageous statements the candidate had made on the campaign trail. Following the final Goldwater quotation ("I don't see how [nuclear war] can be avoided") Jamison cued "explosion" percussions from the studio timpanis and then faded to black. For liberal viewers, expectations ran high that *TW3* would continue its Goldwater jibes in the fall. Unfortunately for them, NBC cancelled its second-season premiere in order to broadcast a paid political announcement by the Republican National Committee. Over the next six weeks, NBC preempted *TW3* five times in order to broadcast GOP-sponsored ads or speeches on behalf of their presidential candidate.[19] If the Democratic National Committee had not purchased ad time on *TW3*'s forestalled September 29 premiere, the GOP would have occupied every *TW3* slot before the November election. A Columbus, Ohio, woman spoke for many other disgruntled fans who sensed a conspiracy when she wrote her local NBC affiliate,

I had been looking forward to *TW3* and was totally amazed that your network had the nerve to substitute a program saluting Barry Goldwater . . . Are you afraid of satire? Or on principle do you want to abolish all TV programs requiring a mental age of 21 plus? It is so obvious that I can hardly believe it and I guess I should look around to see if Big Brother is watching me![20]

When, at the behest of the Democratic Party, *TW3* did finally premiere, it proved to be one of NBC's biggest embarrassments of the 1964–65 season. Despite all the claims producer Leland Hayward and NBC made regarding *TW3*'s political neutrality, the September 29 premiere was noticeably hard on Republicans. With their multiple partisan jabs at Goldwater (with references to his trigger-happiness and "His Southern supporters . . . still wearin' sheets!") and his running mate William Miller, *TW3*'s writers betrayed an unmistakable bitterness toward the party responsible for its preemption. While it was no secret that its writers were liberal—Gerald Gardner was even moonlighting as a joke writer for Robert Kennedy's Senate campaign at the time—few expected Hayward or NBC to allow the number of jokes made at the GOP's expense. "Only when the fact was finally revealed that Johnson was your cold-cash sponsor," a Tulsa woman wrote the *TW3* staff, "did I realize how you had prostituted yourself." It was a shame, this woman argued, that not a word was spoken "about the hundreds killed in Vietnam due to the stupidity of the present administration . . . You have destroyed a program that I thought showed rare integrity. I feel as if I had been raped by the minister . . ."[21]

In the end, what doomed *TW3* in the eyes of viewers and critics was not its satiric daring but the unevenness of its material. Apart from the occasional sharp song or clever sketch, a majority of the segments performed on *TW3* during late 1964 were tired, smug, and corny. *TW3* by this time was paying more attention to inanities involving, among other things, celebrities (Doris Day, Sophia Loren, Ethel Merman), youth fads, *Playboy* playmates, and New York's Lincoln Center. A joke delivered by guest star Steve Allen during the November 17 broadcast ("You know the little white fuzz used in Bufferin bottles . . . it's now Joseph Cotten they have in there.") says much about the decline in the level of *TW3*'s writing. Even David Frost, with his hopeless addiction for bad puns and English music hall gags, began apologizing for the quality of the material he delivered. Segments addressing, for example, the design of foreign flags smacked more of *MAD* than *Monocle*—a fact not surprising since two *MAD* writers, Larry Siegel and Dick DeBartolo, had become regular *TW3* contributors by late 1964. In response, critics and viewers complained that *TW3* had grown sophomoric and even a little dirty. A segment in the November 10 broadcast in which Phyllis Newman proclaimed the "benefits of ménage à trois" prompted *Variety* to wonder "why poor old honest Lenny Bruce is in court." A few weeks earlier *Variety* suggested that *TW3*'s major problem "seems to be that the writing is done by professional comedy writers instead of angry or slightly crazed young men." In order to survive, *Variety* declared, *TW3* had to "quit trying to be likable." A longtime *TW3* fan concurred. "Take off the wraps," this man wrote the *TW3* staff, "hit them where it hurts, and you won't have to worry about ratings." An astute Brooklyn viewer likewise informed Hayward in late November 1964 that *TW3* had grown "cheap and it is shallow . . ." *TW3* "lacks real political courage," he argued, "but suggests great daring; it is sensational, but quite meaningless; it tears down the enemies that seem quite gigantic, but leaves intact those giants that are much more inimical to progress." Such criticism took its toll on Leland Hayward, who confessed to NBC president Robert Kintner that "[t]he problem of *TW3* haunts me day and night . . ."[22] On February 16, 1965 Robert Kintner put Hayward out of his misery when he announced that NBC was canceling *TW3*.

*　　*　　*

By the time NBC executives pulled the plug on *TW3,* the program's ratings had already fallen significantly. While the decline in ratings undoubtedly reflected the problems *TW3* experienced, there were signs that by late 1964 Americans' appetite for hard-hitting political satire was waning. When the drama critic for *Commonweal* reviewed the October opening of *The Committee* on Broadway, he observed that the "satire-sated" audiences of New York and the Eastern seaboard have "already undergone enough satire in the past few seasons to last [a] . . . lifetime." "All the targets are down," he contended, "and shock has become a distant memory in these parts."[23] Although some New York–area fans of *The Big Tune Out* appreciated Richard Neuweiler's new fall production, *A Show of Force* (billed as an "hour of political and social satire and other forms of unrelieved self-indulgence"), audience interest in the program in the weeks following Lyndon Johnson's election dwindled to the point that WBAI-FM was forced to terminate it in December.[24] *Monocle* likewise foundered. Just prior to the election, it had switched from a quarterly to a monthly. "Not that we could afford it," Navasky quipped in his "Publisher's Notes," "but then we can't afford Barry Goldwater either." As it turned out, however,

Monocle's November 1964 issue was its last. With his financial resources seriously depleted and his enthusiasm for more fund-raising exhausted, Navasky decided that he would only publish *Monocle* in the future as an "Emergency Bulletin." [25]

More significant than the loss of *Monocle,* perhaps, was the disappearance of Mort Sahl, whom many considered the dean of modern American liberal satire. Although Sahl could still be counted on to hit Republicans such as Barry Goldwater and Richard Nixon in 1964, he reportedly encountered stiff resistance when he trained his guns on President Johnson. Sahl claims that it was his material on President Johnson and the fear of the reprisals that it might bring that led to the quick cancellation of his WNEW-TV talk show in 1965 and a two-year stalemate with Capitol Records. As a result of what he described as a liberal "whitelist," Sahl found work hard to get. "The same people who like jokes about John Foster Dulles and Goldwater," he explained to a reporter from the *New York Times,* "suddenly freeze when they hear satirical humor about Vietnam or the War on Poverty." [26]

Although Sahl's increasingly radical critique of President Johnson undoubtedly encountered resistance within the entertainment industry, it alone did not precipitate Sahl's fall from grace. Sahl by 1964 had clearly outgrown his persona as the wisecracking graduate student. Moreover, he appeared to have succumbed to the same maladies that had dogged television comedians of the midfifties—contentment and overexposure. Word of Sahl's relationships with movie actresses and his close friendship with Hugh Hefner—the two men shared, in addition to adjoining bedrooms in Chicago's Playboy mansion, interests in luxury automobiles and hi-fi equipment, among other things—prompted some to suggest that Sahl had "sold out" and "gone Hollywood." While columnist Herb Caen, a man who had done much to help launch Sahl's career in the midfifties, questioned "Has Success Spoiled Mort Sahl?" *Beyond the Fringe*'s Jonathan Miller complained that like the millionaire, establishment comedian Bob Hope, Sahl had become more "of a name-dropper than a satirist." [27] From the perspective of Miller and numerous other critics the problem with Sahl's political satire by 1964 was not that it was too sharp or penetrating but that it had lost its intelligence and its edge. One *Variety* critic spoke for other disappointed Sahl fans when he noted that year, "Whereas in the past one always had the feeling Sahl was a step ahead of his audience, that he had read or observed just a little bit more than anyone else in the room and one would be enriched and rewarded by his cerebral alertness, no such admiration is aroused by his current routine, which seems neither up-to-date nor informative enough."[28]

Noticeably backward, in fact, was Sahl's material on American women. Like Jules Feiffer, Sahl had always devoted much of his attention to "the relationship of men and women and how they are competing for domination." Underwriting Sahl's attention to relationships between men and women, however, was a strong and often ugly streak of misogyny. In recordings from the early sixties, most notably his album *Mort Sahl on Relationships,* Sahl mocked a woman's concern over the issue of birth control and belittled competitive, aggressive, domineering "career chicks." Modern women "don't want to be girls," Sahl quipped, "but they don't have the courage to be men." "I'm not worried about Negroes," Sahl liked to quip, "I'm worried about women . . . They've been liberated—without a map." Joining Norman Mailer and other male intellectuals and writers for a 1962 *Playboy* panel on "The Womanization of America," Sahl delivered his screed against the modern woman, describing her as "cold" and "predatory." Yet Sahl's ruminations even proved too much for *Playboy's* readers, some of whom wrote in to complain in *Playboy's* September 1962 issue.[29]

More than the modern woman, it was the assassination of John Kennedy that became Mort Sahl's principal and, in the end, most costly obsession. Dedicated to informing the American public of the truth behind John Kennedy's assassination, Sahl began disputing the conclusions of the Warren Report (released in September 1964) onstage. For most Americans, certainly, the details surrounding the fallen president's murder were hardly the stuff of a comedy routine. Billing himself as "The Nation's Conscience," Sahl began to urge Americans to engage in "guerilla warfare" in order to "save America." Yet in the end, Sahl's brand of populist politics appeared less quixotic than confused. He opposed the March on Washington and refused to endorse SNCC on the grounds that such symbolic support was typically motivated by "the individual neuroses of those Jewish girls who belong to the NAACP." "Let 'em take it out on their husbands," Sahl added, "like they used to." In a 1963 interview with Paul Krassner, Sahl stated that his liberalism should "be left up to the audience. They can decide for themselves." The audience and nightclub owners ultimately did decide, and work became even more difficult for Sahl to find. In 1965 he earned $13,000—a steep drop from the $600,000 to $1 million annual incomes he formerly enjoyed.[30]

*　　*　　*

A worse fate awaited Lenny Bruce. When called to appear before the New York judges deciding his obscenity case on November 4, 1964, Bruce arrived in court dressed, for the first time, in suit and tie. Bruce's change in appearance did not impress the Honorable John M. Murtagh, the presiding judge in the case. Neither did Bruce's decision to fire his attorneys and represent himself before the court. "Please, your honor, I so desperately want your respect," Bruce begged. "Let me testify, please . . . Don't finish me off in show business." In a last-ditch effort to defend himself, Bruce called the judges' attention to "2,130 word-errors in the prosecution transcript," denied doing the key "Jackie Kennedy haul ass bit," cited his drastic loss of revenue, recalled how his attorneys had told him that lower-court judges were "assholes," and told of how he did not wish to become the "darling of the liberals." Finally, in a move that left his few remaining supporters incredulous, Bruce stated, "My thinking is I believe in censorship. I believe, as I said, in prior restraint. I don't believe a building has to burn down for the building inspector to look at the wires." After sternly reprimanding Bruce for making his unorthodox appeals, Murtagh declared Bruce's case closed. He then pronounced the bench's guilty verdict, declaring (in the face of several recent U.S. Supreme Court rulings) that the monologues in question were obscene since they were "chaotic, haphazard, and inartful" and "contained little or no literary or artistic merit." Stripped to their bare essentials, Murtagh suggested, Bruce's monologues were nothing but a device that enabled "Bruce to exploit the use of obscene language." In a move that confirmed the suspicion of some Americans that the country's leading sicknik was indeed sick, Murtagh then ordered Bruce to undergo a psychiatric examination before his sentencing hearing in December.[31]

Lenny Bruce's obscenity conviction prompted him to begin pouring nearly all of his remaining resources and energies into his legal defense. While his benefactor Hugh Hefner retreated to the confines of his Playboy mansion bedroom to pound out his labored, pretentious defense of "The Playboy Philosophy," Bruce holed himself up in his Los Angeles home and pored over a stack of legal texts in preparation for his legal appeal. With a supply of candy bars, soda, and methedrine at the ready, Bruce worked tirelessly, looping himself in hundreds of hours of tapes he had collected of his performances and trial proceedings. Over time, Bruce developed into an amateur legal scholar, and by December he was prepared to take his case to the U.S. Court of Appeals. In New York, on December 15, he appeared before a distinguished panel of Court of Appeals judges—including future Supreme Court Justice Thurgood Marshall—to appeal a U.S. District Court's decision to deny his request for an injunction against the judges and district attorney who convicted him in New York. Bruce here finally got his chance to perform his act in front of men who would decide his fate. According to defense attorney Martin Garbus, Bruce performed his sketch about the kind of justice white men could expect from black juries in the future. "He concluded," Garbus remembers, "with his imitation of the outraged liberal saying, 'They gave me twenty years for raising my voice—those niggers!' Marshall's head jerked up and he nearly dropped a pen from his hand. Bruce saw Marshall's face, stumbled, tried bravely to explain the joke, but could not. Then he knew he had lost the case and sat down."[32]

Six days later, at his formal sentencing, Bruce had his chance to address the judges who had convicted him in November. Wearing a dirty blue trench coat over faded dungarees and T-shirt, Bruce launched into a seventy-two-minute rambling discourse on obscenity that verified the adage that "a person who represents himself has a fool for a client." The most relevant portion of what eyewitness Paul Krassner described as Bruce's "special one-time-only matinee performance" was legal evidence Bruce had uncovered about the 1931 New York statute under which he was tried. Even though Bruce demonstrated that Governor Franklin Roosevelt had then provided an amendment to it which effectively immunized stage actors from its provisions, the three judges and Assistant District Attorney Richard Kuh were not deterred. Kuh asked for immediate imprisonment because of Bruce's "notable lack of remorse," to which Bruce hit back angrily, "I am a Jew before this court [and] I would like to set the record straight that the Jew is not remorseful. I come before the court not for mercy but for justice . . ." Bruce then charged that Kuh had a personal vendetta against him and that Kuh's failure to relate stemmed from an age-old misunderstanding between Christians and Jews. Unmoved, as ever, by Bruce's case, Judge Murtagh then sentenced Bruce to four months on Riker's Island.[33]

*   *   *

For Paul Krassner, as for many other liberal satirists, Bruce's conviction in late 1964 was a profoundly disturbing event. In an attempt to make sense of what happened to Bruce and gauge the climate for satire in the United States, Krassner gathered the Committee's Garry Goodrow, critic Nat

Hentoff, and *Monocle*'s Marvin Kitman in late November for a public "Speak Out" at the Village Vanguard in New York. Before a packed audience, Krassner and his colleagues debated the question "Is Satire Futile?" Indicative of the pessimism surrounding the event, Hentoff mused that with Bruce in deep legal trouble it had once again become a lean time for satire. He later speculated that "maybe everything today is so absurd you just can't make it any more absurd." Kitman concurred, arguing that in the present environment you "have a hard time making a mockery of things." In this way, both Hentoff and Kitman were ratifying Jules Feiffer's remark that "Satire is no longer a comment on the way we live; it is the way we live." Not everyone in the Village Vanguard audience followed this line of argument. When given their opportunity to speak out, several young audience members complained that they simply did not "relate to satire anymore." One young man added that satire "might be not merely futile but positively evil, in that it provides . . . a safety valve for righteous indignation."[34]

Clearly, for those young Americans indignant over the war in Southeast Asia, the lack of voting rights in Mississippi, and restrictions on free speech on college campuses, there were more effective modes of protest than satire. Though many students at the University of California at Berkeley greatly admired Lenny Bruce, they would not rely on him to defend their right to free speech. As Lenny Bruce appeared before the U.S. Court of Appeals in mid-December, thousands of UC Berkeley students were actively engaged in the Free Speech Movement—one of the seminal student protests of the 1960s. For one disenchanted *Monocle* reader, at least, the escalating tensions of the time called for engagement, not the ironic distance afforded by satire. Writing in *Monocle*'s final regular issue, this reader reasoned that "[a]ny magazine dedicated to satire in such an era as this is missing its vocation. It may not be possible to win this game of life, but one thing is sure; only those who get in the game will win or lose. There is no room in this society at this time for people who sit in the grandstand throwing pop bottles at the umpire."[35]

Dick Gregory had already decided to "get in the game," and he had no plans to turn back. By the summer of 1964 he had been arrested eight times, spent a total of two months in jail, and contributed $250,000 of his own money to the cause. He had won much respect from civil rights activists for helping focus attention on the movement and for putting his body on the line in places such as Birmingham, Alabama. Gregory also received praise for his oratorical skills. "None of the Negro leadership talks more tellingly than Gregory," a newspaper editor from Pine Bluff, Arkansas, noted of Gregory in early 1964, "and few sound more bitter." Like many African Americans in the movement, Gregory had grown more militant by the mid-1960s (Gregory confesses that he "got crazy" after Medgar Evers was murdered in June 1963), and as a result his appeals grew more urgent, his tone more angry. At the May 1965 Vietnam Day teach-in at UC Berkeley and numerous subsequent campus appearances, Gregory addressed young white college students, whom he soon called America's "new niggers," in a manner that belied his reputation as a "race-friendly" comedian.[36]

Predictably, Gregory's more serious, confrontational demeanor did not always play well with white audiences. Just as his advisors had predicted, Gregory's metamorphosis into the "Lone Ranger" of the civil rights movement alienated erstwhile liberal supporters who found little to laugh at in Gregory's performances. The author of a profile on Gregory in the June 1964 issue of *Rogue* magazine spoke for many other white fans of liberal satire when he contended that the comedian had "been swallowed by his material . . . lost perspective, lost balance, and, worst of all, lost his sense of humor." "[T]he question of suburban morality probably could have been approached by the old Dick Gregory with a great deal of perception and humor," the critic continued. The "new" Dick Gregory, on the other hand, "has a glacial arrogance, an open contempt, for the people who pay to see him." In May 1964, Jerry Talmer, a *New York Post* columnist and former *Village Voice* critic, saw Gregory perform as an act with the Second City in New York. After spending fifteen minutes of "fun and games" surrounding his multiple arrests and jailings, Tallmer reported, the "once 'comedian Dick Gregory'" invited questions from his audience. When asked about the future of school integration, Gregory set off on a "hot-eyed personal injunction" and forty-five-minute address on Malcolm X. While Gregory's satire could still sting, Tallmer concluded, his "editorials" were a "hang-up." "Boilerplate is boilerplate . . ." The mainstream American press, for its part, did little to dispel the impression that Gregory had become a publicity-seeking firebrand. *Time,* the magazine that helped publicize Gregory shortly after he debuted at Chicago's Playboy Club in 1961, criticized his presence in Greenwood, Mississippi, by remarking how the "uninhibited jeers and gibes he aimed at the cops and other whites" had been "noisily and embarrassingly out of key with the quiet, deliberately passive tone of the student leaders."[37]

Many people in the entertainment business believed that Gregory was

48. Dick Gregory, handcuffed to his joke writer and companion James Sanders, was arrested for demonstrating in Chicago during the summer of 1963. In the minds of show business insiders, scenes like this were being repeated all too often as Gregory shifted his attention to the cause of racial justice. Library of Congress, Prints & Photographs Division, NYWT&S Collection.

becoming, as the trade publication *Variety* put it, "too serious" and that his commitment to the civil rights cause was ruining his career. This impression became widely shared by white nightclub owners. In April 1963, the owner of a supper club in Queens fired Gregory because he was reportedly donating his $5,500 salary to student activists in SNCC. Concerns that nightclub owners such as this one shared over Gregory's new activism were only exacerbated when Gregory vowed, in *Variety,* that he would "leave a nightclub at any time if an important demonstration came up." In the end, whether motivated by disapproval over Gregory's politics or by the fear of what a canceled engagement might cost them, nightclub owners stopped hiring Gregory. The situation was much the same in television. During 1961 and 1962, Gregory made fourteen appearances on NBC television programs such as *The Jack Paar Show.* In 1963, however, he made only two. By the end of the next year, Gregory had virtually disappeared from network television, had reportedly lost $100,000 in nightclub bookings, and was on the verge of bankruptcy.[38]

With increasing frequency Gregory was asked whether his participation in demonstrations was hurting his career, to which he would respond,
"Funny you should ask. I keep asking myself, 'Is my career interfering with
my demonstrations?'" By 1964, Gregory decided that "the Negro movement was the only hope for us—I mean all of us—so I had to risk everything for it . . . Everybody—my manager, my press agent, nightclub owners—they told me to stay out of it. They said nobody would laugh at a
guy who was running around being *serious.*" They were right, of course, but
this mattered little to Gregory. Gregory had once validated humor as a
weapon against oppression; now he dismissed it as a "narcotic." In the
face of growing dissention and militancy within the movement, invective
appeared more appropriate than satire to activists like Gregory. Langston
Hughes, acutely aware of these tensions, decided to terminate his *Simple*
column and retire its protagonist to the suburbs. "No more Simple stories," Hughes told colleagues at the *New York Post* in 1965. "[T]he racial climate has gotten so complicated and bitter that cheerful and ironic humor
is less understandable to many people."[39]

*   *   *

It was not only America's racial climate that had grown so complicated
and bitter. America's escalating presence in Vietnam also began provoking
the type of indignation that allowed little room for humor. When Jerry
Doolittle described the "mess in Washington" in an April 1964 issue of the
Outsider's Newsletter, there was no irony in his voice when he asked, "Did
you catch that news picture of the little four-year-old South Vietnamese
boy carried by his father? The little fellow can't walk by himself any more,
you see, because his entire body is scorched black by a napalm bomb
dropped from a South Vietnamese bomber."[40]

Shortly after President Lyndon Johnson decided to commit troops to
Vietnam in March 1965, Tom Lehrer responded in kind by writing "Send
the Marines," a satiric ditty performed on the final episode of *TW3*. It
proved to be one of the last satirical songs that Lehrer performed and
recorded. Surveying the American scene in 1965, Lehrer saw little demand
for satire and therefore decided to terminate his performing career.
Reflecting back on his decision to retire, Lehrer maintains that the frac-
turing of the liberal consensus, a process well underway by 1965, made it
much more difficult to produce the type of satire that was popular in the

fifties and early sixties. In an age that encouraged "exhortation," he mused, liberal satire appeared to have outlived its usefulness.[41]

By the time Lehrer recorded his final LP, there were unmistakable signs that liberal satire's star was rapidly fading. Not only had Lehrer, Mort Sahl, Lenny Bruce, Dick Gregory, and *Monocle* disappeared from the scene, the Second City, one of only two surviving improvisational revues, had become, in the estimation of troupe member Robert Klein, "extraordinarily apolitical." Second City's loss of critical bite did not escape the notice of its fans and critics. "It wasn't long ago that this troupe had something to say about people and the times," a *Variety* reviewer complained tellingly in 1964. Sheldon Patinkin, Paul Sills's successor, evidenced little interest in ushering satiric commentary to the stage. In 1965 "comedy was getting sillier, because Vietnam was getting worse, and Kennedy was shot, and it was just getting harder and harder to do satire that could make an audience laugh," Patinkin has explained. By the following year, Patinkin admits, Second City was just a commercial venture "trying to stay above water."[42]

*　　*　　*

As Patinkin suggests, American comedy in the mid-1960s veered away from the topical and toward the more gently humorous and silly. Entertainment entrepreneurs and media industry executives believed that American audiences had grown weary of topical, satiric humor. With many of the venues that had once featured stand-up satirists closing or facing financial difficulties, nightclub owners began pursuing a more conservative booking strategy. At Budd Friedman's Improvisation Cafe in New York, one of most prominent showcases for stand-up comedic talent in the midsixties, a more gentle and occasionally zany breed of stand-up comedian began appearing onstage. Critical attention in the midsixties focused not on angry satirists but on Bill Cosby, Dick Cavett, Steve Rossi and Marty Allen, Soupy Sales, and the Smothers Brothers—entertainers who would have agreed with Woody Allen's 1965 prescription that "a comedian strictly should go for laughs, and as far as a social meaning or anything like that, that's purely secondary."[43]

The smart, political edge that liberal satire brought to American humor in the two decades after World War II may have waned by the mid-1960s, but its ironic spirit and irreverence permeated American popular culture. In the ubiquitous "creative" advertising of agencies such as Doyle

Dane Bernbach; in youth-oriented television comedies such as *Get Smart;* in film parodies such as *What's New Pussycat?* (1965); in the insouciant, flip wit of the Beatles; in the black humor fiction of Kurt Vonnegut, Thomas Pynchon, and others; in Pop art and the style identified as "camp," irony, the spoof, and the "put-on" reigned supreme. At a time when generational rifts were intensifying, the art of putting down the "squares" and the hypocrites—soon exemplified by Mike Nichols' box office hit *The Graduate* (1967)—*MAD* magazine flourished, achieving ever-rising sales, embarking on new merchandising ventures, and even initiating a long-running Broadway revue.[44]

Young Americans who participated in the protest movements and the counterculture of the 1960s heavily imbibed the irreverent spirit communicated by *MAD* magazine and Lenny Bruce. Jules Feiffer, an artist who objected to *MAD's* lack of politics, nevertheless acknowledges that the magazine influenced young people in the 1960s far more than his own satiric cartoons. "In terms of being effective and changing things for the better," Feiffer states, "I think *MAD* is a much stronger force than anything I've accomplished over the years." While *MAD*, as Theodore Roszak argued in 1968, gave America's young dissenters experience in treating "the stuff of their parents' lives as contemptible laughing stock," Lenny Bruce served as a model of righteous rebellion. Two young activists in particular, Jerry Rubin and Abbie Hoffman, idolized Bruce and aimed to incorporate his confrontational wit into the political arena. As Rubin recounted in his autobiography, he had fallen under the spell of Bruce when he saw him perform one night in Dayton, Ohio. "Someday, I told myself, I would be like Lenny Bruce," Rubin recalled, "speaking out the truth about our society."[45] Together with a third Bruce acolyte, Paul Krassner, Rubin and Hoffman set out to became the court jesters of the sixties youth rebellion. In 1968 they initiated the Yippie Party and, in a gesture that far exceeded Marvin Kitman's innocent satiric campaign of 1964, nominated a pig for president. With a slogan inspired by Jean Shepherd, "Abandon the creeping meatball!" the Yippies brought their antic protests to the streets of Chicago during the Democratic National Convention.

Some American liberals, particularly those whose politics shaded to the left, expressed regret that the morally earnest, critically attuned satire of the early sixties had been eclipsed by new modes of irreverence. Albert Goldman, writing in the *Nation* in early 1965, observed that "where once there was the continual shock of surprise as one sacred cow after another fell over, impaled by a shaft of wit," comic irreverence had "degenerated into the ritual slaughter of dead horses," its jaded practitioners violating "taboos with the lobotomized glee of Mickey Mouse." Several months later critic Pauline Kael distinguished between satire and the new vogue in spoofing. "Unlike satire," Kael wrote, "spoofing has no serious objectives: it doesn't attack anything that anyone could take seriously; it has no cleansing power. It's just a technique of ingratiation: the spoof apologizes for its existence, assures us that it is harmless . . ."[46]

In the end, the obituaries written for satire in 1965 proved premature. During that year, Jules Feiffer gradually regained his bearings and began to subject Lyndon Johnson to his sharp satiric scrutiny. Meanwhile, a young amateur playwright and Free Speech Movement veteran named Barbara Garson conceived the idea of a satiric play aimed at Johnson while she was addressing an antiwar student rally on the Berkeley campus. *MacBird,* a burlesque of Shakespeare's *MacBeth,* done in Elizabethan blank verse, would soon stand out as one of the most provocative and controversial satirical works of the sixties. When it premiered off-Broadway at the Village Gate in early 1967, it savaged Lyndon and Lady Bird Johnson and the Kennedy family and even suggested, following the plotline of its model, that President Johnson murdered his predecessor. Critic Dwight Macdonald approvingly described it as a "tasteless, crude, wholly destructive satire which roughs up everybody and everything." "Its viewpoint is so thoroughly, consistently alienated from every statistically significant group or trend in American political life today," Macdonald continued, "that only an anarchist like me could find much comfort in it, and cold comfort at that." Also in San Francisco in 1965, the Committee provided Bay Area audiences with a steady diet of provocative, hard-hitting satiric commentary, much of it centered on America's involvement in Vietnam. As former Committee member Garry Goodrow remembers, "We kept after Vietnam very, very strongly."[47] Along with Garson and Feiffer, the Committee continued to demonstrate that satire, far from being futile or obsolete, had something substantial to add to the chorus of outrage building in the sixties.

CONCLUSION

Notes

The following abbreviations for archival collections have been used throughout the notes.

AAA   Archives of American Art, Smithsonian Institution, Washington, D.C.

AAEC   Presidential Papers and Correspondence, the Association of American Editorial Cartoonists Archive, Cartoon Research Library, The Ohio State University, Columbus, Ohio.

BM   Bill Mauldin Collection, Manuscript Division, Library of Congress, Washington, D.C.

BMC   Bill Mauldin Cartoon Collection, Prints and Photographs Division, Library of Congress, Washington, D.C.

BRT   Billy Rose Theater Collection for the New York Public for the Performing Arts, New York.

CA   Comic Art Collection, Special Collections Division, Michigan State University Library, East Lansing, Michigan.

CES   The Caroline and Erwin Swann Collection of Caricature and Cartoon, Prints and Photographs Division, Library of Congress, Washington, D.C.

DRS   Division of Recorded Sound, Library of Congress, Washington, D.C.

GRVV   The G. Robert Vincent Voice Library, Michigan State University, East Lansing, Michigan.

JF   Jules Feiffer Collection, Manuscript Division, Library of Congress, Washington, D.C.

LHP   Leland Hayward Papers, Billy Rose Theater Collection for the New York Public for the Performing Arts, New York.

LM   Lewis Mumford Papers, Department of Special Collections, Van Pelt-Dietrich Library, University of Pennsylvania, Philadelphia.

MBC   Museum of Broadcast Communications, Chicago.

MBRS   Motion Picture, Broadcasting and Recorded Sound Division, Library of
      Congress, Washington, D.C.
MD   Manuscript Division, Library of Congress, Washington, D.C.
MTR   Museum of Television and Radio, New York.
PPD   Prints of Photographs Division, Library of Congress, Washington, D.C.
RO   Robert Osborn Collection, Beinecke Library, Yale University, New Haven,
      Connecticut.
SCA   Second City Archives, The Second City, Chicago.
TFC   The Theodore J. Flicker Collection, Cinema-Television Library, University
      of Southern California, Los Angeles.
USNA   United States National Archives Northeast, New York.
WK   Walt Kelly Collection, Cartoon Research Library, The Ohio State Univer-
      sity, Columbus, Ohio.

INTRODUCTION

1. Kathleen Tynan, ed., *Kenneth Tynan: Letters* (London: Weidenfeld and Nicolson, 1994), 229; Kenneth Tynan, "Dead Spot in Drama," *London Observer,* October 23, 1960, 26; Kenneth Tynan, *Tynan Right and Left: Plays, Films, People, Places and Events* (New York: Atheneum, 1967); and Kathleen Tynan, *The Life of Kenneth Tynan* (London: Weidenfeld and Nicolson, 1987).

2. Kenneth Tynan, "A Note on Satire," in *Tynan Right and Left: Plays, Films, People, Places and Events,* 129. Literary, theater, and humor scholars have devoted much ink to defining the genre of satire. The study of satire, in fact, experienced a renaissance during the period considered in this study. In addition to scholarly journals such as the *Satire Newsletter,* a number of important articles and books addressing the purpose and effects of satire appeared in print at this time, including Maynard Mack, "The Muse of Satire," *Yale Review* 41 (1951):80–92; W. H. Auden, "Notes on the Comic," in *Dyer's Hand and Other Essays* (New York: Random House, 1962); Robert C. Elliott, *The Power of Satire: Magic, Ritual, Art* (Princeton: Princeton University Press, 1960); Ellen Douglas Leyburn, *Allegory: Mirror of Man* (New Haven: Yale University Press, 1956); Northrop Frye, "The Mythos of Winter: Irony and Satire," in *The Anatomy of Criticism* (Princeton: Princeton University Press, 1957), 223–39; Alvin Kernan, *The Cankered Muse* (New Haven: Yale University Press, 1959); Edward W. Rosenheim, *Swift and the Satirist's Art* (Chicago: University of Chicago Press, 1963); Gilbert Highet, *The Anatomy of Satire* (Princeton: Princeton University Press, 1962); Alvin B. Kernan, *Modern Satire* (New York: Harcourt, Brace & World, 1962); Charles A. Allen and George D. Stephens, eds., *Satire: Theory and Practice* (Belmont, Calif.: Wadsworth, 1962); and Leonard Feinberg, *The Satirist: His Temperament, Motivation, and Influence* (Ames, Ia.: Iowa State University Press, 1963). In addition to these works, I have relied principally on George Test, *Satire: Spirit and Art* (Tampa: University of South Florida Press, 1988); Michael Seidel, *Satiric Inheritance: Rabelais to Sterne* (Princeton: Princeton University Press, 1979); and Louis Bredvold, "A Note in Defense of Satire," *ELH* 7 (December 1940):260. My understanding of the social function of humor has been informed by Russell Middleton

and John Moland, "Humor in Negro and White Subcultures: A Study of Jokes among University Students" *American Sociological Review* 24 (February 1959):61–69; and Richard M. Stephenson, "Conflict and Control Functions of Humor," *American Journal of Sociology* 56 (1951):569–74. For other arguments claiming the importance of humor's social role, see Leslie F. Malpass and Eugene D. Fitzpatrick, "Social Facilitation as a Factor in Reaction to Humor," *Journal of Social Psychology* 50 (November 1959):295–303; Jacqueline D. Goodchilds, "Effects of Being Witty on Position in the Social Structure of a Small Group," *Sociometry* 3 (September 1959):261–72; Walter E. O'Connell, "The Social Aspects of Wit and Humor," *Journal of Social Psychology* 79 (December 1969), 183–87; Henry Grady Pitchford, "The Social Functions of Humor" (Ph.D. diss., Emory University, 1960); Antonin J. Orbdlik, "'Gallows Humor'—A Sociological Phenomenon," *American Journal of Sociology* 47 (March 1942):709–16; Joyce Hertzler, *Laughter: A Socio-Scientific Analysis* (New York: Exposition Press , 1970); Orrin E. Klapp, "Heroes, Villains and Fools as Agents of Social Control," *American Sociological Review* 19 (February 1954):56–62; and Morris C. Goldman, "The Sociology of Negro Humor" (Ph.D. diss., New School for Social Research, 1960). The most recent call for a new sociology of humor is made in Marvin R. Koller, *Humor and Society: Explorations in the Sociology of Humor* (Houston: Cap and Gown Press, 1988).

3. Jeff Sorensen, *Bob Newhart* (New York: St. Martin's Press, 1988), 87.

4. Gary Gerstle, "The Protean Character of American Liberalism," *American Historical Review* 99 (October 1994):1045.

5. The importance of racial and ethnic consciousness to the work of liberal satirists informing this book cannot be overstated. There are many studies on the relationship between racial and ethnic consciousness and humor, but I have relied mainly on Joseph Boskin, *Sambo: The Rise & Demise of an American Jester* (New York: Oxford University Press, 1986); Mel Watkins, *On the Real Side: A History of African American Comedy from Slavery to Chris Rock* (Chicago: Lawrence Hill Books, 1999); Lawrence Levine, *Black Culture and Black Consciousness: Afro-American Folk Thought from Slavery to Freedom* (New York: Oxford University Press, 1977), 298–366; Philip Sterling, ed., *Laughing on the Outside: The Intelligent White Reader's Guide to Negro Tales and Humor* (New York: Grosset & Dunlap, 1965); Joseph Boskin and Joe Dorinson, "Ethnic Humor," in *American Humor,* ed. Arthur Dudden (New York: Oxford University Press, 1978); Thomas Jemielty, "Divine Derision and Scorn: The Hebrew Prophets as Satirists," *Cithara* 25 (1985):47–68; Albert Goldman, "Sick Jew Black Humor," in *Freakshow: The Rocksoulbluesjazzsickjew-blackhumorsexpoppsych Gig and Other Scenes from the Counter-Culture* (New York: Atheneum, 1971); Stephen J. Whitfield, "Jules Feiffer and the Comedy of Disenchantment," in *From Hester Street to Hollywood: The Jewish-American Stage and Screen,* ed. Sarah Blacher Cohen (Bloomington: Indiana University Press, 1983); Joseph Dorinson, "The Gold-Dust Twins of Marginal Humor: Blacks and Jews," *Maledicta* 8 (1984–85):163–92; and Elliott Oring, "The People of the Joke: On the Conceptualization of a Jewish Humor," *Western Folklore* 42 (October 1983):261–71.

6. Ann Douglas, *Terrible Honesty: Mongrel Manhattan in the 1920s* (New York: Farrar, Straus and Giroux, 1995), 33.

7. Jackson Lears discusses modernism and its claims on authenticity in *Fables of*

Abundance: A Cultural History of Advertising in America (New York: Basic Books, 1994): 345–50.

8. For a brief but insightful description of how *Playboy* marketed "male rebellion" in the 1950s, see Barbara Ehrenreich, *The Hearts of Men: American Dreams and the Flight from Commitment* (New York: Anchor Press/Doubleday, 1983), 42–51.

9. Arthur M. Schlesinger, Jr., *A Thousand Days: John F. Kennedy in the White House* (Boston: Houghton Mifflin Company, 1965), 727; Douglas T. Miller and Marion Nowak, *The Fifties: The Way We Really Were* (Garden City, N.Y.: Doubleday, 1977), 6.

10. Ellen Schrecker, *Many Are the Crimes: McCarthyism in America* (Princeton: Princeton University Press, 1998), xii; Jackson Lears, "A Matter of Taste: Corporate Cultural Hegemony in a Mass-Consumption Society," in *Recasting America: Culture and Politics in the Age of Cold War,* ed. Lary May (Chicago:University of Chicago Press, 1989), 38–57; Stephen J. Whitfield, *The Culture of the Cold War* (Baltimore: Johns Hopkins University Press, 1991), 55; Alan Trachtenberg, "Picturing History in the Morgue," in *The Tumultuous Fifties: A View from the New York Times Photo Archives,* ed. Alan Trachtenberg and Douglas Dreishpoon (New Haven: Yale University Press, 2001), 28. See also Elaine Tyler May, *Homeward Bound: American Families in the Cold War Era* (New York: Basic Books, 1988); Alan Brinkley, "The Illusion of Unity in Cold War Culture," in *Rethinking Cold War Culture,* ed. James Gilbert and Peter Kuznick (Washington, D.C.: Smithsonian Institution Press, 2001); and Roland Marchand, "Visions of Classlessness, Quests for Dominion: American Popular Culture, 1945–1960," in *Reshaping America: Society and Institutions 1945–60,* ed. Robert H. Bremner (Columbus: Ohio State University Press, 1982), 163–90.

11. C. Wright Mills, *The Sociological Imagination* (New York: Grove Press, 1961), 11; Lewis Coser, "American Notebook: Portraits and Problems," *Dissent* 4 (Summer 1957): 212; Margaret Halsey, "Beware the Tender Trap," *New Republic* 138 (January 13, 1958):7; and John Patrick Diggins, *The Proud Decades: America in War and Peace* (New York: W. W. Norton & Company, 1988), 259–61. George Cotkin admirably summarizes the popularity of existentialism in America in *Existential America* (Baltimore: Johns Hopkins University Press, 2002).

12. Lary May, introduction to *Recasting America: Culture and Politics in the Age of Cold War* (Chicago: University of Chicago Press, 1989), 13.

13. Todd Gitlin, *The Sixties* (New York: Bantam Books, 1987), 19; Daniel Horowitz, *Vance Packard & American Social Criticism* (Chapel Hill: University of North Carolina Press, 1994), 157; Morris Dickstein, *Leopards in the Temple: The Transformation of American Fiction, 1945–1970* (Cambridge: Harvard University Press, 2002), 146; See also Morris Dickstein, *Gates of Eden: American Culture in the Sixties* (New York: Basic Books, 1977), 51–88. In the 1980s, historians convincingly demonstrated that the bulk of this popular social criticism was psychologically oriented, evasive, and elitist. It may be too easy, as Thomas Frank has more recently reminded us, to dismiss their criticisms as "elitist," yet it is nevertheless true that these authors' gripes about mass culture and the suburbs betrayed a measure of snobbery and condescension. See Christopher Lasch, "Mass Culture Reconsidered," *Democracy* 1 (October 1981):7–22; James Gilbert, *A Cycle of Outrage* (New York: Oxford University Press, 1986); Fred Siegel, *Troubled*

Journey: From Pearl Harbor to Ronald Reagan (New York: Hill and Wang, 1984); Richard Pells, *The Liberal Mind in a Conservative Age: American Intellectuals in the 1940s and 1950s* (Cambridge: Harper & Row, 1985); James L. Baughman, "The National Purpose and the Newest Medium: Liberal Critics of Television, 1958–1960," *Mid-America* 64 (April–July 1982):41–55; Lears, "A Matter of Taste: Corporate Cultural Hegemony in a Mass-Consumption Society"; and Thomas Frank, *The Conquest of Cool: Business Culture, Counterculture, and the Rise of Hip Consumerism* (Chicago: University of Chicago Press, 1997), 11.

14. George Cotkin "No Exit?" *Intellectual History Newsletter* 21 (1999):70–75; Daniel Belgrad, *The Culture of Spontaneity: Improvisation and the Arts in Postwar America* (Chicago: University of Chicago Press, 1998); Sally Banes, *Greenwich Village 1963: Avant-Garde Performance and the Effervescent Body* (Durham: Duke University Press, 1993); Barbara Haskell, *Blam! The Explosion of Pop, Minimalism and Performance 1958–1964* (New York: Whitney Museum of American Art, 1984); Thomas Doherty, *Teenagers and Teenpics: The Juvenalization of American Movies in the 1950s* (Boston: Unwin Hyman, 1988; Joel Foreman, ed., *The Other Fifties: Interrogating Midcentury American Icons* (Urbana: University of Illinois Press, 1997); Gitlin, *The Sixties*, 28; Margot A. Henriksen, *Dr. Strangelove's America: Society and Culture in the Atomic Age* (Berkeley: University of California Press, 1997), 9. See also W. T. Lhamon, Jr., *Deliberate Speed: The Origins of a Cultural Style in the American 1950s* (Washington: Smithsonian Institution Press, 1990).

15. Ed Sikov, *Laughing Hysterically: American Screen Comedy of the 1950s* (New York: Columbia University Press, 1994), xii; Sigmund Freud, *Jokes and Their Relation to the Unconscious*, trans. James Strachey (New York: W.W. Norton, 1963), 105; Henriksen, *Dr. Strangelove's America*, 245.

16. Lears, *Fables of Abundance*, 257–58; Gitlin, *The Sixties*, 28–36; Howard Brick, *The Age of Contradiction: American Thought and Culture in the 1960s* (New York: Twayne Publishers, 1998), 59–60. Stephen J. Whitfield has also written sporadically but astutely about the black humor and satire of the period. Historian Joseph Boskin in 1979 contributed a valuable study of 1950s comic expression titled *Humor and Social Change in the Twentieth Century* (Boston: Trustees of the Public Library of the City of Boston, 1979), although it was aimed primarily at "folk and constituent humor." Since then, two comic writers, Tony Hendra and Gerald Nachman, have written informative, although largely celebratory books on 1950s satire. Tony Hendra, *Going Too Far* (New York: Doubleday, 1988), and Gerald Nachman, *Seriously Funny: The Rebel Comedians of the 1950s and 1960s* (New York: Pantheon Books, 2003).

17. Packard quoted in Horowitz, *Vance Packard and American Social Criticism*, 115.

18. Because the black humor fiction of the 1950s and early 1960s has been the subject of much scholarship and criticism, I am confining this study mainly to *nonliterary* forms of satire.

19. Robert Brustein, "The Healthiness of Sick Comedy," *New Republic* 147 (December 15, 1962):28–30. As Wini Brienes reminds us, 1950s popular culture did not foreclose the possibility of American girls and young women identifying with male patterns of rebellion. See Wini Breines, *Young, White, and Miserable: Growing Up Female in the Fifties* (Boston: Beacon Press, 1992).

20. Michael Kazin and Maurice Isserman, *America Divided: The Civil War of the 1960s* (New York: Oxford University Press, 2000), 49–56.

21. Roger Bowen quoted in Jeffrey Sweet, *Something Wonderful Right Away: An Oral History of The Second City and The Compass Players* (New York: Limelight Editions, 1986), 42.

CHAPTER ONE

1. For an understanding of the tradition of graphic satire and comic art in Europe and the United States, I have relied on Stephen D. Becker, *Comic Art in America: A Social History of the Funnies, the Political Cartoons, Magazine Humor, Sporting Cartoons, and Animated Cartoons* (New York: Simon and Schuster, 1959); Coulton Waugh, *The Comics* (New York: Macmillan Company, 1947); Martin Sheridan, *Comics and Their Creators: Life Stories of American Cartoonists* (Boston: Hale, Cushman & Flint, 1942); Stephen Hess, *The Ungentlemanly Art: A History of American Political Cartoons* (New York: Macmillan Company, 1968); M. Thomas Inge, "The Comics as Culture," *Journal of Popular Culture* 12 (Spring 1979):630–754 and "Comic Strips," in *Handbook of American Popular Culture,* ed. M. Thomas Inge (New York: Greenwood Press, 1989):205–28; William Murrell, *A History of American Graphic Humor* (New York: Whitney Museum of American Art, 1933–1938); Jerry Robinson, *The Comics* (New York: Putnam, 1974); Robert C. Harvey, *The Art of the Comic Book: An Aesthetic History* (Jackson: University Press of Mississippi, 1996); Steven Heller, ed., *Man Bites Man: Two Decades of Drawings and Cartoons by 22 Comic and Satiric Artists 1960 to 1980* (New York: A & W Publishers, 1981); E. H. Gombrich and Ernst Kris, *Caricature* (Middlesex, England: King Penguin Books, 1940); Brown University Department of Art, *Caricature and Its Role in Graphic Satire: An Exhibition by the Department of Art, Brown University at the Museum of Art, Rhode Island School of Design April 7 through May 9, 1971* (Providence: Museum of Art, Rhode Island School of Design, 1971); Ralph E. Shikes and Steven Heller, eds., *The Art of Satire: Painters as Caricaturists and Cartoonists from Delacroix to Picasso* (New York: Pratt Graphics Center and Horizon Press, 1984); Ralph E. Shikes, *The Indignant Eye* (Boston: Beacon Press, 1969); and W. G. Rogers, *Mightier Than the Sword: Cartoon, Caricature, Social Comment* (New York: Harcourt, Brace & World, 1969). For examples of how martial metaphors were applied to cartoons and humor more generally during World War II, see *Writers' Congress: The Proceedings of the Conference Held in October 1943 under the Sponsorship of the Hollywood Writers' Mobilization and the University of California* (Berkeley: University of California Press, 1944), 105–111, 220–238.

2. "Mauldin and Patton Clash on GI Thinking," *New York Times,* June 27, 1945, 21; Bill Mauldin, "The Eisenhower I'll Always Remember," *Reporter* 11 (September 23, 1954): 45; "Bill, Willie and Joe," *Time,* June 18, 1945, 16–18; Bill Mauldin, "I Don't Like to See Uncommon Men Suppressed: Bill Mauldin," in *Getting Angry Six Times a Week,* ed. Alan Westin (Boston: Beacon Press, 1979), 86–87. Mauldin later stated that Patton was "one of the few men in the Army with the perspicacity to see what I was really up to . . ." Bill Mauldin, "Foreword" to his *What's Got Your Back Up?* (New York: Harper & Brothers Publishers, 1961), unpaginated.

3. The GI is quoted by his mother, Mary Lovejoy, in a letter to Bill Mauldin, March 16, 1945, BM, box 4, general correspondence.

4. James P. Barney to Bill Mauldin, July 17, 1945, BM, box 2, general correspondence.

5. Herbert Lyons, "Mauldin's Book," *New Republic* 112 (June 18, 1945):847–48; "Mauldin Meets Son," *Life,* July 9, 1945, 30–31. Actor Ronald Reagan was one of many people who attempted to capitalize on Mauldin's fame. In 1945, he appealed to Mauldin to join the American Veterans Committee—an organization that, judging by the pamphlet Reagan enclosed, advocated, among other progressive causes, "industrial democracy." Ronald Reagan to Bill Mauldin, June 27, 1945, BM, box 6, general correspondence.

6. Bill Mauldin, *Back Home* (New York: William Sloane Associates, 1947), 90, 102, 80, 155.

7. In a speech titled "See Here, Private Enterprise," delivered to a restive crowd of 3,400 National Association of Manufacturers members in December 1945, Hargrove condemned American industry's latest attempts at reversing the New Deal.

8. "The Glacier Moves," *Time,* December 17, 1945, 79; Mauldin quoted in John Kuenster, "The Responsible Editorial Cartoonist," *Voice of St. Jude* (March 1961):48; "*New York Herald Tribune* Forum Speech," typed manuscript, BM, box 8, speeches.

9. Mauldin quoted in Richard Samuel West, "Mauldin: From Willie and Joe to Ronnie," *Target* 3 (Winter 1984):12.

10. Mauldin, *Back Home,* 154.

11. Mauldin, *Back Home,* 169, 187, 304.

12. Mauldin, *Back Home,* 238, 223; Bill Mauldin cartoon no. 1297, B size, BMC.

13. Edward Weeks, "Amateur Citizen," *Atlantic Monthly* 180 (November 1947):160; Dennis R. Oliver to Bill Mauldin, August 12, 1952, BM, box 5, general correspondence; Milton Asher to Bill Mauldin, August 23, 1954, BM, box 2, general correspondence.

14. J. Edgar Hoover to unnamed agent, January 14, 1949 and M.A. Jones to Mr. Nichols, March 21, 1956, FBI Office memorandum, Bill Mauldin File, Federal Bureau of Investigation, U.S. Department of Justice, Washington, D.C. In 1949, Mauldin was placed under U.S. Army surveillance when he visited Fort Bliss in Texas. By this time, journalist Herbert Mitgang relates, Mauldin had become, in the eyes of Hoover and the FBI, "Security Matter—C" (C for COMMUNIST). Herbert Mitgang, *Dangerous Dossiers: Exposing the Secret War against America's Greatest Authors* (New York: Donald I. Fine, 1988), 255–57.

15. As the esteemed liberal editorial cartoonist Daniel Fitzpatrick later cracked, "It was as if [the syndicate] had invited Zero Mostel to amuse the customers and [instead] he had delivered a serious address on the Single Tax." D. R. Fitzpatrick, "Mauldin's Healthy Thunder," *New York Herald Tribune Weekly Book Review,* November 2, 1947, 6.

16. "Mauldin Reconverts," *Time,* September 24, 1945, 61; "Education of a GI," *Time,* July 7, 1947, 62; Mauldin, *Back Home,* 271; "In War & Peace," *Time,* September 26, 1960, 49.

17. Mauldin, *Back Home,* 272.

18. Mauldin, *Back Home,* 272, 311, 314.

19. "Education of a GI," 62.

20. West, 4–13; Eric Swenson to Bill Mauldin, September 15, 1953, BM, box 6, general correspondence.

21. "Bill Mauldin Abandons Ike to Aid Stevenson Campaign," *Cincinnati Enquirer,* October 24, 1952.

22. Mauldin, *Back Home,* 239–240; Bill Mauldin, "A Reverie of Revenge," *Reporter* 8 (April 14, 1953):30; Mrs. R. E. Thompson to the *Reporter,* May 19, 1953, BM, box 6, general correspondence.

23. Bill Mauldin, "The Era of the Cop," *Reporter* 9 (December 22, 1953):39. "2 State G.O.P. Congressmen in Lively Races," *New York Times,* October 18, 1956, 26; "St. George Hits Rival On 'Left Wing' Links," *Newburgh News,* October 26, 1956. See also Bill Mauldin, "A Cartoonist Goes Campaigning," *Collier's,* September 28, 1956, 38–39.

24. Frederick Voss, "Mauldin Dons His Mufti," paper delivered at the Library of Congress, Washington D.C., May 16, 1998. I am indebted to Mr. Voss for sharing his unpublished work with me.

25. Arthur Schlesinger, Jr., "The Highbrow in American Politics," in *The Politics of Hope* (Boston: Houghton Mifflin Company, 1963), 227.

26. Richard H. Minear, *Dr. Seuss Goes to War: The World War II Editorial Cartoons of Theodor Seuss Geisel* (New York: New Press 1999); Seuss cartoon, *New Republic* 116 (July 28, 1947):7.

27. Heinz Politzer, "From Little Nemo to Li'l Abner," *Commentary* 8 (October 1949):346.

28. *Li'l Abner* made its enterprising creator enormously successful and wealthy. Capp's satiric "Shmoo" character, licensed by Capp Enterprises in the late 1940s, spawned a $25 million line of Shmoo-related products. Arthur Asa Berger, *Li'l Abner: A Study in American Satire* (Jackson: University Press of Mississippi, 1994); "Die Monstersinger," *Time,* November 6, 1950, 72–78; Nanette Kutner, "li'l abner's mistuh capp," *Esquire* 47 (April 1957):71, 151–52; "Taming of the Shmoo," *Newsweek,* September 5, 1949, 49–50.

29. Al Capp, "It's Hideously True," *Life,* March 31, 1952, 101–108 passim; "Li'l Abner, Broadway and Dogpatch," *Life,* January 14, 1957, 74–78; "The Shmoo's Return," *New Yorker,* October 26, 1963, 39–40.

30. Harrington's good friend Langston Hughes similarly used a comic everyman figure in his Jesse B. Semple stories, which the *Chicago Defender* began publishing in 1943. Michael Denning appropriately identifies Harrington's Bootsie and Hughes's Jesse B. Semple characters as "two of the most popular imaginative creations of the African American Popular Front." Michael Denning, *The Cultural Front: The Laboring of American Culture in the Twentieth-Century* (New York: Verso, 1996), 219.

31. After the 1943 Detroit race riots, for example, Harrington drew a cartoon depicting a white boy showing a friend his father's hunting trophies, among them the head of an African American male. The caption read, "Dad got that one in Detroit last week." Langston Hughes, introduction to Oliver Harrington, *Bootsie and Others* (New York: Dodd, Mead & Company, 1958), unpaginated.

32. M. Thomas Inge, introduction to *Dark Laughter: The Satiric Art of Oliver W. Harrington,* ed. M. Thomas Inge (Jackson: University Press of Mississippi, 1993), vii–xliii; Oliver Harrington, "View from the Back Stairs," *Inks* 1 (February 1994):26–32; and Oliver Harrington, "Why I Left America," in *Why I Left America and Other Essays,* ed. M. Thomas Inge (Jackson: University Press of Mississippi, 1993):96–109. Harrington deserves and awaits a full biography.

33. Oliver Wendell Harrington File, Federal Bureau of Investigation, U.S. Department of Justice, Washington, D.C.; Harrington, "Why I Left America," 96–109; Chester Himes, *My Life of Absurdity: The Later Years: The Autobiography of Chester Himes* (New York: Paragon House, 1990), 34–37.

34. Oliver Harrington, "Look Homeward Angel," in *Why I Left America and Other Essays,* 68.

35. Kenneth Rexroth, "The Decline of American Humor," *Nation* 184 (April 27, 1957):376.

36. Gladwill Hill, "Two Film Leaders Deny They Are Red," *New York Times,* September 25, 1951, 25. Details regarding Ship's life are taken from Gerry Gross, "Reuben Ship," *Canadian Writers, 1920–1959,* vol. 88 of *Dictionary of Literary Biography* (Detroit: Gale Research, 1989), 288–90.

37. Reuben Ship, *The Investigator: A Political Satire in Documentary Form,* Discuriosities, 1954.

38. Jack Gould, "Radio in Review," *New York Times,* December 31, 1954, 20; Marya Mannes, "Channels: Radio's Rut," *Reporter* 12 (February 10, 1955):44–45. Ironically, an experimental 1955 study at the University of Illinois—one of several experimental studies conducted on the effectiveness of "satire" during the 1950s—concluded that among the group of undergraduate subjects tested, *The Investigator* actually prompted more sympathy than mistrust for the disgraced senator. See David K. Berlo and Hideya Kumata, "The Investigator: The Impact Of a Satirical Radio Drama," *Journalism Quarterly* 33 (Summer 1956):287–98

39. Jerome Beatty Jr., "Humor vs. Taboo," *Saturday Review of Literature* 40 (November 23, 1957):11–13. For more on the *New Yorker's* influence on American cartooning, see Robert M. Coates, "Contemporary American Humorous Art," *Perspectives USA* No. 10 (1956):100–15, and John Galbraith, "*New Yorker* Cartoons: The Last Quarter Century," *Reporter* 6 (January 8, 1952):37–39. In addition to direct political and editorial pressures, another significant factor explaining cartoonists' increased cautiousness stemmed from the comic book controversy of the early 1950s. As historian James Gilbert has demonstrated, American "horror" comic books became the target of an intense public debate during the early 1950s. The parents, social scientists, and critics who joined in opposition to these comics argued that they had a powerful and subversive impact on the nation's youth. As a result of intense public scrutiny and the U.S. Senate Subcommittee investigation into comic books, cartoonists grew increasingly anxious about their artistic freedom. Faced with the threat of censorship, cartoonists banded together in their professional organization, the National Cartoonists Society, and spoke out on behalf of "good taste," "decency," and artistic freedom. The effects of the comic book controversy are difficult to gauge, but there is little doubt that it

intimidated and chastened a considerable number of American cartoonists. James Gilbert, *A Cycle of Outrage* (New York: Oxford University Press, 1986). I am also indebted to Professor Lucy Caswell of Ohio State University's Cartoon Research Library for generously sharing her insights into the effects of the comic book controversy as well as the politics of comic art in the 1950s.

40. Scott Long, "Writing Editorials with a Brush," *Harvard Alumni Bulletin* 62 (April 2, 1960):511.

41. By the early 1960s, in fact, only 125 editorial cartoonists were drawing for the nation's 1,700 newspapers. Because the most successful syndicated cartoonists were routinely published in over one hundred markets, *Time* magazine reported in 1958, their work was forced to "straddle current controversies or join all mankind in approving mother love and condemning sin." To illustrate this trend, *Time* profiled the Associated Press's John Milton Morris. Morris, *Time* claimed, "has brought equivocation to such a fine art that he can sometimes make one cartoon do two jobs." Now and then, *Time* continued, "Morris knocks out a vicious cartoon on some pet peeve or political devil, exhibits it around the office, tears it up and, refreshed in spirit, returns to the job of producing six inoffensive cartoons a week." As Scott Long understood, the growing trend toward syndication and "standardization" had forced cartoonists such as Morris to tailor their criticism to wider and wider markets. Editorial cartoonists, he claimed, "find it increasingly difficult to be courageous and . . . controversial for the simple reason that most newspapers are big businesses and anguished cries from the counting rooms must be heeded more and more." "Saying It Safely," *Time*, October 20, 1958, 56; and Scott Long, "The Cartoon Is a Weapon," reprinted from *The Masthead* in *AAEC News* 3 (May 1962):unpaginated.

42. Henry Ladd Smith, "The Rise and Fall of the Political Cartoon," *Saturday Review of Literature* 37 (May 29, 1954):7–9, 28–29. See also Charles O. Bissell, "Bissell Notes Use of Dated Symbolism," *AAEC News* 1 (November 1959); Bill Sanders, "Sanders Sounds Off," *AAEC News* 3 (November 1962):unpaginated; Karl Hubenthal, "Editorial Cartoons: The Role They Play in a Modern Paper," *California Publisher* (September 1965):22–36; Don Hesse, "The Ungentlemanly Art," *Quill* (December 1959):7–8, 17; Audrey Handelman, "Political Cartoonists As They Saw Themselves during the 1950s," *Journalism Quarterly* 61 (Spring 1984):137–41; and Jack H. Bender, "The Outlook for Editorial Cartooning," *Journalism Quarterly* 40 (Spring 1963):175–80. Such criticism rankled members of the professional editorial cartoonists' fraternity, particularly those in the profession's moderately conservative mainstream who devoted many of their single-panel commentaries to the Red Menace and the threat of Soviet "imperialism." The staunch anticommunist Bruce Russell of the *Los Angeles Times*, for example, castigated the "self-appointed critics of the press" and "carping ultra-liberal writers" who criticized his colleagues' work. The *Birmingham News*'s Chuck Brooks, one of several conservative cartoonists who fervently defended the South, told his colleagues that "the efforts of many of our top-flight conservative cartoonists" were quite respectable. "I, for one," Brooks argued, "am getting fed up with reading what a lousy cartoonist I am. Of course I'm never called by name but I'm told over and over that six-sevenths of all American cartoonists are lacking in brains, talent and energy." Bruce Russell, "A

Russell of Wind," and Chuck Brooks "Comments" in *AAEC News* 4 (March 1963): unpaginated.

43. John Stampone to Milt, n.d., AAEC, box AAEC Pres1. In the long run, the AAEC appeared far more interested in courting the political establishment than in bucking it. During the period from 1958 to 1963, it repeatedly solicited the participation of Eisenhower and Kennedy administration officials at its national conventions. Moreover, it regularly conferred honorary memberships and "Golden Doghouse" Awards to government officials such as Vice President Nixon, Senator Barry Goldwater, and Secretary of Defense Charles Wilson—"good sports" who demonstrated that they could take a joke just like any red-blooded American. Throughout the 1950s and early 1960s, the vast majority of AAEC members continued producing cartoons that reflected the moderately conservative, anticommunist editorial outlook of the newspapers that employed them.

CHAPTER TWO

1. Schrecker, *Many Are the Crimes: McCarthyism in America,* 369.

2. Dickstein, *Leopards in the Temple,* 140. Other valuable assessments of McCarthyism's impact on American politics and culture include Stephen Whitfield, *The Culture of the Cold War* (Baltimore: Johns Hopkins University Press, 1991); Richard M. Fried, *Nightmare in Red: The McCarthy Era in Perspective* (New York: Oxford University Press, 1990); and David Caute, *The Great Fear: The Anti-Communist Purge under Truman and Eisenhower* (New York: Simon & Schuster, 1977).

3. Ronald Searle and Robert Osborn, "The Emasculation of American Humor," *Saturday Review of Literature* 40 (November 23, 1957):16–17.

4. "This Is One of My Best of 1957," clipping in AAEC, box AAEC Pres2; Peter Gilmore to author, July 19, 2004; Stephen Hess, "The Art Usually Comes Second," *Cleveland Plain Dealer,* June 28, 1989. For an example of Daniel Fitzpatrick's work, see his anthology *As I Saw It* (New York: Simon and Schuster, 1953). Frances K. Pohl briefly mentions Shahn's cartoon work in her study *Ben Shahn: New Deal Artist in a Cold War Climate, 1947–1954* (Austin: University of Texas Press, 1989).

5. Jean Shepherd, "The Last Stronghold," *Cartoonist* (Winter 1956):20.

6. Steven Heller, "A Dancer, Bernard Mergendeiler," *Target* 2 (Winter 1983):5.

7. Peter Lyon, "The World of Herblock," *Holiday* 31 (April 1962):118; "Gimlet Eye, Talented Hand," *Woman's Home Companion* 83 (November 1956):27.

8. Herbert Block, *A Cartoonist's Life* (New York: Macmillan Publishing Company, 1993), 9–124.

9. H. L. Block, "Thomas Nast, Symbol-Maker," *New York Times Magazine,* September 22, 1940, 5–6, 19.

10. Block, "Thomas Nast, Symbol-Maker."

11. "Block Party," *Time,* January 23, 1950, 38; Richard Rovere, "Letter from Washington," *New Yorker,* February 11, 1950, 61.

12. Frank Getlein, "In Herblock, the World Is Almost Exclusively Political," *Commonweal* 81 (November 27, 1964):332–34; Block, *A Cartoonist's Life,* 182, 309.

See also Elmer Davis, "Words as Weapons," *New Republic* 134 (March 12, 1956):17.

13. Herbert Block, *Special for Today* (New York: Simon and Schuster, 1958), 25.

14. Block, *Special for Today,* 154.

15. Herbert Block, *The Herblock Book* (Boston: The Beacon Press, 1952), 106.

16. Herbert Block, *Herblock's Here and Now* (New York: Simon and Schuster, 1955), 211.

17. Eric Foner, *The Story of American Freedom* (New York: W.W. Norton & Company, 1998), 161.

18. Block, *Herblock Book,* 129; Block, *Herblock's Here and Now,* 9–10.

19. Block, *Herblock Book,* 145, 156; Block, *Here and Now,* 102.

20. Block, *Herblock Book,* 137, 143.

21. Roger Butterfield, "Political Cartoons—The Old Days," *New Republic* 134 (March 12, 1956):13–16.

22. Block, *A Cartoonist's Life,* 140.

23. Block, *Herblock Book,* 55, 57.

24. Block, *Special for Today,* 54; Saul Pett, "Nixon Tells of His Work: A Life without Relaxing," *New York Times,* January 14, 1973, 38. To appreciate how easily hackles were raised over caricatures of the vice president in the middle of the decade, one need only consider the case of Victor Arnautoff's "Dick McSmear." When Arnautoff, an assistant professor of art at Stanford, submitted his ten-by-fourteen-inch drawing of Nixon to the 1955 San Francisco Art Festival, it was ordered removed. "Coast Art Festival Bans Satire on Nixon, Titled 'Dick McSmear' and Priced at $25," *New York Times,* September 17, 1955, 10.

25. Block, *Here and Now,* 114, 70.

26. Block, *Here and Now,* 116; Block, *The Herblock Book,* 77.

27. Herbert Block, *Herblock Looks at Communism* (Washington D.C.: United States State Department, 1950).

28. Block, *A Cartoonist's Life,* 127; "Herblocked," *Time,* October 24, 1955, 72. The CBS television program that was to feature Herblock was originally the idea of Fund for the Republic president and ex-president of the University of Chicago, Robert Hutchins.

29. Anonymous (name withheld) to J. Edgar Hoover, June 10, 1957 and June 19, 1957, contained within the Herbert L. Block File, Federal Bureau of Investigation, U.S. Department of Justice, Washington, D.C.

30. Herbert L. Block file.

31. Herbert L. Block file; Katherine Graham, *Personal History* (New York: Alfred A. Knopf, 1997), 203; Herb Block, "As I See the Democrats," *New Republic* 134 (June 4, 1956):13; Block, *Herblock's Here and Now,* 6–7.

32. Julian Krawcheck, "Be Watchdogs of U.S., Newspapers Told," *Cleveland Press,* October 26, 1957; Block, *Here and Now,* 3–4, 44.

33. Robert C. Osborn, "Homage to Herblock," *New Republic* 134 (March 12, 1956):11.

34. Robert Osborn, *Osborn on Osborn* (New Haven: Ticknor & Fields, 1982), 3–42; Robert Chesley Osborn, *The Exaggerated View* (Tucson, Ariz.: Learning Plans, 1969),

sound cassette; Russell Lynes, "Osborn's Americans," *Horizon* 3 (September 1960):41–48; Robert Osborn interview with Paul Cummings, October 21, 1974, Salisbury, Connecticut, tape recording at AAA.

35. Osborn, *Osborn on Osborn,* 44–79; Robert Osborn interview with Paul Cummings; Robert Osborn to Lewis Mumford, November 27, 1970, LM, folder 3738; Keith Wheeler, "Lighthearted View of Serious Air History: By Osborn, Natch," *Smithsonian* 6 (December 1976):57.

36. Robert Osborn interview with Paul Cummings; Osborn, *Osborn on Osborn,* 84.

37. Osborn, *Osborn on Osborn,* 84; Robert Osborn, *War Is No Damn Good!* (Garden City, N. Y.: Doubleday & Company, 1946); Mel Gussow, "Robert Osborn Is Dead at 90: Caricaturist and Satirist," *New York Times,* December 22, 1994, sec. D, p. 19; Stephen Heller, "Osborn on Conflict," *Target* 4 (Summer 1985):10–14; Steven Heller, "Robert Osborn," in *Man Bites Man: Two Decades of Drawings and Cartoons by 22 Comic and Satiric Artists 1960 to 1980,* ed. Steven Heller (New York: A & W Publishers, 1981), 10–14.

38. Searle and Osborn, "The Emasculation of American Humor," 16–17; Osborn, *Osborn on Osborn,* 95–96; Robert and Elodie Osborn, "Who Cut the Comedy?" in *Film,* book 1, ed. Robert Hughes (New York: Grove Press, 1959):161–75.

39. Lynes, "Osborn's Americans," 43.

40. Garry Trudeau, foreword to *Osborn on Osborn,* 7.

41. Robert Osborn, "U.S. Foreign Policy," *New Republic* 118 (April 19, 1948):9.

42. Robert Osborn, "Osborn Views the Republicans," *New Republic* 135 (October 29, 1956):9; "No Man Is an Island Entire of Itself," *New Republic* 139 (November 3, 1958):12; "Robert Osborn Views the Campaign," *New Republic* 135 (October 15, 1956):16.

43. Robert Osborn, "Robert Osborn Views the Campaign," 16–17.

44. On the reverse side of this original drawing, Osborn later wrote, "that monster from Appleton, Wisc! No one would print this then. Scared!" RO, box uncat 2a 911008-e.

45. Beacon Press chose to use a slightly tamer version of this drawing for the cover of *Trial by Television.* Osborn's original is contained within the Caroline and Erwin Swann Collection of Caricature and Cartoon, PPD.

46. Catalog for the exhibit, *Robert Osborn, Mischa Richter: August 13–September 29, 1958* (Hartford: Wadsworth Atheneum, 1958), 9; Gussow, "Robert Osborn Is Dead at 90"; Osborn, *Osborn on Osborn,* 9; Leo Lionni, "A Portfolio of Drawings by Osborn," *Print* 10 (October–November 1956):25. For more on Osborn and his influence on modern cartooning see also Steven Heller's excellent anthology of modern graphic satire, *Man Bites Man: Two Decades of Drawings and Cartoons by 22 Comic and Satiric Artists* and his *The Savage Mirror: The Art of Contemporary Caricature* (New York: Watson-Guptill, 1992). In many respects, Osborn's cartoons exemplify Art Spiegelman's claim that cartoons are capable of acting as unconscious projections or Rorschach tests in which "the most fundamental processes of cognition" and feeling can be stripped bare. See Art Spiegelman, "Mightier Than the Sorehead," *Nation* 258 (January 17, 1994):4–5.

47. Walt Kelly, "Cartoons," *Art in America* 47 (1959):42–43; Walt Kelly, "A Crying Need for the Cleansing Lash of Laughter," *New York Times Book Review,* August 10, 1952, 5.

48. Kelly, "A Crying Need," 5; Walt Kelly to Dale Hale, January 27, 1959, WK, box WKFAN 4; Walt Kelly, "Herblock: Two Fisted Observer," *Progressive* 22 (December 1958):43–44; Walt Kelly, "Pogo Looks at the Abominable Snowman," *Saturday Review of Literature* 41 (August 30, 1958):9; "Pogo's Papa Treads on Only a Few Toes," *Milwaukee Journal,* December 16, 1958, 1, 14.

49. "Our Archives of Culture: Enter the Comics and Pogo," *Newsweek,* June 21, 1954, 66; Gene Grove, "What's So Funny?" *New York Post,* June 16, 1963, 5.

50. Walt Kelly, "A Crying Need for the Cleansing Lash of Laughter," 5; Walt Kelly, "So far as I am concerned . . . ," Untitled essay, WK, box WK8.

51. Walt Kelly, "Cartoons," 41; Walt Kelly, "It's Easy to Say It in Pictures," *New York Times Book Review,* November 30, 1958, 7, 38; Hall Syndicate Inc., "Walt Kelly: Biographical Sketch," typed manuscript, WK, box WK2; George J. Lockwood, "Walt Kelly," *Cartoonist Profiles* 67 (September 1985):48–49.

52. Nancy Beiman, "Interview with Selby Kelly," *Cartoonist Profiles* 60 (December 1983):26–31; Linda Greenhouse, "Cartoonists Honor Walt Kelly in Memorial Service at Lambs," *New York Times,* November 1, 1973, 46; Walt Kelly, "The Land of the Elephant-Squash," and Selby Kelly, "Snippy Snaps and Snappy Snips of Walt Kelly's Life," in *Walt Kelly: A Retrospective Exhibition to Celebrate the Seventy-Fifth Anniversary of His Birth,* ed. Lucy Caswell (Columbus: Ohio State University Libraries, 1988), 13–19, 21–35; Walt Kelly, "Walt Kelly," in *Five Boyhoods: Howard Lindsay, Harry Golden, Walt Kelly, William K. Zinsser and John Updike,* ed. Martin Levin (Garden City, N.Y.: Doubleday & Company, 1962), 114; Susan Progen, "The World of Pogo," *Cartoonist Profiles* 24 (December 1974):44–45; Don Maley, "Kelly Muses on His 20 Years of Playing Possum," *Editor & Publisher* 102 (April 19, 1969):20–48 and passim.

53. "Waste Not, Want Not," *Editor & Publisher* 81 (November 6, 1948):6; Steve Thompson, *Nibbled To Death by Ducks: Walt Kelly's Editorial Cartoons* (Comic Arts Conference, 1994). For examples of Kelly's work that appeared in *Life,* see in particular *Life,* September 13, 1954, 53–54 and *Life,* June 21, 1954, 124.

54. Progen, 43–45; Carl Brucker, "Walt Kelly's Pogo: The Eye of the Whole Man," *Studies in American Humor* 2 (Winter 1983–1984):161–69; "Police Seize 28 in Wild Harvard Riot," *Boston Post,* May 16, 1952. I am indebted to Richard Ohmann, a Harvard student in the 1950s, for bringing this to my attention. Evidence of the "I Go Pogo" campaign's popularity in 1952 and 1956 is abundantly clear in Kelly's fan correspondence. Amazingly, Kelly kept hundreds of requests that students made for his "I Go Pogo" promotional buttons.

55. The day after Kelly was sworn in as NCS president, he testified before the U.S. Senate Subcommittee to Investigate Juvenile Delinquency. See United States Senate Committee on the Judiciary, *Juvenile Delinquency Hearings before the Subcommittee to Investigate Juvenile Delinquency of the Committee on the Judiciary, United States Senate, Eighty-third Congress, second session, April 21, 22, and June 4, 1954* (Washington, D.C.: U. S. Government Printing Office, 1954).

56. Pogo's popular appeal is addressed in greater detail in David Segal, "Feiffer, Steinberg, and Others," *Commentary* 32 (July 1961):431–35; Selby Kelly, *Pogo Files for Pogophiles: A Retrospective on 50 Years of Walt Kelly's Classic Comic Strip* (Richfield, Minn.:

Spring Hollow Books, 1992); Edward Mendelson, "Possum Pastoral," *Yale Review* 67 (Spring 1978):470–80; "Speaking of Pictures," *Life,* May 12, 1952, 12–14; R. C. Harvey, "More on Pogo (and Not a Minute Too Soon)," *Comics Journal* 76 (October 1982):52–56; Daniel Mishkin, "Pogo: Walt Kelly's American Dream," *Journal of Popular Culture* 12 (Spring 1979):681–90; Lucy Shelton Caswell, introduction to *Walt Kelly: A Retrospective Exhibition to Celebrate the Seventy-Fifth Anniversary of His Birth,* 9–11; "Our Archives of Culture: Enter the Comics and Pogo," 65; Kalman Goldstein, "Al Capp and Walt Kelly: Pioneers of Political and Social Satire in the Comics," *Journal of Popular Culture* 25 (Spring 1992):82–90; Walt Kelly "Ka-Platz: The Delight in the Unexpected," *Atlantic* 211 (March 1963):96; Bill Watterson, "Some Thoughts on POGO & Comic Strips Today," *Cartoonist Profiles* 80 (December 1988):12–19; Arthur Asa Berger, *The Comic-Stripped American* (New York: Walker and Company, 1973), 174–77; Eric Larrabee, "If Not Pogo, Who?" *Reporter* 7 (October 28, 1952):38–40. University of Chicago sociologist Reuel Denney described Kelly's work and the comic strip's shift toward representationalism in his essay, "The Revolt against Naturalism in the Funnies," in *The Funnies: An American Idiom,* ed. David Manning White and Robert H. Abel (New York: Free Press of Glencoe, 1963), 56–71.

57. "Pogo's Papa," *Collier's,* March 8, 1952, 20–21, 64; Walt Kelly, *Ten Ever-Lovin' Blue-Eyed Years with Pogo* (New York: Simon and Schuster, 1959), 73; Don Reckseen to Walt Kelly, July 23, 1953, and Walt Kelly to Don Reckseen, July 23, 1953, WK, box WKFAN 2; Jack Sullivan to Walt Kelly, November 22, 1959, and Walt Kelly to Jack Sullivan, December 22, 1959, WK, box WKFAN 5.

58. John Hastings to Walt Kelly, February 7, 1953, WK, box WKFAN 2. Throughout his career, Kelly received thousands of letters like this from Americans of all ages and from all parts of the country. Remarkably, he usually responded to each of these letters with a personal note and an original strip, "I Go Pogo" button, or a complimentary copy of his latest *Pogo* book. Because of the toll his strenuous working habits took on his health, Kelly was finally ordered by his physician in the late 1950s to curtail his correspondence with fans.

59. Murray Kempton, "Pogo's So-So Stories (So, So Wonderful)," *New York Post,* June 21, 1953, in WK, box WK 1; Hubert H. Humphrey to William Cole, November 25, 1959, WK, box WK 6.

60. Vivian Wood to Walt Kelly, September 25, 1957, WK, box WKFAN 4; Jim White to Walt Kelly, n.d., WK, box WKFAN 3.

61. Mrs. J. J. Burkhardt to Walt Kelly, August 28, 1958, WK, box WKFAN 4; Helen Birdwell to Walt Kelly, March 19, 1952, WK, box WKFAN 1.

62. Kelly, "So far as I am concerned . . ."; Kelly, "Pogo Looks at the Abominable Snowman," 7–8.

63. John L. Stewart to Walter C. Paine, August 8, 1958, WK, box WK3.

64. Joseph L. Featherstone, "Pogo's Black Boot," *Harvard Crimson,* May 22, 1962, 2; Mendelson, "Possum Pastoral," 475; Kelly, *Ten Ever-Lovin' Blue-Eyed Years with Pogo,* 41.

65. R.C. Harvey, "Walt Kelly and the Witch-Hunters: First Encounter," and Walt Kelly, *Pogo,* 13 June–10 July 1950, in Walt Kelly, *Pogo,* vol. 4, ed. Gary Groth (Seattle: Fantagraphic Books, 1995), i–vi, 10-21.

66. Walt Kelly, *Pogo,* October 30, 1951, to November 20, 1951, and March 11, 1952, reprinted in Walt Kelly, *Pogo,* vol. 7, ed. Gary Groth (Seattle: Fantagraphic Books, 1997), 7–16, 64.

67. Walt Kelly, *Pogo,* April 21–22, 1952 and September 13, 1952, reprinted in Walt Kelly, *Pogo,* vol. 8, ed. Gary Groth (Seattle: Fantagraphic Books, 1997), 5, 67; Walt Kelly, *Pogo,* March 3, 1953, reprinted in Walt Kelly, *Pogo,* vol. 9, ed. Gary Groth (Seattle: Fantagraphic Books, 1997), 64; R. C. Harvey, "The Elf of Okefenokee and the Scarlet Pimpernel," in Walt Kelly, *Pogo,* vol. 11, ed. Gary Groth (Seattle: Fantagraphics Books 2000), ix; Kelly, *Ten Ever-Lovin' Blue-Eyed Years with Pogo,* 80.

68. Barbara Beddoe to Walt Kelly, n.d., and Walt Kelly to Barbara Beddoe, December 20, 1951, WK, box WKFAN 1; Walt Kelly, untitled manuscript, dated 1952, WK, box WK8.

69. Walt Kelly, *Pogo,* May 1–19, 1953, reprinted in Walt Kelly, *Pogo,* vol. 10, ed. Gary Groth (Seattle: Fantagraphics Books, 1998), 21–28. Kelly would surely have appreciated the favorite joke circulating among the Washington press corps in early 1953. As related to Bill Mauldin by a *Life* correspondent, the joke involves a rabbit who scurries into the forest, "hysterically seeking shelter." A chipmunk sees him and asks what is wrong. "Haven't you heard?" asks the rabbit, "McCarthy is about to investigate antelopes." "Antelopes?" asks the chipmunk, "Why worry, you're a rabbit?" "I know," says the rabbit, diving for cover, "but how can I prove it?" Bill Lang to Bill Mauldin, March 23, 1953, BM, box 4, general correspondence.

70. Walt Kelly, *Pogo,* May 30, 1953, reprinted in Kelly, *Pogo,* vol. 10, 33.

71. Walt Kelly, *Pogo,* June 2, 1953, reprinted in Kelly, *Pogo,* vol. 10, 34.

72. Walt Kelly, *Pogo,* June 3–12, 1953, reprinted in Kelly, *Pogo,* vol. 10, 35–39; Kelly, *Ten Ever-Lovin' Blue-Eyed Years with Pogo,* 141.

73. "Out Goes Pogo," *Time* 72 (December 1, 1958):40; Kelly, *Ten Ever-Lovin' Blue-Eyed Years with Pogo,* 141; Frank J. Donner, *The Age of Surveillance* (New York: Alfred A. Knopf, 1980), 112; Robert Ellis Smith et al., *The Big Brother Book of Lists* (Los Angeles: Price/Stern/Sloan, 1984); Selby Kelly, *Pogo Files for Pogophiles;* Kempton, "Pogo's So-So Stories (So, So Wonderful)," in WK, box WK1.

74. Watterson, "Some Thoughts on *Pogo,*" 16; Jules Feiffer, telephone interview by author, tape recording, December 6, 1996; Heller, "A Dancer, Bernard Mergendeiler," 5; Jules Feiffer, "Strip-Time: The Comics Observed," in the *Catalogue for the 1986 Festival of Cartoon Art,* ed. Lucy Caswell (Columbus: Ohio State University Libraries, 1986), 25. John D. Morris, "Political Scientist Hits 'Malarkeyism,'" *New York Times,* September 11, 1953, 10. For good background descriptions of the Malarkey and other significant *Pogo* episodes, see Steve Thompson, "Highlights of *Pogo,*" in *Walt Kelly: A Retrospective Exhibition to Celebrate the Seventy-Fifth Anniversary of His Birth,* 41–45.

75. Hugh Byfield to Walt Kelly, n.d., WK, box WKFAN 2.

76. Hugh Byfield to Walt Kelly, June 9, 1953, WK, box WKFAN 2.

77. Walt Kelly to Hugh Byfield, May 22, 1953, WK, box WKFAN 2.

78. Kay Reis to Walt Kelly, October 24, 1958, WK, box WKFAN 4; Mrs. Roger Ernesti to Walt Kelly, November 17, 1953, WK, box WKFAN2.

79. Walt Kelly, foreword to *The Pogo Papers* (New York: Simon and Schuster, 1953).

CHAPTER THREE

1. Herbert Block, *Herblock's Here and Now* (New York: Simon and Schuster, 1955), 1–10.

2. Liberal intellectuals' preoccupation with cultural concerns and the inner life of the (male) individual are best highlighted in Richard Pells, *The Liberal Mind in a Conservative Age;* Daniel Horowitz, *Vance Packard and American Social Criticism;* and Morris Dickstein, *Leopards in the Temple.*

3. Ann Douglas discusses the ways young moderns of the 1920s used "terrible honesty" in her brilliant study *Terrible Honesty: Mongrel Manhattan in the 1920s* (New York: Farrar, Straus and Giroux, 1995).

4. Jesse Bier, *The Rise and Fall of American Humor* (Chicago: Holt, Rinehart and Winston, 1968), 63, 55; Richard Koppe, William Irvine, and John Burns eds., *A Treasury of College Humor* (New York: William Penn, 1950); Dan Carlinsky, *A Century of College Humor: Cartoons, Stories, Poems, Jokes and Assorted Foolishness from Over 95 Campus Magazines* (New York: Random House, 1971).

5. Norman Anthony and George T. Delacorte Jr., eds., *The Book of Ballyhoo* (New York: Simon and Schuster, 1931). Norman Anthony recounts *Ballyhoo* and other publications he pioneered during the 1930s—including the 1939 antifascist satire *Der Gag Bag*—in his autobiography *How to Grow Old Disgracefully* (New York: Duell, Sloan and Pearce, 1946). The 1930s witnessed, in addition to Anthony's magazines, the splendid satiric anarchy of radio comedian Raymond Knight and the Marx Brothers. For discussions of the anarchic radio and film comedy of the 1930s see Henry Jenkins, *What Made Pistachio Nuts?: Early Sound Comedy and the Vaudeville Aesthetic* (New York: Columbia University Press, 1992), and Arthur Frank Wertheim *Radio Comedy* (New York: Oxford University Press, 1979). Of the two great satirists whose work was aimed at middle-class American culture and life during the 1920s, H. L. Mencken and Sinclair Lewis, much has been written. See in particular Richard R. Lingeman, *Sinclair Lewis: Rebel from Main Street* (New York: Random House, 2002); Terry Teachout, *The Skeptic: The Life of H.L. Mencken* (New York: Harper Collins, 2002); and Arthur P. Dudden, *Assault of Laughter* (New York: Thomas Yoseloff, 1962).

6. Robert Taylor, *Fred Allen: His Life and Wit* (Boston: Little, Brown and Company, 1989); Fred Havig, *Fred Allen's Radio Comedy* (Philadelphia: Temple University Press, 1990); Michele Hilmes, *Radio Voices: American Broadcasting, 1922–1952* (Minneapolis: University of Minnesota Press, 1997), 209–210. Defeated and disillusioned, Allen at this time began to address his concerns over the fate of comedy in modern-day commercial broadcasting. As a guest on NBC's documentary program *Living-1949,* he speculated on "The State of American Humor" and concluded that "the real humorist"— the humorist who was not a "mouthpiece of his writers" but a person who wrote his own material and grounded it in real, lived experience—was "fast disappearing." "Mechanized" and mass produced as if it had been "turned out on the assembly line," Allen remarked, modern-day radio humor had become thin and had "lost all spontaneity." In his 1954 best-selling book *Treadmill to Oblivion,* Allen similarly argued that machine-age radio comedy, as a "by-product of advertising," mindlessly set as its pri-

mary goal the attraction of the largest possible audience. As a result, radio comedy lost its distinctiveness and character. In the end, Allen bitterly concluded, all that the comedian like him "has to show for his years of work and aggravation is the echo of forgotten laughter." *Living-1949,* broadcast on NBC, January 30, 1949; Fred Allen, *Treadmill to Oblivion* (Boston: Little, Brown and Company, 1954), 238–40.

7. Robert Lewis Taylor, "Henry Morgan," *Life,* April 14, 1947, 59–66; Henry Morgan, *Here's Morgan* (New York: Barricade Books, 1994), 158.

8. Murray Schumach, "Triple-Threat Morgan," *New York Times Magazine,* September 14, 1947, 54–55; Arthur Frank Wertheim, "'The Bad Boy of Radio': Henry Morgan and Censorship," *Journal of Popular Culture* 12 (Fall 1978):350; Clair Schulz, "Here's Morgan!" *Nostalgia Digest* (August-September 1998):2–5.

9. Morgan, 135; Taylor, "Henry Morgan," 63. For further examples of Morgan's comic antagonism toward advertising see his book (co-authored with Gary Wagner), *And Now a Word from Our Sponsor* (New York: Citadel Press, 1960).

10. Schumach, "Triple-Threat Morgan," 54. Morgan ruminates on the differences between "satirists" and "humorists" in his introduction to the Ring Lardner anthology (coedited by Morgan and Babette Rosmond) *Shut Up, He Explained* (New York: Charles Scribner's Sons, 1962).

11. Eric Barnouw, *Tube of Plenty: The Evolution of American Television* (New York: Oxford University Press, 1975), 118–30; *Red Channels: The Report of Communist Influence in Radio and Television* (New York: American Business Consultants, 1950); Jeff Kisseloff, *The Box: An Oral History of Television, 1920–1961* (New York: Viking, 1995), 403–407, 423, 427.

12. Morgan, *Here's Morgan,* 200–201, 205–206; Gilbert Seldes, *The Public Arts* (New York: Simon and Schuster, 1956), 75; "Henry Morgan," *Variety,* June 12, 1946, 31. In his 1967 memoir *Due to Circumstances beyond Our Control . . . ,* the esteemed radio and television producer Fred Friendly related an anecdote that illustrates how Morgan intimidated sponsors. As producer of the 1949 NBC news quiz show *Who Said That?* Friendly had been informed by the program's sponsor (an oil company) that Morgan and other potential guests such as Norman Thomas and Oscar Levant should not appear because "in a live, ad-lib broadcast 'they just might say something.'" Fred Friendly, *Due to Circumstances beyond Our Control . . .* (New York: Random House, 1967), 25.

13. Stan Freberg, *It Only Hurts When I Laugh* (New York: Times Books, 1988):23, 78–79.

14. Stan Freberg, "It Only Hurts When I Laugh," *Collier's,* May 28, 1954, 74–79.

15. Freberg, "It Only Hurts When I Laugh," 75–79.

16. Freberg, "It Only Hurts When I Laugh," 76, 78.

17. Freberg, "It Only Hurts When I Laugh," 77.

18. Freberg, *It Only Hurts When I Laugh,* 106–107.

19. As discussed in chapter 9, the premiere broadcast featured a skit titled "Incident at Los Voraces," which concluded, much to the chagrin of network officials, with the detonation of an atomic bomb.

20. "Elderly Man River," *The Best of the Stan Freberg Shows* (Capitol, 1958).

21. Gilbert Millstein, "He Makes Crime Gay," *New York Times Magazine,* October 18, 1953, 14; "Gray Flannel Hatful of Teenage Werewolves" and "Freberg in Advertisingland," *The Best of the Stan Freberg Shows.* Freberg's parodies of Madison Avenue were mirrored to an extent by two films released the same year in which *The Stan Freberg Show* debuted on CBS—Frank Tashlin's *Will Success Spoil Rock Hunter* and Elia Kazan's *A Face in the Crowd.* In the latter, an intriguing and largely forgotten film, Kazan and screenwriter Budd Schulberg took aim at the Arthur Godfrey–type pitchman (played by Andy Griffith) and the crass techniques ad agencies deployed to plug consumer products—in this case, a libido-boosting pep pill called Vitajex.

22. Arthur Frank Wertheim, *Radio Comedy* (New York: Oxford University Press, 1979), 380–95; Peter Fornatale and Joshua E. Mills, *Radio in the Television Age* (Woodstock, N.Y.: Overlook Press, 1980) 6; Alfred Bester, "The New Age of Radio," *Holiday* 33 (June 1963):56–73; Erik Barnouw, *The Golden Web* (New York: Oxford, 1968): 288; Gene Klavan, *We Die at Dawn* (Garden City, N.Y.: Doubleday & Company, 1964), 19, 170; Jack Gould, "Radio and Television," *New York Times,* November 14, 1952, 29.

23. "Jean Shepherd: Radio's Noble Savage," *Harper's* 232 (January 1966):88–89; "The Night People," *Time,* October 1, 1956, 71; Jean Shepherd, "The Night People vs. Creeping Meatballism," *MAD* 32 (March–April 1957), unpaginated. Shepherd and his late-night fans collaborated in 1956 on one of the most successful literary hoaxes of the fifties: the merchandising of a fake novel titled *I, Libertine.* Supposedly authored by a British civil servant who happened to be an expert on eighteenth-century erotica, *I, Libertine* created a great stir and was rumored to have been banned by the Archdiocese of Boston. Much to the delight of Shepherd and others "in" on the joke, large numbers of intellectual posers and would-be sophisticates around New York actually claimed to have read it. A Ballantine paperback version of the book, coauthored by Shepherd and Theodore Sturgeon, appeared in 1957.

24. Whitney Balliett, "Profiles: Bob and Ray," *New Yorker,* September 24, 1973, 42–63 and passim; George Sessions Perry, "Funniest Pair on the Air?" *Saturday Evening Post,* December 25, 1954, 21–61 and passim; "Talkers Extraordinary," *Newsweek,* August 27, 1962, 56.

25. Kurt Vonnegut, introduction to Bob Elliott and Ray Goulding, *Write If You Get Work: The Best of Bob and Ray* (New York: Random House, 1975), v–vii.

26. Balliett, "Profiles: Bob and Ray," 42–44; J. Fred MacDonald, *Don't Touch That Dial!: Radio Programming in American Life from 1920 to 1960* (Chicago: Nelson-Hall, 1979), 149; John Dunning, *Tune in Yesterday* (Englewood Cliffs, N.J.: Prentice-Hall, 1976):81–83; Richard Gehman, "Mr. Elliott (Bob) and Mr. Goulding (Ray)," *Cosmopolitan* 141 (August 1956):114–17; "The Boys from Boston," *Newsweek,* September 10, 1951, 52–57; Ray Barfield, *Listening to Radio, 1920–1950* (Westport, Conn.: Praeger Publishers, 1996), 147.

27. Barry Putterman, *On Television and Comedy: Essays on Style, Theme, Performer and Writer* (Jefferson, N.C.: McFarland & Co., 1995), 136–38; J. Hoberman, *Vulgar Modernism: Writing on Movies and Other Media* (Philadelphia: Temple University Press, 1991), 32–39.

28. William A. Henry III, "The Topsy-Turvy in the Everyday World: The Unsur-

passed Career of Ernie Kovacs," and J. Hoberman, "It's Been Real: Ernie Kovacs, Post-modernist," in *The Vision of Ernie Kovacs, The Museum of Broadcasting, May 30–September 4, 1986* (New York: Museum of Broadcasting, 1986), 9–34.

29. Steve Allen, *Hi-Ho, Steverino!: My Adventures in the Wonderful Wacky World of TV* (Fort Lee, N.J.: Barricade Books, 1992), 43–116.

30. Gilbert Millstein, "Portrait of an M.A.L.," *New York Times Magazine*, January 9, 1955, 17, 67; Helen Lawrenson, "Look Ma, I'm Thinking," *Esquire* 48 (November 1956): 79–81. In the early, more experimental days of network television, Fred Allen, Bob and Ray, and Henry Morgan were each given a chance to match the success enjoyed by Steve Allen. But for all of them—and for Fred Allen in particular—finding a niche in television proved frustrating and, ultimately, elusive. It did not help that these performers regarded the new medium with some contempt. Television, Allen believed, limited the imagination and distracted viewers from the literary quality of good comedy. In several widely quoted remarks Allen quipped that television was a "medium" because "nothing on it is ever well done" and, better yet, a device "that permits people who haven't anything to do to watch people who can't do anything." His attempt at producing a puppet version of "Allen's Alley" on *The Colgate Comedy Hour* failed miserably. Allen's friend and fellow radio satirist Henry Morgan was slightly more successful. In 1948, Morgan began hosting a variety program titled *On the Corner* for the fledgling ABC network. After five weeks the program's sponsor, the Admiral Corporation, canned Morgan and his program because he refused to stick to the commercial announcement's script. NBC offered Morgan an opportunity to host his own variety program, *The Henry Morgan Show,* for two months in 1949. For another five months in 1951 it ran *Henry Morgan's Great Talent Hunt,* a parodic twist on its own *Original Amateur Hour.* NBC also recruited Bob and Ray in 1951. Beginning that year and continuing throughout the next, they ran several daytime variations of their popular radio program and a short-lived variety program titled *Embassy Club.* In 1953 they created short fifteen-minute segments for ABC. Information regarding television programming here as in other spots within this chapter has been culled from two indispensable reference works: Alex McNeil's *Total Television: A Comprehensive Guide to Programming from 1948 to 1980* (New York: Penguin Books, 1980), and Tim Brooks and Earle Marsh, *The Complete Directory To Prime Time Network TV Shows, 1946–Present,* 3d ed. (New York: Ballantine Books, 1985).

31. As contributing writer Mel Tolkin has recalled, he and his *Your Show of Shows* collaborators "didn't write gags. We didn't think in terms of gags. We were almost a little snobbish about it." Likewise, Caesar has commented that *Your Show of Shows* deliberately went "against the trend in the Catskills" and did not rely "on the slapstick and pratfalls everyone else was doing in TV comedy." Kisseloff, *The Box,* 309–316; Ted Sennett, *Your Show of Shows* (New York: Macmillan Publishing , 1977), 26; Sid Caesar, *Where Have I Been: An Autobiography* (New York: Crown Publishers, 1982), 101.

32. Caesar, *Where Have I Been,* 88; Max Liebman, "A Broadway Revue Every Week," *Theatre Arts* 37 (May 1953):74–77; "Mr. Caesar, Mr. Liebman," *Newsweek,* March 19, 1951, 56–57; "Playboy Interview: Mel Brooks," *Playboy* 22 (February 1975):47–68.

33. Jack Gould, "Radio and Television," *New York Times,* September 8, 1952, 30; Seldes, *The Public Arts,* 139.

34. "Lonely Saturday Nights?" *Newsweek,* February 15, 1954, 83; Jack Gould, "Television in Review: Ave Caesar," *New York Times,* March 1, 1954, 22; Kisseloff, *The Box,* 316. Not surprisingly, a great deal of speculation continues to surround the conditions that actually prompted the split. Of the three new ventures, Caesar's, a program titled *Caesar's Hour* (1954–57), fared best since he stuck close to the original *Your Show of Shows* formula and managed to supplement his writing staff—most of whom remained with Caesar—with the talents of Gary Belkin and Larry Gelbart.

35. "Bloody Mary, Anyone?" *Time,* October 21, 1957, 27; Brian Sutton-Smith, "Shut Up and Keep Digging," *Midwest Folklore* 10 (Spring 1960):11–22; Max Rezwin, *The Complete Book of Sick Jokes* (Secaucus, N.J.: Citadel Press, 1981), 12–17.

36. All quotes taken from Gerald Walker, "Sick Jokes," *Esquire* 48 (December 1957): 151–53, and Gerald Walker, "The Way Those Joke Cycles Start," *New York Times Magazine,* October 26, 1958, 36.

37. Dickstein, *Leopards in the Temple,* 90; Henriksen, *Dr. Strangelove's America,* 73–118; Paul Goodman, *Growing Up Absurd: Problems of Youth in the Organized System* (New York: Random House, 1960); Belgrad, *The Culture of Spontaneity,* 230.

38. Robert Ruark, "Let's Nix the Sickniks," *Saturday Evening Post,* June 29 to July 6, 1963, 38–39; Jonathan Miller, "The Sick White Negro," *Partisan Review* 30 (Spring 1963):149–55; Benjamin DeMott, "The New Irony: Sickniks and Others," *American Scholar* 31 (Winter 1961–62):108–19.

39. "The Sickniks," *Time,* July 13, 1959, 42, 44.

40. Robert Brustein, "The Healthiness of Sick Comedy," *New Republic* 147 (December 15, 1962):28–30. The so-called black humor of novelists Joseph Heller, Kurt Vonnegut, Vladimir Nabokov, and Thomas Pynchon—writers with whom liberals satirists shared much in common—were open to the same charges of nihilism throughout the fifties and early sixties. Some of these writers defended themselves from their critics by arguing that their novels' focus on absurdity was not an end unto itself but, as Heller explained in relation to his dark masterpiece *Catch-22* (1961), a vehicle for comment. See Paul Krassner, "An Impolite Interview with Joseph Heller," *Realist* 39 (November 1962):18.

41. Jeremy Bernstein, "Tom Lehrer: Having Fun," *American Scholar* 53 (Summer 1984):295–302; Peter Tauber, "The Cynic Who Never Soured," *New York Times Magazine,* November 2, 1997, 50; Dr. Demento, liner notes to *Songs & More Songs by Tom Lehrer* (Rhino, 1996); Tom Lehrer, interview by author, tape recording, Cambridge, Mass., September 24, 1996; Tom Lehrer, liner notes to *Songs by Tom Lehrer* (Lehrer Records, 1953), reissued on *Songs & More Songs by Tom Lehrer.* Other information regarding Lehrer's background is taken from a longer, unedited version of Peter Tauber's article. I am indebted to Peter Tauber for sharing this material with me. The song Lehrer omitted from his first album was "I Got It from Agnes," a ditty about venereal disease.

42. Tom Lehrer, liner notes to *Songs by Tom Lehrer.*

43. Tom Lehrer, "I Wanna Go Back to Dixie," *The Tom Lehrer Song Book* (New York: Crown Publishers, 1962), 15–20.

44. Tom Lehrer, "Be Prepared," *The Tom Lehrer Song Book,* 47–50.

45. Tom Lehrer, "When You Are Old and Gray," *The Tom Lehrer Song Book,* 27–32.

46. Tom Lehrer, "I Hold Your Hand in Mine," *The Tom Lehrer Song Book,* 33–36.

47. Laura Z. Hobson, "Thumbing Around," *Good Housekeeping* 138 (June 1954):13.

48. "Tom Lehrer," *Boston Herald,* November 16, 1957, Tom Lehrer clipping file, BRT; Rolf Malcolm, "The Old Dope Peddler," *Playboy* 2 (May 1955):33–34; Tom Lehrer, interview by author, tape recording, Cambridge, Mass., September 24, 1996.

49. Gerald Nachman, *Seriously Funny,* 236–54; Albert Goldman, "Lindy's Law," *New Republic* 150 (June 13, 1964):34–35; "If You're Not Sick . . ." *Time,* October 13, 1958, 54–56. Always on, Winters even ran through New York nightclubs with a hand grenade shouting, "Everybody goes when the whistle blows."

50. Charles Marowitz, "Who Is Theodore, What Is He—Loon, Ham, or Drama's 'Genius of the Sinister'?" *Village Voice,* February 15, 1956, 56; Gottlieb quoted in "A Pudgy Pile of Mud," *Playboy* 5 (August 1958):22.

51. Jerry Tallmer, "Theatre: Brother Theodore," *Village Voice,* July 2, 1958, 6

52. The cartoons of Shoemaker, Wilson, and Silverstein appeared often in *Playboy* magazine, a venue that proved amenable to sick humor. *Playboy* trumpeted Gahan Wilson in particular, declaring him a "master of mirthful macabre" and a "real wierdee who deserves to be better known in sick circles over here." Although Silverstein's cartoons were not sick in the same way as Wilson's or Shoemaker's were, his illustrated "Uncle Shelby" primers evidenced the same juvenile cruelty as "meanie" jokes. "Playbill," *Playboy* 6 (March 1959).

53. Dwight Macdonald, "Charles Addams, His Family, and His Friends," *Reporter* 8 (July 21, 1953):37. To appreciate the true extent of Addams's sick fascination with the macabre, see his compilation of cartoons and disturbing images in *Dear Dead Days: A Family Album* (New York: G.P. Putnam's Sons, 1959).

54. Paul Buhle, "Interview: Harvey Kurtzman," *Schmate* 6 (Summer 1983):24–25; Paul Buhle, "Beware of Imitations!: The Jewish Radicalism of *Mad* Comics," *Genesis* 2 (Summer 1987):32–34; Paul Buhle, "Harvey Kurtzman, *Mad* Genius," paper presented at the American Studies Association Annual Meeting, Montreal, Canada, October 30, 1999; Jud Hurd, "H. Kurtz," *Cartoonist Profiles* 26 (June 1975):48–49; Kim Thompson and Gary Groth, "An Interview with the Man Who Brought Truth to the Comics: Harvey Kurtzman," *Comics Journal* 67 (October 1981):68–69.

55. Harvey Kurtzman with Howard Zimmerman, *My Life as a Cartoonist* (New York: Minstrel Books, 1988), 15; Buhle, "Interview: Harvey Kurtzman," 24–25; John Benson, "Harvey Kurtzman Interview" in *The Complete Mad* (West Plains, Mo.: Russ Cochran, 1986), unpaginated.

56. While serving in the army, Kurtzman was so irked by the omnipresent racism that he once called his fellow soldiers to attention when a black officer passed by, thus forcing them to salute. "That was my outstanding blow against racism," he later told

Paul Buhle. "It was a radical act at that time. I might have been lynched for it." Buhle, "Interview: Harvey Kurtzman," 24.

57. Harvey Kurtzman, *From Aargh! to Zap!: Harvey Kurtzman's Visual History of the Comics* (New York: Prentice Hall Press, 1991), 27; John Benson, *A Talk with H. Kurtz* (New York: John Benson, 1966), 5; Harvey Kurtzman, interview by Maria Reidelbach, tape recording, New York, October 21, 1989; "Hey Look!," *Rogue* 10 (December 1965):70. Much to the chagrin of Gaines and his artist collaborator Al Feldstein, driven entrepreneurs bent on churning out horror comics to meet the extraordinary demand, Kurtzman spent days, even weeks at the New York Public Library researching backgrounds for his work. Kurtzman's obsession with authenticity confused Gaines and Feldstein. In their minds, Kurtzman's fastidiousness was proof that Kurtzman was an effete liberal intellectual. Gary Groth and Dwight R. Decker, "An Interview with William M. Gaines," *Comics Journal* 81 (May 1983):53–84.

58. Kurtzman, *From Aargh! to Zap!*, 31; Benson, "Harvey Kurtzman Interview," unpaginated. As with many elements of the early history of *MAD*, details concerning exactly who was responsible for suggesting and then naming *MAD* comics are still hotly contested. For Bill Gaines's version of the events leading to *MAD's* founding, see Groth and Decker, "An Interview with William M. Gaines," 53–84.

59. Harvey Kurtzman, "Mad Mumblings," *MAD* 1 (October–November 1952), unpaginated; John Benson, "A Conversation with Harvey Kurtzman and Bill Gaines," *Squa Tront* 9 (1983):82–92.

60. In 1954, Dr. Wertham and the Hartford (Connecticut) *Courant* accused Bill Gaines and his E.C. suspense and horror comics of contributing to the rise in juvenile delinquency. In retaliation, Gaines and his business manager Lyle Stuart used mock ads and editorials in their publications to ridicule Wertham and his fellow "do-gooders." In their most notorious editorial, Gaines and Stuart implied that opponents to E.C. comics were "Red Dupes." On April 21, 1954, Gaines voluntarily testified before the U.S. Senate Hearings before the Subcommittee to Investigate Juvenile Delinquency. Before Senator Estes Kefauver and several of his colleagues, Gaines weakly explained that he intended his "Red Dupe" editorial as a joke. The climax of his testimony came when Senator Kefauver asked him whether he believed an E.C. cover illustration depicting a man with a bloody ax gripping the severed head of a woman was in "good taste." Much to the dismay of Kefauver, his colleagues, and National Cartoonist Society president Walt Kelly, who testified immediately after Gaines, the publisher answered "yes." Gaines's testimony is recorded in the United States Senate Committee on the Judiciary, *Juvenile Delinquency Hearings before the Subcommittee to Investigate Juvenile Delinquency of the Committee on the Judiciary, United States Senate, Eighty-Third Congress, Second Session, April 21, 22, and June 4, 1954* (Washington, D.C.: U.S. Government Printing Office, 1954), 97–109. For further background on Gaines and his appearance before the Senate Subcommittee to Investigate Juvenile Delinquency, see Amy Kiste Nyberg, "William Gaines and the Battle over EC Comics," *Inks* 3 (February 1996): 2–15. See also James Gilbert's excellent discussion of Wertham and his crusade in *Cycle of Outrage*, 91–108.

61. John Benson, "A Conversation with Harvey Kurtzman and Bill Gaines," 82–92.

62. Much to Kurtzman's chagrin, Bill Gaines attempted to further capitalize on *MAD*'s sudden success by publishing a sister publication named *Panic.* Edited by Al Feldstein and bearing the slogan "Humor in a Varicose Vein," *Panic* premiered in late 1953.

63. Buhle, "Harvey Kurtzman, *Mad* Genius"; Will Elder, interview by Maria Reidelbach, tape recording, New York, May 12, 1990.

64. With their use of tchotchkes, Elder and Kurtman may have been influenced by Walt Kelly's *Pogo* comic strip. Throughout the early 1950s, Kelly inserted small signs into the landscape of the Pogofonokee Swamp and at times had his characters playfully engage the conventions of the comic strip medium.

65. Benson, "A Conversation with Harvey Kurtzman and Bill Elder," 67.

66. While humorously chronicling his evolution into a "miserable two-bit hack" comic book cartoonist in *MAD*'s "Special Art Issue," Elder pays homage to Duchamp's *Nude Descending a Staircase* with a piece he titles *I Dreamed I Descended a Staircase in My Playtex Underwear!*

67. Benson, "A Conversation with Harvey Kurtzman and Bill Elder," 71–72.

68. "Harvey Kurtzman, interviewed by T. Durwood," *Crimmer's* 3 (Spring 1976): 24–25.

69. "Cowboy!" *MAD* 20 (February 1955):unpaginated.

70. Critic J. Hoberman identifies the sensibility informing this technique as "vulgar modernism" and links several other postwar artists—among them Kovacs, cartoonist Tex Avery, and his disciple, director Frank Tashlin—to it. Hoberman, *Vulgar Modernism,* 32–39.

71. "Woman Wonder," *MAD* 10 (April 1954):unpaginated; "Bringing Back Father," *MAD* 17 (November 1954):unpaginated.

72. "Howdy Dooit," *MAD* 18 (December 1954):unpaginated; "What's My Shine!" *MAD* 17 (November 1954):unpaginated.

73. "Gopo Gossum!" *MAD* 23 (May 1955):unpaginated.

74. "Mickey Rodent!" *MAD* 19 (January 1955):unpaginated.

75. Buhle, "Beware of Imitations!: The Jewish Radicalism of *Mad* Comics," 33; Art Spiegelman, "H.K. (R.I.P.)," *New Yorker,* March 29, 1993, 76; "Mad Mumblings," *MAD* 21 (March 1955):unpaginated; "Mad Mumblings," *MAD* 16 (October 1954):unpaginated; "Mad Mumblings," *MAD* 15 (September 1954):unpaginated. Another gauge of *Mad's* predominantly male readership is provided by the multiple fanzines that popped up during the fifties. See Ron Parker, ed., *Hoohah!: The Best of E.C.'s Finest Fanzine* (Oakland: Ron Parker, 1984).

76. "Julius Caesar!" *MAD* 17 (November 1954):unpaginated.

77. Robert Warshow "Paul, the Horror Comics, and Dr. Wertham," in *The Immediate Experience: Movies, Comics, Theatre and Other Aspects of Popular Culture* (Garden City, N.Y.: Doubleday & Company, Inc. 1962), 83; "Mad Mumblings," *MAD* 17 (November 1954):unpaginated.

78. Harvey Kurtzman, "Editorial Statement," *MAD* 23 (May 1955):unpaginated.

79. The story of Kurtzman's departure from *MAD* has been contested for years.

According to Kurtzman, he left because he and his staff were not receiving the salaries, autonomy, and respect they deserved. When he demanded in the spring of 1956 that Bill Gaines grant him a majority stake in his *MAD*'s ownership, Gaines refused. Gaines by this time could not afford to lose control of *MAD* since, under the pressure of fellow comics publishers, comics distributors, and the American public, he had been forced to abandon his lucrative suspense and horror comics.

80. Rolf Malcolm, "The Little World of Harvey Kurtzman," *Playboy* 4 (December 1957) 51–86 and passim; Hurd, "H. Kurtz," 48–49; Thompson and Groth, "An Interview with the Man Who Brought Truth to the Comics: Harvey Kurtzman," 68–107. In his autobiography, Kurtzman reflected that he "never did get to do the perfect humor magazine. But *Trump* came the closest, even though it only ran for two issues." Kurtzman with Zimmerman, *My Life as a Cartoonist,* 85. Sadly, Kurtzman never again matched the success he had enjoyed with *MAD.* Following *Trump*'s collapse, he and his stalwart artists Will Elder, Jack Davis, and Arnold Roth pooled their financial resources together and launched a satiric magazine titled *Humbug.* Like *Trump, Humbug* published memorable parodies and satires but eventually ran aground in 1958. A year later, Ballantine Books published *Harvey Kurtzman's Jungle Book,* a collection of pieces written and drawn by Kurtzman. In addition to depicting a lynching in a "degenerate" Southern town of Rottenville (inspired by his artillery training in Texas during World War II) and satirizing the infusion of pop psychology into television westerns, Kurtzman here took revenge on Bill Gaines and the world of magazine publishing in a piece titled "Organization Man in the Grey Flannel Executive Suite." In August 1960, Kurtzman launched his last satiric magazine, *Help!* During its intermittent, five-year run, Kurtzman worked with Will Elder on a series of picaresque satiric stories revolving around the experiences of Goodman Beaver, the innocent young protagonist Kurtzman had created earlier for "Organization Man in the Grey Flannel Executive Suite." Together with other talented *Help!* staff—the writers Gloria Steinem and John Cleese, artist Terry Gilliam, and the pioneering underground cartoonists Robert Crumb, Gilbert Shelton, Jay Lynch, and Skip Williamson—Kurtzman filled the pages of *Help!* with *fumettis* (photographs appended with humorously captioned text) and an assortment of other novel comic features. Also in the early sixties, Kurtzman contributed illustrated stories to *Esquire* magazine and, together with his longtime collaborator, Will Elder, created a lavishly illustrated strip for *Playboy* titled "Little Annie Fanny." A female version of Goodman Beaver, the buxom and, by the conclusion of each strip, topless young blond Little Annie Fanny resembled the sexy, tongue-in-cheek Candide that Terry Southern and Mason Hoffenberg created for their hit underground novel *Candy* (1958). Though providing Kurtzman with a steady income, "Little Annie Fanny," *Playboy*'s "delightfully dizzy damsel," proved a dead end for Kurtzman and his unique and enormously influential brand of satire. For a complete listing of Kurtzman's published work, see Glenn Bray, *The Illustrated Harvey Kurtzman Index* (Sylmar, Calif.: Glenn Bray, 1976).

81. In *MAD*'s version of this ad, "Park-David" ("Pioneers in bigger medical bills") features *Presenting the Bill,* "one of a series of original oil paintings, 'Practicing Medicine for Fun and Profit,'" that it has commissioned for the public. "Great Moments in Medicine," *MAD* 48 (July 1959):inside back cover.

82. Al Feldstein, interview by Maria Reidelbach, tape recording, New York, October 9 and 14, 1989.

83. T. J. Ross, "The Conventions of the Mad," *Dissent* 8 (1961):503–504; Dwight Macdonald, "A Caste, a Culture, a Market-II," *New Yorker,* November 29, 1958, 76.

84. Al Feldstein, interview by Maria Reidelbach, tape recording, New York, October 9 and 14, 1989.

85. "Crazy Like a Fox," *Newsweek,* August 31, 1959, 57.

86. *MAD's* initial and, admittedly unsuccessful, foray into network television was *The Tony Randall Show Mad Revue,* premiering on NBC's *Pontiac Star Parade* on February 24, 1960.

87. "Special Sophistication Issue: Bad," *Esquire* 62 (August 1964):52–56.

88. Fred Pietarinen, Jr. to Jules Feiffer, October 30, 1961, JF, box 9.

89. Tom Hayden, *Reunion: A Memoir* (New York: Random House, 1988), 15.

CHAPTER FOUR

1. Louis Kronenberger, "The Season in New York," *The Burns Mantle Yearbook: The Best Plays of 1952–1953,* ed. Louis Kronenberger (New York: Dodd, Mead and Company, 1953), 6–7; Louis Kronenberger, "The Season on Broadway," *The Burns Mantle Yearbook: The Best Plays of 1958–1959,* ed. Louis Kronenberger (New York: Dodd, Mead and Company, 1959), 20; Harold Clurman, "No Time for Comedy," *Nation* 186 (April 26, 1958): 376–78. Michael Denning discusses Popular Front cabaret and revue in *The Cultural Front,* 295–347.

2. In 1952, for example, many of these critics greeted a revival of James Thurber's *The Male Animal,* a comedy that made pointed references to academic freedom at a time when such freedom was imperiled by McCarthyism. They were later cheered by productions of George S. Kaufman's *Solid Gold Cadillac* (1953), George Axelrod's *Will Success Spoil Rock Hunter* (1955), Harold Clurman's *Tiger at the Gates* (1955), and Peter Ustinov's *The Love of Four Colonels* (1953) and *Romanoff and Juliet* (1957). The 1956 musicals *Candide* and *Li'l Abner* poked fun at big business, politics, Hollywood, war, and cold war diplomacy.

3. Clurman, "No Time for Comedy," 376–77; Martin Esslin, *The Theatre of the Absurd* (New York: Anchor Books, 1961), 292. Theater historian Sally Banes celebrates the Open Theater and other off-off-Broadway venues in her book, *Greenwich Village 1963: Avant-Garde Performance and the Effervescent Body.* Banes oddly omits consideration of the satiric improvisational troupes working in New York during the period but nevertheless demonstrates the irreverent and satiric edge of Greenwich Village theater groups such as the Judson Poets' Theater.

4. Belgrad, *The Culture of Spontaneity,* 1–2.

5. Claudia Cassidy, "The Season in Chicago," *The Burns Mantle Yearbook: The Best Plays of 1952–53,* 21.

6. Lee Gallup Feldman, "A Brief History of Improvisational Theatre in the United States," *Yale/Theatre* 5 (Spring 1974):128–30; Janet Coleman, *The Compass: The Improvi-*

sational Theatre That Revolutionized American Comedy (Chicago: University of Chicago Press, 1991), 42–48; David Shepherd, interview by author, tape recording, New York, July 22, 1996.

7. Beverly Fields, "Playwrights Theater," *Chicago Magazine* 1 (April 1954):47–51; Jeffrey Sweet, *Something Wonderful Right Away: An Oral History of The Second City and The Compass Players* (New York: Limelight Editions, 1986), xv–xxi.

8. David Shepherd, telephone interview by author, tape recording, May 28, 1999; Peter Bryan, "First Nights in a Barroom," *Chicago* 1 (January 1955):59–60. For background on the rise of postwar European cabaret, see Franz Spelman, "The Return of the Political Cabaret" *Show* 2 (May 1962):86–89.

9. Coleman, *The Compass*, 21–38; Charles L. Mee, "The Celebratory Occasion: An Interview with Paul Sills," *Tulane Drama Review* 9 (Winter 1964):167, 171–73. Sills's mother, Viola Spolin, has been dubbed the "High Priestess of Improvisation." Her classic text on improvisation and theater games is *Improvisation for the Theater: A Handbook of Teaching and Directing Techniques* (Evanston: Northwestern University Press, 1963).

10. Coleman, *The Compass*, 83; David Shepherd, "From Brochure 1954," duplicated copy of unpaginated original manuscript sent to author by David Shepherd.

11. Roger Bowen, "Enterprise," duplicated copy of unpaginated, original scenario manuscript sent to author by David Shepherd.

12. Coleman, *The Compass*, 88; Bowen, "Enterprise."

13. Coleman, *The Compass*, 66, 85–99; Gordon Cotler, "For the Love of Mike—and Elaine," *New York Times Magazine*, May 24, 1959, 71; Robert Wool, "Mike and Elaine: Mirrors to Our Madness," *Look Magazine*, June 21, 1960, 46–52; "Two Characters in Search . . ." *Time*, September 26, 1960, 61–62. In significant respects, May fits the model of female rebel described by Wini Breines in *Young, White, and Miserable: Growing Up Female in the Fifties*.

14. Coleman, *The Compass*, 102; "Commedia dell'arte in a 55th Street Saloon," *Chicago* 2 (September 1955):60–62; Sweet, *Something Wonderful Right Away*, 28–31. Isaac Rosenfeld's detailed and often humorous description of Hyde Park is contained in his posthumous article "Life in Chicago," *Commentary* 23 (June 1957):523–34. Before he died, Rosenfeld contributed a scenario to the Compass titled *The Liars*.

15. David Shepherd, telephone interview by author, tape recording, May 28, 1999.

16. Sweet, *Something Wonderful Right Away*, 29–30.

17. Elaine May, "The Real You," duplicated copy of unpaginated, original scenario manuscript sent to author by David Shepherd. According to various former Compass Players, the work of Riesman, Whyte, Paul Goodman, and other social critics was part of the air that they and many other people associated with the University of Chicago breathed during the mid-1950s. Riesman and his coauthor on *The Lonely Crowd*, Reuel Denney, were even known to show up in the Compass's audience from time to time. Andrew Duncan to author, June 18, 1999.

18. Elaine May, "Georgina's First Date," duplicated copy of unpaginated, original scenario manuscript sent to author by David Shepherd; Sweet, *Something Wonderful Right Away*, 30–31.

19. David Shepherd, "Five Dreams for Five Actors," duplicated copy of unpaginated, original scenario manuscript sent to author by David Shepherd.

20. Paul Sills remembers that the public discourse surrounding elected officials was so restricted in the 1950s that merely mentioning the name of the president on stage was a rebellious act. "We mentioned Eisenhower," Sill recalls, "and shook in our boots. It was the first time that a name was actually mentioned in the ordinary theater world." Paul Sills, telephone interview by author, tape recording, June 3, 1999.

21. Duncan quote in Sweet, *Something Wonderful Right Away,* 47.

22. Omar Shapli, telephone interview by author, tape recording, May 24, 1999; Belgrad, *The Culture of Spontaneity,* 180–235.

23. Coleman, *The Compass,* 143; Mark Gordon, telephone interview by author, tape recording, June 3, 1999; Rocco Landesman, "A Conversation with David Shepherd," *Yale/Theatre* 5 (Spring 1974):59. The image of the smart, hip, funny Jew found enormous appeal among the Compass's non-Jews. David Shepherd, for example, was attracted to Jews and Jewish culture while he was in the army. Every six months or so, he recalls, he came into contact with a Jew who was smart, sexy, and played the guitar. "I realized they were the salt of the earth," he explains. Shepherd was informed of radical politics by Sumner Rosen, a New York Jew, on a liberty ship headed back to the United States. David Shepherd, telephone interview by author, tape recording, June 2, 1999. Del Close, a performer who later joined the Compass in St. Louis, was almost spellbound by what he perceived as Elaine May's hip, exotic Jewishness. "I began to think of myself as Jewish or at least a Jewish fellow traveler," Close remembers, "because I thought the Jews were the hip people." Del Close, interview by author, tape recording, Chicago, September 11, 1996. Although cultural outsiders by dint of their ethnic backgrounds, Compass Players Severn Darden and Mike Nichols came from families that were relatively well established. Darden was the son of the New Orleans District Attorney who, before enrolling in the University of Chicago, attended a prep school in upstate New York. Nichols, born Michael Igor Peschkowsky, was the son of a Jewish physician from Berlin and the grandson of Gustav Landauer, the former head of the German Social Democrats. Like Shepherd, Nichols grew up in wealthy Manhattan neighborhoods and attended prestigious private schools. Although he initially planned to become a psychoanalyst, he was drawn to the theater at the University of Chicago and later studied acting with Lee Strasberg in New York. Shelley Berman shared little in common with Nichols, Darden, and Shepherd. The child of working-class immigrants, Berman grew up in a Jewish neighborhood on Chicago's West Side. He did not attend the University of Chicago or any other prestigious academic institution. By his own admission, he never even read a book until he was eighteen years old. After being discharged from the navy, he studied acting at Chicago's Goodman Theater. He later worked as a social director at a Daytona Beach resort and as an Arthur Murray dance instructor. He joined the Compass Players only after struggling for several years as a stock theater actor. Robert Rice, "A Tilted Insight," *New Yorker,* April 15, 1961, 47–70; Wool, "Mike and Elaine: Mirrors to Our Madness," 46–52; Jack Roth, "Road to Success," *New York Times,* January 31, 1960, sec. 2, p. 11; Edwin Miller, "Berman off the Record," *Seventeen* 17 (July 1962):76–77, 116–17.

24. Severn Darden, an eccentric wit who specialized in outrageous and absurd comedy, created a character named Professor Walter von der Vogelweide, which jabbed at the obscurantism and pomposity of emigré intellectuals at the University of Chicago. In his parody of Dada art, Darden would wrap audience members with toilet paper while reading a Tristan Tzara poem in German. When he had finished, he would scream at his audience in English, "You stupid swine. Why are you sitting there taking this shit?" Coleman, *The Compass*, 168–98, 231; Theodore Flicker, telephone interview by author, tape recording, May 28, 1999. Darden liked to parody University of Chicago emigré scholar Bruno Bettelheim (reportedly a Compass fan) by reading a lecture titled "Some Positive Aspects of Anti-Semitism." Sweet, *Something Wonderful Right Away*, 92.

25. Coleman, *The Compass*, 196; "After Hours," *Playboy* 3 (August 1956):6.

26. John Limon, "Analytic of the Ridiculous: Mike Nichols and Elaine May," *Raritan* 16 (Winter 1997):102–22; Sweet, *Something Wonderful Right Away*, 130.

27. Coleman, *The Compass*, 161, 149–50; Helen Markel, "Mike Nichols and Elaine May," *Redbook* 116 (February 1961):98.

28. Mike Nichols and Elaine May, "Disk Jockey," performed on "Sunday Evening with Mitch Miller," broadcast on CBS Radio, June 29, 1958. Recording available at DRS.

29. Theodore Flicker, telephone interview by author, tape recording, May 28, 1999; Myles Standish, "Ted Flicker—Prophet of 'Saloon Theater,'" *St. Louis Post Dispatch*, November 23, 1958, sec. 12, p. 4j; Coleman, *The Compass*, 182–84; Rocco Landesman, "Interview: Ted Flicker," *Yale/Theatre* 5 (Spring 1974):67.

30. Theodore Flicker, telephone interview by author, tape recording, May 28, 1999; Jay Landesman, *Rebel without Applause* (London: Bloomsbury Publishing, 1987), 184. The hip cultural scene that existed around St. Louis's Olive Street is described in John Keisler, "Off-Beat Business Brothers," *St. Louis Post Dispatch*, October 12, 1958, sec. 12, p. 1. The Compass's new home suited Flicker, Darden, and Close particularly well since they prided themselves on their discriminating, offbeat tastes. Like a number of other liberal satirists, these young cultural renegades betrayed a certain snobbery and elitism in their dissent from American middle-class life. All three of these friends were peculiarly susceptible to aristocratic pretensions. Darden, for example, wore a cape and drove a Rolls-Royce while he was still a student at the University of Chicago. He was tellingly described by a friend as a "man of station with perfect contempt." Close, a native of Manhattan, Kansas, and second cousin to Dwight D. Eisenhower, left home as a teenager in order to apprentice under a fire-eating carnival magician named Dr. Dracula. Close was a restless subterranean rebel who managed to gain some experience acting in summer stock and small theaters before he joined the Compass at the age of twenty-three. In addition to his enthusiasm over science fiction, Buddhism, the occult, and L. Ron Hubbard's *Dyanetics*, Close harbored a fascination with aristocracies. He was a self-proclaimed monarchist who wished he could be called "Sir Del." Del Close, interview by author, tape recording, Chicago, September 11, 1996.

31. Del Close, interview by author, tape recording, Chicago, September 11, 1996; "Two Loves—A Mime" is contained in *The Premise Handbook*, TFC, box 1. Titles and descriptions of other St. Louis Compass scenes are taken from TFC, box 1, Compass

scenes folder; Myles Standish, "Compass Players Act in a Rococo Barroom," *St. Louis Post Dispatch,* April 7, 1957, 4j. Women in the St. Louis Compass were occasionally exposed to violent outbursts from the male colleagues, particularly Flicker and Close. While Close began strangling Henderson on stage during one improvisation, Flicker once vented his rage on stage by pounding Nancy Ponder's head against the floor. Coleman, *The Compass,* 224.

32. Del Close, interview by author, tape recording, Chicago, September 11, 1996; Standish, "Ted Flicker," 4j; Theodore Flicker to Ruth, February 13, 1957, TFC, box 2, Compass correspondence folder; Theodore Flicker to Abel Green, February 15, 1957, TFC, box 2, Compass correspondence folder; Theodore Flicker to Arthur Kovner, July 29, 1957, TFC, box 2, Compass correspondence folder. Jay Landesman, a former publisher of the notorious avant-garde journal *Neurotica* and a friend to Beat writers such as Jack Kerouac, enthusiastically supported what the Compass Players were doing in his nightclub. On the same stage where Landesman, St. Louis's "beatnik spokesman," had once discoursed on sex, culture, and middle-class conformity for his Crystal Palace Advance School of Cultural Analysis, the Compass Players excelled. "They took the audience suggestions on topical issues or personal experiences of the most embarrassing kind," Landesman marveled, "and turned them into sharp, biting, satirical commentary on contemporary manners and morals that left no doubt something new was happening in entertainment in America." Keisler, "Off-Beat Business Brothers," 1; Jay Landesman, *Rebel without Applause,* 198–99, 203.

33. Flicker described his role in "The Compass Theatre: Suggestion for a Half-Hour Television Program, Originating LIVE from St. Louis," TFC, *The Premise Handbook,* box 1.

34. Theodore J. Flicker to Severn Darden, October 16, 1957, TFC, box 2, Compass correspondence folder. For more on the Compass's acrimonious split, see also Coleman, *The Compass,* 208–38 and passim.

35. Max Lerner, liner notes to *The Sex Life of the Primate* (Verve, 1964). In his attention to the small annoyances one encounters in daily life, Berman anticipated later "observational" comics such as Jerry Seinfeld and Richard Lewis. Descriptions of Berman's routines are taken from his comedy albums: *Inside Shelley Berman* (Verve, 1959); *Outside Shelley Berman* (Verve, 1959); *The Edge of Shelley Berman* (Verve, 1960); *A Personal Appearance* (Verve, 1961); *New Sides* (Verve, 1963); and *The Sex Life of the Primate* (Verve, 1964).

36. "Confession Comedy," *Time,* January 12, 1959, 56; Louis Untermeyer, liner notes for *A Personal Appearance* (Verve, 1961). At times, Berman's confessional tone contributed to the impression that he was a needy, fragile, and insecure person. In an embarrassingly contrite conclusion to his performance on *The Edge of Shelley Berman,* he tells his audience, "I have gotten to the point where so help me God I don't know whether I am talking sincerely to you or conning the hell out of you." "You don't need me," he tells the hushed crowd, "but I sure need you . . . You can laugh without me . . . But I can't be funny without you. Alone I am not funny." Shelley Berman, *The Edge of Shelley Berman* (Verve, 1960).

37. "Alone on the Telephone," *Time*, January 20, 1961, 66–67; "An Evening with Shelley Berman," videotape production at the Museum of Broadcast Communications, February 19, 1990, MBC; "Berman, Inside and Out," *Newsweek*, February 15, 1960, 103.

38. Jeff Sorensen, *Bob Newhart* (New York: St. Martin's Press, 1988); "'Button-Down' Benchley," *Newsweek*, October 10, 1960, 96; Pete Martin, "Backstage with Bob Newhart," *Saturday Evening Post*, October 14, 1961, 118–21. Christopher Lasch astutely assessed the "sophisticated" tone of the New Frontier and liberal intellectuals' attraction to it in *The New Radicalism in America: 1889–1963: The Intellectual as Social Type* (New York: Alfred A. Knopf, 1965), 311–43.

39. Martin, "Backstage with Bob Newhart," 118; Newhart quoted in Sorensen, *Bob Newhart*, 40. Like Shelley Berman, Newhart resisted the "satirist" tag since it implied certain expectations and responsibilities he did not feel he could meet. "I'm no deep thinker," he told the *New York Times*, "but I think comedy's a dangerous weapon. Ridicule can sway people and you better be sure you're right." "Frankly," he admitted elsewhere, "I don't feel qualified to sway people's opinions . . . I don't go for this idea that comics should be social critics . . . I don't see anything wrong with a routine that's just funny, with no comment at all." Gilbert Millstein, "New Sick and/or Well Comic," *New York Times Magazine*, August 7, 1960, 36; "'Button-Down' Benchley," 96.

40. Martin, "Backstage with Bob Newhart," 121; Bob Newhart, "The Retirement Party" on *The Button-Down Mind Strikes Back* (Warner Brothers, 1960).

41. Bob Newhart, "Abe Lincoln vs. Madison Avenue," on *The Button-Down Mind* (Warner Brothers, 1960). Newhart concluded this routine in a way that surely offended opponents of "sick" humor. "Listen Abe," the agent says, "why don't you take in a play?"

42. Martin, "Backstage with Bob Newhart,"118; Millstein, "New Sick and/or Well Comic," 22.

43. *Omnibus* broadcast, January 14, 1958, videotape viewed at Motion Picture and Television Reading Room, MBRS.

44. Robert Brustein, "Comedians from the Underground," *New Republic* 143 (October 31, 1960):13. Robert Brustein, a former student of Lionel Trilling's at Columbia University, began serving as the *New Republic*'s drama critic in 1959. Like Gore Vidal and several other prominent young, liberal writers and critics, Brustein was clearly disillusioned by Broadway's timeworn and predominantly conservative comedies. In 1960 he argued that satire had been disappearing from the stage "at an alarming rate." This, he claimed, was due less to the lingering effects of McCarthyism than to Americans' new sensitivity to the harmful potential of ethnic and racial jokes. A year earlier in *Harper's* Brustein argued more plausibly that mainstream Broadway producer's preference for pretentious, evasive, and formulaic plays severely limited the possibilities of producing incisive drama and comedy. Americans "have a theater," Brustein concluded ruefully, "which will not admit the simple truths that everyone discusses in the living room." Robert Brustein, "Why American Plays Are Not Literature," reprinted in *American Drama and Its Critics*, ed. Alan S. Downer (Chicago: University of Chicago Press, 1965), 253. Years later, Brustein reevaluated the stifling influence of McCarthyism when he argued, "Undoubtedly the most dismal days in the history of our own theatre were

the fifties, when the stage, along with movies and television, was subjected to scrutiny by the home-grown yahoos of the House Un-American Activities Committee." Robert Brustein, "Freedom and Constraint in the American Theater," *The Culture Watch: Essays on Theatre and Society, 1969–1974* (New York: Alfred A. Knopf, 1975).

45. Coleman, *The Compass*, 267; Markel, "Mike Nichols and Elaine May," 32–33, 98–101; Rice, "A Tilted Insight," 47–70 and passim; John Crosby, "Theater: Revues on the Fringe," *Show Magazine* 1 (December 1961):7.

46. Cotler, "For the Love of Mike—and Elaine," 71; John McClain, "Merely Magnificent," *New York Journal-American,* October 10, 1960, Nichols and May clipping file, BRT; Wool, "Mike and Elaine: Mirrors to Our Madness," 46; Whitney Bolton, "Nichols, May Click Most of the Way," *New York Morning Telegraph,* October 11, 1960, Nichols and May clipping file, BRT.

47. Nichols and May, "Cocktail Piano" on *Improvisations to Music* (Mercury, 1958).

48. Michael Braun, "Mike and Elaine: Veracity-Cum-Boffs," *Esquire* 54 (October 1960):204.

49. Another talented young Jewish New Yorker, Allen Konigsberg, was similarly inspired by Nichols and May. As a boy and teenager growing up in Brooklyn, he was drawn to the comic writing of Max Shulman, Robert Benchley, and S. J. Perelman and became an early fan of radio comedians Bob and Ray. After he turned sixteen, Konigsberg changed his name to Woody Allen and began contributing jokes and one-liners to newspaper columnist Earl Wilson. Within a few years Allen was writing material for Herb Shriner and other television and nightclub comics. Together with Larry Gelbart, Allen created parody sketches for an award-winning 1958 *Chevy Show* starring Sid Caesar. With his attraction to parody and "sophisticated" comedy, Allen was understandably enthusiastic about the emergence of Nichols and May. In 1960 he even approached their managers with the idea of supplying them new material for their act. Instead, Rollins and Jaffe convinced him to develop a stand-up nightclub routine of his own. Introduced by Shelley Berman on the stage of New York's Blue Angel in October 1960, Allen auditioned before a small group of approving patrons. A short time later Allen played the Upstairs at the Duplex in Greenwich Village and then a string of hip nightclubs such as St. Louis's Crystal Palace, Chicago's Mister Kelly's, and the hungry i in San Francisco, where his free-form "age-of-anxiety patter" focused mainly on the challenges faced by the late-fifties, sensitive, educated, frustrated, psychoanalytically oriented urban male. By 1963 Allen was regarded by critics as one of America's top "cerebral" comics, the heir apparent to Nichols and May and their fellow Compass alumni. Eric Lax, *Woody Allen* (New York: Alfred A Knopf, 1991), 25–190. For a good example of the praise Allen earned from critics during his early career, see Charles L. Mee, Jr., "On Stage: Woody Allen," *Horizon* 5 (May 1963):46.

50. Michiko Kakutani, "Jules Feiffer," in *The Poet at the Piano: Portraits of Writers, Filmmakers, Playwrights, and Other Artists at Work* (New York: Peter Bedrick Books, 1988):158–59; Jules Feiffer, "Strip-Time: The Comics Observed," in the *Catalogue for the 1986 Festival of Cartoon Art* (Columbus: Ohio State University Libraries, 1986), 7–8; Jules Feiffer, *The Great Comic Book Heroes* (New York: Dial Press, 1965), 189; Jules Feiffer, "Speech before Newspaper Features Council in New York City, October 1988,"

Cartoonist Profiles 82 (June 1989):54–59; Jules Feiffer, "Jerry Siegel: The Minsk Theory of Krypton," *New York Times Magazine,* December 29, 1996, 14–15.

51. Feiffer, *Comic Book Heroes,* 41; Gary Groth, "Memories of a Pro Bono Cartoonist," *Comics Journal* 124 (August 1988):40–43. *Clifford* hints at a certain rebelliousness that Feiffer felt as a youth. Its most amusing episode, from December 31, 1950, parodied *The Spirit.* See this and Robert Fiore's informative preface in Jules Feiffer, *Feiffer: The Collected Works,* vol. 1 (Seattle: Fantagraphic Books, 1988), vii–viii.

52. Jules Feiffer, "The Furious Five," *Civilization* 5 (June/July 1998):73; Jules Feiffer, "Drawing on Experience," *Civilization* 5 (June/July 1998):47. Osborn, as his friend Russell Lynes pointed out, "has never been one to observe too closely the distinction between cartooning and pure [modern] painting." Indeed, Osborn maintained a close connection to New York's postwar art scene. He counted artists such as Alexander Calder and Robert Motherwell among his best friends, and his wife Elodie had been a curator at New York's Museum of Modern Art. Russell Lynes, "The Sight That Music Makes," *Horizon* 4 (May 1962):120.

53. William Steig entered therapy with Wilhelm Reich in the 1930s while Robert Osborn was being saved "from going bonkers" by Carl Jung. Robert Osborn to Charles Nagel, November 9, 1985, RO, box Za, MS 298. Mike Nichols discussed his engagement with psychoanalysis with Terry Gross in a "Fresh Air" broadcast of March 21, 2001, WHYY, Philadelphia.

54. Jules Feiffer, telephone interview by author, tape recording, December 12, 1996.

55. Jules Feiffer, *Sick, Sick, Sick, Village Voice,* May 14, 1958, reprinted in Jules Feiffer, *Feiffer: The Collected Works,* vol. 3 (Seattle: Fantagraphic Books, 1992), 44.

56. Jules Feiffer journal entry, June 11, 1957, JF, Box 23; Belgrad, *The Culture of Spontaneity,* 146–49; C. Wright Mills, *The Sociological Imagination* (New York: Grove Press, 1961), 12; Jules Feiffer, *Sick, Sick, Sick, Village Voice,* March 13, 1957, reprinted in *Feiffer: The Collected Works,* vol. 1, 14.

57. Jules Feiffer, "Couch-as-Couch-Can School of Analysis," *New York Times Magazine,* May 18, 1958, 6–20 and passim. In an October 1961 strip in the *Voice,* Feiffer demonstrated how the drive toward "psychological adjustment" might adversely impact women as much as it did men. Here a housewife stares blankly to the right, allowing readers to enter her thoughts and hear her explain how one day her husband Arnie pointed out that every word she said "sounded *exactly* like my mother." "So he sent me back into analysis and I worked on it for a year." As soon as she thought she was cured, her mind relates, Arnie told her that she sounded "exactly like" her father and then her analyst. "Now it's over six months and every word I say sounds exactly like my husband," she concludes. "Arnie thinks I'm cured." Jules Feiffer, *Feiffer, Village Voice,* October 19, 1961, 1.

58. Jules Feiffer, "Couch-as-Couch-Can School of Analysis," 6–20 and passim; Elaine Tyler May, *Homeward Bound: American Families in the Cold War Era,* 94; Feiffer quoted in Otis L. Guernsey, Jr., *Broadway Song and Story: Playwrights/Lyricists/Composers Discuss Their Hits* (New York: Dodd, Mead & Company, 1985), 381; Jules Feiffer, telephone interview by author, tape recording, December 6, 1996; "The Playboy Panel: Hip Comics and the New Humor," *Playboy* 8 (March 1961):42; Jules Feiffer, "Men Re-

ally Don't Like Women," *Look,* January 11, 1966, 60; Jules Feiffer, "Jerry Siegel," 15; Henry Allen, "Jules Feiffer: The Ever Dissenting Cartoonist at 50: Still Drawing on Bronx Angst," *Washington Post,* November 17, 1979, B1.; For more on the "sexual containment" of the 1950s see Wini Breines, *Young, White, and Miserable: Growing Up Female in the Fifties,* and Betty Friedan, *The Feminine Mystique* (New York: Norton, 1963).

59. As a young man, Jules Feiffer was himself coming to terms with feelings of narcissism and a latent misogynist impulse. "I can't resist attention," he confided to himself in June 1957, "and this has been the cause of hostility between me and at least several young ladies who suddenly found themselves abandoned at parties because I had found a circle . . . It's as if my body is a huge window soaking in light and glaring brightly—bouncing brilliant reflections off its surface." A week after he made this journal entry, Feiffer confessed the "dreary truth" about women: "women either for sex or companionship serve me as void fillers—as seducers of my apathy—and (so far) they have little other reason for being around." This probing self-analysis, coupled with his acute observation of other men, no doubt helped inform the caricatures he created during the period. Jules Feiffer, journal entries, June 4, 1957, June 11, 1957, JF, box 23.

60. Jules Feiffer, "The Age of the Urban Chick," *Playboy* 8 (April 1961):84–85; Jules Feiffer, "The Lover," *Playboy* 7 (July 1960):21.

61. Arthur M. Schlesinger Jr., "The Crisis of American Masculinity," in *The Politics of Hope* (Boston: Houghton Mifflin Company, 1963), 237–46; Barbara Ehrenreich, *The Hearts of Men: American Dreams and the Flight from Commitment* (New York: Anchor Press/Doubleday, 1983), 42–51.

62. Richard Eder, "Jules Feiffer Draws from Both His Anger and Humor," *Los Angeles Times,* November 7, 1982, part 5, pp. 1, 9; Jules Feiffer, *Sick, Sick, Sick, Village Voice,* July 3, 1957, reprinted in *Feiffer: The Collected Works,* vol. 3, 22; Jules Feiffer, "Superman," in *Feiffer's Album* (New York: Random House, 1963), 66–68; Jules Feiffer, "Kept," *Rex* 1 (December 1957):42–48. For examples of Feiffer's caricatures of women see his strips "The Student," *Playboy* 8 (October 1961):123, *Jules Feiffer, New Republic* 145 (July 31 1961):26, and the untitled strips in Jules Feiffer, *Boy, Girl, Boy, Girl* (New York: Signet Books, 1963). For more examples of Feiffer's relationship cartoons from the late 1950s and early 1960s published mainly outside *Playboy,* see *The Unexpurgated Memoirs of Bernard Mergendeiler* (New York: Random House, 1965). Many women critics and writers have accused Feiffer of hating women, particularly after he and Mike Nichols adapted his screenplay *Carnal Knowledge* into a motion picture in 1971. For an ungenerous (and exaggerated) critique of Feiffer's treatment of women over the course of his career see Debra Claire Schwartz, "The Satire of Jules Feiffer: Changing Form and Ideology" (master's thesis, McGill University, 1975).

63. Hugh Hefner to Jules Feiffer, April 16, 1958, and April 30, 1958, JF, box 17. Perhaps the best advice Hefner gave Feiffer early on was for the artist to abandon the idea of trading his trademark hand lettering for type. "It is a very real part of the direct and personal approach that your work has," Hefner remarked to Feiffer, "and it adds considerably to the charm." Hugh Hefner to Jules Feiffer, October 6, 1958, JF, box 17.

64. Robert Muller, "The Disenchanted World of Feiffer," *(London) Daily Mail,* October 12, 1959.

65. Jules Feiffer, *Feiffer, Village Voice,* October 22, 1964, 3.

66. Jules Feiffer, telephone interview by author, tape recording, December 6, 1996.

67. Jules Feiffer, *Jules Feiffer's America: From Eisenhower to Reagan,* ed. Steven Heller (New York: Alfred A. Knopf, 1982), 11.

68. Julius Novick, "Jules Feiffer and the Almost-In-Group," *Harper's* 223 (September 1961):58; Jules Feiffer, *Sick, Sick, Sick, Village Voice,* May 29, 1957, reprinted in *Feiffer: The Collected Works,* vol. 3, 20.

69. Feiffer, *Boy, Girl, Boy, Girl;* Susan M. Black, "Sokolsky, Meet Feiffer," *New Republic* 142 (June 6, 1960):17.

70. Jules Feiffer, *Sick, Sick, Sick, Village Voice,* September 25, 1957, reprinted in *Feiffer: The Collected Works,* vol. 3, 27. Like the Compass Players, Feiffer attempted to demonstrate that consensus values were often bred at home by anxious parents who want their children to "fit in." In several strips dating from the late fifties and early sixties, Feiffer showed fathers instructing their sons on modern America's updated Rules for Life. The key to growing up, one father insisted, entailed "Never expect[ing] too much . . . Never talk[ing] politics," and "Learning to be happy at doing what you don't want to do!" A strip appearing in the *Voice* in 1958 depicted a boy reciting his "What I Believe" composition to his father. Included in the composition's catalogue of virtue — culled, no doubt, from his father's teaching — is the advice to not "get *too* far ahead of your companions *too* quickly" and "Let others give the first opinion." After brooding over his son's propositions, the father states, "I think that's almost it. Why not leave it for a few days and let your mother and me kick it around." Feiffer, *The Explainers,* unpaginated; Jules Feiffer, *Sick, Sick, Sick, Village Voice,* February 19, 1958, reprinted in *Feiffer: The Collected Works,* vol. 3, 37.

71. Feiffer, *Boy, Girl, Boy, Girl,* unpaginated.

72. Jules Feiffer, telephone interview by author, tape recording, December 12, 1996; Jules Feiffer, *Sick, Sick, Sick, Village Voice,* January 15, 1958, and May 7, 1958, reprinted in *Feiffer: The Collected Works,* vol. 3, 35, 43; Feiffer, *The Explainers,* unpaginated.

73. Robert Osborn, *Low & Inside* (New York: Farrar, Strauss & Young, 1953), unpaginated; Robert Osborn, *Osborn on Leisure* (New York: E.R. Squibb & Sons, 1956), 90–92. Osborn originally presented the latter for the 1955 International Design Conference at Aspen, Colorado.

74. Arthur Schlesinger Jr., "The Challenge of Abundance," *Reporter,* 13 (May 3, 1956):8–11; Richard H. Pells *The Liberal Mind in a Conservative Age: American Intellectuals in the 1940s and 1950s,* 117–261; Daniel Horowitz's *Vance Packard and American Social Criticism.* See also John Patrick Diggins, *The Proud Decades* (New York: W. W. Norton & Company, 1988); Fred Siegel, *Troubled Journey: From Pearl Harbor to Ronald Reagan* (New York: Hill and Wang, 1984); and Jackson Lears, "A Matter of Taste: Corporate Cultural Hegemony in a Mass-Consumption Society," in *Recasting America: Culture and Politics in the Age of Cold War,* ed. Lary May, 38–57.

75. Elizabeth Frank, "Jules Feiffer: Articulate Rage," *Art News* 73 (February 1974):

80; George Melly, "The Whole Essence of Feiffer," *Peace News,* January 12, 1962; Robin Brantley, "'Knock, Knock' 'Who's There?' 'Feiffer,'" *New York Times,* May 16, 1976, 192.

76. Faye Hammel, "The World of Jules Feiffer," *Cue* 18 (March 1961):11; "Polk News Plaque Won by 7 Persons," *New York Times,* March 7, 1962, 27.

77. Novick, "Jules Feiffer and the Almost-In-Group," 58; "Oh-So-Sensitive," *Newsweek,* November 13, 1961, 93; "Sick, Sick, Well," *Time,* February 9, 1959, 52; Sam Maloff, "'Give, Give, Give—or Die,' She Said, Expiring," *New York Times Book Review,* June 30, 1963, 4; Russell Lynes, "Jules Feiffer's Wicked Eye and Ear," *Horizon* 4 (November 1961):48, 57; Nat Hentoff, "Jules Feiffer: Holding the Mirror Up to What Nature Has Become," *Mayfair* 32 (September 1958):30.

78. Gilbert Millstein, "You Are His Target," *Saturday Evening Post* 237 (October 3, 1964):38–40.

79. Paul Carroll, "Letter to the Editor," *Village Voice,* June 1, 1961, 4–5.

80. Gore Vidal, "The Unrocked Boat," *Nation* (April 26, 1958):373; Larry Dubois, "Playboy Interview: Jules Feiffer," *Playboy* 18 (September 1971):94; Jules Feiffer, telephone interview by author, tape recording, December 6, 1996; David Segal, "Feiffer, Steinberg, and Others," *Commentary* 32 (July 1961):435.

CHAPTER FIVE

1. Shepherd quoted in Lee Gallup Feldman, "A Brief History of Improvisational Theatre in the United States."; Close quoted in Sweet, *Something Wonderful Right Away,* 43; Del Close, interview by author, tape recording, Chicago, September 11, 1996; "Crystal Palace, St. Louis," *Variety,* October 5, 1960, 69; Coleman, *The Compass,* 235–60. Close challenged (and often lost) audiences with his highly unusual stage material. In one of his favorite bits, he jokingly proselytized "Resistentialism"—a philosophy preoccupied with "the inherent perversity of inanimate objects." Darden, a virtuoso of highbrow parody and verbal Dada, recorded *The Sound of My Own Voice and Other Noises* in 1961.

2. "Park Plaza, St. Louis," *Variety,* August 6, 1958, 211; Theodore Flicker, telephone interview by author, tape recording, May 28, 1999; Jay Landesman, *Rebel without Applause,* 211–28; Brooks Atkinson, "Beat Picnic," *New York Times,* May 13, 1959, 43; Myles Standish, "Stage Is Set for Civic Aid to Creative Theater," *St. Louis Post Dispatch,* May 21, 1963, 3D. See also Marya Mannes, "Hunger for a Grand Theme," *Reporter* 20 (June 11, 1959):35–36.

3. Bernard Asbell, "The Cultural Renaissance: Chapter Two," *Chicago Magazine* 3 (September 1956):46–50; Linda Winer, "Second City Is Still First in Comedy," *New York Times,* August 19, 1979, sec. 2, p. 5; Paul Sills, telephone interview by author, tape recording, June 3, 1999; Bernard Sahlins, telephone interview by author, tape recording, May 22, 1999. Michael Denning highlights the role of Café Society in 1930s Popular Front culture in *The Cultural Front: The Laboring of American Culture in the Twentieth-Century,* 323–28.

4. A. J. Liebling, "Second City," *New Yorker,* January 19, 1952, 33, and January 26, 1952, 36; Joanne Stang, "Alan Arkin: Brooding about How Happy He Is," *New York*

Times, February 28, 1965, sec. 2, p. 3; Coleman, *The Compass,* 253–62.

5. Paul Sills, telephone interview by author, tape recording, June 3, 1999; Charles L. Mee, "The Celebratory Occasion: An Interview with Paul Sills," *Tulane Drama Review* 9 (Winter 1964):177; Duncan quoted in Sweet, *Something Wonderful Right Away,* 54; Andrew Duncan to author, June 27, 1999.

6. Sheldon Patinkin, interview by author, tape recording, Chicago, September 12, 1996; "Centaurs," transcribed scene in unpaginated *Off the Road* binder, SCA; Del Close, interview by author, tape recording, Chicago, September 11, 1996; "Just Rehearsing, Dear," quoted from Lee Gallup Feldman, *A Critical Analysis of Improvisational Theatre in the United States from 1955–1968* (Ph.D. diss., University of Denver, 1969), 140.

7. "First Affair," in *The Second City Revue,* videotape of program produced by the International Telemeter Company, 1961, viewed at SCA; John Beaufort, "Purlie Victorious and Second City," *Christian Science Monitor,* September 30, 1961, 6; The Second City, "Family Reunion," unpublished drama manuscript, MD.

8. "Museum Piece," on *From the Second City* (Mercury, 1961).

9. "Lekathoy," transcribed scene in unpaginated *Alarums and Excursions* binder, SCA.

10. "Fresh Revue of Second City, Chi, Plenty Caustic but Stirs Less Impact," *Variety,* August 2, 1961, 92; "Great Books," on *Comedy From the Second City* (Mercury, 1961).

11. Bowen quoted in Sweet, *Something Wonderful Right Away,* 32; Bruce Cook, "Satirists à la Sartre," *Rogue* 5 (December 1960):28–77 and passim. Even in the songs Second City actors occasionally sang to help bridge different scenes one heard the plaintive cry of the alienated, frightened outsider. In the tune "Everybody's In the Know," for example, a Second City actress admitted, "Everybody's in the know but me ... Everybody seems to know what to do and what to say ... Me, I'm not so sure of myself ... I'm not ready to make my statement yet ... Can you find me a way to go?" *The Second City,* videotape recorded by WFMT, Chicago on March 28, 1961, viewed at SCA. Lyrics also taken from the unpaginated *Third Program* binder, SCA. To appreciate how the quest for authenticity animated the student New Left, see James Miller, *"Democracy Is in the Streets": From Port Huron to the Siege of Chicago* (New York: Simon and Schuster, 1987), and Doug Rossinow, *The Politics of Authenticity: Liberalism, Christianity, and the New Left in America* (New York: Columbia University Press, 1998).

12. "Vend-a-Buddy" cited in Feldman, *A Critical Analysis of Improvisational Theatre in the United States from 1955–1968,* 144–47; "Phono Pal," in *The Second City Revue,* videotape of program produced by the International Telemeter Company, 1961, viewed at SCA; Sand quoted in Sweet, *Something Wonderful Right Away,* 211; "How to Win a Boyfriend," in *The Second City Revue,* videotape of program produced by WNEW-TV, July 31, 1963, New York, viewed at MTR.

13. Paul Sills, telephone interview by author, tape recording, June 3, 1999; Bernard Sahlins, telephone interview by author, tape recording, May 22, 1999; Avery Schreiber, telephone interview by author, tape recording, May 24, 1999; Richard Schaal, telephone interview by author, tape recording, June 3, 1999; Omar Shapli, telephone interview by author, tape recording, May 24, 1999. Many former performers in The Second

City believe that "Peep Show for Conventioneer: Looking for the Action" represented the best work the troupe ever did during its first five years. Professional critics, particularly British critics, were likewise impressed by this scene, even though they were not entirely sure of its meaning. The critic for London's *Daily Express,* for example, stated that it had "more hard things to say about the American way of life than two Mort Sahls or a Lenny Bruce." Quoted in "Liked in London," *New York Daily News,* April 25, 1963.

14. The results of the Feiffer–Second City collaboration were mixed. Along with several critics, even Feiffer doubted whether his cartoons really worked onstage. Mike Nichols, on the other hand, was so impressed with it that he began to make preparations for a similar production in New York, one which would include musical accompaniment by Stephen Sondheim. In the end, Feiffer balked. Feiffer did, however, see his *Crawling Arnold* staged at Gian-Carlo Menotti's Festival of Two Worlds at Spoleto, Italy, in the summer of 1961. Jules Feiffer, telephone interview with author, tape recording, December 6, 1996. For more on Feiffer and *The Explainers,* see "Pied Feiffer," *Time,* May 26, 1961, 42, 44; and Jerry Demuth, "The Explainers," *Village Voice,* June 25, 1961, 11.

15. Theodore Flicker, telephone interview by author, tape recording, May 28, 1999. In addition to this core group, The Premise over the next several years employed Gene Hackman, George Morrison, Al Mancini, Sandy Baron, Francis Dux, and several other professional actors.

16. John Crosby, "Tolerance in the Sticks," *New York Herald Tribune,* March 8, 1961, 25; *Playgram,* March 1961, The Premise program folder, BRT; Judith Crist, "'Instant Theater' for Off-Broadway," *New York Herald Tribune,* November 20, 1960, sec. 4, p. 2; Theodore Flicker, *The Premise—Rough Draft,* undated manuscript, p. 10, TFC, box 1; "Teenage Fantasy," described in Feldman, *A Critical Analysis of Improvisational Theatre in the United States from 1955–1968,* 116–17.

17. Bamber Gascoigne, "American Quartet," *Spectator* 209 (August 3, 1962):159; "The Chess Story," on *Off Broadway: The Premise* (Vanguard, 1961); Nat Hentoff, "Instant Theater," *Reporter* 24 (March 30, 1961):46–47.

18. Jerry Talmer, "'Premise Actress," *New York Post,* December 7, 1962, 55. Elaine May, a woman who dated and married several prominent psychoanalysts, was one of the many improvisational performers who maintained close personal connections with modern-day, Freudian psychiatry.

19. Nat Hentoff, "The Relevance of Irreverence," *Reporter* 27 (November 22, 1962):44, 46. Compass founder David Shepherd had similar reservations over the psychoanalytic orientation of the late Compass and its descendents. As he explained to playwright Jeffrey Sweet, he believed that too many of these performers were "living out their liberation from their families. They were in analysis and they were using the stage of The Compass to liberate themselves from a whole lot of shit they had fallen into." Shepherd quoted in Sweet, *Something Wonderful Right Away,* 6.

20. When Feiffer explained his cartooning technique for the March 1961 *Playboy* panel on the "Hip Comics and the New Humor," he claimed that his own strip creations were like improvisations on paper. Indeed, as John Hollander noted in the *New York Review of Books,* Feiffer produced "'routines' . . . more like dramatic improvisations

than cartoon strips . . ." "The Playboy Panel: Hip Comics and the New Humor," *Playboy* 8 (March 1961):42; John Hollander, "Sick Hix in Pix," *New York Review of Books* 1 (February 25, 1963).

21. Belgrad, *The Culture of Spontaneity*, 1–40; Banes, *Greenwich Village 1963: Avant-Garde Performance and the Effervescent Body*, 156–57; Sweet, *Something Wonderful Right Away*, 265–66; Jeanette A. Sarkisian, "Director by Instinct," *Chicago Daily News-Chicago Life Magazine*, August 12, 1961, 12–14. For another consideration of improvisation's key place within America's postwar popular arts, see W. T. Lhamon, Jr., *Deliberate Speed: The Origins of a Cultural Style in the American 1950s*.

22. Belgrad, *The Culture of Spontaneity*, 142–56; Flicker quoted in Rocco Landesman, "Interview: Ted Flicker," 71.

23. Harris quoted in Coleman, *The Compass*, 289–90.

24. Viola Spolin, *Improvisation for the Theater: A Handbook of Teaching and Directing Techniques* (Evanston: Northwestern University Press, 1963), 3–13 and passim.

25. Feiffer, *Jules Feiffer's America*, 12.

26. Liner notes, *Off Broadway: The Premise*.

27. Arkin quoted in Sweet, *Something Wonderful Right Away*, 225; Theodore Flicker, telephone interview by author, tape recording, May 28, 1999; Liner notes, *Off Broadway: The Premise*.

28. *The Premise*, tape recorded performance, March 25, 1961, New York, TFC; "A Place in the Sun," on *Off Broadway: The Premise*; Feldman, *A Critical Analysis of Improvisational Theatre in the United States from 1955–1968*, 70.

29. Louis Calta, "Theatre: Strange Doings," *New York Times*, November 23, 1960, sec. 1, p. 22. Walter Kerr similarly asked in opening night review, "Why insist on improvising . . . so much of the time when you can consolidate your gains by trimming and tightening until you get the thing right?" Walter Kerr, "First Night Report: 'The Premise,'" *New York Herald Tribune*, November 23, 1960, 12.

30. Feldman, *A Critical Analysis of Improvisational Theatre in the United States from 1955–1968*, 65. The Premise's dedication to true improvisation is a matter of some disagreement among former Premise actors. According to Garry Goodrow, an actor hired for a Premise replacement cast, he was actually handed a script for the scenes in which he would appear. Garry Goodrow, telephone interview by author, tape recording, June 9, 1999.

31. Charles Marowitz, "False Premises and Doubtful Propositions," *Village Voice*, August 9, 1962, 7; Theodore Flicker to David Dorsen, June 13, 1962, TFC, box 3, Premise correspondence folder. One British critic compared The Premise to a contrived magic act. "One is so busy trying to spot hidden pouches and rabbity bulges in their technique," this critic wrote, "that one doesn't enjoy the sketches as uninhibitedly as one would if they were frankly rehearsed." Roger Gellert, "No Kidding," *New Statesman*, August 3, 1962, 154–55.

32. Bowen has even dismissed improvisation—unfairly—as a "mindless" cult. Looking back on Second City improvisations, Bowen remarks,

> It's very rare that you get something that, in addition to being funny and displaying virtuosity, also makes some kind of statement, has some point of view. You could listen to

tapes of hundreds and hundreds of spot improvs and maybe once or twice the actors would stumble on something that was beautifully pointed and had something to say. When you look for the heavyweight stuff, you look in the prepared scenes where someone began with a good idea (Bowen quoted in Sweet, *Something Wonderful Right Away,* 36–38).

Although he had much greater faith in improvisation than his colleague, even Del Close has admitted that the "democratic mess" of collaborative improvisation cannot yield the type of "synoptic vision" necessary in cogent satire. Del Close, interview by author, tape recording, Chicago, September 11, 1996.

33. Duncan quoted in Lee Gallup Feldman, *A Critical Analysis of Improvisational Theatre in the United States from 1955–1968,* 72.

34. "Instant Theater," *Newsweek,* June 26, 1961, 60; Andrew Sarris, "A View from under the Bridge," *Village Voice,* August 13, 1964, 11.

35. Stanley Green, "Overture: American Musical Revues," in *Musical Theatre in America,* ed. Glenn Loney (Westport, Conn.: Greenwood Press, 1984), 143–48; Leonard Sillman, "Who Said the Revue Is Dead?" *Theatre Arts* 45 (March 1961):17–19, 76; Nancy Walker, "Bring On the Comedians," *Theatre Arts* 43 (October 1959):58–60; Charles Winick, *Taste and the Censor in Television* (New York: Fund for the Republic, 1959), 10; Arthur and Barbara Gelb, "'On the Town' with Comden and Green," *New York Times Magazine,* December 11, 1960, 39, 61–71; *Popular Arts: Betty Comden and Adolph Green,* transcript of an interview conducted by R. C. and J. Franklin for the Oral History Research Office at Columbia University, 1959.

36. John Crosby, "Celebrations and Coffee," *New York Herald Tribune,* January 30, 1961, 13.

37. Robert Hatch, "Theatre," *Nation* 193 (October 14, 1961):254–55; Julius Novick, "The Improvisation Bit," *Nation* 203 (December 5, 1966):613

38. F. H., "Satire's the Thing," *Cue* 32 (May 11, 1963):12

39. Jean Martin, "Letter from Chicago," *Nation* 190 (May 14, 1960):429.

40. One of the more curious sideline activities engaged in by Second City performers was fashion modeling. In the summer of 1963, Ann Alder and Sally Hart helped model the latest fashions in beach, sports, and city wear. Their colleague Dick Schaal provided the fashion commentary. A year later, Omar Shapli and David Steinberg participated in *Playboy* magazine's annual back-to-school fashion shoot.

41. Andrew Duncan to author, July 30, 1999.

42. Although he told his backers and former associates such as George Segal that The Premise was barely breaking even, Flicker made windfall profits from his satiric entertainment—enough, in fact, to support purchases of rare antique automobiles and a new venture in filmmaking. Flush with success, Flicker in 1962 appeared worried that The Premise was in danger of "selling out." In a letter to Buck Henry he warned that "the big shinney [sic] commercial world would make us rich and temporarily successful. They would exploit us without extracting the core of the truth of what we would say or do." Six months later, however, he proposed to Bernard Sahlins and Paul Sills that they join him in forming an improvisational theater cartel. "Money, money, money, money, money," Flicker wrote his counterparts at The Second City. "I think it's there in

large quantities for both of us if we get smart." Since there is a "drain" on talent, he suggested, The Second City and Premise ought to "divide up the country with a Premise here, a Second City there." Theodore Flicker to Paul Sills and Bernard Sahlins, June 9, 1962, TFC, box 3, Premise correspondence folder. Sahlins has in recent years earned the enmity of people who believe he turned The Second City into a little more than a spawning ground for television and film comedians. On this occasion, however, Sahlins wisely resisted Flicker, sarcastically encouraging him with the words "young man, go forth. The country is yours." Bernard Sahlins to Theodore Flicker, n.d., TFC, box 3, Premise correspondence folder.

43. Ronald Bergan, *Beyond the Fringe . . . and Beyond: A Critical Biography of Alan Bennett, Peter Cook, Jonathan Miller and Dudley Moore* (London: Virgin, 1989), 1–20; Steven Watts, "Four on 'Fringe,'" *New York Times,* October 21, 1962, sec. 2, p. 3; Christopher Hitchens, "Kings of Comedy," *Vanity Fair* 58 (December 1995):94. See also Humphrey Carpenter, *A Great, Silly Grin: The British Satire Boom of the 1960s* (New York: Public Affairs, 2000).

44. Kenneth Tynan, "English Satire Advances into the Sixties," *(London) Observer,* May 14, 1961, Weekend Review, p. 27. Tynan had previously become an enthusiastic supporter of satirical cabaret when he lived in the United States, the place he called "the prime incubator of nonconformist night club wit." While serving as interim drama critic for the *New Yorker* during 1959 and early 1960, Tynan had witnessed performances by Nichols and May, The Second City, and other American satirists. Shortly after returning to London, Tynan informed *Observer* readers (many of whom were then enjoying the syndicated strip of Jules Feiffer) that compared with the United States Britain lacked "a place in which intelligent, like-minded people can spend a cheap evening listening to forthright cabaret that is socially, sexually, and politically pungent." "Where else but in a small room, late at night, before an audience more notable for its mind than its money," he asked, "can the true satirist—whether writer or performer or both—practice his art and polish his weapons?" Kenneth Tynan, "Dead Spot in Drama," *London Observer,* October 23, 1960, 26. For further background on Kenneth Tynan and changes in postwar British theater, see Charles Marowitz, Tom Milne, and Owen Hale, eds., *New Theatre Voices of the Fifties and Sixties: Selections from* Encore *Magazine* (London: Eyre Methuen, 1981); Kenneth Tynan, *Tynan Right and Left: Plays, Films, People, Places and Events* (New York: Atheneum, 1967); and Charles Marowitz, *Burnt Bridges: A Souvenir of the Swinging Sixties and Beyond* (Toronto: Hodder & Stoughton, 1990). Perceptive critiques of Tynan are available in Alfred Kazin, "Tynan's Stages," *Reporter* 24 (March 30, 1961):51–53; and Robert Brustein, *Dumbocracy in America: Studies in the Theatre of Guilt, 1987–1994* (Chicago: Ivan R. Dee, 1994), 225–30.

45. Harry Thompson, *Peter Cook: A Biography* (London: Hodder & Stoughton, 1997), 121; Bergan, *Beyond the Fringe,* 38–44, 242–45; Nicholas Luard, "The Man Who Lit a Bonfire," in *Something Like Fire: Peter Cook Remembered,* ed. Lin Cook (London: Methuen, 1996), 39–50; William North Jayne, "The Fringe Generation," *Esquire* 58 (October 1962):48–49.

46. Christopher Hitchens and Joseph Heller, "Heller's Version," in *Something Like Fire,* 78–79. For others such as future Monty Python members Eric Idle and Michael

Palin, witnessing The Fringe perform was a cathartic experience. "It was as if I had suddenly woken up and found that everything that had been oppressing me, restricting me, terrifying me, was now joyously, liberatingly funny," Idle remembers. "It is not easy nowadays," Palin comments about his first brush with The Fringe, "to convey the sensational audacity, the explosively liberating effect of hearing the prime minister of the day impersonated, or judges, bishops, police chiefs and army officers mocked." Eric Idle, "The Funniest Man in the World," in *Something Like Fire,* 139; Michael Palin, "I Had That Peter Cook in the Back of My Car," in *Something Like Fire,* 213. Other chroniclers of British life during the sixties corroborate these descriptions of satire's impact. According to Christopher Booker and Ronald Bergen, the irreverent, dissenting mood whipped up by The Fringe, The Establishment Club, and *Private Eye* "marked a new stage in [Britain's] social revolution" and "started the ball of the Permissive Society rolling." Christopher Booker, *The Neophiliacs: A Study of the Revolution in English Life in the Fifties and Sixties* (London: Collins, 1969), 165; Bergan, *Beyond the Fringe,* 24. For other descriptions of the Anglo-American "satire boom," see Bernard Levin, *The Pendulum Years: Britain and the Sixties* (London: Jonathan Cape, 1971), 321–24; Bernard Hollowood, "This Is the Satire That Is," *New York Times Magazine,* July 7, 1963, 13, 34–36; and Roger Wilmut, *From Fringe to Flying Circus* (London: Eyre Methuen, 1980).

47. Determined that he would produce his own "satire" on Broadway, Merrick first approached Second City's Bernard Sahlins in January 1960. He finally succeeded in bringing a satiric revue, Joan Littlewood's *Oh What a Lovely War,* to the mainstream American theater in late 1964.

48. Like many people associated with satiric cabarets and revues of the early 1960s, Peter Cook's American partner, John Krimsky, had an appreciation for Bertolt Brecht. In 1933, he staged the first American production of *The Threepenny Opera.*

49. Description of "Civil War" taken from The Fringe's appearance on *The Jack Paar Show,* NBC, March 1, 1963, videotape viewed at MTR; Howard Taubman, "The Theatre: Satire as a Silver Lining," *New York Times,* October 29, 1962, 36.

50. Harold Clurman, "Theatre," *Nation* 195 (November 17, 1962):334; Robert Brustein, "The Healthiness of Sick Comedy," *New Republic* 147 (December 15, 1962):28–30. Because both The Fringe and Establishment aimed a greater majority of their material at conventional politics, rather than alienation and male-female relationships, a number of critics credited them for being more "adult" and daring than their American counterparts. "There is no point in even shopping for comparisons," *Commonweal's* Richard Gilman declared, "we have been left abysmally behind, 'Second City,' 'Premise' and the rest." Richard Gilman, "When the Real Thing Comes Along," *Commonweal* 77 (November 16, 1962):201. See also Stephen P. Ryan, "Beyond the Fringe," *Catholic World* 197 (April 1963):75–76; "John Bull's Eye," *Newsweek,* November 12, 1962, 62; Anthony West, "Theater: For Laughs," *Show* 3 (January 1963):24–25; Henry Hewes, "Unstrung Quartet," *Saturday Review of Literature* 45 (November 17, 1962):48; "Openings: New York," *Theatre Arts* 46 (December 1962):10–11; "High Imp Quotient," *Time,* November 9, 1962, 64; and Kenneth Tynan, "Quartet with a Touch of Brass," *Holiday* 30 (November 1962):127–32. Further information about Jonathan Miller and his post-

Fringe career is available in Michael Romain, *A Profile of Jonathan Miller* (New York: Cambridge University Press, 1992).

51. Nancy Walker, "Bring On the Comedians," 58–60; H. E. F. Donohue, "After Dark Satire Goes to Town," *Horizon* 4 (January 1962):66. See also "Intimate and Topical Humor," *Life,* April 7, 1961, 92a–94. Nightclub owners found the idea of staging revues particularly attractive since television had driven the cost of hiring big-name acts beyond what they could afford. With performers such as Dinah Shore asking $10,000 a week, club owners had a hard time making a profit. Therefore, Chicago nightclub owners Oscar and George Marienthal began cashing in on the new cabaret craze with an upscale Rush Street theater called the Happy Medium. With material partially adapted from successful New York revues, the Marienthals, director William Penn, and performers such as Jerry Stiller and Anne Meara, the Happy Medium ran a series of successful, though reportedly tame, productions including *Medium Rare, Put It in Writing* and *3 Cheers for the Tired Businessman.* Beginning in 1960, not far from the future locations of The Premise and Square East's Second City, Phase 2, Take 3, and the Village Showplace began presenting low-budget satiric revues to New York audiences. Performers from Take 3's *Stewed Prunes*—Lynda Segal, MacIntyre Dixon, and Richard Libertini—received such wide acclaim that they were soon hired to become members of the better-known Second City troupe. Further west, satiric revues received warm welcomes at St. Louis's Crystal Palace (*New Directions 1960,* billed as "a wry look at our fashionable world") and at the San Francisco nightclub the Purple Onion (*The Macaroni Show*). In Washington, D.C., Arch Lustberg, a drama instructor at Catholic University, recruited a research mathematician and two housewives for a troupe he called The Uniquecorn. Throughout 1961 and 1962, Lustberg's group performed irreverent revue material in the upper level of a Georgetown bar. Joining The Uniquecorn on M Street were two more, although less notable, revues: The Subcommittee Room and Chez Nous. Henry Hewes, "Fresh Grounds for Theatre," *Theatre Arts* 45 (April 1961):20, 22; "Capital Laps Up Political Satire," *Business Week* 1692 (February 3, 1962):26–27; Happy Medium Theater Programs, Chicago Historical Society, Chicago; William Leonard, "Theatre USA: Chicago," *Theatre Arts* 45 (February 1961):24–72 and passim.

52. A trained pianist, Monk began working in several of the most elite nightclubs in New York and Europe during the 1930s. In the early 1940s he began working as the entertainment director for the modish New York nightclub, Le Ruban Bleu. There he directed Imogene Coca and other performers in parodic and topical sketch material.

53. "Mr. Monk and the Numbers Game," *Show Magazine* 4 (November 1964):38; "The Madness Upstairs," *Newsweek,* October 10, 1960, 93; James Gavin, *Intimate Nights: The Golden Age of New York Cabaret* (New York: Grove Weidenfeld, 1991), 152–170, 201–26, 267–72.

54. "The Monk Stamp," *Newsweek,* January 20, 1964, 57; "Mr. Monk and the Numbers Game," 38–41, 98, 101; Arthur Gelb, "Cabaret Theatres Take on Broadway Look," *New York Times,* October 13, 1960, 40; "That Rumpus Upstairs," *Newsweek,* October 5, 1959, 58; "Julius Monk Gets Job at the Plaza," *New York Times,* May 17, 1962, 31; Julius

Monk, introduction to *Baker's Dozen* (New York: Random House, 1964), xiii; Monk quoted in Gavin, *Intimate Nights,* 203.

55. Eugene Boe, "Some Measured Pleasures," *Cue* 32 (December 14, 1963):58; Judith Crist, "A Revue for Relaxing and Smiling" *New York Herald Tribune,* December 4, 1963, 19; Richard F. Shepard, "Humor in 'Twice Over Nightly' Offers an Offbeat View of Life," *New York Times,* December 4, 1963, 53.

CHAPTER SIX

1. "Second City Reunion," *Cue* 31 (27 January 1962):11; Harold Clurman, "Theatre," *Nation* 192 (June 10, 1961):504. References and comparisons to the editorial pages of mainstream newspapers were not uncommon in critics' praise of The Second City and its cohort. Critic Emory Lewis appreciated Premise actors because they were people "who actually read the editorial pages of the newspapers." "At their best," John Crosby likewise wrote of The Premise in 1961, "these are marvelous editorial expressions of opinion, some of them freer and more lucid and certainly more liberal than you'll find in your local newspaper." Emory Lewis, "The Good, the Bad, and the Awful," *Cue* 32 (April 27, 1963):15; Crosby, "Theater: Revues on the Fringe," 6–7.

2. Although commentators never mentioned Charlie Chaplin in conjunction with McCarthyism and its effects on humor, it is worth noting that America's foremost comedic star during the first half of the twentieth century was himself a casualty of red-baiting. After being hounded by J. Edgar Hoover and the FBI, Chaplin was effectively deported in 1952 through the auspices of the United States Immigration and Natural-ization Service.

3. Richard Strout, "Foe of the Bon Mot: Politics," *New York Times Magazine,* April 22, 1956, 13–58 and passim; T. V. Smith, "Serious Problem of Campaign Humor," *New York Times Magazine,* September 28, 1952, 53. Historian Daniel Wickberg has demonstrated that the idea that humor could find legitimate use within the serious, complex realm of politics only began to gain currency during the early decades of the twentieth century. During this period, writers such as Finley Peter Dunne, Will Rogers, and H. L. Mencken delighted a large audience of Americans with their satirical treat-ment of politicians and their programs. By the 1930s, the idea that humor and the sense of humor were key ingredients in the conduct and preservation of American democ-racy found a voice in sources ranging from President Franklin Roosevelt—a politician well-known for his wit—to popular periodicals such as *Harper's.* Daniel Wickberg, *Senses of Humor: Self and Laughter in Modern America* (Ithaca: Cornell University Press, 1997), 196–206. See also Joseph Boskin, "American Political Humor: Touchables and Taboos," in *The Humor Prism in Twentieth-Century America,* ed. Joseph Boskin (Detroit: Wayne State University Press, 1997), 71–85.

4. Stevenson quote in Gladwin Hill, "'New' Stevenson Using Old Jokes," *New York Times,* May 20, 1956, 1; and Leon A. Harris, *The Fine Art of Political Wit* (New York: E. P. Dutton & Co., 1964), 248–50. For further examples and analyses of Stevenson's wit, see Bessie R. James and Mary Waterstreet eds., *Adlai's Almanac: The Wit and Wisdom of Stevenson of Illinois* (New York: Henry Schuman, 1952); Bill Adler, *The Stevenson Wit*

(Garden City, N.J.: Doubleday, 1966); Wilma H. Grimes, *A Theory of Humor for Public Address* (Ph.D. diss., University of Illinois, 1953); Mary Emily Hannah, *A Comparative Study of the Uses of Humor in Selected Political Speeches of Abraham Lincoln and Adlai E. Stevenson* (Ph.D. diss., University of Illinois, 1967).

5. Quoted in "No Laughter, Please," *Reporter* 12 (February 10, 1955):2–3.

6. Harris, *The Fine Art of Political Wit,* 223–24; Leonard C. Lewin, ed., *Treasury of American Political Humor* (New York: Delacorte Press, 1964), 19; Arthur Schlesinger Jr., "Comedy: Has She a Future?" *Show Magazine* 3 (May 1963):23; Arthur P. Dudden, *The Assault of Laughter,* 35; Malcolm Muggeridge, "America Needs a Punch," *Esquire* 49 (April 1958):59–61. For more on the predicament of American political humor during the 1950s, see Arthur Dudden's "Record of Political Humor," *American Quarterly* 37 (Spring 1985):50–70, and Henry Carlisle Jr.'s introduction to his anthology *American Satire in Prose and Verse* (New York: Random House, 1962).

7. James Thurber, "The Case for Comedy," *Atlantic* 206 (November 1960):98; Kenneth Rexroth, "The Decline of American Humor," *Nation* 184 (April 27, 1957):376. For more of Thurber's views on humor's predicament see also Henry Brandon, "Everybody Is Getting Very Serious: A Conversation with James Thurber," *New Republic* 138 (26 May 1958):11–16.

8. Clayton Fritchey, "A Politician Must Watch His Wit," *New York Times Magazine,* July 3, 1960, 8, 30–31; Roscoe Drummond, "What Makes Ike Laugh?" *Collier's,* January 8, 1954, 15–19; Seymour Topping, "Premier Shows Proverbial Wit," *New York Times,* September 24, 1959, 23.

9. Eric Goldman, "Good-by to the 'Fifties—And Good Riddance," *Harper's Magazine* 220 (January 1960):27–29.

10. Margaret Halsey, "Beware the Tender Trap," *New Republic* 138 (January 13, 1958):7–9; Gore Vidal, "The Unrocked Boat," *Nation* (April 26, 1958):371–73. *Visit to a Small Planet,* a lark involving a space alien who lands on Earth and is confronted with the lunacy of war and the military, may have appeared somewhat daring with its jokes aimed at the military and the follies of earthlings, but it pulled many of its punches. Several months after it opened on Broadway, Vidal explained that he had been forced to extract his play's "sharper (and not always carious) teeth." In order to "protect" his play, an eight-thousand-dollar investment, he had "deliberately dull[ed] the edge of the satire . . . obscured meanings, softened blows, and humbly turned wrath aside." Gore Vidal, "Putting On 'Visit to a Small Planet,'" in *Rocking the Boat* (Boston: Little, Brown and Company, 1962), 268–72.

11. Pierce Fredericks, "The Cartoonist's Bite," *Saturday Review of Literature* 40 (November 23, 1957):1; "The Hell-Raisers," *Time,* April 28, 1958, 66; Bill Mauldin to Robert Lasch, February 24, 1958, BM, box 6, general correspondence.

12. "In War and Peace," *Time,* September 26, 1960, 49; "Hit It If It's Big," *Time,* July 21, 1961, 50–54; Jack Star, "The Idea Factory," *Look,* July 30, 1963, 71–73.

13. Mauldin quoted in John Kuenster, "The Responsible Editorial Cartoonist," *Voice of St. Jude* (March 1961):10; Bill Mauldin, foreword to his *What's Got Your Back Up?* unpaginated.

14. Mauldin, *What's Got Your Back Up?* 13.

15. Mauldin, *What's Got Your Back Up?* 73, 9, 33; Bill Mauldin cartoons nos. 1423–1428, B Size, BMC.

16. Vidal, "The Unrocked Boat," 371; Thurber, "On the Brink of Was," *New York Times Magazine,* December 7, 1958, 26; "Mort Sahl: The Loyal Opposition," broadcast by PBS, September 18, 1989, and viewed at Motion Picture and Television Reading Room, MBRS; "Interview with Mort Sahl," *Fresh Air,* broadcast on WHYY radio, Philadelphia, December 23, 2003.

17. Kenneth Allsop, "Those American Sickniks," *Twentieth Century* 170 (July 1961): 101; Jonathan Miller, "Can English Satire Draw Blood?" *London Observer,* October 1, 1961, 21. For more on the impact of Sahl's early sallies, see Enrico Banducci's liner notes for Mort Sahl, *Mort Sahl at the hungry i* (Verve, 1960).

18. Sahl quoted in Eric Lax, *Woody Allen* (New York: Alfred A Knopf, 1991), 138; Sahl quoted in "An Impolite Interview with Mort Sahl," *Realist* 43 (September 1963):20. So vexed was Sahl that the *Hollywood Close-Up* had called him a communist that he successfully sued the publication for libel.

19. Mort Sahl, *Heartland* (New York: Harcourt Brace Jovanovich, 1976), 150; "Interview with Mort Sahl"; Gerald Nachman, "Mort Sahl: Smiting Hip and Thigh," *New York Post,* November 21, 1965, Mort Sahl Clipping File, BRT; Pierre Berton, "Mort Sahl," in *Voices from the Sixties: Twenty-Two Views of a Revolutionary Decade* (Garden City, N.Y.: Doubleday & Company, 1967), 103–108.

20. Sahl, *Heartland,* 10–11; Joe Hyams, "Beat Generation Defined," *New York Herald Tribune,* July 11, 1958, 10; Nate Hokum, liner notes for Mort Sahl, *Mort Sahl 1960 or Look Forward in Anger* (Verve, 1959).

21. Sahl quoted in Lax, *Woody Allen,* 139. It is important to keep in mind that to some within the entertainment industry, Sahl's choice of casual attire represented a serious breach of etiquette. After the owner of the Black Orchid in Chicago hired Sahl in 1954, he required that Sahl wear a tuxedo. Sahl refused to follow his mandate. The owner told Sahl that he had "no class" and then instructed him that he could only enter his establishment through the kitchen. Sahl's tenure at the Black Orchid was, not surprisingly, brief. Sahl, *Heartland,* 19; Irv Kupcinet, *Kup's Chicago* (Cleveland: World Publishing Company, 1962), 77.

22. Allen quoted in Lax, *Woody Allen,* 138.

23. Rolf Malcolm, "A Real Free-Form Guy," *Playboy* 4 (June 1957):50; Herb Caen, liner notes to Mort Sahl, *The Future Lies Ahead* (Verve, 1958).

24. "Impolite Interview with Mort Sahl," 27.

25. Joe Hyams, "Beat Generation Defined," *New York Herald Tribune,* July 11, 1958, 10; John Springer Associates, "Biography of Mort Sahl," Mort Sahl clipping file, BRT; John Weaver, "San Francisco: Hungry i," *Holiday* 29 (April 1961):125–38 and passim; Joe Hyams, "Mort Sahl Explains Mort Sahl," *New York Herald Tribune,* February 8, 1960, 13; Mort Sahl, "Mort Sahl on Hollywood: It Isn't Even Evil," *Look* 26 (September 25, 1962), 54d; Sahl quoted in Marrie Torre, "Marrie Torre Reports," *New York Herald Tribune,* April 5, 1960, 33.

26. "Impolite Interview with Mort Sahl," 27; Sahl, *At the hungry i;* Mort Sahl, *A Way*

of Life (Verve, 1959); Miller, "Can English Satire Draw Blood?" 21; Mort Sahl, *The Next President* (Verve, 1960).

27. Sahl quoted in Malcolm, "A Real Free-Form Guy," 54; Sahl quoted in William Zinsser, "American Humor, 1966," *Horizon* 8 (Spring 1966):117; Mort Sahl, *Mort Sahl on Relationships* (Reprise, 1961).

28. Walter Kerr, "The Next President," *New York Herald Tribune,* April 10, 1958, 19; John Crosby, "The Sacred Cows," *New York Herald Tribune,* April 16, 1958, sec. 2, p. 1.

29. Robert Legare, "Hip Wits Disc Hits," *Playboy* 7 (September 1960):83; Alfred Bester, "Mort Sahl: The Hip Young Man," *Holiday* 24 (September 1958):91, 100–102; Robert Rice, "The Fury," *New Yorker,* July 30, 1960, 31–52 and passim; Nat Hentoff, "Iconoclast in the Nightclub," *Reporter* 18 (January 9, 1958):35–36.

30. Playboy *Jazz Festival Yearbook* (Chicago: Playboy Jazz Festivals, 1959), 35; "Playboy Club News," *Playboy* 8 (December 1961):39.

31. Mort Sahl, *The Future Lies Ahead;* Mort Sahl, *At the Sunset* (Fantasy, 1958); Mort Sahl, liner notes to *The Future Lies Ahead.*

32. Tim Taylor, "After Dark," *Cue* 28 (September 5, 1959):39; "An Impolite Interview with Henry Morgan," *Realist* 19 (July–August 1960):14.

33. Bob Salmaggi, "Mort Sahl Makes It Big," *New York Herald Tribune,* January 17, 1960, sec. 9, p. 3. The phenomenon of audience members flattering themselves by picking up on Sahl's jokes was widely noted during the 1950s and early 1960s. It appears true that in a nightclub audience packed with hip, well-informed patrons, one withheld laughter at Sahl's esoteric jabs at one's own peril. Listening to recordings of Sahl performances from the period, one often detects an unmistakable delay between Sahl's delivery and the response of audience members.

34. Throughout 1960, Sahl's allegiance to Stevenson occasionally put him at odds with people aligned with the Kennedy campaign. When Sahl cohosted his freewheeling program on the presidential conventions in 1960, he was suddenly interrupted on the air by his sponsor Bart Lytton, a prominent Los Angeles banker and Democratic Party contributor, who reportedly charged Sahl by saying "I'm not running a Stevenson rally." Sahl, *Heartland,* 84.

35. Sahl, *Heartland,* 80; Arthur Gelb, "Sahl Cooking with Less Pepper," *New York Times,* June 7, 1961, 47.

36. Sahl quoted in Salmaggi, "Mort Sahl Makes It Big," 3; Sahl, *The Next President;* Sahl quoted in Tony Hendra, "Politicos: The Tonight Show . . . and Other Political Platforms," in *Stand Up Comedians on Television* (New York: Harry N. Abrams, 1996), 93; Stevenson quoted in Charles Grutzner, "Stevenson Calls Campaign Urgent," *New York Times,* October 18, 1960, sec. 1, pp. 1, 31.

37. Gore Vidal, "The Best Man," *Theatre Arts* 45 (September 1961):27; Gore Vidal, "Notes on 'The Best Man,'" *Theatre Arts* 44 (July 1960):8–9; Gore Vidal, *Palimpsest: A Memoir* (New York: Random House, 1995), 334–54; Fred Kaplan, *Gore Vidal: A Biography* (New York: Doubleday, 1999), 463–79. Ira Henry Freeman, "The Playwright, the Lawyer and the Voters," *New York Times,* September 15, 1960, sec. 1, p. 20. Like Bill

Mauldin four years earlier, Vidal lost his bid for a Congressional seat in the heavily Republican upstate New York.

38. Vidal quoted in Kaplan, *Gore Vidal,* 482. Ronald Brownstein thoroughly addresses John Kennedy's connections with Hollywood celebrities such as Frank Sinatra in *The Power and the Glitter: The Hollywood-Washington Connection* (New York: Pantheon Books, 1990), 141–74. Vidal was related to John Kennedy through Kennedy's wife Jackie, with whom shared he shared the same stepfather.

39. Arthur Schlesinger Jr., "The New Mood in Politics," reprinted in *The Politics of Hope* (Boston: Houghton Mifflin Company, 1963), 81–86.

40. According to comedian Jerry Lewis, Kennedy once even turned to him for advice on how he might add some humor to his prepared speech. See Jerry Lewis with Herb Gluck, *Jerry Lewis, In Person* (New York: Atheneum, 1982), 237–49.

41. Theodore C. Sorensen, *Kennedy* (New York: Harper & Row, 1965), 63; Kennedy quoted in Rowland Evans, "That Wit in the White House," *Saturday Evening Post,* September 2, 1961, 52.

42. Evans, "That Wit in the White House," 52; Gerald C. Gardner, *All the Presidents' Wits: The Power of Presidential Humor* (New York: Beech Tree Books, 1986), 209–58; Gerald C. Gardner, *Campaign Comedy: Political Humor from Clinton to Kennedy* (Detroit: Wayne State University Press, 1994), 269–79; Timothy G. Smith, ed., *Merriman Smith's Book of Presidents* (New York: W. W. Norton & Company, 1972), 130; Gene Graham quoted in Pierre Salinger and Sander Vanocur, eds., *A Tribute to John F. Kennedy* (Chicago: Encyclopedia Britannica, 1964), 88; Arthur Hoppe, *Having a Wonderful Time: My First Half Century as a Newspaperman* (San Francisco: Chronicle Books, 1995), 13.

43. William S. White, "Humor in Politics," *Harper's* 220 (February 1960):97–102; Merriman Smith, "Lament for the Campaign Joke," *New York Times Magazine,* April 3, 1960, 78; Kathleen Hall Jamison, *Packaging the Presidency: A History and Criticism of Presidential Campaign Advertising,* 3d ed. (New York: Oxford University Press, 1996), 129.

44. Richard N. Goodwin, *Remembering America: A Voice from the Sixties* (Boston: Little, Brown and Company, 1988), 104–105; Sorensen, *Kennedy,* 177; Kennedy quoted in W. Gail Hudson, *The Role of Humor in John F. Kennedy's 1960 Presidential Campaign* (Ph.D. diss., Southern Illinois University, 1979), 77.

45. Jamison, *Packaging the Presidency,* 146, 158. At the conclusion of a 1960 press conference, President Eisenhower was asked by a reporter if he could provide an example of a major idea of Nixon's that his administration had implemented, to which he responded, "If you give me a week I might think of one. I don't remember [laughter]"

46. "In War and Peace," 60; Herbert Block, *A Cartoonist's Life,* 176; Block, *Straight Herblock,* 14, 11.

47. "Robert Osborn Views the Campaign," *New Republic* 135 (November 5, 1956):9; "Robert Osborn Views the Campaign," *New Republic* 143 (October 10, 1960):15; "Robert Osborn Views the Campaign," *New Republic* 143 (November 7, 1960):15; "Nixon, the Instinct for the Jugular," contained in the Caroline and Erwin Swann Collection of Caricature and Cartoon, PPD.

48. "Robert Osborn Views the Campaign," *New Republic* 143 (October 31 1960):12.

49. "In the Darkening Woods," *America* 104 (October 15, 1960):66.

50. Robert Osborn, *The Vulgarians* (Greenwich, Conn.: New York Graphic Society, 1960), unpaginated. Similar criticisms of billboards and other features of modern American life can be found in Daniel Boorstin, *The Image* (New York: Atheneum, 1962), Peter Blake, *God's Own Junkyard: The Planned Deterioration of America's Landscape* (New York: Holt, Rinehart and Winston, 1964); and John Kenneth Galbraith, *The Affluent Society* (Boston: Houghton Mifflin, 1958).

51. Back cover, *The Vulgarians;* William Cole, "Eight Deadly Sins," *New Republic* 143 (19 September 1960):16–17.

52. Osborn, *The Vulgarians,* unpaginated.

53. Norman Mailer, "Superman Comes to the Market," *Esquire* 54 (November 1960):119–27 and passim. Several years later, when Mailer included "Superman Comes to the Supermarket" among *The Presidential Papers,* he described it as "act of propaganda" that helped win Stevenson's supporters to the side of Kennedy and, in the end, swing the election in the Democrats' favor. "I had created an archetype of Jack Kennedy in the public mind which might or might not be true, but which would induce people to vote for him," Mailer wrote. Norman Mailer, *The Presidential Papers* (New York: G. P. Putnam's Sons, 1963), 61. The ironies abundant in Mailer's short-lived infatuation with John Kennedy did not escape the notice of critics. John Kenneth Galbraith in his review of *The Presidential Papers* noted that Mailer was "evidently one who prefers a healthy, spontaneous, uncalculated and uncerebral response to Castro . . ." Indeed, it was exactly Kennedy's attraction to the "conquistadorial" that contributed to the Bay of Pigs fiasco—a fiasco that abruptly ended Mailer's support of Kennedy. John Kenneth Galbraith, "The Kennedys Didn't Reply," *New York Times Book Review,* November 17, 1963, 6. See also the parody of *The Presidential Papers* in Xavier Prynne, "The 6th Vice-Presidential Note," *New York Review of Books* 1 (November 28, 1963):23. For more on the contributions writers such as Vidal and Mailer made to *Esquire* and the role this important publication had in the creation of the "New Journalism" of the 1960s, see Nancy Polsgrove, *It Wasn't Pretty, Folks, but Didn't We Have Fun?: Esquire in the Sixties* (New York: W. W. Norton & Company, 1995).

54. Russell Baker, "Cultural Explosion in Washington," *Theatre Arts* 47 (April 1963): 14–15, 70; Harris, *The Fine Art of Political Wit,* 255; Richard B. Morris, "A Presidential Sense of Humor," *New York Times Magazine,* April 30, 1961, 47; Andrew Sarris, "No Biz Like Show Biz, And No Prexy Like JFK," *Village Voice,* May 24, 1962, 17; Schlesinger, *A Thousand Days,* 728. Typical of the romantic view that the Kennedys were personally responsible for the sudden escalation of political satire is that held by author and Kennedy family friend Gerald Gardner. "With the coming of JFK to the White House and the arrival of the Kennedy clan in Washington," Gardner has recently written, "the political climate for humor changed markedly for the better. Suddenly political humor ended its long hibernation and made its appearance in nightclubs, coffeehouses, books, and record albums . . . Humor and whimsy had risen Phoenix-like, and it was no longer subversive to kid the president of the United States." Gardner, *Campaign Comedy,* 281. For more on Kennedy's use of humor, see Evans, "That Wit in the White House," 19, 52–53; Harris, *The Fine Art of Political Wit,* 267–68; and Gardner,

All the Presidents' Wits, 251–56. Examples of Kennedy's wit were well preserved in Bill Adler's *The Kennedy Wit* (New York: Citadel Press, 1964); *The Kennedy Wit* (RCA, 1964) (with introductory remarks by Adlai Stevenson); and the television special "The John F. Kennedy Humor," broadcast on ABC, October 5, 1966, at GRVV.

55. Block, *Straight Herblock,* 41, 44, 148; Block, *A Cartoonist's Life,* 179; Bill Mauldin cartoon no. 709, A size, BMP.

56. Walt Kelly, *The Jack Acid Society Black Book* (New York: Simon and Schuster, 1962); Mrs. Kline L. Roberts to Walt Kelly, August 15, 1961, WK, box WKFAN 6. Not surprisingly, Kelly's exaggerated comic portraits of the John Birch Society greatly antagonized America's conservative right. A Texas man who followed the Jack Acid Society episode in his local paper warned Kelly that America was "in the middle of losing a war with a conspiracy which, if victorious, would not allow your type of satire to exist." A woman from Midland, Michigan, claimed that satire is "a wonderful and powerful weapon," but "[w]rongfully used" could "hinder the work of . . . useful organizations." "I shall be watching for 'Pogo,'" she warned Kelly, "to reflect a change in your attitude, for the only properly informed people who continue to attack us are the Communists." Remarkably, Kelly often attempted to clarify his intent with those who offered such criticism. To a woman from Dallas, for instance, he explained that it "should be apparent that many of us are not so much against anti-communists as we are against all who would hamper the free exchange of speech in the United States. When any organized group chooses to set up a black list of suspects for the edification of the press and others, it is time for true Americans to protest." Lamar Bordelon to Walt Kelly, September 1, 1961, WK, box WKFAN 6; Linda Locke to Walt Kelly, n.d., WK, box WKFAN 6; Walt Kelly to Mrs. O DeAcutis, September 3, 1961, WK, box WFAN 5.

57. Mauldin, *What's Got Your Back Up?,* 133; Mauldin cartoon no. 566, A size, BMP; "The Pogo Problem," *Commonweal* 76 (June 8, 1962):267–68, and "No Go, Pogo" *America* 107 (June 2, 1962):337.

58. Quoted in "Political Humor, 1962," *Time,* February 9, 1962, 72.

59. Robert Hatch, "Theatre," *Nation* 193 (October 14, 1961):254.

60. "Art for Humor's Sake," *Newsweek,* December 4, 1961, 86–87; Howard Langer, "Man with a Hunting License: An Interview with Art Buchwald," *Social Education* 48 (February 1984):103–106; "Playboy Interview: Art Buchwald," *Playboy* 12 (April 1965): 51–62; Art Buchwald, "They Need Each Other," in *I Chose Capitol Punishment* (New York: World Publishing Company, 1963), 161–62.

61. Hoppe, *Having a Wonderful Time,* 63; "Horselaughs in the Times," *Time,* September 14, 1962, 73–74; Russell Baker, *The Good Times* (New York: William Morrow and Company, 1989).

62. David Halberstam, *The Powers That Be* (New York: Alfred A. Knopf, 1979), 422; "The Viewers' Choice," *Time,* July 25, 1960, 42; "Crisis, Conflict and Change in TV News," *Look,* November 7, 1961, 48–62 and passim; Richard Rovere, "The American Establishment" *Esquire* 57 (May 1962):106–108; Noel Parmentel Jr., "Folk Songs for Conservatives," *Esquire* 60 (December 1963):160–61; Noel Parmentel Jr., "The Acne and the Ecstasy," *Esquire* 58 (August 1962):44–114 passim; Mark Eparnay's "The McLandress Dimension," "The McLandress Solution," "The American Sociometric Peerage,"

and "The Fully Automated Foreign Policy" are reprinted in *The McLandress Dimension* (Boston: Houghton Mifflin Company), 1963.

63. Victor Navasky, interview by author, tape recording, New York, July 24, 1996. Like Mort Sahl, Navasky was stationed in Alaska and fought boredom by distributing an "information sheet"—in Navasky's case, the *Moose Hornblower*—to fellow soldiers. Victor Navasky, *A Matter of Opinion* (New York: Farrar, Straus and Giroux, 2005), 17–27.

64. "Editorial," *Monocle* 1(1) (1957):2.

65. "Satire through a Cocked Eye," *Time*, March 13, 1964, 47; Marvin Kitman, "Monocle," *Harper's* 221 (August 1960):23–24; Victor Navasky, interview by author, tape recording, New York July 24, 1996.

66. Victor Navasky, "Introduction" to Leonard C. Lewin, *Report from Iron Mountain: On the Possibility and Desirability of Peace* (New York: Free Press, 1996), vi. Two exceptions to the list of liberal contributors were William F. Buckley (who wrote about his friend, journalist Murray Kempton) and William B. Sprague Jr. (Director of Public Relations for the Republican National Committee).

67. Victor Navasky, interview by author, tape recording, New York July 24, 1996.

68. "To Philatelomania, with Love," *Outsider's Newsletter* 1(6) (1962):6–7; Bognor Q., "Vicuña on My Back," *Monocle* 2 (Winter 1958–59):16; "Future Lies Ahead for Dick Nixon. Chucks Family, Choiner, Checkers," *Outsider's Newsletter* 1(5) (1962):1; Dan Wakefield, "Thunder in the Middle," *Monocle* 5 (Summer–Fall 1963):34–43; Frank Thompson, Jr., "A Modest Proposal for the Return to Conservatism through Decentralization," *Monocle* 4(2) (1961):16; C. D. B. Bryan, "Tarzan and the Lost Safari," *Monocle* 5 (Spring 1964):38–48; Robert Grossman, "That Phoenix Cowboy," *Monocle* 5 (Summer–Fall 1963):8.

69. Victor Navasky, interview by author, tape recording, New York July 24, 1996; "Editorial," *Monocle* 5(1) (1962):5; C. D. B. Bryan to author, August 19, 1999; Navasky quoted in "Edited for Jack," *Newsweek*, June 4, 1962, 92.

70. Russell Baker, "To the Editor," *Monocle* 5(1) (1962):2; Navasky quoted in "Edited for Jack," 92; Navasky quoted in "Satire through a Cocked Eye," 47; "Editorial," *Monocle* 2 (Winter 1958–59):1.

71. Hoppe, *Having a Wonderful Time*, 64. Episodes of "Just Plain Jack" are reprinted in Arthur Hoppe's *The Love Everybody* Crusade* (Garden City, N.Y.: Doubleday & Company, 1963).

72. Martin Gottfried, "Theatre Afield: Compass, Hyannis," *Village Voice*, July 26, 1962, 9; Jesse Gross, "Do It Yourself Legit Rash," *Variety*, July 18, 1962, 53.

73. Addressing the subject of the 1962 stock market slump, for example, The Second City's Kennedy sidesteps an analysis of its cause and effect and instead thanks the American public for having allowed him to convert all of his stocks and bonds. Arthur Gelb, "Cabaret Menu: Roast Politician," *New York Times*, June 4, 1962, 32.

74. Jeffrey Sweet, *Something Wonderful Right Away*, 300.

75. Arch Lustberg, telephone interview by author, tape recording, January 24, 2000.

76. Arch Lustberg, telephone interview by author, tape recording, January 24, 2000.

77. Peter Bunzel, "A Kennedy Spoof Full of 'Vigah,'" *Life,* December 14, 1962, 84. Roulette Records attempted to cash in on *The First Family* craze by issuing *At Home with That Other Family,* a spoof of the Khrushchev family featuring Second City and Premise alumni George Segal, Joan Rivers, and Buck Henry. "Politics Was Never This Funny As Khrush Joins JFK on Comedy Wax," *Variety,* December 12, 1962, 52. For more on the early-sixties adult coloring book fad see Milton Bracker, "These Are Coloring Books: Gold Is the Color," *New York Times,* August 11, 1962, 15; James Reston, "New Orleans," *New York Times,* April 22, 1962, sec. 4, p. 10.

78. Joel Schechter, *Satiric Impersonations: From Aristophanes to the Guerrilla Girls* (Carbondale: Southern Illinois University Press, 1994), 4; Avery Schreiber, telephone interview by author, tape recording, May 24, 1999; Bunzel, "A Kennedy Spoof Full of 'Vigah,'" 84.

79. Quoted in "A Kennedy Spoof Full of 'Vigah,'" 84.

80. Theodore Flicker to George Segal, August 3, 1961, TFC, box 3, Premise correspondence folder. Members of The Premise, like the members of The Uniquecorn, became privy to the sexual indiscretions of politicians (including President Kennedy's) but refused to mention any of them onstage. Even when offered the name of an "excessively well-known mistress of a public figure" during an improvisation, the *Times of London* noted, The Premise cast chose to veer off in a different direction. When Flicker was asked why his troupe did not follow up on such audience suggestions, he told the paper, "We don't do gossip." Theodore Flicker, telephone interview by author, tape recording, May 28, 1999; Arch Lustberg, telephone interview by author, tape recording, January 24, 2000; "American Preferences in the New Satirical Revue," *Times of London,* September 19, 1962, 16.

81. Arthur Gelb, "Political Satire Invades Capital," *New York Times,* January 30, 1962, 22; John V. Lindsay, "Theatre: The Premise, D.C.," *Village Voice,* March 1, 1962, 11. "Holiday along the Potomac," *Cue* 31 (May 19, 1962):9; Rocco Landesman, "Interview: Ted Flicker," *Yale/Theatre* 5 (Spring 1974):69.

82. Liz Carpenter to Theodore Flicker, n.d., TFC, box 3, Washington Premise publicity folder. Carpenter would later serve as the head of the Johnson Administration's "Humor Group," the small think tank responsible for devising jokes for President Johnson's public addresses. Liz Carpenter, *Ruffles & Feathers* 3d ed. (College Station, Tex.: Texas A&M University Press, 1993), 251–56.

83. Arch Lustberg, telephone interview by author, tape recording, January 24, 2000.

84. Bergan, *Beyond the Fringe,* 46; Harry Thompson, *Peter Cook: A Biography,* 141–45. In a letter to his mother, Cook recounted one visit the First Lady had made to The Establishment: "She kept shrieking with delight, and saying how naughty it all was, and how Jack would never allow her up to New York again."

85. Paul Sills, telephone interview by author, tape recording, June 3, 1999; Barbara Harris, telephone interview by author, tape recording, June 2, 1999; Mayor Richard Daley to Lord Mayor of London, October 5, 1962, SCA.

86. Del Close, interview by author, tape recording, Chicago, September 11, 1996. London *Sunday Times* critic Harold Hobson was impressed by the way Close and his

colleagues handled the crowd. "Well, I do not suppose that America will hear of this evening," Hobson wrote, "but if she did she could be proud of it." Harold Hobson, "Almost a Battlefield," *Sunday Times,* October 28, 1962, Premise clippings folder, BRT.

87. Bergan, *Beyond the Fringe,* 28; "Premise Sketches Banned in London," typed manuscript, TFC, box 4, publicity folder No. 1; Harold Hobson, "Stage Tradition Quietly Broken," *Christian Science Monitor,* July 31, 1962, sec. 2, p. 4; Kenneth Tynan, "Joyce Lost in the Words," *New York Herald Tribune,* August 5, 1962, sec. 4, p. 2; James Feron, "Quips on Kennedy Barred in London," *New York Times,* July 21, 1962, 10; Theodore Flicker, telephone interview by author, tape recording, May 28, 1999. This minor uproar erupted again in October when the Lord Chamberlain banned a scene parodying the First Lady. See James Feron, "Mrs. Kennedy Skit Banned," *New York Times,* October 13, 1962, 16; James Feron, "Britain Curbing American Revue," *New York Times,* October 20, 1962, 13.

88. Russell Baker, "Observer," *New York Times,* December 13, 1962, 6; Norman Mailer, "Reflections on the Fate of the Union: Kennedy and After," *New York Review of Books* 1 (December 26, 1963):6.

CHAPTER SEVEN

1. Robert Legare, "Hip Wits Disc Hits," *Playboy* 7 (September 1960):83.

2. Nat Hentoff, "Satire, Schmatire," *Commonweal* 74 (July 7, 1961):376; Nat Hentoff, "New Comedy: The Grand Illusion," *Gent* 7 (December 1962):36; Gordon Rogoff, "First Nights/New York," *Plays and Players* (September 1963):33; John Chapman, "Revue, 'From 2nd City,' Is Semi-Pro in the 1st," *New York Daily News,* September 27, 1961, The Second City clipping file, BRT; "Satire's Last Stand," *Theatre Arts* 45 (December 1961):57.

3. Mailer, "Superman Comes to the Market," 119–27 and passim. Following the Bay of Pigs debacle in the spring of 1961, Mailer published in the *Village Voice* an "Open Letter to John Fitzgerald Kennedy" in which he lambasted the President for holding to the center "like no Republican ever could." The following year, feeling snubbed by the First Lady because of his "Open Letter," Mailer compared her to a "wooden horse" and "royal phony" in a controversial article for *Esquire.* Norman Mailer, "An Open Letter to John Fitzgerald Kennedy and Fidel Castro" and "An Evening with Jackie Kennedy, or, The Wild West of the East" in *The Presidential Papers,* 63–98.

4. Vidal, *Palimpsest: A Memoir,* 361, 395.

5. *The Kennedy Wit* was eventually published in 1964 and remained on the bestseller list for six months. Bill Adler, *Inside Publishing* (Indianapolis: Bobbs-Merrill Company, 1982), 102–103.

6. To delegates attending the 1960 Democratic National Convention in Los Angeles, Sahl reported that Vice President Nixon had sent Joseph Kennedy a telegram reading, "Congratulations. You have not lost a son. You have gained a country." Russell Baker, "Convention Show Moves Outdoors," *New York Times,* July 16, 1960, sec. 1, p. 6; Mort Sahl, *Heartland,* 82. According to Sahl, Kennedy also questioned him about his support for Castro, a position that also put Sahl at odds with Adlai Stevenson.

7. Murray Schumach, "Mort Sahl Satire Knows No Party," *New York Times,* June 2, 1960, 27.

8. Sahl, *Heartland,* 89; Mort Sahl, *The New Frontier* (Reprise, 1961). Although outside of Sinatra's notorious "Rat Pack," Sahl shared an association with the singer that was forged during the 1960 presidential campaign. According to Sahl, Sinatra approached Sahl that year for material that he could use while out campaigning for Kennedy. Sinatra, of course, was one of John Kennedy's most valuable connections to the entertainment business during 1960. For more on Sinatra's relationship to and, later, estrangement from John Kennedy, see Brownstein, *The Power and the Glitter,* 145–67.

9. "Jerry Lewis Blasts 'Incompetent Idiots' at ABC For Censoring Script," *Variety,* October 2, 1963, 31.

10. Pierre Berton, "Mort Sahl," in *Voices from the Sixties,* 106; Sahl, *Heartland,* 93; "Mort Sahl: The Loyal Opposition," broadcast by PBS, September 18, 1989, and viewed at Motion Picture and Television Reading Room, MBRS.

11. "Oh-So-Sensitive," *Newsweek,* November 13, 1961, 93; Sahl quoted by Hugh Hefner in Hugh Hefner to Jules Feiffer, September 29, 1958, JF, box 17; Richard E. Ashcraft, "Confessions of a Cockeyed Artist," *Harvard Crimson,* May 12, 1959, 2; "Jules Feiffer Talks to Denis Hart in New York," *Manchester Guardian Weekly,* January 10, 1963, 14.

12. Feiffer, like Herblock, Bill Mauldin, and Robert Osborn, was indeed fortunate to have the support of the *New Republic,* whose editor Gil Harrison expressed a preference for cartoons with "bite" rather than the "'less controversial' type" that the Hall Syndicate would on occasion submit. Gil Harrison to Edward Riley, March 7, 1961, JF, box 8.

13. Jules Feiffer, "Comments on Mimi's Death," Plaza Memorial Chapel, New York, March 28, 1988, JF, box 3. For other information concerning Jules Feiffer's life and career I rely on three taped telephone interviews I conducted with Feiffer on December 6, 12, and 19 of 1996. Gary Groth's excellent interview "Memories of a Pro Bono Cartoonist," *Comics Journal* 124 (August 1988):37–95, and Steven Heller's insightful discussion with Feiffer, "A Dancer, Bernard Mergendeiler," 4–11 have also proved invaluable to this study. See also Holly Finn, "Jules Feiffer: Sketching Sophistication," in *In the Vernacular: Interviews at Yale with Sculptors of Culture,* ed. Melissa E. Biggs (Jefferson, N.C.: McFarland & Company, 1991):92–102.

14. "The Sick Little World of Jules Feiffer," *Playboy* 5 (August 1958):25; Black, "Sokolsky, Meet Feiffer," 17; Feiffer quoted in Groth, "Memories of a Pro Bono Cartoonist," 86; Jules Feiffer, telephone interview by author, tape recording, December 6, 1996; Donald W. Kramer, "Feiffer: 'An Ambivalent Character,'" *Daily Princetonian,* October 22, 1958.

15. Jules Feiffer, telephone interview by author, tape recording, December 6, 1996; Feiffer quoted in Groth, "Memories of a Pro Bono Cartoonist," 44; Feiffer quoted in Henry Allen, "Jules Feiffer: The Ever Dissenting Cartoonist at 50: Still Drawing on Bronx Angst," *Washington Post,* November 17, 1979, sec. b1, p. 3; Rick Friedman, "Feiffer—Cartoonist with a Point of View," *Editor & Publisher* 94 (June 10, 1961):17, 79;

"What's So Funny," *Bell & Howell's Close-Up!,* ABC-TV, June 12, 1962, videotape viewed at Motion Picture and Television Reading Room, MBRS.

16. Feiffer, *Jules Feiffer's America: From Eisenhower to Reagan,* 11; Steven Heller, "A Dancer, Bernard Mergendeiler," 6; "Jules Feiffer Talks about the Diminishing Size and Importance of the Comic Strip," Broadcast on NET, April 1, 1976, audiotape at GRVV; Jules Feiffer, "Feiffer," *Village Voice,* October 22, 1958, 4.

17. Heller, "A Dancer, Bernard Mergendeiler," 6; Jules Feiffer, *Feiffer, Village Voice,* November 3, 1960, 4.

18. Feiffer quoted in Larry Dubois, "Playboy Interview: Jules Feiffer," 90.

19. Feiffer, *Jules Feiffer's America,* 71.

20. Jules Feiffer, *Jules Feiffer, New Republic* 147 (October 9, 1962):26.

21. Paul Sills, telephone interview by author, tape recording, June 3, 1999; Andrew Duncan to author, June 27, 1999.

22. Theodore Flicker in Landesman, "Interview: Ted Flicker," 68–69; Howard Taubman, "Adorning the News," *New York Times,* June 18, 1961, sec. 2, p. 1; Harris quoted in Michael Smith, "Nymphet with Sex—and Something More," *Village Voice,* May 31, 1962, 8; Jerry Talmer, "Premise Actress," *New York Post,* December 7, 1962, 55; Avery Schreiber, telephone interview by author, tape recording, May 24, 1999. The recollections of several Second City members are marked with considerable ambiguity over the nature and extent of their political commitments. Del Close, for example, has said that Second City only made topical and political references "to remind audiences that we were not Borscht Belt," yet he has also admitted that he and Severn Darden, both ardent supporters of Adlai Stevenson, took issues involving civil rights and the proliferation of nuclear weaponry very seriously. During the early 1960s, Close was even a member of the Fair Play for Cuba Committee and participated in "Ban the Bomb" demonstrations. Del Close, interview by author, tape recording, Chicago, September 11, 1996; Sweet, *Something Wonderful Right Away,* 299.

23. Bowen quoted in Sweet, *Something Wonderful Right Away,* 41.

24. Richard J. Daley to Omar Shapli and Ian Davidson, November 2, 1964; copy of letter sent to author.

25. Michael Myerson, *These Are the Good Old Days: Coming of Age As a Radical in America's Late, Late Years* (New York: Grossman Publishers, 1970); Alan Myerson, telephone interview by author, tape recording, July 12, 1999.

26. Del Close, interview by author, tape recording, Chicago, September 11, 1996.

27. Alan Myerson, telephone interview by author, tape recording, July 12, 1999.

28. Richard Watts Jr., "A Group of Bright Young Visitors," *New York Post,* September 17, 1964, The Committee clipping file, BRT.

29. Liner notes for *The Committee: An Original Cast Album* (Reprise, 1964).

30. *The Committee: An Original Cast Album;* Michael Smith "The First Week," *Village Voice,* September 24, 1964, 14; Rexroth quoted in Donovan Brass, "The Committee," *Ramparts* 3 (December 1964):13; Harold Clurman, "Theatre," *Nation* 199 (October 5, 1964):202–203.

31. Garry Goodrow, telephone interview by author, tape recording, June 9, 1999; Brass, "The Committee," 11.

32. Nat Hentoff, "The Liberals Hissed," *Reporter* 31 (October 22, 1964):46–49; Garry Goodrow, telephone interview by author, tape recording, June 9, 1999; Walter Kerr, "The Dark Days of Comedy," *New York Herald Tribune,* October 4, 1964, sec. 6, p. 17.

33. Alan Myerson, telephone interview by author, tape recording, July 12, 1999; Garry Goodrow, telephone interview by author, tape recording, June 9, 1999.

34. Judith Crist, "A Brassy, Sassy, New 'Establishment," *New York Herald Tribune,* November 1, 1963, 12; Henry Hewes, "The Season in New York," in *The Best Plays of 1962–1963,* ed. Henry Hewes (New York: Dodd, Mead & Company, 1963), 20; Michael Smith, "Cabaret Theatre: The Establishment," *Village Voice,* January 31, 1963, 14; "The Establishment," *Variety,* October 17, 1962, 54–55; Ward S. Just, "Who Is That Laughing?" *Reporter* 28 (February 14, 1963):50; John Wilcox, "Bits and Pieces," *Village Voice,* June 11, 1964, 2.

35. Norman Dorsen, "Letters to the Editor," *Village Voice,* February 14, 1963, 4; Norman Sturgis, "Unstatusing the Quo," *Theatre Arts* 46 (December 1962):8; Harold Clurman, "Theatre," *Nation* 196 (March 2, 1963):187. The Establishment also presented material written by noteworthy contributors such as Kenneth Tynan, novelist John Braine, and the playwright Peter Shaffer.

36. Geidt quoted in Lawrence E. Davies, "Audiences Vary, Satirists Find," *New York Times,* August 31, 1961, 9; Just, "Who Is That Laughing?" 50.

37. Victor Navasky, interview by author, tape recording, New York, July 24, 1996.

38. "Kennedy Foundation Shares Wealth," *Outsider's Newsletter* 1(1) (1962):1; L.L. Case, "Ordeal of Rhetoric," *Monocle* 5 (Summer–Fall 1963):44–47; "Our Own Oscars," *Outsider's Newsletter* 1(25) (1963):2; "Why Jackie Kennedy Never Visited Hazard, Kentucky," *Outsider's Newsletter* 1(51) (1963):6; C. D. B. Bryan, "Jack and Jackie: A Perfect Day for Honeyfitz," *Monocle* 5(1) (1962):14–22; "Non-Fiction Department," *Outsider's Newsletter* 1(35) (1963):4.

39. Dan Wakefield, "Thunder in the Middle," *Monocle* 5 (Summer–Fall 1963):34–43.

40. Feiffer, *Jules Feiffer's America,* 74; Feiffer, *Jules Feiffer, New Republic* 146 (January 22, 1962):19; Jules Feiffer, *Feiffer, Village Voice,* October 24, 1963, 4.

41. Fred Gardner, "Jules Feiffer," *Harvard Crimson,* February 23, 1962; Jules Feiffer, untitled manuscript, 1962, JF, box 55; Jules Feiffer, "Satire Must Skirt Its Own Clichés," (Harvard) *Crimson Bookshelf,* March 23, 1962, 13.

42. Jules Feiffer, "Satire," manuscript, n.d., JF, box 55.

43. Jules Feiffer, untitled manuscripts, 1962, JF, box 55.

44. Jules Feiffer, "You Should Have Caught Me at the White House," *Holiday* 34 (July 1963):66–67; "An Impolite Interview with Jules Feiffer," *Realist* 23 (February 1961):1, 12–15 and passim; Jules Feiffer, "A Feiffer's-Eye-View of Satire," *Chicago Sun-Times,* May 7, 1961, sec. 3, p. 1; Jules Feiffer, telephone interview by author, tape recording, December 12, 1996; Alta Maloney, "His Satire No Stereotype," *Boston Traveler,* February 26, 1962, 28.

45. Jules Feiffer, untitled manuscript, 1962, JF, box 55.

46. Jules Feiffer, untitled manuscript, 1962, JF, box 55.

47. Paul Krassner, "An Impolite Interview with Mort Sahl,"1–28 and passim.

48. Roy Newquist "Magic, Madness of Feiffer," *Chicago Sunday American,* October 27, 1963; Krassner, "An Impolite Interview with Mort Sahl," 17; Jonathan Miller, "Can English Satire Draw Blood?" 21; Harry Thompson, *Peter Cook: A Biography,* 114. The debate over whether or not Peter Cook intended to injure establishment figures and politicians with his satiric bits has survived Cook himself. Those who argue that Cook was capable and willing to shock his targets point to the night when Cook improvised an impersonation of the prime minister while he was in attendance. The audience that night reportedly fell silent when Cook stated, "And when I've a spare evening, there's nothing I like better than to wander over to a theatre and sit there listening to a group of sappy, urgent, vibrant young satirists, with a stupid great grin spread all over my silly old face." Cook quoted in *Something Like Fire,* 170.

49. Alan Brien, "The London Scene," *Theatre Arts* 46 (January 1962):64; Malcolm Muggeridge, "The Hollow Tooth," *New Statesman,* August 24, 1962, 36.

50. "The Anne Fremantle Show," tape Recording of WNBC radio program, June 12, 1963, TFC.

51. Landesman, "Interview: Ted Flicker," 69.

52. Flicker quoted in Feldman, *A Critical Analysis of Improvisational Theatre in the United States from 1955–1968,* 32.

53. Theodore J. Flicker, "Safe and Unsafe Satire at The Living Premise," (Ossining, NY) *Citizen Register,* July 27, 1963, clipping in TFC, box 4, publicity folder no. 1.

54. Flicker, "Safe and Unsafe Satire at the Living Premise."

55. Theodore Flicker, telephone interview by author, tape recording, June 2, 1999; Joan Darling, telephone interview by author, tape recording, August 25, 1999.

56. Ossie Davis, introduction to *Purlie Victorious: A Commemorative* (New Rochelle, N.Y.: Emmalyn Enterprises, 1993), 1–6; Ossie Davis and Ruby Dee, *With Ossie and Ruby: In This Life Together* (New York: William Morrow), 291–97.

57. As Sally Banes reminds us, improvisational revues were hardly the only forms of avant-garde culture based in Greenwich Village during the early 1960s that lacked the participation of African Americans. Banes points out that the Village avant-garde, no matter how much it spoke about "community" and defended civil rights, never involved more than a small minority of blacks. Banes, *Greenwich Village 1963,* 153–57.

58. Flicker, "Safe and Unsafe Satire at The Living Premise"; "Pre-Rehearsal Period and First Day," untitled handwritten notes, April 30, 1963, and May 11, 1963 in TFC, box 2, Living Premise folder; Joan Darling, "Premise 'Erasing The Line,'" *New York Herald Tribune,* June 9, 1963, clipping in TFC, box 4, publicity folder no. 1; "Integrated Thought," *New Yorker,* June 22, 1963, 22–23.

59. Quoted in Leonard Harris, "Races Mix in 'Premise,'" *New York World Telegram,* June 14, 1963, Living Premise clipping file, BRT; and Judith Crist, "There Are Limits," *New York Herald Tribune,* June 14, 1963, TFC, box 5, Living Premise folder.

60. Theodore Flicker, telephone interview by author, tape recording, June 2, 1999; Al Freeman Jr., telephone interview by author, tape recording, July 3, 1999; Sandra Schmidt, "Theatre: The Living Premise," *Village Voice,* July 4, 1963, 7; Richard Shepard,

"'Living Premise,' a New Revue, Tackles Integration Problems," *New York Times,* June 14, 1963, 34; Gene Feist, "On and Off Broadway," *Chelsea News,* September 12, 1963, 8, clipping in TFC, box 4, publicity folder no. 1.

61. Joan Darling, telephone interview by author, tape recording, August 25, 1999; Flicker, "Safe and Unsafe Satire at The Living Premise"; Landesman, "Interview: Ted Flicker," 70.

62. Audiences were particularly uncomfortable at the moment when Godfrey Cambridge, playing the role of the black militant, exclaims, "I want to see how that faggot Kennedy reacts when he sees a redneck standing with his foot on his pregnant wife's neck." Joan Darling, telephone interview by author, tape recording, August 25, 1999.

63. Harold Stern, "One-Note Satire Spoils Full Effect at 'Premise,'" *Brooklyn Eagle,* June 17, 1963, 7, clipping in TFC, box 4, publicity folder no. 1; Crist, "There Are Limits."

64. Al Freeman Jr., telephone interview by author, tape recording, July 3, 1999; Joan Darling, telephone interview by author, tape recording, August 25, 1999.

65. Theodore Flicker, telephone interview by author, tape recording, June 2, 1999.

CHAPTER EIGHT

1. Harry Golden, *Only in America* (Cleveland: World Publishing Company, 1958), 15–17, 118–23; Ted Solotaroff, "Harry Golden and the American Audience," in *Red Hot Vacuum and Other Pieces on the Writing of the Sixties* (New York: New York: Atheneum, 1970), 52–70; "Virginia Library Shift," *New York Times,* December 2, 1960, 22.

2. Jules Feiffer, "The Interview," *Harper's* 224 (June 1962):74–75.

3. Jules Feiffer, "Jules Feiffer," *New Republic* 147 (October 1, 1962):27.

4. Jules Feiffer, *Feiffer on Civil Rights* (New York: Anti-Defamation League of B'nai B'rith, 1966), 48–50.

5. Feiffer, *Feiffer on Civil Rights,* 32–34.

6. Bayard Rustin, foreword to *Feiffer on Civil Rights,* 5; Feiffer, *Jules Feiffer, New Republic* 144 (June 19, 1961):27; Feiffer, *Jules Feiffer's America,* 52.

7. Block, *Special for Today,* 80; Bill Mauldin, *What's Got Your Back Up?,* 7.

8. Walt Kelly, *Ten Ever-Lovin' Blue-Eyed Years with Pogo,* 256–62. In the opinion of several Southern newspaper editors, Kelly's treatment of race transgressed the thin line dividing politics and entertainment. In late November 1958, the editor of the conservative *Richmond (Virginia) Times-Dispatch,* John H. Colburn, discontinued *Pogo* because, as he explained to readers, "the artist became more involved in editorial expression than entertainment." Facing Colburn later at a Newspaper Comics Council meeting, Kelly argued, "A cartoonist . . . is a commentator on the day's events. There is nothing outside his province." Colburn reportedly told newspaper executives assembled at the same meeting that he represented "an influential group of editors who feel it is basically indefensible for comic-strip artists to take off on their own prejudices in the fields of politics, economics and whatnot." One man from Tulsa who wrote Kelly agreed with editors like Colburn. "Please continue," he wrote, "to do what you accom-

plish so well—lighten the hearts of the American people—and stay the hell out of the integration problem." Many other *Pogo* readers disagreed. They appreciated Kelly's ability to integrate the issue of segregation into his plots. "Keep up the anti-segregation work," a man from La Porte, Indiana, wrote Kelly in 1961. "You probably inspire more people than you realize." Selby Kelly, *Pogo Files for Pogophiles: A Retrospective on 50 Years of Walt Kelly's Classic Comic Strip* (Richfield, Minn.: Spring Hollow Books, 1992), 147; "The 'Non-un-de-censored,'" *Newsweek,* January 26, 1959, 92; James L. Collings, "Colburn, Kelly Debate Comic-Strip Editing," *Editor & Publisher* 92 (January 24, 1959):58–59; Norman M. Hulings Jr. to Walt Kelly, August 1, 1963, WK, box WKFAN 6; R. C. Stevenson to Walt Kelly, November 6, 1961, WK, box WKFAN 5.

9. Block, *Straight Herblock,* 191, 142; Mauldin cartoon no. 530, A size, BMP; Bill Mauldin, *I've Decided I Want My Seat Back* (New York: Harper & Row, Publishers, 1965), 26.

10. Block, *Straight Herblock,* 192; Mauldin, *I've Decided I Want My Seat Back,* 56.

11. Mauldin cartoons nos. 998, 957, 965, A size, BMP. Historical literature on the modern civil rights movement is broad in scope and vast in quantity. No better introduction to this literature exists than Harvard Sitkoff's *The Struggle for Black Equality: 1954–1980* (New York: Hill and Wang, 1981).

12. Black and Rodell were also contributors to *Monocle.* See, for example, Black's poems (written under the name of Charles Lund) "The White Citizen Considers a Fearful Possibility," in *Monocle* 3(1) (Summer 1959), and Rodell's "Nine-a-Court" limericks in *Monocle* 6(3) (November 1964).

13. "The Innert Story," *Monocle* 1(1) (1957):3–9.

14. Charles J. Prentiss, "American Statehood for West Berlin," *Monocle* 3 (Summer 1959):6; "Civil War's Second Century Begins; Ceremonies in Oxford," *Outsider's Newsletter* 1(4) (1962):2; "Alternatives to Tax Reform," *Outsider's Newsletter* 1(14) (1963):3; "South Turns Back Calendar," *Outsider's Newsletter* 1(34) (1963):1–2.

15. "Clay Report: Stop U.S. Aid to Miss.," *Outsider's Newsletter* 1(26) (1963):1.

16. Victor Navasky, interview by author, tape recording, New York, July 24, 1996.

17. Calvin Trillin, "Letters to Other Editors," *Outsider's Newsletter* 1(3) (1962):5; "The Black District Plan," *Monocle* 5 (Summer–Fall 1963):7; "White Moderates for Militant Non-Action," *Monocle* 6 (November 1964):8; "North vs. South" and Charles Alverson, "Every Neighborhood Needs One," *Outsider's Newsletter* 1(42) (1963):1–3, 7.

18. Victor Navasky, introduction to Lewin, *Report from Iron Mountain: On the Possibility and Desirability of Peace:* vi; "Negro Violates Federal Marshall's Civil Rights," *Outsider's Newsletter* 1(8) (1962):2; "South Turns Back Calendar,"2; "Bobby Kennedy Diary Published!" *Outsider's Newsletter* 1(22) (1963):2; "People Are Talking about . . ." *Outsider's Newsletter* 1(42) (1963):8.

19. "Outsider's Newsreal," *Outsider's Newsletter* 1(47) (1963):3–4; "Outsider's Newsreal," *Outsider's Newsletter* 1(31) (1963):6–7.

20. Henry Hewes, "People in Search of Characters in Search of . . ." *Saturday Review of Literature* 45 (June 16, 1962):27.

21. *Comedy from the Second City* (Mercury, 1961); Roger Bowen, "The Further Adventures of Businessman," unpublished revue sketch, July 5, 1960, MD.

22. *From the Second City* (Mercury, 1961); *Off Broadway: The Premise* (Vanguard, 1961); The Premise, "A Street," in *The Premise—Rough Draft,* 4–10, TFC, box 1.

23. Garry Goodrow, telephone interview by author, tape recording, June 9, 1999. The type of sly irony The Committee used in this tune also informed Bob Dylan's more accomplished "Talkin' John Birch Blues" (on his 1963 album *The Freewheelin' Bob Dylan*) and several other cuts from *Another Side of Bob Dylan* (1964). Dylan was reportedly a fan of the early Committee and a friend of troupe member Larry Hankin. For The Committee's opening performance in San Francisco, Dylan gave Hankin permission to premiere "Hard Rain's A Gonna Fall," later recorded on *The Freewheelin' Bob Dylan.*

24. "The Committee," *Variety,* December 25, 1963, 59; "The Committee, S.F.," *Variety,* April 17, 1963, 61, 62; Howard Taubman, "Theater: 'The Committee' in Premiere," *New York Times,* September 17, 1964, 53.

25. "The Last Laugh," *Ebony* 16 (December 1961):130; "Racial Fur Flies," *Newsweek,* June 1, 1959, 28; Watkins, *On the Real Side: A History of African American Comedy from Slavery to Chris Rock;* Levine, *Black Culture and Black Consciousness: Afro-American Folk Thought from Slavery to Freedom,* 298–366; DuBois quoted in *Laughing on the Outside: The Intelligent White Reader's Guide to Negro Tales and Humor,* 25; Ralph Ellison, "An Extravagance of Laughter," in *Going to the Territory* (New York: Random House, 1986), 145–97. John H. Burma drew attention to the "well concealed malice" behind African American jokes in his influential study "Humor as a Technique of Race Conflict," *American Sociological Review* 11 (December 1946):710–15. For more on the rich tradition of African American jokelore and vernacular humor see Roger D. Abrahams, *Deep Down in the Jungle . . . : Negro Narrative Folklore from the Streets of Philadelphia* (Hatboro, Penn.: Folklore Associates, 1964), and Alan Dundes, ed., *Mother Wit from the Laughing Barrel: Readings in the Interpretation of Afro-American Folklore* (Englewood Cliffs, N.J.: Prentice-Hall, 1973).

26. Langston Hughes, "White Folks Do the Funniest Things," *Common Ground* 4 (Winter 1944):42–46; Langston Hughes, introduction to *The Best of Negro Humor,* ed. John H. Johnson and Ben Burns (Chicago: Negro Digest Publishing, 1945), iii.

27. Arnold Rampersad, *The Life of Langston Hughes v. 2: 1941–1967, I Dream a World* (New York: Oxford University Press, 1988), 113; Darryl Dickson-Carr, *African American Satire: The Sacredly Profane Novel* (Columbia: University of Missouri Press, 2001), 8–99; Arthur P. Davis, "Jesse B. Semple: Negro American," *Phylon* 15 (First Quarter 1954) 21–28; James David Bryant, *Satire in the Work of Langston Hughes* (Ph.D. diss., Texas Christian University, 1972); Emmanuel Gomes, "The Crackerbox Tradition and the Race Problem in Lowell's The Bigelow Papers and Hughes's Sketches of Simple," *College Language Association Journal* 27 (March 1984):254–69.

28. Oliver Harrington, "Why I Left America," in *Why I Left America and Other Essays,* 98; Harrington, "View from the Back Stairs," 28.

29. Langston Hughes, introduction to *Bootsie and Others* (New York: Dodd, Mead & Company, 1958), unpaginated.

30. Harrington, *Bootsie and Others,* unpaginated.

31. Harrington, *Bootsie and Others,* unpaginated.

32. Oliver Harrington, "Look Homeward Angel," in *Why I Left America and Other Essays*, 68.

33. In the 1960s Harrington published cartoons in *Eulenspigel* and *Das Magazine*. He began contributing cartoons to the leftist *People's Daily World* in 1968.

34. Levine, *Black Culture and Black Consciousness*, 318–20; Goldman, *The Sociology of Negro Humor*, vi; Boskin, *Sambo: The Rise & Demise of an American Jester*, 212. For further discussion of how African American humor evolved during the late 1950s and early 1960s, see Norine Dresser, "The Metamorphosis of the Humor of the Black Man," *New York Folklore Quarterly* 26 (September 1970):216–28; Louis E. Lomax, "The American Negro's New Comedy Act," *Harper's* 222 (June 1961):41–46; Joseph Boskin, "Good-By, Mr. Bones," *New York Times Magazine*, May 1, 1966, 31–36; William Schechter, *The History of Negro Humor in America* (New York: Fleet Press, 1970); Redd Foxx and Norma Miller, *The Redd Foxx Encyclopedia of Black Humor* (Pasadena, Calif.: Ward Ritchie Press, 1977); Joseph Boskin "Humor in the Civil Rights Movement: Laughter in the Outer Sanctuaries," *Boston University Journal* 18 (Spring 1970):2–7; and Irwin D. Rinder, "A Note on Humor as an Index of Minority Group Morale," *Phylon* 26 (Summer 1965): 117–21.

35. Elsie Arrington Williams, *Jackie Moms Mabley: African American, Woman, Performer* (Ph.D. diss. University of Maryland at College Park, 1992); Studs Terkel, *The Spectator: Talk about Movies and Plays with the People Who Make Them* (New York: New Press, 1999), 276; *Jackie Moms Mabley at the Playboy Club* (Chess, 1961); Arthur Gelb, "Harlem Night Club Flourishing," *New York Times*, 15 May 1961, 34; Watkins, *On the Real Side*, 492.

36. Gilbert Millstein, "A Negro Says It with Jokes," *New York Times Magazine*, April 30, 1961, 34; Nat Hentoff, "Goodbye Mistah Bones," *Show Business Illustrated* 1 (October 17, 1961):89.

37. Dick Gregory with Shelia P. Moses, *Callus on My Soul: A Memoir* (Atlanta, Ga.: Longstreet Press, 2000), 3–27; Dick Gregory with Robert Lipsyte, *Nigger: An Autobiography* (New York: Pocket Books, 1965), 81, 88–91.

38. Gregory, *Nigger*, 105, 111–40.

39. *Bell & Howell Close Up!* broadcast by ABC-TV, September 29, 1960, and viewed at MBC.

40. Gregory, *Callus on My Soul*, 45.

41. Gregory, *Nigger*, 142–44.

42. Gregory, *Callus on My Soul*, 47.

43. Gregory, *Callus on My Soul*, 47; "Humor, Integrated," *Time*, February 17, 1961, 68; Dick Gregory with Robert Orben, *From the Back of the Bus* (New York: E.P. Dutton, 1962), 21.

44. Arthur Gelb, "Comic Withers Prejudice," *New York Times*, March 20, 1961, 34.

45. "Dick Gregory," *Ebony* 16 (May 1961):68.

46. Gregory, *Nigger*, 132; Lawrence Mintz, Art Buchwald, Jeff MacNally, Robert Orben, and Mark Russell, "Perspectives on American Political Humor," *American Humor: An Interdisciplinary Newsletter* 5 (Fall 1978):1–13. In addition to Orben, Gregory relied on

the joke writing of Jimmy Sanders, a fellow African American and his traveling companion throughout the early 1960s. In his second autobiography, *Up from Nigger,* Gregory stated, "I just couldn't miss with material salted by Bob [Orben] and peppered by Jim [Sanders]." Dick Gregory with James R. McGraw, *Up from Nigger* (New York: Stein and Day, 1975), 15.

47. Hentoff, "Goodbye Mistah Bones," 94; Gregory, *Up from Nigger,* 49; Gregory, *Nigger,* 132; Gregory quoted in Thomas B. Morgan, "The Two Worlds of Dick Gregory," *Holiday* 36 (December 1964):127.

48. Gregory, *From the Back of Bus,* 80; Dick Gregory, *So You See . . . We All Have Problems* (Colpix, 1964); Dick Gregory, *Dick Gregory in Living Black and White* (Colpix, 1961); Dick Gregory, *East and West* (Colpix, 1961).

49. Robert Lipsyte, "You Gits a Little Uppity and You Lands in Jail," *Esquire* 68 (August 1967):72–73.

50. Gregory quoted in Millstein, "A Negro Says It with Jokes," 30; Robert C. Ruark, "The Will Rogers of the Atomic Age," *New York World-Telegram,* September 15, 1961, Dick Gregory Clipping File, BRT; "Humor, Integrated," 68; Hugh Hefner, introduction to *From the Back of the Bus,* 11; Alex Dreier, liner notes for *Dick Gregory in Living Black and White* (Colpix, 1961).

51. Gregory, *Nigger,* 132.

52. Gregory, *Nigger,* 132.

53. A number of people have commented that a number of Gregory's more poignant comic observations were taken directly from African American joke cycles. Arthur Steuer, for example, claimed in the profile of Gregory he contributed to *Esquire* that many of Gregory's jokes "are the same comic postcards Negroes have been sending to themselves for years." Arthur Steuer, "The Space for Race in Humor," *Esquire* 56 (November 1961):147. Another source for Gregory's material were the routines of other black comics. According to Nipsey Russell, Slappy White, and Timmie Rogers, Gregory blatantly pirated their jokes. When Gregory opened the Blue Angel in New York, these three sat at a front table with a large tape recorder so that they could find out, as White later wrote Gregory, "which of our material not to use any more." Hentoff, "Goodbye Mistah Bones," 90.

54. Gregory, *Nigger,* 132.

55. Dick Gregory, *Dick Gregory in Living Black and White;* Dick Gregory, *The Two Sides of Dick Gregory* (Vee Jay, 1963); Gregory quoted in "Humor, Integrated," 68; Millstein, "A Negro Says It with Jokes," 37.

56. "Godfrey Cambridge," *Current Biography,* 1969, ed. Charles Moritz (New York: H. W. Wilson, 1969), 67–69; Gregory quoted in Mel Gussow, "Laugh at This Negro, but Darkly," *Esquire* 62 (November 1964):94; Godfrey Cambridge, *Ready or Not, It's Godfrey Cambridge* (Epic, 1964); Jose, "Godfrey Cambridge," *Variety,* April 22, 1964, 142.

57. Gregory, *Nigger,* 159–60.

58. "Yankee, Go Home," *Time,* April 12, 1963, 26; Claude Sitton, "Mississippi Town Seizes 19 Negroes," *New York Times,* April 4, 1963, 22; "Locked Out," *Newsweek,* April 15, 1963, 30–31; Gregory, *Nigger,* 170; Howard Zinn, *The New Abolitionists* (Boston: Beacon Press, 1964), 150–51.

59. Milton Esterow, "Dick Gregory Comes Marching In," *New York Times,* September 9, 1963, 23; Gregory, *Callus on My Soul,* 20; Gregory, *Nigger,* 79, 155; Gregory quoted in Redd Foxx and Norma Miller, *The Redd Foxx Encyclopedia of Black Humor,* 180–81; Bob Ellison, "Dick Gregory: Last Man at the Lunch Counter," *Rogue* 9 (June 1964):28; James A. Wechsler, "The Tragedian," *New York Post,* May 8, 1963, 44.

CHAPTER NINE

1. Dickstein, *Gates of Eden,* 119–21; Joseph Heller, "Joseph Heller Replies," *Realist* 50 (May 1964):30. While many historians have argued that Americans accommodated themselves to the prerogatives of the cold war and the presence of nuclear weapons during the 1950s, others have recently characterized a more troubled response. Maurice Isserman, Allan Winkler, and Elaine Tyler May, among others, have charted movements and protests that were coordinated during this period—the formation of the National Committee for a Sane Nuclear Policy (SANE) in 1957 and the more militant Committee for Nonviolent Action in 1958, the orchestration of the Women's Strike for Peace in 1961, and the grassroots protests against civil defense, for example—that directly confronted the government's nuclear diplomacy and cold war policies. Maurice Isserman, *If I Had a Hammer: The Death of the Old Left and the Birth of the New Left* (Urbana: University of Illinois Press, 1993); Allan Winkler, *Life under a Cloud: American Anxiety about the Atom* (New York: Oxford University Press, 1993); and Elaine Tyler May, *Homeward Bound: American Families in the Cold War Era.* Historian Paul Boyer has argued that a "mood of diminished awareness and acquiescence in the developing arms race" settled in during the early 1950s but that it "soon gave way to a new and very different stage" in the period 1955–63. Paul Boyer, *By the Bomb's Early Light,* 352. In the realm of cold war culture, examples of resistance to the bomb during the 1950s have only recently caught the attention of historians. In her important study *Dr. Strangelove's America,* Margot Henriksen argues that while the atomic bomb became the "unifying symbol of American safety and security in the culture of consensus," it also spawned an "alternative culture of dissent, a rebellious counterculture that conflicted with the culture of consensus and its new understanding of life with this new revolutionary weapon of death and destruction." Indeed, Henriksen convincingly demonstrates that representations of cold war culture ranging from science fiction films to Beat poetry, while they did not go so far as Allen Ginsberg's notorious injunction to "Go fuck yourself with your atom bomb," reflected the American public's ambivalence over the superpowers' annihilating capacity. Henriksen, *Dr. Strangelove's America,* xx, 81. Valuable critical evaluations of Joseph Heller's masterpiece include, in addition to Henriksen's book, Robert Brustein, "The Logic of Survival in a Lunatic World," *New Republic* 145 (November 13, 1961):11–13; Dickstein, *Leopards in the Temple,* 41–48; and Stephen J. Whitfield, "Still the Best Catch There Is: Joseph Heller's Catch-22" in *Rethinking Cold War Culture,* ed. James Gilbert and Peter Kuznick (Washington, D.C.: Smithsonian Institution Press, 2001), 175–200.

2. Boyer, *By the Bomb's Early Light,* 352.

3. Tom Lehrer, "The Wild West Is Where I Want to Be," *The Tom Lehrer Song Book* (New York: Crown Publishers, 1962), 56–59.

4. Charles Bazerman, "Nuclear Information: One Rhetorical Moment in the Construction of the Information Age," *Written Communication* 18 (July 2001):259–95.

5. Tom Lehrer, "We Will All Go Together When We Go," *The Remains of Tom Lehrer* (Warner Brothers, 2000).

6. Tom Lehrer, interview by author, tape recording, Cambridge, Massachusetts, September 24, 1996; Larry Dubois, "Playboy Interview: Jules Feiffer," 81–96, 206–207; Jules Feiffer, telephone interview by author, tape recording, December 6, 1996.

7. Jules Feiffer to Rhoda and David Feiffer, n.d., and Mimi Feiffer to Jules Feiffer, August 27, 1951, JF, box 2; "Up against the Wall!: Jules Feiffer," in Westin, ed. *Getting Angry Six Times a Week: A Portfolio of Political Cartoons,* 15; Feiffer quoted in Jan Henry, "Jules Feiffer: The Boy Cartoonist No Longer," *Brooklyn Heights Press,* February 28, 1963, 1; Feiffer quoted in Groth, "Memories of a Pro Bono Cartoonist," 46.

8. Feiffer quoted in Henry Allen, "Jules Feiffer: The Ever Dissenting Cartoonist at 50," B1; Jules Feiffer, *Munro,* in *Passionella: and Other Stories* (New York: McGraw-Hill Book Company, 1959). Feiffer's animated version of *Munro,* directed by Gene Dietch, won him an Academy Award in 1961.

9. Jules Feiffer, telephone interview by author, tape recording, December 6, 1996; Feiffer quoted in Groth, "Memories of a Pro Bono Cartoonist," 46, 65.

10. Feiffer quoted in Groth, "Memories of a Pro Bono Cartoonist," 49; Jules Feiffer, *Boom,* in *Passionella: and Other Stories;* "Cartoonist Stages Whopper," *Boston Globe,* February 26, 1962.

11. Jules Feiffer, *Feiffer: The Collected Works,* vol. 3 (Seattle: Fantagraphics Books, 1992), 39; Jules Feiffer, *Feiffer, Village Voice,* February 10, 1960, 7.

12. Jules Feiffer, *Boy, Girl, Boy, Girl,* unpaginated.

13. Jules Feiffer, *Feiffer, Village Voice,* July 30, 1958.

14. Jules Feiffer, *Feiffer, Village Voice,* August 18, 1960, 4.

15. Jules Feiffer, *Feiffer, New Republic* 145 (December 11, 1961):27; Jules Feiffer, *Feiffer, Village Voice,* May 4, 1960, 1.

16. Jules Feiffer, *Crawling Arnold, Horizon* 4 (November 1961):49–56; Greg Connolley, "Hands Off CBC despite the Critics," *Ottawa Citizen,* February 15, 1962.

17. Jules Feiffer, *Sick, Sick, Sick, Village Voice,* September 17, 1958, 4; Jules Feiffer, *Feiffer, New Republic* 145 (September 4, 1961):27; Jules Feiffer, "Feiffer," *Village Voice,* October 13, 1960, 4.

18. Feiffer, *Feiffer: The Collected Works,* 6, 22; Jules Feiffer, *Feiffer, Village Voice,* March 23, 1960, 4.

19. Jules Feiffer, "Good By, Satire, Good By," *New York Herald Tribune,* May 15, 1959; Jules Feiffer, *Feiffer, New Republic* 144 (April 10, 1961):25.

20. Jules Feiffer, *Feiffer, Village Voice,* June 11, 1958; reprinted in Jules Feiffer, *Feiffer: The Collected Works,* vol. 3, 46.

21. Jules Feiffer, *Feiffer, Village Voice,* July 13, 1961, 4.

22. Jules Feiffer, "Jules Feiffer," *New Republic* 145 (August 21, 1961):25. Much to Feiffer's chagrin, Arthur M. Schlesinger Jr., calling himself an "inveterate Feiffer fan," wrote to Feiffer and requested an original of this cartoon. Arthur M. Schlesinger Jr. to Jules Feiffer, August 28, 1961, JF, box 9.

23. Jules Feiffer, *Jules Feiffer, New Republic* 146 (March 19, 1962):29.

24. Jules Feiffer, *Jules Feiffer, New Republic* 146 (April 2, 1962):27.

25. Todd Gitlin to Jules Feiffer, April 3, 1962, JF, box 9.

26. Nancy Pogel and Paul Somers Jr. have claimed that Herblock's "Mr. Atom" "ranks among the most effective cartoon symbols of the mid-twentieth century." Nancy Pogel and Paul Somers Jr., "Editorial Cartoons," in *Handbook of American Popular Culture,* ed. M. Thomas Inge (New York: Greenwood Press, 1989):374. Herblock intended "Mr. Atom" to be sinister, and he was flattered when people told him it gave them "the shivers." Unfortunately, some Americans considered the character more "cute" than menacing. One enterprising clothier even proposed to license it for a new line of neckwear. Block, *The Herblock Book,* 35; Block, *A Cartoonist's Life,* 125.

27. Block, *Special for Today,* 179, 14, 30.

28. Mauldin, frontispiece for *I've Decided I Want My Seat Back;* Robert Osborn, cover illustration for the *New Republic* 148 (April 27, 1963); Robert Osborn, "The Balance of Terror," *New Republic* 145 (August 7, 1961):19; Mauldin cartoons nos. 576 and 728, A size, BMP.

29. Cover illustration for *New Republic* 146 (January 15, 1962); Mauldin cartoons nos. 848, 919, 767, A size, BMP.

30. Mauldin cartoons nos. 1039, 764, 829, A size, BMP.

31. Mauldin cartoon no. 732, A size, BMP; Mauldin, *I've Decided I Want My Seat Back,* 34; Block, *A Cartoonist's Life,* 195; Mauldin, *What's Got Your Back Up?* 113.

32. Bob Bone, "Hallelujah I'm a Bomb or Singing in the Bathtub," *Monocle* 1(2) (1957):5–6; John Putnam, "The Pleasure Principle," *Monocle* 3 (Summer 1959):15; "A Plan to Save WNDT," *Outsider's Newsletter* 1(26) (1963):4–5; Allan Danzig, "Outcast of Yucca Flat," *Monocle* 2 (Summer 1958):4.

33. Untitled cartoon, *Monocle* 5(1) (1962):84; Ed Koren, "Superkahn, Government Contractor," *Outsider's Newsletter* 1(30) (1963):10–11; Friedrich, "The Ultimate Solution: An Interview with Dr. Grubble," *Monocle* 5(1) (1962):38–41; "Col. C.C. Chesnut's Column," *Outsider's Newsletter* 1(14)(1963):5; "Col. C.C. Chesnut's Column," *Outsider's Newsletter* 1(18) (1963):2.

34. Victor Navasky to the editor of the *Saturday Review,* reprinted in *Monocle* 5(1) (1961):82; Kurt Vonnegut Jr. and Karla Kuskin, "'Hole Beautiful': Prospectus for a Magazine of Shelteredness," *Monocle* 5(1) (1961):45–51.

35. Y, "Self Containment: A New Foreign Policy," *Monocle* 3 (Summer 1959):7–9; Carleton Beals, "Such a Little Country," *Monocle* 2 (Winter 1958–59):19; Edward Sorel and Seymour Chwast, "Cold War Cut-Outs," *Monocle* 5 (Summer–Fall 1963):57–60; C. D. B. Bryan, "Lord of the Hawks," *Monocle* 5 (Summer–Fall 1963):16–25.

36. "Cuban Exiles to Be Unleashed," *Outsider's Newsletter* 1(27) 27 (1963):1–3; "Broadway on the Go," *Outsider's Newsletter* 1(47) (1963):5, 12; "Time-Incer, Burned-Up, Burns Up," *Outsider's Newsletter* 1(50) (1963):7; "Excerpts from the Diary of Mme. Nhu," *Outsider's Newsletter* 1(50) (1963):2–4; "Outsider's Newsreal," *Outsider's Newsletter* 1(46) (1963):8–9, 12.

37. "Co-Existence Love Songs" *Outsider's Newsletter* 1(49) (1963):4.

38. Dan Greenburg, "Inter-Office Memorandum: Change of CIA's Image," *Monocle* 5 (Winter 1963–64):40–43.

39. Richard R. Lingeman, "CIA House Organ: For Your Eyes Only," *Monocle* 5 (Winter 1963–64):15–22. According to Navasky, the assassination of President Kennedy deterred Simon and Schuster from distributing most of the 75,000 copies of the "CIA Issue" that were printed. Members of the CIA's Office of Security managed to procure a copy and subsequently deemed it "not entertaining or humorous . . . in fact several of the cartoons are vulgar and in extremely poor taste . . ." Navasky, *A Matter of Opinion,* 81.

40. "The Madness at Monk's Place," *Horizon* 3 (July 1961):77

41. Quoted in Gelb, "Cabaret Menu: Roast Politician," 32.

42. The Second City, "Brainwashing in Berlin," transcribed scene in unpaginated *Alarums and Excursions* binder, SCA.

43. The Second City, "My Friend Art Is Dead," tape recording, July 4, 1962, SCA; "Partial Show Prior to 12/63 with Del Close, Jack Burns, Avery Schreiber," tape recording, n.d., SCA; "Political Humor, 1962," 72.

44. Description of "The Button Room" taken from *The Premise,* unpublished drama manuscript, August 21, 1961, MD; Hentoff, "Instant Theater," 47.

45. *The Jack Paar Show,* NBC-TV, March 1, 1963, videotape viewed at MTR. According to critic Robert Brustein, it was "under the shadow of [the bomb's] monstrous birth" that the entire Fringe revue was played out. Brustein, "The Healthiness of Sick Comedy," 28–30.

46. Henriksen, *Dr. Strangelove's America,* 210–33; The Second City, "Fallout Shelter Salesman," in *The Second City Revue,* videotape of program produced by WNEW-TV, July 31, 1963, New York, viewed at MTR.

47. "Playboy after Hours," *Playboy* 9 (February 1962):15; "The Contaminators: A Statement by the Editors of Playboy," *Playboy* 6 (October 1959); Seymour Chwast and Ed Sorel, "How to Stop Worrying about the Bomb," *Playboy* 9 (March 1962):80–81.

48. Description of "Laos" taken from *The Premise,* unpublished drama manuscript, August 21, 1961, MD; and Feldman, *A Critical Analysis of Improvisational Theatre in the United States from 1955–1968,* 123; "Fresh Revue of Second City, Chi, Plenty Caustic but Stirs Less Impact," *Variety,* August 2, 1961, 92. Descriptions of and quotations from The Second City's "General's Headquarters" or "Technical Assistance in Vietnam" are taken from *My Friend Art Is Dead,* tape recording, July 4, 1962, SCA; "Partial Show prior to 12/63 with Del, Jack Burns, Avery Schreiber," tape recording, n.d., SCA; and "What's So Funny," *Bell and Howell's Close-Up!,* ABC-TV, June 12, 1962 videotape viewed at the Motion Picture and Television Reading Room, MBRS. The impression one gets from viewing "Technical Assistance in Vietnam" as it was performed in front of an audience is that relatively few in attendance dared laugh at this ironic commentary about Christianity and war.

49. Paul Gardner, "Nothing Sacred," *New York Times,* March 29, 1964, sec. 2, p. 13; Judith Crist, "A Brassy, Sassy, New 'Establishment," *New York Herald Tribune,* November 1, 1963, 12; "Strollers, NY," *Variety,* September 18, 1963, 65.

50. "The Incident at Los Voraces" and other selected segments from "The Stan

Freberg Show" are taken from Stan Freberg, *The Best of the Stan Freberg Shows* (Capitol, 1990), sound cassettes.

51. Freberg, *It Only Hurts When I Laugh,* 111.

52. "Stan, the Man," *Time,* July 29, 1957, 66.

53. Henriksen, *Dr. Strangelove's America,* 265.

54. Henriksen, *Dr. Strangelove's America,* 304–31; Lee Hill, *A Grand Guy: The Art and Life of Terry Southern* (New York: HarperCollins, 2001), 98–128; John Molleson, "Kubrick's Apocalyptic Comedy," *New York Herald Tribune Magazine,* January 26, 1964, 28–30; Whitfield, *The Culture of the Cold War,* 219–25; Peter Lyon, "The Astonishing Stanley Kubrick," *Holiday* 35 (February 1964):101–105, 146–50; Lawrence Suid, "The Pentagon and Hollywood: *Dr. Strangelove or: How I Learned to Stop Worrying and Love the Bomb,*" in *American History/American Film: Interpreting the Hollywood Image,* ed. John E. O'Connor and Martin A. Jackson (New York: Frederick Ungar Publishing, 1979), 220–35; Paul Boyer, *Fallout: A Historian Reflects on America's Half-Century Encounter with Nuclear Weapons* (Columbus: Ohio State University Press, 1998), 95–102; Charles Maland, "*Dr. Strangelove* (1964): Nightmare Comedy and the Ideology of Liberal Consensus," in *Hollywood as Historian,* ed. Peter C. Rollins (Lexington: University of Kentucky Press, 1983), 190–210; Vincent LoBrutto, *Stanley Kubrick: A Biography* (New York: Donald I. Fine Books, 1997), 227–51; Terry Southern, "Strangelove Outtake: Notes from the War Room," *Grand Street* 13 (Summer 1994):64–80.

55. "How Would You Make a Film about the H-Bomb?" *Show Magazine* 2 (June 1962):78–81.

56. Kubrick quoted in Whitfield, *The Culture of the Cold War,* 219–20; Kubrick quoted in Eugene P. Walz, "Dr. Strangelove, Or: How I Learned to Stop Worrying and Love the Bomb" in *Frames of Reference: Essays on the Rhetoric of Film,* ed. Eugene P. Walz, John Harrington, and Vincent DiMarco (Dubuque, Ia.: Kendall/Hunt Publishing Company, 1972), 69; LoBrutto, *Stanley Kubrick,* 229.

57. Jules Feiffer, telephone interview by author, tape recording, December 19, 1996; Stanley Kubrick to Jules Feiffer, January 25, 1959, JF, box 8.

58. "The Astonishing Stanley Kubrick," 105, 146; Kubrick quoted in Eugene Archer, "How to Learn to Love World Destruction," *New York Times,* January 26, 1964, sec. 2, p. 13, and in "Direct Hit," *Newsweek,* February 3, 1964, 79.

59. Charles Marowitz, "A Short Sprint with Lenny Bruce," in *Burnt Bridges: A Souvenir of the Swinging Sixties and Beyond* (Toronto: Hodder & Stoughton, 1990), 44; Jules Feiffer, telephone interview by author, tape recording, December 19, 1996; Terry Southern, "Dark Laughter in the Towers," *Nation* 190 (April 23, 1960):348–49; Terry Southern, "After the Bomb, Dad Came Up with Ice," *New York Times,* June 2, 1963, 28; Southern, "Strangelove Outtake," 64–80.

60. *Dr. Strangelove, or: How I Learned to Stop Worrying and Love the Bomb* (Columbia Pictures, 1964).

61. The Washington, D.C., Uniquecorn several years earlier performed a routine in which President Kennedy (played by Arch Lustberg) calls Premier Khrushchev to apologize for the mistake of launching U.S. missiles toward Moscow. Arch Lustberg, telephone interview by author, tape recording, January 24, 2000.

62. *Dr. Strangelove, or: How I Learned to Stop Worrying and Love the Bomb.* In the film's original ending, the Soviet ambassador aims a custard pie at General Turgidon but hits President Muffley instead. In an ironic foreshadowing of President's Kennedy's assassination later that year, the president falls to the ground and General Turgidson exclaims, "Gentlemen... The President has been struck down, in the prime of his life and his presidency." A gigantic pie-throwing melee ensues among the Soviets, Joints Chiefs, and technical advisors. Because the actors could not keep their faces straight during filming, Kubrick wisely decided to remove this slapstick scene from the final cut. Southern, "Strangelove Outtake," 75–78.

63. May, *Homeward Bound,* 219–20.

64. Marvin Kitman, "By Jingo," *Outsider's Newsletter* 1(5) (1963):4.

65. Henriksen, *Dr. Strangelove's America,* 304–31; Whitfield, *The Culture of the Cold War,* 219–25; Maland, "*Dr. Strangelove* (1964)," 190–210; Boyer, *Fallout: A Historian Reflects on America's Half-Century Encounter with Nuclear Weapons,* 95–102.

66. Anthony F. Macklin, "Sex and Dr. Strangelove," *Film Comment* 3 (Summer 1964):55–57.

67. Fred Kaplan, "Truth Stranger Than 'Strangelove,'" *New York Times* October 10, 2004, sec. 2, p. 21. Herman Kahn was also so struck by the verisimilitude of Kubrick's film that he was motivated to ask the director for a royalty! Whitfield, *The Culture of the Cold War,* 221–22.

68. Southern, "Strangelove Outtake," 78–80; "Inside the Making of *Dr. Strangelove or: How I Learned to Stop Worrying and Love the Bomb,*" dir. David Naylor (Columbia Tristar Home Video, 2000).

69. Lee Russell, "Stanley Kubrick," *New Left Review* 26 (Summer 1964):71–74; Midge Decter, "The Strangely Polite 'Dr. Strangelove,'" *Commentary* 37 (May 1964):75–77; Susan Sontag, "Going to Theater (and the Movies)," *Partisan Review* 31 (Spring 1964):290–92.

70. Moira Walsh, "Films: Dr. Strangelove," *America* 110 (March 28, 1964):462–65; Philip T. Hartung, "What Five-Sided Building?" *Commonweal* 79 (February 21, 1964): 632–33; "Capital Notes a 'Strangelove' Rap," *Variety,* February 26, 1964, 1.

71. Bosley Crowther, "'Dr. Strangelove, a Shattering Sick Joke," *New York Times,* January 30, 1964, 24; Bosley Crowther, "Hysterical Laughter: Further Thoughts on 'Dr. Strangelove,'" *New York Times,* February 16, 1964, sec. 2, p. 9.

72. Lewis Mumford, "The Human Prospect," in *Interpretations and Forecasts: 1922–1972* (New York: Harcourt Brace Jovanovich, 1972), 462.

73. Lewis Mumford, "The Mood of Satire," *Freeman* 8 (November 14, 1923):224–25; Lewis Mumford, in "Strangelove Reactions," *New York Times,* March 1, 1964, sec. 2, p. 8.

74. Gilbert Seldes in "'Patient' Diagnoses 'Dr. Strangelove,'" *New York Times,* April 5, 1964, sec. 2, p. 7; Dwight Macdonald, "Films," *Esquire* 61 (February 1964): 26–28.

75. Stanley Kauffman, "Dean Swift in the 20th Century," *New Republic* 150 (February 1, 1964):26–28; Robert Brustein, "Out of This World," *New York Review of Books* 1 (February 6, 1964):3–4.

76. Nora Sayle, *Running Time: Films of the Cold War* (New York: Dial Press, 1982), 219;

Mumford in "Strangelove Reactions," 8. Historians of American cold war culture have generally agreed with Mumford's assessment. Stephen Whitfield, for example, has written that after *Dr. Strangelove,* the "air of democratic discourse was less thin." Whitfield, *The Culture of the Cold War,* 224. Margot Henriksen likewise views *Dr. Strangelove* as a "cultural tour de force," one of the seminal products of the "culture of dissent" spawned in reaction to the cold war power politics of the 1950s.

> Its attention to accidental nuclear war and the profanity of the nuclear establishment summed up postwar cultural qualms about the corruption of American power and leadership and undermined the sacred Cold War institutions of the bomb and its military and political bureaucracy . . . With a revisionist, imaginative, iconoclastic vision symbolic of the cultural renaissance in the 1960s, Dr. Strangelove showed the previously disguised Cold War reality for what it was: immoral, insane, deadly—and ridiculous.
>
> HENRIKSEN, *Dr. Strangelove's America,* 318.

CHAPTER TEN

1. R. W. Emerson, secundus, "Television's Peril to Culture," *American Scholar* 19 (Spring 1950):137–40.

2. Barnouw, *Tube of Plenty,* 115–30; Jack Gould, "Let's Slow Down: TV 'Clean Up' Threatens to Get out of Hand," *New York Times,* April 9, 1950, Sec. 2, p. 11; "Boston Prelate Blasts TV Comics for 'Committing (Video) Suicide," *Variety,* February 28, 1951, 26; Alfred Towne, "The New Taste in Humor," *American Mercury* 73 (September 1951): 27; "Highlights of Television B'casters Code of Program Standards," *Variety,* October 24, 1951, 36; Fred MacDonald, *One Nation under Television* (New York: Pantheon Books, 1990), 101–12; Matthew Murray, "Television Wipes Its Feet: The Commercial and Ethical Considerations behind the Adoption of the Television Code," *Journal of Popular Film and Television* 21 (Fall 1993):128–38; Thomas Doherty, *Cold War, Cool Medium: Television, McCarthyism, and American Culture* (New York: Columbia University Press, 2003); Lynn Spigel, *Make Room for TV: Television and the Family Ideal in Postwar America* (Chicago: University of Chicago Press, 1992), 147–51; Horace Newcomb, "TV Situation Comedies," *TV: The Most Popular Art;* David Marc, *Comic Visions: Television Comedy and American Culture* (New York: Routledge, 1992), 24–27; Mark Crispin Miller, "Deride and Conquer," in *Watching Television,* ed. Todd Gitlin (New York: Pantheon Books, 1987), 198; George Lipsitz, *Time Passages: Collective Memory and American Popular Culture* (Minneapolis: University of Minnesota Press, 1990), 39–75; David Marc, *Demographic Vistas: Television in American Culture* (Philadelphia: University of Pennsylvania Press, 1996). It is easy to caricature mid- and late-1950s sitcoms and omit mention of those few programs that did not adhere to the pattern of *Ozzie and Harriet.* One such program was Nat Hiken's spoof of military life, *You'll Never Get Rich*—also known in syndication as *The Phil Silvers Show* (CBS, 1955–59). Hiken, formerly a comedy writer for Fred Allen and Milton Berle's *Texaco Star Theater* who, like Henry Morgan, was also listed in *Red Channels,* was one of the most talented and respected television comedy writers of the decade. Hiken's interests were in developing comic situations beyond the private domains of the American suburbs. During the premiere season of *You'll*

Never Get Rich he told *Newsweek* magazine that he "picked the Army barracks" as a setting because he "wanted to get as far away . . . as possible" from the traditional sitcoms's "chintzy living room." In a further departure from the trend sitcoms and television in general began taking in the mid-1950s, *You'll Never Get Rich* even continued to feature African American performers. "World of Gags," *Newsweek,* October 24, 1955, 90.

3. Hugh G. Taylor, "What Are We Laughing At?" *Holiday* 28 (May 1960):212; Diamond quoted in Kisseloff, *The Box,* 333; Harold Mehling, *The Great Time-Killer* (Cleveland: World Publishing Company, 1962), 171.

4. Taylor, *Fred Allen: His Life and Wit,* 296; Jack Gould, "Television in Review," *New York Times,* September 11, 1953, 30; Gilbert Seldes, *The Public Arts,* 75. For more on the roles Fred Allen and other comedians played on Goodson-Todman game shows, see Gil Fates, *What's My Line?: The Inside History of TV's Most Famous Panel Show* (Englewood Cliffs, N.J.: Prentice-Hall, 1978).

5. Daniel Dixon, "Laughing at Madison Avenue for Fun and Profit," *Esquire* 51 (February 1959):57; Freberg, *It Only Hurts When I Laugh,* 119–28; Stan Freberg, telephone interview by author, tape recording, June 8, 1996. In 1959, Freberg produced his television pilot in Australia where he had a very devoted following.

6. Marx quoted in Wes D. Gehring, "Television's Other Groucho," *Humor* 5(3) (1992), 278. According to files recently released by the FBI, some American television viewers (and agency officials) still found something "subversive" about Marx and *You Bet Your Life.* Information regarding the FBI's interest into Groucho's political sympathies is provided in Jon Weiner, "The Secret Word on Groucho," *Nation* 267 (September 28, 1998):23–24.

7. Philip Roth, "The Hurdles of Satire," *New Republic* 137 (September 9, 1957):22. In its assumptions about the "mass mind" and "mass audience," Roth's assessment reflected justifications often cited by network and ad agency executives. One CBS official spoke for many of his colleagues in the industry when he explained, "Personally, I think [Caesar] is a very big talent. But the audience for satire just isn't big enough to pay off." A vice president at ABC-TV likewise opined that the only way Caesar could survive on television was by avoiding the "egghead" and "esoteric" and giving it "that old common denominator—empathy." And at NBC, the powerful vice president of television programs, Robert Lewine, declared that "the comedy that succeeds is that which approaches the greatest common denominator, and the comedy that is understood by the most people—on a regional age and educational basis—is the domestic-situation comedy, because it's so readily identifiable." "Decline of the Comedians," *Time,* May 27, 1957, 72; Gilbert Millstein, "TV's Comics Went Thataway," *New York Times Magazine,* February 2, 1958, 14.

8. Steve Allen, *The Funny Men* (New York: Simon and Schuster, 1956), 41; Al Capp, "Can TV Be Saved?" *Esquire* 60 (December 1963):211, 273.

9. Baughman, "The National Purpose and the Newest Medium: Liberal Critics of Television, 1958–1960," 41–55; James L. Baughman, *Television's Guardians: The FCC and the Politics of Programming 1958–1967* (Knoxville: University of Tennessee Press, 1985); Michael Curtin, *Redeeming the Wasteland: Television Documentary and Cold War Politics* (New Brunswick, N.J.: Rutgers University Press, 1995), 7–30; MacDonald, *One Nation*

under Television, 125–41. Barnouw, *Tube of Plenty,* 241–306 and passim; David Marc, *Bonfire of the Humanities: Television, Subliteracy, and Long-Term Memory Loss* (Syracuse, N.Y.: Syracuse University Press, 1995), 87–107; William Boddy, *Fifties Television: The Industry and Its Critics* (Urbana: University of Illinois Press, 1990), 237; "Inside Jack Gould," *Television Magazine* 15 (November 1958):49.

10. Julie D'Acci, "Nobody's Woman?: Honey West and the New Sexuality," and Moya Luckett, "Girl Watchers: Patty Duke and Teen TV," in *The Revolution Wasn't Televised: Sixties Television and Social Conflict,* ed. Lynn Spigel and Michael Curtin (New York: Routledge, 1997), 73–118; William Boddy, "Senator Dodd Goes to Hollywood: Investigating Video Violence," in *The Revolution Wasn't Televised,* 177; Harold Mehling, *The Great Time-Killer,* 32; "Says the Critic," *Television Magazine* 20 (April 1963):58–59, 90; Rufus Crater, "The Restless Viewer," *Television Magazine* 18 (May 1961):39–43; Rufus Crater, "Says the Viewer," *Television Magazine* 20 (April 1963):54.

11. Crater, "Says the Viewer," 54–57, 82.

12. Lynn Spigel, "From Domestic Space to Outer Space: The 1960s Fantastic Family Sit-Com," in *Close Encounters: Film, Feminism and Science Fiction,* ed. Constance Penley et al. (Minneapolis: University of Minnesota Press, 1991), 214. David Marc's reading of *The Dick Van Dyke Show* in his *Comic Visions: Television Comedy and American Culture* remains the best interpretation of this popular, award-winning comedy series. Allan Funt and the enormously popular program he hosted are described in J. M. Flagler's "Student of the Spontaneous," *New Yorker,* December 10, 1960, 59–92. See also Deborah Haber, "Kings among the Jesters," *Television Magazine* 20 (September 1963):54–65 and passim.

13. Lax, *Woody Allen,* 111–14; Stan Freberg, telephone interview by author, tape recording, June 8, 1996; "Stan Freberg Presents: Chinese New Year's Special," *Show Magazine* 2 (February 1962):22.

14. Denning, *The Cultural Front,* 420–22; Keith Scott, *The Moose That Roared: The Story of Jay Ward, Bill Scott, a Flying Squirrel, and a Talking Moose* (New York: St. Martins Griffin, 2001).

15. Hal Erickson, *Television Cartoon Shows: An Illustrated Encyclopedia, 1949 through 1993* (Jefferson, N.C.: McFarland & Company, 1995), 412–20, "Bullwinkle Show," *Variety,* September 27, 1961, 36; "Of Moose and Men," *Newsweek,* December 4, 1961, 79; Bullwinkle Clipping File, CA; Jules Feiffer, "Bullwinke, A Moose with Bezazz," *Show Business Illustrated* 1 (November 28, 1961):8.

16. Erickson, *Television Cartoon Shows,* 413–19; "Bullwinkle vs. NBC: To the Network, No Moose was Good Moose," *TV Guide,* August 11, 1962, 22–26; "The Horns of Bullwinkle Moose's Dilemma," *TV Guide,* January 20, 1962, 22–24. NBC's decision to remove *The Bullwinkle Show* from its Sunday 7 p.m. slot was made with the assent and possibly the encouragement of the program's sponsor, General Mills. According to *TV Guide,* executives at General Mills and its advertising agency were never happy that NBC pitted *The Bullwinkle Show* against CBS's popular *Lassie.*

17. "Television Comedy," *Television Magazine* 18 (February 1961):37; Crater, "Says the Viewer," 86.

18. Information regarding comedians' guest appearances was obtained from "NBC

Program Analysis Files: Personality," catalogued at the Motion Picture and Television Reading Room, MBRS.

19. Mary Ann Watson, *The Expanding Vista: American Television in the Kennedy Years* (New York: Oxford University Press, 1990), 99–100.

20. Richard Gehman, "Same to You, Fella," *TV Guide,* January 27, 1962, 8; Dwight Whitney, "Bob Newhart Unbuttons His Mind," *TV Guide,* June 9, 1962, 4.

21. Watson, *The Expanding Vista,* 42; Pete Martin, "Backstage with Bob Newhart," *Saturday Evening Post,* October 14, 1961, 118–21.

22. Gehman, "Same to You, Fella," 8; Miller, "Deride and Conquer," 10. See also, "All Buttoned Down," *Newsweek,* January 15, 1962, 56.

23. Martin Williams' *Village Voice* review appears in his anthology *TV: The Casual Art* (New York: Oxford University Press, 1982):42–43; Richard F. Shepard, "Bob Newhart on TV: Problems, Pleasures of Weekly Show Are Explored by the Comedian," *New York Times,* April 29, 1962, sec. 2, p. 17; Sorensen, *Bob Newhart,* 66.

24. Whitney, "Bob Newhart Unbuttons His Mind," 5; Jack Gould, "A Comedian's Problems and a Controversy," *New York Times,* May 6, 1962, sec. 2, p. 17.

25. Val Adams, "'Candid Camera' Cancels Skit That Spoofed Soap Commercials," *New York Times,* November 1, 1963, 67; Val Adams, "Carney's TV Skit On Kennedy Is Off," *New York Times,* January 13, 1961, 58; "Jerry Lewis Blasts 'Incompetent Idiots' at ABC For Censoring Script," *Variety,* October 2, 1963, 31.

26. Videotape of Museum of Broadcasting Seminar Series: BBC Seminar: Television Satire with David Frost, Museum of Broadcasting, New York, December 2, 1986 viewed at MTR; David Frost, *David Frost: An Autobiography* (London: Harper Collins, 1993), 47; "The BBC's 'TWTWTW,'" *Variety,* December 19, 1962, 32; Clive Barnes, "Britain's 'TWTWTW,'" *New York Times,* September 22, 1963, sec. 2, p. 19.

27. James Feron, "'That Was the Week That Was' Is Now Only a Memory in Britain," *New York Times,* December 30, 1963, 41; Sydney Gruson, "B.B.C. Satire Show to Take Breather," *New York Times,* May 2, 1963, 5.

28. Grace Wyndham Goldie, *Facing the Nation: Television and Politics 1936–1976* (London: Bodley Head, 1977), 220–38; David Frost and Ned Sherrin, eds., *That Was the Week That Was* (London: W. H. Allen, 1963); Angus Wilson, "TW to the Third Power," *Show* 3 (June 1963) 18–19; John Crosby, "Old Auntie's Triumph," *New York Herald Tribune,* November 20, 1963, 25.

29. "What's Going On," *New Yorker,* May 11, 1963, 34–35; "What's Going On Here," *Variety,* May 12, 1963, 39; John Horn, "Wacky Newsreel — Inconclusive Satire," *New York Herald Tribune,* May 13, 1963, 17. The dialogue is quoted in "'What's Going on Here?'" *New York Post,* May 19, 1963, magazine section, p. 6.

30. Jack Gould, "British-Style Satire," *New York Times,* May 13, 1963, 59; "Satire in America," *Times of London,* July 13, 1963, 5; "Something's Going On Here," *Time,* May 24, 1963, 72.

31. Calvin Trillin, telephone interview by author, tape recording, December 19, 1997; Seminar on *That Was the Week That Was* sponsored by the Museum of Television and Radio, New York, June 3, 1997.

32. *The Ed Sullivan Show* aired on CBS on October 13 and 20, 1963. Both programs were viewed at MTR.

33. Hayward had became a power broker in the entertainment business as far back as the 1930s. It was then that he acquired a reputation as a hard-driving yet smooth and charismatic "gentleman's agent." After he sold his "stable" of talent to Jean vanden Heuvel's father, Jules Stein, at MCA in the mid-1940s (by this time it included Greta Garbo, Jimmy Stewart, Judy Garland, Fred Astaire, Ernest Hemingway, and dozens of other big-name clients), he began producing a string of blockbuster plays and musicals on Broadway including *South Pacific, Mr. Roberts,* and *The Sound of Music.* During the late 1950s, when his reputation as a stage and film producer was at its peak, Hayward began weighing prospects for translating theater-caliber entertainment to television. Television fascinated Hayward, and it lured him with the promise of large financial returns. He produced his first television "spectacular," *The Fabulous Fifties,* in 1960 on CBS for his friend William Paley. Anchored by two Nichols and May scenes and a Shelley Berman monologue, *The Fabulous Fifties* was a critical and popular success and the winner of Emmy and Peabody Awards. Brooke Hayward, *Haywire* (New York: Alfred A. Knopf, 1977); Slim Keith with Annette Tapert, *Slim: Memories of a Rich and Imperfect Life* (New York: Simon and Schuster, 1990); Sonia Berman, *The Crossing: Adano to Catonsville: Leland Hayward's Producing Career* (Lanham, Md.: Scarecrow Press, 1995); Jack Gould, "TV: 'Fabulous Fifties,'" *New York Times,* February 1, 1960, 51.

34. In 1962 Hayward had attempted to tap the "Camelot" fever in a Broadway production titled *Mr. President.* With the directorial services of Joshua Logan, music and lyrics provided by Irving Berlin, and enormous preopening publicity, *Mr. President* had all the ingredients, Hayward hoped, of a smash hit. Despite its initial strong sales, *Mr. President* drew bad reviews and ended up a box-office flop. Sally Bedell Smith, *Reflected Glory: The Life of Pamela Churchill Harriman* (New York: Simon & Schuster, 1996), 195–242; Christopher Ogden, *Life of the Party: The Biography of Pamela Digby Churchill Hayward Harriman* (Boston: Little, Brown, and Company, 1994), 270–95.

35. "That Was the Week That Was: A Presentation for a network half hour television program," LHP, box 14.

36. See, for example, Gardner's *Who's in Charge Here* (New York: Pocket Books, 1962), *Miss Caroline* (Greenwich, Conn.: Fawcett Publications, 1963), and *Gerald Gardner's News-Reals News-Reals* (New York: Pocket Books, 1963). Early on, Hayward expressed interest in soliciting material from witty liberal writers, commentators, and critics such as Art Buchwald, Gore Vidal, Murray Kempton, Marya Mannes, Ken Tynan, Russell Lynes, Norman Mailer, Dwight Macdonald, Bill Mauldin, Dorothy Parker, and S. J. Perelman.

37. Robert Emmett, telephone interview by author, tape recording, July 25, 1997; "That Was the Week That Was: A Presentation for a network half hour television program," LHP, box 14; Marshall Jamison to Leland Hayward, June 21, 1963, LHP, box 1.

38. Kintner was a commanding presence at NBC, hailed by many as the kinetic force responsible for turning the network into an efficient, ratings-hungry, profitable enterprise. Although many critics complained about Kintner's replacement of televi-

sion pioneer Pat Weaver, stockholders of NBC's parent company RCA were no doubt pleased by the financial returns brought in by Kintner's entertainment-heavy prime-time formula. During the notorious quiz show scandal and the subsequent Dodd Senate Judiciary Committee Hearings on Juvenile Delinquency, Kintner was implicated as a major force in the networks' turn toward sleaze and deception. In the early 1960s, he overcame some of the personal embarrassment caused by the scandals by expanding (with much fanfare) NBC's news bureau. As a veteran newsman who cut his teeth as a reporter for the Washington bureau of the *New York Herald Tribune* during the 1930s, Kintner resolved to upgrade network news coverage. "NBC's Kintner: First Comes News," *Printers' Ink* 80 (August 3, 1962):52–56; "The Man Who Had It Made," *Newsweek,* December 20, 1965, 94; "The Kinetic Mr. Kintner," *Television Magazine* 14 (May 1957):62, 121, 123. An unflattering, fictional portrait of Kintner was provided by former Kintner colleague David Levy in his novel *The Chameleons* (New York: Dodd, Mead, 1964).

39. *That Was the Week That Was,* NBC promotional brochure, LHP, box 44.

40. Harold Stern, "Topical Satire English Style, Tested by NBC," *Philadelphia Inquirer,* November 8, 1963; Rex Polier, "British-Type Satire Gets a Tryout Today," *Philadelphia Inquirer Sunday Bulletin,* November 10, 1963, 2; Paul Gardner, "'That Was the Week That Was' Tonight," *New York Times,* November 10, 1963, sec. 2, p. 23.

41. *That Was the Week That Was,* originally broadcast by NBC, November 10, 1963, Videotape viewed at MTR.

42. *That Was the Week That Was,* originally broadcast by NBC, November 10, 1963, Videotape viewed at MTR.

43. John Horn, "Satire: A Splendid Debut," *New York Herald Tribune,* November 11, 1963, 15; Barbara Delatiner, "'That Was the Week That Was,'" New York *Newsday,* November 11, 1963; Harriet Van Horne, "That Was the Night That Was," *New York World Telegram,* November 11, 1963; Jack Gould, "TV: 'That Was the Week That Was,'" *New York Times,* November 11, 1963, 63; Jack Gould, "Turning Point," *New York Times,* November 17, 1963, sec. 2, p. 17.

44. "Telephone Conversation with Hedda Hopper—California," transcribed telephone conversation between Leland Hayward and Hedda Hopper, November 13, 1963, LHP box 1. This particular joke appears to have been Hayward's creation since he told Hopper that he had tried it out on "one of the Negro actors . . . and the band leader." Wisely, they recommended that Hayward revise the black actor's response from "We is" to "We are."

45. Transcribed "Telephone Conversation with Katherine Cole—NBC," November 13, 1963, LHP, box 1; "Report on the Mail Response to 'That Was the Week That Was,'" n.d., LHP, box 44.

46. John Kernell to Leland Hayward, November 19, 1963, LHP, box 3; Patricia Houston to *TW3,* November 28, 1963, LHP, box 3; Virginia Durr to Leland Hayward, November 11, 1963, LHP, box 3.

47. Murray Kiteley to Leland Hayward, n.d., LHP, box 3; Arno Boder to Leland Hayward, November 11, 1963, LHP, box 3; Dr. Howard Mackey to Leland Hayward, November 11, 1963, LHP, box 3.

48. Research and interviews conducted for this study reveal that President Kennedy's death was a shattering blow for many liberal satirists. In the weeks following the assassination, The Second City in Chicago consciously omitted all mention of politics and refused to rise to the bait of audience member Bill Mauldin when he suggested "President Kennedy" as the subject of an improvisation. The Second City arguably never regained its nerve. *Monocle* and the *Outsider's Newsletter* also suffered from this sobering event. The distribution of *Monocle*'s hard-hitting "CIA Issue," which appeared on newsstands just two days prior to the tragic event in Dallas, was particularly ill timed, since its cover and frontispiece featured illustrations of a feline Madame Nhu (a favorite target of both publications), drowning swine, a CIA operative with his hand concealed within his breast pocket, and a large smoking gun. Worse yet, a counterfeit news item in the November 24 issue of the *Outsider's Newsletter* reported that President Kennedy was missing from the White House. Omar Shapli, telephone interview by author, tape recording, May 24, 1999.

49. Val Adams, "That Was the Week That Was' Will Become Regular Series," *New York Times,* December 8, 1963, sec. 2, p. 17; George Rosen, "Something New Happening in TV," *Variety,* December 11, 1963, 21, 36.

50. Ed Friendly, telephone interview by author, tape recording, September 22, 1997; Thomas Ryan, telephone interview by author, tape recording, September 19, 1997; Robert J. Dunne to Thomas Ryan, June 25, 1963, LHP, box 1; "NBC Agreement," typed draft dated December 18, 1963, box 1. One of the many devices networks such as NBC used to consolidate their control over programming in the early 1960s was to eliminate the influence of single sponsors. By selling advertising time in "spots," networks were able to restrict the meddling of sponsors who previously attached their names to programs. Indeed, as *Variety*'s George Rosen reported, a number of "astute Madison Avenue observers" interpreted the scheduling of *TW3* as an important signal that "NBC has decided to assume sole and absolute control over its own schedule."

51. Hayward's correspondence to Jamison sheds light on one of the most glaring paradoxes behind *TW3,* namely, that the impresario behind one of television's "hippest" prime-time programs was thoroughly out of touch with American youth culture and the rapid social changes overtaking the United States. In reference to The Beatles, for example, Hayward suggested that "we could play one of their horrid records and say that there is a disease—a serious disease—sweeping the Continent . . ." Leland Hayward to Marshall Jamison, December 23, 1963, LHP, box 1.

52. "As Broadcast" script for January 24, 1964, LHP, box 15. "As Broadcast" scripts were kept by Hayward and his legal counsel Thomas Ryan in case a lawsuit was filed against them. As such, they were usually very accurate accounts of what transpired on *TW3.* Since NBC has destroyed all but four of the *TW3* episodes, these scripts are one of the few sources available for reconstructing the program. I have also benefited from the generous assistance of *TW3* fan Art Chimes and former *TW3* performer Stanley Grover. In addition to providing insight into specific segments of the program, they provided me with a collection of audiotaped excerpts taken from *TW3* broadcasts.

53. "As Broadcast" script for February 28, 1964, LHP, box 17; "As Broadcast" script for February 7, 1964, LHP, box 16.

54. "As Broadcast" script for March 6, 1964, LHP, box 18; See especially July 3 and 10, 1964, "As Broadcast" scripts, LHP, box 26. The description of the "Good Ole Summertime" segment is taken from the NBC audience survey, William Schwartz, "Results of Audience Reaction Studies," September 24, 1964, p. 4 in LHP, box 2. It is interesting to note that for this same broadcast, lines in the "Newsflashes" segment referring to racist murder and Philadelphia, Mississippi, as the "city of brotherly hate" were inexplicably deleted from the broadcast script. See "As Broadcast" and preliminary scripts for June 21 in LHP, box 25; Willard Levitas, telephone interview by author, tape recording, April 22, 1998. *TW3*'s attention to the cause of civil rights reflected the tolerant, liberal point of view shared by the program's writers and performers. At times, *TW3* performers even made their objections to the segregationist South public. Nancy Ames, a former Southern debutante and a descendant of Maryland gentry, lashed out at the South claiming, in a *Life* magazine profile on her, that "they ought to take a big scoop and just shove Southerners into the Gulf of Mexico." On the whole, *TW3*'s writers and performers enthusiastically supported racial integration, as evidenced, for example, by the inclusion of a song titled "The Lord Is Color Blind" on the May 15 broadcast. At the same time, however, they were suspicious of African American separatists and radicals such as Malcolm X. "What this country needs," a line from the April 17 broadcast quipped with tragic, unknowing irony, "is an X Malcolm." On the February 21 broadcast, Henry Morgan delivered a commentary on George Washington that counseled restraint on civil rights. In a heavy, moralizing tone that occasionally crept into *TW3*'s delivery, Morgan stated that two hundred years following Washington's birthday "there are still many among us who lose patience with the slow democratic process and turn to violence." "We believe with Washington," Morgan concluded, "that no man is above the law." "That Was the Deb That Was," *Life,* June 26, 1964, 87. *That Was the Week That Was,* originally broadcast by NBC, April 17, 1964; videotape viewed at MTR; "As Broadcast" script for February 21, 1964, LHP, box 17.

55. Excerpt from *That Was the Week That Was* broadcast, February 21, 1964, on tape recording provided by Stanley Grover. The use of the word "damn" here was improvised. The "As Broadcast" script denies that Brown substituted "damn" for "mighty."

56. In one of the most well received sketches from *TW3*'s first season, former *Kukla, Fran and Ollie* puppeteer and *TW3* regular Burr Tillstrom performed a melancholy "hand puppet scene" involving two family members separated by the Berlin Wall. *That Was the Week That Was* originally broadcast by NBC, January 10, 1964; videotape viewed at MTR. This performance won Tillstrom an Emmy Award in 1964.

57. *That Was the Week That Was,* April 17, 1964; Jack Gould, "TV: Finding the Target," *New York Times,* January 25, 1964, 49.

58. Visual clips from the February 21 boxing segment taken from an unidentified videotape recording at MTR. At the conclusion of this filmed segment, actor Roscoe Lee Brown told viewers that 244 boxers had died since 1945 and that Clay was in great danger of being added to the list. The January 24 sequence was reprised on May 5, 1965, during *TW3*'s farewell broadcast. *That Was the Week That Was,* originally broadcast by NBC, May 5, 1965; videotape viewed at MTR. In the days leading up to *TW3*'s January 24 airing, sponsor Brown & Williamson threatened to pull its ad if Hayward, Jami-

son, and NBC did not scrap the Martin segment. NBC, for its part, expertly milked the praise of critics by refusing to buckle to Brown & Williamson's pressure.

59. *That Was the Week That Was,* January 10, 1964; "As Broadcast" script for July 10, 1964, LHP, box 26; "As Broadcast" script for May 15, 1964, LHP, box 22. Frost first proposed to recite a list of Goldwater quotations for the *TW3* premiere, but, according to press reports, these lines were ordered cut by NBC.

60. Robert Emmett, telephone interview by author, tape recording, July 25, 1997; *That Was the Week That Was,* January 10, 1964; "As Broadcast" script for April 3, 1964, LHP, box 19; "The White House 'Week That Was,'" *Newsweek,* February 3, 1964, 15–16.

61. "As Broadcast" script for February 28, 1964, LHP, box 17.

62. One Portland woman, for example, explained to Hayward that Vietnam should be off limits since "men were murdered [there], and U.S. skirts are not clean in this matter." Harriett V. Stevens to Leland Hayward, November 11, 1963, LHP, box 3.

63. "As Broadcast" script for February 14, 1964, LHP, box 17; "As Broadcast" script for April 10, 1964, LHP, box 20.

64. "As Broadcast" script for May 1, 1964, LHP, box 21.

65. Frank Sauers, "*TW3* Brings Rain to Wasteland," *Villanovan,* February 19, 1964; Harriet Van Horne, "That Week Hits Its Stride—Fast, Funny," *New York World Telegram,* February 7, 1964, 47.

66. John Horn, "*TW3* This Is the Satire That Isn't," *New York Herald Tribune,* June 7, 1964, 33; Jack Gould, "Airwaves: The Week That Was," *New York Times,* April 19, 1964, sec. 2, p. 13; Jack Gould, "TV: Paar vs. '*TW3*,'" *New York Times,* May 25, 1964, 67. See also Albert Goldman, "British and American Satire: '*TW3*,'" *New Republic* 150 (February 22, 1964):27–28; Martin Levin, "Was That the Week That Was?" *Show* 4 (April 1964):38.

67. Robert Emmett, telephone interview by author, tape recording, July 25, 1997. This was difficult for viewers to ignore. "Audience reaction studies" undertaken by NBC at the end of the first season revealed that a considerable number of people who quit watching *TW3* thought its humor had become "silly." As one viewer from Pennsylvania wrote Leland Hayward at the end of April, *TW3* no longer contained "enough true satire." "I'm afraid," this viewer concluded, that "it's become just another TV gag show . . ." William Schwartz, "Results of Audience Reaction Studies," 2; C. Camarota to Leland Hayward Productions, April 27, 1964, LHP, box 3.

68. Marshall Jamison, telephone interview by author, tape recording, July 22, 1997; Leland Hayward to Marshall Jamison, March 27, 1964, LHP, box 1.

69. Frank B. Gibney to Leland Hayward, June 22, 1964, LHP, box 1; Howard Estabrook to Leland Hayward, June 7, 1964, LHP, box 1.

70. Charles Spitzer to Leland Hayward, March 2, 1964, box 1.

71. Leland Hayward to David Frost, March 13, 1964, box 1; Cynthia Lowry, "From 2 to 13 on TV," *(Plainfield NJ) Courier News,* May 9, 1964.

72. Leland Hayward to Marshall Jamison, March 25, 1964, LHP, box 1; Leland Hayward to Marshall Jamison, March 13, 1964, LHP, box 1; Cynthia Lowry, "Phyllis Newman: A Forum for Her Satire," *Newark Sunday Star-Ledger,* January 10, 1965; "As Broadcast" script for May 29, 1964, LHP, box 23.

73. Harry Harris, "U.S. Isn't Really Stupid, Concedes Morgan, the Mordant," *Philadelphia Inquirer,* February 9, 1964, 2; Leland Hayward to Marshall Jamison, March 13, 1964, LHP, box 1; Leland Hayward to Marshall Jamison, March 25, 1964, LHP, box 1; Leland Hayward to Marshall Jamison, March 27, 1964, LHP, box 1; Peter Bogdanovich, "That Was the Week That Was for That Was the Week That Was," *TV Guide,* April 4–10, 1964, 24–27.

74. Matt Massina, "Cast Changes Due for *TW3,*" *New York Daily News,* April 23, 1964, 102.

75. Ed Friendly, telephone interview by author, tape recording, September 22, 1997.

76. Alex Freeman, "TV Closeup," *TV Time,* January 21, 1964; Henry Harding, "For the Record," *TV Guide,* January 25, 1964, a-3; Bob Williams, "'Week That Was'—An Uncensored Row," *New York Post,* April 5, 1964. Ames, a performer who confessed to *Life* magazine that her "main trouble" was "keeping my mouth shut" greatly angered Hayward with her lack of restraint. It is interesting to note that he and NBC executives were not the only people she accused of discouraging *TW3*'s political satire. During the January 1964 Panama crisis, her grandfather Ricardo Alfaro, the former president of Panama, reportedly instructed his daughter to "keep quiet" on American intervention. For more on Ames, see "That Was the Deb That Was," 83–89.

77. Industry insiders speculated that pulling *TW3* from its original position was first and foremost a sop to NBC star Jack Paar. Paar despised *TW3* (they maintained a vituperative exchange during the early months of 1964) and resented NBC for not yielding its thirty minutes to his *Jack Paar Show.* When Paar finally gave up on the idea of expanding his program, he argued that he must have a strong comedy "lead-in" program. According to *Variety,* he finally threatened to leave NBC if it did not replace *TW3* with something else. "Jack Benny, *TW3* Switch Slots as Sop to Paar," *Variety,* February 26, 1964, 40; "Show Deplores," *Show* 4 (May 1964):35; "'That Was the Cast That Was' As NBC Plans Fresh Show for Fall," *Variety,* April 22, 1964, 105, 120.

78. Ed Friendly, telephone interview by author, tape recording, September 22, 1997.

79. Dean Shaffner to Ed Friendly, July 30, 1964, LHP, box 1; Willard Levitas to Leland Hayward, February 25, 1964, LHP, box 44; "'That Was the Cast That Was' As NBC Plans Fresh Show for Fall," 120.

80. Robert Dunne to Thomas Ryan, May 28, 1964, LHP, box 1; Thomas Ryan, "Confidential File Memo," June 4, 1964, LHP box 1.

81. On the ties between Kintner and Johnson, see Baughman, *Television's Guardians: The FCC and the Politics of Programming 1958–1967,* 145, and Robert Dallek, *Flawed Giant: Lyndon Johnson and His Times 1961–1973* (New York: Oxford University Press, 1998), 298.

82. Tom Mackin, "D.C. Helped Kill 'Week,'" *Newark Evening News,* May 5, 1965, 51; Marshall Jamison, telephone interview by author, tape recording, July 24, 1997.

83. Richard K. Doan, "*TW3*—A Revelation," *New York Herald Tribune,* June 16, 1964; "Jamison Exits *TW3* in Hassle," *Variety,* June 17, 1964, 26, 42; "Jamison Quits 'T.W.3,'" *New York Times,* June 16, 1964, 79.

84. Paul Gardner, "'Week That Was' Won't Stay As Is Next Season," *New York Times,* July 10, 1964, 59; Paul Gardner, "'Week That Was' Trips on Politics," *New York Times,* September 25, 1964, 81.

CHAPTER ELEVEN

1. Thomas Ryan, "Confidential memo for files," October 14, 1964, LHP, box 1; Gloria Steinem, telephone interview by author, tape recording, December 19, 1997; Tom Lehrer, interview by author, tape recording, Cambridge, Massachusetts, September 24, 1996.

2. When *Panic, MAD's* sister publication at E.C. Comics, parodied "The Night before Christmas" and pictured Santa Claus as "just divorced" in its December 1953 issue, Massachusetts attorney general George Feingold threatened to bring criminal proceedings against E.C. owner Bill Gaines unless he withdrew it from stores and newsstands. Five years later, Capitol Records initially refused to release Stan Freberg's protest over yuletide overcommercialization, "Green Chritma." "Comic Book Ban Fought," *New York Times,* December 28, 1953, 9; Stan Freberg, telephone interview by author, tape recording, June 8, 1996.

3. Anonymous to J. Edgar Hoover, Bill Mauldin file, Federal Bureau of Investigation, U.S. Department of Justice, Washington, D.C.; Sheldon Patinkin, interview by author, tape recording, Chicago, Illinois, September 12, 1996; Avery Schreiber, telephone interview by author, tape recording, May 24, 1999. Quotes from the "Faith Healer" are taken from Feldman, *A Critical Analysis of Improvisational Theatre in the United States from 1955–1968,* 238–44 and passim.

4. Alan Myerson, telephone interview by author, tape recording, July 12, 1999; Henry Hewes, "Intramural Sport," *Saturday Review of Literature* 47 (January 25, 1964): 25; John Simon, "Theatre Chronicle," *Hudson Review* 16 (Spring 1963):272; Stuart Little, "'Establishment' Skit Forced Out," *New York Herald Tribune,* May 20, 1963, 12; "Establishment Skit Dumped," *Village Voice,* May 23, 1963, 1, 2; "Ottawa, Toronto Censor Crucifixion," *Variety,* August 14, 1963, 65; Barbara Delatiner, "Off-Color Tones Mar New Satire," *New York Newsday,* March 31, 1964, The Establishment clipping file, BRT; "The Establishment," *Variety,* October 17, 1962, 54; Melvin Maddocks, "Establishment," *Christian Science Monitor,* January 26, 1963, 10.

5. Paul Krassner, *Confessions of a Raving, Unconfined Nut: Misadventures in the Counterculture* (New York: Simon & Schuster, 1993), 14–41.

6. Krassner was a fan of *MAD* magazine and had even sold several ideas there, yet he believed its orientation after Harvey Kurtzman left was too juvenile. When he suggested that Al Feldstein publish a satire on labor unions, Feldstein declined by arguing that the topic was "too adult." Krassner's motivation for creating a magazine of adult satire was only strengthened after the appearance of several articles during 1958 (such as Malcolm Muggeridge's "America Needs a Punch" in *Esquire*) that lamented satire's poor fate in contemporary America. Krassner, *Confessions of a Raving, Unconfined Nut,* 39, 42.

7. Paul Krassner, "An Angry Young Magazine . . ." *Realist* 1 (June–July 1958):1–2; Paul Krassner, "A Wee Bit O' Soul-Searching or, The Fine Art of Self-Defense," *Realist* 5 (December 1958):3.

8. A proponent of enlightened, active citizenship, Krassner used the *Realist* to recruit volunteers for various community programs and to drum up support and dona-

tions for the *Realist*'s short-lived integrated Summerlane Camp and School. Perhaps the most unusual causes pursued by Krassner related to the working and reproductive rights of women. In June 1962, the *Realist* featured "An Impolite Interview with an Abortionist," and in a later issue Krassner asked his readers, "Is there a doctor out there who performs abortions and would be willing to serve as a test case to establish the moral/legal right to do so?" In September 1959, Krassner spelled out the *Realist*'s editorial position on women: "We hadn't felt it necessary to include a disclaimer, but, just for the record, let us say here and now that we are completely in favor of equal rights for women—both in theory and in practice." George von Hilsheimer, "People: Regress Report #4," *Realist* 42 (August 1963):21–22; "Regress Report #5: A Self-Appointed Messiah," *Realist* 43 (September 1963):29–31; "Summations of a Self-Appointed Messiah," *Realist* 47 (February 1964):21–22; Paul Krassner, "Sordid Announcements," *Realist* 47 (February 1964):4; Paul Krassner, "Editorealisms," *Realist* 11 (September 1959):6.

9. Perhaps the most successful of the *Realist*'s early hoaxes involved a letter-writing campaign Krassner and his readers directed at various television sponsors. Intended as a protest against the manner in which commercial sponsors restricted the content of television programs, this hoax called for people to complain very vaguely about some offense committed on the *Masquerade Party* television program. Although Krassner admitted that this was a rather nonconstructive way to approach the problem of television censorship he asked his readers whether "hoaxwise—doesn't it give you a nice warm feeling inside just to picture all these TV officials, sponsor representatives and advertising men sitting around this screening room in their gray flannel ulcers, watching a kinescope of *Masquerade Party* and trying to find something offensive . . ." Paul Krassner, "A Stereophonic Hoax," *Realist* 16 (March 1960):6.

10. Paul Krassner, "Sex and the Cold War: Three Views—or Lucky Paul, He's in the Middle," *Realist* 29 (September 1961):24; Paul Krassner, "How Yellow Was My Journalism," *Realist* 43 (September 1963):3. *Esquire* magazine might have similarly raised eyebrows when in January 1963, it published "Versailles-on-the-Potomac: A Report to the Bourgeoisie," a cheeky guide to the cultural renaissance taking place in the nation's capital under John Kennedy. Sarel Eimerl here playfully alluded to the president's "policy of concealing the amount of government business which is done around the pool." Sarel Eimerl, "The Kennedy Water Syndrome," *Esquire* 59 (January 1963):41–47.

11. Krassner, for example, published numerous and lengthy articles written by Albert Ellis, a psychotherapist and the author of several sensationalist books (published by Lyle Stuart) including *The American Sexual Tragedy* (1954), *Sex without Guilt* (1958), *Art and Science of Love* (1960), *If This Be Sexual Heresy* (1963), and *Sex and the Single Man* (1963). Not surprisingly, the *Realist*'s devotion to free love and male liberation caught the eye of Hugh Hefner. Hefner hired Krassner to work as an assistant editor at *Playboy*, thus providing him and his homemade publication with a means of support throughout the early 1960s. As one of *Playboy*'s resident satirists, Krassner in 1961 moderated a lengthy roundtable discussion on "Hip Comics and the New Humor."

12. Paul Krassner, "A Fable for Our Time: The Second Coming," *Realist* 20 (October 1960); 1–2; Paul Krassner, "Rumor of the Month," *Realist* 35 (June 1962):13, and *Realist* 47 (February 1964):4.

13. "Letters to the Editor," *Realist* 49 (April 1964):24; "Sir Realist," *Realist* 23 (February 1961):2; Paul Krassner, "A Wee Bit O' Soul-Searching," 2–3; "Sir Realist," *Realist* 14 (December–January 1960):2; Sahl quoted in "An Impolite Interview with Mort Sahl," 18. Similarly, a Catholic college student from Baltimore responded to a cartoon drawn by Frank Cieciorka in which God sodomizes Uncle Sam with a caption reading," . . . one nation, under God . . . ,": "I mean, it really disgusted the hell out of me—not as a Catholic, not as a Christian, but as a human being who usually seeks an intelligent motive in the actions of others." "Letters to the Editor," *Realist* 49 (April 1964):17.

14. Paul Krassner, "A Matter of Taste," *Realist* 35 (June 1962):7; "The Cause and Cure of the Realist," *Realist* 29 (September 1961):3; Paul Krassner, "The Power of Kinky Thinking," *Realist* 30 (December 1961):18.

15. "Sir Realist," *Realist* 8 (May 1959):3; "An Impolite Interview with Joseph Heller," *Realist* 39 (November 1962):19.

16. Paul Sills, telephone interview by author, tape recording, June 3, 1999; Pat Englund, telephone interview by author, tape recording, May 13, 1998.

17. "Modern Times with Larry Josephson: Lenny Bruce Remembered," KCRW radio broadcast, 1991, audiotape heard at MTR; "One Night Stand: The World of Lenny Bruce," NTA Television, broadcast May 11, 1959, videotape viewed at MTR; Lenny Bruce, *How to Talk Dirty and Influence People* (Chicago: Playboy Press, 1965; reprint New York: A Fireside Book, 1992), 1–24; Gilbert Millstein, "Man, It's Like Satire," *New York Times Magazine,* May 3, 1959, 28, 30; Albert Goldman, from the journalism of Lawrence Schiller, *Ladies and Gentlemen—Lenny Bruce!!* (New York: Random House, 1974), 84–113.

18. Arthur Steuer, "How to Talk Dirty and Influence People," *Esquire* 54 (November 1960):155; Bruce, *How to Talk Dirty and Influence People,* 30.

19. Bruce's biographer Albert Goldman claimed in 1974 that Bruce had begun emulating the perspective of the smart, irreverent, jazz-loving, socially marginal hipster before he headed to the West Coast. By Goldman's account, Bruce first fell under the spell of the hipster when he began mingling with wisecracking, lower-middle-class Jews from Brooklyn. It was here, Goldman wrote, in the "Bensonhurst-Boro Park Delta of Jewish humor, the Basin Street of Jewish jazz, the Beale Street of Jewish blues, [that] Lenny first learned to be funny—to see funny, think funny, talk funny. To believe that being funny was the greatest quality a human being could have, that once a person possessed this precious gift, he would find everything in the whole world was funny, funny being equivalent to vital, strong, ethnic, honest and soulful." Goldman and Schiller, *Ladies and Gentlemen—Lenny Bruce!!* 126.

20. Phil Berger, *The Last Laugh: The World of the Stand-Up Comics* (New York: William Morrow & Company, 1975), 77–81; Honey Bruce with Dana Berenson, *Honey: The Life and Loves of Lenny's Shady Lady* (Chicago: Playboy Press, 1976), 213–16; Buckley quoted in John Carpenter's liner notes to *Bad Rapping of the Marquis de Sade* (World Pacific, 1969); "The Gettysburg Address" and "The Nazz," both recorded in 1951, are available on Crestview Records' *The Best of Lord Buckley.* Other Buckley recordings on World Pacific include *Way Out Humor* (1959), *Blowing His Mind (and Yours, Too)* (1960), and *Buckley's Best* (1968). Buckley's routines were admired by African American jazz musicians such as Dizzy Gillespie and Thelonious Monk, but they also offended many

other black civil rights leaders who took offense to Buckley's use of old "Amos 'n' Andy"-type racial stereotypes. Buckley suffered a fatal stroke in November 1960. For more on Buckley see Albert Goldman, "Lord Buckley," in *Freakshow: The Rocksoulblues jazzsickjewblack-humorsexpoppsych Gig and Other Scenes from the Counter-Culture* (New York: Atheneum, 1971), 252–55; and Berger, *The Last Laugh*, 52–65. Buckley was not the only comedian at work during the late 1940s and early 1950s who impersonated square characters speaking hip. Steve Allen, who during this period was working as a disk jockey on Los Angeles station KNX, delighted many of his early fans by telling children's stories such as "Little Red Riding Hood" in jazz lingo. Steve Allen, *Funny People* (New York: Stein and Day, 1981), 80.

21. Bruce, *How to Talk Dirty and Influence People*, 7; Lenny Bruce, "Masked Man" and "Father's Flotsky's Triumph," in John Cohen, ed., *The Essential Lenny Bruce* (New York: Ballantine Books, 1967), 70–75, 179–83. Also contributing to the impression that Bruce was a "sick" comedian were the bits he performed involving twisted freaks—a glue-sniffing nine-year-old boy asking for two thousand tubes of airplane glue at a local toy store, a strung-out Bela Lugosi Dracula coping with his nagging wife and kids, a junkie jazz musician applying for work in Lawrence Welk's band. Bruce's "Enchanting Transylvania" and "The Interview" both appear on Lenny Bruce's first album, *Interviews of Our Time* (Fantasy, 1958).

22. Albert Goldman, "What Lenny Bruce Was All About," *New York Times Magazine*, June 27, 1971, 16. "Religions Incorporated" appears on *The Sick Humor of Lenny Bruce* (Fantasy, 1959) and in Cohen, *The Essential Lenny Bruce*, 61–67.

23. Portions from these performances are taken from recordings made by Wally Heider at the Peacock Lane, Los Angeles, in January 1958 and at the Facks, San Francisco, on January 1–2, 1959; audiotapes heard at the Recorded Sound Reference Center, MBRS. During his early career, Bruce's performances onstage often proceeded as acts of provocation. At times Bruce would even deliver cheap jokes in order to weed out his hip followers from the "American Legion types" and *The Lawrence Welk Show* squares seated in the audience. On one occasion, Bruce even tested his audience and employer by appearing onstage completely nude.

24. Ralph Gleason, liner notes to *The Real Lenny Bruce* (Fantasy, 1975).

25. Ralph Gleason, liner notes to *The Sick Humor of Lenny Bruce*.

26. Charles Marowitz, "The Confessions of Lenny Bruce," in *The Encore Reader* (London: Methuen, 1965), 253; Millstein, "Man, It's Like Satire," 28, 30; Bamber Gascoigne, "Unmentionabilia," *Spectator* 208 (May 4, 1962):585; Jonathan Miller, "The Sick White Negro," *Partisan Review* 30 (Spring 1963):149–55.

27. Cohen, *The Essential Lenny Bruce*, 101–102. As was the case with many other satiric performers of the late 1950s and early 1960s, Bruce's loose, free-form technique onstage added significantly to the sense of intimacy he achieved with his audience. Dark, slender, well-dressed, prowling the stage "like a nervous cat," Lenny Bruce by the late 1950s was an exciting, alluring presence onstage. Jules Feiffer, an early fan, remembers that there was indeed something "operatic" and seductive about Bruce when he was onstage. As one art critic caught by Bruce's magnetism explained to a friend, "Screw the comedy. I don't come to laugh. I just want to be in his presence." The intensely per-

sonal, confessional approach Bruce often took onstage added significantly to his appeal. Sincere, direct, and vulnerable, Bruce won audiences over easily. And when he sensed that an audience was behind him, when he believed he had won their love, respect, and understanding, he reciprocated with frank expressions of his affection. Bruce explained in interviews that "when I'm swinging and I feel that warmth coming up at me, I'd like to ball the whole audience." "I feel like I want to hug 'em and kiss 'em" and "talk to them in the uninhibited way I do to my family and friends." John D. Weaver, "The Fault, Dear Bruce, Is Not in Our Stars, but in Ourselves," *Holiday* 44 (November 1968):72; Jules Feiffer, telephone interview by author, tape recording, December 12, 1996; Charles Marowitz, "How Much of the Lust Is Real?—'All of It!'" *Village Voice,* May 24, 1962, 15; Bruce quoted in Larry Siegel, "Rebel with a Caustic Cause," *Playboy* 6 (February 1959): 66; Bruce quoted in "The Playboy Panel: Hip Comics and the New Humor," 41; Bruce quoted in Steuer, "How to Talk Dirty and Influence People," 155.

28. Max Gordon, *Live at the Village Vanguard* (New York: St. Martin's Press, 1980), 77; Steuer, "How to Talk Dirty and Influence People," 153.

29. Cohen, *The Essential Lenny Bruce,* 76; Lenny Bruce, performance recorded at the Crescendo, September 16, 1960, Los Angeles; audiotape heard at the Recorded Sound Reference Center, MBRS; Bruce's opinions about Eisenhower and his administration are evident in a routine that he performed onstage throughout 1958. Relating to the vicuña coat scandal involving Sherman Adams, Bruce in this scene envisioned a White House meeting in which "Ike" and "Sherm" call on Vice President Nixon ("Nick") to travel to Lebanon. "How'd you like to go to hell, Ike?" Nixon responds petulantly. "Is that a way to talk, Nick?" Eisenhower responds. "After all I've done for you, you have the *chutzpah* to tell me to go to hell?" When Nixon reminds his superior that he was spat upon in Caracas, Venezuela, he responds that he "did good in Biloxi." "They like *you,*" he continues, "it's your old lady . . . She overdresses." Bruce quoted in Siegel, "Rebel with a Caustic Cause," 78; Cohen, *The Essential Lenny Bruce,* 94.

30. Lenny Bruce, performance recorded at the Crescendo, September 16, 1960; Lenny Bruce, *Lenny Bruce, Carnegie Hall* (United Artists, 1972).

31. "An Interview with Studs Terkel" in *The (Almost) Unpublished Lenny Bruce: From the Private Collection of Kitty Bruce* (Philadelphia: Running Press, 1984), 17; Cohen, *The Essential Lenny Bruce,* 26–27; Bruce quoted in Steuer, "How to Talk Dirty and Influence People," 153.

32. Lenny Bruce, "How to Relax Colored Friends at Parties," on *Lenny Bruce— American* (Fantasy, 1960). In early 1964, Bruce would again marvel onstage at the lamentable lack of understanding between American whites and blacks. To illustrate this point, he would create fictional dialogues between either Republican presidential candidate Barry Goldwater or President Lyndon B. Johnson and a group of hip, jive-talking Northern Negroes. He would then comment, "How about that? I mean, we piss away a million dollars on Radio Free Europe, and don't know anything about the country within the country—don't know *anything* about these people." Bruce might extend this routine by imagining the consequences of African Americans' eventual access to the ballot—notably, the creation of all-black juries and the appointment of black judges. And when that happened, he would add, whites would scream at the injustice

and then promptly remind blacks of their role in the civil rights movement. "Are you *kidding?*" he impersonated one white liberal. "I was *before* those marches . . . I was so liberal—I'll show you canceled checks, for Chrissakes! I've been since 1939 with that integration shit. Are you kidding with that?" Cohen, *The Essential Lenny Bruce*, 18–19.

33. "An Interview with Studs Terkel," 17; Bruce quoted in Millstein, "Man, It's Like Satire," 30.

34. Lenny Bruce, Performance recorded at the Crescendo, September 16, 1960. With this, as with other pronouncements, Bruce was unintentionally prophetic. As Maurice Isserman, Michael Kazin, and other historians relate, there was indeed a religious revival in the 1960s, one that largely took place outside of traditional denominational structures. See their study *America Divided: The Civil War of the 1960s* (New York: Oxford University Press), 249–67.

35. Ralph J. Gleason, "Total Satire: The Comedy of Dissent," *Contact* 5 (June 1960): 148. In his autobiography, Bruce justified his involvement in a fraudulent charity organization (he was arrested in Miami in 1951 for soliciting funds in full vestment) by referring to religious leaders as "hustlers." "I knew in my heart by pure logic that any man who calls himself a religious leader and owns more than one suit," Bruce argued, "is a hustler as long as there is someone in the world who has no suit at all." "All so-called 'men of God' are self-ordained," he reasoned. "The 'calling' they hear is just their own echo." Bruce, *How to Talk Dirty and Influence People*, 58, 53.

36. Lenny Bruce, performance recorded at the Crescendo, September 16, 1960.

37. Bruce, *Lenny Bruce, Carnegie Hall.*

38. To knowing, appreciative (and often Jewish) audiences throughout the early 1960s, Bruce illustrated the stark divide between the Jewish and goyish worlds, lumping together urban living, jazz, Ray Charles, Negroes, Italians, and "Irishmen who have rejected their religion" with the former, while assigning Eddie Cantor, folk singers, the name "Steve," lime Jell-O, white bread, and TV dinners to the latter. Variations of Bruce's Jewish/goyish categorizations are contained on Lenny Bruce, *Live at the Curran Theater* (Fantasy, 1971). Critic Charles Marowitz once wryly observed, "Of Bruce the Jew one could write a Torah." Indeed, Bruce's Jewish identity is a complex subject—one that deserves more scrutiny. In his various writings on Bruce, Albert Goldman has focused closely on his Jewishness. Though normally quite perceptive about the life and career of Bruce, however, Goldman's analysis of Bruce's Jewishness proves disappointing, particularly since Goldman views it in the light of what he sees as Bruce's self-hatred. For a better treatment, see Joseph Dorinson, "Lenny Bruce, A Jewish Humorist in Babylon," *Jewish Currents* 35 (February 1981):14–32.

39. In his autobiography Bruce tells how he "related very strongly" to Christ and Moses "because it seemed to me that I thought so much like them in so many ways." "They had a deep regard for education and they continually gave, with no motivation other than to give." Elsewhere, Bruce wrote, "I have read the Bible many times, and if Christ were alive today, I would devote my life to him. He represents all the truths and beauty." Bruce, *How to Talk Dirty and Influence People,* 57; Lenny Bruce, "In the Beginning" in *The (Almost) Unpublished Lenny Bruce,* 9.

40. Lenny Bruce, performance recorded at the Crescendo, September 17, 1960, Los Angeles; audiotape heard at the Recorded Sound Reference Center, MBRS; Gascoigne, "Unmentionabilia," 585; Albert Goldman, "The Comedy of Bruce," *Commentary* 36 (October 1963):315–16; Bruce, *Live at the Curran Theater;* Cohen, *The Essential Lenny Bruce,* 117; Paul Krassner, "Lenny Bruce Revisited," *Realist* 22 (December 1960): 15; Bruce quoted in Goldman and Schiller, *Ladies and Gentlemen—Lenny Bruce!!* 439. Bruce's low regard for old-school comedians bordered on contempt. In an interview with Paul Krassner, Bruce criticized Bishop for "doing the same thirty minutes of cafe comedy for the last ten years." Paul Krassner, "An Impolite Interview with Lenny Bruce," *Realist* 15 (February 1960):3.

41. Bruce quoted in Goldman and Schiller, *Ladies and Gentlemen—Lenny Bruce!!* 578; Bruce, *Lenny Bruce, Carnegie Hall;* Caen quoted in Siegel, "Rebel with a Caustic Cause," 22; Alpert quoted in Nat Hentoff, "The Inert Machine," *Village Voice,* April 12, 1962, 7.

42. Jerry Tallmer, "Mr. Bruce Comes Back," *New York Post,* March 30, 1964, Lenny Bruce clipping file, BRT; Jerry Tallmer, "Known Truth," *Village Voice,* May 18, 1961, 11; Jerry Tallmer, "A Meeting of the B'Nai B'rith," *Village Voice,* May 18, 1960, 9; Nat Hentoff, "The 'New' Lenny Bruce," *Village Voice,* January 10, 1963, 25; Nat Hentoff, "Satire, Schmatire," 376.

43. Kenneth Tynan, foreword to *How to Talk Dirty and Influence People,* xi–xv; Kenneth Tynan, "Look Back in Quadruplicate," *London Observer,* April 29, 1962, 29; Miller, "The Sick White Negro," 149–50; George Melly, "Bruce the Baptist," *New Statesman* 63 (April 27, 1962):612.

44. Lenny Bruce, ""The Money I'm Stealing" in *The (Almost) Unpublished Lenny Bruce,* 28; Cohen, *The Essential Lenny Bruce,* 112.

45. Bruce, ""The Money I'm Stealing," 28. The entire performance of Bruce's legendary midnight Carnegie Hall concert of February 4, 1961, was structured around Bruce's meditations on the obsolescence of moral absolutes. Not long after Bruce entered the stage that night, he told the audience, "And I'm really getting on this plateau of thinking. There's no right and wrong, just my right and your wrong and vice versa." With that motif set, Bruce later in the evening stated, "I'm not going to moralize . . . Again, neither right nor wrong, what cooks for me." Bruce, *Lenny Bruce, Carnegie Hall.*

46. Cohen, *The Essential Lenny Bruce,* 111; Bruce, *Live at the Curran Theater.*

47. Cohen, *The Essential Lenny Bruce,* 112; Bruce, *Lenny Bruce, Carnegie Hall;* Lenny Bruce, performance recorded at the Crescendo, September 17, 1960.

48. Cohen, *The Essential Lenny Bruce,* 55, 256.

49. It was Americans' peculiar embarrassment over sex, Bruce argued, that prevented vital information about venereal disease—a serious health issue—from being discussed in public. Bruce made this point in an oddly somber moment during his February 1961 Carnegie Hall concert. Relating a fictional episode in which a deceased fourteen-year-old girl sends a letter to the "Dear Abby" advice column, Bruce here made the point that the girl was forced to undergo a deadly abortion because it was impossible for her to tell her religious parents about her pregnancy.

50. Cohen, *The Essential Lenny Bruce,* 288.

51. Lenny Bruce, performance recorded at Facks, January 1–2, 1959; Gascoigne, "Unmentionabilia," 585; Weaver, "The Fault, Dear Bruce, Is Not in Our Stars, but in Ourselves," 72.

52. Reportedly "overwhelmed" when he saw Bruce perform for the first time, Hugh Hefner helped Bruce land his first gig in Chicago in 1959. Four years later, Hefner began serializing Bruce's autobiography *How to Talk Dirty and Influence People.* Bruce made a memorable appearance on the premiere of *Playboy's Penthouse,* broadcast WBKB-TV, October 24, 1959; videotape viewed at MBC.

53. Alan Brien, "Peeping Tom Thumb," *Sunday Telegraph,* April 29, 1962, Lenny Bruce clipping file, BRTC; Ruark, "Let's Nix the Sickniks," 38–39; "Fallen Angel, Pitt," *Variety,* October 12, 1960, 62; "Village Vanguard, NY," *Variety,* January 23, 1963, 68. According to Nat Hentoff, an audience member once threw Bruce through a plate glass window. Bruce himself claimed that he was punched in the face after doing his "Christ and Moses" at a Milwaukee club. Bruce often made matters worse by striking back at audience members. *Variety* reported in April 1962 that he even struck a disgruntled patron while he was performing at the Village Vanguard in New York. Bruce did not limit his retaliatory strikes to men. He did not hesitate to call female hecklers names such as *schlub,* and in 1962 he stunned an Australian audience when he shouted "fuck you" to one disapproving woman seated in the audience. Hentoff, "The Humorist as Grand Inquisitor," 27–29; Bruce, *How to Talk Dirty and Influence People,* 145; "Lenny Bruce Slugs Nitery Heckler," *Variety,* April 18, 1962, 56.

54. "An Impolite Interview with Henry Morgan," 13. In response to his "Let's Nix the Sickniks" article, Groucho Marx wrote Robert Ruark, "Freedom of speech is one thing, but [Bruce and his cohort] are overdoing it. And when I say 'gents,' this is where most of them should be doing their act." Groucho Marx, *The Groucho Letters: Letters from and to Groucho Marx* (New York: Simon and Schuster, 1967), 179.

55. Nat Hentoff, "Where Liberals Fear to Tread," *Reporter* 22 (June 23, 1960):52; Nat Hentoff, "The 'New' Lenny Bruce," *Village Voice,* January 10, 1963, 25.

56. Lenny Bruce, "The Violent Liberals," in *The (Almost) Unpublished Lenny Bruce,* 13; Lenny Bruce, *The Essential Lenny Bruce: Politics* (Douglas, 1969); Bruce, *Live at the Curran Theater;* Lenny Bruce, *Lenny Bruce Is Out Again* (Philles, 1965); Bruce, *How to Talk Dirty and Influence People,* 185.

57. Bruce, *Live at the Curran Theater;* Cohen, *The Essential Lenny Bruce,* 20, 24, 26.

58. Paul Krassner, "Lenny Bruce Revisited," *Realist* 22 (December 1960):15; Steuer, "How to Talk Dirty and Influence People," 155. Police in other cities such as Miami would later periodically use the threat of tape recording to force Bruce to "launder" his act. See "Ill. Would Jail Comic for 'Obscenity'; Lenny Bruce 'Clean' in Fla., Biz OK," *Variety,* April 24, 1963, 60.

59. Goldman and Schiller, *Ladies and Gentlemen—Lenny Bruce!!* 390; Bruce, *How to Talk Dirty and Influence People,* 164; "Lenny Bruce in Philly Alleges 10G 'Fix' Offer to Quash Narcotics Rap," *Variety,* October 11, 1961, 1, 68. Law enforcement officials were particularly disturbed by Bruce's apparent willingness to expose corruption among their ranks. When he told reporters how Philadelphia police officials had offered him

a bribe for his release, Bruce sent a clear signal to law enforcement agencies around the country that he was willing to question and even defy their authority.

60. Ralph J. Gleason, liner notes to Bruce, *Live at the Curran Theater;* Ralph J. Gleason, "Lenny Bruce's Obscene Language Pinch in Frisco after Philly Rap," *Variety,* October 11, 1961, 61; Bruce, *How to Talk Dirty and Influence People,* 111; Bill Steif, "Lenny Bruce Beats Frisco Obscenity Rap, but Contempt Costs Him $100," *Variety,* March 14, 1962, 60.

61. "Lenny Bruce Show Closed amid Criticism in Sydney," *New York Times,* September 8, 1962, 16; Eric Gorrick, "Lenny Bruce Gets Axed by Sydney Hotel: 'Too Dirty,'" *Variety,* September 12, 1962, 2, 50; Cohen, *The Essential Lenny Bruce,* 257; Goldman and Schiller, *Ladies and Gentlemen—Lenny Bruce!!* 472–73.

62. Bruce, *How to Talk Dirty and Influence People,* 142–43; Paul Krassner, liner notes to *Lenny Bruce in Concert* (United Artists, 1967).

63. "Bruce Guilty on Chi Obscenity Rap; Acts See Bad Censorship Precedent," *Variety,* March 6, 1963, 49; "Lenny Bruce Being Tried in Absentia as Chi Gate of Horn Fights for Life," *Variety,* January 30, 1963, 58; Goldman and Schiller, *Ladies and Gentlemen—Lenny Bruce!!* 481.

64. Lenny Bruce, "A Letter to John Brogan, Attorney at Law," reprinted in *The (Almost) Unpublished Lenny Bruce,* 106. Bruce describes "police harassment" and his fight for Constitutional freedoms in his fascinating March 4, 1964, appearance on *The Steve Allen Show*—an episode that was never aired but can be viewed at MTR.

65. Cohen, *The Essential Lenny Bruce,* 298; Johnnie L. Cochran Jr. with Tim Rutten, *Journey to Justice* (New York: Ballantine Books, 1996), 79–81.

66. Goldman and Schiller, *Ladies and Gentlemen—Lenny Bruce!!* 520; "Village Coffeehouse Goes Concert-Theatre for Lenny Bruce Stint," *Variety,* April 1, 1964, 77.

67. This was not the first public response to Lenny Bruce's legal harassment. In May 1963, a group of Minneapolis college students initiated a movement and began circulating "Hands Off Lenny Bruce" pins and petitions across the country.

68. Michael Smith, "Drizzle Does Not Dim Ardor of Arts Marchers," *Village Voice,* April 30, 1964, 1. It is important to remember that New York City at the time of Bruce's arrest was experiencing a "pornography scare." A campaign named Operation Yorkville, organized by a Jesuit priest and a rabbi, was presently exerting pressure on news dealers, bookstore owners, and film exhibitors to cleanse their operations of smut. Aligned with this campaign, many believed, were Cardinal Spellman, Robert Moses, and various real estate interests, all of whom who were eager to "clean up" New York City before the summer World's Fair. The tasks of padlocking theaters, closing down coffeehouses, and making arrests were undertaken by the New York City Police Department Vice Squad, fire and municipal building authorities, and the Department of Licenses, along with the New York State Division of Motion Pictures. The most notorious arrests involved the Living Theatre's Julian Beck and Judith Malina, both of whom were convicted for defying the Internal Revenue Service and then jailed for contempt of court in May 1965, and Film-Makers Cooperative founder and *Village Voice* columnist Jonas Mekas, who had been arrested, tried and convicted for showing Jack

Smith's *Flaming Creatures* and Jean Genet's *Un Chant d'Amour.* Martin Garbus, *Ready for the Defense* (New York: Avon Books, 1972), 94; Stephanie Gervis Harrington, "DA Presses Bruce Case, As Fair Opening Nears," *Village Voice,* April 16, 1964, 2; Albert Goldman, "The Trial of Lenny Bruce," *New Republic* 151 (September 12, 1964):13–14.

69. Goldman and Schiller, *Ladies and Gentlemen—Lenny Bruce!!* 538–39. Signers of Ginsberg's petition spanned nearly all of the liberal and left-liberal quarters of American literary, artistic, and intellectual life, from editors Barney Rossett, Irving Howe, Paul Krassner, Norman Podhoretz, and William Phillips to cartoonists Walt Kelly and Jules Feiffer; writers and critics Henry Miller, James Baldwin, Susan Sontag, John Updike, Robert Brustein, Malcolm Cowley, Terry Southern, Gore Vidal, Michael Harrington, Joseph Heller, Nat Hentoff, Alfred Kazin, and Dwight Macdonald; poets Peter Orlovsky, LeRoi Jones, Frank O'Hara, and Gregory Corso; Columbia University professors Lionel Trilling, Meyer Shapiro, Albert Goldman, Eric Bentley, and F.W. Dupee; actors and performers Bob Dylan, Severn Darden, and Paul Newman; playwrights Lillian Hellman and Jack Gelber; and fellow comedians Woody Allen, Godfrey Cambridge, and Dick Gregory. The two most surprising names on this list, according to news reports, were those of critic Lionel Trilling and theologian Reinhold Niebuhr. Trilling had never seen Bruce perform in person, but after reading transcripts of his performance said he found the comedian "a very remarkable and pointed satirist." Niebuhr had likewise never seen Bruce but signed the petition on the recommendation of close friends. Thomas Buckley, "100 Fight Arrest of Lenny Bruce," *New York Times,* June 14, 1964, 75.

70. Martin Garbus with Stanley Cohen, *Tough Talk: How I Fought for Writers, Comics, Bigots, and the American Way* (New York: Times Books, 1998), 31; Richard Kuh, *Foolish Figleaves?: Pornography in and out of Court* (New York: Macmillan Company, 1967), 181; Court Reporter's Minutes, *The People of the State of New York v. Lenny Bruce,* Criminal Court part 2B, County of New York, Criminal Courts Building, New York, June 17, 1964, 1–141, USNA; Edward de Grazia, *Girls Lean Back Everywhere: The Law of Obscenity and the Assault on Genius* (New York: Random House, 1992), 460–68, Goldman and Schiller, *Ladies and Gentlemen—Lenny Bruce!!* 548; John Cohen, *The Essential Lenny Bruce,* 260, 266.

71. The case of *Jabobellis v. Ohio* involved an Ohio movie theater manager who had exhibited Louis Malle's film *The Lovers.* The U.S. Supreme Court's ruling on this case and others involving Henry Miller's novel *Tropic of Cancer,* both delivered in June 1964, effectively nullified the old "balancing test" that attempted to weigh the social value of a given work against its "prurient" appeal. They also redefined "contemporary community standards" in terms of a *national,* rather than a *local* standard. These landmark decisions forced the Illinois Supreme Court to reconsider Bruce's conviction in Chicago. On November 24, 1964, the Illinois Supreme Court ruled that Bruce's performance, although "thoroughly disgusting and revolting as well as patently offensive" was constitutionally protected. "While we would not have thought that constitutional guarantees necessitate the subjection of society to the gradual deterioration of its moral fabric which this type of presentation promotes, we must concede that some of the topics commented on by defendant are of social importance. Under *Jacobellis* the entire per-

formance is thereby immunized, and we are constrained to hold that the judgment of the circuit court of Cook County must be reversed and defendant discharged." Writ of Error to the Municipal Court of Chicago in the case of *The People of the State of Illinois, Defendant in Error, v. Lenny Bruce, Plaintiff in Error,* Supreme Court of Illinois, 31 Ill. 2d 459; 202 N.E.2d 497; 1964 Ill., November 24, 1964; "Illinois Reverses a Bruce Conviction," *New York Times,* November 25, 1964, 44. For further discussion on the importance of *Jacobellis v. Ohio* and other obscenity trials dating from this period, see Wells D. Burgess, "Obscenity Prosecution: Artistic Value and the Concept of Immunity," *New York University Law Review* 39 (December 1964):1063–86; Thomas Daniel Hart, "Constitutional Law—Obscenity—Weighing Social Import against Prurient Appeal Unconstitutional Test," *American University Law Review* 14 (1965):226–30; and de Grazia, *Girls Lean Back Everywhere,* 243–495.

72. Garbus, *Ready for the Defense,* 118; Stephanie Gervis Harrington, "How Many 4-Letter Words Can a Prosecutor Use?" *Village Voice,* July 16, 1964, 3, 6; "Bruce's Trial," *Newsweek,* July 20, 1964, 76.

73. Killgallen quoted in O. John Rogge, "Obscenity Litigation," *American Jurisprudence Trials* 10 (Rochester, N.Y.: Lawyer's Co-Operative Publishing Company, 1965), 232–49 and Goldman and Schiller, *Ladies and Gentlemen—Lenny Bruce!!* 555–56.

74. Marya Mannes, *More in Anger* (Philadelphia: J.B. Lippincott Company, 1958), 14–16; Marya Mannes, "Plea for Fairer Ladies," *New York Times Magazine,* May 29, 1960, 16, 26; Garbus, *Ready for the Defense,* 133.

75. Jules Feiffer, telephone interview by author, tape recording, December 12, 1996; Garbus, *Tough Talk,* 37; Goldman, "The Comedy of Bruce," 312–17; Albert Goldman, "Stand-Up Shaman," *New Leader* 46 (March 4, 1963):31; Jules Feiffer, telephone interview by author, tape recording, December 19, 1996. The question over Bruce's feelings toward his liberal intellectual supporters has caused considerable debate since his death. One of the most interesting (and condescending) interpretations came from Jonathan Miller, a young intellectual who normally possessed a keen understanding of Bruce and the cultural impact of satire. In his rueful obituary for *New York Review of Books,* Miller gave the impression that Bruce was too impressionable, too gullible to achieve independence from his intellectual benefactors. "Bruce was in many ways a willing sucker for the sort of martyrdom upon which affluent, free-thinking liberals vicariously thrive," Miller wrote. Bruce, as described by Miller, was "intellectually underprivileged" and therefore so keen "to be accepted and admired by educated people" that he was "sometimes deceived by the over-complicated program which certain missionary intellectuals read into his act." With considerable regret Miller admitted that he and other liberal intellectuals had tricked Bruce into doing "our dubious dirty work of evangelical shock therapy." Jonathan Miller, "On Lenny Bruce," *New York Review of Books* 7 (October 6, 1966):10, 12. See also Lionel Trilling's reply to Miller in his letter to the editors, *New York Review of Books* 7 (November 17, 1966):39–40.

76. Garbus, *Tough Talk,* 30; Goldman and Schiller, *Ladies and Gentlemen—Lenny Bruce!!* 541; Ralph J. Gleason, "Obituary on Lenny Bruce," *Ramparts* 5 (October 1966): 36; Nat Hentoff, "The Onliest Lenny Bruce," *Village Voice,* February 5, 1991, 23. Bruce's resolve was no doubt strengthened by the agony he endured while seated at the defense

table. It may not have mattered much to his attorneys, but the way in which his act was being represented in court by Inspector Ruhe was an insult to Bruce and his craft. To the press Bruce quipped that it was like hearing "Ezra Pound reading the Bible," but in a "Supplemental Memorandum of Law for the Defendant Lenny Bruce" he later prepared for the judges deciding his verdict he agonized over Ruhe's misplaced punctuation, his bad rhythm, and his complete misunderstanding of the black vernacular. In a long dissertation on the argot of 1930s black jazz musicians, for example, Bruce explained that "'This is not my stick' is a paraphrase of 'this is not my axe'" and that "'that's not my stick' [only] means 'that's not my specialty.'" Bruce was able to contain his frustration in the trial's early phase, but as it stretched into July signs of his exasperation and depression became increasingly visible. Stephanie Gervis Harrington, "Supreme Court Decision May Affect Obscenity Rap," *Village Voice,* June 15, 1964, 13, 15; Lenny Bruce, "Supplemental Memorandum of Law for the Defendant Lenny Bruce," typed statement in Lenny Bruce Trial Materials, USNA, Folder 1.

CONCLUSION

1. Jerome L. Rodnitzky, "The Sixties between the Microgrooves: Using Folk and Protest Music to Understand American History, 1963–1973," *Popular Music and Society* 23 (Winter 1999):106.

2. Godfrey Cambridge, *Ready or Not, It's Godfrey Cambridge* (Epic, 1964).

3. Bill Mauldin cartoon no. 1112, A size, BMC; Block, *Straight Herblock,* 64–67. Herblock displayed his dislike of Goldwater earlier than most liberal satirists. In a cartoon dating from December 6, 1961, Herblock pictured Senator Goldwater ("the champion of the overdog") telling a poverty-stricken family, "If you had any initiative, you'd go out and inherit a department store." *Time* magazine reportedly called this cartoon "one of the lowest blows in [Herblock's] editorial-cartooning career."

4. John Crosby, "Theater: Revues on the Fringe," *Show* 1 (December 1961):6–7; Noel E. Parmentel, Jr., and Marshall J. Dodge, III, *Folk Songs for Conservatives* (New York: Unicorn Press, 1964).

5. "Gag Disks Kidding Politicos Wax Hot As Presidential Campaign Intensifies," *Variety,* 16 September 1964, 1. As *Variety* here reported, even Goldwater conservatives were getting in on the act. While California podiatrist Nathan Stein released "The Administration," a clean-cut college quartet calling themselves the Goldwaters cut an LP titled *Folk Songs to Bug the Liberals.* Recorded in Nashville, the album was heavily promoted by Goldwater clubs and the Young Americans for Freedom and sold 200,000 copies. The Goldwaters may appear to be a kitschy curiosity, but they represented a real attempt on the part of some New Right conservatives to deploy popular modes of satire to score political points with young people. That was certainly the intent behind *Goodbye Lyndon* (1964), a book of captioned photographs done in the style of *Gerald Gardner's News-Reals* and published by Kent Courtney, National Chairman of the Conservative Society of America.

6. Val Adams, "WNEW Bans Political Lampoons," *New York Times,* July 29, 1964,

sec. 1, p. 67; "LP Ribbing Goldwater Candidacy Banned by WNEW as 'Poor Taste,'" *Variety*, July 29, 1964, 1, 68; Val Adams, "2 Stations Decry WNEW Ban on Satirical Disks," *New York Times*, July 30, 1964, sec. 1, p. 53.

7. Jules Feiffer, telephone interview by author, tape recording, December 12, 1996; Judy Sheftel to Rhoda Feiffer, July 24, 1964, JF, box 2; "Paper Apologizes for 'Extremism' of Jules Feiffer," *San Francisco Examiner*, August 16, 1964. Several newspapers, including the *Philadelphia Bulletin* and *Tucson Daily Citizen*, refused to run Feiffer's satires on Goldwater. "[W]hen he does political cartoons lambasting Goldwater we can't run him," the editor of the *Bulletin's Sunday Magazine* informed Feiffer's syndicate. "He's had two Goldwater strips we had to kill although [the editorial staff] couldn't agree more with him." B.A. Bergman to Robert Walton, August 4, 1964, JF, box 10.

8. Paul Gardner, "WBAI's Convention," *New York Times*, July 17, 1964, sec. 1, p. 55; Paul Gardner, "New NBC Team for Conventions," *New York Times*, July 6, 1964, sec. 1, p. 49; Richard Neuweiler, telephone interview by author, tape recording, May 27, 1999; *The Big Tune Out*, audiotapes in author's possession.

9. "Memos Revealed," *Outsider's Newsletter* 2 (January 31, 1964):2; "Goldwater A-Bomb Statement Clarified," *Outsider's Newsletter* 2 (June 26 1964):1; "Obituary," *Outsider's Newsletter* 2 (March 20, 1964):6; Michael and Stephanie Harrington, "The Poverty Pavilion," *Monocle* 6 (Summer 1964):10–15.

10. Marvin Kitman, *The Number One Best Seller: The True Adventures of Marvin Kitman* (New York: Dial Press, 1966); Rocco Landesman and Joel Schechter, "Satire Is Alive and Hiding in Argentina: An Interview with the Editors of *Monocle* Magazine," *Theater* 10 (Spring 1979):111.

11. Landesman and Schechter, "Satire Is Alive and Hiding in Argentina," 112; Marvin Kitman, "The Making of a Presidential Candidate," *Monocle* 5 (Spring 1964):12–22.

12. "The Making of a Presidential Candidate, Chapter 2," *Monocle* 6 (Summer 1964):8–9; Marvin Kitman, "My Last Hurrah," *Monocle* 6 (November 1964); "'I Won Also' Kitman Says," *Outsider's Newsletter* 2 (March 27, 1964):1–3; John H. Fenton, "A 'Lincoln Man' Enters Politics," *New York Times*, March 1, 1964, sec. 1, p. 52.

13. "Power of the Pen," Jules Feiffer interviewed by Terrence Smith on *The News Hour with Jim Lehrer*, PBS broadcast, August 10, 2000.

14. Brian O'Doherty, "'Third Ear' Opens at Premise Theater," *New York Times*, May 29, 1964, 16; Mark Gordon, telephone interview by author, tape recording, June 3, 1999. According to cast member Mark Gordon, *The Third Ear's* devotion to "the political struggle of the times and a clarification of what was happening" was ultimately compromised by May's interest in exploring male-female relationship scenes. In the end, what was perhaps most interesting and significant about *The Third Ear* was the attention it paid to issues of gender. With Elaine May's encouragement, *The Third Ear's* Louise Lasser and Renée Taylor asserted themselves strongly and, according to Mark Gordon, turned material around "from a woman's point of view." In one scene, for example, Taylor played a mother providing her bride-to-be daughter the straight dope about husbands. As many members of The Second City and other troupes would admit, female improvisational satirists—with the notable exception of Elaine May, Joan

Darling, and Barbara Harris—were constantly ignored or belittled by their male colleagues. Gordon, not accustomed to having his authority challenged by women, remembers that Taylor in particular was "scaring the hell out of me."

15. Navasky and Lingeman had announced their intentions to keep after Johnson only weeks after he took the oath of office. In late December 1963, the two men declared that they had "held a pep rally for satirists." "We have discarded suggestions that we go into something non-controversial like the dry-cleaning business," they stated. "You see we thought of Lyndon Johnson's voting record . . . we thought of Bobby Baker . . . and other Texas public servants who have sojourned in Washington in the past, we thought of the curious attempts to sanitize history [regarding Kennedy's presidency] . . . well, we decided we were needed after all." "On Continuing," *Outsider's Newsletter* 2 (December 20, 1963):3.

16. "Johnson's Wax," *Outsider's Newsletter* 2 (March 27, 1964):3; "Posters Spur War Effort," *Outsider's Newsletter* 2 (April 10, 1964):1–3; "Interviews of Glory: Robert Strange McNamara," *Outsider's Newsletter* 2 (May 29, 1964):8–10; PX, "Observers in Laos," *Outsider's Newsletter* 2 (June 26, 1964):15.

17. Richard Neuweiler, telephone interview by author, tape recording, May 27, 1999; *The Big Tune Out,* audiotapes in author's possession.

18. Robert Shelton, "Concert Offers Social Comment," *New York Times,* September 28, 1964, sec. 1, p. 19; Louis Calta, "Democrats Plan Revue for Votes," *New York Times,* September 30, 1964, sec. 1, p. 39; Richard Neuweiler, telephone interview by author, tape recording, May 27, 1999.

19. "As Broadcast" script for June 5, 1964, LHP, box 23; "As Broadcast" script for May 8, 1964, LHP, box 21.

20. Mrs. Marilyn Hirshler to Channel 4, Columbus, Ohio, September 9, 1964, LHP, box 3.

21. Mrs. Doran Johnson to *TW3,* n.d., LHP, box 3.

22. "As Broadcast" script for November 17, 1964, LHP, box 27; "Lament of 'TW3' Writer: 'Save Us from Friends,'" *Variety,* December 23, 1964, 20, 36; "Tele Follow-Up Comment," *Variety,* November 18, 1964, 33; "'That Was the Week That Was,'" *Variety,* October 7, 1964, 26; G.T. Amodeo to *TW3,* December 15, 1964, LHP, box 5; John Van Pelt Lassoe Jr. to Leland Hayward, November 25, 1964, LHP, box 4; Leland Hayward to Robert Kintner, January 29, 1965, LHP, box 2.

23. Wilfred Sheed, "Housebroken Satire," *Commonweal* 81 (October 9, 1964):73.

24. WBAI's decision to cancel *A Show of Force* was aided, Neuweiler contends, by complaints the station received over Peter Boyle's portrayal of a Catholic priest. Richard Neuweiler, telephone interview by author, tape recording, May 27, 1999

25. Victor Navasky, "Publisher's Notes," *Monocle* 6 (November 1964):1. In 1965 Navasky and his colleagues published a "Brushfire War Issue on Vietnam," which was "designed to fit into the pocket of U.S. Army fatigue pants." In it, they juxtaposed proclamations issued by "distinguished satirists" such as Secretary of State Dean Rusk, Ambassador Henry Cabot Lodge, and Secretary of Defense Robert McNamara with the stark, harrowing cartoons of Lou Myers. In one of these cartoons, McNamara is shown in a naked embrace with a female corpse. With the last of their sporadic attacks

on the American military establishment and the escalating war in Vietnam—an illustrated allegory titled *Animal Ranch: The Great American Fable* and a well-crafted satiric
hoax titled *Report from Iron Mountain: On the Possibility and Desirability of Peace,* both
published in 1966—Navasky and his colleagues permanently suspended a spirited
round of satiric criticism that, regrettably, has rarely been replicated since. *Monocle:
Politics, Polemics and Satire for the Sub-Influential* 6 (4) (1965); Jack Newfield, Victor
Navasky, Richard Lingeman, Karla Kuskin, and Marvin Kitman, *Animal Ranch: The
Great American Fable* (New York: Monocle Periodicals and Parallax Publishing, 1966).
For background information about the genesis and continuing success of *Monocle's* fi-
nal publication, see Victor Navasky's introduction to the reprint of Leonard C. Lewin's
Report from Iron Mountain and his article "Anatomy of a Hoax," *Nation* 260 (June 12,
1995):1. See also Navasky, *A Matter of Opinion,* 73–81.

26. "Onward! and Downward! with Mort Sahl," *National Review* 18 (August 9,
1966):760; Sahl, *Heartland,* 131; Peter Bart, "Mort Sahl Gets Own Nightclub on the
Coast as Outlet for Satire," *New York Times,* June 15, 1966, 42. Gerald Nachman claims
that Sahl was fired from WNEW-TV in 1965 for saying, "The problem with Hitler
wasn't that he killed six million Jews, but that he missed the ones at [the station's parent company] Metromedia." Nachman, *Seriously Funny: The Rebel Comedians of the 1950s
and 1960s,* 85.

27. "Mort Sahl: The Observer Profile," *London Observer,* July 16, 1961, 5; Herb
Caen, "Has Success Spoiled Mort Sahl?" *Houston Chronicle,* March 26, 1961, 7; Miller
quoted in Nat Hentoff, "Relevance of Irreverence," *Reporter* 27 (November 22, 1962):
44–46.

28. "Mort Sahl," *Variety,* May 6, 1964.

29. Bob Thomas, "Sahl Spiel," *Newark Evening News,* November 16, 1959, Mort Sahl
clipping file, BRT; Joe Hyams, "Mort Sahl Explains Mort Sahl," *New York Herald Tribune,*
February 8, 1960, 13; "An Impolite Interview with Mort Sahl," 26; Jerry Talmer, "Mort
Sahl and Roger Bannister," *New York Post,* June 21, 1964, Mort Sahl clipping file, BRT;
"The Playboy Panel: The Womanization of America," *Playboy* 9 (June 1962):136.

30. "Mort Sahl: The Loyal Opposition," broadcast by PBS, September 18, 1989, and
viewed at the Motion Picture and Television Reading Room, MBRS; "An Impolite Interview with Mort Sahl," 21–24; Gerald Nachman, "Mort Sahl: Smiting Hip and Thigh,"
New York Post, November 21, 1965, Mort Sahl clipping file, BRT.

31. Decision of the Criminal Court of the City of New York, part 2B, County of
New York, November 4, 1964, in Lenny Bruce Trial Materials, USNA, folder 2; de
Grazia, *Girls Lean Back Everywhere: The Law of Obscenity and the Assault on Genius,* 464–
65. Judge Creel was the lone dissenter on this decision. According to the attorney and
legal scholar Edward de Grazia, the third judge, an African American who throughout
the trial could be seen stifling his laughter, was sympathetic to Bruce but was told by
Murtagh that he would have to serve in traffic court for the remainder of his term if he
voted to acquit the comedian. de Grazia, *Girls Lean Back Everywhere: The Law of Obscenity and the Assault on Genius,* 479. The personal motives behind the judges' and district attorney's actions in this trial have been periodically called into question over the
past thirty-five years. In 1974, Nat Hentoff successfully thwarted Richard Kuh's run for

New York City district attorney when he reminded readers of the *Village Voice* of what Kuh had done to Bruce. For the latest exchange between Richard Kuh and his enemies, see Martin Garbus, "When the Censor Was in the Statehouse," *New York Times,* September 20, 1998, sec. 2, p. 27, and the follow up in the "Letters" section of *New York Times,* October 4, 1998, sec. 2, p. 4. In 2004, David M. Skover and Ronald K. L. Collins, authors of *The Trials of Lenny Bruce: The Fall and Rise of an American Icon* (Naperville, Ill.: Sourcebooks, 2002), successfully petitioned New York governor George Pataki for a posthumous pardon of Lenny Bruce.

32. Martin Garbus quoted in Goldman and Schiller, *Ladies and Gentlemen—Lenny Bruce!!* 587.

33. Paul Krassner, "Lenny the Lawyer," in *How a Satirical Editor Became a Yippie Conspirator in Ten Easy Years* (New York: G.P. Putnam's Sons, 1971), 113; Goldman and Schiller, *Ladies and Gentlemen—Lenny Bruce!!* 588–89; Henry Paul, "Final Performance Nets 4 Months at Hard Labor," *Village Voice,* December 24, 1964, 1, 19, 20. In the last twenty months of his life, Bruce inundated the courts with petitions and reams of other legal material in a desperate attempt to save himself and his career. Although he ultimately managed to elude the workhouse, he became a prisoner to his legal obsessions. Confining himself to his Hollywood Hills home, he buried himself in stacks of legal texts and scattered notes like some "mad Talmudist," as Albert Goldman described him. Lacking both the venues and, in some instances, the motivation to perform in public, Bruce was soon beset by severe financial troubles. By October 1965 he was declared legally bankrupt. When he did appear onstage in San Francisco or Los Angeles, the only cities in America where he then could find work, he subjected audiences to recitations of court transcripts and various witless ruminations concerning obscenity law. Writer John Weaver, who saw Bruce perform in Los Angeles in February 1966, tellingly compared the experience to "watching Joe DiMaggio muff a fly ball." "Lenny stumbled," Weaver wrote, "chanting a lewd litany that had long since lost its capacity to shock or to edify." Likewise, Ralph Gleason, one of Bruce's earliest and strongest supporters, described seeing Bruce, "deep in the search for some slender logical thread," suddenly forget he had an audience. "One night," Gleason remembered, "he mentioned his father's name and lost the point of the story he was telling. Finally he insisted on going down to the basement to play back the tape he was making, in order to find his place and return to reality." In the end, badly injured by his fight with the law, his senses impaired by paranoia and his worsening dependence on drugs, Bruce sadly surrendered his acute awareness of himself and his surroundings. Forever eliminating the possibility of becoming what he called a sad "old hipster," Bruce died of a morphine overdose on August 3, 1966. Albert Goldman, "Comics," *New York Review of Books* (January 20, 1966); Weaver, "The Fault, Dear Bruce, Is Not in Our Stars, but in Ourselves," 75; Ralph Gleason, "An Obituary" in *The (Almost) Unpublished Lenny Bruce,* 128; Lenny Bruce, *How to Talk Dirty and Influence People,* 35.

34. Paul Krassner, "Three Obituaries," *Realist* 55 (December 1964), 24; "Over and Out," *New Yorker,* December 19, 1964, 29–31; John Pekkanen, "Nation Soured on Its Dream," *Middleton Press,* April 11, 1964, 11.

35. "Communications," *Monocle* 6 (November 1964):4.

36. Gregory and McGraw, *Up from Nigger,* 24; Patrick Owens, "Gregory Came to Town," *New Republic* 150 (March 28, 1964):10.

37. Gregory and Moses, *Callus on My Soul: A Memoir,* 79; Bob Ellison, "Dick Gregory: Last Man at the Lunch Counter," *Rogue* 9 (June 1964):27; Jerry Tallmer, "Question and Answer Man," *New York Post,* May 20, 1964, 54; "Yankee Go Home," *Time,* April 12, 1963, 26.

38. "hungry i, S.F.," *Variety,* July 22, 1964, 80; "Square East, N.Y.," *Variety,* May 27, 1964, 59; "Nitery Fires Dick Gregory in Show Row," *New York Journal American,* April 17, 1963, BRTC; "Cabaret in Queens Drops Dick Gregory," *New York Times,* April 18, 1963, sec. 1, p. 38; "Dick Gregory Makes L.A. Wait," *Variety,* August 28, 1963, 49; "NBC Program Analysis Files: Personality," Index File, Motion Picture and Television Reading Room, MBRS; Lipsyte, "You Gits a Little Uppity and You Lands in Jail," 74.

39. "Dick Gregory Working As Jail Paper Reporter," *New York Times,* August 18, 1963, sec. 1, p. 50; Dick Gregory quoted in Morgan, "The Two Worlds of Dick Gregory," 128; Gregory quoted in Allan Morrison, "Negro Humor: An Answer to Anguish," *Ebony* 22 (May 1967):105; Hughes quoted in Faith Berry, *Langston Hughes: Before and beyond Harlem* (Westport, Conn.: Lawrence Hill & Company, 1983), 326.

40. Jerry Doolittle, "The Mess in Washington," *Outsider's Newsletter* 2 (April 10, 1964):6–7.

41. Tom Lehrer, interview by author, tape recording, Cambridge, Massachusetts, September 24, 1996.

42. Klein quoted in Sweet, *Something Wonderful Right Away,* 346; "Second City, Chi," *Variety,* January 29, 1964, 65–66; Patinkin quoted in Donna McCrohan, *The Second City: A Backstage History of Comedy's Hottest Troupe* (New York: Perigree Books, 1987), 137–38; Sheldon Patinkin, interview by author, tape recording, Chicago, September 12, 1996.

43. "Woody Allen and His Impolite Interview," *Realist* 28 (April 1965):11. Supporters of Bill Cosby in particular explained that his brand of comedy represented a "healthy" reaction against the racially charged routines of Dick Gregory. As Brooks Johnson noted in *Negro Digest* in 1966, Cosby "represents a relief to the consciences of people after Gregory's constant bombardment against the state of racial affairs in America." Brooks Johnson, "In the Wake of Gregory, Cosby Becomes a Star," *Negro Digest* 15 (October 1966):41–42.

44. *MAD*'s path had been cleared by the U.S. Court of Appeals in March 1964 when it ruled that its parodies did not infringe on the copyright of popular songs. Writing on behalf of the three-judge panel, Irving Kaufman declared that although "our individual tastes may prefer a more subtle brand of humor," they believed that *MAD*'s parodies were worthy of protection. In language that it and New York state courts ignored later in the case of Lenny Bruce, the Court concluded that "parody and satire are deserving of substantial freedom—both as entertainment and as a form of social and literary criticism." "Parody of Songs Upheld by Court," *New York Times,* March 24, 1964, 37; "Parody and Satire Deserve Substantial Freedom," *Publishers Weekly* 186 (October 5, 1964):42.

45. Jules Feiffer, telephone interview by author, tape recording, December 19, 1996; Theodore Roszak, *The Making of a Counter Culture* (Garden City, N.Y.: Doubleday & Company, 1968), 24; Marty Jezer, *Abbie Hoffman: American Rebel* (New Brunswick: Rutgers University Press, 1992), 31, 107, 124; Larry Sloman, *Steal This Dream: Abbie Hoffman and the Countercultural Revolution in America* (New York: Doubleday, 1998), 22; Jack Hoffman and Daniel Simon, *The Lives of Abbie Hoffman: Run, Run, Run* (New York: G.P. Putnam's Sons, 1994), 71; Jerry Rubin, *Growing (Up) at Thirty-Seven* (New York: M. Evans and Company, 1976), 66.

46. Albert Goldman, "The Comic Prison," *Nation* 200 (February 8, 1965):142–44; Pauline Kael, "Spoofing and Schtik," *Atlantic Monthly* 216 (December 1965):84–85.

47. Dwight Macdonald, "Birds of America," *New York Review of Books,* December 1, 1966, 14; Garry Goodrow, telephone interview by author, tape recording, June 9, 1999.

Bibliography

SELECTED DISCOGRAPHY

The Best of Washington Humor, Cameo, 1961.

The Kennedy Wit, RCA, 1964.

Berman, Shelley. *The Edge of Shelley Berman.* Verve, 1960.

——. *Inside Shelley Berman.* Verve, 1959.

——. *New Sides.* Verve, 1963.

——. *Outside Shelley Berman.* Verve, 1959.

——. *A Personal Appearance.* Verve, 1961.

——. *The Sex Life of the Primate.* Verve, 1964.

Beyond the Fringe. *Beyond the Fringe: The Original Broadway Cast.* Capitol, 1962.

——. *Beyond the Fringe '64, Volume II: Original Broadway Cast.* Capitol, 1964.

Bruce, Lenny. *The Berkeley Concert.* Reprise, 1969.

——. *Carnegie Hall.* United Artists, 1972.

——. *The Essential Lenny Bruce: Politics.* Douglas, 1969.

——. *I Am Not a Nut, Elect Me!* Fantasy, 1960.

——. *Interviews of Our Times.* Fantasy, 1958.

——. *Law, Language and Lenny Bruce.* Warner Spector, 1974.

——. *Lenny Bruce—American.* Fantasy, 1960.

——. *Lenny Bruce Is Out Again.* Philles, 1965.

——. *Lenny Bruce Live at the Curran Theater.* Fantasy, 1971.

——. *Let the Buyer Beware,* Shout! Factory Records, 2004.

——. *The Real Lenny Bruce.* Fantasy, 1975.

——. *The Sick Humor of Lenny Bruce.* Fantasy, 1959.

——. *Thank You Masked Man.* Fantasy, 1972.

——. *What I Was Arrested For.* Douglas, 1971.

Buckley, Lord. *Bad Rapping of the Marquis de Sade.* World Pacific, 1969

——. *The Best of Lord Buckley.* Elektra, 1969.

——. *Blowing His Mind (and Yours, Too).* World Pacific, 1960.

——. *Buckley's Best.* World Pacific, 1968.

——. *Way Out Humor.* World Pacific, 1959.

Cambridge, Godfrey. *Ready or Not, It's Godfrey Cambridge.* Epic, 1964.

Chad Mitchell Trio. *The Best of the Chad Mitchell Trio.* Kapp, 1963.

——. *The Chad Mitchell Trio at the Bitter End.* Kapp, 1962.

Close, Del. *The Do-It-Yourself Psychoanalysis Kit.* Hanover, 1959.

Cook, Peter, et al. *Peter Cook Presents: The Establishment.* Riverside, 1963.

The Committee. *The Committee: An Original Cast Album.* Reprise, 1964.

Darden, Severn. *The Sound of My Own Voice and Other Noises.* Mercury, 1961.

Freberg, Stan. *The Best of Stan Freberg.* Capitol, 1964.

——. *The Best of the Stan Freberg Shows.* Capitol, 1958.

——. *Child's Garden of Freberg.* Capitol, 1957.

——. *Stan Freberg Presents the United States of America.* Capitol, 1961.

——. *Stan Freberg with the Original Cast.* Capitol, 1959.

The Goldwaters. *The Goldwaters Sing Folk Songs to Bug the Liberals.* Greenleaf, 1964.

Gregory, Dick. *Dick Gregory Talks Turkey.* Vee Jay, 1962.

——. *East and West.* Colpix, 1961.

——. *In Living Black and White.* Colpix, 1962.

——. *So You See . . . We All Have Problems.* Colpix, 1964.

——. *The Two Sides of Dick Gregory.* Vee Jay, 1963.

Jordan, Will. *Ill Will.* Jubilee, 1960.

Lehrer, Tom. *An Evening Wasted with Tom Lehrer.* Lehrer Records, 1959.

——. *More of Tom Lehrer.* Lehrer Records, 1959.

——. *Songs and More Songs by Tom Lehrer.* Rhino, 1996.

——. *Songs by Tom Lehrer.* Lehrer Records, 1953.

——. *The Remains of Tom Lehrer.* Warner Brothers, 2000.

——. *Tom Lehrer Revisited.* Lehrer Records, 1960.

——. *That Was the Year That Was.* Reprise, 1965.

Mabley, Jackie. *Jackie Moms Mabley at the Playboy Club.* Chess, 1961.

Maxwell, Len, et al. *I'd Rather Be Far Right than President.* Divine Right, 1964.

Meader, Vaughn. *The First Family.* Cadence, 1962.

——. *Bob Booker and Earle Doud present Vaughn Meader and the First Family. Volume Two.* Cadence, 1963.

Morgan, Henry. *The Best of Henry Morgan,* Judson, n.d.

——. *The Best of Henry Morgan: Excerpts and Commercials from His ABC Radio Program, 1946–1947.* Command Performance, n.d.

——. *The Saint and the Sinner.* Offbeat, 1962.

Newhart, Bob. *Behind the Button-Down Mind.* Warner Brothers, 1961.

——. *Bob Newhart Faces Bob Newhart.* Warner Brothers, 1965.

——. *The Button-Down Mind.* Warner Brothers, 1960.

——. *The Button-Down Mind on TV.* Warner Brothers, 1962.

——. *The Button-Down Mind Strikes Back.* Warner Brothers, 1960.

Nichols, Mike and Elaine May. *Highlights from the Broadway Production* An Evening with Mike Nichols and Elaine May. Mercury, 1961.

——. *Improvisations to Music*. Mercury, 1958.

——. *Mike Nichols and Elaine May Examine Doctors*. Mercury, 1962.

The Premise. *Off Broadway: The Premise*. Vanguard, 1961.

Sahl, Mort. *A Way of Life*. Verve, 1959.

——. *Anyway . . . Onward*. Mercury, 1967.

——. *At the Sunset*. Fantasy, 1958.

——. *The Future Lies Ahead*. Verve, 1958.

——. *Mort Sahl 1960 or Look Forward in Anger*. Verve, 1959.

——. *Mort Sahl at the hungry i*. Verve, 1960.

——. *Mort Sahl on Relationships*. Reprise, 1961.

——. *The New Frontier*. Reprise, 1961.

——. *The Next President*. Verve, 1960.

The Second City. *Comedy from the Second City*. Mercury, 1961.

——. *From the Second City*. Mercury, 1961.

Segal, George, et al. *At Home with That Other Family*. Roulette, 1962.

Shepherd, Jean. *Jean Shepherd and Other Foibles*. Elektra, 1959.

——. *Will Failure Spoil Jean Shepherd?* Elektra, 1960.

Ship, Reuben. *The Investigator: A Political Satire in Documentary Form*. Radio Rarities, Inc., 1954.

Winters, Jonathan. *Another Day, Another World*. Verve, 1961.

——. *Down to Earth*. Verve, 1960.

——. *Here's Jonathan*. Verve, 1961.

——. *The Wonderful World of Jonathan Winters*. 1960.

SELECTED BIBLIOGRAPHY

Allen, Fred. *Treadmill to Oblivion*. Boston: Little, Brown and Company, 1954.

Allen, Steve. *Hi-Ho, Steverino!: My Adventures in the Wonderful Wacky World of TV*. Fort Lee, N.J.: Barricade Books, 1992.

Anthony, Norman, and George T. Delacorte, Jr., eds. *The Book of Ballyhoo*. New York: Simon and Schuster, 1931.

Baker, Russell. *The Good Times*. New York: William Morrow and Company, 1989.

Banes, Sally. *Greenwich Village 1963: Avant-Garde Performance and the Effervescent Body*. Durham: Duke University Press, 1993.

Barnouw, Eric. *Tube of Plenty: The Evolution of American Television*. New York: Oxford University Press, 1975.

Baughman, James L. *Television's Guardians: The FCC and the Politics of Programming 1958-1967*. Knoxville: University of Tennessee Press, 1985.

Becker, Stephen D. *Comic Art in America: A Social History of the Funnies, the Political Cartoons, Magazine Humor, Sporting Cartoons, and Animated Cartoons*. New York: Simon and Schuster, 1959.

Bedell Smith, Sally. *Reflected Glory: The Life of Pamela Churchill Harriman*. New York: Simon & Schuster, 1996.

Belgrad, Daniel. *The Culture of Spontaneity: Improvisation and the Arts in Postwar America.* Chicago: University of Chicago Press, 1998.

Bergan, Ronald. *Beyond the Fringe . . . and Beyond: A Critical Biography of Alan Bennett, Peter Cook, Jonathan Miller and Dudley Moore.* London: Virgin, 1989.

Berger, Arthur Asa. *Li'l Abner: A Study in American Satire.* Jackson, Miss.: University Press of Mississippi, 1994.

Berger, Phil. *The Last Laugh: The World of the Stand-Up Comics.* New York: William Morrow & Company, 1975.

Berman, Sonia. *The Crossing: Adano to Catonsville: Leland Hayward's Producing Career.* Lanham, Md.: Scarecrow Press, 1995.

Berton, Pierre, ed. *Voices from the Sixties: Twenty-Two Views of a Revolutionary Decade.* Garden City, N.Y.: Doubleday & Company, 1967.

Bier, Jesse. *The Rise and Fall of American Humor.* Chicago: Holt, Rinehart and Winston, 1968.

Block, Herbert. *A Cartoonist's Life.* New York: Macmillan Publishing Company, 1993.

———. *The Herblock Book.* Boston: Beacon Press, 1952.

———. *Herblock's Here and Now.* New York: Simon and Schuster, 1955.

———. *Special for Today.* New York: Simon and Schuster, 1958.

———. *Straight Herblock.* New York: Simon and Schuster, 1964.

Blum, John Morton. *Years of Discord: American Politics and Society, 1961–1974.* New York: W.W. Norton, 1991.

Boddy, William. *Fifties Television: The Industry and Its Critics.* Urbana: University of Illinois Press, 1990.

Booker, Christopher. *The Neophiliacs: A Study of the Revolution in English Life in the Fifties and Sixties.* London: Collins, 1969.

Boskin, Joseph. *Humor and Social Change in the Twentieth Century.* Boston: Trustees of the Public Library of the City of Boston, 1979.

———., ed. *The Humor Prism in Twentieth-Century America.* Detroit: Wayne State University Press, 1997.

———. *Sambo: The Rise and Demise of an American Jester.* New York: Oxford University Press, 1986.

Boyer, Paul. *By the Bomb's Early Light.* New York: Pantheon Books, 1985.

———. *Fallout: A Historian Reflects on America's Half-Century Encounter with Nuclear Weapons.* Columbus: Ohio State University Press, 1998.

Breines, Wini. *Young, White, and Miserable: Growing Up Female in the Fifties.* Boston: Beacon Press, 1992.

Bremner, Robert H., ed. *Reshaping America: Society and Institutions 1945–60.* Columbus: Ohio State University Press, 1982.

Brick, Howard. *The Age of Contradiction: American Thought and Culture in the 1960s.* New York: Twayne Publishers, 1998.

Brownstein, Ronald. *The Power and the Glitter: The Hollywood-Washington Connection.* New York: Pantheon Books, 1990.

Bruce, Kitty, ed. *The (Almost) Unpublished Lenny Bruce: From the Private Collection of Kitty Bruce.* Philadelphia: Running Press, 1984.

Bruce, Lenny. *How to Talk Dirty and Influence People.* Chicago: Playboy Press, 1965; reprint, New York: Fireside Book, 1992.

Brustein, Robert. *The Culture Watch: Essays on Theatre and Society, 1969–1974.* New York: Alfred A. Knopf, 1975.

Buchwald, Art. *I Chose Capitol Punishment.* New York: World Publishing Company, 1963.

Caesar, Sid. *Where Have I Been: An Autobiography.* New York: Crown Publishers, 1982.

Carlisle, Jr., Henry, ed. *American Satire in Prose and Verse.* New York: Random House, 1962.

Carpenter, Humphrey. *A Great, Silly Grin: The British Satire Boom of the 1960s.* New York: Public Affairs, 2000.

Caswell, Lucy, ed. *Walt Kelly: A Retrospective Exhibition to Celebrate the Seventy-Fifth Anniversary of His Birth.* Columbus: Ohio State University Libraries, 1988.

Cohen, John, ed. *The Essential Lenny Bruce.* New York: Ballantine Books, 1967.

Cohen, Sarah Blacher, ed. *From Hester Street to Hollywood: The Jewish-American Stage and Screen.* Bloomington: Indiana University Press, 1983.

Coleman, Janet. *The Compass: The Improvisational Theatre That Revolutionized American Comedy.* Chicago: University of Chicago Press, 1991.

Cook, Lin, ed. *Something Like Fire: Peter Cook Remembered.* London: Methuen, 1996.

Cotkin, George. *Existential America.* Baltimore: Johns Hopkins University Press, 2002.

Curtin, Michael. *Redeeming the Wasteland: Television Documentary and Cold War Politics.* New Brunswick, N.J.: Rutgers University Press, 1995.

Davis, Ossie, and Rubie Dee. *Purlie Victorious: A Commemorative.* New Rochelle, N.Y.: Emmalyn Enterprises, 1993.

de Grazia, Edward. *Girls Lean Back Everywhere: The Law of Obscenity and the Assault on Genius.* New York: Random House, 1992.

Denning, Michael. *The Cultural Front: The Laboring of American Culture in the Twentieth-Century.* New York: Verso, 1996.

Dickson-Carr, Darryl. *African American Satire: The Sacredly Profane Novel.* Columbia: University of Missouri Press, 2001.

Dickstein, Morris. *Gates of Eden: American Culture in the Sixties.* New York: Basic Books, 1977.

———. *Leopards in the Temple: The Transformation of American Fiction, 1945–1970.* Cambridge: Harvard University Press, 2002.

Diggins, John Patrick. *The Proud Decades: America in War and Peace.* New York: W.W. Norton & Company, 1988.

Doherty, Thomas. *Cold War, Cool Medium: Television, McCarthyism, and American Culture.* New York: Columbia University Press, 2003.

———. *Teenagers and Teenpics: The Juvenalization of American Movies in the 1950s.* Boston: Unwin Hyman, 1988.

Douglas, Ann. *Terrible Honesty: Mongrel Manhattan in the 1920s.* New York: Farrar, Straus and Giroux, 1995.

Dudden, Arthur P. *The Assault of Laughter.* New York: Thomas Yoseloff, 1962.

Ehrenreich, Barbara *The Hearts of Men: American Dreams and the Flight from Commitment.* New York: Anchor Press/Doubleday, 1983.

Elliott, Bob, and Ray Goulding. *Write If You Get Work: The Best of Bob and Ray.* New York: Random House, 1975.

Feiffer, Jules. *Boy, Girl, Boy, Girl.* New York: Signet Books, 1963.

——. *Feiffer on Civil Rights.* New York: Anti-Defamation League of B'nai B'rith, 1966.

——. *Feiffer: The Collected Works.* Vol. 1. Seattle: Fantagraphic Books, 1988.

——. *Feiffer: The Collected Works.* Vol. 3. Seattle: Fantagraphic Books, 1992.

——. *The Great Comic Book Heroes.* New York: The Dial Press, 1965.

——. *Jules Feiffer's America: From Eisenhower to Reagan.* Edited by Steven Heller. New York: Alfred A. Knopf, 1982.

——. *Passionella: And Other Stories.* New York: McGraw-Hill Book Company, 1959.

Foner, Eric. *The Story of American Freedom.* New York: W.W. Norton & Company, 1998.

Foreman, Joel, ed. *The Other Fifties: Interrogating Midcentury American Icons.* Urbana: University of Illinois Press, 1997.

Frank, Thomas. *The Conquest of Cool: Business Culture, Counterculture, and the Rise of Hip Consumerism.* Chicago: University of Chicago Press, 1997.

Freberg, Stan. *It Only Hurts When I Laugh.* New York: Times Books, 1988.

Freud, Sigmund. *Jokes and Their Relation to the Unconscious.* Translated by James Strachey. New York: W.W. Norton, 1963.

Frost, David, and Ned Sherrin, eds. *That Was the Week That Was.* London: W. H. Allen, 1963.

Galbraith, John Kenneth. *The Affluent Society.* Boston: Houghton Mifflin, 1958.

Garbus, Martin, and Stanley Cohen. *Tough Talk: How I Fought for Writers, Comics, Bigots, and the American Way.* New York: Times Books, 1998.

Garbus, Martin. *Ready for the Defense.* New York: Avon Books, 1972.

Gardner, Gerald C. *Campaign Comedy: Political Humor from Clinton to Kennedy.* Detroit: Wayne State University Press, 1994.

——. *Who's in Charge Here?* New York: Pocket Books, 1962.

Gavin, James. *Intimate Nights: The Golden Age of New York Cabaret.* New York: Grove Weidenfeld, 1991.

Gilbert, James. *A Cycle of Outrage.* New York: Oxford University Press, 1986.

Gilbert, James, and Peter Kuznick, eds. *Rethinking Cold War Culture.* Washington, D.C.: Smithsonian Institution Press, 2001.

Gitlin, Todd. *The Sixties.* New York: Bantam Books, 1987.

Golden, Harry. *Only in America.* Cleveland: World Publishing Company, 1958.

Goldman, Albert, and Lawrence Schiller. *Ladies and Gentlemen—Lenny Bruce!!.* New York: Random House, 1974.

Goldman, Albert. *Freakshow: The Rocksoulbluesjazzsickjewblack-humorsexpoppsych Gig and Other Scenes from the Counter-Culture.* New York: Atheneum, 1971.

Goodman, Paul. *Growing Up Absurd: Problems of Youth in the Organized System.* New York: Random House, 1960.

Goodwin, Richard N. *Remembering America: A Voice from the Sixties.* Boston: Little, Brown and Company, 1988.

Gregory, Dick, and James R. McGraw. *Up from Nigger.* New York: Stein and Day, 1975.

Gregory, Dick, and Robert Lipsyte. *Nigger: An Autobiography.* New York: Pocket Books, 1965.

Gregory, Dick, and Robert Orben. *From the Back of the Bus.* New York: E. P. Dutton, 1962.

Gregory, Dick, and Shelia P. Moses. *Callus on My Soul: A Memoir.* Atlanta, Ga.: Longstreet Press, 2000.

Halberstam, David. *The Powers That Be.* New York: Alfred A. Knopf, 1979.

Harrington, Oliver. *Bootsie and Others.* New York: Dodd, Mead & Company, 1958.

———. *Dark Laughter: The Satiric Art of Oliver W. Harrington.* Edited by M. Thomas Inge. Jackson: University Press of Mississippi, 1993.

———. *Why I Left America and Other Essays.* Edited by M. Thomas Inge. Jackson: University Press of Mississippi, 1993.

Harris, Leon A. *The Fine Art of Political Wit.* New York: E. P. Dutton & Co., 1964.

Haskell, Barbara. *Blam! The Explosion of Pop, Minimalism and Performance 1958–1964.* New York: Whitney Museum of American Art, 1984.

Havig, Fred. *Fred Allen's Radio Comedy.* Philadelphia: Temple University Press, 1990.

Heller, Steven, and Gail Anderson. *The Savage Mirror: The Art of Contemporary Caricature.* New York: Watson-Guptill, 1992.

Heller, Steven, ed. *Man Bites Man: Two Decades of Drawings and Cartoons by 22 Comic and Satiric Artists 1960 to 1980.* New York: A & W Publishers, 1981.

Hendra, Tony. *Going Too Far.* New York: Doubleday, 1988.

Henriksen, Margot A. *Dr. Strangelove's America: Society and Culture in the Atomic Age.* Berkeley: University of California Press, 1997.

Highet, Gilbert. *The Anatomy of Satire.* Princeton: Princeton University Press, 1962.

Hill, Lee. *A Grand Guy: The Art and Life of Terry Southern.* New York: HarperCollins, 2001.

Hilmes, Michele. *Radio Voices: American Broadcasting, 1922–1952.* Minneapolis: University of Minnesota Press, 1997.

Hoberman, J. *Vulgar Modernism: Writing on Movies and Other Media.* Philadelphia: Temple University Press, 1991.

Hoppe, Arthur. *Having a Wonderful Time: My First Half Century as a Newspaperman.* San Francisco: Chronicle Books, 1995.

———. *The Love Everybody* Crusade.* Garden City, N.Y.: Doubleday & Company, 1963.

Horowitz, Daniel. *Vance Packard and American Social Criticism.* Chapel Hill: University of North Carolina Press, 1994.

Isserman, Maurice. *If I Had a Hammer: The Death of the Old Left and the Birth of the New Left.* Urbana: University of Illinois Press, 1993.

Jamison, Kathleen Hall. *Packaging the Presidency: A History and Criticism of Presidential Campaign Advertising.* 3d ed. New York: Oxford University Press, 1996.

Jezer, Marty. *Abbie Hoffman: American Rebel.* New Brunswick: Rutgers University Press, 1992.

Kaplan, Fred. *Gore Vidal: A Biography.* New York: Doubleday, 1999.

Kazin, Michael, and Maurice Isserman. *America Divided: The Civil War of the 1960s.* New York: Oxford University Press, 2000.

Kelly, Selby. *Pogo Files for Pogophiles: A Retrospective on 50 Years of Walt Kelly's Classic Comic Strip.* Richfield, Minn.: Spring Hollow Books, 1992.

Kelly, Walt. *Pogo.* Vol. 4. Edited by Gary Groth. Seattle: Fantagraphic Books, 1995.

——. *Pogo.* Vol. 7. Edited by Gary Groth. Seattle: Fantagraphic Books, 1997.

——. *Pogo.* Vol. 8. Edited by Gary Groth. Seattle: Fantagraphic Books, 1997.

——. *Pogo.* Vol. 9. Edited by Gary Groth. Seattle: Fantagraphic Books, 1997.

——. *Pogo.* Vol. 10. Edited by Gary Groth. Seattle: Fantagraphics Books 1998.

——. *Pogo.* Vol. 11. Edited by Gary Groth. Seattle: Fantagraphics Books 2000.

——. *Ten Ever-Lovin' Blue-Eyed Years with Pogo.* New York: Simon and Schuster, 1959.

——. *The Jack Acid Society Black Book.* New York: Simon and Schuster, 1962.

——. *The Pogo Papers.* New York: Simon and Schuster, 1953.

Kernan, Alvin B. *Modern Satire.* New York: Harcourt, Brace & World, 1962.

Kisseloff, Jeff, ed. *The Box: An Oral History of Television, 1920–1961.* New York: Viking, 1995.

Kitman, Marvin. *The Number One Best Seller: The True Adventures of Marvin Kitman.* New York: Dial Press, 1966.

Krassner, Paul. *Confessions of a Raving, Unconfined Nut: Misadventures in the Countercul-ture.* New York: Simon & Schuster, 1993.

——. *How a Satirical Editor Became a Yippie Conspirator in Ten Easy Years.* New York: G. P. Putnam's Sons, 1971.

Kuh, Richard. *Foolish Figleaves?: Pornography in and out of Court.* New York: Macmillan Company, 1967.

Kurtzman, Harvey, and Howard Zimmerman. *My Life as a Cartoonist.* New York: Minstrel Books, 1988.

Kurtzman, Harvey. *From Aargh! to Zap!: Harvey Kurtzman's Visual History of the Comics.* New York: Prentice Hall Press, 1991.

Landesman, Jay. *Rebel without Applause.* London: Bloomsbury Publishing, 1987.

Lasch, Christopher. *The New Radicalism in America: 1889–1963: The Intellectual as Social Type.* New York: Alfred A. Knopf, 1965.

Lax, Eric. *Woody Allen.* New York: Alfred A. Knopf, 1991.

Lears, Jackson. *Fables of Abundance: A Cultural History of Advertising in America.* New York: Basic Books, 1994.

Levin, Martin, ed. *Five Boyhoods: Howard Lindsay, Harry Golden, Walt Kelly, William K. Zinsser and John Updike.* Garden City, N.Y.: Doubleday & Company, 1962.

Lewin, Leonard C., ed. *Treasury of American Political Humor.* New York: Delacorte Press, 1964.

——. *Report from Iron Mountain: On the Possibility and Desirability of Peace.* New York: Free Press, 1996.

Lhamon, W. T. Jr., *Deliberate Speed: The Origins of a Cultural Style in the American 1950s.* Washington: Smithsonian Institution Press, 1990.

Lipsitz, George. *Time Passages: Collective Memory and American Popular Culture.* Minneapolis: University of Minnesota Press, 1990.

LoBrutto, Vincent. *Stanley Kubrick: A Biography.* New York: Donald I. Fine Books, 1997.

MacDonald, J. Fred. *One Nation under Television.* New York: Pantheon Books, 1990.

Mailer, Norman. *The Presidential Papers.* New York: G. P. Putnam's Sons, 1963.

Mannes, Marya. *More in Anger.* Philadelphia: J. B. Lippincott Company, 1958.

Marc, David. *Comic Visions: Television Comedy and American Culture.* New York: Routledge, 1992.

———. *Demographic Vistas: Television in American Culture.* Philadelphia: University of Pennsylvania Press, 1996.

Marowitz, Charles. *Burnt Bridges: A Souvenir of the Swinging Sixties and Beyond.* Toronto: Hodder & Stoughton, 1990.

Mary, Lary. *Recasting America: Culture and Politics in the Age of Cold War.* Chicago: University of Chicago Press, 1989.

Mauldin, Bill. *Back Home.* New York: William Sloane Associates, 1947.

———. *I've Decided I Want My Seat Back.* New York: Harper & Row, 1965.

———. *What's Got Your Back Up?* New York: Harper & Brothers Publishers, 1961.

May, Elaine Tyler. *Homeward Bound: American Families in the Cold War Era.* New York: Basic Books, 1988.

McCrohan, Donna. *The Second City: A Backstage History of Comedy's Hottest Troupe.* New York: Perigree Books, 1987.

Miller, James. *"Democracy is In the Streets": From Port Huron to the Siege of Chicago.* New York: Simon and Schuster, 1987.

Mills, C. Wright. *The Sociological Imagination.* New York: Grove Press, 1961.

Mumford, Lewis. *Interpretations and Forecasts: 1922–1972.* New York: Harcourt Brace Jovanovich, 1972.

Nachman, Gerald. *Seriously Funny: The Rebel Comedians of the 1950s and 1960s.* New York: Pantheon Books, 2003.

Navasky, Victor. *A Matter of Opinion.* New York: Farrar, Straus and Giroux, 2005.

Osborn, Robert. *Low and Inside.* New York: Farrar, Straus & Young, 1953.

———. *Osborn on Osborn.* New Haven: Ticknor & Fields, 1982.

———. *The Vulgarians.* Greenwich, Conn.: New York Graphic Society, 1960.

———. *War Is No Damn Good!* Garden City, N.Y.: Doubleday & Company, 1946.

Pells, Richard. *The Liberal Mind in a Conservative Age: American Intellectuals in the 1940s and 1950s.* Cambridge: Harper & Row, 1985.

Polsgrove, Nancy. *It Wasn't Pretty, Folks, but Didn't We Have Fun?: Esquire in the Sixties.* New York: W.W. Norton & Company, 1995.

Putterman, Barry. *On Television and Comedy: Essays on Style, Theme, Performer and Writer.* Jefferson, N.C.: McFarland & Co., 1995.

Rampsersad, Arnold. *The Life of Langston Hughes v. 2: 1941–1967, I Dream a World.* New York: Oxford University Press, 1988.

Rollins, Peter C., ed. *Hollywood as Historian.* Lexington: University of Kentucky Press, 1983.

Rossinow, Doug. *The Politics of Authenticity: Liberalism, Christianity, and the New Left in America*. New York: Columbia University Press, 1998.

Roszak, Theodore. *The Making of a Counter Culture*. Garden City, New York: Doubleday & Company, 1968.

Sahl, Mort. *Heartland*. New York: Harcourt Brace Jovanovich, 1976.

Sanders, Barry. *Sudden Glory: Laughter as Subversive History*. Boston: Beacon Press, 1995.

Schechter, Joel. *Satiric Impersonations: From Aristophanes to the Guerrilla Girls*. Carbondale: Southern Illinois University Press, 1994.

Schechter, William. *The History of Negro Humor in America*. New York: Fleet Press, 1970.

Schlesinger, Jr., Arthur M. *A Thousand Days: John F. Kennedy in the White House*. Boston: Houghton Mifflin Company, 1965.

———. *The Politics of Hope*. Boston: Houghton Mifflin Company, 1963.

Schrecker, Ellen. *Many Are the Crimes: McCarthyism in America*. Princeton: Princeton University Press, 1998.

Scott, Keith. *The Moose That Roared: The Story of Jay Ward, Bill Scott, a Flying Squirrel, and a Talking Moose*. New York: St. Martins Griffin, 2001.

Seidel, Michael. *Satiric Inheritance: Rabelais to Sterne*. Princeton: Princeton University Press, 1979.

Sennett, Ted. *Your Show of Shows*. New York: Macmillan Publishing, 1977.

Shikes, Ralph E., and Steven Heller, eds. *The Art of Satire: Painters as Caricaturists and Cartoonists from Delacroix to Picasso*. New York: Pratt Graphics Center and Horizon Press, 1984.

Siegel, Fred. *Troubled Journey: From Pearl Harbor to Ronald Reagan*. New York: Hill and Wang, 1984.

Sikov, Ed. *Laughing Hysterically: American Screen Comedy of the 1950s*. New York: Columbia University Press, 1994.

Sitkoff, Harvard. *The Struggle for Black Equality: 1954–1980*. New York: Hill and Wang, 1981.

Sloman, Larry. *Steal This Dream: Abbie Hoffman and the Countercultural Revolution in America*. New York: Doubleday, 1998.

Solotaroff, Ted. *Red Hot Vacuum and Other Pieces on the Writing of the Sixties*. New York: New York: Athenaeum, 1970.

Sorensen, Jeff. *Bob Newhart*. New York: St. Martin's Press, 1988.

Sorensen, Theodore C. *Kennedy*. New York: Harper & Row, 1965.

Spigel, Lynn, and Michael Curtin, eds. *The Revolution Wasn't Televised: Sixties Television and Social Conflict*. New York: Routledge, 1997.

Spigel, Lynn, *Make Room for TV: Television and the Family Ideal in Postwar America*. Chicago: The University of Chicago Press, 1992.

Sterling, Philip, ed. *Laughing on the Outside: The Intelligent White Reader's Guide to Negro Tales and Humor*. New York: Grosset & Dunlap, 1965.

Sweet, Jeffrey. *Something Wonderful Right Away: An Oral History of The Second City and The Compass Players*. New York: Limelight Editions, 1986.

Test, George. *Satire: Spirit and Art.* Tampa: University of South Florida Press, 1988.

Tynan, Kenneth. *Tynan Right and Left: Plays, Films, People, Places and Events.* New York: Athenaeum, 1967.

Vidal, Gore. *Palimpsest: A Memoir.* New York: Random House, 1995.

——. *Rocking the Boat.* Boston: Little, Brown and Company, 1962.

Warshow, Robert. *The Immediate Experience: Movies, Comics, Theatre and Other Aspects of Popular Culture.* Garden City, N.Y.: Doubleday & Company, 1962.

Watkins, Mel. *On the Real Side: A History of African American Comedy from Slavery to Chris Rock.* Chicago: Lawrence Hill Books, 1999.

Whitfield, Stephen J. *The Culture of the Cold War.* Baltimore: Johns Hopkins University Press, 1991.

——. *In Search of American Jewish Culture.* Hanover, N.H.: Brandeis University Press, 1999.

Wickberg, Daniel. *Senses of Humor: Self and Laughter in Modern America.* Ithaca: Cornell University Press, 1997.

Winkler, Allan. *Life under a Cloud: American Anxiety about the Atom.* New York: Oxford University Press, 1993.

Index